A

GENEALOGICAL REGISTER

OF THE

FIRST SETTLERS

OF

NEW-ENGLAND;

CONTAINING

AN ALPHABETICAL LIST OF THE

GOVERNOURS,
DEPUTY-GOVERNOURS,
ASSISTANTS or COUNSELLORS, and
MINISTERS OF THE GOSPEL in the several Colonies, from 1620 to 1692;
REPRESENTATIVES OF THE GENERAL COURT OF MASSACHUSETTS, from 1634 to 1692;

GRADUATES OF HARVARD COLLEGE to 1662;
MEMBERS OF THE ANCIENT AND HONOURABLE ARTILLERY COMPANY to 1662;
FREEMEN admitted to the Massachusetts Colony from 1630 to 1662; with many other of the early inhabitants of New-England and Long-Island, N. Y., from 1620 to the year 1675:

TO WHICH ARE ADDED

VARIOUS GENEALOGICAL AND BIOGRAPHICAL NOTES,

COLLECTED FROM ANCIENT RECORDS, MANUSCRIPTS,

AND PRINTED WORKS.

BY JOHN FARMER,

REPRINTED WITH
ADDITIONS AND CORRECTIONS
By Samuel G. Drake

Originally published: Lancaster, Massachusetts, 1829
Reprinted with Additions and Corrections from
The New England Historical and Genealogical Register,
Volume I, No. 2 (April 1847)
Genealogical Publishing Co., Inc.
Baltimore, 1964, 1969, 1976, 1979, 1983, 1989, 1994
Library of Congress Catalogue Card Number 64-19761
International Standard Book Number 0-8063-0108-2
Made in the United States of America

PREFACE.

THE following Register is designed as an introduction to a biographical and genealogical dictionary, which shall comprehend concise sketches of those individuals who have been known and distinguished in the annals of New-England. If the health of the compiler should admit of the completion of such a work in the manner contemplated, it will contain biographical accounts of many persons here but slightly noticed, and a continuation of eminent persons from the close of the seventeenth century to the present time.

An arrangement of names like the following, in this age of antiquarian research and inquiry, seemed to be wanted. We are all curious to know something respecting those who have preceded us on the stage of action ; and there has begun a curiosity among many of the present generation to trace back their progenitors, in an uninterrupted series, to those who first landed on the bleak and inhospitable shores of New-England. And it is not improbable that the arrival of the puritan fathers of New-England will form a more memorable epoch in history than the Conquest of England does in that country, and that posterity, a few centuries hence, will experience as much pleasure in tracing back their ancestry to the New-England colonists, as some of the English feel in being able to deduce their descent from the Normans.

There is a satisfaction in recognizing our first ancestor from the European continent ; in knowing from what part of Great-Britain he came ; where he settled, and the circumstances and condition of his family. Owing to the trials and hardships endured by the first settlers of New-England, the uncertainty of their remaining in the country, and the little time afforded them for recording family data and genealogical facts, there are but few families, who have full and complete satisfaction in each of these particulars. But some facts, even at this late period, might be known of almost every individual who settled in any of the colonies, if suitable patience, research, and industry were employed in collecting them. Our earliest records and memorials are full of information, and in regard to minuteness and accuracy will bear a comparison with those of modern date ; and it is somewhat remarkable that so large a portion of them have escaped the many perils to which fire and the aboriginal wars exposed them. But many town records are in a decaying state, and those in whose hands they are deposited are highly culpable that they do not use their efforts to have them fairly and correctly transcribed.

The following work is intended to contain the names of a large portion of the First Settlers, of the most prominent, as well as the more humble ; of those who had " to level forests, where savage beasts and savage men had roamed for ages, and to make comfortable dwelling places amidst a wide and gloomy wilderness." But no one can reasonably expect it to contain the names of all who early came to New-England. To bring the names of all from their musty and moth-eaten concealment would be a labour beyond the power of a single individual. The object in the progress of the undertaking has been to give,

I. The names of the Magistrates, and Ministers of the Gospel, in all the New-England colonies from 1620 to 1692.

II. The Deputies or Representatives of the General Court, of the colony of Massachusetts, from 1634 to the commencement of government under the new charter of 1692.

III. The Graduates of Harvard College, and the Members of the Ancient and Honourable Artillery Company, from the date of those institutions until 1662.

IV. The Freeman admitted to the Massachusetts colony, in the colony records, from 1630 to 1662.

V. The names of all such Emigrants, both freemen and non-freemen, as could be collected, who had come over to the several colonies before 1643.

Besides those coming under these several heads, there have been given the names of many others, especially those who were the first of the name and family in the country, down to Philip's war in 1675. The four first objects (excepting a complete list of the counsellors of Rhode-Island) have been principally attained, and some idea of the deficiencies of the last may be had from a consideration of the number of persons, who had come to New-England from the first arrival at Plymouth to the year 1643, to which period it was originally the aim of the compiler to limit his inquiries.

Former writers have differed in their statements of the number who had come to this section of the country before 1640, when, according to Johnson, emigration "*only* for enjoyment of exercising the ordinances of Christ, and enlargement of his kingdom," ceased. But other causes operated to draw people from England, and it is not unlikely that there continued to be accessions of new settlers for, at least, the first half century from the beginning. Governour Hutchinson, in the preface to the first volume of his history of Massachusetts, says, " In the first ten years, about twenty thousand souls had arrived in Massachusetts." " Since then," he observes, " it is supposed more have gone from hence to England than have come from thence hither." Dr. Cotton Mather, who wrote in 1697, says, " the number who did actually arrive at New-England before the year 1640, have been computed about four thousand," which we must charitably suppose to mean *families*, for before that period three fourths of that number of *individuals* had come over in a single year. He also says, that after 1640 far more went out of the country than came into it. But Johnson, who wrote in 1651, within eight years of the time to which he makes his computation, and who had better means of knowing the truth than either Mather or Hutchinson, says, the number " for fifteen years space, to the year 1643, of men, women, and children, passing over this wide ocean, as near as at present can be gathered, is supposed to be 21,200, or thereabouts." This calculation of Johnson seems to embrace the whole of New-England, from the time of Endecott's arrival at Salem, in 1628, to 1643, while Hutchinson gives nearly the same number of emigrants to Massachusetts alone, within two thirds of the period mentioned by Johnson. Allowing five persons to have constituted a family, the number of male heads of families, if we regard Johnson's computation as correct, would exceed 4000, whose names should find a place in a perfect register of the emigrants to New-England during the first twenty-three years from the settlement at Plymouth. But, as many of the earliest settlers returned to England, or removed to other places, their proportion to those who remained can never be ascertained, and some deduction should therefore be made. Of the most of those who left, nothing very satisfactory can be obtained ; and as they quitted the country at a time when their aid and services were most needed, we feel less solicitous to know their history, than of those who endured the heat and burden of the day.

The assertion so often made, that more persons have gone from New-England to England since 1640, than have come from thence hither, probably originated with Mather, who misunderstood the language of Johnson, and was perpetuated by Hutchinson, and has been adopted by succeeding writers of reputation. A little reflection may satisfy almost any one that if the remark was true in 1651, only eight years after the check given to emigration by the more favourable condition of the puritans in England, a lapse of forty-six years would be likely to affect the truth of it in 1697, and it would appear still further from the truth in 1760, when Governour Hutchinson wrote his history.

The first settlers of Plymouth colony were separatists from the Church of England. Some of them had early embraced the sentiments of Robert Brown, but were reduced to milder principles under the, tolerant and catholick Robinson. Those who settled the colony of Massachusetts were Puritans, *who had not seceded from the established church.* They were of that class of Episcopalians who had long laboured for reform in the rites and ceremonies of the church, and had contended that these should be regulated " by the rules of Scripture, and that nothing should be maintained which did not rest on that authority." ' They had been chiefly born and brought up in the National Church, and had, until their emigration, lived in communion with her. Their ministers had been ordained by her bishops, and had officiated in her parochial churches, and had made no secession from her until they left their native land.' They had long desired to establish churches in their worship, form, matter, and discipline, after what they conceived to be the model of the New Testament. They had long been persecuted by grievous impositions, by fines and imprisonments. But it seems that they did not relinquish the principles of a National Church, and of the power of the civil magistrate in matters of faith and worship. We know that in exercising this power our fathers greatly erred, but they erred in common with others of that age. The mild and forbearing principles of toleration were then hardly known, and had seldom been practised.

On the character of the great body of the following list, the compiler has not time nor ability to dwell. With a late writer, he believes that " the early colonists of New-England were on the whole a highly respectable community. Many of them were among the best specimens of what was then, and is now, the better class of society in England—its well educated commoners—men superior, perhaps, to any of their successors in deep and extensive learning, and second to none for fervent piety, for their integrity and disinterested patriotism. But that all the early settlers of New-England were of this description is a supposition which, though it sometimes seems to have been taken for granted, is manifestly absurd. There were some in humble circumstances; poor, but respectable; and there were others needy adventurers, who depended on finding in a remote settlement the subsistence which they were unwilling to procure by honest exertion in their native land."

It is needless to observe to those acquainted with such labour, that much time has been bestowed on the compilation. The colony records of Massachusetts and Plymouth, the county records of Suffolk, Essex, Middlesex, and the ancient county of Norfolk, (now extinct) the ancient records of New-Hampshire, and those of many of the most ancient towns in Massachusetts and Plymouth have been partially examined ; and a large number of books and pamphlets, from which information could be gleaned, have been consulted. The compiler would not pretend that he has personally examined all the records named. It has been principally through the aid afforded by his friends and correspondents in the places where those publick records are kept, that he has been able to avail himself of the facts they contain. To Mr. FRANCIS JACKSON, one of the representatives of Boston, he is particularly indebted, not only for the list of freeman from 1630 to 1662, and the list of representatives or deputies to the General Court of Massachusetts from 1634 to 1692, but for various other information respecting the early families of Boston, and most of the towns in its immediate vicinity. He is also under many obligations for the assistance afforded by their communications, to Mr. JOSHUA COFFIN, of Newbury, Mr. ALONZO LEWIS, of Lynn, Rev. JOSEPH B. FELT, of Hamilton, and Mr. LEMUEL SHATTUCK, of Concord. Had the plan of the work allowed, the authorities for the different facts stated would have been given, but restricted to such narrow limits, it would have been impossible to cite every author, manuscript, and record which have been used. It will be proper to state that the names of the members of the Ancient and Honourable Artillery Company are derived from the history of the company by Z. G. WHITMAN, esq., of Boston.

The authors cited, whose works have been reprinted, are the following, to which is added the edition which has been consulted :

BELKNAP, History of New-Hampshire, 2d edit. 3 vols. Dover, 1812.

CALAMY, Account of Ejected Ministers, &c., 2d edit. 2 vols. 8vo. London, 1713.

CALEF, More Wonders of the Invisible World. Salem edit. 12mo. 1823.

CHURCH, History of King Philip's War, (by S. R. Drake) edit. 12mo. 182-.

DUGDALE, Antiquities of Warwickshire, 2d edit. 2 vols. folio. London, 1730.

HOLMES, American Annals, 2d edit. 2 vols. 8vo. Cambridge, 1829.

HUBBARD, Narrative of Indian Wars, 1st edit. 4to. Boston, 1677.

HUTCHINSON, History of Massachusetts, 3d edit. 2 vols. 8vo Boston, 1795.

JOHNSON, History of New-England, 1st edit. 4to. London, 1654.

LEMPRIERE, Universal Biography, (by E. Lord) 2 vols. 8vo. New-York, 1825.

MATHER, Magnalia Christi Americana, 2d edit. 2 vols. 8vo. Hartford, 1820.

MORTON, New-England's Memorial, (by John Davis) 5th edit. 8vo. Boston, 1826.

NEAL, Hist. of the Puritans, (by Joshua Toulmin, D. D.) 5 vols. 8vo. Newbury-port, 1817.

PRINCE, Annals New-England, 1st edit. 2 vols. 12mo. Boston, 1736 and 1755.

SNOW, History of Boston, 1st edit. 8vo. Boston, 1825.

WINTHROP, History of New-England, (by James Savage) 2 vols. 8vo. Boston, 1825 and 1826.

WOOD, History of the Towns on Long-Island, N. Y., revised edition, 8vo. Brooklyn, N. Y., 1828.

The other works from which information has been drawn will appear in the course of the work.

See additional explanations at the end of the Appendix.

ALPHABETICAL LISTS OF TOWNS,

SETTLED BEFORE 1692 IN THE SEVERAL COLONIES OF NEW-ENGLAND.

The towns in Massachusetts and Plymouth Colonies, with those in Maine, are arranged in the same list. Those in the two are distinguished by P. for Plymouth and M. for Maine. Excepting Falmouth, Saco, Scarborough, and Northfield, it is believed that the following were represented in the first General Court, assembled at Boston, 8 June, 1692, under the province charter, granted by King William and Queen Mary, 7 Oct. 1691.

IN MASSACHUSETTS.

	SETTLED.	INCORP.		SETTLED.	INCORP.
			Hatfield		1670
Amesbury		1668	Haverhill	1641	1645
Andover	1643	1646	Hingham	1633	1635
Attleborough, P.		1694	Hull	1641	1644
Barnstable, P.	1639	1639	Ipswich	1633	1634
Beverly	1626	1668	‡Isles of Shoals, M.		
Billerica	1653	1655	Kittery, M.	1632	
Boston	a. 1626	1630	Lancaster	1643	1653
Boxford		1685	◊Little Compton, P.	1674	1682
Bradford	a. 1643	1675	Lynn	1629	1630
Braintree	1630	1640	Malden	1648	1649
Bridgewater, P.	1651	1656	Manchester	1640	1645
*Bristol, P.			Marblehead	1631	1649
Brookfield	1660	1673	Marlborough		1660
Cambridge	1630	1630	‖Martha's Vineyard		
Charlestown	1628	1629	Marshfield, P.	a. 1640	1640
Chelmsford	1653	1655	Medfield		1651
Concord	1635	1635	Medford	1630	1630
Dartmouth		1664	Mendon	1667	1667
Dedham	1635	1636	Middleborough, P.		1660
Deerfield	a. 1668	1682	Milton		1662
Dorchester	1630	1630	Monamoy, P.		1686
†Dunstable		1673	Nantucket	1659	1659
Duxbury, P.	1637	1637	Newbury	1635	1635
Eastham, P.	1644	1646	Newton		1691
Falmouth, P.		1686	Northampton	1654	1654
Falmouth, M.		1718	Northfield	1673	1713
Freetown, P.		1683	Plymouth, P.	1620	1620
Gloucester	1639	1639	Reading	1640	1644
Groton	a. 1655	1655	Rehoboth, P.	1644	1645
Hadley	1647	1661	Rochester, P.		1686
Harwich		1694	Rowley	1639	1639

* Now belonging to Rhode-Island.
† The greater portion and the principal settlement now in New-Hampshire.
‡ Sent two representatives in 1692.

◊ Now belonging to the State of Rhode-Island.
‖ Comprising Edgartown and Tisbury, both incorporated in 1671.

	SETTLED.	INCORP.
Roxbury	1630	1639
Saco, M.	1635	
Salem	1626	1628
Salisbury	1639	1640
Sandwich, P.		1639
Scarborough, M.		
Scituate, P.	1633	1636
Sherburne		1674
Springfield	1635	1645
Stow		1683
Sudbury	1638	1639
Swanzey, P.		1667
Taunton, P.		1639
Topsfield	1642	1650
Watertown	1630	1630
Wells, M.	1643	
Wenham	1639	1643
Westfield	1659	1669
Weymouth	1624	1635
Woburn	1640	1642
Woodstock		*1686
Worcester	1685	1684
Wrentham		1673
Yarmouth, P.	1639	1639
York, M.	1630	

IN NEW-HAMPSHIRE.

Dover	1623	1633
Exeter	1638	1639
Hampton	1638	1638
Portsmouth	1623	†1653

IN CONNECTICUT 1690.

Branford	1644	
Canterbury	1690	1703
Derby	a. 1660	
Fairfield	1639	
Farmington	1640	

	SETTLED.	INCORP.
Glastonbury		
Guilford	1639	
Greenwich	a. 1640	
Haddam	1663	1668
Hartford	1635	
Killingworth	1663	
Lyme	a. 1636	1667
Middletown	1651	
Milford	1638	
New-Haven	1638	
New-London	1646	
Norwalk	1651	
Norwich	1660	
Plainfield	1689	1699
Pomfret	1686	
Preston	1686	
Saybrook	1635	
Simsbury	1671	
Southbury	1672	
Stamford	1641	
Stonington	1658	
Stratford	1639	
Wallingford	1669	
Waterbury	1686	
Weathersfield	1635	
Windham	1686	1692
Windsor	1635	
Woodbury	1674	

IN RHODE-ISLAND 1690.‡

East-Greenwich	b. 1677	1677
Kingston	a. 1679	1674
Newport	1638	
New-Shoreham		1672
Providence	1636	
Portsmouth	before 1663	
Warwick	1643	
Westerly	1665	

* Granted this year by Massachusetts, and called New-Roxbury. It now belongs to Connecticut, although it paid taxes, and sent representatives to the General Court of Massachusetts until the year 1748.

† By Massachusetts. Until then it had been known by the name of Strawberry-Bank. It had exercised the privileges of a distinct corporation from its early settlement.

‡ The towns of Bristol, Tiverton, and Little-Compton were then settled, but were considered as belonging to Massachusetts and Plymouth.

A

GENEALOGICAL REGISTER

OF THE

FIRST SETTLERS OF NEW-ENGLAND.

EXPLANATIONS.

Those having this mark § were Governours ; those with a † were Deputy Governours ; with a ‡ Assistants ; with a * Representatives of the General Court of Massachusetts ; with a ‖ Members of the Ancient and Honourable Artillery Company. Ministers of the Gospel are in italick capitals. The year following the town denotes the time when first residence (so far as has been ascertained) commenced. The year when first elected Representative, or Assistant, is given, and, in most cases, the whole term of service is mentioned. The abbreviations are ar. co. for member of the Ancient and Honourable Artillery Company ; H. C. for Harvard College ; D. C. for Dartmouth College ; Y. C. for Yale College ; b. for born ; m. for married ; d. for died, &c.

ABBOT, ARTHUR, Marblehead, of which place he was an early inhabitant. Rev. A. Abbot. DANIEL, admitted freeman 18 May, 1631, was of Cambridge in 1634. He was fined five shillings for neglecting his watch in 1630. GEORGE, Rowley, d. 1647, leaving sons, George, of Andover ; Nehemiah, of Ipswich and Rowley ; and Thomas, (who d. without issue) of Rowley. Rev. A. Abbot. GEORGE, Andover, son of the preceding, was born a. 1630, freeman 1675, d. 22 March, 1689, leaving sons, 1. George, b. 8 Feb. 1659, m. Elizabeth Ballard, and had 5 sons ; 2. John, b. 6 Sept. 1662, d. leaving no family ; 3. Nehemiah, b. 31 July, 1667, resided in Andover, was a deacon of the church and representative, d. 8 Oct. 1750 ; Samuel, b. 10 June, 1678 ; and 4 daughters. His widow m. Henry Ingalls. Ibid. GEORGE, came, it is said, from Yorkshire, England, and settled in Andover in 1647, was admitted freeman and d. 4 Jan. 1682, æ. 66. He m. Hannah Chandler in 1647, by whom (who d. June 1711, the widow of Rev. Francis Dane) he had, 1. John, b. 13 March 1648, a deacon of the church, and who d. 30 March, 1721 ; 2. Joseph, who d. young ; 3. Joseph 2d, who was killed by the Indians, 8 April, 1676 ; [see Hubbard's Indian Wars, 83] 4. George, a captain, b. 18 June, 1655, d. 9 March, 1736 ; 5. William, born 29 Nov. 1657, d. 13 Nov. 1713 ; 6. Benjamin, b. 31 Dec. 1662, d. at Andover, 10 April, 1703 ; [see

2   9

Calef's More Wonders] 7. Timothy, b. 28 Nov. 1663, d. 20 Sept.
1730; 8. Thomas, b. 17 May, 1666, d. 9 May, 1728; 9. Edward;
10. Nathaniel, b. 15 July, 1671, d. 12 Dec. 1749, the ancestor of
one branch of the Abbot families in Concord, N. H.; 11. Hannah;
12. Sarah; 13. Elizabeth. Descendants are very numerous. Thirty-
one persons of the name of Abbot had grad. at the N. E. Colleges
in 1828, all of whom descended from the preceding, excepting those
of the name who grad. at H. C. in 1720, 1764, 1787, and 1826.
Ibid. JOSEPH, New-Haven 1683, had a son who settled at Wallingford, Conn. one of whose two sons settled in Ridgefield, Conn.
and was father of Hon. Joel Abbot, M. C. from Georgia. Ibid.
NEHEMIAH, freeman 1669, was son of George Abbot, of Rowley, and resided in Ipswich, and was probably the deacon of Topsfield, chosen 24 May, 1686. Rev. J. B. Felt. ROBERT, Watertown, whose name is *Abbitt* in the colony records, was admitted
freeman in 1634. THOMAS, Andover, a. 1663, had sons, Thomas, Joseph, Nathaniel, and John. WALTER, a vintner of New-
Hampshire in 1640.

ABELL, ROBERT, Weymouth, freeman 1631, had a son Abraham, buried Nov. 1639. Elijah and James Abell grad. at Y. C.
1760 and 1819.

ABINGTON, WILLIAM, Maine 1642. Coffin.

ACRES, JOHN, Boston 1656.

ADAMS, ‖ALEXANDER, Boston, freeman 1648, member of
the ar. co. 1652, m. Mary, sister of Tristram Coffin, and had sons,
John, b. 1652; Samuel, b. 1656, and probably others. CHARLES,
Dover 1665, Oyster-River, now Durham, 1669, was a grand-jury-
man 1688. CHRISTOPHER, was a petitioner, with Henry Adams
sen. and jr., Thomas and Samuel Adams, for land in Massachusetts,
in 1644. Coffin. *EDWARD, Medfield, son of Henry Adams,
senior, was admitted freeman in 1654, and was probably the representative at two sessions of the court in May, 1689. His wife was
Lydia, and his children were, Jonathan, b. 4 April, 1655; Eliashib,
b. 1658; James, b. 4 Jan. 1662; Elizabeth, who d. 1661; Elisha,
and perhaps others. FERDINANDO, Dedham, freeman 1640, had
permission to go to England in 1641; [Worthington, Hist. Dedham,
103] but if he went thither at that time, he probably returned, as
his son Nathaniel was b. 16 March, 1643. HENRY, Braintree,
came from Devonshire, England, it is said by Alden and others,
in 1630, but probably not so early; settled at Braintree, where he
d. 8 Oct. 1646, leaving sons, Henry, Samuel, Thomas, Peter, Joseph, Edward, and two others. To his memory is erected in Quincy, by his illustrious descendant, John Adams, a monument with an
inscription, from which the following is extracted : " In memory of
HENRY ADAMS, who took his flight from the Dragon persecution, in
Devonshire, England, and alighted with eight sons near Mount Wollaston. One of the sons returned to England, and, after taking some
time to explore the country, four removed to Medfield and the
neighbouring towns; two to Chelmsford. One only, Joseph, who
lies here at his left hand, remained here, who was an original [?] pro-

ADAMS.

prietor in the township of Braintree, incorporated in 1639." ‖*HEN-
RY, son of the preceding, was of Braintree in 1640, but removed
to Medfield as early as 1649, where he was town clerk, and representative in 1659, 1665, 1674, and 1675. He was also a lieutenant, and perhaps the same mentioned by Increase Mather, in his
Hist. of Philip's war, as being killed at his own door by the Indians,
21 Feb. 1676, whose wife was soon after accidentally killed by an
Englishman. He m. Elizabeth Paine, 17 Nov. 1643, and his children were, Eleazar, b. 5 August, 1644; Jasper, b. 23 June, 1647;
both at Braintree; Elizabeth, b. 11 Nov. 1649; John, b. 14 July,
1652; Moses, b. 26 Oct. 1654; Henry, b. 19 Nov. 1657, and Samuel, b. 10 Dec. 1661, the last five at Medfield. JEREMY, Cambridge 1632, [1 Coll. Mass. Hist. Soc. vii. 10.] may have accompanied the first emigrants to Connecticut. JOHN, Plymouth 1621,
came over in the ship Fortune in 1621, d. in 1633. James Adams,
his son, m. Frances, daughter of William Vassall, and d. at sea in
1651, on board the James, of London, leaving a son William, born
at Scituate, 13 March, 1648, and other children. JOHN, Cambridge, whose wife was Anne, had children, Rebecca, born in England; Mary; John, b. 1 May, 1653; Joseph; Hannah; Daniel, 1662.
There was a John Adams of Concord, in 1650, and of Chelmsford
in 1654 [Shattuck] who is supposed to have been one of the 8 sons
of Henry Adams. JOSEPH, son of Henry Adams, was b. in England in 1626, settled in Braintree, (now Quincy) and was admitted
freeman in 1653, d. 6 Dec. 1696, æ. 68. He m. Abigail Baxter,
[Alden erroneously says *Mary*] 26 Nov. 1650, by whom, who d. 27
Aug. 1692, æ. 58, he had, 1. Henry, [?] b. 13 Nov. 1652; 2. Joseph,
b. 24 Dec. 1654; 3. John, who d. Feb. 1657; 4 and 5. John and
Bethia, (twins) b. 8 Dec. 1661; 6. Samuel, b. Sept. 1665; 7. Peter, b. 7 Feb. 1670; 8. Jonathan, b. 31 Jan. 1671; 9. Deliverance;
10. Mary. Joseph, the 2d child, m. Hannah, daughter of John Bass,
and d. 12 Feb. 1737, æ. 82, leaving several children, of whom
John, b. 8 Feb. 1692, was a deacon of the church of Braintree, and
d. 25 May, 1761, æ. 69, the father of the patriot of the revolution,
and second president of the U. S., and Joseph, b. 1 Jan. 1689 or
1690, grad. at H. C. 1710; was the minister of Newington, N. H.
from 16 Nov. 1715 to his death, 26 May, 1783. This family still
retains the paternal seat at Quincy. It has been rendered illustrious,
by having furnished two presidents of our country, who, with their
distant relative, Gov. Samuel Adams, will ever be remembered by
the friends of our civil and political institutions. NATHANIEL,
Weymouth 1642, had a son Abraham, b. 16 Jan. 1643. NATHAN-
IEL, Boston, freeman 1647, had a wife Mary, and children, Nathaniel, b. 10 Sept. 1653; David, b. 30 June, 1659; Joseph, b. 19 Dec.
1661; Benjamin, b. 10 Dec. 1665, and daughters, Mary, Sarah,
and Elizabeth. A Nathaniel Adams d. at Boston, 30 March, 1690.
PETER, Medfield, freeman 1650, son of Henry Adams, had children
by Rachel his wife, Hannah, b. 1658; Jonathan, b. 1663; Jonathan, 2d b. 15 May, 1664, and others. PHILIP, Massachusetts,
was admitted freeman in 1652. *RICHARD, Weymouth, free-

11

man 1635, representative at two sessions, Nov. 1637 and March, 1638, had a son Samuel, b. 6 June, 1639, and daughters Sarah and Ruth. RICHARD, Salem 1637, may have d. at Malden, 6 Oct. 1674. ROBERT, was b. in 1601, and came from Holderness, in Yorkshire, or as others say from some place in Devonshire, and settled at Newbury before 1649, where he d. 12 Oct. 1681. He was a tailor by occupation. Coffin. SAMUEL, one of the 8 sons of Henry Adams, was admitted freeman 1643, was of Charlestown, where his son Samuel was b. 3 July, 1647; removed to Chelmsford, where he was a captain and d. 24 Jan. 1688, over 70 years. He or his son Samuel m. Hester Sparhawk, 7 May, 1668. *THOMAS, brother of the preceding, was of Braintree in 1642, where his daughter Mary was b. 24 July, 1643; removed to Concord, and had sons, Jonathan and Pelatiah, (twins) b. 1646; Timothy, b. 1648; George, b. 1650; removed to Chelmsford, where he was the first town clerk, and representative at the second session in 1673, and d. 20 July, 1688, æ. 76. WILLIAM, Cambridge, 1635, freeman 1639, may have removed to Ipswich, where was a William Adams, who d. in 1661, and who was probably father of William Adams, jr. who d. in Jan. 1659. The senior left a son Nathaniel. Samuel Adams was of Ipswich in 1665. *WILLIAM*, the first graduate at H. C. of the name of Adams, was the second minister of Dedham; grad. 1671, was ordained 3 Dec. 1673, d. 17 August, 1685. Worthington, Hist. Dedham, 104.

ADDINGTON, ISAAC, Boston was admitted freeman 1650. Whitman gives the name of Israel Addington, member of the ar. co. in 1652. ‡*ISAAC, Boston, son of the preceding, was b. in Boston, 22 Jan. 1645, admitted freeman 1673, was representative and speaker of the house, 1685, assistant 1686, and many years secretary of the province under the new charter. He d. 19 March, 1715, æ. 70, and his funeral was attended by 20 of the counsellors of the province.

AGAR, WILLIAM. (See AUGER.)

AINSWORTH, DANIEL, Roxbury, d. 13 Nov. 1680.

ALBEE, BENJAMIN, Braintree 1641, freeman 1642, was of Medfield in 1653, where his son Benjamin was b. that year. He had daughters born in 1641 and 1642. Whitney [Hist. Quincy] spells this name *Alber*. JOHN, Salem 1637, freeman 1643. d. in 1690. A John Albee was of Braintree in 1640, whose servant Francis Brown d. that year.

ALBOROW, ‡JOHN, Rhode-Island, was one of Sir Edmund Andros' council 1687. Hutchinson, i. Hist. Mass. 317.

ALCOCK, *GEORGE, Roxbury, freeman 1631, was a deacon of the church, and a representative at the first general court, 14 May, 1634. He d. 30 Dec. 1640. JOHN, son of Deacon George Alcock, grad. at H. C. 1646, lived in Roxbury, and is believed to have been a physician. His son George was born 25 March, 1655, graduated at H. C. 1673, and died before 1699. JOHN and SAMUEL, were of Kittery, and admitted freemen in 1652. SAMUEL, grad. at Harvard College in 1659, was admitted freeman 1676, and

d. before 1698. THOMAS, Boston, freeman 1631, d. 14 Sept. 1657. His son John was b. 2 July, 1651. THOMAS, Dedham, freeman 1635, had 4 daughters b. between 1638 and 1644.

ALCOT, JOHN, is named by Douglas as one of the first council under the charter of William and Mary 1692.

ALDEN, ‡DAVID, Duxbury, son of the following, was a representative several years ; an assistant of Plymouth colony in 1690 ; had sons, Benjamin and Samuel, and one daughter Alice, the wife of Judah Paddock, of Yarmouth.   ‡JOHN, one of the first pilgrims of Plymouth 1620, and one of the first settlers of Duxbury 1640, was representative 1641 to 1649 ; an assistant of Plymouth colony from 1633 to 1639, excepting 1637, and from 1651 to 1686, excepting 1653, in all, 42 years. He m. Priscilla, daughter of William Mullins, and his children were, 1. John ; (see next article) 2. Joseph of Duxbury, who d. 8 Feb. 1697, aged a. 73, leaving Isaac, Joseph, and John ; 3. David, above named ; 4. Jonathan, of Duxbury, who d. Feb. 1697, æ. about 70, leaving Andrew, Jonathan, John, and Benjamin ; 5. Elizabeth, who m. William Paybody, of Little-Compton ; 6. Sarah, who m. Alexander Standish ; 7. Ruth, who m. John Bass, of Braintree ; 8. Mary, who m. Thomas Delano. John Alden d. 12 Sept. 1687, aged a. 89. An elegy on his death is in the iii. vol. of Alden's Collection of Epitaphs, 271—274. JOHN, son of the preceding, went from Duxbury to Boston as early as 1659, and d. 14 March, 1702. His children were, John, b. 1663 ; William, b. 1664 ; William, 2d, b. 5 March, 1666 ; Nathaniel ; Zechariah, b. 18 Feb. 1673, grad. at H. C. 1692 ; Anna ; Elizabeth. He is named in ii. Hutchinson ; iii. Alden ; in Hubbard ; and in Calef.

ALDERMAN, JOHN, Salem 1637, freeman 1639, was admitted to the church 17 Feb. 1637, d. 1657. One Alderman of Bear-Cove is mentioned by Winthrop under 1634.

ALDIS, NATHAN, Dedham, freeman 1640, was deacon of the church, and d. 15 March, 1676.

ALDRIDGE, HENRY, Dedham 1644, freeman 1645, d. 23 Feb. 1646. His son Samuel was b. 10 March, 1644. GEORGE, Dorchester, freeman 1636, removed to Braintree, and had born there, sons, John, 2 April, 1644 ; Peter, 14 April, 1648 ; Jacob, 28 Feb. 1653 ; Mattithijah, 10 June, 1656, and several daughters.

ALEWORTH, FRANCIS, freeman 1631, was chosen lieutenant at a court of assistants, [Prince, ii. Annals, 32] but returned to England in March, 1632. ROBERT, Pemaquid 1631.

ALEXANDER, GEORGE, was one of the first proprietors of Northampton 1653. Nathaniel Alexander d. at Hadley, 29 Oct. 1742, æ. 90 1-2 years.

ALFORD, WILLIAM, Salem 1657, and perhaps as early as 1637. Felt, Annals Salem, iii. WILLIAM, Boston, had a son John b. 1658.

ALLEN, ANDREW, Lynn 1642, m. Faith Ingalls, and went to Andover. Sixty-five persons of the name of Allen had grad. at the N. E. Colleges in 1825, of whom 17 have been clergymen. ||*BO-

ALLEN.

ZOUN, came from Lynn, England, and settled at Hingham as early as 1638, was a representative 1643, 8 years, and member of the ar. co. 1650. Lincoln says he was "often a deputy, a military officer, and an influential citizen of Hingham." He removed to Boston, and there d. 14 Sept. 1652. His widow m. Joseph Jewett, of Rowley, 13 May, 1653. Bozoun Allen, his son, was representative of Boston a number of years. EDWARD, Ipswich, came from Scotland to N. E. in 1636, m. a Kimball, and had 15 sons and 3 daughters [MS. letter of Hon. Joseph C. Allen.] Hubbard mentions the burning of his barn by lightning, in 1670. Hist. N. E. 628. GEORGE, Weymouth 1641, was admitted freeman in 1645. A George Allen of Lynn 1636, is supposed to have removed to Sandwich. HENRY, a joiner of Boston, was admitted to the church in 1645, freeman 1648, was probably the deacon who d. at Boston, 6 Jan. 1696. Henry Allen was representative for Rowley in 1674. JAMES, minister of the first church in Boston, was A. M. at New College, Oxford, and one of the ejected ministers. He came to N. E. in 1662, admitted freeman 1665; was installed 9 Dec. 1668, d. 22 Sept. 1710, æ. 78. John Dunton, in his journal, says a son of Mr. Allen was a minister in England, and d. in Northampton. James Allen, perhaps another son, grad. at H. C. 1687. James Allen, grandson of Rev. James, of Boston, grad. at H. C. 1717, was a preacher, and d. 8 Jan. 1755, in his 58th year. Allen, Biog. Dict. 2 Coll. Mass. Hist. Soc. ii. 101. Winthrop, MS. Catalogue. JAMES, Dedham 1639, Medfield 1652, freeman, 1647, had children, John, b. 4 Dec. 1639; Sarah, b. 1644; Joseph, 24 June, 1652. JOHN, Scituate 1633. ||*JOHN, Charlestown, freeman 1640, member of the ar. co. 1639; captain; representative 1668, had a son John, b. 16 Oct. 1640. JOHN, Newbury, had sons, John, b. 1656; Samuel, b. 1658. ‡JOHN, was a magistrate of New-Haven colony 1662; of Connecticut 1665; was one of Sir Edmund Andros' council in 1687. ‡*MATTHEW, Cambridge 1632, freeman 1635, representative 1636. He probably removed to Connecticut, where one of this name was magistrate or assistant in 1658 and 1665, and in various other offices. Mather spells the name *Allyn*, but Trumbull writes the name of both Matthew and John, *Allen*. ROBERT, Salem 1637, was received as a member the church, 15 May, 1642. A Robert Allyn was of New-London in 1648. SAMUEL, Braintree, freeman 1635, had a daughter, b. in March, 1639. SAMUEL, Northampton, a. 1666, freeman 1683, d. about the year 1722. [MS. letter of Pres. Allen] His son, deacon Samuel Allen, b. 1688, d. 1739, was the ancestor of Rev. Thomas Allen, H. C. 1762, minister of Pittsfield, Ms. who was b. 17 Jan. 1743, d. 11 Feb. 1810, æ. 67, leaving several sons, of whom is William Allen, D. D., president of Bowdoin College. SAMUEL, Bridgewater, m. a daughter of George Partridge, and has a great number of descendants. *THOMAS*, minister of Charlestown, came to N. E. in 1638, was admitted a member of Boston church, 27 Jan. 1639, and the same year settled at Charlestown. He returned to England, and d. 21 Sept. 1673, æ. 65. Allen, Biog. Dict. TIMOTHY, Marblehead 1648. WALTER, Newbury 1640, perhaps the one who d. at Charlestown, 8 July, 1681. His son Benjamin was b. 1647. WILLIAM, Salem 1627, was born a. 1602, came to N. E. in 1626, and was living in 1664. He had sons, Samuel, b. 8 Jan. 1631 ; Onesiphorus, b. 6 June 1642 ; and several daughters b. between 1630 and 1640. His wife d. in March, 1632, and he m. again. One of this name was one of the first proprietors of Newbury.

ALLERTON, ‡ISAAC, one of the first pilgrims at Plymouth 1620, was an assistant in 1621, lost his wife, 21 Feb. 1621. Hutchinson says the male posterity of this pilgrim settled in Maryland. There appears to have been an Isaac Allerton in Marblehead, in 1648, [Dana] and one in New-Haven in 1650. [Dodd.] Isaac Allerton, the graduate at H. C. in 1650, was probably son of the assistant, or of John Allerton, who was at Plymouth in 1620. 2 Coll. Mass. Hist. Soc. x. Index. Davis, Morton's Memo.

ALLEY, HUGH, Lynn 1650, had a son Hugh. Lewis. JOHN, Lynn 1650, had sons John and Hugh. Ibid.

ALLIN, JOHN, the first minister of Dedham, came to N. E. and was admitted freeman 1638, was ordained 24 April, 1639, and d. 26 August, 1675, æ. 75. A son John is recorded as being b. 4 Dec. 1639. Allen, Biog. Dict. Worthington, Hist. Dedham. 47—49. *JOHN*, was in the second class of graduates, 1643, went to England, and was minister of Great-Yarmouth, in Norfolk, and d. of the plague in 1665.

ALLING, JAMES, the third minister of Salisbury, grad. at H. C. 1679, succeeded Rev. John Wheelright, and d. 3 March, 1696, æ. 37. A Francis Alling d. at Roxbury, 1 Dec. 1692, and a Samuel Alling was of Conn. in 1675, where the name still exists.

ALLIS, WILLIAM, a deacon of the church in Braintree, was admitted freeman 1640, and d. 12 Oct.1653. His sons were, John, b. 5 March, 1642 ; Samuel b. 24 Feb. 1647 ; Josiah, b. 20 Oct. 1651 ; William b. 10 Jan. 165–. Rev. Samuel Allis, H. C. 1724, of Somerset, Conn. was probably of this family.

ALLISON, JAMES, Boston 1644, had a son James, b. in 1650.

ALLISTRE, PAUL, Boston 1650.

ALLYNE, *EDWARD, Watertown, thence to Dedham, was admitted freeman in 1638, was one of the founders of the church, 8 Nov. 1638, representative 1639—1642, 4 years, d. at Boston, 8 Sept. 1642. He wrote his name as above. Worthington, Hist. Dedham, 47. 101. WILLIAM, Massachusetts, was admitted freeman in 1642.

ALMY, WILLIAM, Lynn 1636, Sandwich 1637. Lewis.

ALVORD, ALEXANDER, settled at Northampton as early as 1659. Six of this name had received the honours of the N. E. colleges in 1828.

AMADOWN, ROGER, Salem 1637, Weymouth 1640, Boston 1643.

AMBLER, RICHARD, Watertown, 1639, had a son Abraham b. in 1642.

AMBROSE, HENRY, freeman 1642, appears to have been an early proprietor of Hampton, but was of Boston in 1654, and was living in 1679. His wife was Susanna. A daughter Abigail was b. in 1654. *JOSHUA*, grad. at H. C. 1653, went to England, and was admitted to the degree of A. M. at Oxford. He settled, according to Calamy, at Darby, in Lancashire, from whence he was ejected. Calamy, ii. Account, 419. From Mather's catalogue, it appears that he was living in 1697. *NEHEMIAH*, grad. 1653 at H. C., of which he was a fellow. He went to England, and was settled at Kirkby, in Lancashire, from whence he was ejected after the restoration. Calamy.

AMEREDITH, JOHN, was an inhabitant of Kittery in 1688.

AMES, JOHN, son of Richard Ames, of Bruton, in Somersetshire, came to N. E. and settled at Bridgewater, and died leaving no children. WILLIAM, Braintree, 1641, brother of the preceding, was admitted freeman 1647, unless the following was the freeman, and d. 11 March, 1654. His son John, b. 24 May, 1647, settled in Bridgewater, and had 5 sons, John, Nathaniel, Thomas, William, and David. Nathaniel, who was b. 1677, and died in 1736, was father of Dr. Nathaniel Ames, long known by the reputation of his almanacks, which were published 40 years successively. Dr. Ames was b. in 1708, and d. in 1765, leaving several sons liberally educated, of whom the distinguished orator, Fisher Ames, LL. D., was one, several of whose sons have grad. at H. C. Those who have given notices of this eminent statesman [Pres. Kirkland, in his elegant sketch of his life and character, and Dr. Holmes, ii. Annals, 440] mistake in deducing his descent from the author of the Medulla Theologiæ. *WILLIAM*, son of Rev. William Ames, D. D. professor of the university of Francker, in Holland, who d. in Nov. 1633, æ. 57, grad. at H. C. 1645, went to England, and was the minister of Wrentham, where he d. in 1689, æ. 66. His mother, Joane Ames, came to N. E., lived sometime in Salem, and d. at Cambridge, 23 Dec. 1644.

AMSDEN, ISAAC, Cambridge, d. 7 April, 1659. He had a son Jacob, b. in 1657.

ANDERSON, GAWEN, Massachusetts, was admitted freeman in 1640. There was a John Anderson of Boston in 1647, and one of the same name at Ipswich in 1665.

ANDREW, SAMUEL, Cambridge 1654, was son of Mr. William Andrew, [Cambridge Chh. records] and by Elizabeth, his wife, had sons, Samuel, b. 1656; William, b. June, 1658; John, b. 2 March, 1652; Thomas, b. 1665; Thomas, 2d, b. 1668. *SAMUEL*, minister of Milford, Conn. was son of the preceding, and was b. 29 Jan. 1656, grad. at H. C. 1675, was ord. 18 Nov. 1685, and d. 24 Jan. 1738, æ. 82. WILLIAM, a schoolmaster of Ipswich and other places, d. 19 July, 1683.

ANDREWS, *DANIEL, was a representative of Salem-Village in 1689. JOHN, Ipswich, probably the freeman of 1642, had a son John of Ipswich in 1642 and 1687. [See Revolution in N. E. justified, 14.] There was a John Andrews, of Lynn in 1650, who d.

in 1662, and a John Andrews, of Boston, had sons, John b. 21
Nov. 1656; James b. 1 Dec. 1664, and Edmund, b. 1665. *JO-
SEPH, Hingham 1635, freeman 1636, was the first town clerk, and
representative 3 years from 1636 to 1638. Lincoln, Hist. Hingham,
42, 163. RICHARD, Ipswich, died a. 1644, leaving a son John.
ROBERT, Ipswich, was admitted freeman in 1635. SAMUEL,
Cambridge. (See ANDREW.) THOMAS, Hingham 1635, and
perhaps the representative in 1678. There was a Captain Thomas
Andrews, of Hingham, whose son Jedediah was b. 7 July, 1674,
grad. at H. C. 1695, and was minister in Philadelphia. Lincoln,
Hist. Hingham, 116. THOMAS, of Cambridge 1646, and a proprietor of Watertown, had a daughter Rebecca, b. 18 April, 1646.
WILLIAM, Lynn 1634. There were three of the name of William Andrews, who were admitted freemen in 1634, 1635, and
1640, one of whom was of Cambridge in 1635; the preceding of
Lynn in 1634, and the other may have been the schoolmaster, William Andrew, or William Andrews, of New-Haven in 1639.

ANDROS, ∫EDMUND, Boston, was appointed, by James II,
governour for the whole of N. E. and arrived at Boston, 20 Dec.
1686, and remained in office, exercising an oppressive and tyrannical
sway over the people, until 18 April, 1689, when he was seized by
the inhabitants around Boston, and confined; and the next year was
sent to England for trial. He escaped publick censure, and was
appointed governour of Virginia in 1692. He is said to have d. in
London, 24 Feb. 1714.

ANGIER, *ARTHUR, was representative of Scarborough in
1671 and 1672. A Lieutenant Andrew Angier, of Scarborough, is
mentioned by Hubbard, Hist. N. E. 600. EDMUND, Cambridge
1636, freeman 1640, m. Ruth, daughter of Rev. William Ames,
D. D., and had children, Ruth, Ephraim, Samuel, (see following
article) and John, b. 21 June, 1656. His wife d. 3 July, 1656, and
he m. Ann Pratt, 12 June, 1657, and had Edmund, b. 20 Sept.
1659; Hannah, b. 1660; Mary, b. 1663; John, b. May, 1664;
Nathaniel, b. May, 1665; and Elizabeth. JOHN, graduated at H. C.
in 1653. SAMSON, Kittery, was admitted freeman in 1652.
SAMUEL, minister of Rehoboth and Waltham, was son of Edmund Angier, and was b. at Cambridge, 17 March, 1655, grad. at
H. C. 1673, was ord. at Rehoboth, 15 Oct. 1679, from whence he
was dismissed; was installed at Waltham, 25 May, 1697, d. 24 Jan.
1719, æ. 65. Two of his sons were Ames, b. at Rehoboth, 29
June, 1681, grad. at H. C. 1701, and John, H. C. 1720, the minis-
ter of East-Bridgewater, who d. 14 April, 1787, æ. 86. Samuel and
Oakes Angier, who grad. at H. C. 1763 and 1764, were sons of
Rev. John Angier.

ANNABLE, ANTHONY, came to Plymouth in 1621, in the
ship Fortune, was one of the first settlers of Scituate 1633, removed
to Barnstable, and d. 1673. 2 Coll. Mass. Hist. Soc. x. Index.
JOHN, Ipswich, 1648, d. 8 Oct. 1664. [Coffin.] John Annable
H. C. 1744, was a native of Ipswich, became a preacher and d. 18
April, 1762, æ. 41.

3   17

APPLEGATE, THOMAS,Weymouth 1641. Coffin.

APPLETON, *SAMUEL, a descendant of John Appleton, who d. at Great-Waldingfield, in Suffolk, England, in 1436, was b. at Little-Waldingfield in 1586, came to N. E. in 1635, and settled at Ipswich. He was admitted freeman in May, 1636, and was representative at the May and Sept. sessions of the general court in 1637. He d. in June, 1670, leaving John, Samuel, (see next articles) Sarah, who m. Rev. Samuel Phillips; Judith, who m. Samuel, son of Rev. N. Rogers; and Martha, who m. Richard Jacob. Eight of his descendants of the family name had grad. at H. C. in 1828, besides 6 at Dartmouth and Bowdoin. *JOHN, Ipswich, son of the preceding, was b. at Little-Waldingfield, in 1622. He was elected representative 19 years between 1656 and 1679, and was a captain at Ipswich. He was fined and imprisoned under the administration of Sir Edmund Andros, for resisting the principle of taxation without representation—probably one of the first instances in the annals of N. England. He d. in 1700, æ. 78. He m. Priscilla, daughter of Rev. Jesse Glover, by whom he had two sons, John, b. 1652, and Jesse, or Jose, b. 1660, a merchant in Boston, who d. 1721, cœlebs. John, a counsellor under the charter of William and Mary, and 20 years judge of probate for Essex, m. Elizabeth, daughter of President Rogers, and d. in 1739, leaving Nathaniel, b. 9 Dec. 1693; Daniel, the register of probate in Essex; and 3 daughters. Nathaniel grad. at H. C. 1712, was ordained at Cambridge, 9 Oct. 1717, and d. 9 Feb. 1784, æ. 91, having had educated at H. C. Nathaniel, A. A. S. in 1749, a loan officer, who d. 1798; John, 1757, a merchant of Salem, who d. March, 1817, æ. 62, and Henry, 1755, a merchant of Portsmouth, who d. 5 Sept. 1768, æ. 31. Nathaniel W., H. C. 1773, was son of Nathaniel, A. A. S., and d. 16 April, 1795, æ. 40. ‡*SAMUEL, Ipswich, brother of the preceding, was b. at Little-Waldingfield, in 1625, was representative in 1669, 1675, 1677, and 1680, captain of the militia; a major, and the commander in chief in Philip's war 1676. He was elected assistant from 1681 to 1686, six years, and was one of the first council under the charter of William and Mary 1692, d. 15 May, 1696, æ. 70. He m. (1) Hannah, daughter of William Paine, and had issue; (2) Mary, daughter of John Oliver, 2 Dec. 1656. She was b. 7 June, 1640. [Newbury records.] By both he had sons, 1. Samuel, b. 1654, a merchant of Boston, one of the council most of the time from 1703 to 1714, a colonel and commissioner at Quebec; 2. John, who left issue; 3. Isaac, a major, b. 1664, m. Priscilla Baker, a grand-daughter of Dep. Gov. Symonds, and d. 1747; 4. Oliver, of Haverhill, who left issue; and 3 daughters. Isaac had 6 daughters, and one son, Isaac, who was b. 1704, and d. at Ipswich 1794, having had sons, 1. Isaac, of New-Ipswich, b. 1731, d. 1806, the father of Samuel, Nathan, and Ebenezer Appleton, distinguished merchants of Boston; 2. Francis, of New-Ipswich, the father of Rev. Jesse Appleton. D. D., president of Bowdoin College, b. 17 Nov. 1772, grad. at D. C. 1792, and d. at Brunswick, 12 Nov. 1819; 3. Samuel; 4. Thomas; 5. John; 6. Daniel; 7. William; 8. Jo-

seph, Brown Univ. 1772, the minister of North-Brookfield, Ms., ord.
30 Nov. 1776, d. 24 July, 1795.   The 4, 5, and 6, settled in Maine;
William d. young in Portsmouth.

ARCHER, HENRY, Ipswich 1641.   Six of this name had grad.
at New-Jersey and the N. E. Colleges in 1828.   SAMUEL, a carpenter, who requested freedom 1630, lived in Salem, and d. in 1667,
aged a. 60.   Hubbard, [Indian Wars] mentions a Layton Archer,
and his son of Rhode-Island, who were killed by the Indians, 25
June, 1675.

ARMITAGE, GODFREY, Lynn 1634, Boston, freeman 1638,
had sons, Samuel, b. 7 Oct. 1645 ; Samuel, 2d, b. 1651.   JOSEPH,
Lynn 1637, d. 27 June, 1680, æ. 80.   Lewis.   MANASSEH,
grad. at H. C. 1660, and d. before 1698.   Mather, ii. Magnalia, 24.
THOMAS, Lynn 1635, removed to Sandwich 1637.   Lewis.

ARMSTRONG, GREGORY, Plymouth, died in 1650.   2 Coll.
Mass. Hist. Soc. iii. 184, 185.

ARNOLD, BENEDICT, Providence 1639, was president of
Rhode-Island in 1663, and continued in office 8 years.   He d. in
1678.   EDWARD, Boston, d. 8 August, 1657.   Son Barachiah, b.
in 1653. ||JOHN, Cambridge, freeman 1635, member of the ar.
co. 1644, was probably the same who owned an estate in Boston.
JOSEPH, Braintree 1658, had sons born there.   RICHARD,
Rhode-Island, was one of Sir Edmund Andros' council 1687.
Hutchinson, i. Hist. Mass. 317.   SAMUEL, the first minister of
Rochester, Mass. was ordained in 1684, and d. before 1717.   2.
Coll. Mass. Hist. Soc. iv. 259, 262.   THOMAS, Watertown, free-
man 1640, had sons, Ichabod, b. 1640, Richard, b. 1642.   WIL-
LIAM, Hingham, 1635, perhaps one of the founders of the first
Baptist Church in Rhode-Island.

ASHBY, ANTHONY, Salem 1665.   2 Coll. Mass. Hist. Soc.
viii. 106.

ASHLEY, ROBERT, Springfield 1639.   David Ashley, perhaps
a son, was one of the settlers of Westfield, Ms., as early as 1666,
and is the ancestor of several distinguished men.   Emerson Davis,
Hist. Westfield.

ASLETT, JOHN, Newbury, m. Rebecca Ayer in 1648.

ASPINWALL, PETER, Muddy River [Brookline, Ms.] 1653,
came from Lancashire, England, and is the ancestor of the respectable family bearing this name in Massachusetts.   Savage, i. Win-
hrop, 33.   Snow, Hist. Boston, 137.   *||WILLIAM, Boston, was
on a jury, 28 Sept. 1630; representative 1637; member of the
ar. co. 1643; was afterwards of Watertown.   He removed to
Rhode-Island, and was the first secretary of the colony, but returned to Boston, and finally to England, where he died.   His children
recorded in Boston records, were Edward, b. and d. 1630; Hannah, b. 25 Dec. 1631; Elizabeth, (the name of his wife) b. 30
Sept. 1633; Samuel. b. 30 Sept. 1635; Ethlan, b. 1 March, 1637;
Dorcas, b. 14 Feb. 1640.   Savage, i. Winthrop, 33.   2. Coll. Mass.
Hist. Soc. x. Index.

ASTWOOD, JAMES, Dorchester, freeman 1639, was probably one of the founders of the 2d church in Boston. Sons, John, and Joseph were b. in 1640 and 1644. ‡JOHN, Massachusetts, freeman in 1636, removed to New-Haven colony, and settled at Milford as early as 1639, and was elected one of the assistants or magistrates in 1653.

ATHERTON, ‡‖*HUMPHREY, Dorchester, came, it is supposed, from Lancashire; was admitted freeman 1636; member of the ar. co. 1638, its captain in 1650; representative 1638, nine years, until 1651; assistant 1654 to 1661, eight years, major-general on the death of Robert Sedgwick in 1656. He d. 17 Sept. (" about one o'clock, A. M." says a manuscript note of John Hull) 1661. Boston records also say he d. the 17th, although the inscription copied into Alden's Coll. of Epitaphs, says the 16th. Tradition reports his death to have been caused by a fall from his horse, in consequence of riding over a cow, while attending a military review on Boston common. His children were, Jonathan; Rest, b. 1639; Increase, b. 1641; Thankful, b. 1644; Hope, b. 1646; Consider; Watching, b. 1651; Patience, b. 1654. Johnson describes Major Atherton as " one of a cheerful spirit, and intire for the country." His descendants still remain in the county of Norfolk. *HOPE*, minister of Hatfield, was son of the preceding, and was baptized at Dorchester, 30 August, 1646. He grad. in 1665, at H. C. in the catalogue of which his name is *Sperantius*. He was a chaplain of the forces under Captain Turner, in Philip's war, and was at the battle of the falls of Montague, Ms., 18 May, 1676, and was lost in the woods in the retreat of the troops, but finally returned in safety to Hatfield. The tradition in the family reports that he became deranged. JAMES, an inhabitant of Dorchester, of Lancaster in 1654, of Milton in 1678, and subsequently of Sherburne, where he d. in 1707. He had sons, James, b. 13 May, 1654, and Joshua, b. 13 May, 1656, both b. at Lancaster. Joshua m. Mary Culliver, of Milton, and their sixth son, Peter, b. 12 April, 1705, a colonel and magistrate, of Harvard, Ms., was father of the Hon. Joshua Atherton, H. C. 1762, a senator, and attorney general of New-Hampshire, and Dr. Israel Atherton, H. C. 1762, of Lancaster, Ms., who d. in July, 1822, æ. 82. Joshua, who d. 3 April, 1809, was father of Hon. Charles H. Atherton, H. C. 1794, of Amherst, N. H., member of congress from New-Hampshire from 1815 to 1817.

ATKINS, ‖ABRAHAM, was a member of the ar. co. in 1642. Three of the name of Dudley Atkins grad. at H. C. in 1748, 1781, and 1816, the second of whom is now Dudley Atkins Tyng, a distinguished gentleman of Newburyport. Two of the name of Elisha Atkins have grad. at Y. C. and one at Brown Univ.

ATKINSON, JOHN, Newbury 1663, son of the following, m. Sarah Mireck, 27 April, 1664. His sons were, Thomas, b. 27 Dec. 1669, possibly the graduate at H. C. 1691; Theodore, b. 1672, drowned 1685; Samuel, b. 16 Jan. 1676; Nathaniel, b. 29 Nov.

1677; Joseph, b. 1 May, 1682. He had also several daughters. ‖THEODORE, came from Bury, in Lancashire, a. 1634, and settled at Boston; became a member of the ar. co. 1644, and d. in August, 1701, æ. 90. Theodore, his son, who was b. 10 April, 1644, had a son Theodore, b. 3 Oct. 1669, and d. at Boston in May, 1676. Nathaniel, another son, was b. 28 Oct. 1645, and grad. at H. C. 1667, and d. before 1698. Theodore, the third in succession, and b. in 1669, was a counsellor of N. H., and d. in 1719, æ. 55, leaving a son, Theodore, who was b. at New-Castle, N. H., 20 Dec. 1697, grad. at H. C. 1718, was a counsellor, judge, and secretary of N. H., and d. 22 Sept. 1779, æ. 82, having had a son Theodore, H. C. 1759, a counsellor of N. H., who d. before his father, 28 Oct. 1765, without issue. THOMAS, freeman 1636, lived in Boston, and also in Concord, where he died a. 1646. Two of his children were, Susanna, who m. Caleb Brooks in 1660, and Hannah, b. in 1643. THOMAS, Plymouth 1638. Davis, Morton's Memo. 384.

ATWATER, JOSHUA, was elected an assistant or magistrate of Connecticut in 1658. Eleven of the name had grad. at the N. E. Colleges in 1828.

ATWELL, BENJAMIN, Maine 1675. Hubbard, Wars with the Eastern Indians, 33. Two of the name of Atwell have grad. in N. E., both at Brown Univ.

ATWOOD, ‖HARMAN, Massachusetts, member of the ar. co. 1644, was admitted freeman in 1645. Thomas Atwood, of Mass., d. 3 April, 1694. Philip Atwood was one of the first proprietors of Bradford, Ms., and John Atwood, from Boston, was there early in the last century. Four of the name had grad. at Yale College in 1827. JOHN, Plymouth, was an assistant of Plymouth colony in 1638, and d. in 1644, having brought to N. E. a large estate. Davis, Morton's Memo. 121. WILLIAM, Charlestown, was admitted freeman in 1652.

AUDLEY, EDMUND, Lynn 1641. Lewis.

AUGER, NICHOLAS, a learned physician of New-Haven in 1638, had brothers, John and Robert. Dodd, East-Haven Register. WILLIAM, admitted freeman in 1631, lived in Salem in 1637, and d. in 1654. Jonathan Ager or Auger was of Salem in 1665.

AULT, JOHN, Pascataqua 1631, was living in 1652.

AUSTIN, ANTHONY, Rowley, had a son Anthony b. in 1667 Seventeen of the name of Austin had grad. at the N. E. colleges in 1828. FRANCIS, Dedham 1638. JONAS, Hingham 1635, removed to Taunton. Lincoln, Hist. Hingham. There was a Jonas Austin of Cambridge in 1634, who may have been the one at Hingham the next year.

AVERILL, WILLIAM, Ipswich, died in 1652 or 1653.

AVERY, CHRISTOPHER, was one of the selectmen of Gloucester in 1646. Felt. A Thomas Avery, a blacksmith, was of Salem in 1659. Ibid. Seventeen of the name of Avery had grad. at the N. E. colleges in 1828. JAMES, New-London 1648. Trumbull, i. Hist. Conn. 169. *JOHN*, a minister, was wrecked, and perished in a storm, 15 August, 1635, with his wife and 8 children, in going from Newbury or Ipswich to Marblehead, where he was about to settle. Mather, Magnalia. Alden. JOHN, Boston, d. 31 July, 1654. WILLIAM, received a grant of land at Ipswich in 1638. A William Avery was member of the ar. co. in 1654, and representative for Springfield 1669.

AVIS, WILLIAM, Boston, had a son John, b. in 1664.

AUBREY, WILLIAM, a merchant of Boston, m. Rachel, daughter of Secretary Rawson, 18 Jan. 1653. He may be the same whom Whitman [Hist. Sketch of Ar. Co., 157] calls William Auberg.

AWKLEY, MILES, Boston, had a son Miles, b. in 1638.

AXEY, *JAMES, Lynn 1636, was representative in 1654, and d. in 1669. Frances, his wife, d. in 1669, leaving an estate of £232. 9. 6. Lewis.

AXTELL, HENRY, an inhabitant of Sudbury, and in 1660, of Marlborough, was killed by the Indians in 1675. Rev. Henry Axtell, D. D., grad. at New-Jersey College in 1796.

AYER, JOHN, Salisbury 1640, Ipswich 1648, d. at Haverhill in 1657. Descendants are numerous in Massachusetts, and are in Concord, N. H. *PETER, Haverhill, was admitted freeman in 1666, and was chosen representative in 1683, 1685, 1689, and 1690. ROBERT, and THOMAS, were of Haverhill, and admitted freemen in 1668.

AYLET, JOHN, Boston, 1655.

BABB, PHILIP, Isle of Shoals, N. H. 1658. The name still exists in New-Hampshire.

BABCOCK, GEORGE, Boston, d. 2 Sept. 1695. Twelve of the name had grad. at the N. E. colleges in 1828, besides two at Harvard of the name of Badcock.

BACHELLER, JOHN. (See BATCHELOR.)

BACKUS, ————, Saybrook 1637. Twelve persons of this name had grad. at Yale and Dartmouth in 1828. Rev. Isaac Backus, a distinguished Baptist minister, died in 1806, æ. 82.

BACON, GEORGE, Hingham 1635. Lincoln, Hist. Hingham, 43. Ten of the name of Bacon had grad. at the N. E. colleges in 1828. NATHANIEL, Plymouth colony, was an assistant in 1667. WILLIAM, Salem, died a. 1653.

BADGER, GILES, NATHANIEL, and RICHARD, were inhabitants of Newbury in 1647. Giles d. 17 July, 1648, leaving issue. Eight of the name had grad in N. E. in 1828.

BAGLEY, SAMUEL, Weymouth 1658.

BAILEY, JOHN, minister of Watertown and Boston, was b. 24 Feb. 1644, in Lancashire, England, came to N. E. about 1683, was settled at Watertown, 6 Oct. 1686; removed to Boston 1692, and became assistant minister of the first church, 17 July, 1693, and d. 12 Dec. 1697, in his 54th year. JOHN, Newbury and Salisbury. (See BAYLEY.) RICHARD, Lynn 1647, removed to Salem and died a. 1648. Theophilus Bailey, of Lynn 1645, d. in 1694. Lewis. THOMAS, Weymouth, freeman 1640. *THOMAS*, brother of Rev. John Bailey, was his assistant in the ministry several years, and d. at Watertown, in Jan. 1689.

BAKER, ALEXANDER, Boston, freeman 1646, had sons, Alexander, b. 1635; Samuel, b. 1637; John, b. 1640; Joshua, b. 1642; William, b. 1647; Benjamin, b. 1652; and Josiah, b. 1654. Eighteen of the name had grad. at the N. E. colleges in 1828. EDWARD, Lynn, freeman 1638, d. in March, 1687, leaving sons, Edward and Thomas. Lewis. An Edward Baker was of Northampton in 1658. FRANCIS, Boston, had a son Nathaniel b. in 1642. JOHN, Ipswich 1634, probably the freeman of that year. JOHN, Boston 1640, removed to Newbury. He was one of the two, of this name, admitted freeman 1641. Winthrop, ii. Hist. N. E. 29. *JOHN, representative for Dover, may be the freeman of 1647. JOHN, Dedham, freeman 1641. JOHN, Boston, had sons, John; Thomas, b. 1653; Samuel, b. 1654; Nathaniel, b. 1656. A John Baker was member of the ar. co. 1644; and a John Baker was admitted freeman 1642. LANCELOT, Boston 1644. NATHANIEL, Hingham 1635. *NICHOLAS*, Hingham, freeman 1636, representative 1636 and 1638, removed to Scituate, and was the third minister of the 1st church, and d. 22 Aug. 1678, æ 68, leaving widow Grace, and sons, Samuel, Nathaniel, and Nicholas. RICHARD, Dorchester, member of the church 1639, freeman 1642. A Richard Baker was member of the ar. co. in 1658. ROBERT, Salem 1640. Savage, ii. Winthrop, 24. Felt, MS letter. THOMAS, Boston, freeman 1649, died 3 Jan. 1699. He had sons, John, b. 1654; Joseph, b. 1657, and perhaps Thomas, who d. at Boston 1703. THOMAS, East-Hampton, L. I. 1650. ‡THOMAS, was elected one of the magistrates of Connecticut in 1658. *THOMAS, Topsfield, freeman 1669, was representative 1686, 1689, and 1690, and a military officer. THOMAS, Roxbury, d. 28 Jan. 1684. Thomas Baker, jr., of Roxbury, was killed by the Indians with Capt. Wadsworth, 27 April, 1676. WILLIAM, Charlestown, freeman 1634. One of this name was in Boston 1652, and had sons John and William, b. there in 1653 and 1655. A William Baker d. in Concord in 1679.

BALCH, JOHN, came from Bridgewater, in Somersetshire, and having resided at Cape Ann, as early as 1625, settled at Salem in 1626, and died there in 1648. He left three sons, one of whom, John, was drowned in crossing the ferry to Beverly in Jan. 1662. His wives were Margaret and Agnes. Felt, Annals Salem, 6, 7. 179. Rev. William Balch, H. C. 1724, of Bradford, Ms., who d. 12 Jan. 1792, æ. 87, was one of his descendants.

BALDWIN, GEORGE, Boston, had a son John, b. in 1639, d. 1643. He may have been the George Baldwin, who was at Huntington, L. I. in 1672. The name of Baldwin is an ancient one, and may be traced beyond A. D. 672, when Baldwinus was consecrated bishop of North-Elmham. See Bloomfield's Topog. Hist. Norfolk. Forty-two persons of the name had grad. at the N. E. colleges in 1826, besides several at New-Jersey College. HENRY, Woburn, freeman 1652, came, it is supposed, from Devonshire, England. He m. Phebe Richardson in 1649, and had sons, Henry; John, b. 1656; Daniel, b. 1659. Henry had 3 sons, Henry, who d. 20 Dec.

1753; David, and James. David was father of William Baldwin, H. C. 1748, a magistrate of Sudbury, and Samuel Baldwin, H. C. 1752, minister of Hanover, Ms. James was father of Loammi Baldwin, member of the American Academy, and the friend and correspondent of Count Rumford. JOHN, with his wife Joanna, was living in Dedham in 1635, and had a son John, b. there that year. There was a John Baldwin of Hadley in 1671. JOHN, was a petitioner for the grant of Chelmsford in 1653, and probably the same who settled in Billerica, where he d. 25 Sept. 1687. His descendants are numerous in Billerica and other places. John Baldwin, a colonel and magistrate of Billerica, is one of them. RICHARD, Braintree 1637, [Winthrop, ii. Hist. N. E. 348] may be the same named by Trumbull in the 1st vol. Hist. Conn.

BALL, ALLING, New-Haven 1644. Ten of the name of Ball had grad. at the N. E. colleges in 1827. FRANCIS, Springfield 1644. Sprague, Hist. Discourse. JOHN, Concord, came from Wiltshire, England, and was admitted freeman 1650, d. 1 Nov. 1655. His children were, John, who was of Watertown and Lancaster, and Nathaniel, who settled in Concord, and had sons, Nathaniel, Ebenezer, Eleazar, and John. Shattuck. RICHARD, Salisbury 1650.

BALLANTINE, WILLIAM, Boston 1653, had sons, John, b. 1653, member of the ar. co. 1682, its captain 1703; David, b. 1658; Benjamin, b. 1661; William, b. 1665. His grandson John, H. C. 1694, a member of the ar. co. 1694, representative of Boston, and clerk of the court of common pleas, was father of Rev. John Ballantine, of Westfield, who grad. at H. C. 1735.

BALLARD, WILLIAM, Lynn 1637, freeman and member of the ar. co. 1638, removed to Andover, and had sons, Joseph, William, and John, who settled there. There was a Nathaniel Ballard of Lynn 1650.

BALSTONE, JOHN, Boston, d. 6 June, 1706, æ. 86. JONATHAN, Boston, had sons, John, b. 1645; Jonathan, b. 1651; James, b. 1657; Robert, b. 1662; Benjamin, b. 1663. WILLIAM, Boston, was admitted freeman 1631, went to Rhode-Island. 2 Coll. Mass. Hist. Soc. vii. 98.

BAMBRIDGE, GUY, Cambridge 1634, freeman 1635. Sometimes written Banbridge.

BANCROFT, JOHN, Lynn, died a. 1637, having had sons, John, Thomas, and Ebenezer. Some of the family settled in Reading. Mather [ii. Magnalia, 32] relates a remarkable anecdote of Thomas Bancroft, who was a deacon of the church in 1697. Six of the name had grad. at Harvard and Williams, and one at Brown, in 1828. ROGER, Cambridge 1636, freeman 1642, d. 28 Nov. 1653.

BAND, GEORGE, freeman 1650. There is some doubt whether this is Band or Rand. ROBERT, Connecticut, was elected a magistrate in 1659.

BANGS, EDWARD, was born at Chichester, England, in 1592, arrived at Plymouth, in the ship Ann, in July, 1623. He was a ship-wright, and tradition in the family reports that he superintended the construction of the first ship built at Plymouth. He removed, with Gov. Prince and others, to Eastham, in 1644, and there d. in 1678, æ. 86. His son Jonathan was b. at Plymouth, 1640, went with his father to Eastham, m. Mary Mayo, 16 July, 1664, d. at Harwich, now Brewster, in 1728. Edward, son of Jonathan, was b. at Eastham, 30 Sept. 1665, d. 22 May, 1746, leaving a son Edward, b. in 1694, d. 3 June, 1755, whose son Benjamin was father to Edward D. Bangs, esquire, secretary of the commonwealth of Mass. JOHN, Plymouth 1637.

BANKES, RICHARD, was a member of the church at York in 1673.

BANNISTER, CHRISTOPHER, Marlborough 1657, d. 30 March, 1678. Thomas Banister grad. at H. C. 1700.. John Bannister grad. at H. C. 1764. Hon. W. B. Banister grad. at D. C. 1797.

BARBER, EDWARD, Dorchester, d. 9 June, 1677, æ. 80. ||*GEORGE, Dedham 1643, member of the ar. co. 1646, was representative in 1668, 1669, and 1682, of Medfield, in which place he was the principal military officer. JOHN, Salem 1637, admitted to the church 3 April, 1646, is styled a carpenter. *JOHN, Medfield, representative 1677. RICHARD, Dedham, freeman 1640, d. 18 June, 1644. This name is written Barbore. WILLIAM, Marblehead 1648.

BARDEN, JOHN, was in the class of graduates at Harv. Coll. of 1647. He went to England.

BAREFOOTE, WALTER, New-Hampshire 1660, was a counsellor in 1682, deputy governour 1685.

BARKER, EDWARD, Boston 1650, had a son Thomas, b. 1657. Twelve of this name had grad. at the N. E. colleges in 1827. JAMES, Rowley, freeman 1640. One of this name went early to Rhode-Island. 2 Coll. Mass. Hist. Soc. vii. 93. RICHARD, Andover 1645, d. 1695, had five sons, who settled in Andover, viz. John, Ebenezer, Richard, Stephen, and Benjamin. THOMAS, Massachusetts, freeman 1640.

BARLOW, GEORGE, Exeter 1639, Saco 1652. JOHN, Fairfield 1668. Joel Barlow, LL. D., a native of Reading, Conn. grad. at Y. C. 1778, died in Poland in 1812, æ. 54. Holmes ii. Annals, 451. THOMAS, Boston, d. 13 Oct. 1661.

BARNARD, FRANCIS, is reported to have removed from Hartford to Hadley as early as 1662 ; was admitted freeman 1663. He is the great ancestor of all the divines of the name of Barnard who have grad. at H. C., excepting John, H. C. 1700, of Marblehead, and Jeremiah, H. C. 1773, of Amherst, N. H. MASSACHEL, Weymouth 1637, had daughters Mary and Sarah, b. in 1637 and 1639. The first Minister of Weymouth, according to Prince, [i. Annals, 151] was a Rev. Mr. Barnard. ||MATTHEW, Boston, Member of the ar. co. 1660, freeman 1673. His wife Sarah d. 31 August, 1659. Sons, John, b. 29 Sept. 1654, member of the ar. co. 1677 ; Thomas, b. 4 April, 1657 ; Benjamin, b. 6 Jan. 1662. ||RICHARD, Boston, member of the ar. co. 1662, d. 20

4   25

Dec. 1706. ROBERT, one of the founders of the church in Andover, in 1645. Two of his sons, John and Stephen, settled in Andover. Rev. Jeremiah Barnard, H. C. 1773, is one of his descendants. *THOMAS*, third minister of Andover, was son of Francis Barnard, [Alden] and grad. at H. C. in 1679. He was ordained as colleague with Rev. Francis Dane in 1682, and d. 13 Oct. 1718, and was succeeded by his son John, H. C. 1709, who d. 14 June, 1757, æ. 69, leaving sons, Thomas, H. C. 1732, minister of Newbury and Salem; and Edward, H. C. 1736, minister of Haverhill. Thomas d. 5 August, 1776, æ. 60, leaving a son Thomas, H. C. 1766, minister of the north church in Salem, who d. 1 Oct. 1814, æ. 67. Edward d. 26 Jan. 1774, æ. 54, leaving a son Edward, H. C. 1774, a physician of Salem, who d. Dec. 1822, æ. 67, leaving an only son Edward, and a grandson Edward, both of Salem. TOBIAS, one of the graduates in the first class at H. C. 1642, went to England. Johnson, Hist. N. E. 165.

BARNES, DANIEL, New-Haven 1644. Thirteen of the name of Barnes and Barns had grad. at the N. E. colleges in 1826. JOSHUA, East-Hampton, L. I. 1650. MATTHEW, Braintree 1640, Boston 1653. Snow, Hist. Boston. RICHARD, Marlborough 1660. THOMAS, Hingham 1637, freeman 1645. THOMAS, New-Haven 1644, was brother of Daniel, and had sons, Thomas, b. 1653; Daniel, and Maybee. Dodd, East-Haven Reg. WILLIAM, freeman 1641, was one of the proprietors of Salisbury in 1640.

BARNET, ———, was an early minister of New-London. Mather, i. Magnalia, 216. THOMAS, Salisbury 1640. Felt.

BARNEY, *JACOB, Salem, freeman 1634, was representative in 1635, 1638, 1647, and 1653, d. 1673. Felt, Annals Salem.

BARRELL, GEORGE, Boston, freeman 1643, d. 11 Sept. 1643, ‖JOHN, Boston, member of the ar. co. 1643, its ensign in 1656, d. 29 August, 1658. He had sons, John, b. 1645; John, 2d, b. 1652; William, b. 1654; John, 3d, b. 1656. THOMAS, Massachusetts, was admitted freeman 1645. WILLIAM, Boston, d. 20 August, 1639.

BARRETT, HUMPHREY, Concord 1640, freeman in 1657, d. in Nov. 1662. His children were, Thomas, drowned in Concord River 1660; Humphrey, a representative of Concord 1691, who had sons, Joseph and Benjamin; and John, who settled in Marlborough. Shattuck, MS Hist. Concord. THOMAS, d. at Chelmsford, 6 Oct. 1668, leaving a son Thomas, and others.

BARRON, DANIEL, Woburn 1653. William A., Oliver, and Thomas Barron grad. at H. C. in 1787, 1788, and 1796. ELLIS, Watertown, who, from the colony records, is called by Mr. Savage, *Barrow*, was admitted freeman 1641, had a wife Grace; a daughter of this name b. 1640, and a son Moses, b. 1643, who probably settled at Chelmsford, and was ancestor of Oliver Barron, H. C. 1788, a physician, who died in the Isle of Man, in 1809. W. Winthrop.

BARSHAM, JOHN, son of the following, was born at Watertown 1635, grad. at H. C. 1658. There was a John Barsham who lived in New-Hampshire, whose children were, Annabell, Mary, Dorothy, Sarah, and William, born between 1669 and 1678. WILLIAM, Watertown, came to N. E. in 1630, was admitted freeman 1637, had sons John and Joshua, b. in Watertown in 1635 and 1639.

BARSTOW, ||GEORGE, was a member of the ar. co. 1644. Five persons, uniting the name as above, and Bastow, had grad. in N. E. in 1827. *MICHAEL, Watertown, was representative in 1653. WILKIN, Dedham 1636. See Worthington's Hist. Dedham, p. 42, where the name is spelled *Bearstowe*. WILLIAM, Dedham, where his son Joseph was born; was afterwards of Scituate.

BARTHOLEMEW, *HENRY, was born in 1606, came from London to N. E. 7 Nov. 1635; settled at Salem, which he represented in 1635, and 18 years afterwards. He was admitted freeman in 163-; d. 1692. Two of his children were baptized in 1641 and 1643. Felt. ||RICHARD, Salem, was admitted to the church 31 July, 1640, freeman 1641, member of the ar. co. 1643. d. 1646. Ibid. *WILLIAM, brother of Henry, of Salem, elected representative in 1635, and 7 years afterwards, appears to have been of Marblehead in 1674, and may have d. at Charlestown, 18 Jan. 1681.

BARTLETT, CHRISTOPHER, Newbury, was born a. 1623, m. his first wife in 1645, his second, Mary Hoyt, in 1660, and d. 15 March, 1670, æ. 47. His children were, Christopher, b. 11 June, 1655, m. Deborah Weed 1677; Jonathan, b. 1657, d. 1659; John, who d. young; Mary, and Martha. Forty persons of the name of Bartlett have received the honours of the N. E. colleges. JOHN, Newbury 1637, d. 5 Feb. 1679, æ. 66. Joan, his wife, d. 13 Sept. 1678. RICHARD, Newbury 1637, d. 25 May, 1647, leaving sons, Richard and Christopher. *RICHARD, son of the preceding, was born 1621, settled in Newbury, which he represented from 1679 to 1681, and in 1684. He d. in 1698, æ. 77. Abigail, his wife, died 1 March, 1687. His sons were, Samuel, b. 20 Feb. 1646, m. Elizabeth Titcomb, 1671; Richard, b. 21 Feb. 1649, m. Hannah Emery, 18 Nov. 1673, and had 9 sons and 2 daughters; Thomas, b. 7 Sept. 1650, m. Tirzah Titcomb, 1685; John, b. 2 June, 1655, m. Mary Rust, 1680. Richard, the eldest of the 9 sons of Richard, was b. 20 Oct. 1676, and was the grandfather of Dr. Richard Bartlett, of Pembroke, N. H., a grandson of whom is Richard Bartlett, secretary of state of N. Hampshire. Stephen, the sixth son of Richard Bartlett, was father of Gov. Josiah Bartlett, one of the signers of the Declaration of Independence. He was b. at Amesbury, in Nov. 1729, and d. at Kingston, 19 May, 1795, æ. 64, leaving three sons, Levi, Josiah, and Ezra, who have been members of the senate or council of New-Hampshire, and the 2d a member of congress, and president of the N. H. Med. Soc. ROBERT, Plymouth 1623. Davis, Morton's Memo. 385. ROBERT, Northampton 1658. A Robert Bartlett was of Conn. in 1646, and is named in a note to the 1st vol. of Trumbull. THOMAS, Dedham 1636, may have been the ensign of Watertown in 1639, and who d. there, 26 April, 1654, æ. 60.

27

BARTOLL, JOHN, Marblehead 1648.

BARTON, RUFUS, Providence, 1648.   Winthrop, ii. Hist. N.
E. 323.   THOMAS, Massachusetts 1646.   Davis, Morton's Memo.
236.

BASCOM, THOMAS, Northampton 1658.   Ten persons of the
name of Bascom had grad. in N. E. in 1826.

BASS, JOHN, Braintree, m. Ruth, daughter of John Alden, of
Plymouth, 12 April 1657, and had children, John, b. 26 Nov. 1658;
Samuel, b. 25 March, 1660; Ruth; Joseph; Sarah; and perhaps
others.   JOSEPH, Braintree 1648.   *SAMUEL, Braintree, freeman 1634, the first deacon of the church, and in office above 50
years, was representative 1641, 12 years, d. 3 Dec. 1694, æ. 94,
having seen 162 descendants.   Ann, his wife, d. 5 Sept. 1693.
SAMUEL, Massachusetts, was admitted freeman 1648.   THOMAS,
was admitted freeman 1656.   WILLIAM, Massachusetts, freeman
1638.

BASSETT, WILLIAM, Plymouth 1623, Duxbury 1639, representative 1640 and 1644.   WILLIAM, Lynn 1659, had sons, William and Elisha.   Lewis.

BATCHELOR, JOHN, Salem, came, according to tradition, from
Dorsetshire, was admitted to the church, 23 June, 1639, freeman in
1640, and died in 1646.   His descendants write the name Batchelder, of whom is John. P. Batchelder, M. D., late president of the
Berkshire Medical Institution.   JOHN, Dedham, probably one of
the early proprietors of Watertown, had sons, Samuel, b. 8 Jan.
1640; Jonathan and David, (gemini) b. 14 Dec. 1643.   *JOSEPH,
Salem, freeman 1638; was afterwards of Wenham, which he represented in 1644.   *STEPHEN*, the first minister of Lynn and
Hampton, was born in England, a. 1561, arrived at Boston, with
Rev. Thomas Weld, 5 June, 1632; was the next year settled at
Lynn, and in 1638 or 1639, became the minister of Hampton, but
was dismissed in 1641.   He is supposed to have returned to England in 1655 or 1656, leaving in America, a wife, Mary, who in
1656, petitioned the general court for a divorce, stating that her
husband, Rev. S. B., upon some pretended ends of his own, had
gone to England, and had taken a new wife, and expressing her
wish to be at liberty to marry, if she should have a good opportuni-
ty, and the Lord should incline her heart.   She also stated that she
had two children, who were diseased.   Mr. B. must therefore have
been between 95 and 100 years when he died.   His grandson Nathaniel was a respectable inhabitant of Hampton, and living in 1690,
and descendants of the minister are said to be numerous in Rockingham county, N. H.   WILLIAM, Charlestown, freeman 1644, d.
22 Feb. 1668.   His son Joseph was b. 20 August, 1644.

BATEMAN, NATHANIEL, Watertown 1640.   THOMAS,
Concord, was admitted freeman 1642, d. 6 Feb. 1669, æ. 55, leaving sons, Thomas; Peter, who d. in Woburn 1676; John, and Ebenezer.   Shattuck, MS Hist. Concord.   WILLIAM, Concord,
brother of the preceding, was admitted freeman 1641, and removed

to Chelmsford. WILLIAM, perhaps the father of the preceding,
was admitted freeman 18 May, 1631.

BATES, CLEMENT, was admitted freeman 1636. Seventeen
of the name of Bates had grad. at the N. E. colleges in 1827.
*EDWARD, Boston, a. 1636, freeman 1638, and the representative
of Weymouth, where he probably settled, from 1638 to 1641, and
1660. GEORGE, Boston, freeman 1636. Belknap, i. Hist. N. H.
36. *JAMES, Dorchester and Hingham, freeman 1636, representative 1641 from Hingham.

BATT, *CHRISTOPHER, Newbury, freeman 1638, removed
to Salisbury, which he represented in 1640, 1641, 1643, and 1650;
removed to Boston, and was accidentally killed by his son, 10 Aug.
1661. EDWARD, Weymouth 1639, had sons, Increase and Edward, b. in 1641 and 1655. NICHOLAS, a linen-draper of Newbury, was admitted freeman in 1638, and d. 27 June, 1662.

BATTEN, HUGH, Dorchester, d. 8 June, 1659.

BATTER, *EDMUND, Salem, representative 1637, and 16
years afterwards; d. 1685, æ. 76.

BATTLE, THOMAS, freeman 1657, should perhaps be *Brattle*.
ROBERT, Boston, d. 23 Dec. 1658.

BAUDOUIN, PIERRE, a physician at Rochelle, in France, escaped thence on the revocation of the edict of Nantes, 8 Oct. 1685,
to Ireland, and thence soon after to Casco, now Portland, Me., and
from Casco went to Boston, in 1690. He left several children, one
said to have been the ancestor of the Bowdoins in Virginia, and
another, Hon. James Bowdoin, an eminent merchant of Boston, and
a member of the council, who d. in 1747, leaving five children,
William, Mary, Elizabeth, Judith, and James. William was b. 14
June, 1713, grad. at H. C. 1735, d. 24 Feb. 1773, leaving one child,
Sarah Bowdoin Dearborn. James the youngest, was b. 7 Aug.
1726, grad. at H. C. 1745, was member of the council from 1757
to 1769; president of the convention which formed the constitution
of Mass.; a founder and the first president of the American Academy; and governour of Mass. in 1785 and 1786. He d. at Boston,
6 Nov. 1790, æ. 64, leaving two children, James, H. C. 1771, minister plenipotentiary from the U. S. to Spain, and d. without issue,
25 Oct. 1811, æ. 59, and Elizabeth, who m. Sir John Temple, con-
sul general and minister resident to the U. S. from Great Britain,
and d. in 1809, leaving 2 sons and 2 daughters. One of the daughters m. Hon. Thomas L. Winthrop, lieut. gov. of Mass., one of
whose sons, James Bowdoin Winthrop, at the request of his uncle,
has dropt the name of Winthrop, and is now the only male representative of the Bowdoin family in New-England.

BAXTER, GEORGE, an arbitrator for settling the line between
New-Haven and the Dutch 1650. Hutchinson, i. Hist. Mass. 149,
but in the appendix, p. 447, his signature to the determination is
Theo. Baxter. GREGORY, Roxbury 1630, Braintree freeman
1632, d. 24 June, 1659. By Margaret, his wife, who d. 13 March,
1662, he had 1. Abigail, who m. Joseph Adams; 2. Dearing; 3.
John, b. 1 Dec. 1639, m. Hannah White 1660, was a lieutenant,

and d. at Braintree, 29 April, 1719, æ. 81, the father of Rev. Joseph Baxter, b. 4 June, 1676, grad. at H. C. 1693, was the minister of Medfield, and d. 2 May, 1745, having had, by his wife Mary Fiske, of Braintree, 6 children, of whom Joseph, H. C. 1724, a physician, was b. 14 May, 1706, and d. of the small pox on his passage to England. Shattuck. NICHOLAS, Boston 1639. A Nicholas Baxter d. at Boston, 10 Jan. 1692.

BAYES, THOMAS, Dedham 1643, Boston 1645, where his son Thomas was b. 1645.

BAYLEY, JOHN, came from Chippenham, Wilshire, a. 1639, and on his passage was wrecked at Pemaquid. He settled at Salisbury, from thence removed to Newbury, a. 1650, and d. 2 Nov. 1651. Coffin. Twenty-six of the name Bailey and Bayley had grad. in N. E. in 1828. JOHN, son of the preceding, came with his father to N. E. and settled at Newbury, where he d. 22 July, 1662. His children were Sarah, b. 1641; Joseph, b. 4 April, 1648; James, b. 12 Sept. 1650; Joshua, b. 17 Feb. 1653. Rev. Abner Bailey, H. C. 1736, of Salem, N. H., was one of his descendants.

BAYNLY, THOMAS, Concord, d. 18 March, 1643.

BEACH, RICHARD, Cambridge 1635, Watertown 1639; may have removed to New-Haven, where John, son of Richard Beach, was b. 1639. Rev. Abraham Beach, D. D. grad. at Y. C. 1757.

BEADSLEY, WILLIAM, Massachusetts, was admitted freeman 1638.

BEAL, *JOHN, a shoemaker, who, with his wife, five sons, and three daughters and two servants, came from Hingham, England, and settled in Hingham, Ms., which he represented in 1649. Judge Sewall records the death of a Mr. Beal in 1688, aged 100 years. JEREMIAH, Hingham 1652, freeman 1657. *NATHANIEL, Hingham 1654, was representative 1676, 1677. THOMAS, Cambridge 1634, freeman 1636. WILLIAM, Plymouth 1623.

BEAMAN, GAMALIEL, 1659, d. 1707, leaving a son John, whose son Gamaliel was b. 1684, d. 1745, at Sterling, Ms. Worcester Magazine, ii. 39.

BEAMSLEY, WILLIAM, Boston 1632. (See BENSLEY.)

BEAN, PHILIP, Salem 1638. Six of the name had grad. at Harv. and Dart. in 1828.

BEARD, THOMAS, Massachusetts, was admitted freeman 1643. WILLIAM, Dover 1643.

BEAUCHAMP, EDWARD, Salem, freeman 1643, admitted to the church, 29 Dec. 1639. Prince, ii. Annals, 118. Felt. RICHARD, Massachusetts, freeman 1641. ROBERT, Ipswich 1648. Spelled also Beacham.

BECK, ALEXANDER, freeman 1634, had sons Ephraim, Strange, and Deliverance, all born 1 June, 1640; Manasseh, b. 1645. Four of the name had grad. at Union College in 1828.

BECKFORD, JOHN, Dover 1659, Oyster-River, now Durham, N. H. 1669. Thomas Beckford, or Bickford, whose bravery is noticed by Mather, [Magnalia, ii. 544] and named by Haven, [Remains, 20] was probably a son.

BEEBE, JAMES, Hadley 1668. Eight of the name had, in 1828, grad. at the N. E. colleges.

BEECHER, *THOMAS, Charlestown, freeman 1632, was a representative at the first general court, 14 May, 1634 and the 6 courts in 1635 and 1636. Rev. Lyman Beecher, D. D., of Boston, grad. at Y. C. in 1797.

BEERS, ANTHONY, Massachusetts, freeman 1657. Four of the name of Beers have received the honours of Yale College. *RICHARD, Watertown, freeman 1637, was representative from 1663 to 1675, 13 years, and captain in Philip's war. He was killed in battle with the Indians at Northfield, Ms., 4 Sept. 1675. His name is spelled *Beares* in colony records.

BEETFIELD, SAMUEL, Boston, d. 1 Sept. 1660.

BELCHER, ||ANDREW, Sudbury 1640, Cambridge 1646, was member of the ar. co. 1642. He m. Elizabeth, daughter of Nicholas Danforth, and his children were Elizabeth, Jemima, Martha, Anna, and Andrew. Andrew was b. at Cambridge, 1 Jan. 1647, removed to Boston 1703, was a captain, and several years counsellor, and d. in the autumn of 1717, leaving one son, Jonathan Belcher, b. in Jan. 1681, grad at H. C. 1699, the governour of Mass. and N. H. from 1730 to 1741, and afterwards of New-Jersey, and 4 daughters, Sarah Fay, of Charlestown, Elizabeth Oliver, Martha Stoddard, and Anna Noyes, of Charlestown. Dr. Holmes [i. Amer. Annals, 425] erroneously makes *Thomas* Belcher father of the governour. EDWARD, Boston, freeman 1631. Satisfaction, b. 1656, and John, b. 1657, were sons of Edward Belcher, of Boston, but perhaps not of Edward Belcher the freeman. GREGORY, Braintree, freeman 1640, d. 21 June 1659. Sons, Samuel, b, 24 Aug. 1637 ; Joseph, b. 25 Dec. 1641. Dea. Gregory Belcher, perhaps his grandson, d. 4 Nov. 1727, æ. 63. JEREMY, Ipswich, was born 1612, freeman 1638, and was living in 1665. *SAMUEL*, was a native of Ipswich, and probably son of the preceding, grad. at H. C. 1659, was a preacher at the Isle of Shoals ; afterwards settled at West-Newbury, and died in 1714, æ. 74, at Ipswich, to which place he removed several years before his death.

BELDING, SAMUEL, Hadley 1661, was admitted freeman 1673. Sixteen of the name of *Belden* had grad. at Yale college in 1828.

BELKNAP, ABRAHAM, Lynn 1637; Salem, died a. 1643. Felt. Lewis. Joseph Belknap, of Boston, was probably his son. He was a member of the ar. co. 1658, and was admitted freeman in 1669. His children were, Joseph, b. 26 Jan. 1659 ; Nathaniel, b. 13 Aug. 1663 ; Thomas ; John ; Abraham ; Joseph; Jeremiah, b. 1 Jan. 1687. The historian of N. Hampshire was a descendant from one of these brothers.

BELL, THOMAS, Roxbury, was admitted freeman in 1636. Savage, ii. Winth. 39. Eight persons of the name of Bell have grad. at the N. E. colleges, of whom Hon. Samuel Bell, LL. D., of Chester, New-Hampshire, is grandson of John Bell, an early inhabitant of Londonderry, N. H. ||THOMAS, member of the ar. co. 1654, may have been the one who d. in Boston, 7 June, 1654. His son Joseph was b. in 1653.

BELLINGHAM, †‡*§RICHARD, Boston, representative 1635; assistant 1636, 14 years; deputy governour 1635, 13 years; governour 1641, 10 years; major-general 1664. He d. 7 Dec. 1672, having lived to be the only surviving patentee named in the charter. He had a number of children. His son James was b. in May, 1656. John, H. C. 1642, was probably his son. SAMUEL, one of the first graduates of H. C. 1642, appears to have been living, of Rowley, in 1643, and, from the Magnalia, was living in 1697. WILLIAM, Rowley, brother of Richard, was admitted freeman 1640, died a. 1650.

BELLOWS, JOHN, Concord 1655, m. Mary Wood, of Marlborough, where he removed. His children were Mary, Samuel, Abigail, Daniel, and Benjamin.

BEMAN, GAMALIEL, Dorchester 1658. [See BEAMAN.)

BEMIS, JOSEPH, Watertown, 1640. Three of the name of Bemis, had, in 1828, grad. at H. C. and one, Rev. Stephen Bemis, at D. C.

BENDALL, ||EDWARD, Boston, freeman 1634, member of the ar. co. 1638. Prince, ii. Annals, 69. Sons, Freegrace, b. 1636; Reform, b. 1639; Hopefor, b. 1641.

BENHAM, JOHN, Massachusetts, was admitted freeman 1631.

BENJAMIN, JOHN, Watertown, freeman 1632, one of the proprietors of Cambridge. Holmes, Hist Cambridge. He d. June, 1645. John was his eldest son. Savage, i. Winth. 185. RICHARD, Watertown 1640.

BENNET, DAVID, a physician, d. at Rowley, 4 Feb. 1719, æ. 103. His wife d. 26 March, 1712. His son, Hon. Spencer Phipps, was baptized at Rowley, 9 Aug. 1685; grad. at H. C. 1703, was lieutenant governour of Mass. and d. 4 April, 1757, æ. 72. EDMUND, Weymouth, freeman 1636. GEORGE, Boston, drowned 27 March, 1652. HENRY, Ipswich 1665. 2 Coll. Mass. Hist. Soc. viii. 107. JAMES, Concord, freeman 1638; removed to Fairfield Sept. 1644. Thomas, his son, was b. 16 Nov. 1642. JOHN, Salem 1638; Marblehead 1648. RICHARD, Boston 1645. Snow, Hist. Boston, 137. ||SAMUEL, Lynn 1637, a carpenter, was member of the ar. co. 1639. WILLIAM, Salem 1637, born 1603, died 1683.

BENNING, RALPH, Boston, d. 14 Nov. 1663.

BENSLEY or BEAMSLEY, WILLIAM, freeman 1638, died at Boston 29 Sept. 1658.

BENT, JOHN, Sudbury, freeman 1640, was one of the proprietors of Marlborough, d. at Sudbury, 27 Sept. 1672. PETER, Sudbury 1656.

BENTON, EDWARD, Guilford, Conn. 1650.

BENYTHON, RICHARD, was one of the first settlers of Saco. Sullivan, Hist. Maine. (See BONIGHTON.)

BERKLEY, RICHARD, New-Haven 1651.

BERNARD, JOHN, Watertown, was admitted freeman 1634. His son Joseph b. 1639. JOHN, Cambridge 1634, freeman 1635.

BERRY, WILLIAM, Pascataqua 1632, freeman 1642, was probably one of the grantees of Newbury.

BESBEDGE, THOMAS, Scituate 1637. Written also Besbeech, and now spelled Bisbee.

BESSEY, ANTHONY, Lynn; removed to Sandwich 1637. Lewis.

BETTS, THOMAS, Guilford, Conn. 1650. RICHARD, Ipswich 1648. JOHN, Cambridge 1640, was a proprietor of Lexington 1642. Boston News-Letter, i. 266.

BETSHAM, RICHARD, freeman 1637.

BEWETT, HUGH, Massachusetts; removed to Providence. Savage, ii. Winth. 19.

BIBLE, THOMAS, Malden, died July, 1653.

BICKNELL, *JOHN, Weymouth 1658, representative 1677.

BIGELOW or BIGGELY, JOHN, Watertown 1642, had a son John, b. 1643. Of the name of Bigelow and Biglow, 24 had grad. at the N. E. colleges in 1828.

BIGGS, ||JOHN, Boston, freeman 1634; Ipswich 1635; member of the ar. co. 1641.

BILL, JOHN, Boston, d. Dec. 1638.

BILLINGS, JOHN, Portsmouth 1640. Belknap, i. Hist. N. H. 47. NATHANIEL, Concord, was admitted freeman 1641, and d. 24 Aug. 1673, leaving sons, Nathaniel, and John, who married Elizabeth Hastings, 1661, and d. 1704. Shattuck, MS Hist. Concord. ROGER, Dorchester, member of church 1640, freeman 1643. WILLIAM, one of the proprietors of Lancaster 1654.

BILLINGTON, JOHN, one of the first settlers of Plymouth 1620, hanged in 1630, leaving sons John and Francis, who lived in Plymouth. Savage, i. Winthrop, 36.

BINGLEY, WILLIAM, Newbury 1665.

BIRCHER, THOMAS, was admitted freeman in 1637.

BIRD, JOHN, Massachusetts, admitted freeman 1645. JATHNELL, received a grant of land in Ipswich in 1641. SIMON, Braintree, freeman 1644, one of the proprietors of Billerica, where he died, 7 July, 1667. THOMAS, Scituate 1639. THOMAS, Dorchester 1642.

BIRDLEY, GILES, Ipswich 1648.

BISBEE, THOMAS, Duxbury a. 1645. (See BESBEDGE.)

BISCOE, JOHN, Watertown, an early proprietor. Shattuck. NATHANIEL, Watertown 1642. (See BRISCOE.)

BISHOP, ‡‡JAMES, Connecticut, secretary of New-Haven 1661; assistant of Conn. 1668, deputy governour 1683, d. 22 June, 1691. JOHN, Newbury, had sons, John, b. 1648; Jonathan, 1657; Noah, 1658; David, 1660. *JOHN*, the minister of Stamford, Conn. died in 1694. JOHN, jr., Guilford, Conn. 1650. NATHANIEL, had a houselot in Ipswich in 1638, was admitted freeman in 1645, when he appears to have lived in Boston. He had sons, Joseph, b. 1642; Benjamin, b. 1644; John, b. 1646; Samuel, b. 1647; all

5   33

born in Boston. RICHARD, freeman 1642, Salem 1647, d. 30
Dec. 1674. Felt, MS Annals. Edward Bishop was one of the
founders of the church in Beverly in 1667. SAMUEL, son of Nathaniel Bishop, was born in Boston, 7 March, 1647, and grad. at
H. C. 1665. STEPHEN, Guilford, Conn. 1650. *THOMAS,
Ipswich 1636, representative 1666, died 1671, leaving widow, Margaret ; children, Samuel, John, Thomas, Job, and Nathaniel. His
estate amounted to £5000. 1. 1. Felt. *TOWNSEND, Salem,
freeman 1635, representative 1636. Leah, his daughter, baptized
19 June, 1637 ; John, his son, bapt. 31 July, 1642. Felt, Annals
Salem, 171. EDWARD, Salem 1645.

BIXBY, JOSEPH, Ipswich 1648.

BLACK, HENRY, Massachusetts, was admitted freeman 1645.
(See BLAKE.) JOHN, born 1609, lived in Salem, was admitted
freeman 1632, d. in Beverly, 16 March, 1675. Freeborn, his wife,
d. 1631, æ. 46. RICHARD, was admitted freeman in 1645.

BLACKBORNE, ||WALTER, freeman in 1639 ; member of
the ar. co. in 1638.

BLACKLEACH, *JOHN, Salem, admitted freeman 1635 ; representative in 1636. In 1637 he had a family of 9 persons. He
had a grant of 300 acres of land in 1636. His son John, of Boston,
had a son John, b. 1660. This name is written Blackleeche on the
records of Salem. [Felt, MS Annals.] Hudson Blackleach grad.
at Y. C. in 1757.

BLACKMAN, ADAM, minister of Strafford, Conn. preached
a short time at Scituate, came early to N. E. and died in 1665.
BENJAMIN, grad. at H. C. 1663 ; was a preacher at Malden 1675.
He m. Sarah Scottow, 1 April, 1675, and left Malden about 1678.
JOHN, Dorchester, admitted member of the church 1658, free-
man 1669, had sons Jonathan and Joseph.

BLACKMER, ————, Lynn ; removed to Sandwich 1637.
Lewis.

BLACKSTONE, WILLIAM, Boston a. 1626 ; freeman 1631.
He removed, a. 1635, to a place near Rhode-Island, and d. 26 May,
1675. The records of Boston state that he was m. to widow Sarah
Stephenson, 4 July, 1659. She d. June, 1673. Savage, i. Winth.
44, 45. See an interesting note of him in Holmes' Annals, i. 377.

BLAGG, HENRY, Braintree 1643. Son Philip b. 24 March,
1643.

BLAISDELL, RALPH, Salisbury 1640. Silas and Daniel Blaisdell grad. at D. C. in 1817 and 1827.

BLAKE, GEORGE, Gloucester 1649. Ten of the name of
Blake had grad. at H. C. in 1824. HENRY, Boston, d. 26 July,
1662 ; perhaps the Henry Black made freeman in 1645. *JAMES,
Dorchester, freeman 1652, representative 1677, a deacon and ruling elder of the church, d. 28 June, 1700, æ. 77. JASPER, Hamp-
ton, d. 11 Feb. 1673. ||JOHN, Dorchester, freeman 1644, mem-
ber of the ar. co. 1642. ||WILLIAM, Dorchester, freeman 1638,
member of the ar. co. 1646. One of the first settlers of Springfield,
it is presumed. *WILLIAM, Milton, freeman 1651, admitted a

member of the church in Dorchester, 1652, representative 1689. His son Nathaniel was b. 1659. Rev. T. M. Harris, D. D.

BLAKESLEY, EDWARD, Roxbury, d. Nov. 1637. Solomon and Tillotson Blakesley grad. at Yale College in 1785.

BLANCHARD, JOHN, freeman 1649, was probably one of the founders of the church at Dunstable, 16 Dec. 1685. Nathaniel Blanchard was of Weymouth in 1662. JOSEPH, Boston, d. Dec. 1637. THOMAS, Charlestown, came to N. E. in the ship Jonathan, in 1639, and died 21 May, 1654. WILLIAM, admitted member of the church of Salem, 7 Feb. 1641, freeman 1641. A William Blanchard d. at Boston Oct. 1652.

BLANDFORD, JOHN, Sudbury 1641. Son John b. 1646.

BLANTON, WILLIAM, Boston, freeman 1643. Snow [Hist. Boston] spells the name Blaintaine. He died 15 June, 1662.

BLANY, JOHN, Lynn 1656, had a son John. Lewis.

BLATCHLEY, SAMUEL, Guilford, Conn. 1650.

BLINMAN, RICHARD, a minister of Gloucester, came to N. E. 1641, and was admitted freeman the same year. He went thence to New-London 1648, to New-Haven in 1658, whence he returned to England, and died in the city of Bristol, " in a good old age." Calamy. Allen.

BLISS, GEORGE, Lynn, removed to Sandwich 1637. Lewis. Twenty-five persons of the name of Bliss had grad. at the N. E. colleges in 1826, of whom Rev. Daniel Bliss, of Concord, Ms., a native of Springfield, grad. at Yale. JOHN, Northampton 1658. NATHANIEL, Springfield, 1646, d. 18 Sept. 1654. Moses and Jonathan Bliss were barristers at law in Springfield in 1774. THOMAS, was admitted freeman in 1642. LAURENCE, Springfield, d. 1676.

BLY, THOMAS, Boston 1658, had a son Thomas, b. in 1656.

BLODGETT, DANIEL, Chelmsford 1654, freeman 1652. This name was anciently written *Bloghead*, [see I. Mather's Indian Wars] and was so pronounced within 30 years. Five of the name have grad. at Dart., Midd., and Vermont colleges. THOMAS, Cambridge, freeman 1636.

BLOISE, EDMUND, Watertown, was admitted freeman in 1639. FRANCIS, Cambridge, freeman 1641. The name is spelled Bloss on Cambridge records. He d. Sept. 1646.

BLOOD, JAMES, Concord 1639, was brother of Colonel Blood, known in English history for his designs on Charles II; had sons, Richard, of Groton, who d. 30 August, 1692; Robert, and James. *JAMES, Concord, son of the preceding, m. Hannah Purchis, dau. of Oliver Purchis, 1657. He was representative for Sudbury, 1660, deacon of the church, and died 20 Nov. 1692. Shattuck. ROBERT, Lynn 1647, Concord 1653, m. Elizabeth, daughter of Major Simon Willard, 8 April, 1653, and had Mary; Elizabeth; Sarah; Simon, b. 5 July, 1662; John, b. 29 Oct. 1666; Ellen; James, b. 1673; Ebenezer, b. 1676; and four others. He d. 27 Oct. 1692.

BLOTT, ROBERT, Boston, freeman 1635. Snow, Hist. Boston, 118.

BLOWERS, JOHN, Boston 1654, sons, John, b. 1659; Thomas, b. 1665.

BLUMFIELD, THOMAS, Newbury 1638, removed to Woodbridge, N. J., before 1668. Coffin. He had children, Mary, ; Sarah, b. 1643; John, b. 15 March, 1646; Thomas, b. 12 Dec. 1648; Nathaniel, b. 1651; Ezekiel, b. 1653; Ruth, b.1659; Timothy, b. 1664.

BLUNT, WILLIAM, was admitted freeman in 1635. WILLIAM, Andover, came from Ireland a. 1668, d. 1709, æ. 67. He had 3 sons, William, John, and Hanborough. [Rev. A. Abbot.] William had 2 sons, David, b. 1699; and John, who grad. H. C. 1727; ord. at New-Castle, N. H. 20 Dec. 1732; d. 7 Aug. 1748, æ. 41. He is the ancestor of the Blunt families in Portsmouth and New-Castle.

BOLTON, WILLIAM, Newbury, d. 27 March, 1697.

BOND, JOHN, one of the grantees of Newbury, had sons, John, b. 10 June, 1650; Thomas, b. 1652; Joseph, b. 1653. His wife was Hester Blakely. NICHOLAS, was admitted freeman in 1652. ROBERT, Connecticut, elected a magistrate in 1659. [*SAMPSON?*] Having preached a sermon not composed by himself, which being considered highly disreputable, and being discovered, he removed to Barbadoes. i. Hutch. 377. *WILLIAM, Watertown, representative 1689, speaker of the house 1691, one of the council of safety 1689, d. 15 Dec. 1695.

BONHAM, GEORGE, Plymouth, died 1704, aged a. 93.

BONIGHTON, JOHN, Casco-Bay 1658. RICHARD, Saco, was appointed assistant of the plantation at Saco, 2 Sept. 1639. Gov. Sullivan [Hist. Maine] spells his name Benython.

BONNEY, THOMAS, one of the proprietors of Bridgewater 1645.

BOOSY, JAMES, one of the deputies of the first general assembly of Connecticut, 1639. Trumbull, i. Conn. 103.

BOOTFISH, ROBERT, Lynn, freeman 1635, removed to Sandwich 1637, where descendants now write the name *Bodfish*. ROBERT, jr., Lynn 1635.

BOOTH, *ROBERT, Exeter 1645, representative of Saco 1659. He was born a. 1604.

BORDMAN, WILLIAM, Cambridge, freeman 1652. His children were Moses, Rebecca, Andrew, Aaron, Francis, Martha, Mary, William, and Elizabeth. THOMAS, Lynn 1637; removed to Sandwich. Lewis.

BOREMAN, *THOMAS, Ipswich, freeman 1635, representative 1636, probably d. 25 May, 1679. WILLIAM, Guilford, Conn. 1650.

BOSWELL, JONATHAN, Cambridge 1632. Holmes, Hist. Cambridge. This name should probably be Bosworth.

BOSWORTH, HANIEL, Ipswich 1648. JOHN, was admitted freeman in 1634. JONATHAN, Cambridge 1634. *NATHANIEL, representative of Hull 1680. ||ZACCHEUS, Boston, freeman 1636, member of the ar. co. 1650, d. 28 July, 1655. Bellamy Bosworth grad. at H. C. 1736.

BOULTER, NATHANIEL, Hampton, was living in 1685, æ. 60 years. Adams, Annals Portsmouth, 397. THOMAS, Weymouth 1661.

BOULTON, NICHOLAS, Dorchester, admitted member of the church 1644, freeman 1644. A William Boulton, of Massachusetts, d. 27 March, 1697.

BOUND, WILLIAM, Salem, admitted freeman 1637. Rev. Ephraim Bownd was the first minister of the 2d Baptist church in Boston, ord. 7 Sept. 1743 ; d. 18 June, 1765, æ. 46.

BOURNE, GARRETT, Boston, a. 1640, had a son John born 1643. Snow, History Boston, 118. HENRY, Scituate 1637 ; removed to Barnstable. JOHN, Salem 1637 ; went to Barbadoes after 1644. Felt, MS letter. ||NEHEMIAH, Boston, freeman 1641 ; member of the ar. co. 1638. He was a shipwright ; returned to England, was an officer in Cromwell's army, and attained the rank of major. His son Nehemiah was b. in 1640. Whitman, MS letter. RICHARD, of Lynn 1637, according to Lewis, removed to Sandwich, was a teacher among the Indians at Marshpee ; was ordained by Eliot and Cotton 1670 ; d. 1685. Morton, Holmes. Davis. Lord, i. Lempriere, 270. THOMAS, Plymouth, and also of Marshfield. 2 Coll. Mass. Hist. Soc. iv. 248.

BOUTWELL, JAMES, Salem and Lynn, freeman 1638 ; died a. 1651, leaving children, Samuel, Sarah, and John. John Boutwell was of Cambridge 1646, and a Thomas Boutwell is mentioned 2 Coll. Mass. Hist. Soc. iv. 110.

BOWDIN, or BODIN, AMBROSE, Casco-Bay 1658. His son Ambrose was there in 1658. WILLIAM, was of Maine in 1642.

BOWDITCH, ———, Salem. His wife, Sarah, joined the church, 10 May, 1640. Felt, Annals Salem 174.

BOWDOIN, PETER, (See BAUDOUIN.)

BOWEN, GRIFFITH, Boston, freeman 1639. Snow, Hist. Boston, 118. Son Peniel, b. 1644. Rev. Penuel Bowen, H. C. 17— was a minister in Boston.

BOWERS, GEORGE, Cambridge 1644. George, son of Benjamin and Elizabeth Bowers was b. Cambridge, 3, Feb. 1654. *JOHN*, Derby, Conn. was son of George Bowers, of Cambridge ; grad. at H. C. 1649 ; settled in the ministry at Derby. W. Winthrop, MS Catalogue. MATTHEW, Cambridge, d. 30 Jan. 1645.

BOWINGE, THOMAS, Marblehead 1648.

BOWKER, ||EDMUND, member of the ar. co. 1646, d. March, 1666. ROBERT, Salem, was received as an inhabitant July, 1637.

BOWLES, ||JOHN, Roxbury, freeman 1640 ; member of the ar. co. 1645. His wife d. in 1648. This name appears to be Bowelis in the the colony records. *JOHN, Roxbury, perhaps son of the preceding, grad. at H. C. 1671 ; was elected representative 1689 ; speaker of the House of Reps. 1690. He d. 30 March, 1691.

BOWMAN, NATHANIEL, Watertown 1687. Son Nathaniel, b. 1640. Harvard College has eleven of this name on its catalogue.

BOWSTREE, WILLIAM, Concord ; d. 31 Oct. 1642.

BOYDEN, THOMAS, Watertown 1639 ; freeman 1647, had sons, Thomas b. 1639 ; Jonathan b. 1651.

BOYES, JOSEPH, Salem ; born a. 1608, was admitted member of the church, 7 Feb. 1641, and freeman in 1642. An Antipas

Boyes was of Boston in 1665. *MATTHEW, Rowley, freeman 1639 ; representative 1641, 1644, 1645 and 1650.

BOYKIM, JARVIS, New-Haven 1639. John Boykim grad. at New-Jersey College, in 1811.

BOYLSTON, THOMAS, was a physician, who, after obtaining the degree of Doctor of Medicine at Oxford, came to N. E. and settled at Brookline in 1635. Thacher, Med. Biog. i. 185. He was father or grandfather to the celebrated Dr. Zabdiel Boylston, F. R. S., born at Brookline 1680, and d. 1 March, 1766, in his 87th year.

BOYNTON, WILLIAM, Rowley, admitted freeman 1640. He was born in 1605. JOHN, Rowley 1643.

BRACKENBURY, JOHN, Boston, had a son John, b. 1657. Samuel Brackenbury grad. at H. C. in 1664, and William Brackenbury d. at Malden in 1668. RICHARD, requested to be made free 1630, and was admitted to the oath 1634. He arrived at Salem with Gov. Endicott, Sept. 1628; was one of the founders of the church in Beverly, and d. 1684, æ. 84. Prince, i. Annals, 174.

BRACKETT, ANTHONY, Portsmouth 1640. Belknap, i. Hist. N. H. 47. Hubbard, Wars with Eastern Indians. *PETER, Braintree, freeman 1643, representative 1644—1646, 1653, 1660—1662, 7 years. Representative for Scarborough 1673 and 1674. He had sons, John, b. 1641 ; Joseph, b. 1643. *RICHARD, Boston, freeman 1636; dismissed from Boston church to Braintree 1642, ordained deacon, 21 July, 1642; member of the ar. co. 1639 ; was the 3d captain of the militia in Braintree ; town clerk many years. He died 3 March, 1691, æ. 80. Alice, his wife, died in 1690, æ. 76. WILLIAM, Pascataqua 1631. Adams, Annals Portsmouth.

BRADBURY, *THOMAS, Salisbury, freeman 1639, was representative in 1651, 7 years. His children were, Wymond, b. 1637, died in the Isle of Mœvis 1669 ; Thomas b. 28 Jan. 1640; Mary, b. 1642 ; Jane, b. 1645 ; Judith ; Jacob, b. 1647, d. at Barbadoes, 1669 ; William, b. 1649 ; Elizabeth, b. 1651 ; John, b. 1654; Ann, b. 1656, and d. 1659 ; Jabez, b. 1658.

BRADBROOK, JOHN, Newbury, d. 28 June, 1662.

BRADFORD, JOHN, was son of Governour Bradford by his first wife, and lived in Duxbury and Marshfield, both which he represented at the Plymouth court. JOSEPH, Plymouth, son of Gov. B. d. in 1715, in his 85th year, and left a son by the name of Elisha. The catalogues of the N. E., N. Y., and N. J. colleges contain the names of 31 Bradfords, who had grad. at their various institutions in 1828. ROBERT, Boston, member of the church 1640, freeman 1642, had a son Moses, b. in 1644, who was a member of the ar. co. 1677, and died in Boston, 23 March, 1692. ‡WILLIAM, Plymouth 1620, one of the first pilgrims, was born at Ansterfield, a village in the north of England, in 1588; came to N. E. 1620; was elected governour of Plymouth colony in 1621, and was in office more than 30 years. He d. 9 May, 1657, in his 69th year. His first wife d. in Cape Cod Harbour, Dec. 1620. He m., 14 April, 1623, widow Alice Southworth, who lived till 1670, æ. 80, and had two sons, William and Joseph. ‡WILLIAM, Plymouth, son of the preceding, was born 17 June, 1624; was assistant 1658, and deputy governour of Plymouth colony many years; one of Sir Edmund Andros' council 1687; d. 20 Feb. 1704, in his 80th year. By his first wife he had 4 sons, Israel, Ephraim, Samuel, and John; by the 2d, one son, Joseph, who settled in Conn.; by the 3d, 4 sons, William, Thomas, David, Hezekiah. He had also three daughters. Samuel had 3 sons; 1. Perez, H. C. 1713, a member of the council of Massachusetts; 2. Gershom, of Kingston; 3. Gamaliel, a judge and counsellor, whose son Gamaliel, a colonel in the revolutionary army, and representative, and who d. in 1806, was father of Alden Bradford, esq., late secretary of Massachusetts. Alden, iii. Coll. Ep. 246, 247.

BRADLEY, DANIEL, Haverhill, was killed by the Indians, 13 Aug. 1689. Daniel and Hannah Bradley, and their children Mary and Hannah, were killed 15 March, 1697. Joseph Bradley, and his children Joseph and Martha, were killed 11 March, 1697. NATHAN, Dorchester, d. 26 July, 1701, æ. 70. Eighteen persons of the name of Bradley have grad. at the N. E. colleges. RICHARD, Boston 1651.

BRADISH, ROBERT, Cambridge 1635. Wife Vashti; sons, John, b. 3 Dec. 1645, probably d. at Boston, 12 Oct. 1696; Samuel, b. 28 Nov. 1648. Three persons of the name of Bradish had grad. at Harvard College in 1828.

BRADSHAW, ‖HUMPHREY, Cambridge, member of the ar. co. 1642. Son John b. 24 June, 1656. John Bradshaw lived in Medford in 1699, and his son, Samuel, was born 29 Aug. 1700. Benjamin Bradshaw, of Stoughton, Ms., was b. 11 Dec. 1741, grad. at H. C. 1769, d. 25 Jan. 1779. Parkman Bradshaw grad. at H. C. 1780.

BRADSTREET, *DUDLEY, Andover, son of Gov. Bradstreet, was b. 1648, representative 1677; colonel of the militia; one of the council of safety 1689. [Hutch. i. Mass. 340.] He married Ann Price 12 Nov. 1673, and had Dudley, b. April, 1678; grad. H. C. 1698; and Margaret, b. 1680, who d. in infancy. *HUMPHREY, Ipswich, freeman 1635; representative 1635, d. 1655. JOHN, Salem, died a. 1659. *SAMUEL, probably the son or a nephew of Governour Bradstreet, grad. in 1653, at H. C. of which he was one of the fellows. He was admitted freeman in 1656; was representative of Andover in 1670. He lived sometime in Boston, and two of his daughters were b. there in 1663 and 1665. §‡†SIMON, Cambridge; Ipswich; Andover, a. 1645; Boston; Salem, to which place he removed 18 Sept. 1695. He was born in Horbling, Lincolnshire, England, March, 1603; was one year at Emmanuel College; arrived at Salem 1630; the place where he died 27 March, 1697, at the age of 94. He was elected assistant, March, 1630, and was 48 years in office; secretary of the colony, 23 Aug. 1630 to 1643, deputy governour 1673—1678; governour 1679 to May, 1686; and again governour after the imprisonment of Andros, from May, 1689, to May, 1692. His first wife, by whom he had 8 children, was Ann, daughter of Gov. Thomas Dudley. She was a woman of much literary celebrity, and d. 16 Sept. 1672. His 2d wife, daughter of Emanuel Downing, was living in 1695. *SIMON*, minister of New-London, son of the preceding, graduated at H. C. 1660 ; was ordained 5 Oct. 1670, d. 1685, aged a. 45.

BRAGDEN, ARTHUR, Kittery 1652, was born a. 1597. This name still exists in Maine.

BRAKIN, WILLIAM, Pascataqua 1631.

BRANCH, WILLIAM, admitted freeman 1648.

BRAND, BENJAMIN, Massachusetts, came to N. E. in 1630, and was admitted freeman 18 May, 1631.

BRANDISH, JOHN, admitted freeman in 1635.

BRANKER, JOHN, was admited freeman in 1632.

BRANSON, GEORGE, Masssachusetts, k. by a bull, 25 July, 1657. Coffin.

BRATCHER, AUSTIN, died on Cradock's plantation, and his death was supposed to have been caused by violence, and a jury was empanelled to inquire into the cause of it.

BRATTLE, ||*THOMAS, Boston 1657 ; was probably made freeman 1657 ; (see Thomas Battle) member of the ar. co. 1672 ; representative 1671 and 1672 for Lancaster, 1678 and 1679 for Concord. His son Thomas, b. at Boston, 5 Sept. 1657 ; grad. at H. C. 1676, was treasurer of the college ; and his son William, b. in 1662, grad. at H. C. 1680, was the learned minister of Cambridge, a fellow of the Royal Society in England and d. 15 March, 1717, æ. 54.

BRAY, JOHN, was a ship-wright at Kittery, 1663. His daughter married William Pepperell, father of Sir William Pepperell.

BRAYBROOK, JOHN, Watertown 1640, had sons, John. b. 1642; Thomas, b. 1643. WILLIAM, Lynn, removed to Sandwich 1637. Lewis.

BRECK, EDWARD, Dorchester, a member of the church in 1636 ; admitted freeman 1639. His son, Captain John Breck, was father of Rev. Robert Breck, of Marlborough, who was born in Dorchester, 7 Dec. 1682, died 6 Jan. 1731. Sprague, Hist. Disc. 79. ROBERT, Boston, freeman 1649, probably son of Edward. His son Robert was b. 1658.

BREED, ALLEN, Lynn, born 1601, was one of the grantees named in the Indian deed of South-Hampton, L. I. 1640. He died at Lynn, 17 March, 1691. His children were Allen, Timothy, Joseph, and John. Lewis. JOHN, Lynn 1640, died 1678. Ibid.

BREEDEN, THOMAS, Boston 1665. 2 Coll. Mass. Hist. Soc. viii. 105.

BRENTON, *§WILLIAM, Boston, admitted freeman 1634, representative 1635. It appears that he went to Rhode-Island, where he was president between 1647 and 1663, and governour in 1666, 1667, and 1668. He died at Newport 1674. To him, it is not improbable, was granted, a. 1658, the large and beautiful tract of land on Merrimack River, in N. H., long known by the name of "Brenton's Farm," and now constituting the township of Litchfield.

Several of his descendants held important offices in R. I. colony. Those who were living at the period of the revolution adhered to the royal government. Jahleel Brenton, a late admiral in the British navy, was born in Newport, and another of the same name received the order of knighthood about 1810.

BRETT, WILLIAM, one of the proprietors of Bridgewater 1645, was representative in 1661 at Plymouth court.

BREWER, DANIEL, Roxbury, freeman 1634, d. 9 Jan. 1689, æ. 84. His son Nathaniel, b. 1635, d. 26 Feb. 1693. *DANIEL,* minister of West-Springfield, son of Daniel Brewer, of Roxbury, grad. at H. C. 1687, was ord. 16 May, 1694; d. 5 Nov. 1733, æ. 66. His wife whom he m. 23 Aug. 1699, was Catharine Chauncy, of Northampton. She d. 15 May, 1754, æ. 78. They had 8 children. JOHN, Cambridge 1644, had a daughter Hannah, by Ann, his wife, b. in 1644. *OBADIAH, Gloucester, representative 1647 —1649, 3· years. This name may be Obadiah Bruen, who, it appears, was an early preacher at Gloucester. THOMAS admitted freeman 1652.

BREWSTER, JONATHAN, Plymouth, 1623, son of elder William Brewster, removed to New-London, thence to Norwich, Conn., and died 1659. Wood, 48. JOHN, Portsmouth, 1665. There have been many families of the name in Portsmouth. LOVE, Plymouth 1623, afterwards of Duxbury, was son of Elder William Brewster. *NATHANIEL,* grad. in the first class of H. C. 1642; went to England, and was settled in the ministry at Norfolk, and of good report : [Hutchinson, Hist. Mass. i. 107.] Received from Dublin the degree of Bachelor of Divinity; returned to America, and settled in 1656, at Brookhaven, L. I.; and died in 1690, leaving 3 sons, John, Timothy, and Daniel, whose descendants are still respectable on Long Island. Hon. Silas Wood, MS letter. WILLIAM, Plymouth 1620. One of the first pilgrims, and a ruling elder in the church. He died 16 April, 1644, in his 84th year. His children were Patience, Fear, Love, Wrestling, Jonathan, Lucretia, William, Mary. Davis, Morton's N. E. Memo. Allen, Biog. Dict.

BRIDEMORE, ||————, member of the ar. co. 1639.

BRIDGE, EDWARD, Roxbury, freeman 1639, d. 20 Dec. 1683, æ. 82. *JOHN, Cambridge 1632; freeman 1635, representative 1637. Winthrop, ii. N. E. 347. MATTHEW, Cambridge, son of the preceding, member of the ar. co. 1643, m. Anna, daughter of Nicholas Danforth, and had children, John, b. 15 June, 1645; Anna; Martha, 1648; Matthew, b. 5 May, 1650; Samuel, b. 17 Feb. 1653; Thomas, b. 1 June, 1656; Elizabeth. Ten of the name of Bridge are on the Harvard catalogue; five of whom were clergymen. ||THOMAS, Cambridge, 1648, was member of the ar. co. 1643. His wife was Deborah. *THOMAS,* minister of the first church in Boston, was born at Hackney, in England, in 1657; came to America in 1682; ord. 10 May, 1705; died 26 Sept. 1715, æ. 58. WILLIAM, Charlestown, freeman 1647. His sons Samuel and Peter were born in 1643 and 1647, the latter at Boston.

BRIDGES, ‡*ROBERT, Lynn, freeman 1641, representative 1644; speaker of the House 1646; assistant 1647 to 1656. His house was burnt down in April, 1648. He d. in 1656. Savage, ii. Winthrop, 53, 237. EDMUND, Lynn, 1637, was admitted freeman 1639, d. 1686. His sons were John and Josiah. Lewis.

BRIDGHAM, ‖HENRY, Dorchester 1641, freeman 1643; Boston; member of the ar. co. 1644; captain; constable 1653. Snow. Hist. Boston, 137. His sons were John, b. 1645; Joseph, b. 1651; Benja. b. 1654; Hopestill, 1658; Samuel, b. in 1660; Nathaniel, b. 1662; James, b. 1664. *JOSEPH, representative in 1690 of Northampton, was probably son of the preceding. *SEBASTIAN, Cambridge, 1636; removed to Rowley, where he was captain of the military band 1644; and representative 1646 and 1647. John, his son, grad. at H. C. 1669. Johnson, Hist. N. E., 193. Coffin, MS letter.

BRIDGMAN, JAMES, Northampton 1654. JOHN, Salem d. a. 1655.

BRIGDEN, THOMAS, Charlestown, was admitted freeman 1636, and d. 20 June, 1668. ZECHARIAH, who grad. at H. C. 1657, was a preacher at Stonington, Conn. and d. 1663. W. Winthrop, MS Catalogue.

BRIGGS, CLEMENT, Plymouth 1623; Weymouth 1633; had sons, Thomas, Jona., David, Clement, born from 1632 to 1642. JOHN, Lynn; removed to Sandwich 1637. Lewis. WILLIAM, Boston 1642.

BRIGHAM, *JOHN, Marlborough; representative 1689, son of Mr. Brigham, of Sudbury, who m. Mercy Hurd. Nine of the name, and some of them his descendants, had grad. in N. E. 1826. THOMAS, Cambridge 1636, freeman 1637, afterwards of Watertown and Sudbury. His son John, by Mercie his wife, was b. 9 March, 1644.

BRIGHT, FRANCIS, a puritan minister, who arrived in N. E. 1629; remained in Charlestown about a year, and returned to England. HENRY, Charlestown, 1632; Watertown 1637, had several children, and d. 14 Sept. 1673, æ. 109. Henry Bright, probably a descendant, grad. at H. C. 1770, and the family still remains at Watertown and its vicinty. HENRY, jr. Watertown, 1642. John, son of Henry Bright, was b. 14 May, 1641.

BRIMSMEAD, JOHN, Dorchester, freeman 1638, Charlestown 1640. His son John b. 1640. WILLIAM, the first minister of Marlborough, was member of the class at Harv. Coll. which grad. in 1648, but left college in 1647, without his degree. He first preached at Plymouth; went to Marlborough as early as 1660, but was not ordained until 3 Oct. 1666. He d. July 3, 1701, having never been married. Allen, Biog. Dict. 112.

BRINLEY, FRANCIS, Rhode-Island 1651, was b. in Oct. 1633, was an assistant in 1672, and living in 1709. 1 Coll. Ms. Hist. Soc. 252.

BRISCOE, DANIEL, freeman 1642. There was a Briscoe, a tanner, who lived in Watertown 1644. Hutch. i. Hist. Mass. 377. JOSEPH, Boston, was drowned 1 Jan. 1658. Son Joseph b. 1658.

Boston Records.   NATHANIEL, Watertown, 1642, was perhaps the usher or tutor of Harvard College, while under Nathaniel Eaton Winthrop, i. Hist. N. E. 308.   WILLIAM, freeman, 1641, was a member of the church in Boston.

BRISTOW, JOHN, Cambridge 1642.   RICHARD, Guilford, Conn. 1650.

BRITTERIDGE, RICHARD, Plymouth, one of the first pilgrims, d. 21 Dec. 1620.

BRITTON, JAMES, Woburn, d. 3 May, 1655.

BROCK, JOHN, minister of Reading, was born at Stradbrook, Eng. 1620: came to N. E. 1637 ; grad. at H. C. 1646 ; ord. 13 Nov. 1662; Allen says 1668; d. 18 June, 1688, æ. 68.   He may be the John Brock who was admitted freeman in 1642.   RICHARD, Watertown, d. 24 Oct. 1673.   WILLIAM, Salem 1639.   W. Gibbs.

BROCKLEBANK, SAMUEL, Rowley, a captain, was born in 1628, and was killed in battle with the Indians, 14 April, 1676, æ. 46, leaving children, Samuel, Hannah, Mary, Elizabeth, Sarah, and Joseph.

BROCKHOLT, ANTHONY, one of Sir Edmund Andros' council, and entrusted by him with the command of the forts in the eastern country in 1688.   Hutchinson, i. Hist. Mass. 331.

BROOKS, CALEB, Concord, son of Capt. Thomas Brooks, was admitted freeman in 1654, removed, to Medford 1672, and d. 29, July, 1696.   He m. (1) Susanna Atkinson 1660, who died 1668, and had 4 daughters ; (2) Ann, by whom he had Ebenezer, b. in 1670, the ancestor of Governour John Brooks, and Samuel, ancestor of Hon. Peter C. Brooks.   Shattuck, MS Hist. Concord.   GERSHOM, Concord, brother of the preceding, m. Hannah Eckels 1665, and had Joseph, Daniel, and 4 daughters.   Ibid.   GILBERT and WILLIAM, were of Scituate between 1633 and 1657.   HENRY, Concord, was probably the freeman in 1638 under the name of *Brook*, unless the name of Mr. Brock is *not* mistaken for Mr. Brook, who is represented in Allen's Hist of Chelmsford as preaching at Wenham in 1654.   Henry Brooks had a son Joseph, born in 1641. HUGH, Woburn, d. 1683, leaving sons John, Timothy, and Isaac. There was a John Brooks of Woburn, who was admitted freeman in 1651, whose son John was b. in 1653.   JOSHUA, Concord, son of Capt Thomas Brooks, was admitted freeman in 1652, m. Hannah Mason of Watertown, and had, Noah, b. 1655 ; Daniel, b. 1663, the great-grandfather of the Hon. Eleazar Brooks, of Lincoln ; (See Allen's Biog. Dict.) Thomas, b. 1666 ; Joseph ; Job ; Hugh, and two daughters.   Shattuck, MS Hist. Concord.   RICHARD, Lynn, 1637, removed to East-Hampton, L. I. where he was one of the first settlers 1650.   *THOMAS, Concord, freeman 1636, was a captain, and representative 1642, seven years, and d. 22 May, 1667, leaving sons, Joshua, Caleb, and Gershom already noticed.   Grace, his wife d. 12 May, 1664.   Nineteen of the name had grad. at the N. E. colleges in 1828.

BROOME, GEORGE, Boston, d. in Feb. 1662.

BROUGHTON, THOMAS, Watertown 1643, Boston 1652, where his sons Thomas and Nathaniel were born. He d. 12 Nov. 1700, æ. 87. Thomas d. at Boston, 4 Dec. 1702. There was a John Broughton of Northampton in 1653, and a George Broughton is mentioned by Hubbard, Indian Wars, as of Salmon-Falls River in 1675.

BROWN, ABRAHAM, Watertown, freeman 1632, had sons, Jonathan and Abraham, b. in 1635 and 1639. His wife was Lydia. The name of Brown is frequently written in ancient records with the addition of the *e*, and several families, as those in Salem, have ever retained this orthography. The number of graduates at the colleges of N. E., N. J., and Union in N. Y. of this name, in 1828, was more than 100, of whom 22 had been clergymen. *CHAD*, went from Massachusetts to Rhode-Island, in 1636, and was ordained over the Baptist church as successor of Rev. Roger Williams in 1642. His grandson, James Brown, was born in Providence, and was minister of the same church. From him are descended the respectable families of Browns in R. I. Four of the grandsons of James have been distinguished patrons of Brown University, viz. Nicholas, who d. 1791, æ. 62; Joseph LL. D., who d. Dec. 1785; John, and Moses. Benedict, i. Hist. Baptists, 477. CHARLES, Rowley, before 1652. *EDMUND*, the first minister of Sudbury, came over in 1637, was admitted freeman 1640, was ordained in August, 1640, and d. 22 June, 1677. EDMUND, Dorchester, freeman 1650, had a son Samuel b. in 1661. EDWARD, Salem, perhaps the freeman of 1635, died a. 1659. EDWARD, Ipswich, freman 1641. Joseph Brown was of Ipswich in 1665. FRANCIS, New-Haven 1639, had sons, Eleazar, Samuel, Ebenezer and John. FRANCIS, Newbury 1665. GEORGE, a carpenter of Newbury 1638, was admitted freeman 1640, d. 1 April, 1642. *GEORGE, Haverhill, a lieutenant, was a representative in 1672, 1675 and 1680. HENRY, a proprietor of Salisbury, was b. 1615. HUGH, Salem 1637, perhaps afterwards, of Boston, where several sons of Hugh Brown were b. before 1653. Isaac, Newbury, d. 3 Jan. 1675, æ. 36. JACOB, was one of the proprietors of Billerica 1659. There was subsequently a George Brown there, the ancestor of the present families of that name in Billerica. JAMES, the son of Joseph Brown, came from Southampton in England, and was one of the first settlers of Newbury. Coffin. JAMES, Boston, freeman 1636, was member of the ar. co. 1643. His son James was b. 1635. ||JAMES, Charlestown, freeman 1634, member of the ar. co. 1639, had sons, John, b. 1637; James; James, 2d, b. 1647; Nathaniel, b. 1648. JAMES, Swanzey, son of John Brown, of Plymouth, was elected assistant 1665. Davis, Morton's Memo. 297. *JAMES*, one of Mather's *third* classis of ministers, was the minister of Swanzey after 1662. JOHN, Salem, one of the patentees of Massachusetts, and one of the first assistants of the company, came over in 1629, but returned the next year to England, from whence he again came to this country. Morton. Mather. Prince. Bentley. JOHN, an assistant of Plymouth colony, to which office he was elected 17 years from 1636,

d. (probably at Rehoboth) in 1668. Davis, Morton's Memo. 163, 164. JOHN, an elder of the church in Salem, was probably the freeman of 1638. He d. 1685. John and James, his sons, were baptized in 1638 and 1640. JOHN, Watertown, freeman 1634, had a son John, b. 1636. JOHN, Ipswich, 1648. *JOHN, Reading, was b. 1634, a captain, freeman 1679, representative in 1679, 1680, 1682, and 1683, m. for his 2d wife, Elizabeth, widow of Rev. Joseph Emerson, of Mendon. *NATHANIEL, Salisbury, freeman 1685, representative 1691. *NICHOLAS, Lynn, freeman 1638, representative 1641, afterwards removed to Reading. His son Thomas of Lynn 1650, d. 28 Aug. 1693, leaving sons, Thomas and Joseph. OBADIAH, perhaps *Bruen* of Gloucester, was admitted freeman in 1642. (See BREWER and BRUEN.) PETER, one of the first pilgrims at Plymouth 1620. *RICHARD, a ruling elder of the church of Watertown, came over 1630, freman 1631, representative at the first general court, May, 1634, and from 1635 to 1639, and 1647 to 1655, excepting 1653. Savage, i. Winthrop, 58. RICHARD, Newbury 1635, brother of George Brown, died a. 1661. He had sons, Joshua, b. 10 April, 1642; Caleb, b. 1645; Richard, b. 18 Feb. 1651; Edmund, b. 17 July, 1654. Richard had an only son, Rev. Richard Brown, H. C. 1697, the minister of Reading, who d. 29 Oct. 1732, æ. 57. ROBERT, Cambridge, freeman. ‡SAMUEL, brother of John Browne, of Salem, was one of the patentees of Massachusetts, and came over in 1629. He was elected 30 April, 1629, by the Mass. company in London, one of Gov. Endicott's council. Morton, 76. Prince, i. Annals, 185. *SAMUEL, Salem, representative 1675. THOMAS, one of the proprietors of Newbury, 1638, freeman 1639, d. 1686. THOMAS, Concord 1640, removed to Cambridge. He had sons Thomas, town clerk of Concord, who d. 4 April, 1718, æ. 67; and Boaz, b. 1640, who removed from Concord to Stow, 1690. Shattuck, MS Hist. Concord. WILLIAM, Sudbury 1643. His son Thomas was b. 1644. ‡*WILLIAM, a merchant of Salem, freeman 1641. He was born in England, 1 March, 1608; representative 1654; 1659 and 1666; assistant 1680—1683; one of Sir Edmund Andros' council 1687; d. 20 Jan. 1688, æ. 80. Hutchinson [i. Hist. Mass., 36] mistakes in considering him as living in 1691. Two of his sons were distinguished; William and Joseph; the last of whom grad. 1666, at H. C. where he had a fellowship, which he resigned 15 Sept. 1673; and died 9 May, 1678; having a short time before received a call to settle at Charlestown. ‡*WILLIAM, Salem, son of the preceding, born 14 April, 1639; freeman 1665; representative 1680; one of the council of safety, 1689; counsellor under the charter of William and Mary; d. 14 Feb., 1716, æ. 77. His grandson, Hon. William Browne, grad. at H. C. 1727, and d. 27 April, 1763, æ. 54. Hon. William Browne, a great-grandson, grad. at H. C. 1755; was judge of the sup. court of Mass., left the country in 1775—6, and was afterwards governour of Bermuda. WILLIAM, freeman 1649, perhaps of Salisbury. WILLIAM, freeman 1660. WILLIAM, Gloucester, was one of the selectmen in 1647.

BROWNING, THOMAS, Salem, freeman 1637, was b. 1587; d. 1671. Felt, MS Annals. MALACHI, d. at Boston, 27 Nov. 1658.

BRUEN, or BROWN, OBADIAH, was of Gloucester in 1642, and appears to have been a preacher there, and probably went to Connecticut. Trumbull, i. 249.

BRUCY, ———, the minister of Branford, Conn. before the year 1660. Mather, i. Magnalia, 214, 536.

BRYANT, JOHN, Scituate, a. 1640. William Bryant d. at Boston in 1697.

BRYAN, ALEXANDER, Connecticut, was elected assistant in 1665; Mather says 1668.

BRYER, RICHARD, Newbury 1665.

BUCK, ISAAC, Scituate, was the 2d town clerk in that place. 2 Coll. Mass. Hist. Soc. x. Index. JAMES, Hingham 1638. ROGER, Cambridge 1643, had sons, John, b. 1644; Ephraim, b. 26 July, 1646. His daughter Mary was b. 1638.

BUCKLAND, THOMAS, Massachusetts, was admitted freeman in 1635. WILLIAM, Hingham 1635.

BUCKMINSTER, JAMES, was one of the proprietors of Sudbury in 1640. Shattuck. THOMAS, written *Buckmaster* in colony records, came from some part of Wales to N. E. [Alden, ii. Coll. 180] and was made free 1645; died at Boston, 28 Sept., 1658. He had several sons, of whom were, perhaps, Zachariah, John, and Joseph, who were living in Boston, or Brookline, in 1660. Joseph, the son of Joseph, was b. 1666, and was one of the earliest settlers of Framingham, and died there, æ. 84. His son, Colonel Joseph, who was born in 1697, d. 1780; was father of Rev. Joseph, of Rutland, Ms., who grad. at H. C. 1739; grandfather of Rev. Joseph, D. D., of Portsmouth, N. H., Y. C. 1770; whose son, Rev. Joseph Stevens Buckminster, H. C. 1800, was the minister of Brattle-Street church in Boston.

BUCKINGHAM, THOMAS, New-Haven 1639. Rev. Thomas Buckingham, according to a MS note of Mr. Savage, was minister of Saybrook in 1669. Rev. Thomas Buckingham, H. C. 1690, and Rev. Stephen Buckingham, H. C. 1693, were the ministers of Hartford and Norwalk, Conn.

BUCKNAM, WILLIAM, Charlestown 1647. John Bucknam was of Boston in 1653.

BUFFUM, JOSHUA, Salem 1658; went to England 1659. He had a son Joseph.

BUGBY, RICHARD, freeman 1631. Samuel and Francis Bugbee grad. at Brown and Yale Colleges in 1802 and 1818. EDWARD, Roxbury 1642, Edward and John Bugby died at Boston 1703.

BULGAR, RICHARD, Boston, freeman 1631. Belknap, i. Hist. N. H. 36. He was a member of Boston church.

BULFINCH, JOHN, Salem, was admitted freeman 1641, removed from Salem.

46

BULKLEY, EDMUND, freeman 1635. This name should perhaps be Edward. *EDWARD*, early admitted a member of Boston church, was son of Rev. Peter Bulkley. He was several years the minister of Marshfield, and succeeded his father at Concord, a. 1659. He died at Chelmsford, 2 Jan. 1696, and was buried at Concord. *GERSHOM*, minister of New-London, son of Rev. Peter, grad. H. C. 1655; married Sarah, daughter of President Chauncy, 26 Oct. 1659; settled at New-London, from whence he removed a. 1666, and d. 1713, æ. 78. His son Rev. John, H. C. 1699, was the minister of Colchester, Conn., and the father of the Hon. John Bulkley, a physician, lawyer, and judge of the Superiour court of Connecticut. *JOHN*, son of Rev. Peter, was one of the first class of graduates at H. C. 1642, and the third named in the catalogue. He went to England, and settled at Fordham, from whence he was ejected, a. 1662; retired to Wapping, in the suburbs of London, and practised physick with good success. Calamy, ii. Account, 311. *PETER*, the first minister of Concord, was son of Edward Bulkley, D. D., and was born at Woodhill, in Bedfordshire, England, 31 Jan. 1583; was educated at St. John's College, Cambridge; came to N. E. 1635; settled at Concord, over the church formed 5 July, 1636, with Rev. John Jones as a colleague or assistant, and d. 9 March, 1659, æ. 76. His 1st wife was daughter of Mr. Thomas Allen, of Goldington, by whom he had 11 children; his 2d was a dau. of Sir Richard Chitwood, by whom he had 3 sons and one daughter.. The names of his children, so far as known, were Edward, John, Thomas, Eleazar, Gershom, Peter, Dorothy, Elizabeth. ‡*PETER, Concord, was one of the youngest sons of the preceding, and was born at Concord, 12 Aug. 1643, [Shattuck] grad. 1660, at Harv. College, of which he was a fellow. He was made a freeman 1670; was a captain and major; representative 1673—1676; speaker of the House, assistant 1677—1684, 8 years; sent to England 1676, as agent, to answer complaints made by the heirs of Gorges and Mason. He d. 24 May, 1688, in his 45th year. His children were Edward, b. 18 March, 1668; Joseph b. 7 Oct. 1670; John b. 10 July, 1673; Rebecca b. 1681. WILLIAM, an inhabitant of Ipswich in 1648. THOMAS, Concord, son of Rev. Peter, was admitted freeman in 1638; removed in 1644 to Fairfield with Rev. John Jones, whose daughter he married. He died a. 1652. Shattuck. A Thomas Bulkley was of Rowley in 1643.

BULL, ⟨HENRY, Boston, freeman 1637, was born in South Wales, in 1609; came to N. E. about 1636; removed to R. I. and was one of the original purchasers of Aquidneck, now Rhode-Island. He settled at Newport 1638; was governour of the colony in 1685, and again in 1689. He died in 1693, æ. 84. Lord, ii. Lempriere's Biog. Dict. Addenda. WILLIAM, Cambridge 1644, had children, Rebecca, b. 1644; John, b. 9 March, 1647; Mary; William, b. 1652; Samuel, b. 1654; Elisha, b. 1657. The name of his wife was Blyth.

BULLARD, BENJAMIN, was a proprietor of Watertown, a. 1644. GEORGE, Watertown, freeman 1641. His wife d. 1639. His son Jacob, by another wife, was b. 1642. JOHN, Dedham, freeman 1640, had a son Joseph, b. in 1643. WILLIAM, Cambridge, admitted freeman 1640, m. Mary, daughter of Francis Griswold.

BULLEN, SAMUEL, Dedham, freeman 1641, whose son Samuel was b. in 1644.

BULLIVANT, BENJAMIN, was physician in Boston in 1688.

BULLOCK, HENRY, Salem, died a. 1657. RICHARD, was admitted freeman 1646.

BUMPUS, EDWARD, Plymouth 1623, Duxbury 1645.

BUMSTEAD, EDWARD, Boston, freeman 1640, had a son Joseph, b. 1653. ||THOMAS, Boston, member of the ar. co. 1647, d. 1677. Savage, ii. Winth. N. E. 203. Son Gerard, b. at Roxbury, 1643.

BUNKER, GEORGE, Charlestown, freeman 1634 ; disarmed in 1637 ; died a. 1658. Savage i. Winth. N. E. 248. *BENJAMIN*, minister of Malden, son of preceding, grad. at H. C. 1658 ; died 3 Feb. 1670. John Bunker, d. at Malden, 10 Sept. 1672.

BURBANK, JOHN, Rowley, freeman 1640. There had been seven graduates of the name at the N. E. Colleges in 1826.

BURCHAM, EDWARD, Lynn 1636, was admitted freeman 1638, was clerk of the writs. ||WILLIAM, member of the ar. co. 1644.

BURCHER, EDWARD, Plymouth 1623.

BURDEN, GEORGE, Boston, a shoemaker, was a member of the church 1636, freeman 1637 : disarmed 1637. Sons, Thomas, b. 1637 ; Elisha, b. 1638 ; Ezekiel, b. 1641. This name exists in Pennsylvania.

BURDITT, GEORGE, a minister, came from England about 1635, in which year he was admitted freeman ; became a member of the church at Salem, where he preached more than a year, and received grants of land in 1635 and 1637 ; removed to Dover, a. 1637, from thence to Maine, and finally returned, it is supposed, to England. ROBERT, Malden, d. 16 June, 1667.

BURDSALL, HENRY, freeman 1638, was admitted member of the church in Salem 1636.

BURGATT, PETER, Lynn 1638. Lewis. (See BUSGATT.)

BURGE, THOMAS, Lynn; removed to Sandwich 1637. Lewis.

BURGES, JAMES, Boston, died 27 Nov. 1690. He had sons, John, b. 1654 ; Benja., b. 1655. RICHARD, was of York 1660. Coffin.

BURGESS, THOMAS, Concord 1666.

BURNHAM, JOHN, Ipswich 1638. ROBERT, Boston, had a son Robert, b. 1647. A Robert Burnham was of New-Hampshire in 1665. *THOMAS, Ipswich, was b. in 1617, freeman 1671 ; representative 1684, d. June 1694.

BURNAP, ISAAC, Reading, d. 18 Sept. 1667. He was ancestor of Rev. Jacob Burnap, D. D., of Merrimack, N. H., who d. 26

Dec. 1821, æ. 75, two of whose sons have grad. at Harv. College.
ROBERT, Roxbury 1642.

BURNELL, WILLIAM, Boston, had a son John, b. 1644.

BURR, JEHU, Springfield 1638, was a carpenter, and among
the first settlers. Sprague, Hist. Disc. 13, 15. JOHN, Ipswich
1665. 2 Coll. Mass. Hist. Soc. viii. 106. JOHN, son of Rev. Jonathan Burr, settled in Fairfield, Conn. *JONATHAN*, minister
of Dorchester, was born at Redgrave, in Suffolk, England, a. 1604.
He came to N. E. 1639, with his wife and 3 children ; was settled
as colleague with Rev. Richard Mather, in Feb. 1640 ; d. August,
1641, æ. 37. His widow, Frances, m. Hon. Richard Dummer, of
Newbury, where she d. 19 Nov. 1682, æ. 70. His sons were Jonathan, John, and Simon. Peter Burr, H. C. 1690, a judge of the
supreme court of Conn. and Samuel Burr, H. C. 1697, of Charlestown, were his grandsons. Rev. Isaac Burr, Y. C. 1717, was son
of Judge Peter Burr, and father to Rev. Aaron Burr, the learned
president of New-Jersey College. Vice-Pres. Aaron Burr is son of
President Burr. Rev. Dr. Harris, MS letter. Savage, ii. Winth.
N. E. 22. JONATHAN, son of the preceding, was born in England ; grad. at H. C. 1651 ; settled as a physician at Hingham, and,
according to Rev. Dr. Harris, [MS letter to me] died in Canada,
1690 ; although Mr. Savage [ii. Winth. N. E. 22] says he d. at Bristol,
England, 25 July, 1691, æ. 56. Some mistake, however, is appre-
hended, in the last date, as the same place, year, month. and day
are assigned by Calamy [ii. Account, 610] for the death of Dr. Ichabod Chauncy, a class-mate with Mr. Burr. Perhaps a reliance on
Winthrop's MS Catalogue of H. C. may have caused so extraordi-
nary a coincidence. SIMON, a brother of the preceding, settled
in Hingham, a. the year 1646. Harris. Lincoln.

BURRAGE, JOHN, Charlestown, freeman 1642, d. 1 Jan.
1678. Another John Burrage d. at Charlestown 18 Jan. 1681.

BURRILL, GEORGE, came to Lynn soon after its settlement,
was one of the most wealthy farmers of the place, died in 1653,
leaving 3 sons, George, of Boston, who d. 5 July, 1698 ; Francis, b.
1626, d. 10 Nov. 1704, æ. 78; John. Lewis, MS Hist. Lynn. *JOHN,
son of the preceding, born 1631 ; lived in Lynn ; representative
1691 ; d. 24 April, 1703, æ. 72. By Lois, his wife, he had 10
children ; 1. John, b. 15 Oct. 1658 ; 21 times elected representative of Lynn ; was speaker of the House several years ; 30 years
town clerk ; and counsellor at the time of his death, 10 Dec. 1726,
æ. 63, leaving no children ; 2. Sarah ; 3. Thomas, b. 7 Jan. 1663 ;
4. Anna ; 5. Theophilus ; 6. Lois ; 7. Samuel, b. 20 April, 1674 ;
8. Mary ; 9. Ruth ; 10. Ebenezer, b. 1679 ; representative 6 years
from Lynn ; counsellor 1731 and 1746 ; d. Sept. 6, 1761, æ. 82.
His wife was Martha Farrington, by whom he had 10 children, of
whom were Ebenezer, b. 6 Feb. 1702 ; d. 20 May, 1778, æ. 76 ;
town clerk 17 years, and representative 12 years ; Theophilus, a
magistrate, b. 21 May, 1709 ; and Samuel, b. 1 April, 1717 ; representative from Lynn five times. The last named Ebenezer m.
Mary Mansfield, and had 11 children, of whom were John, b. 29

Aug. 1726 ; m. Anna Thompson, had 9 children, and d. 14 Dec. 1793, æ. 67 ; James, b. 11 March, 1744 ; removed to Providence, and whose son, Hon. James, LL. D., a grad. of Brown Uuniv. in 1788, and a senator in Congress, died at Washington city in 1820, æ. 46. Thompson Burrill, esq., son of John, was b. 30 April, 1764, and has been frequently a representative from Lynn. Lewis, MS Hist. Lynn.

BURROUGHS, GEORGE, a minister, who preached at Wells, and other places, grad. at H. C. 1670, was one of the victims at Salem in the witch craft infatuation ; and was executed 19 Aug. 1692. JOHN, Salem, 1637, perhaps the ancestor of the preceding. John Dunton, in his journal, mentions a Mr. Burroughs of Boston in 1686.

BURSLEY, *JOHN, or, as it is spelled in the colony records, Burslin, was one of the early, if not one of the first, settlers of Weymouth. He was admitted free in 1631, and chosen representative 25 March, 1636. He may be the same who, with Jeffrey, was assessed £2 in 1628, for expenses in the campaign against Morton. Savage, i. Winth. N. E. 44. One of this name was of Exeter in 1643 and 1645.

BURT, GEORGE, Lynn 1635, d. 2 Nov. 1661, leaving sons, George, Hugh, and Edward. Lewis. HENRY, Northampton, freeman 1648, one of the early settlers. David Burt, an early settler there, had 15 children. The late Rev. Federal Burt, of Durham, N. H., born at Southampton, Ms., 4 March, 1789, was probably a descendant. HUGH, of Lynn and Salem, brother of George Burt, was born a. 1591 and d. 1650. Lewis.

BURTON, BONIFACE, Lynn, freeman 1635 ; d. 13 June, 1669, æ. 113 years. Hutchinson, i. Mass., 246. Lewis. JOHN, Salem 1637 ; died 1684. Felt, MS letters.

BUSBY, ||ABRAHAM, freeman 1650, was member of the ar. co. 1647. NICHOLAS, Boston 1646, d. 28 August, 1657.

BUSGAT, PETER, Lynn 1638. Lewis.

BUSH, JOHN, Cambridge 1654. Sons, Joseph, b. 16 Aug. 1654; Daniel, b. 4 April, 1659. Six of the name had grad. at Yale and Dartmouth in 1828. RANDOLPH, Cambridge 1642.

BUSHNELL, GOODMAN, Massachusetts. Winthrop, i. Hist. N. E. 387. There was a widow Bushnell of Boston in 1637, mentioned by Snow, Hist. Boston, page 60. A John Bushnell was of Boston in 1665. FRANCIS, Guilford, 1650. Rev. Harvey Bushnell of Conn., is probably a descendant. Seven of the name have grad. at Yale and Williams colleges.

BUSS, JOHN, a physician and preacher, was born a. 1640, and commenced preaching at Durham, in N. H., in 1678, and was a minister there forty years successively, though not settled. He d. in 1736, æ. 96. MS petition, dated 1718, to Gov. Shute, and the General Assembly of N. H., Dr. Belknap, and various other authorities relying on him, state his age to be 108, but the petition just cited seems decisive. In it, he states his age to be 78 in 1718. WILLIAM, Concord, 1640, a lieutenant, d. 31 June, 1698. By his wife Ann, he had, Richard, b. 1640 ; Ann, b. 1641 ; Nathaniel, b. 1646 ; m. Mary Hayes, 1668 ; d. 17 Dec. 1717 ; Joseph, b. 1649 ; m. Elizabeth Jones, 1671, and d. 1681. Lieut. Bass m. widow Dorcas Jones for a 2d wife. Shattuck, MS Hist. Concord.

BUSWELL, ISAAC, Salisbury, freeman 1640. Some of the New-Hampshire branch write the name Buzzell. *WILLIAM, Salisbury, representative in 1679.

BUTLER HENRY freeman 1651. He was born in Kent ; educated at Cambridge ; came to N. E. a. 1650 and was in the ministry 11 or 12 years. He returned to England, and was settled at Yeovil, in Somersetshire, and d. 24 April, 1696, æ. a. 72. Calamy, ii. Account, 611. JOHN, Massachusetts, was admitted freeman 1635. One of this name was member of the ar. co. in 1644. JOHN, Massachusetts, freeman 1649. NICHOLAS, Dorchester, freeman 1638. RICHARD, Cambridge 1632, freeman 1634. Holmes, Hist. Cambridge. THOMAS, Lynn ; removed to Sandwich 1637. Lewis. WILLIAM, Boston and Cambridge, freeman 1635. He married Eunice, sister of Tristram Coffin, who came to N. E. in 1644. Peter Butler, perhaps a son, d. at Boston in 1699.

BUTTALL, THOMAS, Boston, a glover, was admitted member of the church in 1639. Snow, Hist. Boston.

BUTTERFIELD, BENJAMIN, Woburn, freeman 1643 : Chelmsford 1654, is the great ancestor of the Butterfields in Middlesex county, Mass. His son Nathaniel, was b. in 1642. There was a Butterfield near Saybrook, who was taken by the Pequots in 1636, and probably put to death. Winthrop, i. Hist. 198. There was a Samuel Butterfield early at Springfield.

BUTTERWORTH, SAMUEL, admitted freeman 1640. John Butterworth was one of the founders of the first Baptist church in Swanzey 1663. Nathaniel Butterworth d. at Groton in 1682.

BUTTOLPH, THOMAS, Boston, freeman 1641. Snow, Hist. Boston, 105. He had sons, Thomas, b. 1637 ; John, b. 1639. Thomas Buttolph d. in Boston, 30 Nov. 1690.

BUTTON, JOHN, Boston, freeman 1634. Savage, i. Winth. N. E. 248. Snow, Hist. Boston, 105. MATTHIAS, Ipswich 1648. ROBERT, Salem, admitted member of the church 27 Feb. 1642 ; freeman 1642.

BUTTRICK, WILLIAM, Concord 1635, came over with Thomas Flint, m. (1st) Sarah Bateman 1646, who d. 1664, (2d) Jane Goodenow, in 1667. He d. 30 June, 1698. His children were, Mary, William, John, b. 1653, settled in Stow ; Samuel, Edward, Joseph, Sarah, and Mary. Shattuck, MS Hist. Concord.

BUXTON, ANTHONY, Salem, 1637 ; d. 1684. Thomas Buxton, who is styled a husbandman, was of Salem and d. a. 1654.

BYAM, GEORGE, was admitted member of the church in Salem, 27 Sept. 1640 ; freeman 1642.

BYFIELD, ||*NATHANIEL, son of Rev. Richard Byfield, of Long-Ditton, in Sussex and the youngest of 21 children, was b. in 1653, came to Boston in 1674 ; was member of the ar. co. 1679 ; was a proprietor, and one of the principal settlers of Bristol, which he represented in the House of Representatives, of which he was speaker in 1693. He was a colonel, judge of the vice-admiralty, and of the court of common pleas for Bristol county, of the latter 38 years. He d. at Boston, 6 June, 1733, in his 80th year.

BYLES, or BYLEY, HENRY, came from Sarum, in England, and settled at Salisbury as early as 1640. His daughter m. Rev. John Hale.

BYRAM, NICHOLAS, Weymouth 1638, removed to Bridgewater. He died 1687, leaving one son, Nicholas. 2 Coll. Mass. Hist. Soc. vii. 154. Rev. Eliab Byram, H. C. 1740, probably a descendant, was the minister of Hopewell, N. J.

CABELL, JOHN, Springfield 1636. Sprague, Hist. Disc. 14.

CADY, JAMES, came from the west of England with three sons, and settled at Hingham 1635, but appears to have removed from thence to Yarmouth, as early as 1640, and the same year there appears to have been a James Cady of Boston. Nicholas Cady was of Watertown in 1645, and James and Nicholas Cady were early inhabitants of Groton.

CAFFINGE, JOHN, Guilford 1639. Trumbull, i. Hist. Conn.

CAKEBREAD, ||THOMAS, Boston, freeman 1634, member of the ar. co. 1637, removed to Sudbury, and d. 4 Jan. 1643.

CALDWELL, JOHN, Ipswich 1665. Twelve of the name had grad. at the N. E. colleges in 1828.

CALEF, ROBERT, a merchant of Boston, and author of "More Wonders of the Invisible World," printed in London 1700, died at Roxbury, 13 April, 1719. John and Jonathan Calef grad. at D. C. in 1786 and 1787.

CALL, *JONATHAN, Charlestown, representative 1689. PHILIP, Ipswich, died a. 1662, leaving children Philip and Mary. THOMAS, Charlestown, was admitted freeman 1640.

CAMMOCK, THOMAS, nephew to the Earl of Warwick, came to N. E. as early as 1632, lived sometime at Pascataqua, and d. at Scarborough, Me., 1663. 2 Coll. Mass. Hist. Soc. v. 216, 224. Prince, ii. Annals, 70.

CANNEY, THOMAS, Pascataqua 1631, Bloody-Point, in Dover, 1644. Joseph, his son, m. Mary Clements 1670.

CANNON, JOHN, Plymouth 1623. Four of the name had grad. in 1828, at Union and Williams Colleges.

CANTERBURY, CORNELIUS, Hingham 1653.

CANTLEBURY, WILLIAM, Lynn, 1641 ; afterwards of Salem, and died 1663.

CANWELL, JOHN, Massachusetts, was admitted freeman in 1631.

CAPEN, BERNARD, Dorchester, freeman 1636, d. 8 Nov. 1638, æ. 76. His widow, Jane Capen, d. 26 March, 1653, æ. 75. Dorchester Sexton Monitor, 13. ||*JOHN, Dorchester, freeman 1634 ; member of the ar. co. 1646 ; a captain of the militia ; deacon of the church 1656 ; representative 1671, 1673—1678, 6 years. He died 4 April, 1692, æ. 80. *JOSEPH*, minister of Topsfield, son of John Capen, was born at Dorchester, 20 Dec. 1658, grad. at H. C.

1667, ord. at Topsfield, 11 June, 1684 ; died 30 June, 1725, in his 67th year, leaving widow, Priscilla, and several children.

CARDER, RICHARD, Boston, freeman 1636. Savage, i. Winth. N. E. 248. ii. 121, 148.

CARLETON, *EDWARD, Rowley, freeman 1642, representative 1644 to 1647, 4 years. His son Edward was the first person born in Rowley on record. John Carleton, of Haverhill, died in 1669.

CARMAN, JOHN, Lynn 1636, removed to Sandwich in 1637. Lewis. Winthrop [ii. Hist. N. E. 124] mentions a Mr. Carman, the master of a ship.

CARNES, ||JOHN, Boston, member of the ar. co. 1649, and the same year its captain. Mr. Whitman [Hist. Sketch, 20] says he was a captain in the British navy. Rev. John Carnes grad. at H. C. in 1742.

CARPENTER, *WILLIAM, Weymouth, freeman 1640, representative 1641, and 1643. WILLIAM, Providence 1641, was one of the founders of the first Baptist church. 3 Coll. Mass. Hist. Soc. i. 4. Savage, ii. Winth. 85. Benedict, i. Hist. Baptists. JOSEPH, Swanzey, one of the founders of the first Baptist church in Massachusetts. Rev. Ezra Carpenter, H. C. 1720, and Hon. Benjamin Carpenter, lieut. gov. of Vermont, who d. 29 March, 1804, æ. 79, were propabably from this family, both being natives of Rehoboth.

CARR, GEORGE, a ferryman and shipwright, was of Ipswich 1638, Salisbury 1642, d. 4 April, 1682.

CARRIER, THOMAS, Billerica 1665, Andover 1692, died at Colchester, Conn., 16 May, 1735, æ. 109. [Allen, Biog. Dict.] He came from Wales, and m. 7 May, 1664, Martha Allen, who was one of the victims of the witchcraft infatuation at Salem-Village, 19 Aug. 1692. He had several children born in Billerica, where his name is sometimes connected by an alias to *Morgan*, in the town records.

CARRINGTON, EDWARD, Charlestown, was admitted freeman 1636. Four, Edward, Samuel, Abijah, and George Carrington, have grad. at Yale College.

CARSLEY, WILLIAM, Hingham 1637. Perhaps the William Casely of Scituate.

CARTER, JOHN, Woburn, freeman 1644. I. Mather, Indian Wars, 35. Sixteen of the name of Carter had grad. at the N. E. colleges in 1828. JOSEPH, Newbury 1636. Joseph Carter, sen. d. at Charlestown, Dec. 1676. JOSHUA, freeman 1634, perhaps of Northampton 1660. RICHARD, Boston 1641. Perhaps Carder, which see. ||SAMUEL, Charlestown, freeman 1647 ; member of the ar. co. 1648. Sons, Samuel, born 18 Sept. 1642, and probably the graduate of of H. C. 1660 ; Zachary, and others. *THOMAS*, the first minister of Woburn, came to N. E. as early as 1635, and was admitted freeman, 9 March, 1637, lived several years at Dedham, and Watertown ; was ordained at Woburn, 22 Nov. 1642, and d. 5 Sept., 1684, æ. 74. Johnson, Hist. N. E. 177, 181. Chick-

ering, Ded. Sermon. Worthington, Hist. Dedham, 104. THO-
MAS, Charlestown, freeman 1638, was perhaps one of the proprietors of Salisbury. THOMAS, son of the preceding, was admitted
freeman 1647.

CARTLAND, PHILIP and NATHANIEL, Lynn 1638. (See
KIRTLAND.) The name of Cartland exists in New-Hampshire.

CARVER, §JOHN, one of the first pilgrims of Plymouth 1620,
and the first governour of the colony, died in April, 1621. His wife
died 5 or 6 weeks after. Prince, i. Annals, 105. Allen, Biog.
Dict.

CARY, JAMES, came from Bristol, England, and settled at
Charlestown as early as 1639, and died in 1681. His children
were, John ; James, b. 1644 ; Nathaniel, b. 1645 ; Jonathan, b.
1646 ; Elizabeth ; Eleanor. From him descended Rev. Thomas
Cary, of Newburyport, H. C. 1761, whose son, Rev. Samuel Cary,
H. C. 1804, was minister of King's Chapel, and d. 1815, æ. 30.
JOHN, Bridgewater, came to N. E. from Somersetshire, a. 1640,
at the age of 25 ; was one of the first settlers, and the first town
clerk of that town. He d. 2 Nov. 1681. Cary, Genealogy of North-
Bridgewater. NICHOLAS, Salem 1637.

CASELY, EDWARD, Scituate 1638, removed to Barnstable.
2 Coll. Mass. Hist. Soc. iv. 239. WILLIAM, Scituate 1639. Ibid.

CASKIN, WILLIAM, Concord 1642. Daughter Sarah born
1642.

CASS, JOSEPH, Exeter, a. 1680, had children, from one of whom
descended Major Jonathan Cass, father of Hon. Lewis Cass, governour of Michigan, a native of New-Hampshire.

CAULKIN, *HUGH, Lynn, admitted freeman 1642 ; went to
Gloucester as early as 1643 ; representative in 1650 and 1651.
John Caulkins grad at Y. C. 1788.

CAYNE, CHRISTOPHER, Cambridge. (See KEAINE.)

CHADBOURNE, *HUMPHREY, Pascataqua 1631, Kittery
1652, was representative 1657 and 1659. Ichabod R. Chadbourne,
esq., D. C. 1808, and Thomas Chadbourne, M. D., of Conway, N.
H., are descendants from him or the following. WILLIAM, Pascataqua 1631, may have been the one of Boston in 1644. WIL-
LIAM, son of the preceding, Pascataqua 1631, Kittery 1652.

CHADDOCK, THOMAS, Newbury, m. Sarah Woolcott, 6.
April, 1674.

CHADWELL, RICHARD, Lynn 1636, removed to Sandwich
1637. Lewis. THOMAS, Lynn 1648; died Feb. 1683. He had
sons Thomas, Moses, and Benjamin. Ibid.

CHADWICK, *CHARLES, Watertown, freeman 1631, representative 1657 and 1659 ; died 10 April, 1682, æ. 86. Shattuck.
JOHN, Watertown, son of the preceding, freeman 1655, was called
Sergeant Chadwick, had 5 sons and 3 daughters, and d. 5 Feb.
1711. THOMAS, Watertown, brother of the preceding, had 4
sons and 3 daughters. Ibid.

CHAFFY, MATTHEW, a ship-carpenter, was admitted member of the church in Boston, 1636 ; freeman 1637. Descendants

write the name *Chaffee.* THOMAS, Hingham 1637 ; removed to Swanzey. Lincoln, Hist. Hingham.

CHAFLIN, MICHAEL, Salem 1637, was admitted freeman 1643.

CHAMBERLAIN, EDMUND, Chelmsford 1655, had a son Edmund, b. 20 May, 1656, and probably other children. Descendants remain. HENRY, Hingham, a blacksmith, was admitted freeman 1638, and left sons, Henry, perhaps the freeman of 1645, and William. JOHN, Charlestown, d. 3 March, 1653. John, a currier, perhaps the same admitted townsman of Boston, 28 July, 1651. RICHARD, Braintree 1644. RICHARD, Portsmouth, counsellor under the provincial government 1682. THOMAS, Woburn, freeman 1644 ; removed to Chelmsford. WILLIAM, Billerica 1654, perhaps son of Henry of Hingham, had sons Jacob, Thomas, and Edmund. He d. 31 May, 1706, æ. 86.

CHAMBERS, THOMAS, Scituate 1639. Rev. Joseph Chambers, grad. at N. J. College in 1765.

CHAMPERNOON, ‡FRANCIS, York, Me., 1665, a captain and magistrate, and in 1684 one of the provincial counsellors of New-Hampshire. Hubbard, Hist. N. E. 584. Belknap.

CHAMPNEY, JOHN, Cambridge 1635. Joseph Champney was admitted freeman in 1654. RICHARD, Cambridge 1635, freeman 1636, an elder of the church, d. 26 Nov.1669. By Jane, his wife, his children were, Esther, born in England ; Samuel ; Daniel, born 9 March, 1645, admitted to the church 1663 ; Lydia. *SAMUEL, Cambridge, admitted member of the church 1661, freeman 1663, was son of the preceding. He lived in Billerica several years, and five of his children were born there. Joseph and Daniel were b. at Cambridge. He was representative of Cambridge 1686 and 1689.

CHANDLER, EDMUND, Duxbury, one of the first settlers a. 1645. Thirty-six of the name had grad. at the N. E. colleges in 1828. JOHN, one of the proprietors of Concord, was admitted freeman in 1640. One of the same name was admitted townsman of Boston 31 May, 1647. *THOMAS, Andover 1645, son of William Chandler, was representative in 1678, and at the 2d session 1679. His sons were John, William, Thomas, Henry, and Joseph, who all settled in Andover. WILLIAM, Roxbury, was admitted freeman in 1640, and d. 19 June, 1641. WILLIAM, Newbury, a cooper, had several children, and d. 5 March, 1702, æ. 85. Mary, his wife, died 1666.

CHAPIN, *HENRY, Springfield, representative 1689. Twenty-three of the name of Chapin had grad. at the N. E. colleges in 1826. *JOSIAH Weymouth 1659, Braintree, freeman 1678, representative for Mendon 1689. SAMUEL, Braintree, freeman 1644, when he appears to have settled in Springfield, where he was a deacon, d. 11 Nov. 1675.

CHAPLAIN, *CLEMENT, Cambridge 1635, was admitted freeman and elected representative in 1636 ; probably went to Weathersfield, where was a Chaplain in the early settlement.

CHAPLIN, HUGH, Rowley, son of Ebenezer Chaplin, b. 10 May, 1572, and grandson of Jeremy Chaplin of Bradford in Yorkshire, b. 4 Aug. 1541, was born 22 May, 1603, came to N. E. as early as 1638, and was admitted freeman in 1642. He is the ancestor of Rev. Daniel Chaplin, D. D. of Groton. His son Joseph was b. in 1643, and settled in Attleborough, Mass.

CHAPMAN, JOHN, Massachusetts, was admitted freeman in 1634. Jacob Chapman was admitted a resident or townsman in Boston, 28 March, 1642. RICHARD, Braintree 1647, was killed by the Indians. He had daughters, Susan, Hope, and Mary. Dea. Samuel Chapman was a proprietor of Westfield in 1660. ‡ROBERT, Connecticut, was elected a magistrate in 1683. Twelve of the name, and probably his descendants, had grad. at Y. C. in 1828.

CHAPPELL, NATHANIEL, Massachusetts, freeman 1639. One of this name received an honorary degree from Midd. Coll. in 1819.

CHARD, WILLIAM, Weymouth, admitted freeman 1654, was town clerk. Thomas Chard, born in 1657, lived in Boston in 1680.

CHARLES, WILLIAM, Marblehead 1648.

CHASE, AQUILA, Newbury, was born 1618, removed to Hampton. His children born in Newbury were, Aquila, b. 26 Sept. 1652; Thomas, born 1654; John, b. 2 Nov. 1655, Daniel, 1661; Moses, b. 24 Dec. 1664, and several daughters. He is the ancestor of Hon. Dudley Chase, a U. S. senator from Vermont, and of Rev. Philander Chase, D. D., bishop of the Ohio diocese. Descendants are very numerous. Thirty of the name had grad. at the N. E. colleges in 1828. THOMAS, an early settler of Hampden, d. in 1652. Coffin. WILLIAM, Massachusetts, requested to be made freeman 1630, and was admitted 14 May, 1634.

CHATFIELD, GEORGE, Guilford 1650. John Chatfield grad. at Y. C. 1735.

CHATTERTON, MICHAEL, Portsmouth 1640. Belknap, i. Hist. N. H. 47. THOMAS, Pascataqua 1631. Adams, Annals Portsmouth, where the name is Chatherton.

CHAULKLEY, ROBERT, Charlestown, was admitted freeman 1647, d. 2 Sept. 1672.

CHAUNCY, BARNABAS, son of the following, was admitted member of the church in Cambridge, 10 Dec. 1656, grad. at H. C. 1657, and died according to W. Winthrop [MS Catalogue] in middle age. *CHARLES*, the second president of Harvard College, was the 5th son of George Chauncy, of Hertfordshire, who died in 1627. He was baptized at Yardley, 5 Nov. 1592, educated at Trinity College, Cambridge; settled at Marstow, then at Ware, came to N. E. in 1638, arrived at Plymouth, where he preached 3 years, settled at Scituate 1641; became president of H. C. 27 Nov. 1654, died 19 Feb. 1672, in his 80th year, or, according to Mather and others, in his 82d year. His wife was Catharine, daughter of Robert Eyre, esq. of Wiltshire, and she d. 4 Jan. 1668. His children were Isaac, Ichabod, Barnabas, Nathaniel, Elnathan, Israel, Sarah, and Hannah. Sarah, admitted member of the church, 10

Dec. 1656, became the wife of Rev. Gershom Bulkley. *CHARLES*, minister of Fairfield, Conn., grandson of the preceding, grad. at H. C. 1686, and died 4 May, 1711. He was father of Rev. Charles Chauncy, D. D., of Boston. ELNATHAN, son of President Chauncy, was baptized at Scituate, grad. at H. C. 1661, and settled as a physician in Boston. *ICHABOD*, brother of the preceding, born in England 1635, grad. at H. C. 1651; went to England, and was chaplain to Sir Edward Harley's regiment, at Dunkirk, was afterwards physician in Bristol, and of " good note." He went to Holland 1684; returned to England 1686, and d. at Bristol, 25 July, 1691, æ. 56. Mary, his widow, died a. 1736, æ. 90. *ISAAC*, brother of the preceding, was born 23 August, 1632, grad. at H. C. 1651; went to England, where he settled in the ministry; was ejected from office after the restoration : settled then in London, where he d. 28 Feb. 1712, in his 80th year. His children were, 1. Isaac; 2. Uzziel, who died 1696; 3. Charles, before named; 4. Elizabeth, who m. John Nisbet, of London, 10 Dec. 1689, and died 1727. *ISRAEL*, brother of the preceding, was born at Scituate, grad. at H. C. 1661, was ordained the minister of Stamford, Conn., 1665; d. 14 March, 1703, æ. 59. He had two sons, Charles and Isaac, whose posterity are in England. *NATHANIEL*, minister of Hatfield, was brother of the preceding, and was bapt. at Scituate; grad. 1661, at H. C. of which he was fellow; died 4 Nov. 1686. His children were, 1. Catharine, who m. Rev. Daniel Brewer; 2. Abigail, who m. 1st, Dr. Hudson, 2d, Edward Burroughs; 3. Isaac, who died without issue; 4. Nathaniel, who had 3 sons and 3 daughters; 5. Sarah, who m. Rev. Samuel Whittelsey, of Wallingford, Conn.

CHEATER, JOHN, Newbury 1644, went to Wells, Maine.

CHECKETT, JOSEPH, Scituate 1638.

CHECKLEY, ||ANTHONY, Boston, a captain, elected member of ar. co. 1662. Capt. Samuel Checkley was the ancestor of the graduates of this name at Harvard College. JOHN, Boston, freeman 1648. Son John, born 1653.

CHEDSEY, JOHN, New-Haven 1644, a dea. of the church, d. 31 Dec. 1688, æ. 67. This name is now written Chidsey in this country.

CHEESEHOLME, ||THOMAS, Cambridge, freeman 1636; member of ar. co. 1638, deacon of the church. The name of *Chisolm* exists in N. E.

CHEESEBOROUGH, WILLIAM, Boston, freeman 1631, resided in Braintree, Rehoboth, and Stonington, Conn. to which place he removed in 1649. His descendants are in Connecticut, where three have grad. at Yale college, and several have been ministers. His son Joseph was b. at Braintree, 18 July, 1640. Savage, i. Winth. N. E. 55, 76. Holmes, i. Amer. Annals, 580.

CHEESHAHTEAUMUCK, CALEB, an Indian, and the only one who grad. at H. C. the first century, received the degree of A. B. in 1665, and died at Charlestown the next year.

CHEEVER, BARTHOLOMEW, Boston, came from Canterbury, England, a. 1637, admitted freeman 1647, died 18 Dec. 1693, æ. 88, leaving no children. He made his nephew Richard, 3d son of Daniel Cheever, of England, his heir, who came to N. E. in 1668, and died in France on his return to England in 1704. Boston Magazine, 1826, p. 619. DANIEL, Cambridge 1647, member of the church, with Esther his wife. His children were Lydia, b. 1647; James; Daniel; Mary; John, bapt. 1659; Esther; Israel, bapt. 1661; Hannah; Elizabeth; Gamilla; [?] Elizabeth, 2d. EZEKIEL, the celebrated schoolmaster, of whom an early poet says,

" 'Tis Corlet's pains, and Cheever's, we must own,
" That thou, New-England, art not Scythia grown,"

was born in London, 25 Jan. 1615, came to N. E. in 1637, and settled at New-Haven; removed to Ipswich, Dec. 1650, to Charlestown, Nov. 1660, to Boston, 6 Jan. 1670, where he died 21 August, 1708, æ. 93. Ezekiel Cheever of Salem was admitted freeman in 1681. *SAMUEL*, the first ordained Minister of Marblehead, was son of the preceding, and was born at New-Haven, 22 Sept. 1639; grad. at H. C. 1659; ordained 13 August, 1684; d. 29 May, 1724, æ. 85. Rev. Ames Cheever, his son, grad. at H. C. 1707, and was the minister of Manchester, Mass. *THOMAS*, brother of the preceding, grad. at H. C. 1677, freeman 1680; ordained at Malden, from whence he removed and was settled the first minister of Chelsea, 19 Oct. 1715, died in Nov. 1749, æ. 93.

CHELETT, NICHOLAS, Boston, admitted freeman 1645.

CHELLIS, *PHILIP, was born a. 1617, came to N. E. and settled in Salisbury; was representative in 1662. Coll. N. H. Hist. Soc. ii. 222, where the name is spelled *Chalice*.

CHENEY, JOHN, Newbury, freeman 1637, had a son Nathaniel and other children, died 17 Jan. 1672. There was a John Cheney at Watertown at an early period, who d. 5 Sept. 1675. Seven of the name have grad. at the N. E. colleges. WILLIAM, Roxbury 1639, died 30 June, 1667, æ. 73. Son John was born 1640.

CHESLEY, PHILIP, Dover 1642. Thomas Chesley was of Dover in 1663.

CHESTER, LEONARD, Weathersfield 1635, came to N. E. 1633, from Leicestershire, and d. 11 Dec. 1648, æ. 39. His son John died 23 Feb. 1607, in his 62d year; his grandson John, esq., d. 14 Dec. 1711, æ. 56. Col. John Chester, son of the last, was b. 30 June, 1703, and died 11 Sept. 1771, leaving son, Hon. John Chester, b. 29 Jan. 1749. d. 4 Nov. 1809. Eleven of the name have grad. at the N. E. colleges.

CHICHESTER, JAMES, Salem 1651, removed from thence. WILLIAM, Marblehead 1648.

CHIDLEY, ||JOHN, member of the ar. co. 1639.

CHICKERING, ||*Francis, Dedham, freeman 1640, member of ar. co. 1643; representative 1644 and 1653. He was chosen one of the first deacons at Dedham in 1650. Worthington, Hist. Dedham, 104. *HENRY, Dedham, freeman 1641, representative 1642—1644, 1647, and 1651, 5 years. Four of this name, two of them clergymen, had grad. at Harv. College in 1826.

CHILD, *EPHRAIM, Watertown, was admitted freeman in 1631, having come to N. E. the preceding year. He was elected representative in the years 1635, 1646, 1649, 1650, and from 1652 to 1662, excepting 1653 and 1658. He was a deacon of the church, and d. 13 Feb. 1663, æ. 70. Twelve of the name, and seven spelling it Childs, had grad. at the N. E. colleges in 1826. JOSEPH, Massachusetts, was admitted freeman in 1654. ROBERT, a physician, who received the degree of Doctor of Medicine from Padua, came twice to N. E. and gave considerable disturbance to the government. [Winthrop, ii. Hist. N. E. Index. Winslow, N. England's Salamander Discovered, 1647.] Robert Child was one of the petitioners for the grant of Lancaster in 1644. Willard, Hist. Lancaster. WILLIAM, Massachusetts, was admitted freeman 1634.

CHILLINGWORTH, THOMAS, Lynn; removed to Sandwich 1637. Lewis.

CHILTON, JAMES, one of the first pilgrims at Plymouth 1620, died 8 Dec. 1620.

CHINE, GEORGE, Marlborough 1648.

CHITTENDEN, THOMAS, Scituate 1638. WILLIAM, New-Haven 1639, Guilford 1650. He was probably the ancestor of Thomas Chittenden, the first governour of Vermont, who was a native of East-Guilford, Conn. Hon. Martin Chittenden, his son, grad. at D. C. 1789, and has been governour of Vermont.

CHOATE, JOHN, Ipswich 1648. Benjamin, Amos, George, and Augustus Choate have grad. at Harvard, and Rufus Choate, D. C. 1819, was a tutor at Dartmouth College.

CHUBB, THOMAS, was born in Crewhorn, in Somersetshire, came to N. E. as early as 1636, settled in Salem, and afterwards lived in Beverly, where he d. 17 Oct. 1688, æ. 82. Beverly Town Records.

CHUBBUCK, THOMAS, Hingham 1634. Jeremiah Chubbuck grad at H. C. 1725.

CHURCH, BENJAMIN, Little-Compton, the celebrated warrior, was son of Joseph Church, and was born at Duxbury 1639; [Judge Davis says at Plymouth] m. Alice Southworth, by whom he had Thomas, Constant, Edward, Benjamin, Charles, and one daughter. Col. Church d. 17 Jan. 1718, æ. 77. For an account of him and some of his descendants, see S. G. Drake's edition of Church's Memoirs. Eighteen of the name had grad. at the N. E. Colleges in 1825. GARRETT, Watertown 1636; freeman 1649, had sons, John, b. 10 March, 1637; Samuel, b. 12 June, 1640. JOSEPH, Duxbury, 1639, had sons Joseph, Caleb, and Benjamin, and perhaps others. Caleb lived in Watertown; the other two at Little-Compton. Life of Church in his memoirs, 159. RICHARD, Massachusetts, requested freedom 19 Oct. 1630, and was probably the same who was afterwards at Hingham, and possibly the Richard Church, one of the first settlers of Duxbury, whom Mr. Bradford [2 Coll. Mass. Hist. Soc. x. 66] makes to be the father of the "great warriour against the Indians." But the Life of Church, in his Memoirs, quoted above, says Joseph was the father of Benjamin.

CHURCHMAN, HUGH, Lynn 1640 ; died 1644. Lewis.

CHUTE, LIONEL, a schoolmaster of Ipswich, d. about 1645, leaving a son James, and perhaps other children. Daniel and James Chute grad. at D. C. in 1810 and 1813.

CLAP, EDWARD, Dorchester, freeman 1636, deacon of the church 26 years, d. 8 Jan. 1644, leaving no issue. Twelve of the name had grad. at Harv. and Yale in 1828. NICHOLAS, Dorchester 1636, was a deacon of the church. His son Nathaniel was b. 15 Sept. 1640. ||*ROGER, Dorchester 1630,.was born at Salcolm, in Devonshire, 6 April, 1609, came to N. E. with Messrs. Maverick and Warham; was admitted freeman 1634 ; member of the ar. co. 1646, lieutenant of the same 1655 ; captain of the militia ; representative 1652—1665, excepting one year, and 1671, 14 years. He d. 2 Feb. 1691, in his 82 year. His sons were, Samuel, b. 11 Oct. 1634, a representative in 1689 ; died 15 Oct. 1708 ; William and Waitstill who both d. young ; Preserved, one of the first settlers of Northampton, who d. 20 Sept. 1720 ; Hopestill ; Desire. THOMAS, Weymouth, brother of Nicholas Clap, freeman 1638, removed to Hingham, and from thence to Scituate, and d. 1684. Son Thomas born at Weymouth 1639.

CLARK, ARTHUR, Hampton, was admitted freeman 1640. The name of Clark is a very common one ; it is sometimes spelled Clarke, but more frequently the *e* is omitted. One hundred and four persons of the name had grad. at the New-England and at Princeton and Union colleges in 1826, of whom 28 have been settled ministers. Kelly, MS Catalogue. DANIEL, Ipswich, 1635. Hutchinson (i. Hist. Mass. 385] names a Daniel Clarke, and Rev. Mr. Felt gives me the name of David Clark, of Ipswich, at an early period. ‡DANIEL, a magistrate of Connecticut, in 1662, secretary of the colony in 1660. EDMUND, Lynn 1636; removed to Sandwich 1637. Lewis. ‡HENRY, Connecticut, was a magistrate in 1648, and many years afterwards. ||HUGH, Watertown 1640, three of whose children were, John, born 13 Oct. 1641 ; Uriah, b. 5 April, 1644 ; Elizabeth, b. 6 Nov. 1647. There was a Hugh Clark, probably the same, who was admitted freeman in 1660, member of ar. co. 1666, and who d. at Roxbury, 20 July, 1693. Elizabeth, his wife, died in 1692. ‡JEREMIAH, Rhode-Island, was president of the colony in 1648. He was probably one of the brothers of John Clark, one of the founders of the colony. JOHN, Cambridge, freeman 1632, probably went with Rev. Thomas Hooker to Connecticut, where several of the name were early in publick life. JOHN, a physician, and one of the founders of the R. I. colony, came, according to tradition, from Bedfordshire, and settled in Massachusetts, from whence he was driven before 1638. He was treasurer of R. I. colony, and a minister. He died 20 April, 1676. See an account of him in Allen's Biog. Dict. 190—192. He had 3 brothers, ancestors to a large family in Rhode-Island. *JOHN, the first physician in Newbury, was born a. 1598, settled in Newbury in 1638 ; admitted freeman 1639, representative at the Sept. session that year ; removed to Boston, where he was much distinguished as a physician, and died in Jan. 1665, æ. 66. Thacher, i. Med. Biog. 222. Coffin, MS letter. *JOHN, son of the preceding, was a physician, and admitted freeman 1673 ; representative 1689 and 1690, and d. 17 Dec. 1690. His son John was born 27 Jan. 1668, grad. at H. C. 1687, was rep. of Boston from 1708 to 1714, and 1720 to 1724 ; chosen speaker 1709, 1720—1723 ; was also a counsellor, and d. 6 Dec. 1728. Ibid, 223. JOHN, Massachusetts, admitted freeman 1635, may have been the John Clark who removed to R. Island. JOSEPH, Dedham, freeman 1635 ; had sons, Joseph, b. 1642 ; Benjamin 1643, and Ephraim 1645. JOSEPH, Newport 1644 ; one of the founders of the first Baptist church in that place. JONAS, Cambridge, freeman 1647, had by his first wife, Sarah and Jonas ; by the 2d, Elizabeth, whom he m. 1650, his children were, Elizabeth ; Thomas, b. 1653 ; Jno. born 1655 ; Timothy ; Samuel, b. 1659 ; Abigail ; Mary ; Jno. b. 1665 ; Nath'l, 1677. NATHANIEL, Plymouth, was one of Sir Edmund Andros' council in 1687, d. 1717, æ. 73, leaving no children. Nathaniel Clark, of Newbury, d. 25 Aug. 1690. NICHOLAS, Cambridge 1634. RICHARD, one of the first pilgrims at Plymouth, died in 1621. A Richard Clark was an early settler at Rowley. ROBERT, Boston, was assistant minister of King's Chapel in 1686. ‡‖*THOMAS, Boston, admitted freeman, and member of ar. co. 1638 ; captain of ar. co. 1651 ; major of the Suffolk regiment ; representative 1651, 18 years ; speaker of the house 1662, '65, '69, '70, and '72 ; elected assistant 1673 to 1677, 5 years. He died 13 March, 1683. He was one of the two who entered their dissent against the law of 1656 punishing with death all quakers who should return to Massachusetts after banishment. THOMAS, jr., Boston, probably son of the preceding, was representative from 1673 to 1676, 4 years. THOMAS, blacksmith, of Boston, was admitted a townsman 25 Nov. 1639, member of the church 1640, freeman 1641. Cornelius and Jacob, sons of Thomas Clark, were b. in 1639 and 1642. THOMAS, Dorchester, member of the church 1636. There was a Thomas Clark of Ipswich in 1648, and another in 1674, who was admitted freeman that year. There was a Thomas Clark of Lynn 1640, who removed to Reading. *THOMAS*, the second minister of Chelmsford, son of Jonas Clark, was born at Cambridge, 2 March, 1653 ; grad. at H. C. 1670, succeeded Rev. John Fiske in 1677 ; d. 7 Dec. 1704, æ. 52. His children were, Jonas, a colonel and magistrate, born 20 Dec. 1684, died 8 April, 1770 ; Thomas, b. 28 Sept. 1694 ; Elizabeth, who m. Rev. John Hancock, of Lexington ; Lucy, who m. Major William Tyng, of Dunstable ; and several who died in infancy. Mary his first wife, d. 2 Dec. 1700, and he m. Elizabeth Whiting in 1702. THOMAS, Newport, one of the founders of the first Baptist church in that place in 1644. THOMAS, Plymouth, d. 24 March, 1697, æ. 98. There was a Thomas Clark of Scituate in 1676. ‡WALTER, Rhode-Island, was speaker of the house of deputies; one of Sir Edmund

Andros' council 1687, and governour in 1676, 1686, 1696, and 1697. WILLIAM, Ipswich, one of the first settlers 1633, and probably admitted freeman in 1631. He is mentioned by Prince, who omits his name of captain, which is supplied by the Ipswich town records. There was a William Clark of Watertown in 1631 ; another of Dorchester, and member of the church in 1636 ; one of Salem, who died a. 1647 ; and one who was admitted freeman in 1639. WILLIAM, Lynn 1646 ; perhaps the member of the ar. co. in 1647 ; died 5 March, 1683. His children were, Hannah ; John, who d. 1684 ; Lydia ; Sarah ; Mary ; and Elizabeth. Lewis. *WILLIAM, Northampton, representative in 1663. URIAH, Watertown, son of Hugh Clark, was born at Watertown, 5 April, 1644, admitted freeman 1685. He was father of Rev. Peter Clark, H. C. 1712, a learned minister of Danvers, whose sons, Peter and William, grad. at H. C. 1739 and 1759, the latter an Episcopal minister of Dedham. [See Worthington's Hist. Dedham, 119, and Whitney's Hist. Hingham, 42.] A descendant of the sixth generation from Rev. Peter Clark, the whole series being of that name, is a member of Dartmouth College.

CLARY, JOHN, Hadley 1671.

CLAYS, JOHN, Casco 1665. Hutchinson, Coll. 398. (See CLOYES.)

CLEMENT, AUGUSTINE, Dorchester, freeman 1636. Sons, Samuel, b. 1635 ; John, b. 1639. ‡JOB, Dover, a mandamus counsellor of New-Hampshire 1682. He m. Joanna Leighton, 16 July, 1673. *JOHN, Haverhill, m. 1st, Margaret Dummer 1647 ; 2d, m. Sarah Osgood, 1649 ; died, it is supposed, in 1659. He was representative 1654. *ROBERT, brother of the preceding, came from London 1642, and settled in Haverhill, which he represented 1648 to 1653, 6 years. He died a. 1658. Robert Clement, prob. his son, d. in 1712. WILLIAM, Cambridge 1636. A William Clement was member of the ar. co. 1662.

CLEVERLY, JOHN, Braintree, a. 1660, was a lieutenant, and perhaps d. in Boston, 1703. Rev. John Cleverly, who grad. at H. C. 1715, was minister of Elizabeth-Town, N. J.

CLEVES, *GEORGE, Falmouth 1658, came to N. E. as early as 1637 ; was representative in 1663. Winthrop, i. Hist. N. E. 237. ii. 256.

CLIFFORD, ‖GEORGE,‘ Massachusetts, member ar. co. 1644. JOHN, Lynn, d. 17 June, 1698, in his 68th year. Lewis.

CLIPTON, THOMAS, Massachusetts, admitted freeman 1641.

CLOUGH, ISAAC, Massachusetts, admitted freeman 1642. JOHN, one of the proprietors of Salisbury, and perhaps also of Watertown, was admitted freeman 1642.

CLOYES, JOHN, Watertown 1637. Sons, John, b. 1638 ; Peter, b. 1639 ; Nathaniel, b. 1642. Nathan Cloyes, of Massachusetts, was admitted freeman 1660.

COALBORN, NATHANIEL, Dedham, freeman 1641. Son, Nathaniel, b. 1644.

COATES, THOMAS, Lynn 1658, had sons John, James, and Thomas. Lewis.

COBB, HENRY, came to Plymouth as early as 1629; was at Scituate 1633, removed to Barnstable, where he died in 1679, leaving 7 sons and 4 daughters. His descendants, says the antiquary of Plymouth, [2 Coll. Mass. Hist. Soc. iv. 247] are "as numerous, figuratively, as the sands on the sea shore." Nineteen of the name had grad. at the N. E. colleges in 1828.

COBBETT, JOSIAH, Cambridge 1636, freeman 1640, appears to have been one of the proprietors of Salisbury in 1640. One of the same name was of Hingham in 1635. SAMUEL, who graduated in 1663, is supposed to have been the eldest son of the following. He was admitted freeman in 1674, and was living in 1698. *THOMAS*, the fourth minister of Ipswich, was born at Newbury, England, in 1608; was sometime a student at Oxford, arrived in N. E. 26 June, 1637; was colleague with Rev Samuel Whiting, of Lynn, a. 20 years. He was settled in Ipswich in 1656, and there d. 5 Nov. 1685, æ. 77, leaving sons, Samuel; Thomas, of whose capture by the Indians in 1676 Hubbard gives an account; John, and one daughter, Elizabeth. Samuel was probably the graduate at H. C. in 1663, and living in 1698.

COBURN, EDWARD, (See COLBURN.)

COCKERILL, WILLIAM, Hingham 1635, afterwards of Salem, where he died 1661.

COCKERUM, WILLIAM, Hingham, freeman 1638. He sailed on his return to England, 3 Oct. 1642. Peter Hobart, MS Diary.

CODDINGTON, JOHN, Boston, d. 18 August 1655. Son John b. 1653. STOCKDALE, Roxbury, 1644, removed from thence, and died a. 1650. His wife died at Roxbury, 1644. Coffin. ‡§*WILLIAM, came from Boston, in Lincolnshire, in 1630, and settled at Boston. He was assistant 1630 and 1632 to 1638, 6 years; representative 1637; removed to Rhode-Island, where he was governour 1674, 1675, 1683, and 1684. He d. 1 Nov. 1678, æ. 77.

CODMAN, ROBERT, 1637, at which time his family consisted of four persons. He had land granted to him in Salisbury in 1641. The Codmans in New-Hampshire are descended from William Cod, who came from Ireland before 1743, and settled at Amherst. The additional syllable was added by his sons, one of whom was Dr. Henry Codman, who died in 1812, æ. 68. RICHARD, York, 1653, was son-in-law of Richard Bonighton. STEPHEN, Charlestown, a. 1680, died in 1706. His son John died in Charlestown 1755. John Codman, esq., a merchant in Boston, who died in 1792, was father of the Hon. John Codman, of Boston, who d. 17 May, 1803, in his 49th year, and grandfather of Rev. John Codman, D. D., of Dorchester. WILLIAM, a lieutenant and deputy for Portsmouth, R. I. in 1672.

COE, MATTHEW, Portsmouth 1640. Belknap, i. Hist. N. H. 47. Rev. Curtis Coe, of N. H. grad. at Brown in 1777. ROBERT, freeman in 1634, removed to Weathersfield, thence to

Long-Island, and settled at Hempstead, as early as 1643, and might be the high sheriff in 1669, mentioned by Wood, Hist. Sketch, L. I. 150.

COFFIN, JAMES, son of Tristram Coffin, lived some time in New-Hampshire, but removed to Nantucket in 1660. His wife was Mary Severance of Salisbury, whom he m. Dec. 1663. He had 14 children. He is the ancestor of Admiral Sir Isaac Coffin. *‡PETER, Dover, brother of the preceding, was born in 1631; admitted freeman in 1666; representative 1672, 1673, 1673, appointed counsellor of the province of N. H. in 1692. His wife was Abigail Starbuck. His children were Abigail, b. 1657; Peter, b. 20 August, 1660; Jethro, b. 16 Sept. 1663; Tristram, b. 8. Jan. 1665; Edward b. 20 Feb. 1669; Judith, b. 1672; Elizabeth. TRISTRAM, son of Peter Coffin, of Brixton, England, came to N. E. in 1642, with his mother, (who d. May, 1661, æ. 77) his wife, and 4 children, Peter, Tristram, Elizabeth, and James. He settled at Salisbury, whence he removed to Haverhill, where his children, Mary and John, were born in 1645 and 1647; thence to Newbury, where Stephen was b. 11 May, 1652, and in 1660 went to Nantucket, where he died in 1681, æ. 76. Twenty-six of his descendants of the name of Coffin have been educated at the different colleges in N. E. Seven of them were born in the same house in Newbury. J. Coffin, MS letter. TRISTRAM, Newbury, son of the preceding, was b. in 1632, m. Judith, widow of Henry Somerby, in 1652, and had 10 children. He was admitted freeman in 1668; was deacon of the church 20 years, and acted as a magistrate. He died 4 Feb. 1704, æ. 72.

COGGAN, ||JOHN, Boston, was admitted freeman 1633, member of the ar. co. 1638. He m., 10 March, 1651, Martha, the widow of Governour Winthrop, and died in 1658. Son Joshua was b. 1652. JOHN, Boston, son of the preceding, was admitted freeman 1642.

COGGESHALL, *JOHN, Boston, freeman 1632, was representative at the first general court 1634; was banished the colony of Massachusetts in 1638; retired to Rhode-Island, where he was assistant in 1641, and in 1647, president of the colony. His descendants are still in repute in R. I. Savage, 1 Winth. N. E. 130, 296 and Index.

COGSWELL, JOHN, Ipswich, came to N. E. in 1635, and was admitted freeman in 1636. In his passage he was wrecked at Pemaquid. He d. 29 Nov. 1669. He had 3 sons, John, b. 1623, and died in 1653, leaving 3 children; William, who lived in Ipswich in 1648; and Edward, born a. 1629. Coffin. Felt.

COIT, JOHN, Gloucester 1649, was one of the selectmen. Felt. Rev. Joseph Coit grad. at H. C. 1697. Eleven others of the name had grad. at Harvard and Yale in 1828.

COKER, ROBERT, Newbury 1638, was born in 1606, and d. 19 Nov. 1680. Sons, Joseph, b. 1640; Benjamin, b. 1650. Theodore Coker grad. at H. C. 1726.

COLAMORE, ISAAC, Boston, whose name is *Colimer* in the colony records, a ship-carpenter, was admitted freeman in 1643.

Peter Colamore, of Scituate, a. 1650, is probably the ancestor of those of the name in Plymouth county, where the name is common.

COLBRON, *WILLIAM, Boston, freeman 1631 ; representative 1635, and a ruling elder of the church, d. 1 Aug. 1662. Savage, i. Winth. N. E. 37. ii. Index, 404.

COLBURN, EDWARD, Chelmsford 1675, the ancestor of the Dracut Colburns, or Coburns. Hubbard, Ind. Wars. NATHANIEL. (See COALBORN.) ROBERT, Ipswich 1648, had a son Robert. SAMUEL, Salem 1637.

COLBY, ANTHONY, Cambridge 1632, freeman 1634, removed to Salisbury, and died 1663, leaving 8 children. Coffin. *SAMUEL, Amesbury, representative 1689.

COLCORD, EDWARD, Exeter 1638, when he was one of the witnesses of the Indian deed to Rev. John Wheelwright. He was killed by the Indians, 18 June, 1677, æ. 61. [Belknap, i. Hist. N. H. 128.] His descendants are still in N. H., and one of them, Ebenezer Colcord, d. at Brentwood in 1824, æ. 99.

COLDAM, CLEMENT, Lynn 1630, went to Gloucester. Lewis. ||CLEMENT, son of the preceding, was b. 1622 ; member of ar. co. 1645, and d. 8 April, 1675. Ibid. THOMAS, Lynn 1630, freeman 1634, d. 8 April, 1675, æ. 74. Ibid.

COLE, GEORGE, Lynn 1637 ; removed to Sandwich, and died about 1653. ISAAC, Charlestown, freeman in 1638, d. 10 June, 1674. He had sons Abraham and Jacob, born in 1636 and 1641. ||JOHN, Boston, member of ar. co. 1642, had sons, John, b. 1643, and Samuel, b. 1646. There was a John Cole, of Lynn, according to Mr. Lewis, in 1642, who d. 8 Oct. 1703. RICE, or RISE, Charlestown, freeman 1633, d. 15 May, 1646. ROBERT, Salem, freeman 1631, came to N. E. in 1630. He also appears to have resided at Ipswich, and may be the same who was one of the founders of the first Baptist church in Rhode-Island. Savage, ii. Winth. Index. Benedict, Hist. Baptists. SAMUEL, Boston, came over in 1630, set up the first house of entertainment in Boston in 1633, and d. in 1666 or 7. [Winthrop, i. N. E. 124.] He may be the same person who requested to be made freeman in Oct. 1630, and whose name is read, by Prince, in the colony records, *Poole*, and by Savage, *Coole*. WILLIAM, Boston 1653, might be the same who was a witness to the Indian deed to Rev. John Wheelwright in 1638, and the same who d. at Hampton, a. 1663.

COLEMAN, THOMAS, Newbury 1635, was admitted freeman 1637 ; went to Nantucket, and d. 1685. His sons were, Benjamin, b. 1 May, 1640 ; Joseph, b. 2 Dec. 1642 ; Isaac, b. 20 Feb. 1647. John and Noah Coleman were of Hadley about 1665.

COLLICOTT, *EDWARD, was representative of the general court of Massachusetts in 1642. Coll. N. H. Hist. Soc. ii. 214. ||*RICHARD, Dorchester, freeman 1633 ; member of the ar. co. 1637 ; representative 1637, and perhaps the representative of Saco in 1672. He removed to Boston, where he d. in 1686. His wife, Joanna, d. 5 Aug. 1660. His children by Thomasin, another wife, weře, Experience, a daughter, b. 1641 ; Dependence, a son, b. 5 July, 1643. Savage, ii. Winth. N. E. 336.

COLLIER, Moses, Hingham, was admitted freeman in 1652. THOMAS, Hingham, freeman 6 May, 1646. A Thomas Collier, of Hingham, is said to have d. 6 April, 1646. ‡WILLIAM, Plymouth colony, came to N. E. 1633, was elected assistant from 1634 to 1665, excepting 1638, '52, and '53, 28 years ; was one of the commissioners of the United Colonies in 1643. Morton, N. E. Memo. 91. Savage, i. Winth. N. E. 139.

COLLINS, *EDWARD, Cambridge 1640, a deacon of the church, representative 16 years, from 1654 to 1670, excepting 1661. Mather [ii. Magnalia, 116] says he lived to see " several most worthy sons become very famous persons in their generation." The church records of Cambridge give the names of his children, viz : Daniel, who lived in Koningsberg, in Prussia, in 1658 ; John, H. C. 1649 ; Samuel, who went to Scotland, and was living there with his wife and son Edward in 1658 ; Martha ; Nathaniel, H. C. 1660 ; Abigail ; Sybil, and Edward. Fifteen graduates at the N. E. colleges of this name. FRANCIS, Salem 1665. HENRY, Lynn, freeman 1637, d. Feb. 1687, leaving sons, John, Henry, and Joseph. Lewis. JOHN, Gloucester, selectman 1646. Felt. ||JOHN, Boston, member of the church, admitted freeman 1646 ; member of ar. co. 1644. Son Thomas b. 1645. *JOHN*, son of Deacon Edward Collins, was born in England, whence, after having graduated at H. C. in 1649, he returned and not long after went to Scotland, and in 1658, was a minister in Edinburgh ; was chaplain to General Monk, when he went from Scotland to England. He afterwards was minister in London, where he d. 3. Dec. 1687. *NATHANIEL*, brother of the preceding, was born at Cambridge, grad. at H. C. 1660, and was ordained the minister of Middletown, in Conn., 4 Nov. 1668. He died 28 Dec. 1684, æ. 42.

COLLISHAW, WILLIAM, Massachusetts, freeman 1634.

COLMAN, EDWARD, Boston 1651. Son Joseph b. 1656. Twelve of the name of Colman had grad. at the N. E. colleges in 1826. JOSEPH, Scituate, 1638. NOAH, Hadley 1667. Coffin. THOMAS, Newbury. (See COLEMAN.) ||WILLIAM, Boston, member of the ar. co. 1676, was born in Satterly, in Suffolk, England, and was father of Rev. Benjamin Colman, D. D. of Boston. Coffin.

COLT, WILLIAM, Salem, admitted freeman 1648.

COLTON, *GEORGE, Springfield 1644, representative 1669. Nine of the eleven graduates at Yale College of this name have been clergymen.

COMBS, GEORGE, Charlestown, d. 27 July, 1659.

COMES, ISAAC, Weymouth 1662.

COMY, or COMEE, David, Concord 1664, d. 31 March 1676. Shattuck.

COMINS, ISAAC, Watertown. (See CUMMINGS.) MATTHEW, Boston, d. 4 Dec. 1654.

COMPTON, JOHN, Boston, freeman 1634; disarmed 1637. Savage, i. Winth. N. E. 248. Snow, Hist. Boston, 108.

CONANT, CHRISTOPHER, Plymouth 1623. Davis, Morton's Memo. 379. *EXERCISE, son of Roger Conant, was baptized at Salem, 24 Dec. 1637; was admitted freeman 1663; was one of the founders of the church in 1667, in Beverly, which he represented 1682—1684. *ROGER, supposed to be son of Richard and Agnes Conant, and brother of Dr. John Conant, of Exeter College, one of the assembly of divines, was born at Budleigh, a market town in Devonshire, in April, 1591. His grandfather was John Conant, " descended from ingenious parents of Gittisham, near Honiton, whose ancestors, for many generations, have been fixed there, but were originally of French extraction." Gibbs. He came to N. E. in 1623, lived at Plymouth, Nantasket, Cape Ann, and Salem, where he built the first house, about 1626. He was admitted freeman 1631, was representative at the first general court in 1634; was a worthy and useful character, and d. at Beverly, 19 Nov. 1679, in his 89th year. [Coffin.] Joshua Conant, who d. at Salem, in 1659, and Lot Conant, born 1624, one of the founders of the church in Beverly, 1667, living in Marblehead in 1674, were probably sons of Roger Conant. ROGER, son of the preceding, was the first child born in Salem, and from that circumstance had a grant of 20 acres of land in Jan. 1640. He appears to have been living at Marblehead in 1674. Felt, Annals Salem, 127.

CONDY, JAMES, Braintree, 1640, had sons, Joshua, Experience, and James. Rev. Jeremiah Condy, H. C. 1726, was a minister in Boston.

CONEY, ||JOHN, Boston, member of ar. co. 1662, died 24 Dec. 1690. See 2 Coll. Mass. Hist. Soc. viii. 105, where the name is spelled *Conney.*

CONKLING, ANANIAS, Salem, admitted member of the church 29 Dec. 1639; freeman 1642, removed to East-Hampton, L. I. Rev. Benjamin Conkling grad. at Princeton, N. J. 1755, and several others of the name have been publickly educated.

CONNER, WILLIAM, Plymouth 1623.

CONVERS, ALLEN, Woburn, was admitted freeman 1644. *JAMES, Woburn, freeman 1671, representative 1679, 1684—1686, and 1689, was the distinguished officer in the Indian war, mentioned by Mather, Magnalia, Book vi. JOSIAH, Woburn, was admitted freeman 1651.

CONVERSE, *EDWARD, came to N. E. in 1630, was admitted freeman, resided in Charlestown, and had a grant of the ferry there. He removed, as early as 1643, to Woburn, which he represented in 1660. Savage, ii. Winth. N. E. 349.

COOKE, *AARON, admitted freeman 1635, was of Northampton 1659, and a representative in 1668. Forty-four persons of the name of Cook and Cooke had grad. at the N. E. colleges in 1826, of whom 11 have been clergymen. ‡*ELISHA, Boston, son of Richard Cooke, was born in Boston, 16 Sept. 1637; grad. at H. C. 1657; admitted freeman 1673; representative 1681 to 1683; assist-

ant 1684—1686; one of the council of safety 1689; an agent for
Massachusetts in England 1690 and 1691. He d. 31 May, 1715, æ.
78., leaving son Elisha, a distinguished political character, who grad.
H. C. 1697, and d. at Boston, in August, 1737, æ. 59, whose son
Middlecott grad. at H. C. in 1723. *‖GEORGE, Cambridge, was
admitted freeman 1636; representative 1636, 1642—1645, five
years; speaker of the house of reps. 1645; captain of the company
at Cambridge 1642; a member of the ar. co. and its captain 1643.
He returned to England, and was afterwards a colonel in the time
of the civil wars. Mr. Savage says "he probably died in Oliver's
service." Johnson. Winthrop. FRANCIS, one of the first pilgrims at Plymouth 1620. JOHN, Salem 1637, admitted member
of the church 1641; freeman 1642, removed from Salem, perhaps
to Boston, where a John Cooke d. in May, 1643. ‖*JOSEPH,
Cambridge, freeman 1636, representative 1636—1640, 5 years;
member of ar. co. 1640. His children were, Joseph; Elizabeth, b.
1645; Mary; Grace; Ruth. His wife was Elizabeth. JOSEPH,
Cambridge, son of the preceding, grad. at H. C. 1660 or 1661, was
admitted member of the church at Cambridge, 18 May, 1665, freeman 1666. His son John was baptized in 1667. JOSIAH, Eastham 1644. PHILIP, Cambridge, freeman 1647, d. 10 Feb. 1667.
Sons, Samuel, b. 1659; Philip, b. 1661; John, b. 1663; Barnabas,
b. 1665. ‖*RICHARD, tailor, Boston, member of the church 1634,
freeman 1635; member of the ar. co. 1643, and perhaps the representative for Dover in 1670, unless he was the Richard Cooke who
d. at Malden, 14 Oct. 1658. His sons were, Elisha; Elkanah, b.
1642; Joseph, b. 1 May, 1642, who grad. at Harvard College and
d. before 1698. ROBERT, Charlestown, freeman 1641, had a son
Samuel b. in 1644. THOMAS, Guilford, Conn., 1650. WAL-
TER, Weymouth 1643, freeman 1653, had sons, Ebenezer, Walter, and Nicholas.

COOLEDGE, *JOHN, Watertown, freeman 1636, representative 1658. Sons Stephen and Obadiah b. in 1639 and 1642. He
was one of the petitioners for the grant of Dedham.

COOLEY, BENJAMIN, Springfield 1646, Westfield 1660.
Sprague, Hist. Discourse, 52, 83. He d. 17 Aug. 1674. JOHN,
Salem, d. a. 1654.

COOPER, ANTHONY, Hingham 1635. Lincoln, Hist. Hingham. JOHN, Cambridge, freeman 1636, perhaps also of Lynn
1637, and one of the grantees named in the Indian deed of South-
Hampton, L. I., 1640. JOHN, jr., Cambridge, freeman 1642, was
a constable, selectman, and deacon of the church. He m. Anna,
daughter of Nathaniel Sparhawk, and had children, Anna; Mary;
Samuel, b. 1654; John, b. 1656; Nathaniel, b. 1659; Lydia;
Hannah. PETER, Rowley 1643. Coffin. THOMAS, Hingham,
freeman 1638, perhaps removed to Rehoboth. See Davis, Morton's
Memo. 442. THOMAS, freeman 1638, may be the one who removed from Windsor to Springfield in April, 1641, and d. 5 Oct.
1675. Sprague, Hist. Discourse, 52. TIMOTHY, Lynn 1637, d.
March, 1659. He had sons, John, b. 1647; Timothy, b. 1651,

and 4 daughters. Lewis. WILLIAM, Pascataqua 1631. He is probably the person whom Winthrop, i. Hist. N. E. 120, calls Cowper.

COPELAND, LAWRENCE, Braintree, d. 30 Dec. 1699, "a very aged man, born in the reign of our gracious sovereign Queen Elizabeth, of blessed memory." Records. Judge Sewall says he was 110. He m. Lydia Townsend in 1653, and had sons, Thomas, b. 1654; William, b. 1656; John, b. 1658. Alexander, Benjamin, and George Copeland grad. at Yale and Brown Colleges.

COPIE, JAMES, was admitted freeman 1640.

COPP, WILLIAM, shoemaker, the earliest proprietor of Copp's Hill, Boston, was admitted freeman 1641. His son Jonathan was b. 1640. Snow, Hist. Boston, 105. Elder David Copp d. at Boston, Nov. 1713, æ. 78. Rev. Jonathan Copp grad. at Y. C. 1744.

CORBIN, ROBERT, Casco-Bay 1658. Pliny M. Corbin grad. Vermont Coll. 1822.

CORLETT, ELIJAH, was educated at Lincoln College, in Oxford, to which he was admitted in 1626 ; came to N. E. and settled at Cambridge as early as 1644, and admitted freeman 1645. He was one of the most eminent schoolmasters in this country, where he taught more than 40 years. He d. 25 Feb. 1687-8, æ. 78. His children were Rebecca, Hepzibah, and Ammi-Ruhamah, who grad. 1670 at H. C., of which he was a fellow, and d. 1 Feb. 1679.

CORNEL, JOHN, Dorchester, d. 31 July, 1675, æ. 64. James Cornall was a witness to the Indian deed to Rev. John Wheelwright 1638.

CORNING, SAMUEL, was admitted freeman in 1641, and was one of the founders of the church in Beverly 1667.

CORNISH, RICHARD, Boston, d. 6 Feb. 1694, perhaps the one whose wife, Catharine, is mentioned by Hutchinson, i. Hist. Ms. 385. SAMUEL, Salem 1637. James Cornish was the first schoolmaster and town clerk of Westfield, where was also Gabriel Cornish in 1667. Thomas Cornish was of Exeter in 1652.

CORWIN. (See CURWIN.)

CORWITHEN, DAVID, Marblehead 1648, was admitted member of the church in Salem 1649. DICKORY, Boston, a ship-master, d. 6 Sept. 1653. SAMUEL, Marblehead 1648.

CORY, GILES, Salem 1659, was one of the victims of the witchcraft infatuation in 1692. He was pressed to death, 16 Sept. that year, at the age of 77. Calef, More Wonders, 217, 218.

COSIN, ||FRANCIS, member of the ar. co. 1640. Isaac Cosin or Cosins was of Rowley a. 1650. Coffin. MATTHEW, Boston 1656.

COSMORE, JOHN, a magistrate of Connecticut in 1647.

COTTERILL, FRANCIS, Wells 1668.

COTTLE, EDWARD, Salisbury, had a son William, of Newbury, who d. in 1668, leaving 4 children.

COTTON, JOHN, the second minister of the first church in Boston, was son of Roland Cotton, esquire, and was born at Derby, in England, 4 Dec. 1585. He was educated at Emmanuel College, Cambridge, was settled the minister of Boston, in Lincolnshire, a.

1612, from whence he came to N. E. where he arrived 4 Sept. 1633, and became teacher of the first church, 10 Oct. 1633. He was admitted freeman in 1634; died 23 Dec. [the records of Boston, old book, say the 15th] 1652, æ. 67. By his first wife, Elizabeth Horrocks, he had no children; by his second, Sarah Story, he had 1. Seaborn, born on his passage to N. E.; 2. Sarah, who d. 20 Jan. 1649; 3. John; 4. Roland, who d. of small pox, 29 Jan. 1649; 5. a daughter, who m. Mr. Eggington; [C. Mather] 6. Maria, who m. Rev. I. Mather, D. D., of Boston. Twenty-one of Mr. Cotton's descendants of the family name, besides a large number in the different female branches, have grad. at H. C., of whom 14 have been clergymen. *SEABORN*, the third minister of Hampton, was son of the preceding, and was born at sea, in August, 1633, and baptized at Boston, 6 September, two days after his father's arrival. He grad. at H. C. 1651; was ordained 1660; died 19 April, 1686, æ. 52. He m. 14 June, 1654, Dorothy, (who d. 26 Feb. 1672) daughter of Governour Bradstreet, and had children, 1. Dorothy, who m. a Smith, of Hampton; 2. John; 3. Ann, b. 23 April, 1661; 4. Sarah, b. 2 July, 1663; 5. Elizabeth, b. 13 Sept. 1665; 6. Mercy, b. 3 Nov. 1666, who m. Capt. Thomas Tufts, whose son, Rev. John Tufts, grad. at H. C. 1708; 7. Abiah, b. and d. 1669; 8. Maria, b. 22 April, 1670, m. 1st, Mr. Atwater, and 2d, Samuel Partridge. One of the daughters m. Richard Pierce, and another a Mr. Carr. *JOHN*, minister of Plymouth, brother of the preceding, was born, 13 March, 1640, grad. at H. C. 1657, was ordained 30 June, 1669; dismissed 5 Oct. 1697; sailed for Charleston, S. C., 15 Nov. 1698, settled there in the ministry, and d. 18 Sept. 1699, in his 60th year. He m. Jane Rosseter, 7 Nov. 1660, (she d. 12 Oct. 1702, æ. 60) and his children were, 1. John, minister of Yarmouth; 2. Elizabeth, wife of (1)Rev. James Alling and (2) Rev. Caleb Cushing, and mother of Rev. James Cushing, of Plaistow, N. H., and Rev. John Cushing, of Boxford; 3. Sarah; 4. Roland, minister of Sandwich; 5. Sarah; 6. Maria; 7. son, who d. an infant; 8. Josiah; 9. Samuel; 10. Josiah, 2d, b. 8. Jan. 1680, grad. at H. C. 1698, a magistrate of Plymouth, where he d. 19 Aug. 1756, æ. 76; 11. Theophilus, minister of Hampton-Falls, N. H., who grad. at H. C. 1701, and d. 18 August, 1726. *JOHN*, minister of Yarmouth, was the eldest son of the preceding, and was born at Plymouth, 3 August, 1661; grad. at H. C. 1681, and d. 21 Feb. 1706, æ. 45. By Sarah, his wife, the daughter of Richard Hubbard, of Ipswich, he had Joanna, Sarah, Elizabeth, Mercy, Maria, Margaret, and Priscilla. *JOHN*, the fourth minister of Hampton, son of the Rev. Seaborn Cotton, was born 8 May, 1658, grad. at H. C. 1678, ordained 1696; d. 27 March, 1710, æ. 52. Mary, one of his daughters, m. Rev. John Whiting, Concord, Ms.; another m. Rev. Nathaniel Gookin, His successor at Hampton. He had but one son, whose name is not ascertained. *ROLAND*, minister of Sandwich, son of Rev. John Cotton, of Plymouth, was born 27 Dec. 1667, grad. at H. C. 1685, ordained 2 Nov. 1694, d. 22 March, 1722, æ. 55. His wife was widow Elizabeth Denison, of Ipswich, only daughter of Hon.

Nathaniel Saltonstall, and sister of Governour S., of Conn.   Their children were, 1. John, minister of Newton, Ms., who had 5 sons and 5 daughters ; 2. Sarah ; 3. Rev. Nathaniel, of Bristol ; 4. Abigail, who m. Rev. Shearjashub Bourne ; 5. Meriel ; 6. Roland, H. C. 1719 ; 7. Rev. Josiah, of Providence, Woburn, and Sandown, N. H. ; 8. Joanna, who m. Rev. John Brown, of Haverhill, whose 4 sons, John, Cotton, Ward, and Thomas grad. at H. C. in 1741, 1743, 1748, and 1752 ; 9. Ward, the minister of Hampton, who grad. at H. C. in 1729. ||WILLIAM, Boston, freeman 1647 ; member ar. co. 1650, had sons, William, b. 1646 ; William, 2d, 1654. There was a William Cotton in Portsmouth in 1685, and a John Cotton in Concord in 1667 and 1679.   GEORGE, Springfield d. 17 Dec. 1699.

COTTA, ROBERT, Salem, was admitted freeman 1635.   The name is spelled *Cotty* in the colony records. Felt, Annals Salem, 172.

COURSER, WILLIAM, Boston, freeman 1636, had a son John, b. in 1642.   Snow, Hist. Boston, 137.   The name of Corser exists in New-Hampshire, and has furnished one graduate, Rev. Enoch Corser, of Loudon, Dart. Coll. 1811.

COURTNEY, ||————, was a member of the ar. co. 1640.

COWDRY, *WILLIAM, Lynn 1637, removed to Reading, which he represented in 1651, and where he was town clerk.   He had a son Nathaniel.   Lewis.

COWELL, EDWARD, Boston 1655, d. 12 Sept. 1691.   His son William was b. in 1655.   John Cowell d. at Boston, Dec. 1693.

COWPER, [WILLIAM] Pascataqua 1633.   Winthrop, i. Hist. N. E. 120.   (See COOPER.)

COX, MOSES, Hampton 1639, d. 28 May, 1687, æ. 93.   His wife Alice, and son John, with six other persons, were drowned in 1657, as they were going out in a boat from Hampton.   John Cox d. at Boston in 1690.   John W. Cox and Henry C. Cox grad. at Dartmouth and Yale Colleges in 1789 and 1806.

COYE, JOHN, Brookfield, was killed by the Indians, 2 August, 1675.   RICHARD, Brookfield 1673.

COYTMORE, *THOMAS, Charlestown, freeman 1640, representative 1640 and 1641, died on the coast of Wales, 27 Dec. 1645. [Boston records.]   He had sons Thomas and William.   Martha, his widow, m. Gov. Winthrop, in Dec. 1647.   Isaac Coytmore was a member of the ar. co. 1639.   Savage, ii. Winthrop, 75.   Hubbard.

CRABB, JOHN, requested to be made freeman 19 Oct. 1630. RICHARD was a deputy at the first general assembly of Connecticut, 1639.

CRABTREE, JOHN, Boston 1639.   Son John born 1639.

CRACKBURNE, GILBERT, admitted freeman 1636, became, with his wife Elizabeth, member of the church in Cambridge 1659, and d. 2 Jan. 1672.

CRACKSTON, JOHN, Plymouth, one of the first Pilgrims, d. 1621.

CRAFT, *GRIFFIN, Roxbury, was·a lieutenant and representative 1663—1667, 5 years.   He had sons, John, b. 1630, m. 1654, and d. 3 Sept. 1685; Samuel, b. 1637, d. 9 Dec. 1709, æ. 72. Moses Craft, of Newton, probably a descendant, was father of Dr. John Staples Crafts, who had 6 sons born in Bridgewater, Thomas, Samuel, John, Moses, Edward, Zibeon. Thomas grad. at H. C. 1783, was the minister of Princeton and Middleborough, Mass., and died 1819, æ. 60. His son Eliphalet Porter Crafts was ordained the minister of East-Bridgewater in 1828.

CRAM, JOHN, Exeter 1639. Rev. Jacob Cram grad. at D. C. 1782.

CRANCH, ANDREW, New-Hampshire 1687.

CRANE, ‡JASPER, New-Haven 1639, assistant or magistrate of New-Haven colony 1658, of Connecticut 1665. Of the name of Crane, 15 have grad. at Princeton and the N. E. colleges. HENRY, Dorchester 1658. CHRISTIAN, Cambridge 1647.

CRANSTON, §JOHN, Rhode-Island, was elected Governour in 1679. Walter Cranston grad. at H. C. 1810. §SAMUEL, Rhode-Island, was the governour of that colony 29 years, from 1698 to 1726, a term of service exceeding that of Governour Eaton, of Connecticut. See a note by Mr. Savage in i. Winth. Hist. N. E. 228.

CRANWELL, JOHN, requested to be made freeman 19 Oct. 1630, and was admitted 4 March, 1634. He is probably the one who d. in Boston in 1639. A Thomas Cranwell was admitted a resident in Boston, 20 August, 1638. (See CROMWELL.)

CRAWFORD, STEPHEN, Massachusetts, d. before 1649.

CRESEY, MIGHILL, Ipswich, died 1670. [Coffin.] Rev. Noah Cresey grad. at Williams College in 1805.

CRICHLEY, RICHARD, a blacksmith, Boston, was admitted freeman 1642. His sons were, Samuel, b. 1640; Joseph, b. 1643; John, b. 1657.

CRISP, BENJAMIN, Watertown 1639, freeman 1646, had sons, Jonathan, b. 1639; Eleazar, b. 1641.

CROAD, JOHN, Salem 1659, was admitted freeman 1663, d. 1670. He married daughter of Walter Price. Felt, Annals, 239. RICHARD, merchant of Salem, was son of Richard Croad, of Hampton, in England, and d. 1689, æ. 61, leaving a wife, Frances, and children, Hannah, Richard, William, John, and Sarah. Felt, Annals, 296. RICHARD, Hingham 1656, had a son John, b. 1657.

CROCKER, JOHN, Scituate 1638. Eleven of the name of Crocker had grad. in 1826 at H. C. and three at Yale. THOMAS, Kittery, freeman 1652.

CROE, JOHN, one of the petitioners for the grant of Billerica in 1654. Rev. John Croes, D. D., was the Bishop of the Episcopal church in New-Jersey.

CROMWELL, GILES, d. at Newbury, at an advanced age, 24 Feb. 1673. His son Philip, a butcher, belonging to Salem, was admitted freeman in 1665. John Cromwell, b. in 1636, lived in Newbury, and m. Joan Butler in 1662. SAMUEL, Massachusetts, was admitted freeman 1634. THOMAS, a mariner, who made a great fortune by privateering, (See ii. Winthrop, 263, 274] died in

Boston in 1649, leaving a widow, who soon married.   Savage, MS note.   THOMAS, Newbury 1637, removed to Hampton.

CROSBY, ANTHONY, a chirurgeon of Rowley before 1652, had sons, Nathaniel, b. 1667, d. 7 March, 1701 ; Nathan, b. 1669, and probably other children.   His widow became the 2d wife of Rev. Seaborn Cotton.   *JOSEPH, Braintree, probably son of Simon Crosby, of Cambridge, was representative 1690, and d. 26 Nov. 1695.   He m. Sarah Brackett 1675, and had sons, Thomas, Simon, Ebenezer, and others.   SIMON, Cambridge 1635, freeman 1636, was one of the selectmen in 1636 and 1638.   Twenty-six of the name, and many of them his descendants, had received degrees at the N. E. Colleges in 1826.   *SIMON, son of the preceding, was the first innholder in Billerica, which he represented in 1691, 1697, and 1698.   He m. Rachel Brackett, 15 July, 1659, and had several sons, whose descendants are scattered through Massachusetts and New-Hampshire.   THOMAS, probably an elder brother of the preceding, grad. at H. C. 1653 ; settled at Eastham, and was living in 1698.   His children were, Simon, b. 5 July, 1665 ; Sarah, 1667 ; Joseph, b. 27 Jan. 1669 ; John, and perhaps others.   THOMAS, was an early inhabitant of Cambridge and Rowley.

CROSS, JOHN, Watertown, d. 15 Sept. 1640.   *JOHN, Ipswich 1635, Hampton, freeman 1639, representative 1640, died a. 1652.   ROBERT, Ipswich 1639, was one of the Pequod soldiers.

CROSSMAN, ∥ROBERT, member of the ar. co. 1644.

CROW, SAMUEL, Hadley 1671.   Coffin.

CROWTHER, JOHN, Portsmouth 1631.   Belknap, i. Hist. N. H. 47.   Adams, Annals Portsmouth, 18.

CRUTTENDEN, ABRAHAM, sen. and jr. were of Guilford in 1650.

CUDWORTH, †JAMES, Scituate, assistant of Plymouth colony in 1656 and 1657, and afterwards deputy governour.   Davis, Morton's Memo. 468.

CULLICK, ‡JOHN, Connecticut, was assistant in 1648.   Capt. John Cullick died in Boston, 23 Jan. 1663, and John Cullick grad. at H. C. in 1668, and died before 1698.

CULVER, EDWARD, Dedham 1640, had sons, John, Joshua, and Samuel.   This name exists in New-Hampshire.

CUMMINGS, ISAAC, whose name is also written *Comins* and *Cummins*, was admitted freeman 1642, was an early proprietor of Watertown, and perhaps lived in Topsfield.   A David Cummins d. at Boston, 12 Dec. 1690.   Eighteen of the name, Cuming, Cumings, Cummens, Cumming, and Cummings, are on the catalogues of the N. E. colleges.   WILLIAM, Salem 1637.

CUNLIFFE, HENRY, Dorchester, where the name in the church records is *Condliffe*, was admitted freeman 1644, and his name is entered *Cunlithe* in the colony records, according to Mr. Savage, but the records of Northampton, where he appears among the first settlers, has the name as above.

CURRIER, RICHARD, Salisbury, was a member of the church 1675.   Rev. Joseph Currier, H. C. 1765, and Seth Currier, a native of Hopkinton, N. H., D. C. 1796, were the only graduates of the name in New-England in 1825.

CURTIS, DEODATE, Braintree, a. 1643, had a son Solomon. Of the name of Curtis, 24 had grad. at the N. E. colleges in 1825. HENRY, Marblehead, came from England. His descendants are in North-Bridgewater. See Cary's Genealogy, 39. HENRY, Sudbury 1641, where he d. 8 May, 1678. Son Ephraim was b. 1642. Henry Curtis was one of the proprietors of Northampton 1653. PHILIP, a lieutenant of Roxbury, was slain by the Indians at Hassanamesset, [Grafton, Ms.] 9 Nov. 1675. RICHARD, Marblehead 1648. WILLIAM, Roxbury, freeman 1633, d. 8 Dec. 1672, æ. 80. Sons, Thomas, who d. 1652; Isaac, b. 1642, and probably others.

CURWIN, *GEORGE, was b. at Workington, in the county of Cumberland, Eng., 10 Dec. 1610, came to N. E. and settled at Salem 1638, was admitted freeman 1665,, a selectman, captain, representative 1666, 9 years, and d. 6 Jan. 1685, æ. 74. He m. (1) Elizabeth, widow of John White, by whom (who d. in 1668) he had, Elizabeth, Abigail, Hannah, John, and Jonathan; (2) Elizabeth Brooks in 1669, by whom he had, Penelope, George, who d. in infancy, and Susanna. Capt. Curwin left an estate of 5964 pounds. His son John, a captain, of Salem, freeman 1665, m. Margaret, daughter of Gov. Winthrop, and d. 12 July, 1683, æ. 45. His wife d. 28 Sept. 1697. Felt, Annals, 274, 279. ‡*JONATHAN, son of the preceding, was bapt. at Salem, 17 Jan. 1641, freeman 1671, was elected representative 1689, one of the first council under the new charter 1691, d. 9 June, 1718, æ. 77. Matthias, Ipswich 1634, probably removed to South-Old, L. I. Wood, Hist. L. I. 34, where the name is spelled *Corwin*. SAMUEL. A Samuel Curwin died at Boston in Nov. 1698.

CUSHING, *DANIEL, Hingham, eldest son of Matthew Cushing, was born in England, came to N. E. in 1638; was representative 1680, 1682, and 1695. His sons were Jeremiah and Theophilus. For information of several persons of this name see 2 Coll. Mass. Hist. Soc. x. Index. *JEREMIAH*, minister of the first church in Scituate, was son of the preceding, and was born 3 July, 1654; grad. at H. C. 1676; ordained 27 May, 1691, and died 22 March, 1706, æ. 51. ‡JOHN, Hingham and Scituate, son of Matthew Cushing, was b. in England, came to N. E. 1638, was a representative, and a. 1690 an assistant of Plymouth colony. He was the first representative from Scituate, under the charter of 1692. His son and grandson were judges of the supreme court of Massachusetts, and the latter, the Hon. William Cushing, was judge of the supreme court of the U. S. He was born in Scituate, March, 1723, grad. at H. C. 1751, and d. 13 Sept. 1810. MATTHEW, Hingham 1638, the great ancestor of the numerous respectable families of Cushings in N. E. arrived at Boston, 10 August, 1638, with his wife, Nazareth Pitcher, and the following children : Daniel, Jeremiah, Matthew, who m. 1652, Deborah, and John. He died 30 Sept. 1660, æ. 72. Lincoln, Hist. Hingham, 46. Thirty of his descendants of the name of Cushing had grad. at H. C. in 1825, of whom 8 were Clergymen, and a large proportion of them publick characters. THEOPHILUS, Hingham, a. 1635, died in March, 1679, at the age of a. 100 years. Lincoln, Hist. Hingham, 41.

CUSHMAN, JAMES, Scituate between 1633 and 1657. 2 Coll. Mass. Hist. Soc. iv. 240. Eleven persons of the name had grad. at the N. E. colleges in 1826. ROBERT, arrived at Plymouth, 10 Nov. 1621, where he tarried only one month; returned to Europe, and d. in 1626. His family came to N. E. after his death, and his descendants are numerous. Allen, Biog. Dict. 238. THOMAS, Plymouth 1623, son of the preceding, m. Mary, daughter of Isaac Allerton, and d. in 1691, æ. 84. His widow d. in 1699, æ. about 90. His son, Rev. Isaac Cushman, was the first minister of Plympton, Mass., was ordained 1698, and d. 1732, æ. 84.

CUTLER, JAMES, Watertown 1635, where his son James was b. that year. Twenty-one of the name had grad. at the N. E. colleges in 1826. *JOHN, Charlestown, was representative in 1680 and 1682. He was probably the Major Cutler, father of Rev. Timothy Cutler, D. D., of Boston, who d. 17 August, 1765, æ. 82. ROBERT, a deacon of the church at Charlestown, died 7 March, 1665. His son Nathaniel, grad. at H. C. 1663, and d. 13 August, 1678.

CUTHBERTSON, CUTHBERT, Plymouth 1623. Davis, Morton's Memo. Hon. Alfred Cuthbert, grad. at Princeton 1803. James and John Cuthbert grad. at Y. C. in 1815 and 1816.

CUTT, JOHN, came from Wales to N. E. before 1646, and was an eminent merchant in Portsmouth. He was appointed president of N. H. in 1679, when this colony became a province, and entered upon the duties of his office early in 1680. He d. 27 March, 1681. President Cutt m. Hannah Star, 30 July, 1662, and their children were, John, b. 30 June 1663; Elizabeth, b. 1664, d. 1665; Hannah, b. 1666; Mary, b. 1669; and Samuel. A 2d wife Ursula, or, as she wrote the name, Ursilla, survived the president, and was killed by the Indians. See Belknap, i. Hist. N. H. President Cutt left an estate of £9723. 9. 6 3-4. *RICHARD, Portsmouth, brother of the preceding, was admitted freeman 1665, representative 1665 and from 1669 to 1676, except 1671. He settled at the Isle of Shoals, and carried on the fisheries there; afterwards lived in Portsmouth in the great house at the bottom of Pitt street. He d. a. 1676. Adams, Annals Portsmouth, 70. ROBERT, brother of the preceding, went to Barbadoes soon after he came to N. E.; from thence came to N. H. and lived at Great Island, now New-Castle. He removed to Kittery, where he established a ship-yard, and carried on the ship-building very extensively. Ibid. 70.

CUTTER, RICHARD, Cambridge, freeman 1641, member of the ar. co. 1643, had children, Samuel, b. 1646; Thomas, b. 19 July, 1648; William, b. 22 Feb. 1650; Ephraim; Gershom; Nathaniel, b. 1663; Mary, Rebecca, and Hepsibah. ROBERT, Massachusetts, was admitted freeman 1638. ||WILLIAM, freeman 1633; perhaps the member of ar. co. 1638. WILLIAM, freeman 1637.

CUTTING, JOHN, Newbury, came from London, and settled at Charlestown, afterwards at Newbury. He was Captain of a vessel and made thirteen voyages across the Atlantick. He d. 20 Nov. 1659. Coffin.

DADY, WILLIAM, Charlestown, freeman 1633, had sons, Zachary, b. 1644; Nathaniel, who d. 25 April, 1665.

DAGGETT, JOHN, Watertown, 1642. Nine of the name of Daggett had grad. at Y. C. in 1828, of whom was Rev. Naphtali Daggett, D. D., president of that institution from 1766 to 1777. He d. 25 Nov. 1780.

DAILLE, PETER, first minister of the French Protestant church in Boston, came to N. E. in 1686, and d. 20 May, 1715, æ. 66. Worcester Magazine, ii. 349. Bowen's Picture of Boston, p. 129, calls him *Paul*. Neal in his Hist. of the Puritans, vol. iv. p. 259, mentions a Daille of Paris.

DAKIN, THOMAS, Concord, 1660, had children, Joseph, John, Samuel, and Sarah. Samuel, a descendant, grad. at D. C. 1797.

DALTON, PHILEMON, Dedham, freeman 1636, went to Hampton, from thence to Ipswich and d. there, 10 Nov. 1661, leaving 3 children. His name is spelled Dolbon in the list of Mr. Savage, ii. Winthrop, 336. *‡SAMUEL, son of the preceding, was born in 1635, settled in Hampton, which he represented 12 years from 1662; was one of the first council under president Cutt in 1680. *TIMOTHY*, the first teacher of the church in Hampton, was brother to Philemon. He d. 28 Dec. 1661, without issue, and Ruth, his widow, d. 12 May, 1666, both leaving wills. The ministerial funds in Hampton and North-Hampton arose from the liberal donation of Mr. Dalton.

DAME, JOHN, Dover, whose name was formerly, and is now sometimes, written *Dam*, had children, Elizabeth, b. 1649; Mary, b. 1651; William, b. 4 Oct. 1653; Judith.

DAMON, JOHN, and ZACHARIAH, were soldiers of Scituate in 1676. Rev. George Daman, of Tisbury, grad. at H. C. 1756. Rev. Jude Damon, of Truro, grad. at H. C. 1776, and d. 19 Nov. 1828, æ. 78. Rev. David Damon, of Amesbury, grad. at H. C. 1811. Edward Damon was of Marblehead in 1674.

DANA, RICHARD, Cambridge, a member of the church, m. Ann Bullard, and had 12 children. He d. suddenly, a. 1695. Four of his sons survived him, and are ancestors to the numerous families of the name in the country. 1. Jacob was b. 2 Feb. 1655, m. Patience, and had a son Jacob, b. in Cambridge 1679; went to Pomfret, Conn., and was ancestor to the late Rev. Joseph Dana, D. D., two of whose sons, Rev. Daniel Dana, a graduate and president of D. C., and Rev. Samuel Dana, are ministers of Newburyport and Marblehead; 2. Joseph was born 21 May, 165–; 3. Benjamin, born April, 1660; 4. Daniel, b. 20 March, 1663, lived in Cambridge, and was ancestor of Richard Dana, H. C. 1718, two of whose sons were Rev. Edmund Dana, H. C. 1759, who d. at Wroxeter, England, in 1823, and Hon. Francis Dana, H. C. 1762, chief justice of Mass. and minister to Russia, who d. at Cambridge, 25 April, 1811. æ. 68.

The Hon. Samuel Dana, of Amherst, N. H., who grad. at H. C.
1755, was a descendant from Daniel, through his son Caleb. The
Hon. Samuel Dana, of Groton, is son, and the late Professor James
F. Dana, and Samuel L. Dana, both M. D.s and graduates of H. C.
in 1813, are grandsons, of Judge Dana, of Amherst. Twenty-one
of the name of Dana had grad. at Harvard, Yale, and Dartmouth
Colleges in 1829.

DAND, JOHN, Massachusetts 1641. Winthrop, ii. Hist. N. E.
262, 292—295.

DANE, FRANCIS, the second minister of Andover, came
over, it is said, with Rev. Nathaniel Rogers in 1636. He was ordained a. 1648, and died 17 Feb. 1697, in his 82d year. Mary, his
wife, d. in March, 1689, and he m. Hannah, the widow of George
Abbot, and she d. in June, 1711. He left two sons, Nathaniel, who
d. 1725, æ. 80, having had 3 sons; and Francis, who d. 1738, æ. 81.
leaving sons, Francis, John, Joseph, and Daniel. JOHN, Ipswich
1648, brother of the preceding, was born a. 1618, and is ancestor
to the Non. Nathan Dane, LL. D., of Beverly, who grad. at H. C.
1778. THOMAS, Concord. (See DEAN.)

DANFORTH, *JONATHAN, Billerica 1653, was son of Nicholas Danforth, and was born at Framlingham, in Suffolk, England,
29 Feb. 1628, came with his father to N. E. in 1634; m. 22 Nov.
1655, Elizabeth, daughter of John Poulter, and had 11 children, of
whom 6 were sons, but only two of them left issue, Jonathan, born
in 1656, and Samuel, b. in 1666. He was the first captain of Billerica, was chosen representative in 1684, town clerk 20 years, and
one of the most eminent land surveyors of his time. He d. 7 Sept.
1712, æ. 84, leaving a widow, who was a second wife. Hist. Memoir Billerica, 5, 14. *JOHN*, the seventh minister of Dorchester,
was son of Rev. Samuel Danforth, of Roxbury, and was born 8 Nov.
1660, grad. at H. C. 1677, was ordained 28 June, 1682; d. 26 May,
1730, æ. 70. Pres. Allen and Dr. Harris erroneously state his age
at 78. He was father of Elijah Danforth, b. 1683, grad. at H. C.
1703, a physician at Castle-William, now Fort Independence, who
died 8 October, 1736, aged 53, and of Hon. Samuel Danforth
H. C. 1715, a counsellor and judge of the court of common pleas,
and of probate in Middlesex county, and a mandamus counsellor
in 1774, who d. 2 Oct. 1777, æ. 81. The last was father of the
late Samuel Danforth, M. D., of Boston, who d. 16 Nov. 1827, æ.
87. *NICHOLAS, Cambridge, came from Framlingham, in Suffolk, to N. E. in 1634, was admitted freeman in 1636, was a representative in 1636 and 1637, and d. in April 1637, leaving sons,
Thomas, Samuel, and Jonathan; and daughters, Anna, who m.
Matthew Bridge, of Cambridge, and Elizabeth, wife of Andrew
Belcher, and grandmother of Gov. Belcher. *SAMUEL*, the third
minister of Roxbury, was son of the preceding, and b. in England,
Sept. 1626; grad. at H. C. 1643; admitted freeman 1648; was ordained as colleague with Rev. John Eliot, 24 Sept. 1650; died 19
Nov. 1674, æ. 48. His wife was a daughter of Rev. John Wilson,
of Boston, whom he m. in 1651, and by whom he had 12 children.

SAMUEL, minister of Taunton, son of the preceding, was born at Roxbury, 18 Dec. 1666, grad. at H. C. 1683, d. 14 Nov. 1727. He was esteemed one of the most learned and eminent ministers of that period. *‡†THOMAS, Cambridge, son of Nicholas Danforth, was born in England in 1622, came with his father to N. E. in 1634; admitted freeman 1643, elected representative 1657 and 1658, assistant from 1659 to 1678, 20 years, deputy governour 1679 to 1686, eight years, and three years after the revolution in 1689, and once, in 1684, came within 61 votes of being elected governour. He was appointed by the general court of Mass. president of Maine, 11 May, 1681, and repaired for a short time to that territory. He was also a judge of the superiour court of Mass. and sustained other important offices. He d. 5 Nov. 1699, æ. 77. He m. Mary, daughter of Henry Withington, 2 Feb. 1644, and had 12 children, of whom were Samuel, b. 5 Oct. 1652, grad. at H. C. 1671, a distinguished scholar, who d. in London, of small pox, 22 Dec. 1676, and Jonathan, b. 10 Feb. 1659, grad. at H. C. 1679, and d. 13 Nov. 1682. President Danforth left posterity in the female line. WILLIAM, Newbury 1667, had sons, William, Jonathan, and others. His descendants are in New-Hampshire, several of whom write the name Danford.

DANIEL, RICHARD, Billerica, 1675, lived also in Andover, and is noticed by Gookin, in his account of the Indians. ROBERT, Watertown and Cambridge, was admitted freeman 1638, and d. at Cambridge, 6 July, 1655. THOMAS, Cambridge, d. Nov. 1644. ‡THOMAS, Kittery 1652, perhaps afterwards of Portsmouth, and one of the first council of N. H. under President Cutt, 1680. WILLIAM, Massachusetts, was admitted freeman in 1648.

DANIELS, WENTWORTH, Lynn 1640. Lewis.

DARLEY, DENNIS, was an early inhabitant of Braintree.

DARLING, JOHN, Braintree, between 1660 and 1690. · Thirteen of the name of Darling had grad. at the N. E. colleges in 1828.

DARMAN, JOHN, Braintree 1644, had sons, John, b. 1644; Joseph, b. 1645; John, 2d, b. 1653.

DART, AMBROSE, Boston 1654.

DARVELL, ROBERT, Sudbury, died 26 Feb. 1662.

DASSET, JOHN, Braintree, freeman 1641, had a son Joseph, b. 6 Dec. 1642. John, perhaps his son, was of Braintree, admitted freeman in 1657, m. Hannah Flint, of Concord, 15 Sept. 1662, and Joseph Dasset, H. C. 1687, was probably their son.

DAUTS, ROBERT, Massachusetts, was admitted freeman in 1643.

DAVENISH, THOMAS, Salem, admitted to the church 1641, and freeman same year.

DAVENPORT, JOHN, the first minister of New-Haven, and the fourth of the first church in Boston, was son of the mayor of Coventry, and probably Henry Davenport, who sustained that office in 1613. See Dugdale's Antiquities of Warwickshire. He was b. in 1597; was educated at the university of Oxford; Rev. Mr. Dodd says, at Brazen-Nose College, came to N. E. 26 June, 1637, and

the next year settled at New-Haven.   He removed to Boston, and
was installed the successor of Rev. John Wilson, 9 Dec. 1668, and
d. 15 or 12 March, 1670, æ. 73.   Twelve of the name had grad. at
the N. E. colleges in 1828.   JOHN, New-Haven, son of the preceding, might be the John Davenport, jr., of Boston, admitted freeman in 1669.   He m. Abigail, daughter of Rev. Abraham Pierson,
27 Nov. 1663, and had John ; Elizabeth ; Abigail, who m. Rev.
James Pierpont ; John, 2d, the following, and Mary.   *JOHN*, minister of Stamford, Conn., son of the preceding, was born 1670, grad.
at H. C. 1687 ; was ordained 1694 ; died 5 Feb. 1731, æ 61.   By
two wives he had 8 children, whose posterity are numerous in Connecticut.   *RICHARD, was born a. 1606, and arrived at Salem
with Governour Endecott in Sept. 1628; was representative in
1637 from Salem, where he resided until 1642.   He was afterwards
commander at Castle-Island, in Boston harbour, many years, and
was killed by lightning, 15 July, 1665, æ. 59.   Capt. Davenport, of
Boston, who was killed by the Indians, 19 Dec. 1675, in taking
Narraganset Fort, was his son.   Prince, i. Annals, 174.   Hutchinson, i. Hist. Mass. 232.   Johnson, Hist. N. E. 194.   THOMAS,
Dorchester, member of the church 1640, freeman 1642, had sons,
Jonathan and Eleazar.

DAVIE, JOHN, was a magistrate of Boston in 1680.   Edmund
Davie grad. at H. C. 1674, went to Europe and took the degree of
M. D. at Padua.   John Davie, grad. at H. C. 1681, became heir to
an estate in England, from which he derived the title of baronet.
Holmes, i. Annals, 511.

DAVIS, DOLOR, Cambridge 1634, a proprietor of Groton in
1656, and according to S. Davis, esq. of Plymouth, an early planter
and freeman at Barnstable, where he d. in 1773.   He m. Margery,
sister of major Simon Willard.   His sons were John, Simon, and
Samuel.   Simon and Samuel lived in Concord, the former of whom
was representative in 1689.   The name of Davis has been very
common in N. E. and in other parts of our country, and had in 1828,
furnished from 50 to 60 graduates at the N. E., N. Y., and N. J.
colleges.   In several ancient records, some of the following names
are spelled *Davies*.   DANIEL, Kittery was admitted freeman 1652.
GEORGE, Boston, freeman 1645, was probably one of the founders
of the 2d church.   Snow, Hist. Boston, 129.   Samuel and John,
sons of George Davis, were b. in Boston, 1651 and 1652.   GEORGE,
Lynn and Reading, freeman 1647, d. at Reading, 4 July, 1667.
ISAAC, was an inhabitant of Beverly in 1659.   *JAMES, Haverhill, was representative at the 2d session in 1660, and probably the
freeman of 1640.   He d. 19 Jan. 1679, æ. 90.   James Davis, supposed his son, d. at Haverhill, 18 July, 1694.   JAMES, Boston, a
mariner, was member of the church, and perhaps the freeman of
1635 ; had a son Jacob, b. in 1639.   JENKIN, Lynn, 1637, was
a joiner, and d. in 1662, leaving one son and one daughter.
Winthrop, ii. Hist. N. E. 45.   Coffin.   Lewis.   JOHN, Boston, a
joiner, was member of the church in 1635, and perhaps member
of the ar. co. 1643.   There was a John Davis of Watertown, a. 1642.

JOHN, Newbury 1644, had sons, John, b. 15 Jan. 1645; Zachary, b. 1646; Jeremy, b. 1648; Cornelius, b. 1653; Ephraim, b. 1655. He had also several daughters. JOHN, from New-Haven, grad. at H. C. 1651, and was lost at sea with Jonathan Ince and Nathaniel Pelham in 1657. Savage, ii. Winthrop, 329. JOHN, Kittery, was admitted freeman and appointed to keep an ordinary there in 1652. JOHN, Dover 1653, had children, Hannah, b. 1653; Jane, b. 1655; Moses, b. 30 Dec. 1657; Joseph, b. 26 Jan. 1659; Jane, 2d, and James, b. 23 May, 1662, a col., who d. 1749, æ. 87, leaving children, James, who d. aged 93; Thomas, 88; Samuel, 96; Daniel, 65; Sarah, 91; Hannah, 77; Elizabeth, 79; Ephraim, 87; and Phebe, 85. Belknap, iii. Hist. N. H. 188, 189. NICHOLAS, Woburn 1643, perhaps the same who was admitted freeman at Kittery in 1652. NICHOLAS, a merchant of Barnstable in 1643, favoured the quakers on their first appearance in 1656; d. in 1673. S. Davis, esq., MS letter. ROBERT, Yarmouth 1638, removed to Barnstable, had sons, John, Robert, Josiah, and Tristram, born from 1650 to 1664. Ibid. ROBERT, Sudbury, 1644. Shattuck. SAMUEL, Boston, freeman 1645, had a son Samuel, b. in 1654. ‡SYLVANUS, Sheepscot, Maine 1675, a captain in the Indian war, was wounded by the Indians, 1675, (Hubbard, 41) and was one of the counsellors under the new charter of William and Mary, granted in 1691. His statement respecting the eastern fisheries and settlements is in the 3 Coll. Mass. Hist. Soc. i. 101. THOMAS, Newbury 1641, was one of the first settlers of Haverhill. THOMAS, an early settler at Biddeford, Me., (then Saco) was assessed for publick worship in 1636. S. Davis, esq. THOMAS, was secretary of the province of N. H. in 1693. WILLIAM, Roxbury 1642, d. 9 Dec. 1683, æ. 66. His son John was b. in 1643, was an officer, and d. 11 March, 1717. Tobias Davis d. at Roxbury in 1690, and John and William Davis d. there in 1706. *‖WILLIAM, Boston, freeman 1645, member of the ar. co. 1643, its captain from 1664 to 1672; was commander of a company of troop in Ninigret's war; represented Springfield in 1652, and perhaps Haverhill in 1668. He m., 5 Dec. 1644, Margaret, daughter of William Pynchon, and his children, by his former wife and by her, were, Thomas, who d. 1636; Tierne, [?] b. 1642; Joseph, b. 1645; Thomas; Benjamin, a major, who lived in Boston, and died 26 Nov. 1704, and William.

DAVISON, ‖DANIEL, Ipswich 1665, removed to Newbury, and was a man of note there, a major of the Essex regiment; member of the ar. co. 1672. He had a number of children.

DAVY, DANIEL, Kittery 1652. George Davy was an inhabitant at, or near, Wiscasset, Me., as early as 1666. ‖‡*HUMPHREY, Boston, freeman 1665, was a non-resident representative of Billerica 4 years, from 1666 to 1669, and for his services received, by vote of the town, the present of "a fat beast;" represented Woburn in 1678; was member of the ar. co. 1665; and was elected assistant from 1679 to 1686. JOHN, Boston, freeman 1637, perhaps the magistrate of Boston in 1680, and father of the preceding and the two graduates at H. C., Edmund and John Davie, was among those disarmed by order of government in 1637. Savage, i. Winthrop, 248.

DAWES, WILLIAM, Boston, freeman 1646, died 24 March, 1703, æ. 86. He had sons, Ambrose, born in Braintree, 25 July, 1642; William and Robert, b. in Boston, a. 1655 and 1656. Three of the name, Thomas, Ebenezer, and Thomas, grad. at H. C. in 1777, 1785, and 1801.

DAWSON, HENRY, Massachusetts, was admitted freeman in 1641.

DAY, MATTHEW, probably the first printer in North-America, and the one mentioned by Gov. Winthrop, who came to N. E. in 1639. His name is found in the imprint of one or more works published before 1648. He was admitted freeman in 1646, and died at Cambridge, 10 May, 1649. NATHANIEL, Ipswich 1637. Kimball, Eccl. Sermon. RALPH, Massachusetts, was admitted freeman 1645. ROBERT, Cambridge, was admitted freeman 1635, and probably went to Connecticut, where ten persons of the name had received the honours of Yale College in 1828, of whom is the president of the institution, Jeremiah Day, D. D., LL. D., who grad. in 1795. ROBERT, freeman 1641, was of Ipswich in 1648. STEPHEN, Cambridge, is considered by Dr. Thomas, in his Hist. of Printing, as the first printer in this country, who commenced business in March, 1639. He d. 22 Dec. 1668, æ. 58. Dr. Thomas gives a catalogue of the books supposed to be printed by him, in vol. ii. p. 231—234 of his History. ||WENTWORTH, was a member of the ar. co. 1640.

DAYTON, RALPH, East-Hampton, L. I., 1650. Three of the name, Jonathan, LL. D., Thomas B. C., and Aaron O. grad. at N. J. College, in 1776, 1806, and 1813.

DEACON, JOHN, Lynn 1637. Lewis. Goodman Deacon, of Hadley, was killed by the Indians in March, 1676. Hubbard.

DEAN, DANIEL, a lieutenant, and an early proprietor of Concord, d. 29 Nov. 1725, æ. 97. Shattuck. JOHN, freeman 1641, may have been the John Dane of Ipswich. Thirteen of the name of Dean and Deane had received the honours of the N. E. colleges in 1828. SAMUEL, Lancaster 1653. STEPHEN, Plymouth 1623. THOMAS, Boston 1665. 2 coll. Mass. Hist. Soc. viii. 105. THOMAS, Concord 1645, whose name is often spelled *Dane*, d. 5 Feb. 1676. Elizabeth, his wife, d. 1673. His son Joseph m. Elizabeth Fuller 1662, and had sons, Thomas, b. 1664; Joseph, b. 1667; and Daniel, b. 1669. Shattuck.

DEARBORN, GODFREY, came form Exeter, England, with his son Henry, "a man grown," and settled at Exeter in 1639. He removed to Hampton, where he m. Dorothy Dalton, probably the widow of Philemon, 25 Nov. 1662. His descendants are abundant in N. H. Gen. Henry Dearborn is from this family.

DEERING, HENRY, was a schoolmaster at Salisbury in 1664. Two of the name of Deering have grad. at H. C. and two writing it

Dering have grad. at Y. C.   SAMUEL, Braintree 1649, had daughters, Bethia, Mary, Hannah, and Sarah, b. from 1648 to 1657.

DELANO, PHILIP, Plymouth 1623. The name was first spelled De la Noye, by which we may conclude that he was a French protestant who had united himself to the church of Leyden. Savage, MS note.

DELL, GEORGE, freeman 1651, had sons, John, b. 1645; Samuel, b. 1647 ; Joseph, b. 1649 ; Benjamin, b. 1652. There is a notice of one Dell in i. Winthrop, 312.

DEMING, JOHN, whose name is *Daming* in the colony records, was admitted freeman in 1645. Eight of the name of Deming had grad. in N. E. in 1828, of whom Rev. David, H. C. 1700, was minister of Medway. John Deming was named in the charter of Connecticut in 1662.

DENISON, ||‡*DANIEL, son of William Denison, was of Cambridge in 1633, freeman 1634, when he removed to Ipswich, which he represented 8 years from 1635. He was a captain in 1637, major in 1648, member of the ar. co. 1660, speaker of the house of reps. 1649 and 1651, major-general, a. 1662, assistant 29 years, from 1654 to 1682. He d. 20 Sept. 1682, æ. 70. He m. Patience, daughter of Gov. Thomas Dudley. Thirteen of the name had grad. at the N. E. colleges in 1828. *EDWARD, Roxbury, was disarmed in 1637, admitted freeman 1648, was representative in 1652 and 1655, and d. 26 April, 1668. He had sons, John, b. 1644 ; Edward, Jeremiah, and Joseph, some of whom d. young. GEORGE, Roxbury, was born in 1621, admitted freeman 1648, is mentioned by Winthrop as "a young soldier lately come out of the wars in England," and as being chosen captain by the young men in Roxbury in 1647. He probably removed to Stonington, Conn., and much distinguished himself in Philip's war in 1675. Hubbard, Indian Wars, 97. JOHN, Ipswich 1648, was probably a brother of Major-general Denison. JOHN, only son of Major-gen. Denison, d. 9 Jan. 1671, leaving a wife Martha, daughter of Deputy-governour Samuel Symonds, and children, John and Martha. Martha m. Matthew Whipple, and d. 12 Sept. 1728, æ. 60. *JOHN*, the sixth minister of Ipswich, was son of the preceding, and grad. at H. C. 1684, was ordained colleague with Rev. William Hubbard in 1687, and d. in Sept. 1689. His wife was Elizabeth, daughter of Hon. Nathaniel Saltonstall, by whom he had one son, Col. John Denison, who grad. at H. C. 1710. She afterwards m. Rev. Rowland Cotton. THOMAS, Kittery 1652. *WILLIAM, Roxbury, freeman 1632, was Representative in 1635, was among the disarmed in 1637, and d. 25 Jan. 1653 or 4, "an old man," say the Roxbury Records. His wife d. in 1646.

DENMARK, PATRICK, New-Hampshire 1664.

DENNET, JOHN, Portsmouth, freeman 1672, had a son Ephraim, b. 2 Aug. 1683, who was one of the counsellors of New-Hampshire, appointed by mandamus in 1732.

DENNING, WILLIAM, Boston, d. 20 Jan. 1654.

DENNIS, EDMUND, Boston, 1640. THOMAS, Boston, had a son Thomas, b. in 1630.

DENNY, EDWARD, was admitted freeman in 1637. Thomas Denny was admitted freeman 1669.

DENSLOW, NICHOLAS, Massachusetts, freeman 1633.

DENT, FRANCIS, Massachusetts, was admitted freeman in 1634.

DENTON, RICHARD, Dorchester, d. 28 Dec. 1658. *RICH-ARD*, minister of Weathersfield and Stamford, in Conn. and Hempstead, L. I., died at the last place in 1663. Johnson erroneously calls him *Lenten*, and Mr. Savage adds this name to his list of ministers in the 2d volume of Winthrop. Wood [Hist. Towns on Long-Island] says that he had been a minister at Halifax, Yorkshire, and that he came to N. E. between 1630 and 1635.

DERBY, JOHN, Beverly, a. 1680, left issue. There was an Edward Derby of Braintree 1690. Of this name there have been several distinguished merchants, and seven have grad. at H. C. and one at Bowdoin college.

DESBOROUGH, ‡JOHN, was a magistrate of New-Haven 1637. Major-general John Desborough is mentioned in 1 Coll. of Mass. Hist. Soc. x. 98. SAMUEL, New-Haven 1639, was one of the first settlers and founders of the church at Guilford 1643. He returned to England in 1651, represented the city of Edinburgh in parliament, and in 1656, was returned as a member of the British parliament for the Sheriffdom of Mid-Lothian. Noble, ii. Memoirs of the Cromwell family, 254. There was a Nicholas Desborough of Hartford in 1683, who is mentioned in the Magnalia, ii. 393.

DEVEL, or DEVELL, WILLIAM, Braintree, had a son John, born there, a. 1643.

DEVEREUX, JOHN, Salem, 1637, Marblehead 1648. John Devereux, freeman in 1683. Burrill and Humphrey Devereux, H. C. 1767 and 1798, are probably his descendants.

DEVOTION, EDWARD, Roxbury, freeman 1645, d. 28 Sept. 1685, æ. 64. Ebenezer Devotion, H. C. 1707, was the minister of Suffield, Conn. and was probably father of Rev. Ebenezer Devotion, Y. C. 1732, and ancestor of Rev. John, Ebenezer, John, and Samuel H. Devotion, graduates at Yale College.

DEWEY, *JONATHAN, Westfield, representative in 1689 and 1691. Jedidiah, Joseph, and Thomas Dewey, were of Westfield in 1679. Ten of the name had grad. at the N. E. colleges in 1828.

DEWING, ANDREW, Dedham, was admitted freeman in 1646.

DEXTER, GREGORY, a native of London, was a stationer, but became a preacher, and settled in Providence over the Baptist church in 1643. He d. in his 91st year. Twelve persons of the name had been educated at Harvard, Yale, and Brown colleges in 1828. RICHARD, Charlestown 1644. THOMAS, Lynn, 1630 was admitted freeman 1631. He owned 800 acres of land, and was commonly called "Farmer" Dexter. He lived near the Iron works on Saugus river. He was one of the proprietors of Sandwich in 1637. Mr. Lewis gives some account of the impetuosity of his temper, and the publick censures to which it exposed him. He had a son Thomas, of Lynn.   Lewis, MS Hist. Lynn.   Savage, i. Winthrop, 53.

DIBBLE, ABRAHAM, Boston, 1648.   Robert Dibble was of Massachusetts, and admitted freeman in 1635.   THOMAS, Dorchester, freeman 1637, removed to Windsor, and was probably ancestor of Rev. Ebenezer Dibble, D. D., of John and John Alexis Dibble, who grad. at Y. C. 1734, 1758 and 1778.

DICKERMAN, THOMAS, Dorchester, 1636, freeman 1638, had a son Isaac b. in 1637.

DICKINSON, JOHN, Salisbury 1640.   Twenty-seven of the name had been educated at the N. E. colleges in 1825. PHILEMON, Salem, freeman 1641, removed from thence.   Nathaniel Dickinson was of Hadley in 1663.   THOMAS, Rowley, 1643, d. 1662, leaving a son James and 4 daughters.

DICKSON, WILLIAM, Cambridge, 1642.   See (Dixon.)

DILLINGHAM, EDWARD, Lynn, 1636, removed to Sandwich 1637. Lewis.   William H. and Charles Dillingham are on the catalogue of Williams College.   JOHN, freeman 18 May, 1631, appears to have been one of the first settlers of Ipswich.

DIMAN, or DIMOND, JOHN, Lynn, 1647.   One of the same name was of Kittery in 1652.   Five persons of the name of Diamond, Diman, and Dimon had grad. at Harv. and Yale in 1828.

DINELY, THOMAS, Boston, d. 15 Jan. 1655.   WILLIAM, Boston, was a member of the church, and admitted freeman in 1635.

DINGLEY, JOHN, Lynn, removed to Sandwich 1637, in the vicinity of which his descendants abound.   Amasa Dingley grad. at H. C. 1785.   *RICHARD*, a Baptist minister of Newport, went to South-Carolina in 1694.   Benedict.

DINNY, EDWARD, perhaps the same as Denny, was admitted freeman in 1637.   (See DENNY.)

DINSDALE, ||WILLIAM, Boston, freeman 1657, member of the ar. co. 1658.   Son John b. in 1644.   Thomas Dinsdale was admitted freeman in 1660.

DISBEROE, ISAAC, Lynn 1638.   [Lewis.]   Samuel Disberough grad. at N. J. College in 1822.

DIVEN, JOHN, Lynn, 1643, d. 4 Oct. 1684.   Lewis.

DIX, ANTHONY, Plymouth, 1623, admitted freeman 1631, Salem 1637.   This is the same person, whose loss, under the name of Dick, is recorded by Winthrop, i. 287.   Savage, MS note.   EDWARD, Watertown, admitted freeman 1635, had a son John, b. in 1640.   Edmund Dix, perhaps the same, was of Watertown in 1637, and d. 9 July, 1660.   There was a Ralph Dix of Ipswich in 1648. Five of the name of Dix had grad. at H. C. in 1828.

DIXEY, JOHN, Salem 1639.   Felt, Annals of Salem, 126. THOMAS, Salem 1637, Marblehead 1674, d. 1691.   WILLIAM, arrived at Cape Ann in June, 1629, settled in Salem, was admitted freeman 1634; was an ensign of the militia, and died 1690, æ. 82.

DIXON, JEREMIAH and JOHN, were of New-Haven in 1639. Five of their descendants have grad. at Yale College. WILLIAM, Cambridge, whose name is Dickson in the colony records, but Dixon in Cambridge town records, was admitted freeman in 1642. His wife was Jane, and his children were Lydia, Abigail, Mary, Hannah, and John. There was a William Dixon of Kittery in 1652, but not the one of Cambridge.

DIXWELL, JOHN, a colonel, and one of the judges, who condemned Charles I to death, came to N. E. and lived at New-Haven under the name of *Davids*, married there and left several children. He d. 18 march, 1689, in his 82d year. Descendants through female lines remain, of whom one, a respectable physician of Boston, has assumed the name of this regicide.

DOANE, ‡JOHN, Plymouth, was an assistant of Plymouth colony in 1633, removed to Eastham, a. 1644, was living there in 1678, very aged. Isaiah, Elisha, George, and Augustus-Sidney Doane grad. at H. C. in 1774, 1781, 1812, and 1825.

DODGE, GEORGE, Concord 1645. Shattuck. *JOHN, born 1636, was an inhabitant of Beverly in 1666, and appears to have been representative of Rowley 1664. See Coll. N. H. Hist. Soc. ii. 222, 226. RICHARD, Salem, was received to the church, 5 May, 1644, and was one of the founders of the church in Beverly 1667, where he probably lived. WILLIAM, Salem, was admitted freeman 1637, was one of the founders of the church in Beverly 1667. He is mentioned by Hubbard, Indian Wars, p. 59. *WILLIAM, son of the preceding, was of Beverly, admitted freeman 1683, representative, 28 May 1690. Daniel Dodge was a graduate at H. C. 1700.

DOE, NICHOLAS, Oyster River, now Durham, N. H., 1669, in the vicinity of which his descendants remain.

DOGGETT, JOHN, Watertown, freeman 1631. (See Daggett.) THOMAS, Concord, d. 23 August, 1642. Shattuck.

DOLE, GEORGE, Lynn 1637, removed to Sandwich 1637. Lewis. RICHARD, was born 1614, came from Somersetshire, England, 1640, with Percival Lowle, and settled at Newbury. He m. Hannah, daughter of widow Rolfe, 3 May, 1647, and had issue, 1. John, b. 10 August, 1648, m. 23 Oct. 1677, Mary, daughter of Capt. William Gerrish; 2. Richard, b. 6 Sept. 1650, m. Sarah Greenleaf, 1677; 3. Anna, b. 1653; 4. Benjamin, b. 1654; 5. Joseph, b. 1657; 6. William, b. 1660; 7. Henry, b. 1663; 8. Hannah, b. 1665; 9. Apphia, b. 1668; 10. Abner, b. 1672. He m. a. 2d wife, Hannah, widow of Capt. Samuel Brocklebank, of Rowley. Coffin.

DONNELL, HENRY, Kittery, was admitted freeman 1652. ‡SAMUEL, was a magistrate of York, judge of the court of common pleas, one of the first council under the charter of William and Mary 1692, d. 9 March, 1718, æ. 72. Douglass by mistake calls him *Daniel*.

DOOLITTLE, JOHN, Lynn 1643, Rumney Marsh [Chelsea] 1653. Lewis. Snow, Hist. Boston, 137. Six of the name had grad. at Y. C. in 1828, of whom Benjamin, 1716, was a clergyman, and Joel, 1799, has been a judge in Vermont.

DORCHESTER, ANTHONY, Springfield, d. 9 Nov. 1649.

DORMAN, EDMUND, New-Haven 1639. THOMAS, one of the first settlers of Ipswich was admitted freeman in 1635, perhaps d. at Topsfield in 1670.

DORR, EDWARD, Roxbury, had a son Edward, who d. in 1683. Fourteen of the name had received their education at the N. E. colleges in 1828, ten of them at Harvard.

DORRIL, JOHN, Boston, d. 3 March, 1704.

DORYFALL, BARNABY, Braintree, was admitted freeman in 1636.

DOTEY, EDWARD, one of the servants of Stephen Hopkins of Plymouth 1620, and one of the combatants in the first duel in N. E. 18 June, 1621. Prince, i. Annals, 105. Samuel Doty grad. at Y. C. 1733.

DOUGHTY, [SAMUEL?] a preacher, it would seem from Lechford, as quoted by Hutchinson, at Taunton in 1639. Charles J. Doughty grad. at Y. C. in 1806.

DOUBLEDAY, ROGER, Boston, d. 22 Nov. 1690.

DOUGLASS, HENRY, Massachusetts, was admitted freeman in 1657. WILLIAM, Boston, freeman 1646, had a son William b. in 1645.

DOW, FRANCIS, came from Salisbury, in England, and settled at Salisbury as early as 1651. Coffin. *HENRY, Watertown, freeman 1642, was probably the same who was representative of Hampton in 1655 and 1656, and where, probably, he d. in 1659. He had sons, Joseph and Daniel, b. in Watertown, in 1638 and 1641. Henry Dow, was a mandamus counsellor of N. H. in 1702.

THOMAS, one of the grantees of Newbury, settled in Salisbury, was admitted freeman 1642, and d. 31 May, 1654, leaving children Thomas, Stephen, and Mary. Jonathan Dow, esq. of Weare, a member of the convention which adopted the constitution of the U. S., and a representative in the N. H. legislature, was from this family.

DOWDY, GEORGE, Massachusetts, was admitted freeman in 1645. HENRY, Guilford, Conn. 1650.

DOWMAN, or DORMAN, THOMAS, d. at Topsfield, 1670, æ. 70.

DOWNHAM, JOHN, Plymouth, a deacon of the church, d. 1668 aged a. 80. Davis, Morton's Memo.

DOWNING, DENNIS, Kittery 1652. *EMANUEL, Salem, was admitted, with Lucy his wife, to the church in Salem, 4 Nov. 1638, freeman Dec. 1638, representative 1639, five years. His children were George ; John, bapt. 1 March, 1640; Dorcas, b. 7 Feb. 1641 ; Theophilus, bapt. 13 March, 1642. A John Downing d. at Boston, 29 April, 1694, and a Richard Downing, of Ipswich, d. there, 3 Nov. 1702. GEORGE, son of the preceding, was born in London, grad. at H. C. 1642, went to England 1645, and sustained various offices under Cromwell and Charles II, and by the last was made a baronet, 1 July, 1662, his residence being then at East Hatley, in Cambridgeshire. [Guillim's Heraldry.] He m.

about 1654, Frances Howard, and d. in 1684, æ. about 59. His son George m. Catharine, eldest daughter of James, Earl of Salisbury. Their son George d. in 1747, without issue, and left a bequest for founding a college at Cambridge, England, now called Downing college, which bequest now amounts to £150,000. Hutchinson, i. Hist. Mass. 107. Savage, ii. Winthrop, 240—242. Felt, Annals Salem, 168.

DOWNS, THOMAS, Boston 1652, perhaps of Dover 1663.

DOWSE, FRANCIS, Boston 1643. Jonathan, Edward, and Joseph Dowse grad. at H. C. in 1715, 1725, and 1766. LAW-RENCE, a carpenter of Boston, was admitted to the church in 1643.

DRAKE, ABRAHAM, Exeter, 1646, removed to Hampton, where he was marshal. There was a Robert Drake of Hampton in 1668, and in 1686, Abraham Drake, jr. and Nathaniel Drake were of New-Hampshire. JOHN, came to N. E. as early as 1630, in which year, on 19 October, he requested to be made a freeman. There was a Thomas Drake of Weymouth in 1660, and a Job Drake of Westfield, a. 1667.

DRAPER, JAMES, one of the proprietors of Lancaster 1654. One of the same name d. at Roxbury in 1697. Nine have been educated at the N. E. colleges. NICHOLAS, Salem 1637. ROGER, Concord 1639, had children Adam and Lydia.

DRAYTON, JOHN, Maine 1642.

DRESSER, JOHN, Rowley 1643, d. 1672. Coffin. *JOHN, freeman 1684, was representative in 1691.

DREW, THOMAS, Oyster River, now Durham, N. H. 1669. This family suffered by the Indians in 1694 or 1695. See Belknap.

DRINKER, PHILIP, Massachusetts, freeman 1637. Edward Drinker was one of the founders of the first Baptist church in Boston, 1665.

DRIVER, ROBERT, Lynn 1630, freeman 1635, d. according to Mr. Lewis, 3 April, 1680, æ. 88. Phebe, his wife, d. in Feb. 1683. The fate of his son Robert is recorded in the Magnalia, B. vi. Lewis.

DRUCE, VINTON, 1639. Lincoln, Hist. Hingham. There was a Vincent Druce of Cambridge, who had a son John, b. there in 1669. John Druce, probably from this family, grad. at H. C. 1738. JOHN, was killed by the Indians, the first year of Philip's war.

DRURY, ||HUGH, member of the ar. co. 1659, was of Boston, where his son John was b. in 1646. Ephraim, John, and Luke Drury grad. at Harvard, Williams, and Brown Colleges in 1776, 1804, and 1813. JOHN, Massachusetts, was admitted freeman in 1654.

DUDLEY, FRANCIS, Concord, m. Sarah Wheeler, 26 Oct. 1665, and had a number of children. HUGH, of Springfield, a. 1654, is named in Sprague's Hist. Discourse. §†‡||*JOSEPH, Roxbury, son of Gov. Thomas Dudley, by his last wife, was b. 23 July, 1647, grad. at H. C. 1665, was representative 1673 to 1675, member of the ar. co. 1677, was elected an assistant 1676 to 1685; appointed president of Mass. and N. H. 1686, a member of Sir Edmund Andros' council 1687, chief justice of Mass., went to England 1682, again in 1689, and was eight years governour of the Isle of Wight. He returned to N. E. 11 June, 1702 as governour of Mass. and N. H. in which office he remained until Nov. 1715. He d. at Roxbury, 2 April, 1720, æ. 72. His wife, who d. 21 Sept. 1722, was Rebecca, daughter of Edward Tyng, and his children were, 1. Thomas, b. 26 Feb. 1670, grad. at H. C. 1685; 2. Edward, b. 4 Sept. 1671, d. Jan. 1683; 3. Paul, b. 3 Sept. 1675, grad. at H. C. 1690, was fellow of the Royal Society, chief justice of Massachusetts, and founder of the Dudleian lecture at Cambridge; d. at Roxbury, 21 Jan. 1751, æ. 75; 4. Samuel, b. Sept. 1677; 5. John, b. 28 Feb. 1679; 6. Rebecca; 7. Catharine; 8. Ann; 9. William, b. 20 Oct. 1686, grad. at H. C. 1704, was a colonel, and member of the council of Mass., and father of Thomas and Joseph Dudley, H. C. 1750 and 1751; 10. Daniel, b. 4 Feb. 1689; 11. Catharine, 2d; 12. Mary. ||PAUL, brother of the preceding, was b. at Roxbury, 8 Sept. 1650, member of the ar. co. 1677, m. Mary, daughter of Gov. John Leverett, and died a. 1681, leaving Paul, b. at Boston, 4 March, 1667; Thomas, b. 10 Feb. 1681. *SAMUEL, eldest brother of the preceding, was b. in England about 1606; came to N. E. and resided in Cambridge, Boston, and Salisbury, and finally settled at Exeter as the minister of that town, and there d. in 1683, æ. 77. He was representative of Salisbury at the March and May sessions 1644. He m. Mary, daughter of Gov. Winthrop. She d. at Salisbury, 12 April, 1643. He afterwards m. a second and third wife. His children were 1. Thomas, bapt. 9 March, 1634, grad. at H. C. 1651, d. 7 Nov. 1655; 2. John, bapt. 28 June, 1635; 3. Samuel. bapt. 2 Aug. 1639, d. 17 April, 1643; 4. Anne, b. at Salisbury, 16 Oct. 1641, m. Edward Hilton, of Exeter; 5. Theophilus, b. 4 Oct. 1644; 6. Mary, b. and d. 1646; 7. Biley, b. 27 Sept. 1647; 8. Mary, b. 1649, m. Samuel Hardy, a schoolmaster of Beverly, 24 Jan. 1676; 9. Stephen; 10. James; 11. Timothy; 12. Abigail; 13 Dorothy; 14. Rebecca; 15. Elizabeth, who m. Kinsley Hall. The descendants of Rev. Samuel Dudley are very numerous in New-Hampshire. §‡†THOMAS, son of captain Roger Dudley, was born at Northampton, England in 1576, came to N. E. in 1630, lived in several places, and finally settled at Roxbury. He was an assistant in 1635, 1636, 1641 to 1644; deputy governour 13 years commencing in 1630; governour 1634, 1640, 1645, and 1650. He d. 31 July, 1653, in his 77th year. Dorothy, his wife, d. 27 Sept. 1643, and he m. again the next year. His widow m. Rev. John Allin, of Dedham. His children by both marriages were Samuel, the preceding; Ann, wife of Gov. Simon Bradstreet. Patience, wife of Major-gen. Daniel Denison; Mercy, b. 27 Sept. 1621, who m. Rev. John Woodbridge; one who m. Major Benjamin Keaine, of Boston; Deborah, b. 27 Feb. 1645; Joseph, b. 1647; Paul, b. 1650. Some of Governour Dudley's descendants have been ambitious to claim their descent from John

Dudley, duke of Northumberland, who was beheaded by order of queen Mary, 22 August, 1653, æ. 51, but the evidence in Dugdale's Antiquities of Warwickshire, and Camden's Remains, is conclusive against such descent.

DUEN, ||ANDREW, was member of the ar. co. 1644. Whitman.

DUMBLETON, JOHN, Springfield, a. 1654. Sprague, Hist. Discourse.

DUMMER, ||JEREMIAH, son of the following, was b. at Newbury, 14 Sept. 1645, settled in Boston, where he was a member of the ar. co. 1671, was one of the council of safety 1689, [Hutch. i. 340] and d. 24 May, 1718, æ. 73. He was father to the celebrated Jeremy Dummer, the agent in England for Mass., who grad. at H. C. 1699, a most distinguished scholar, who d. at Plaistow, in England, 19 May, 1739. ‡*RICHARD, second son of John Dummer, of Bishop-Stoke, England, was b. a 1591, came to N. E. 26 May, 1632, and admitted freeman the same year. He was elected an assistant in 1635 and 1636, being then of Roxbury, from whence he soon removed to Newbury, which he represented in 1640, 1645, and 1647. He d. 14 Dec. 1679, æ. 88. He m. Frances, widow of Rev. Jonathan Burr, by whom, who d. 19 Nov. 1682, he had Jeremiah; Hannah, b. 1647; Richard; William, b. 18 Jan. 1659, who, Mr. Coffin says, was father of Lieut. Gov. William Dummer, who d. in 1761. His son Shubael was by a former wife. RICHARD, Newbury, son of the preceding, was born 13 Jan. 1650, was one of the council of safety 1689, and d. 4 July, 1689, æ. 44. He m. Elizabeth Appleton, 2 Nov. 1673, and had Shubael, b. 10 Jan. 1677; Richard, b. and d. 1678; Richard, 2d, b. 1680; Elizabeth, b. 1682. *SHUBAEL*, minister of York, son of Richard Dummer, was b. 17 Feb. 1636, grad. at H. C. 1656, admitted 1660, commenced preaching at York as early as 1662, was ordained 3 Dec. 1672, and killed by the Indians, 5 Feb. 1692, æ. 56. He m. a daughter of Edward Rishworth. STEPHEN, Newbury, brother of the first Richard Dummer, was born at Bishop-Stoke, came to N. E. about 1636; admitted freeman 1639, returned to England in 1647. His wife was Alice Archer, and his daughter Jane m. Henry Sewall. Mehetabel, another daughter, was b. 1641. THOMAS, brother to the preceding, came to N. E. as early as 1635, admitted freeman in 1640, soon after which he resided in Salisbury.

DUNBAR, ROBERT, Hingham, had a son John b. in 1657. Twelve of the name have received a classical education in N. E., of whom Samuel, Asa, and Elijah, H. C. 1723, 1767, and 1794, were ministers of Stoughton, Salem, and Peterborough.

DUNCAN, ||*NATHANIEL, Dorchester, freeman 1635, was a merchant, a captain, auditor general, and representative, and is described by Johnson [Hist. N. E. 109] as "learned in the Latin and French tongues, and a very good accountant." Nathaniel and Peter, probably his sons, were admitted members of the ar. co. in 1644, and 1654.

DUNHAM, JOHN, Plymouth 1638. Davis, Morton's Memo. 384. (See Downham.)

DUNKIN, SAMUEL, Newbury 1638. John Dunkin was of Billerica, in 1675, where two of his children were killed by the Indians, 1 August, 1692.

DUNN, THOMAS, Massachusetts, was admitted freeman 1647.

DUNSTER, HENRY, the first president of Harvard College, came to N. E. in 1640, was admitted freeman in 1641, was inducted into the office of president 27 August, 1640, resigned 24 Oct. 1654, d. at Scituate 27 Feb. 1659, and was buried at Cambridge. His wife was Elizabeth, widow of Rev. Jesse Glover. He had sons, David, b. 16 May, 1645; Henry, b. 1650, Jonathan, b. 1653.

DUNTON, ROBERT, Reading 1647. Lewis. Samuel Dunton was also of Reading about the same time.

DURAND, JOHN, Scituate 1657.

DURANT, JOHN, Billerica 1675. Memoir Billerica, 11.

DURHAM, HUMPHREY, Maine, was killed by the Indians, 1676. Hubbard, 33.

DUSTIN, JOSIAH, Reading 1647, d. 16 Jan. 1672.

DUSTON, THOMAS, Haverhill, m. Hannah Duston, 3 Dec. 1677, by whom he had 13 children b. before 1699, one of whom Martha, was killed by the Indians, 15 March, 1697, at which time the mother was captured, and the 5 of April following, with Samuel Lennardson and Mary Neff, performed the exploit on Duston's island, in Contoocook River, above Concord, N. H. which has rendered her name so celebrated in the Magnalia, in Hutchinson, Dwight's Travels, and various other works.

DUTCH, ROBERT, Ipswich 1648. Felt. A remarkable account of his resuscitation when supposed to have been killed by the Indians, is given by Hubbard, Ind. Wars, 39. SIMON, Gloucester 1649. Ibid.

DUTTON ———, came to N. E. in 1630. Thomas Dutton, b. in 1621, was of Woburn in 1662; removed to Billerica, and was living there with his sons Thomas and John in 1675.

DWELLEY, RICHARD, Lancaster 1654. A Richard Dwelley was of Scituate in 1676. Willard, Hist. Lancaster, and ii. Coll. Mass. Hist. Soc.- iv.

DWIGHT, JOHN, Dedham 1635, was admitted freeman in 1638, d. in 1653. The Boston records give the death of John Dwight of Dedham, 24 March, 1638, who was perhaps a son. Josiah Dwight, H. C. 1687, was minister of Woodstock, Conn., and Dedham. Over the 3d church of the last place he was installed 4 June 1735. W. Winthrop and Worthington. THOMAS, Dedham, was admitted freeman in 1638. *TIMOTHY, Dedham, freeman 1641, was representative of Medfield in 1652, where he resided many years. *TIMOTHY, Dedham, was a child when his father brought him to Dedham in 1635. He was admitted a member of the church in 1652, elected a representative in 1691 and 1692, and perhaps at a later period. He is described as one " of an excellent spirit, peaceable, generous, charitable, and a promoter of the true interests of the church and town." He d. 31 Jan. 1718, æ. 83. The late Rev. Timothy Dwight, D. D. president of Yale College, was one of his descendants. Worthington, Hist. Dedham, 52. Alden, iii. Coll. Epitaphs, 53. Between 30 and 40 of the name have received the honours of Harvard and Yale colleges.

DYER, GEORGE, Dorchester, was on a jury, 28 Sept. 1630, and was admitted freeman, 18 May, 1631. *THOMAS, Weymouth 1632, freeman 1644, representative 1646, five years, was a member and deacon of the church, and d. 16 Nov. 1676, æ. 64, leaving an estate of £2103. 14. 7. He m. Agnes Reed, who d. 4 Dec. 1667. His children were, 1. Mary, b. 1641, m. Samuel White; 2. John, b. 12 July, 1643, settled in Boston, and left posterity there; 3. Thomas, b. 1645, d. young; 4. Abigail, b. 1647, m. Jacob Nash; 5. Sarah, b. 1649, m. John Ruggles; 6. Thomas, b. 5 May, 1651, settled in Plymouth; 7 and 8. Joseph and Benjamin, twins, b. 6 Nov. 1653. Joseph lived in Weymouth, was deacon of the church, and d. 12 Oct. 1704. He m. (1) Hannah Frary in 1676, who d. 1682; (2) Hannah Baxter, who d. in 1726. He was father of Benjamin Dyer, esq. of Weymouth, who died 12 Feb. 1774, æ. 86, John Dyer, colonel and judge, of Canterbury, Conn., and Thomas Dyer, of Windham, Conn., who was father of Judge Eliphalet Dyer, Y. C. 1740. Shattuck. WILLIAM, admitted freeman 1636, removed from Mass. to Rhode-Island in 1638. Mary Dyer, his wife, became a quaker, and for "rebellious sedition, and presumptuous obtruding herself after banishment upon pain of death," was sentenced to be executed, but upon the petition of William Dyer, her son, was reprieved on condition that she departed the jurisdiction of Mass. in 48 hours, and if she returned to suffer the sentence. She returned and was executed, 1 June, 1660. Hutchinson, i. Hist. Mass. 184.

EAMES, *ANTHONY, Hingham, was a representative in 1637 and 1638. There was a John Eames, who d. at Hingham in 1641, and John, the son of Mark Eames, was b. there in 1649. THOMAS, Dedham 1642, had a son John b. in 1642. There was a Thomas Eames of Sudbury, who had his house, barns, corn, and cattle burned by the Indians, 1 Feb. 1676, and his family captured. Hubbard, Ind. Wars.

EARLE, JOHN, Northampton 1662. Robert Earle d. at Boston in 1698, and Samuel Earle d. there in 1706, æ. 35. Robert Earle of Newport was born 1606, and his wife was living in 1699 at the age of 105 years.

EAST, FRANCIS, Boston, a carpenter, was admitted to the church 1636, freeman 1637. He had sons, Samuel, b. 1639; David, b. 1646; Daniel, b. 1652.

EASTON, §JOHN, Rhode-Island, son of Gov. Nicholas Easton, was elected governour of that colony 5 years, from 1690 to 1694. He d. in 1705, æ. 85. JOSEPH, one of the earliest inhabitants of Cambridge, was admitted freeman in 1635. §*NICHOLAS, one of the first settlers of Ipswich, was admitted freeman 1634, was "unduly" elected representative at the court in March, 1635; soon after, removed to Newbury, and from thence to Newport, where he was president of the R. I. colony, and was elected governour in 1672 and 1673. He d. in 1675, æ. 83.

EASTMAN, ROGER, was b. 1611, came to N. E. and settled at Salisbury in 1640, and d. 16 Dec. 1694, æ. 83. He is the great ancestor of the Eastmans, of whom 15 had grad. at the N. E. Colleges in 1828. *JOHN, probably son of the preceding, was representative of Salisbury in 1691.

EASTOW, *WILLIAM, Hampton, freeman 1638, was representative in 1644, 1648 and 1649.

EASTWICK, EDWARD. (See Estwick.) PHESANT, Portsmouth 1680.

EATON, FRANCIS, Plymouth 1620, was one of the first pilgrims ; removed to Duxbury a. 1645. JOHN, Dedham, freeman 1636, had a son Jacob, b. in 1642. JOHN, a proprietor of Salisbury in 1640, d. in Haverhill 1669. Thomas Eaton, of Haverhill, was killed by the Indians, 15 March, 1697. JONAS, Reading, was admitted freeman 1653, and d. 24 Feb. 1674. *NATHANIEL*, Boston, freeman 1638, had sons, Eleazar and Nathaniel, born in Boston in 1636 and 1639. He was the first head or principal of Harvard College, which was under his care until the accession of President Dunster in 1640. He went to Virginia, and finally to England, where, it is said, he d. in obscurity. *SAMUEL*, minister of New-Haven, came to N. E. in 1637, and d. 9. Jan. 1665, æ. 68. SAMUEL, Duxbury, 1641. ‡SAMUEL, New-Haven, son of the following, was b. a. 1629 ; came with his father to N. E. and grad. in 1649, at H. C. of which he was a fellow. He was elected a magistrate of New-Haven colony in 1654, and d. in that or the succeeding year. §THEOPHILUS, brother of Rev. Samuel Eaton, was a native of Stony-Stratford, Oxfordshire, and held the office of deputy-governour, of the East-India Company, and ambassador to the Court of Denmark, before he came to N. E. in 1637. He was one of the first settlers of the town and colony of New-Haven, and was elected gevernour of the latter in 1639, and continued in office until his death, the 7 Jan. 1657, in his 67th year. WILLIAM, Watertown, where his son Daniel was b. in 1638. There was a William Eaton of Reading, freeman in 1653, who d. 13 May, 1673.

EBORNE, SAMUEL, Salem 1637, Lynn 1640. Felt. Lewis. This name is spelled frequently *Abourne*. THOMAS, Salem, was admitted freeman 1634.

ECKELS, RICHARD, Cambridge, was admitted freeman in 1642. John D. Eccles grad. at Y. C. in 1815.

EDDINGTON, EDWARD, Scituate 1641.

EDDY, BENJAMIN, Watertown 1639. JOHN, Watertown, freeman 1634, had children, Pilgrim ; John, b. 1636 ; Benjamin ; Samuel, b. 30 Sept. 1640. Savage, i. Winthrop, 101. SAMUEL, Plymouth 1638. Davis, Morton's Memo. 384.

EDGECOMBE, NICHOLAS, was an inhabitant of Casco-Bay in 1658. He was probably of the family of Sir Richard Edgecombe, of Mount-Edgecombe, in Devonshire, who was a proprietor of lands near Casco.

EDGERLY, THOMAS, Dover 1665, freeman 1672, was a magistrate of N. H. He m. Rebecca Hallowell in 1665. He is probably the great ancestor of the Edgerlys in New-Hampshire.

EDMUNDS, JOHN, Massachusetts, was admitted freeman in 1631. Two of the name of *Edmond* have grad. in N. E. both at Y. C. in 1777 and 1796. JOSHUA, and SAMUEL, were of Concord in 1745. The first was admitted freeman in 1650. WALTER, Concord, freeman 1639, had a son John b. 1640. WILLIAM, Lynn, freeman 1635, had sons, John, Samuel, and Joseph, and d. 4 August, 1693. Lewis.

EDSALL, ‖THOMAS, Boston, was member of the ar. co. 1652. His son Henry was b. 1654.

EDSON, SAMUEL, Salem, from thence to Bridgewater, where he was a deacon of the church; representative to Plymouth court 1676, d. 9 July, 1692, æ. 80. Susanna, his widow, d. 20 Feb. 1699, æ. 81. Five of the name of Edson, and probably his descendants, have been educated at Harv., Yale, and Dartmouth.

EDWARDS, NATHANIEL, a merchant of Boston, died 2 Jan. 1654. There was a Nicholas Edwards of Boston, who d. at Barbadoes, 12 Oct. 1661. The name of Edwards has furnished some distinguished men; the catalogues of the New-England, Union, and New-Jersey colleges presenting 25 graduates, of whom are the two presidents of the name. ROBERT, Concord, was admitted freeman 1642, and d. a. 1650, leaving several children. THOMAS, Salem 1637, was admitted freeman in 1643. WILLIAM, Lynn 1648, East-Hampton, L. I. 1650.

EELLS, JOHN, whose name is also written Eales and Eels, is styled a bee-hive maker, and was probably the freeman in 1634. He finally settled in Newbury, and there d. 23 Nov. 1653. Of the 12 graduates of this name at Harvard, Yale, and Williams colleges, 10 were clergymen.

EGGLESTON, BIGOT, or BAGOT, Dorchester, was admitted freeman 1631, removed to Windsor, with the first settlers of that town, and was there in 1636. Descendants are in Conn. and N. H. Ambrose and George W. Eggleston grad. at Y. C. and H. C. in 1813 and 1815.

EGLINGTON, EDWARD, Boston, d. 17 Nov. 1696.

ELDERKIN, JOHN, Lynn 1637, Dedham 1641, may have posterity in Conn., where the name exists, and has had four grad. at Yale College.

ELDRID, SAMUEL, Cambridge 1646, had a son Thomas, b. in 1648. Samuel probably another son, lived in Rochester in 1688, and is named in the Revolution in N. E. Justified.

ELFORD, JOHN, Salem 1638. (Perhaps the same as ALFORD, an early name in Salem.)

ELIOT, ANDREW, Beverly. (See ELLIOTT.) FRANCIS, Braintree, freeman 1641, was ord. deacon of the church, 12 Oct.

1653. His son John was b. 17 April, 1650. Whitney, Hist. Quincy. Savage, i. Winth. 203. The various families of Eliot, Elliot, and Elliott had furnished 40 graduates at the N. E. colleges in 1828, of whom 11 were clergymen. JACOB, Boston, brother to Rev. John Eliot, was admitted freeman 1632, was an elder of the church. His son Jacob, b. 1632, freeman 1654, was a captain, and probably died in Boston 16 August, 1693, æ. 61. John, another son, was b. 1634. Savage, ii. Winthrop, Index. JOHN, Watertown 1633, whose name is spelled Ellet, had sons, John b. 1636, and Samuel. *JOHN*, the celebrated apostle among the Indians, arrived in N. E. in 1631, freeman 1632, was ordained the first minister of Roxbury, on Monday, 5 Nov., or as Mr. Prince supposes, on Friday, 9 Nov. 1632. He commenced preaching to the Indians at Nonantum, in Newton, Mass. 28 Oct. 1646, and continued his benevolent labours until his powers were subdued by age. He d. 20 May 1690, in his 86th year, having survived one colleague, Rev. S. Danforth, and received a second, Mr. Walter, in 1688. Anna, his wife, d. 22 March, 1687. His children were John; Joseph (see next articles); Samuel, b. 22 June, 1641, grad. 1660, at H. C. of which he was a fellow; became a preacher, but d. young; Aaron. b. 19 Feb. 1644, d. 18 Nov. 1655; Benjamin, b. 29 Jan. 1647, grad at H. C. 1665, was a preacher, and d. 15 Oct. 1687; in his 41st year. *JOHN*, the first minister of Newton, son of the preceding, was born at Roxbury, 31 August, 1636, grad. at H. C. 1656, was admitted freeman 1660, ordained 20 July, 1664, m. Elizabeth, daughter of Daniel Gookin, 23 May, 1666, and d. 13 (or 11) Oct. 1668, æ. 32, leaving a son John, born 28 April, 1667, who grad. at H. C. 1685. *JOSEPH*, minister of Guilford, brother of the preceding, was born 20 Dec. 1638, grad. at H. C. 1658, was ordained 1664, and d. 24 May, 1694, æ. 55. His son, Rev. Jared Eliot, of Killingworth, who was b. 7 Nov. 1685, grad. at Y. C. 1706, d. 22 April, 1763, æ. 77, was father of John Eliot, who grad. at H. C. 1737, a son of whom was Rev. Richard R. Eliot, H. C. 1774, the minister of Watertown, who d. in 1818. ||*PHILIP, Roxbury, brother of the Rev. John Eliot, of Roxbury, was admitted freeman in 1636, member of the ar. co. 1638, representative 4 years, from 1654 to 1657. He d. 24 Oct. 1657. ‡ROBERT, Portsmouth, was a counsellor of N. H. in 1683.

ELITHORP, THOMAS, Rowley 1643, died in 1709, quite advanced.

ELKINS, HENRY, a tailor of Boston, was admitted freeman in 1635, removed to Hampton, and d. 1669.

ELLERY, *WILLIAM, freeman 1672, was elected representative of Gloucester in 1689. The name of Ellery had, in 1828, furnished 8 graduates at the N. E colleges, of whom William, H. C. 1747, was one of the signers of the declaration of independence, and d. at Newport, 13 Feb. 1820, æ. 94.

ELLINGHAM, WILLIAM, was an inhabitant of Kittery 1652.

ELLINGWOOD, RALPH, was born a. 1610, came to N. E. and settled at Salem as early as 1638; was a member of the church, and one of the founders of the church in Beverly in 1667.

ELLINS, ANTHONY, Pascataqua 1631.   Adams, Annals Portsmouth, 18.

ELLIOTT, *ANDREW, Beverly, came from Somersetshire, was admitted freeman 1683, town clerk 1687, was representative from 1690 to 1692.   In the Coll. of the Mass. Hist. Soc. [2 series, i. 229] is a genealogy of this family, which is very erroneous, so far as it relates to this person and the following.   It does not appear from the Beverly records whether there was a previous ancestor in N. E. or not, although Winthrop [i. Hist. N. E. 151] names an Eliot of Ipswich, sub anno 1634, who *may* be the one said to have come from Wales, [2 Coll. Mass. Hist. Soc. i. 229] but rather improbable. Beverly Records.   ANDREW, the only son of the preceding, was born at East-Coker, in Somersetshire, 1651; m. Mercy, daughter of Samuel Shattuck, 9 Dec, 1680, and was lost at Cape Sables, from on board a ship, belonging to Philip English, while returning to N. E. 12 Sept. 1688, æ. 37, leaving children, Mary, b. 1681; Andrew, b, 11 Sept. 1683; Samuel, b. 11 Feb. 1686; all b. in Beverly.   Andrew, the eldest son, m. Ruth Symonds, and had, 1. Samuel, a bookseller in Boston ; 2. Ruth, who m. Nathaniel Thayer, of Boston, and was mother of Rev. Ebenezer Thayer, of Hampton, H. C. 1753; 3. Andrew, D. D., b. 25 Dec. 1718, grad. at H. C. 1737, was ordained over the North church in Boston, 14 April, 1742, d. 13 Sept. 1778, leaving three sons, who received a publick education, (1) Rev. Andrew, b. 11 Jan. 1743, grad. at H. C. 1762, was ordained at Fairfield, Conn. 1774, d. 1805, æ. 62; (2) Rev. John, D. D. b. 21 May, 1754, grad. at H. C. 1772, succeeded his father at Boston, 3 Nov. 1779, d. 14 Feb. 1813, æ. 59; (3) Ephraim, b. 29 Dec. 1761, grad. at H. C. 1780, was a druggist in Boston, and d. Sept. 1827, æ. 65.   These three brothers were members of the Mass. Hist. Soc.   This name, now spelled Eliot, was written Elliott by the ancestor of the family at Beverly.

ELLIS, ARTHUR, came to N. E. in 1630.   Nine of the name of Ellis had grad. at the N. E. colleges in 1828.   JOHN, Dedham, freeman 1641, was probably of Medfield in 1653, where his wife died.   He m. again in 1656, and had sons, Samuel, Joseph, and Eleazar.   Hon. Caleb Ellis, H. C. 1793, of Claremont, N. H., was of this family.   WILLIAM.   (See ALLIS.)

ELLISON, RICHARD, Braintree 1646, had children, Mary; Hannah; John, b. 21 Aug. 1650; Sarah; Temperance ; Experience, b. 1657.

ELLSWORTH, JEREMIAH, Rowley 1650, d. 6 May, 1704. Six of the name of Ellsworth have received the honours of the N. E. colleges.

ELSLEY, JOHN, one of the first proprietors of Salisbury, was admitted freeman in 1639.

ELMES, RODOLPHUS, Scituate between 1633 and 1657.   2 Coll. Mass. Hist. Soc. iv. 241.

ELMER, EDWARD, Cambridge 1632, one of the first settlers
of Northampton a. 1653. Six of the name, writing it Elmer and
Elmore, had grad. at N. J., Midd., and Union colleges in 1828.

ELSE, ROGER, Charlestown, d. 25 Dec. 1668. John Elzey d.
at Boston 31 Dec. 1702.

ELWELL, ROBERT, Salem, freeman 1640, was received as
member of the church in 1643; removed to Gloucester as early as
1649. Savage, ii. Winthrop, 178.

ELY, NATHANIEL, Cambridge 1635. Samuel and William
Ely were admitted freemen in 1680. Twenty-one of the name had
grad. at Y. C. in 1828, seven of them clergymen, and 5 had grad.
at the other N. E. colleges.

EMBLEN, JOHN, minister of the first Baptist church in Boston,
from 1684 to his death, 9 Dec. 1702.

EMERSON, JOHN, an inhabitant of Ipswich 1648, and probably the son of Thomas Emerson. The name of Emerson has furnished 17 ordained ministers out of the 43 persons who had grad.
at the N. E. colleges in 1828. Several others have been preachers,
but not ordained. *JOHN*, minister of Gloucester, son of Thomas
Emerson, of Ipswich, grad. at H. C. 1656, was ordained 6 October,
1663, and died 2 Dec. 1700, having preached more than 40 years.
He married Ruth, daughter of Deputy-gov. Symonds in 1662. He
had several children, of whom John, grad. at H. C. 1689, was probably the preacher at Manchester, named in the Magnalia, i. 81,
and was afterwards ordained at New-Castle, and installed the first
minister of the 2d church in Portsmouth, 28 March, 1715, died 21
June, 1732, æ. 62. *JOHN*, who grad. at H. C. in 1675, is put in
italicks as being a minister. He was nephew to the preceding, and
was probably the eminent schoolmaster at Newbury in 1681, afterwards at Charlestown, from whence he removed to Salem in 1699,
and there d. in 1712. Wisner, Sermon on Hon. W. Phillips, Appendix. Bentley. *JOSEPH*, the first minister of Mendon, Mass.
was ordained in 1667, [Worcester Magazine, ii. 373] and remained
in office eight years. [Whitney, Hist. Co. Worcester, 56.] He
removed to Concord, and d. there, 3 Jan. 1680. [Shattuck.]
He m. Elizabeth, daughter of Rev. Edward Bulkley, 7 Dec. 1665,
and had 3 sons. [Tradition.] His widow m. Capt. John Brown,
of Reading, and one of her sons by Mr. Emerson, Peter, married a
daughter of Capt. Brown, and was ancestor of Rev. Daniel Emerson,
H. C. 1739, of Hollis, two of whose sons, Joseph and Samuel, grad.
at H. College. Rev. Joseph Emerson, of Malden, was a son of
Edward Emerson, and grandson of Rev. Joseph, of Mendon. He
m. Mary, daughter of Samuel Moody, of York, and had 9 sons and
4 daughters, and d. 13 July, 1767, in his 68th year. Three of the
sons were ministers, Joseph, born 25 August, 1724, grad. at H. C.
1743, settled at Pepperell, and d. 29 Oct. 1773; William, born 21
May, 1743, grad. at H. C. 1761, settled at Concord; was a chaplain in the rev. army, and d. at Rutland, Vt. 20 Oct. 1776; John,
b. 20 Nov. 1745, grad. at H. C. 1764, and d. at Conway, Ms. July,
1826, æ. 81. William had but one son, the late Rev. William

Emerson, of the first church in Boston, H. C. 1789, who d. 12 May, 1811. æ. 42, four of whose sons, William, Ralph Waldo, Edward Bliss, and Charles Chauncy, grad. at H. C. 1818, 1821, 1824, and 1826. The second son was ordained at Boston as colleague with Rev. Henry Ware, 11 March, 1829. ROBERT, Haverhill, freeman 1668, the ancestor of the Haverhill Emersons, of whom was Moses, H. C. 1737 ; Samuel, D. C. 1814, and John S., D. C. 1826 are probably descendants. Thomas Emerson and his wife, and children Sarah and Timothy, of Haverhill, were killed by the Indians, 15 March, 1697. THOMAS, Ipswich 1639, d. 1 May, 1666. His wife was Elizabeth. His children were, Joseph, who had a son Joseph ; Nathaniel ; James, who went to England ; Thomas, who d. before his father, and John, who is named in a codicil to his father's will 1660.

EMERY, ANTHONY, Newbury, removed to Dover as early as 1644, thence to Kittery, where he was admitted freeman in 1652. Ten of this name, three of them clergymen, had grad. at the N. E. colleges in 1828. GEORGE, a physican of Salem, was b. in 1609, and d. 20 Feb. 1687. Mary, his wife, d. in 1673. *JAMES, Kittery, freeman in 1652, was representative in 1676. JOHN, Newbury 1635, brother of Anthony, was b. a. 1598, admitted freeman in 1641, and was living in 1678. He had children, viz : John ; Ebenezer, b. 1648 ; Jonathan, b. 13 May, 1652. John had sons, John, b. 1656 ; Joseph, b. 1663 ; Stevens, b. 1666 ; Samuel, b. 1670 ; Josiah, b. 1681, and eight daughters, b. between 1652 and 1679.

EMMONS, THOMAS, Boston, admitted freeman 1652, d. 11 May, 1664.

ENDECOTT, ‡†§JOHN, came from Dorchester in England, and arrived at Salem, in Sept. 1628. He was elected assistant in 1630 ; nine years ; colonel 1636 ; deputy-governour 1641, 5 years ; governour in 1644, 1649, 1651 to 1653, and from 1655 to 1664, fifteen years ; major-general from 1645 to 1648, four years. He d. at Boston, to which place he removed in 1644, 15 March, 1665, æ. 76. His wife, who. was Anna Gover, d. soon after his arrival, and he was m. by Gov. Winthrop and Rev. John Wilson, to Elizabeth Gibson, 18 Aug. 1630, and she survived her husband. JOHN, son of the preceding, was admitted freeman in 1665, m. 9 Nov. 1653, to Elizabeth, daughter of Jeremy Houchin, of Boston. ZERUBBABEL, Salem, brother of the preceding was admitted freeman in 1665, and d. in 1684, leaving sons, John, Samuel, Zerubbabel, and 5 daughters. He m. (probably a 2d wife) the widow of Rev. Antipas Newman.

ENDRED, ||JOHN, member of the ar. co. 1644. Whitman.

ENGLISH, PHILIP, a merchant of Salem, a. 1670, m. a daugher of Richard Hollingworth, and was a great sufferer in the witchcraft delusion, 1 Coll. Mass. Hist. Soc. x. THOMAS, one of the first pilgrims at Plymouth 1620, died the next year after his arrival.

ENOS, WILLIAM, New-Haven 1639. Pascal Paoli Enos grad. at D. C. 1794.

ENSIGN, JAMES, Cambridge, was admitted freeman in 1635. Edward F. Ensign grad. at H. C. 1815.

EPES, *DANIEL, son of Daniel Epes of Kent, England, came with his mother, who m. Dep. Gov. Symonds, to N. E. and settled at Ipswich, where he was a captain, freeman 1674, and representative 1684. He d. 8 Jan. 1692, æ. 67. He m. Elizabeth, daughter of Dep. Gov. Symonds, 20 May, 1644, and had 11 children, 1. Samuel, b. 24 Feb. 1647, grad. at H. C. 1669, and d. before 1698; 2. Daniel, the following; 3. Nathaniel, b. and d. 1650; 4. John, b. and d. 1651; 5. one, (obliterated) b. 1651; 6. Joseph, b. 1653; 7. Martha, b. 1654; 8. Mary, b. and d. 1656; 9. Lionel, b. 1657; 10. a son, b. and d. 1658; 11. Richard, b. 1659. ‡DANIEL, son of the preceding, was b. 24 March, 1649, grad. at H. C. 1669, was a magistrate and counsellor, and d. in Nov. 1722, æ. 73. He m. Martha, daughter of William Bordman, of Cambridge, 17 April, 1672, and had 2 sons and 7 daughters. The sons were, 1. Daniel, b. 28 Oct. 1679, m. Hannah Higginson, of Boston, in May, 1705, had 7 sons and 2 daughters, of whom Daniel, b. 8 Nov. 1710, was father of Daniel Epes, esq. b. 10 March, 1739, grad. at H. C. 1758, and d. at Portland in May 1799; 2. Samuel, b. 4 Jan. 1681. Dunton mentions, in his Journal, an Epes, who was the " most eminent schoolmaster in N. England," probably Daniel or Samuel, H. C.1669.

ERRINGTON, ABRAHAM, Cambridge, a member of the church, m. Rebecca, daughter of Robert Cutler, and had Rebecca, Hannah, Sarah, Mary, Abraham, b. 8 Nov. 1663, and perhaps others. THOMAS, Lynn 1642. Lewis.

ESSET, WILLIAM, Boston, d. 24 May, 1697.

ESTABROOK, JOSEPH, minister of Concord, was born at Enfield, in Middlesex, England, and came to N. E. a. 1660, with two brothers, one of whom, Thomas, lived in Swanzey and Concord. He grad. at H. C 1664, was ordained a colleague with Rev. Edward Bulkley, a. 1667, and d. 16 Sept. 1711. By Mary, his wife, a daughter of Capt. Hugh Mason, he had children, 1. Joseph, b. 6 May, 1669, settled at Lexington, where he was a deacon from 1716 to his death, 24 Sept. 1733, leaving issue; 2. Benjamin, b. 24 Feb. 1671, grad. at H. C. 1690, was ordained at Lexington, 21 Oct. 1696, d. 28 July, 1697, leaving a widow, Abigail, daughter of Rev. Samuel Willard, whom he m. 29 Nov. 1693; 3. Mary, b. 28 Feb. 1672, m. Jonathan Green, of Newton; 4. Samuel, b. 7 Jan. 1674, grad. at H. C. 1696, was ordained at Canterbury, Conn. 13 Jan. 1711, d. 26 June, 1727, æ. 53; 5. Daniel, b. 14 Feb. 1676, settled at Cambridge, and d. at Sudbury, 7 Jan. 1736; and 6. Anna, b. 30 Jan. 1677, m. Joshua Haynes, of Sudbury, 26 Jan. 1710. Rev. Joseph Estabrook, H. C. 1782, of Athol, is descended from Joseph, the eldest son of Rev. Joseph Estabrook. Shattuck, MS Hist. Concord.

ESTWICK, EDWARD, a mariner of Salem 1649.

ESTY, JEFFREY, an inhabitant of Salem 1637.

EVANS, HENRY, Boston, was admitted freeman 1645. David Evans, of Boston, d. 27 July, 1663. ||JOSIAH, was a member of

the ar. co. 1642. Richard, Dorchester, freeman 1645, had a son
Matthiah, b. in 1643. ROBERT, Portsmouth 1665, had sons,
Robert, Edward, and Jonathan. The late judge Richard Evans,
of N. H. was probably a descendant. WILLIAM, Gloucester, was
one of the selectmen in 1647. Felt.

EVARTS, JOHN, Concord, was admitted freeman in 1638, and
had sons, John and Judah, b. in 1639 and 1649. He may have
removed to Conn., as there was a John Evarts at Guilford in 1650.
Jeremiah Evarts, Y. C. 1802, is probably of this descent.

EVELETH, SYLVESTER, was of Gloucester, and one of the
selectmen in 1647. Rev. John Eveleth, H. C. 1689, a preacher at
Manchester, at Arundel, at Enfield, and the minister of Stow, might
be a descendant.

EVERDEN, WALTER, came from Kent to N. E. and was living in Mass. in 1674. Hutch. Coll. 468.

EVERETT, *JOHN, whose name is written Evered, and in Allen's Hist. of Chelmsford, p. 169, appears, John Webb, alias Everett, was a representative of Chelmsford in 1664; died there, 16
Oct. 1668. (See WEBB, JOHN.) RICHARD, formerly written
Everard, was an inhabitant of Dedham in 1636, and was admitted
freeman in 1646. His children named in records of births, were,
Samuel, b. 30 Sept. 1639 ; Mary, b. 1639 ; Sarah, b. 1641 ; James,
b. and d. 1643. Of his descendants, several have been distinguished for talents. Eighteen of the name had received the honours of
the N. E. colleges in 1828, of whom were, Moses, H. C. 1771, ordained minister of Dorchester, 28 Sept. 1774, d. 14 Jan. 1793 ;
Oliver, H. C. 1779, minister of Summer-street church in Boston ;
ordained 2 Jan. 1782, dismissed, 1792 ; d. at Dorchester, 19 Nov.
1802, æ. 50. leaving sons, Alexander Hill, H. C. 1806 ; Edward, H.
C. 1811 ; Thomas ; John, H. C. 1818. WILLIAM, Kittery 1652.
Stevens Everett grad. at H. C. 1815.

EVERILL, JAMES, Boston, was admitted to the church, 20
July 1634, freeman 3 Sept. 1634, was one of the selectmen and d.
1682 or 1683. Savage, i. Winth. 290, ii. 213.

EWELL, HENRY, Scituate 1638. ii. Coll. Mass. Hist. Soc. x.
Index. JOHN, Newbury, d. 31 July, 1686.

EWER, HENRY, Sandwich 1637. Lewis. Gamaliel Ewer
grad. at D. C. 1777. THOMAS, Massachusetts, was admitted
freeman 1636. Winthrop [Hist. N. E. i. 234] mentions one Ewre,
who indulged in some freedom of speech, which subjected him to
the notice of Lord Ley.

EYER, JOHN, Salisbury 1642. (See AYER.)

EYRE, ||JOHN, son of Simon Eyre, was b. at Boston, 19 Feb.
1654 ; was member of the ar. co. 1682 ; one of the council of safety in 1689, and d. 17 June, 1700. John Eyre, H. C. 1718, was
probably of this family. *SIMON, Watertown, was admitted freeman in 1637, was representative at the Oct. court 1641. This family is of ancient descent ; and may possibly centre in Simon Eyre,
mayor of London in 1445, who was son of John Eyre, of Brandon,
in Suffolk. SIMON, Watertown 1640, perhaps the same as the

preceding, was of Boston in 1652, where he d. 10 Nov. 1658. His
sons, Simon and John were b. in Boston. THOMAS, Watertown
1644. This name perhaps should be Thomas Ewer, who was admitted freeman in 1636, or Ewer should be Eyre.

EYTON, SAMSON, Cambridge as early as 1650. Hutchinion,
[i. Hist. Mass. 108] supposes that he left college before he had his
degree, and went to England, and was made a fellow of one of the
universities there.

FABER, GEORGE, Boston 1639. Winthrop, i. Hist. N. E.326.
Joseph W. Faber, from Charleston,S. C., graduated at H. C. 1824.

FABENS, GEORGE and JOHN, were of N. H. in 1686. The
name exists in Salem, Mass. *Fabgan* is a name in N. H.

FAIRBANKS, ||GEORGE, Dedham and Medfield, probably the
member of the ar. co. in 1644. The name is sometimes spelled
Fairbank, of which two, besides five written *Fairbanks*, had grad.
at the N. E. colleges in 1828. JOHN, Dedham 1642, whose sons,
Joshua and John were b. in 1642 and 1643. Worthington, Hist.
Dedham, 47, 104. JONAS, Lancaster 1659, was killed, with his
son Joshua, aged 15, by the Indians, 10 Feb. 1676. Willard, Hist.
Lancaster. RICHARD, Boston, was admitted freeman in 1634.
Savage, i. Winthrop, 248. One of the same name was member of
the ar. co. in 1654.

FAIRFIELD, DANIEL, Boston 1640 ; Lynn 1641 ; also of
Salem, and perhaps of Weymouth. Winthrop, ii. Hist. N. E. 45.
John Fairfield d. at Boston in 1691. Four of the name, John,
Rev. John, Micaiah, and Josiah, have grad. at Harv., Dart., and
Midd. colleges. JOHN, Salem, was admitted to the church, 25
August, 1639, freeman 1640, and d. a. 1647, leaving a widow
Elizabeth, and sons Benjamin and *Walter, the last a representative
of Wenham in 1689.

FAIRWEATHER, JOHN. (See FAYERWEATHER.)

FALCONER, DAVID, Boston, had a son Thomas, b. in 1656.

FALES, JAMES, Massachusetts, was admitted freeman in 1673.
James, perhaps a son, was admitted freeman in 1683. The names
of both are spelled *Vales* in the colony records. Seven of the
name had grad. at H. C. in 1828, the earliest in 1711.

FANNING, WILLIAM, Newbury, m. Eliz. Allen, in 1668, and
had sons, Joseph, b. 1669 ; William, b. 1673.

FARLEY, GEORGE, settled first at Roxbury, removed early to
Woburn, and from thence to Billerica, before 1656, and d. there
27 Dec. 1693. He was one of the early Baptists, and a member of
the first Baptist church of Boston. He had a number of children,
of whom James was b. at Woburn in 1643, and d. in 1644 ;
Timothy, who was killed with 7 other persons by the Indians at
Brookfield, 4 August, 1675 ; Caleb, who settled in Billerica, whose
descendants are in Mass. and in Hollis and Concord, N. H. and
who may have d. 16 March, 1712, at Roxbury, where a Benjamin
Farley died 12 March, 1719. Nine of the name had grad. at
the N. E. colleges in 1828, of whom Abel and Stephen, D. C. 1798.
and 1804, and Frederick Augustus, H. C. 1818, have been clergy-

men ; the last settled at Providence. MICHAEL, came to N. E. in 1675, and settled at Ipswich, having been sent by Richard Saltonstall to take charge of his fulling-mill. He had two sons, Michael and Meshech, who were of Ipswich in 1682.

FARMER, EDWARD, son of John Farmer, of Ansley, in Warwickshire, came from thence to N. E. as early as 1672, and settled at Billerica, where he d. 27 May, 1727, aged a. 87. Mary, his wife, d. 26 March, 1719, aged 78. His mother, a widow, also came with him, m. Elder Thomas Wiswall, of Newton, and d. at her son's house. His children were, 1. Sarah, who m. Thomas Pollard, of Billerica, had 10 sons and 5 daughters, and d. 3 May, 1725 . 2. John, b. 19 August, 1671, d. at Billerica, 9 Sept. 1736, leaving 6 sons ; 3. Edward, b. 22 March, 1674, m. Mary Richardson, and d. 17 Dec. 1752, æ. 78, leaving one son Andrew ; 4. Mary, b. 3 Nov. 1675, m. a Dean ; 5. Barbary, b. 1677, d. 1681 ; 6. Elizabeth, b. 17 May, 1680, m. William Green, of Malden, and d. 26 Dec, 1761, æ. 81 ; 7. Thomas, b. 8 June, 1683, great-grandfather of William Farmer, who grad. at H. C. in 1819 ; 8. Oliver, b. 2 Feb. 1686, m. Abigail, a grand-daughter of Hon. William Johnson, of Woburn, and d. at Billerica, 23 Feb. 1761, æ. 75, leaving 3 sons and 6 daughters. The sons were, 1. Oliver, b. 31 July, 1728, d. at Billerica, 24 Feb. 1814, leaving sons, Oliver, John, and Jeremiah ; 2. Edward, b. 24 Feb. 1734, a magistrate and the representative of Billerica 14 years, who d. 4 August, 1804, æ. 70, having had sons, Edward, Jona., and Jesse ; 3. John, b. 7 Dec. 1737, d. at Billerica, 9 Jan. 1806, in his 70th year, leaving one son, John, of Boscawen, N. H., a colonel and one of the present representatives of that town. Gena. Memoir of the Farmers of Billerica, 1828. THOMAS, probably a brother, of the preceding, was of Billerica in 1675, and in 1684, but after this period removed, and probably returned to England or settled in some other colony. There were others of the name in N. E. at the close of the seventeenth century, whose descendants are probably in N. H. and Vermont.

FARNUM, ‖HENRY, was a member of the ar. co. 1644. JOHN, Dorchester, was admitted freeman 1640, and probably one of the founders of the 2d church in Boston in 1650. His son, Jonathan was b. in 1638. John and Thomas Farnum were inhabitants of Andover in 1660, and their descendants are numerous, some of whom write the name *Farnham*. Three had grad. at Harv. and Brown in 1828, besides several whose names are spelled Farnham. JOHN, possibly the preceding, or a son, was an early member of the 1st Baptist church in Boston.

FARNWORTH, JOSEPH, Dorchester, was admitted freeman 1638, and may be the same who died there in Jan. 1660. JOSEPH, was admitted freeman 1649. Calamy, in his Account of Ejected Ministers, vol. ii. p. 840, notices a Mr. Farnworth, who returned from N. E. and died in extreme poverty. Nine of the name of *Farnsworth* had received the honours of the N. E. colleges in 1828.

FARR, BARNABAS, d. at Boston, 13 Dec. 1654. GEORGE, Lynn 1630, was admitted freeman in 1635 ; d. 1661, leaving sons,

John ; Lazarus ; Benjamin ; Joseph, freeman 1682 ; and 4 daughters. Elizabeth, his wife, d 1687. [Lewis.] Jonathan Farr grad. at H. C. in 1818.

FARRAR, JACOB, Lancaster 1653 was killed by the Indians 22 Aug. 1675. His son Jacob had, by Hannah, his wife, the following children : 1. Jacob, b. 29 March, 1669 ; 2. George, b. 16 Aug. 1670 ; 3. Joseph, b. 16 Aug. 1672 ; 4. John. George, the 2d son, m. 7 Sept. 1692, Mary How, of Concord, and had sons, 1. Joseph ; 2. Daniel ; 3. George, b. 16 Feb. 1705 ; 4. Samuel, b. 28 Sept. 1708. George had 9 children, of whom were Rev. George Farrar, b. 23 Nov. 1730, and Rev. Joseph Farrar, b. 30 Jan. 1744, graduates of H. C. in 1751 and 1767. Samuel, the 4th son of George, m. Lydia Barrett, of Concord, and had 7 children, of whom were Samuel, the father of Samuel Farrar, H. C. 1797, and Prof. John Farrar, H. C. 1803 ; Rev. Stephen Farrar H. C. 1755, and Hon. Timothy Farrar, H. C. 1767, both of New-Ipswich, N. H. and both distinguished men. L. Shattuck, MS letter. Willard, Hist. Lancaster, 28, 37. JOHN, Lancaster 1653, supposed to be brother of the preceding, d. at Lancaster, 3 Nov. 1669. Willard, Hist. Lancaster, 28. THOMAS, Lynn 1639, d. 23 Feb. 1694. His children were Thomas and 4 daughters. [Lewis.] Twelve of the name had grad. at the N. E. colleges in 1826.

FARRINGTON, EDMUND, Lynn 1640, removed to South-Hampton, L. I. a. 1640. He had a son Matthew. Two of the name, Thomas, and Rev. Daniel, grad. at Harv. and Brown in 1773 and 1775. JOHN, Lynn, removed to South-Hampton, L. I. about 1640.

FARROW, JOHN, Hingham 1635. Nathan, son of John Farrow, was b. in 1654. A George Farrow is named by Hubbard, in his Indian Wars, and John W. Farrow grad. at New-Jersey coll. in 1825.

FARWELL, HENRY, Concord, admitted freeman in 1638, removed to Chelmsford, and there d. 1 Aug. 1670. Sons, Joseph, b. 1640 ; James, and perhaps others. John Farwell, H. C. 1808, probably a descendant, is a lawyer in Tyngsborough, Mass.

FASSETT, JOHN, Massachusetts, admitted freeman in 1654, Nathaniel Fassett was of Concord in 1666.

FAULKNER, EDMUND, Andover, one of the founders of the church in 1645 ; died in Jan. 1687. His wife was Dorothy Robinson, whom he m. 4 July, 1647. Sons, Francis, b. May, 1651, d. 1732, æ. 81 ; John, b. May, 1654, d 1706, æ. 52. From Francis, is descended William Emerson Faulkner, H. C. 1797, Luther Faulkner, H. C. 1802, and Francis Faulkner, esq. of Billerica.

FAUNCE, JOHN, Plymouth in 1623 may be the same who was admitted free by the Mass. colony in 1635. Thomas Faunce, an elder of Plymouth church, d. 27 Feb. 1746, æ. 99. His daughter Patience Kempton, d. in 1779, æ. 105 years and 6 months.

FAWN, JOHN, Ipswich 1639, removed to Haverhill. His wife was Elizabeth. One of his two daughters m. Robert Clement.

FAXON, THOMAS, Braintree, m. Deborah Thayer in 1653, and d. 25 May, 1662. His wife d. 6 days afterwards. James Faxon d. at Braintree, æ. about 76. Richard Faxon was there as early as 1659, and Thomas Faxon was a representative in 1669. Azariah Faxon, of this family, grad. at H. C. 1752, and John Faxon grad. at Brown Univ. in 1787.

FAY, HENRY, Newbury, died without issue, 30 June, 1655. ||JOHN, was a member of the ar. co. in 1678. Ten persons of the name had grad. at the N. E. colleges in 1826.

FAYERWEATHER, *JOHN, son of the following, was born in Boston, Sept. 1634, admitted freeman in 1673, representative in 1684, d. 13 April, 1712, æ. 78. Rev. Samuel Fayerweather, H. C. 1743, an episcopal minister of South-Kingston, R. I., the only graduate of the name in New-England, d. 24 Aug. 1781. THOMAS, Boston, admitted freeman 1634. Prince, ii. Annals, 69. Snow, Hist. Boston, 61.

FEAKE, HENRY, Lynn, was admitted freeman in 1634, and removed, according to Mr. Lewis, to Sandwich in 1637. *ROBERT, came to N. E. as early as 1630, was admitted freeman in 1631, settled at Watertown, and was one of the first deputies of the general court in 1634, and again elected in 1635 and 1636. He was also a lieutenant in 1635. Worthington [Hist. Dedham, 122] makes him an inhabitant of Dedham before 1647, under the name of Robert Feashe, and Trumbull [Hist. Conn. i. 118] gives his name as one of the purchasers of Greenwich in 1640.

FEARING, JOHN, Hingham, came from Cambridge, England, in 1638. One of the same name was admitted freeman in 1652. Six had grad. in N. E. in 1828, of whom the Hon. Paul Fearing, of Ohio, took his degree at H. C. in 1785.

FELCH, HENRY, Reading 1647, perhaps of Boston in 1657. John Felch grad. at Y. C. in 1758.

FELLOWS, SAMUEL, admitted freeman 1644, of Salisbury in 1651. Four had grad. in N. E. in 1828. WILLIAM, Ipswich 1648.

FELT, GEORGE, born a. 1601, lived 21 years on a plantation at Great Cove, in Casco-Bay, from whence he was driven by the Indians. He died at Malden 1693. George Felt, perhaps his son, was killed by the Indians at, or near, Mountjoy's Island, in Maine, in Sept. 1676. Hubbard says that he was much lamented, and that he had been more active than any other man in those parts against the Indians. Indian Wars, 45. Rev. Joseph B. Felt, D. C. 1813, minister of Hamilton, Mass., is descended from this family.

FELTON, BENJAMIN, Salem, was born a. 1604, admitted freeman 1639. NATHANIEL, Salem 1637, died, according to Mr. Felt, 30 July, 1705, æ. about 91.

FEMYS, ||WILLIAM, member of the ar. co. 1638, lieutenant in 1638.

FENN, ‡BENJAMIN, was elected assistant of New-Haven colony in 1654. Five of the name of Fenn had grad. at Yale College in 1828. ROBERT, Boston, whose son Robert was b. in 1644.

FENNER, ARTHUR, Rhode-Island, m. Dec. 1684, Howlong, daughter of WILLIAM HARRIS. Hon. James Fenner, gov. of R. I. grad. at Brown Univ. 1789. JOHN, an inhabitant of New-Haven in 1639.

FENWICK, ‡GEORGE, came to N. E. in 1635, and settled at Saybrook, where his lady died soon after his arrival, and was buried on the margin of Connecticut River, where her monument still remains. He was a magistrate or assistant in 1647, a colonel of the military force, and died in high esteem in England in 1657. Hutchinson, in his Coll., p. 107, gives a letter which he wrote from Saybrook in 1639.

FERMAN, JOHN, admitted freeman 1631. (See FIRMIN.)

FERMSIDE, JOHN, Boston 1642.

FERNALD, RENALD, Pascataqua 1631, was one of Captain Mason's company, and the first surgeon who settled in New-Hampshire. Belknap, i. Hist. N. H. 47. Adams, Annals Portsmouth, 19.

FERNIS, BENJAMIN, Salem 1640. JEFFREY, Massachusetts, was admitted a freeman 1635.

FERSON, THOMAS, Bloody-Point, N. H. a. 1644. William Ferson grad. at D. C. 1797.

FESSENDEN, JOHN, came from Kent, in England, settled in Cambridge, was admitted freeman in 1641, and d. 21 Dec. 1666, leaving no issue. His wife was Jane, and both were members of the church. His relative, Nicholas, came from England and inherited his estate; had a son Nicholas, who grad. at H. C. 1701, and d. in 1719, æ. 38. The descendants of Nicholas are respectable, and 15 of them had graduated in 1826, nine at H. C., 4 of whom have been ministers.

FIELD, ALEXANDER, Salem, was received as member of the church ,Nov. 1648, freeman 1649, and is styled a cordwainer. Felt. DARBY, Exeter 1638, was an Irishman, and probably the first European who ascended the White Mountains in N. H. This was in 1642. He was accompanied by two Indians, and made the journey in 18 days. See Winthrop, and note by Mr. Savage, ii. 67. He lived until about the year 1661. JOHN, Providence, was one of the early settlers of Bridgewater. ROBERT, Boston, tailor, admitted freeman 1644. Sons, Robert, b. 1647; Thomas; Thomas, 2d, b. 1652; Robert, 2d, b. 1653; John b. 1656. WILLIAM, Providence 1641. 2 Coll. Mass. Hist. Soc. vii. 93. 3 ibid, i. 4. Twenty persons of the name, 5 of them clergymen, are on the catalogues of the N. E. colleges.

FIENNES, CHARLES. His name appears to the address signed 7 April, 1630, by John Winthrop and others, but it seems uncertain whether he came over with the company who arrived the next summer. His name to that address is spelled *Fines.* Hutchinson, i. Hist. Mass. 428.

FIFIELD, JOHN, of Massachusetts, d. 18 Aug. 1665. WILLIAM, Newbury, removed to Hampton 1639, and d. 18 Dec. 1700, aged above 80.

FILCHER, ———, Mount Wollaston 1628, was an officer of the settlement under Capt. Wollaston. Prince [i. Annals, 162] writes the name Fitcher, but Morton, [N. E. Memo.138] Increase Mather [Ind. Wars,21] and Whitney, [Hist. Quincy, 9] all spell it as above.

FILER, WALTER, Dorchester, a lieutenant, was admitted freeman 1634, and was of Windsor 1635. GEORGE, was an inhabitant of Northampton as early as 1662. JOHN, was a graduate at H. C. in 1666.

FILLEBROWNE, GORDON, Cambridge 1666, had several children. THOMAS, Cambridge, was admitted freeman in 1668.

FILMINGHAM, FRANCIS, Salem 1637, whose family consisted of 4 persons. This name, as it is variously spelled, may be the same as *Flemingham*, of which name several have grad. at N. J. College.

FINCH, ABRAHAM, Massachusetts, freeman in 1634. DANIEL, came to N. E. as early as 1630, and settled in Massachusetts, where he was admitted freeman in 1631. JOHN, Weathersfield, came to N. E. as early as 1632, was killed by Nepaupuck, a Pequot captain, 30 Oct. 1637. Sherman Finch grad. at Y. C. in 1828. SAMUEL, Massachusetts, freeman in 1634.

FINNEY, ROBERT, deacon of the church at Plymouth, died 1687, æ. 80. Phebe, his widow, d. in 1710, æ. 91. This name may be the same with *Phinney*.

FIRMIN, GILES, came from Sudbury, England, in 1630, and settled at Boston, where he was chosen deacon in 1633. He was admitted freeman 1634, and d. in Sept. the same year. Savage, i. Winthrop's N. E. 114. GILES, freeman 1634, son of the preceding, was b. in Suffolk county, in England, was educated at Cambridge, came to N. E., resided at Ipswich, where, in 1638, he received a grant of 120 acres of land; practised physick, and was a useful man. He returned to England, and was settled in the ministry when more than 40 years old. In a sermon before the house of lords and commons, and the assembly of divines at Westminster, he said, " I have lived in a country seven years, and all that time I never heard one profane oath, and all that time never did see a man drunk in that land." This land was N. England in its days of primitive purity. He died at Ridgewell, England, in April, 1697, at an advanced age. His wife was daughter of Rev. Nathaniel Ward. HENRY, Massachusetts, was admitted freeman in 1641. JOHN, Watertown, was admitted freeman in 1631. The colony records has this name *Ferman*. Gov. Winthrop records the burning of his wigwam, i. Hist. N. E. p. 38. JOSIAH, Massachusetts, admitted freeman in 1641. THOMAS, Ipswich, admitted freeman 1639. This name is *Firmam* in Ipswich records, and *Firman* in Colony records.

FISH, GABRIEL, Exeter 1639, Boston 1643. Son Abel, b. 1644. Winthrop, i. Hist. N. E. 327. Nine of the name of Fish, six of them clergymen, had grad. at the N. E. colleges in 1825. JOHN, Lynn, with Jonathan and Nathaniel, of the same place, removed to Sandwich, according to Mr. Lewis, in 1637.

FISHER, ANTHONY, Dedham, was member of the ar. co. 1644, admitted freeman 1645. Eight out of 21 of the name of Fisher who have grad. in N. E. have been settled ministers. The freemen of the name, besides those mentioned below, were John, 1678; John, 1682; Josiah, 1683, Thomas, 1674; Thomas, 1678. ANTHO-NY, Mass., freeman in 1646. CORNELIUS, Mass., freeman 1649. ‡||*DANIEL, Dedham, admitted freeman and member of the ar. co. 1640, captain of the militia, representative from 1658 to 1682, (excepting 1659 and 1670) speaker of the house of representatives 1680; elected assistant 1683, and d. Nov. 1683. Worthington, Hist. Dedham, 50. ||JOSHUA, Dedham, was admitted freeman, and member of the ar. co. 1640; and d. 14 Nov. 1645. *JOSHUA, Dedham, freeman 1649, representative 1653, 7 years. JOHN, one of the petitioners for the grant of Lancaster in 1644. There was a John Fisher, of Dedham who died 5 Sept. 1637. *OLI-VER, Wrentham, Ms. representative at the Nov. session 1689. *SAMUEL, Wrentham, Ms. representative at the June and Dec. sessions 1689. Hon. Jabez Fisher, b. in 1718, d. 15 Oct. 1806, was of Wrentham, and probably a descendant. Boston Magazine, ii. 27—33. THOMAS, Cambridge, admitted freeman 1635. Stephen Fisher, an old man, d. at Billerica in 1682.

FISKE, DAVID, one of the early proprietors of Watertown, was admitted freeman 1638. This name which is generally spelled *Fisk*, has furnished a good proportion of literary characters, 40 persons, 13 of them clergymen, having graduated at the various colleges in New-England. *DAVID, Cambridge, admitted freeman 1647, perhaps representative 1690, had children, Lydia, b. 1647, David, b. 1648; Seaborn, Elizabeth, Sarah, Hannah. He had two wives, Lydia and Seaborn, the first of whom was mother of Lydia and David. *EDWARD, Cambridge, representative at five courts in 1689. JAMES, Haverhill, where his children were born, viz. James, 8 Aug. 1649, John, 10 Dec. 1651, Anne, b. and d. 1654; Anne, 1656; Samuel, 1 Nov. 1658. *JOHN, Wenham 1654, representative 1669. Coll. N. H. Hist. Soc. ii. 224. *JOHN*, the first minister of Wenham and Chelmsford, and an esteemed physician, was born in St. James, Suffolk, Eng. about 1601, was educated at Emmanuel college, came to N. E. and was admitted freeman in 1637, resided a short time at Cambridge, then at Salem; thence removed to Wenham, where he was ordained, 8 Oct. 1644; removed to Chelmsford 1655, where he d. 14 Jan. 1677, in his 76th year. His 1st wife, Ann, whom he m. 1629, d. 14 Feb. 1672. His 2d wife was Elizabeth, widow of Edmund Hinchman. He left 4 children, Moses, b. 1642; John, of Chelmsford, born at Wenham, 12 Dec. 1654; and two daughters. *MOSES*, the third minister of Braintree, (now Quincy) was son of the preceding, and grad. at H. C. 1662, admitted freeman 1666, ordained 11 Sept. 1672; d. 10 August, 1708, æ. 66. His 1st wife, (who d. 2 Nov. 1692) was daughter of Mr. Symmes of Charlestown, whom he m. 7 Nov. 1672, and by whom he had 7 sons and 7 daughters, the sons were 2 Johns, 2 Samuels, Moses, William, and Edward. His 2d wife was Ann

Quincy, daughter of the second Rev. Thomas Shepard, by whom he had 2 children, one of whom, Shepard, grad. at H. C. 1721, was a physician at Killingly, Conn. and at Bridgewater, Ms., died 14 June, 1779, æ. 77.   The 2d Samuel grad. at H. C. 1708, was minister of the 1st church, and afterwards of the 3d church in Salem, and d. 7 April, 1770, æ. 81.   Descendants are still respectable in various branches of this family.   NATHAN, Watertown, was admitted freeman in 1642.   His wife was Susan.   Sons, Nathan, b. 17 Oct. 1642; David, b. 29 Feb. 1652, and probably others.   Rev. Nathan Fiske, D. D. of Brookfield, a native of Weston, an original part of Watertown, was probably from this family.   *PHINEHAS, Salem, freeman 1642; Wenham 1644, representative 1653, had sons James, John, and Thomas.   *THOMAS, Wenham, son of the preceding, was born a. 1633; representative 7 years, 1671, 1672, 1680, 1686, and 1689 to 1691; captain of the militia.   *WILLIAM, Wenham, admitted member of the church in Salem, 2 July, 1641, freeman in 1643, elected first town clerk of Wenham, 4 Dec. 1644, representative 4 years 1647 and from 1649 to 1650.   He died in 1654.

FITCH, JEREMIAH, Lynn 1634, Boston 1652, died 3 May 1692.   Sixteen persons of the name of Fitch had grad. at the N. E. colleges in 1826.   *JAMES*, the first minister of Saybrook and Norwich, was born in Bocking, in Essex, England, 24 Dec. 1622, came to N. E. 1638; was ordained at Saybrook 1646, removed with the greater part of his church to Norwich in 1660, and there died 18 Nov. 1702, in his 80th year.   By Abigail, his 1st wife, a daughter of Rev. Henry Whitfield, he had, James, Abigail, Elizabeth, Hannah, Samuel, and Dorothy.   By his 2d wife, Priscilla, daughter of Major John Mason, his children, were Daniel, John, Jeremiah, Jabez, b. April 1672, grad. at H. C. 1694; ordained at Ipswich 1703; installed at Portsmouth, N. H. a. 1725, d. 22 Nov. 1746; Ann, Nathaniel, Joseph, and Eleazer.   All his children, excepting the last, lived to have families.   ‡JAMES, Connecticut, probably the eldest son of the preceding, was an assistant in 1681.   JAMES, member of the church in Boston 1634.   JOSEPH, Northampton 1658.   THOMAS, brother of Rev. James Fitch, came to N. E. 1638, settled at Norwalk, and was father to Governour Thomas Fitch.

FITTS, *BENJAMIN, Reading, representative 1689 and 1691. ZACHARY, Reading, admitted freeman 1638.   The two last names are also spelled Fitch.   ROBERT, Salisbury 1640; removed to Ipswich and died a. 1665, leaving a wife Grace and son Abraham.   RICHARD, Newbury, d. 2 Dec. 1672.   This name is also spelled Fitz.

FITZRANDLE, EDWARD, Scituate 1638; removed out of Plymouth colony 1649.   2 Coll. Mass. Hist. Soc. iv. 240.

FLACK, COTTON, Boston, admitted freeman 1640.   Snow, Hist. Boston, 118.   JOSEPH, Cambridge 1637.

FLACKMAN, THOMAS, admitted freeman 1640.   (See FLATMAN.)

FLAGG, GERSHAM, Massachusetts, admitted freeman 1674. There had been 10 graduates of this name at the N. E. colleges in 1828. THOMAS, Watertown 1644. Son John, b. 1643. This and the preceding is spelled *Fleg*.

FLANDERS, STEPHEN, Salisbury 1651.

FLATMAN, THOMAS, Salem 1637; freeman 1640, removed to Braintree, where his son Thomas was b. 23 July, 1643.

FLAVELL, THOMAS, Plymouth 1623, and his son are mentioned in Davis's Morton, 378.

FLEMMING, JOHN, Waterton 1639, d. 4 June, 1657. Son John b. 1642.

FLETCHER, ||EDWARD, Boston, a cutler, was admitted a townsman, 24 Feb. 1640; member of the church, freeman, and member of the ar. co. the same year. *EDWARD*, one of the ejected ministers, who had been settled at Dunsburn, in Gloucestershire, came to N. E. after 1660, and according to Calamy [ii. Account 330] d. in this country. FRANCIS, Concord, freeman 1677, son of Robert Fletcher, m. Elizabeth Wheeler in 1656, and had a large family. JOHN, Portsmouth, admitted freman 1669, was one of the founders of the first church in 1671, and one of the earliest deacons. MOSES, Plymouth, one of the first pilgrims who came over in 1620. Morton gives his name *Joses*, but Prince, from Gov. Bradford, says Moses. ROBERT, Concord 1635, a constable in 1637, d. 3 April, 1677, æ. 85. His sons were, Luke, who d. 1665; Francis; William, and Samuel. Shattuck. WILLIAM, son of the preceding, was admitted freeman in 1643, lived in Concord, where his son Joshua was b. 30 March, 1648; was one of the first settlers of Chelmsford, and one of the selectmen, and d. 6 Nov. 1677. His son William was born 21 Feb. 1657. Others are named in Chelmsford records. His descendants still remain on the paternal farm, near the meeting-house in Chelmsford, which is now [1829] occupied by the sixth generation. Thirteen of the name, and several of them his descendants, had grad. at the N. E. colleges in 1825.

FLINT, EDWARD, Salem 1665. [2 Coll. Mass. Hist. Soc. viii. 106.] Of the 15 graduates of the name of Flint or Flynt, who had received degrees at the N. E. colleges, in 1826, 7 have been clergymen. *HENRY*, one of the first ministers of Braintree, (now Quincy) came from England, and arrived here in 1635, and became member of the church in Boston; admitted freeman, 25 May, 1636; ordained at Braintree, 17 March, 1640; d. 27 April, 1668. His wife, who was Margery Hoar, sister of President Hoar, d. in March, 1687. His children were, Josiah, b. 1645; David, b. and d. 1652; Seth, b. 2 April, 1653; John and Cotton, (twins) b. 16 June, 1656, d. in infancy, and 5 daughters, Dorothy, Anna, Margaret, Joanna, and Ruth. *JOSIAH*, Dorchester, son of the preceding, was born at Braintree, 24 August, 1645; grad. at H. C. 1664, ordained at Dorchester, 27 Dec. 1671; d. 16 Sept. 1680, æ. 35. His son Henry, grad. in 1693, at H. C. of which he was appointed a fellow in 1700, tutor in 1705, and d. 13 Feb. 1760, in his 85th

year. *JOHN, Concord, son of the following, was a lieutenant and
representative in 1677, 1679. He m. Mary, sister of President
Oakes, in 1667, and d. in 1687. Shattuck. ‡*THOMAS, Concord, brother of Rev. Henry Flint, came from Matlock, in Derbyshire, settled in Concord in 1637, admitted freeman in 1638, representative from 1637 to 1640, four years; assistant 1642 until his
death, 8 Oct. 1653. He brought with him, says Rev. Dr. Ripley,
[Dedication Sermon, 35.] £4000 sterling, which he expended
chiefly for the benefit of the town. Mr. Shattuck informs me that
he left several children, of whom were John, above named, and
Ephraim, b. 14 Jan. 1642, m. Jane Bulkley, 20 March, 1684, and
d. 3 Aug. 1722. THOMAS, Salem, d. 15 April, 1663, leaving a
wife and 5 children, Thomas, Elizabeth, George, John, and Joseph.
Shattuck. WILLIAM, Salem 1652, d. May, 1673, leaving a wife
and son Thomas. His estate amounted to £895. Shattuck.

FLOOD, EDMUND, Plymouth 1623. Davis, Morton's Memo.
379. JOHN, Lynn, perhaps the same who was at Salisbury in
1679. PHILIP, Newbury, a. 1660. RICHARD, Boston 1642.

FOBES, JOHN, Bridgwater 1645, the ancestor of Rev. Perez
Fobes, LL. D., of Raynham, Mass., who grad. at H. C. 1762.

FOGG, ‖RALPH, Salem, admitted freeman 1634; member of
ar. co. 1644, returned to England, and d. in London 1674. Felt.
Rev. Jeremiah, Rev. Daniel, Jeremiah, and William Fogg grad. at
H. C. in 1730, 1764, 1768, and 1774. SAMUEL, Hampton, d.
16 April 1672.

FOLGER, JOHN, came from Norwich, England, in the same
ship with Hugh Peters. [Coffin.] Perhaps he was of Watertown.
PETER, son of the preceding, was born 1618, and came to N. E.
in 1635; m. Mary Morrill. He settled first at Martin's Vineyard in
1636 [Coffin]; removed to Nantucket 1662. Dr. Franklin, who
was his grand-son, in a letter dated at London in 1772, supposes
the Folgers were a Flemish family, and migrated to England in the
time of Elizabeth.

FOLLET, WILLIAM, New-Hampshire 1651, where the name
still exists.

FOLSOM, ADAM, Hingham, came over in 1639. Lincoln,
Hist. Hingham, 45. JOHN, Hingham 1638. Ibid. and Savage,
ii. Winth. N. E. 234, where the name is spelled *Foulshame*, its ancient orthography. The Folsoms of New-Hampshire are said to be
descendants of the above. Charles and George Folsom grad. at
H. C. 1813 and 1822.

FOOTE, ‖CALEB, was a member of ar. co. 1648. Twenty of
the name of Foote had grad. at the N. E. colleges in 1826. ‗PASCO,
Salem, member of the church 1652, d. 1672, leaving children, Pasco, Elizabeth, Mary, Samuel, probably of Amesbury, and Abigail.
NATHANIEL, Massachusetts, was admitted a freeman in 1634.
*SAMUEL, captain of the militia, and representative of Amesbu-
ry in 1690.

FOP, DANIEL, Hingham 1635. Lincoln, Hist. Hingham, 42.

FORD, ANDREW, Weymouth, freeman 1654, had sons Samuel and Ebenezer. Twelve graduates of this name had been educated at the N. E. colleges in 1825. ROGER, (Ford or Foord) d. at Cambridge, 24 April, 1644. THOMAS, Dorchester, admitted freeman 1631, removed to Windsor, Conn. WILLIAM, was a proprietor of Bridgewater 1645.

FORDHAM, ROBERT, the second minister of South-Hampton, L. I., came to N. E. before 1641; went to the west part of Long-Island (probably to Hempstead) with Rev. Richard Denton. He settled in South-Hampton in 1648, where he d. in 1674, leaving children whose descendants still reside in that place. Wood, Sketch Long-Island, 38. *JONAH*, a minister, and perhaps a son, or grand-son, of the preceding, grad. at Harv. College in 1658, preached a short time at Brookhaven, L. I., and was living, it would appear from the Magnalia, in 1697. He is probably the same whom Mr. Wood [Hist. Sketch, 39] calls Josiah.

FORMAIS, MARK, Salem, admitted member of the church, 22 Sept. 1639; freeman 1640, removed from Salem. This name may be the same as Fermaes.

FORRETT, JAMES, agent of William, earl of Sterling, and his heirs, was in Boston in 1640. Savage ii. Winth. N. E. 4, 5.

FOSDITCH, STEPHEN, Massachusetts, was admitted freeman 1638. THOMAS, Watertown, d. 21 June, 1650.

FOSS, JOHN, New-Hampshire 1688, one of the grand jury that year, had a son John. Descendants are numerous in N. Hampshire.

FOSTER, ANDREW, Andover, died May, 1685, æ. 106. He had one son, Andrew, who lived in Andover. Abbot, Hist. Andover. Thirty-nine persons of the name of Foster in N. E. had grad. at the different colleges in 1825. ABRAHAM, Ipswich 1648. Rev. J. B. Felt. CHRISTOPHER, Lynn, admitted freeman 1637. One of this name lived on Long-Island in 1670. EDWARD, Scituate, d. in 1643 leaving an only son, Timothy, who settled in the Mass. colony. 2 Coll. Mass. Hist. Soc. iv. 243. ||*HOPESTILL, Dorchester, admitted freeman 1636, member of ar. co. 1642, representative 1652, 20 years, captain of the militia. Sons, John and Comfort. John, who grad. at H. C. 1667, and d. 9 Sept. 1681, æ. 33, designed the arms of the colony of Massachusetts—an Indian with a bow and arrow, &c. Shaw, Hist. Boston. *ISAAC*, minister of Hartford, was born at Charlestown, [W. Winthrop] grad. at H. C. 1671, admitted freeman 1679, ordained after 1677, died 22 August, 1682. JOHN, Massachusetts, freeman 1682, was one of the council of safety in 1689, a colonel, and one of the first counsellors under the charter of William and Mary 1692, died in Jan. 1710. REGINALD, Ipswich, received a grant of land in 1641. *SAMUEL, Chelmsford, was born a. 1619, was a deacon of the church, representative at the second session 1679, d. 10 July, 1702, æ. 82. His son Edward, was born 29 April, 1657. Allen, Hist. Chelmsford. THOMAS, Weymouth, whose sons, Thomas, Increase, and John, were b. between 1639 and 1643. THOMAS, Boston, member of the church 1640, freeman 1642. THOMAS, Braintree, admitted freeman 1647, may be the same who removed to Billerica, was one of the early Baptists, and died 20 April, 1682. Son Hopestill born at Braintree, 28 March, 1650. WILLIAM, Ipswich, received a grant of land in 1635. Rev. Mr. Felt.

FOWKES, HENRY, Massachusetts, admitted freeman 1645.

FOWLE, GEORGE, Concord, freeman 1638, perhaps died at Charlestown, 21 Sept. 1682. Sons, Peter and James, b. in 1641 and 1642. Six graduates of the name of Fowle are on the H. C. catalogue. *JOHN, Charlestown, representative 1689. ||THOMAS, merchant of Boston, member of the ar. co. 1639, removed to Braintree as early as 1643, where one of his children was born. His son John was born in Boston 1641. Snow, Hist. Boston, 118. Savage, ii. Winth. N. E. 291.

FOWLER, JOHN, Gilford 1650. Nineteen of the name of Fowler had grad. at the N. E. colleges in 1826. PHILIP, one of the first settlers of Ipswich, was admitted freeman in 1635. *THOMAS, Amesbury, was representative in 1692. ‡WILLIAM, New-Haven colony, was elected a magistrate in 1637, and was one of the first settlers of Milford 1639.

FOWNELL, JOHN, Charlestown, was admitted freeman in 1645, d. 19 March, 1673.

FOX, GEORGE, the founder of the sect of Quakers, visited New-England in 1672, having arrived in America from England the year before. He returned to England in 1673, and d. 13 of the 11 mo. 1690, æ. 64. *JABEZ*, the second minister of Woburn, was son of Thomas Fox, and grad. at H. C. in 1665. He was ordained colleague with Rev. Thomas Carter, 5 Sept. 1679, and died of the small pox, 28 Feb. 1703, æ. 56. His widow, Judith, m. Col. Jona. Tyng, and d. 5 June, 1736, in her 99th year. [Alden.] His son, Rev. John Fox, H. C. 1698, was his successor, was ordained 4 Oct. 1703, and died 12 Dec. 1756, æ. 76, whose son Jabez, H. C. 1727, was a counsellor of Massachusetts, and d. at Portland, Me., 7 April, 1755, in his 50th year. THOMAS, Cambridge, was admitted freeman in 1638, one of the selectmen in 1670, and living in 1674. His wife was widow Ellen Greene. It is said that he was a descendant from the historian of the martyrs. The martyrologist was born in Boston, Lincolnshire, 1517, and left two sons, Thomas, who was fellow of King's College, Cambridge, and Samuel, fellow of Magdalen College, Oxford, who wrote his father's life. THOMAS, Concord, freeman 1644, m. a second wife, Hannah Brooks, in 1647. He left children, Eliphalet, who m. Mary Wheeler in 1665, and d. 15 Aug. 1711; Hannah, b. 1648; Thomas, b. 1649; Isaac, b. 1657, and some others. Shattuck.

FOXCROFT, ||FRANCIS, Boston, member of the ar. co. in 1679, a colonel, and d. at Cambridge, 31 Dec. 1727. Francis and Thomas Foxcroft, H. C. 1712 and 1714, were his sons. The former, a judge of probate, d. 28 March, 1768, æ. 75, having had a son Daniel, who grad. at H. C. 1746, and d. 30 Jan. 1756, æ. 29.

The latter was ordained over the first church in Boston, 20 Nov. 1717, and d. 16 June, 1769, æ. 73.

FOXERY, WILLIAM, Boston 1652. Savage, MS note.

FOXWELL, RICHARD, a merchant, was of Scituate 1634, went to Saco, where he d. in 1677. Coffin. Folsom. A Foxwell, whose christian name is supposed by Mr. Savage to be Richard, was admitted freeman 18 May, 1631, when he might have been of Salem.

FRAILE, GEORGE, Lynn 1637, d. 9 Dec. 1663, leaving a son George, who was accidentally killed in 1669. Lewis.

FRANCIS, JOHN, Braintree, a. 1650, whose wife Rose died in 1659. RICHARD, Cambridge, freeman 1640, d. 24 March, 1687, æ. 80, leaving sons, Stephen, b. 1644 ; John, b. 4 Jan. 1650.

FRANKLIN, JOSIAH, Boston, was son of Thomas Franklin, of Eaton, in Northamptonshire, who was born in 1598. [Life of Franklin.] He came to N. E. about 1682, and d. at the age of 87. His brother Benjamin, a silk dyer, also came to N. E. and left posterity in Boston. The first wife of Josiah was Anna, by whom he had, 1. Josiah, b. 23 Aug. 1685 ; 2. Anna, b. 1687 ; 3. Joseph, b. 5 Jan. 1688 ; 4. Joseph, 2d, b. 30 June, 1689 ; the 2d wife was Abiah, daughter of Peter Folger, and his children were, 5. John, b. 7 Dec. 1690 ; 6. Peter, b. 22 Nov. 1692 ; 7. Mary, b. 1694 ; 8. James, b. 4 Feb. 1697 ; 9. Sarah, b. 1699 ; 10. Ebenezer, b. 1701, d. 1703 ; 11. Thomas. b. 7 Dec. 1703 ; 12. Benjamin, the philosopher, b. 6 Jan. 1706, d. at Philadelphia, 17 April, 1790, æ. 84 ; 13. Lydia, b. 1708 ; 14. Jane, b. 1712. WILLIAM, Ipswich 1634, thence to Newbury and Boston, was admitted freeman 1638. The particulars of his death in 1644 are given by Winthrop, ii. 183—185. His son William was admitted a townsman in Boston, 28 March, 1642. [Savage.] His children b. in Boston were, Elizabeth 1638 ; John, 14 July, 1642 ; Benjamin, 12 Oct. 1643, who had several children ; Ebenezer, who d. in 1644 ; and Eleazar, b. 4 Oct. 1645.

FRARY, JOHN, Dedham, freeman 1638, one of the founders of the church, 8 Nov. 1638, afterwards removed to Deerfield. [Worthington, Hist. Dedham, 104.] His sons were Isaac, b. 1638 ; Samuel, b. 1641. Samson and Elizur Frary were of Hadley in 1667. JOHN, Massachusetts, admitted freeman in 1636. ||*THEOPHILUS, Boston 1657, member of the ar. co. 1666 ; captain of the same 1682 ; representative 1689, d. 17 Oct. 1700. Son Theophilus was b. 1657.

FREAKE, JOHN, Boston 1665. 2 Coll. Mass. Hist Soc. viii. 105.

FREEBORNE, WILLIAM, Boston, freeman 1634, removed to Rhode-Island. 2 Coll. Mass. Hist. Soc. ix. 179.

FREELAND, WILLIAM, Massachusetts, freeman in 1650.

FREEMAN, ‡EDMUND, Lynn, 1632 ; [Winthrop, ii. Hist. N. E. 342 ; and Lewis] one of the first settlers of Duxbury, [A. Bradford, Notes] and an early settler in Sandwich, was elected an assist-

ant of Plymouth colony seven years from 1640 to 1646.   He died
about 1668, leaving two sons, John and Edmund, who both m.
daughters of Gov. Prince.   Among his descendants, are General
Nathaniel Freeman, of Sandwich, and his son Nathaniel, who grad.
at H. C. 1787, and brother Hon. Jonathan, of Hanover, N. H. a
M. C. 4 years from 1797 to 1801 : Hon. Solomon, a Senator of
Mass.; Edmund, who grad. at H. C. 1733, died 9 March, 1800, æ.
89 ; Edmund, who grad. at H. C. 1767 ; and Jonathan, who grad.
at H. C. 1778, and was lost at sea on his passage from Europe in
1795, æ. 34.⁹ ‡JOHN, Eastham, son of the preceding, was elected
an assistant of Plymouth colony in 1666.   His wife was Mercy
Prince.   Mr. Shattuck informs me that there was a John Freeman
of Sudbury in 1644, and the Boston records under 1645, give the
birth of his son Joseph Freeman, who was probably the representative of Sudbury in 1691.   SAMUEL, admitted freeman 1639, supposed to be brother of Edmund, came from Devonshire, England,
1630, and settled at Watertown, where his house was burnt 11 Feb.
1631. [Winthrop, i. Hist. N. E. 41.]   He is said to have returned
to England, leaving two sons, Henry, who died in 1672, and Samuel, b. in 1638; from one of whom is descended Rev. James Freeman, D. D. of Boston, who grad. at H. C. 1777.   SAMUEL, son of
the preceding, was born 11 May, 1638, and lived in Watertown.
His son Samuel settled in Eastham, was a deacon of the church, m.
a daughter of Constant Southworth, and had 3 sons and 4 daughters.
One of the sons was Samuel, who had 9 sons and 3 daughters.
Enoch, the 8th son of the last Samuel, was born at Eastham, 17
May, 1706, grad. at H. C. 1729 ; settled in Falmouth, (now Portland) was judge of the court of common pleas, and of probate,
register of deeds, and d. 2 Sept. 1788, æ. 82.   Hon. Samuel Freeman, the eldest son of Enoch, was born at Falmouth, 15 June, 1743,
was judge of probate many years, and is well known for various
useful compilations.   His sons, Samuel Deane, William, and George,
grad. at college, the two former at Harvard in 1800 and 1804 ; the
latter at Bowdoin in 1812, and d. 27 May, 1815, in his 20th year.
  FRENCH, EDWARD, Ipswich 1636, probably removed to
Salisbury, and a proprietor there in 1640.   Ten of the name of
French had grad. at Harvard and the other N. E. colleges in 1826.
JACOB, Weymouth, admitted freeman 1652.   JOHN, Cambridge,
freeman 1644, whose children were, Sarah, b. Oct. 1637 ; Joseph,
b. 4 April, 1640, m. Experience Foster and settled in Billerica,
from whence he removed ; Nathaniel, b. 7 June, 1643.   Joanna, his
wife, d. 20 Jan. 1646; his housekeeper d. in Feb. 1646, and he d.
soon after.   JOHN, Dorchester 1639, whose sons John and Thomas were b. 28 Feb. 1641 and 10 July 1643, may have removed to
Braintree, where Dependence, Temperance, William, Thomas, and
Samuel, children of John and Grace French, were b. in 1648, 1651,
1654, 1657, and 1659.   One of these was ancestor of the late
Rev. Jonathan French, of Andover who was b. at Braintree, 30 Jan.
1740; grad. at H. C. 1771 ; d. 28 July 1809.   JOHN, Ipswich
1648.   *STEPHEN, Weymouth, freeman 1634, representative in

1638, was perhaps father of Jacob, freeman 1652. THOMAS, Boston, admitted freeman 1632, member of the church, from whence he was dismissed 27 Jan. 1639 to Ipswich, where he appears to have resided as early as 1634. He may have been the ensign of the ar. co. in 1650. THOMAS, Guilford 1650. WILLIAM, brother of John French, of Cambridge, came to N. E. as early as 1635, was admitted freeman 1636, and settled at Cambridge, from whence he went to Billerica with the first settlers; was a lieutenant, appointed to solemnize marriages, and was the first representative in 1660, and again in 1663. He died 20 Nov. 1681, aged 78. His children were, Elizabeth and Mary b. in England, John b. in Cambridge and settled with his father in Billerica, had a large family and d. Oct. 1712, aged a. 78; Sarah, b. March, 1638; Jacob, b. 16 Jan. 1640, settled in Billerica, had a large family, and d. 20 May, 1713, æ. 73; Hannah, b. 21 Feb. 1641; Samuel, b. 3 Dec. 1645, the five last b. in Cambridge. He had other children by a second wife. His posterity have been numerous in Billerica, and still remain so.

FRIEND, JOHN, a carpenter of Salem, whose family in 1637, consisted of 11 persons, admitted a townsman in Boston, 30 March, 1640, and was member of the ar. co. same year. He d. 1655 or 6. A John Friend is mentioned by Winthrop, i. Hist. N. E. 391. Daniel Friend grad. at H. C. 1779.

FRISK, JOHN, one of the proprietors of Bridgewater 1645. Johnson mentions a Mr. David Frisk, a minister, who arrived in N. E. in 1637, but there may be some errour in the name. See his Hist. N. E. 128.

FRIZELL, JOHN, Braintree, came from Scotland, d. 19 Jan. 1664. John Frizell, a merchant of Boston, grad. at H. C. 1724. William Frizell was of Concord in 1669.

FROST, *CHARLES, Kittery, representative 1658, 1660, 1661, captain of the militia, and probably the same named by Hubbard in his Wars with the Eastern Indians, p. 28, and possibly the major Frost, killed by the Indians at Kittery, 4 July, 1697. Seventeen of the name had grad. in N. E. in 1828. EDMUND, a ruling elder of the church, at Cambridge, came to N. E. in 1635, with Rev. Thomas Shepard, was admitted freeman 1636. His sons were, John, b. in England; Samuel; Joseph; James, who settled in Billerica, was a deacon, and d. 12 Aug. 1711, aged a. 74; Ephraim, and Thomas. His wife was Thomasine. NICHOLAS, Kittery 1652. John Frost was of Dover in 1665, and the name has continued there and in its vicinity with reputation to the present time.

FROTHINGHAM, WILLIAM, Charlestown 1630, was admitted freeman 1632, had sons, John, b. 1633; Peter, b. 1636, admitted freeman 1668; Nathaniel, b. 1640; Stephen, b. 1641; Joseph, b. and d. 1645; Hon. John Frothingham d. at Portland, Feb. 1826, æ. 76.

FRYE, GEORGE, Massachusetts, was admitted freeman 1651. JOHN, Newbury, removed to Andover 1645; freeman 1669, died 1698, æ. 92 years 7 months. His sons, John, Samuel, James, and Benjamin, settled in Andover. Six of the name of Frye, and several, if not all, his descendants, had grad. at the N. E. colleges in 1826. Jonathan, H. C. 1723, was Captain Lovewell's chaplain, and perished at Pequawkett in May, 1725. WILLIAM, Weymouth, d. 26 Oct. 1642.

FRYER, *NATHANIEL, of Boston in 1657, and afterwards a merchant of Portsmouth, representative in 1666, and a counsellor of New-Hampshire in 1683, and captain of the militia, and magistrate. His eldest son, James, is the one of whom Hubbard [Ind. Wars] gives some account. THOMAS, (Fryer or Frior) Salem 1639.

FUGILL, THOMAS, perhaps the one mentioned in a MS of Rev. Thomas Shepard, as of Buttercrambe, about 7 miles from York, England, was of New-Haven in 1639, and in 1641 was secretary of the colony.

FULLER, EDWARD, Plymouth, one of the first pilgrims, died 1621. Twenty-three of the name of Fuller had been educated at the various colleges in N. England in 1826. EDWARD, arrived in Boston 1630, when there were only " seven huts erected." His son John settled in Lynn. Lewis. GILES, Hampton, a. 1646, d. 2 April 1676. JOHN, one of the first proprietors of Salisbury 1640, and perhaps of Ipswich in 1648. *JOHN, Lynn 1644 ; representative 1655 and 1664, d. 29 June, 1666, leaving sons, John, the following, William, and James. *JOHN, Lynn 1645, representative 1674— 1678, 5 years, a lieutenant, d. 29 April, 1695. His sons were, John, Thomas, Edward, Elisha, Joseph, and Benjamin. Lewis. MAT-THEW, Plymouth, a. 1640 ; removed to Barnstable 1652, was surgeon-general of Plymouth colony forces 1673, and styled captain 1675, in which year he d. Thatcher, i. Med. Biog. 18. ROBERT, Dorchester, member of the church 1640 ; freeman 1641 ; had a son Jonathan, b. 1643. SAMUEL, Plymouth 1620, one of the first pilgrims, and the first physician who settled in New-England. He d. in 1633. His son Samuel was of Plymouth in 1623. *THOMAS, Dedham 1643, freeman 1653, representative 1673, 1679, 1686, an ensign of the militia. THOMAS, Woburn, whose son Thomas was b. 1644. WILLIAM, Ipswich 1637, freeman 1641, removed as early as 1646 to Hampton, which he represented in 1667. There was a William Fuller of Concord, a miller, in 1639. JOHN, Cambridge, (Newton) died 1698. He had sons, Joseph, b. 1652 ; Joshua., 1654 ; Jeremiah, 1658, and John. Hon. Abraham Fuller of the 4th generation, b. 23 March, 1720, represented Newton 20 years, commencing in 1764.

FURBER, *WILLIAM, b. 1614, came from London in the ship Angel Gabriel, [Coffin] and settled in Dover, which he represented in 1648, and was living, together with his son William, at Dover in 1684. His name appears as one of the witnesses of the genuine Indian deed to Wheelwright in 1638.

FURNELL, ‖STRONG, Boston, freeman 1643 ; member of ar. co. 1651. Sons, John, b. 1653 ; William, b. 1655. Whitman, in his Hist. of Anc. and Hon. Art. Co. gives his name of baptism, *Strange*. 2 Coll. Mass. Hist. Soc. iv. 199. WILLIAM, Boston 1656. Son Joseph, b. 1656.

GAGE, JOHN, admitted freeman 1634, was one of the first settlers of Ipswich. Benjamin, perhaps a son, freeman 1671, lived in Haverhill. Six of the name have received the honours of the N. E. colleges.

GAGER, WILLIAM, a chirurgeon, and deacon of the first church at Charlestown, came over with Gov. Winthrop in 1630, and died 20 Sept. 1630. Winthrop, i. Hist. N. E. 33. One of the name, William Gager, grad. at Y. C. in 1721.

GAINS, DANIEL, Lancaster 1660, was killed by the Indians, 10 Feb. 1676. Willard, Hist. Lancaster. HENRY, Lynn, was admitted freeman 1638. THOMAS, Lynn 1640.

GALE, AMBROSE, Marblehead 1674, was one of the founders of the church there. HU, Kittery, freeman 1652. RICHARD, Watertown 1640.

GALLOP, JOHN, Boston, was admitted to the church, 5 Jan. 1634, and freeman the same year ; died in Jan. 1650, leaving a wife, and sons, John, Samuel, and Nathaniel. Samuel lived in Boston, and had a son Samuel, b. in 1656. Savage, ii. Winthrop, Index. Snow, Hist. Boston, 125. JOHN, son of the preceding, was of Boston in 1644. Capt. Gallop, of New-London, was one of the six captains slain by the Indians in taking Narraganset Fort, 19 Dec. 1675. HUMPHREY, Dorchester, had a son Joseph, b. in 1643.

GALLY, JOHN, Salem 1637, whose son John, freeman in 1670, lived in Beverly. Florence, his widow, d. at Beverly 1686, æ. 80.

GAMLIN, ROBERT, Concord, admitted freeman 1634, d. 7 Oct. 1642. The name of Gambling, probably the same, has existed in Mass. and N. H., and two named Benjamin grad. at H. C. in 1702 and 1734, the first of whom was a counsellor of N. Hampshire, and d. 1 Sept. 1737, æ. 56. ROBERT, Roxbury, probably son of the preceding, who is styled sen. in colony records, was admitted freeman 3 Sept. 1634. Joseph and Benjamin, sons of Robert Gamlin, were b. in Roxbury, a. 1639.

GANNETT, MATTHEW, Scituate 1650. THOMAS, Bridgewater 1645, brother to the preceding, d. in 1655. Caleb Gannett, esq., of Cambridge, H. C. 1763, born at Bridgewater, 22 August, 1745, was from this family.

GARDE, ROGER, was mayor of York 1644. Winthrop ii. 210.

GARDINER, SIR CHRISTOPHER, a knight, came to N. E., Morton says, in 1632, but Mr. Savage more correctly assigns the date of his arrival to 1630 ; remained at Plymouth and Boston, and their vicinity, two or three years, and returned to England, where he joined the disaffected in preferring complaints against the government of the colonies. Morton. Winthrop. LYON, one of the first settlers of Connecticut, came from Scotland in 1635, and erected the fort at Saybrook under Lord Say and Seal and Lord Brooke. He went to East-Hampton, L. I. 1655 and d. in 1663. His son David, born at Saybrook, 29 April, 1636, was the first born of European parentage in Connecticut, and his daughter Elizabeth, born on Long-Island, 14 Sept. 1641, may have been the first English child born in New-York. Wood, Hist. Long-Island, 66. Mr. Savage [i. Winthrop, 174] gives to the father the name of the son, whose manuscripts might be those to which Trumbull referred. RICH-ARD, Plymouth, one of the first pilgrims who came over in 1620.

GARDNER, *ANDREW, a captain, belonged to Muddy-River, [now Brookline] which he represented in 1689. He was lost in the expedition to Canada 1690. His son Andrew, who grad. at H. C. 1696, was a preacher at Lancaster, where he was accidentally killed by a soldier, 26 Oct. 1704. Rev. Andrew Gardner, H. C. 1712, was minister of Lunenburg, Mass. Forty-one persons of the name had grad. at the N. E. colleges in 1825, besides eleven whose names are spelled *Gardiner*. EDMUND, Ipswich, was admitted freeman 1640. GEORGE, Salem 1637, was admitted to the church 3 Jan. 1641 ; freeman 1642. JOSEPH, Salem, a captain, was killed, with five other officers of the same grade, in battle with the Indians, 19 Dec. 1675. His wife was Anne Downing, who, after his death, m. Gov. Bradstreet. He left no children. Felt, Annals, 251, 252. RICH-ARD, Woburn, was admitted freeman 1652. *SAMUEL, Salem, born a. 1627, freeman 1675, representative 1681 and 1682. SAM-UEL, Roxbury, a lieutenant, and killed by the Indians with Capt. Wadsworth, 27 April, 1676. Eight of the number killed at this time belonged to Roxbury. Samuel, son of Peter Gardner of Rox-bury, was killed six days before. Samuel Gardner was of Hadley in 1663. *THOMAS, came from Scotland, and was an overseer of the plantation at Gloucester 1624, and removed thence to Salem, was admitted freeman 1636, representative 1637. THOMAS, a merchant of Salem, son of the preceding, united with the church 1639, freeman 1641, was a selectman, and d. 1674. His last wife was Damasis Shattuck. His children were, Sarah Balch ; Sceth Grafton ; Thomas ; George ; John, freeman 1675 ; Samuel, free-man 1675 ; Joseph ; Richard, and Miriam. Felt, Annals, 246. THOMAS, Roxbury, d. Nov. 1638. THOMAS, Roxbury 1638, perhaps the freeman under 1646, d. 15 July, 1689. His son An-drew, probably the one at Muddy-River, was b. 1641.

GARFIELD, *BENJAMIN, Watertown, was representative in 1689. EDWARD, Watertown, freeman 1635, had a son Joseph, b. in 1637. SAMUEL, was also of Watertown, and an early pro-prietor.

GARFOARD, JARVIS, Salem 1637, admitted to the church 24 March, 1639 ; freeman same year ; was also resident in Lynn.

GARLAND, PETER, Boston 1654. One of the name grad. at D. C. in 1828.

GARNER, EDMUND, Cambridge 1635.

GARNETT, JOHN, Hingham 1653. This name has existed in N. J., and one grad. at its college in 1803.

GARRETT, JAMES, Charlestown, freeman 1639, had a son James, b. in 1646. RICHARD, Boston, a shoemaker, and mem-ber of the church, came over in 1630, in which year he requested to be admitted freeman. A particular account of the circumstances which occasioned his death, 31 Dec. 1630, is given by Winthrop,

i. Hist. N. E. 39, 40.   Richard Garrett, who d. at Boston, 29 March, 1662, and Robert Garrett living there in 1643, might be his sons.

GASCOYNE, EDWARD, Salem, a member of the church, had children, Samuel, Preserved, and Daniel, who were baptized in 1639 and 1640.

GASKELL, EDWARD, was a ship-carpenter of Salem 1637.

GATCHELL, JOHN, Marblehead 1648, was b. a. 1611. SAMUEL, Salisbury 1651.

GATES, STEPHEN, Massachusetts, was admitted freeman 1653, d. 3 April 1654.

GATLINE, THOMAS, a miller of Braintree 1650, d. 17 May, 1663.

GAUNT, PETER, Lynn, went to Sandwich 1637.   Lewis.

GAY, JOHN, Dedham, was admitted freeman 1635, and the great ancestor of the Gays of Massachusetts and Connecticut, 14 of whom had grad. at the N. E. colleges in 1826, 6 of them having been clergymen.   JOHN, Dedham, freeman 1644.   Samuel, Hezekiah, and Nathaniel, sons of John Gay, were b. at Dedham 1639, 1640, and 1642.   Nathaniel was admitted freeman in 1675.

GAYLORD, JOHN, Dorchester 1632.   Prince, ii. Annals, 60, where the name is spelled Gallard.   *WILLIAM, Dorchester, freeman 1631, representative 1635 and 1636, removed to Windsor with Rev. John Warham in 1636.   He was a deacon before and after his removal.   Rev. William Gaylord, Y. C. 1730; Rev. Nathaniel Gaylord, of Hartland, Conn. Y. C. 1774, and Rev. Flavel S. Gaylord, a graduate of Williams College in 1816, are probably descendants.

GEARY, *WILLIAM, a deacon of the church of Roxbury, was admitted freeman 1652; elected representative 1675, d. 4 Sept. 1712.   Dunton [2 Coll. Mass. Hist. Soc. ii. 103] mentions a captain Gery, who he says was "as eminent for his love to his country, as Junius Brutus and the famous Scævola among the Romans."

GEDNEY, ‡BARTHOLOMEW, Salem, son of the following, was baptized 14 June, 1640, admitted freeman 1669, elected assistant 1680 to 1683, 4 years; one of Sir Edmund Andros' council 1687; one of the first council under the charter of William and Mary 1692; d. 1 March, 1698, æ. 58.   JOHN, Salem, was born 1603, was admitted to the church in Salem, 19 Nov. 1637, and freeman the next year, d. 1688 æ. 85.   His children were, John, Bartholomew, Sarah, Eli, and Eleazar.   His 1st wife was Mary, his 2d Catharine.

GEE, JOHN, Boston, d. 25 July 1693.   Rev. Joshua Gee, H. C. 1717, was a colleague minister with Rev. Dr. Cotton Mather, and d. 22 May, 1748, æ. 50.

GEEREE, ARTHUR, (See GERRY.)   DENIS, Lynn 1635, gave by will to the colony of Massachusetts, £300.   Winthrop, ii. Hist. N. E. 341.   WILLIAM, Salem, admitted to the church 21 Nov. 1640; freeman 1641.   This name, according to Mr. Savage, is spelled *Geares* in the colony records.

GENERE, LAMBERT, Dedham 1636. Worthington, Hist. Dedham, 42.

GEORGE, JOHN, Charlestown, was one of the founders of the first Baptist church in Boston 1665, d. at Charlestown, 12 Sept. 1666. NICHOLAS, Dorchester 1666, d. at Boston, 9 April, 1691. PETER, Braintree 1642, had children, Susan, b. 1642; Mary, 1645; Hannah, 1648; John, 1650; Samuel, 1651; John, 2d, 1653; Peter, 1655. RICHARD, Boston 1656. WILLIAM, Lynn 1637. Lewis.

GERRISH, BENJAMIN, Salem, son of Captain William Gerrish, was born at Newbury, 13 Jan. 1652, freeman 1681, was collector of his majesty's customs. He m. Hannah Ruck, 24 Oct. 1676, and d. 2 July, 1713, æ. 61, having had 5 sons and 6 daughters. Benjamin, his eldest son, b. 17 Jan. 1683, was appointed governour of Bermuda in 1754, and d. in 1755, æ. 72. ‡JOHN, Dover, brother of the preceding, was b. 12 Feb. 1645, counsellor of New-Hampshire 1692, a captain, sheriff, &c. d. in 1714, æ. 69. He m. Elizabeth, daughter of major R. Waldron, and his sons were, Richard, a counsellor of N. H. 1716; John, a captain; Paul, a colonel and counsellor of Mass.; Nathaniel, a captain; Timothy, a colonel, who m. Sarah, daughter of Robert Eliot, and whose sons Robert Eliot Gerrish and Joseph Gerrish grad. at H. C. 1730 and 1752; and Benjamin. A. Gerrish, esq. MS letter, 1828. *JOSEPH*, minister of Wenham, was brother of the preceding, was b. 23 March, 1650, grad. at H. C. 1669, freeman 1673, was ordained succesor of Rev. A. Newman in 1673, d. 20 Jan. 1720, aged 70. He m. a daughter of Major Waldron of Dover, and had 4 sons, Joseph, Paul, John, and Samuel. Joseph was born 25 April, 1676, grad. at H. C. 1700, and settled in the ministry; Samuel was a stationer in Boston, town clerk and register of deeds, and was an elegant chirographer, as was his father. MOSES, Newbury, brother of the preceding was b. 9 May, 1656, m. Jane, daughter of Henry Sewall, 24 Sept. 1677, and d. 4 Dec. 1694, æ. 38. One of his sons was Colonel Joseph Gerrish, representative many years from Newbury, whose son Joseph was also a colonel. Col. Samuel, who was engaged in the battle of Bunker Hill 1775, Colonel Jacob Gerrish of Amesbury, and Colonel Henry Gerrish, of Boscawen, N. H. a senator in the N. H. legislature 1793 and 1799, were descendants from Moses Gerrish. *WILLIAM, Newbury, was born at Bristol, in Somersetshire, 20 August, 1617, and tradition asserts, was an officer under the duke of Buckingham, but as he came to N. E. before the civil wars in England commenced, this may admit of doubt. He was the first captain of the military band in Newbury; [Johnson, Hist N. E. 193] was representative of that place, 4 years, from 1650 to 1653, and of Hampton in 1663 and 1664. He m. 17 April, 1644, Joanna, widow of J. Oliver, by whom (who d. 18 June, 1677) he had 11 children. He m. 2d Ann, daughter of Richard Parker, and had one son, Henry, who lived in Boston, and d. without issue. Capt. Gerrish removed to Boston, and left that place for Salem, 3 August, and d. there, 9 Nov. 1687, aged 70. WILLIAM, the 5th son of the preceding, was a physician, born 1 April, 1658, m. Ann, his wife, in 1674, and d. at Charlestown, 10 May, 1683, æ. 25.

GERRY, ARTHUR, Roxbury, freeman 1638, d. 17 Dec. 1666, æ. 67.   WILLIAM, Roxbury.   (See GEARY.)

GIBBARD, WILLIAM, was secretary of the colony of Connecticut 1657.

GIBBONS, AMBROSE, Pascataqua 1632.   Written also Gibbens.   See Belknap, i. Hist. N. H. App'x.   Savage, i. Winthrop, 7, 410, 423.   JAMES, Saco 1652.   ‡*EDWARD, came to N. E. as early as 1629, was admitted freeman 1631 ; representative of Boston 1635 ; assistant of Massachusetts colony in 1650 ; [Dr. Eliot says 1644] major-general 1649 to 1651 ; d. 9 Dec. 1654.   His sons Jotham and John were b. in Boston in 1633 and 1641.   Savage, i. Winthrop, 192.

GIBBS, ‖BENJAMIN, Boston, was admitted to the first church, 13 July 1662 ; a member of the ar. co. 1666.   He had several children born in Boston.   GILES, Massachusetts, was admitted freeman in 1633.   HENRY, came to N. E. from Hingham, England, and settled at Hingham, Ms. as early as 1635, and d. 7 July, 1676. Lincoln, Hist. Hingham, 22, 41.   *HENRY*, minister of Watertown, was son of Robert Gibbs, of Boston, and was b. 8 Oct. 1668. He grad. at H. C. 1685, was ordained 6 Oct. 1697, d. 21 Oct. 1723, æ. 55.   He m. Mercy, Daughter of William Greenough, and his children were, 1. Elizabeth, b. 12 Jan. 1696, d. 26 May, 1706 ; 2. Mercy, b. 23 Dec. 1696, who was the 2d wife of Rev. Benjamin Prescott, of Danvers, Ms. ; 3. Margaret, b. 3 July, 1699, d. 17 Jan. 1771, who was wife of Rev. Nathaniel Appleton, D. D. of Cambridge, and had 6 children ; 4. Henry, b. 1702, d. 1703 ; 5. William, b. 11 July, 1704, d. at Cambridge, 10 Aug. 1715 ; 6. Mehitabel, b. 8 Jan. 1706, who m. Benjamin Marston, esq. of Salem, and d. 21 Aug. 1727 ; Henry, b. 13 May, 1709, m. (1st) Margaret, daughter of Rev. Jabez Fitch ; (2d) Catharine, daughter of Secretary Josiah Willard, and d. at Boston, 17 Feb. 1759, æ. 50, leaving by the 2d wife, Henry, b. 7 May, 1749, m. Mercy, daughter of Benjamin Prescott, esq. 29 Oct. 1781, and had 3 children, 1. William, of Salem ; 2. Josiah Willard, professor at Y. C., at which he grad. in 1809, the translator of Gesenius's Hebrew Lexicon, and 3. Henry, Y. C. 1814, a merchant in Philadelphia.   Josiah Willard, b. 30 Sept. 1752, d. in Philadelphia, Jan. 1822, æ. 69, having had ten children.   JOHN, arrived at Boston from London in 1637, and was one of the first settlers of New-Haven, where was a Matthew Gibbs in 1639, and where William Gibbs d. in 1654, and a John Gibbs d. in 1690.   MATTHEW, a proprietor of Sudbury 1654, had a son Thomas, b. 10 April, 1660.   His wife was Mary.   ROBERT, an eminent merchant, descended from an ancient family in Devonshire, was born a. 1639 ; came to N. E. as early as 1660, and settled in Boston, where he d. a. 1673.   He m. Elizabeth, daughter of Jacob Sheafe, and had, 1. Margaret, b. 13 May, 1663 ; 2. Robert, b. 20 Sept. 1665, d. at Boston, 7 Dec. 1702, whose wife was Mary Shrimpton, by whom he had, Henry, b. 7 Nov. 1694, lived in Newton ; Robert, b. 29 Nov. 1696, who lived at Boston and Providence, and d. at Providence, 29 June, 1769; Mary, b. 28 May, 1699, m. Rev. John Cotton, of Newton ; 3. Rev. Henry, noticed above, and 4. Jacob, b. 18 Feb. 1672.

GIBSON, CHRISTOPHER, Dorchester, admitted freeman 1631, might be one of the founders of the 2d church in Boston 1650. JOHN, Cambridge 1634, was living in 1688, at the age of about 87. See Hutchinson, i. Hist. Mass. 328. His children were Rebecca, Mary, Martha, John, Samuel, b. 28 Oct. 1644. *RICHARD*, an episcopal minister, and one of the first preachers at Portsmouth, came to N. E. as early as 1640, and probably returned to England. Winthrop, ii. Hist. N. E. 66.

GIDDINGS, *GEORGE, Ipswich, freeman 1638, representative 1641, and 8 years afterwards until his death, 1 June, 1676. He left a widow Jane, and sons, Thomas, John, James, and Samuel. The inventory of his estate was £1021. 12. 6. Felt. *JOHN, Ipswich, representative 3 years from 1653 to 1655.

GIFFORD, JOHN, Lynn 1658, m. Margaret Temple, and had a son Philip, who d. 19 June, 1690. Lewis.

GILBERT, JONATHAN, is mentioned under 1646 in Increase Mather's Indian Wars from 1614 to 1675, pp. 61, 63. Hutch. i. Hist. Mass. 171. JOHN, Northampton 1653. HUMPHREY, Ipswich, d. 13 Feb. 1658. MATTHEW, an assistant of New-Haven colony 1658, was afterwards elected deputy-governour. THOMAS, Springfield, d. 5 June, 1662. *THOMAS*, minister of Topsfield, was a native of Scotland, and arrived at Charlestown from England, in July, 1661, and soon after settled at Topsfield, from whence he was dismissed, and went to Charlestown, where he d. 26 Oct. 1673, æ. 63. Middlesex Co. records. Boston News-Letter.

GILDERSLEVE, RICHARD, one of the first settlers of Stamford. Trumbull, i. 121. Six of the name had in 1828 received the honours of the U. S. colleges.

GILE, or GILES, ANTHONY, a ship carpenter of Boston was admitted to the church in 1642. JOHN, Boston 1654. (See GUILD.) Rev. Samuel Gile grad. at D. C. in 1804. EDWARD, Salem, was admitted freeman in 1634.

GILL, ARTHUR, Boston, freeman 1631, had sons, John, b. 1639; Thomas, b. 1644. JOHN, Dorchester, admitted to the church 1640, perhaps d. before 1648. Willard, Hist. Lancaster, 21. JOHN, Salisbury 1651. THOMAS, Hingham, 1635, had sons Samuel and Nathan. Four of the name had grad. at H. C. in 1828.

GILLAM, Benjamin, Boston, a ship-carpenter, was admitted to the church and freeman in 1635. He may be the same who is mentioned by Morton as going to England in 1664. He had sons, Zachary, b. 1636 ; Joseph, b. 1644, and probably others.

GILLET, JONATHAN, Massachusetts, was admitted freeman 1635. Samuel Gillet was of Hadley in 1668. NATHANIEL, Dorchester, came to N. E. in 1630, with the ministers, Maverick and Warham, and was admitted freeman in 1634. Nine of the name, 6 of them clergymen, had grad. at the N. E. colleges in 1828.

GILLOW, BENJAMIN, Lynn 1637. JOHN, Lynn 1637; d. 1673. Lewis. THOMAS, Lynn 1639. Ibid.

GILLOWAY, JOHN, Lynn 1637. Lewis.

GILMAN, EDWARD, probably came from the county of Norfolk, England, where some of his friends resided, and settled at Hingham; was admitted freeman in 1638; removed early to Ipswich, where he lived in 1647; thence to Exeter before 1652, and there died. Tradition reports that he had 3 sons, Edward, the following, John, and Moses. Two of his daughters m. a Cushing and a Hersey. His son Moses lived in that part of Exeter, now Newmarket, and had sons, Jeremiah, b. 1660; James, b. 1665; John, b. 1672; David; Josiah, and Caleb. EDWARD, son of the preceeding, freeman 1645, was of Ipswich in 1647, of Exeter in 1652. It is said that he went to England in 1653, for mill gear, and was lost at sea. ‡JOHN, Exeter 1657, brother of the preceding, one of the principal men of that place, and one of the first counsellors under the province charter 1680, d. 24 July, 1708, æ. 84. He m. 30 June, 1657, Elizabeth Treworthy, who d. 8 Sept. 1719, æ. 80, by whom he had 6 sons and 10 daughters. Eight of the daughters married. The sons were, 1. James, b. 6 Feb. 1660; 2. John, b. 1663, d. in childhood; 3. Samuel, b. 30 March, 1671; 4. Nicholas, b. 26 Dec. 1672, who m. Sarah Clark, 10 June, 1697; and had 7 sons, of whom were *Daniel*, born 28 June, 1702, the father of Hon. Nicholas Gilman, b. 31 Oct. 1731, a state counsellor of N. H. who d. at Exeter, 7 April, 1783, leaving sons, Nicholas, John Taylor, and Nathaniel, all of Exeter, men much distinguished in the political annals of N. H., and *Nicholas*, born 18 Jan. 1707, grad. at H. C. 1724, was ordained at Durham, N. H. in 1742, and d. 13 April, 1748, leaving sons, Tristram, H. C. 1757, minister of North-Yarmouth, Maine, Joseph, a judge in Ohio, and Josiah; 5. John, 2d, b. 19 Jan. 1677, who, by two wives, had eleven children, six sons, of whom were Peter, b. 6 Feb. 1705, a mandamus counsellor of N. H., who d. 1 Dec. 1788, and Samuel, the grandfather of Rev. Samuel Gilman, H. C. 1811, minister at Charlestown, S. C. *JOSHUA, representative of Hampton in 1669. Coll. N. H. Hist. Soc. i. 224.

GILSON, WILLIAM, Scituate, was elected one of the assistants of Plymouth colony in 1633, and d. at Scituate without issue, Frances, his widow, surviving him.

GINGEN, JOHN, Massachusetts, was admitted freeman in 1646. Savage. ii. Winthrop.

GIRLING, RICHARD, Cambridge 1635. Dr. Holmes [Amer. Annals, i. 230] mentions a Girling, who was master of a ship in 1635.

GLOVER, CHARLES, Salem, was admitted to the church 10 May, 1640; freeman 1641; removed to Gloucester; selectman 1644. HABUKKUK, Boston, freeman 1650. 2 Coll. Mass. Hist. Soc. viii. 105. ‡*JOHN, Dorchester, a captain; representative

1637, 13 years; assistant in 1652 and 1653, died in Jan. 1654. Savage, i. Winthrop, 46, 212. Johnson calls him "a man strong for the truth; a plain, sincere, godly man, and of good abilities." Hist. N. E. 109. He had sons, John, Pelatiah, Nathaniel, who m. Mary Smith, and probably others. JOHN, son of the preceding, grad. at H. C. 1650, and was, as Rev. Dr. Harris believes, a physician at Roxbury. It seems from the H. C. catalogue that he received the degree of M. D. from the university of Aberdeen. JOHN, who grad. at H. C. in 1651, was probably son of Rev. Jesse Glover, who d. in 1639 on his passage to N. E., although Dr. Thomas, in his Hist. of Printing, considers the graduate of 1650, as son of the founder of the first printing establishment in North-America. NATHANIEL, son of the Hon. John Glover, was admitted freeman in 1654. Notice of Nathaniel Glover, of this family, who d. in London, 13 March 1726, is in ii. vol. Boston News-Letter, p. 59. *PELATIAH*, second minister of Springfield, was son of Hon. John Glover, and was born at Dorchester in 1637. He was educated at H. C., but did not receive a degree; was ordained 18 June, 1661, d. 29 March, 1692, æ. 55, leaving several children. His wife d. in 1689. RALPH, Massachusetts, requested to be admitted freeman 19 Oct. 1630, and d. before August, 1633. ||THOMAS, was a member of the ar. co. 1642.

GOARD, RICHARD, Roxbury, admitted freeman 1644, had sons, John, b. 1643; Benjamin, b. 1654.

GOBBLE, JOHN, Concord, with his son John, went to Fairfield with Rev. John Jones in Sept. 1644. This name exists in New-Jersey. Shattuck. THOMAS, Concord, admitted freeman 1634, d. 1657. His son Thomas d. 22 Nov. 1690. Ibid.

GODDARD, JOHN, Pascataqua 1631; Oyster-River [Durham, N. H.] 1669. Adams, Annals Portsmouth, 18. MS records.

GODFREY, EDWARD, Pascataqua 1632; Kittery 1652, was one of the aldermen of Agamenticus, [York] and governour of the province of Maine. Savage, i. Winthrop, 90. FRANCIS, a carpenter, lived in Bridgewater, and d. in 1669. JOHN, born in 1622, was an inhabitant of Andover. PETER, born in 1631, died 5 Oct. 1697. He married Mary Broune, the first native of Newbury, 13 May, 1656. She d. 16 April, 1716, in her 80th year. WILLIAM, Watertown, freeman 1640, perhaps removed to Hampton, where a deacon William Godfrey d. in 1671. His son Isaac was b. at Watertown 1639.

GODSON, FRANCIS, Lynn 1637. Lewis.

GOE, HENRY and RALPH, were among Captain Mason's company at Pascataqua 1631. Peter Goe lived at the Isles of Shoals in 1656.

GOFFE, *EDWARD, came to N. E. 1635. Cambridge, freeman 1636, representative 1646 and 1650, d. 26 Dec. 1658. His children were, Samuel, Lydia, Deborah, Hannah, and Abiah. Samuel was b. in England and left sons, Samuel, John, Nathaniel, and Joseph. JOHN, one of the proprietors and perhaps an inhabitant of Watertown, came to N. E. in 1630, in the fleet with Governour

Winthrop, and was admitted freeman, 18 May, 1631. He probably went to Newbury, and d. 9 Dec. 1641. WILLIAM, a major-general, and one of the judges of King Charles I., arrived at Boston in July 1660, lived at Cambridge a short time, which he left 26 Feb. 1661, for New-Haven, and lived in concealment in various places, and at last, took up his abode with Rev. John Russell at Hadley, where he was concealed 15 or 16 years, and where he is supposed to have died a. the year 1671. Stiles. Hist. of the Judges. Hutchinson, Hist. Mass.

GOLDING, WILLIAM, was present at the Thursday Lecture in Boston, 5 Nov. 1646, and sailed the same month for England. He had been the minister of Bermuda. Winslow, N. E. Salamander Discovered, 17.

GOLDSTONE, HENRY, Watertown, d. 25 July, 1638.

GOLDTHWAIT, THOMAS, Salem, freeman in 1634, was admitted a member of the church, 5 June, 1637.

GOLT, WILLIAM, Salem, was admitted to the church, 25 Aug. 1639, died a. 1660.

GOODALE, RICHARD, came from Yarmouth, England, and settled in Newbury, a. 1638; removed to Salisbury as early as 1644, and d. in 1666. Coffin. ROBERT, Salem, 1637. Written sometimes Goodall and Goodell.

GOODALL, RICHARD, one of the founders of the first Baptist church in Boston 1665.

GOODE, ROBERT, Massachusetts 1646. 2 Coll. Mass. Hist. Soc. iv. 110. One of the name grad. at Midd. Coll. in 1822.

GOODENOW, *EDMUND, Sudbury, freeman 1640, was the first lieutenant of the military band in that town, and afterwards the captain; representative in 1645 and 1650. His son Joseph was b. 1645. Johnson, Hist. N. E. 192. JOHN, Sudbury, freeman 1641, d. 28 March, 1655. John, perhaps his son, was born a. 1635. Revo. in N. E. justified. THOMAS, Sudbury, freeman 1643, was one of the grantees of Marlborough. His son Samuel was b. 1645.

GOODHUE, *JOSEPH, Ipswich, the eldest son of Deacon William Goodhue, was admitted freeman 1674; representative 1672 and 1673, a selectman and deacon, d. 2 Sept. 1697, leaving several children. His wife was Sarah, daughter of John Whipple. Hon. Benjamin Goodhue, H. C. 1766, a native of Salem, and senator in Congress, who d. 28 July, 1814, was his great-grandson. *WILLIAM, Ipswich, was born a. 1615, freeman 1636, selectman, deacon of the church 1658, representative 1666 and 1667, died in 1699 or 1700. His 1st wife was Margery Watson, by whom his children were Joseph, William, and Mary. He was one of the persons fined under the administration of Andros. See Revo. in N. E. justified, p. 16. *WILLIAM, Ipswich, 2d son of the preceding, one of the first deacons of the church at Chebacco, (now Essex) was admitted freeman 1681, representative 1691, selectman, captain, d. 12 Oct. 1712. His wife was Hannah Dane, by whom he had several children. Francis, one of them, was b. 4 Oct. 1678, grad. at H. C. 1699, and was the minister of Jamaica, L. I., and d. at Rehoboth, 15 Sept. 1707.

GOODMAN, JOHN, Plymouth 1620, one of the first pilgrims, d. in 1621. RICHARD, Cambridge 1632, was admitted freeman 1634.

GOODRIDGE, BENJAMIN, JEREMY, and JOSEPH, were inhabitants of Newbury in 1662. Thomas and Sewall Goodridge grad. at H. C. 1726 and 1764. The name of *Goodrich* has furnished 15 graduates at Yale College.

GOODWIN, EDWARD, Massachusetts, was admitted freeman in 1642. John Goodwin, whose four children were supposed to be under the power of witchcraft in 1688, lived in Boston. See Mather, ii. Magnalia, 396—403. *NATHANIEL, Reading, was elected representative in 1689. *WILLIAM, Cambridge, freeman 1632, was representative at the first general court of Massachusetts; removed, it is supposed, to Hadley, and was a ruling elder of the church there. Savage, i. Winthrop, 142. Sixteen of the name of Goodwin had grad. at the N. E. colleges in 1828.

GOODYEAR, STEPHEN, New-Haven colony, of which he was a magistrate in 1637 and deputy-governour in 1641, and generally continued in that office until 1656. His wife was lost in Mr. Lamberton's ship, which sailed in Jan. 1646. He d. in London 1657, leaving a respectable family. George Goodyear grad. at Y. C. in 1824.

GOOKIN, ‡‖*DANIEL, emigrated with his father, in 1621, from the county of Kent to Virginia, [Lord, i. Lempriere, 745] from whence he came to N. E. in 1644, principally on account of the preaching of the missionaries sent thither from N. E. in 1642. The Magnalia regards him as one of the " constellation" of converts made by the labours of Rev. William Thompson.

> " GOOKINS was one of *these :* by *Thompson's* pains,
> CHRIST and NEW-ENGLAND, a dear GOOKINS gains."

He was admitted a member of Boston church, 26 March, 1644, from whence he was dismissed to Cambridge, 3 Sept. 1648. He was admitted freeman 1644; member of the ar. co. 1645; representative of Cambridge 1649 and 1651; speaker of the house 1651, assistant 1652 to 1686, 35 years; elected major-general 11 May, 1681, and d. 19 March, 1687, æ. 75, leaving 3 sons. His daughter Mary m. Edmund Butler, of Salem. Hannah, perhaps his 2d wife, d. 28 Oct. 1689, æ. 48. *DANIEL*, minister of Sherburne, Mass., son of the preceding, was b. in Cambridge, 12 July, 1650, grad. at H. C. 1669, d. 8 Jan. 1718, æ. 67. In his house, accidentally burnt, is said to have perished his father's MS Hist. of New-England. *NATHANIEL*, minister of Cambridge, brother of the preceding, was b. in Cambridge, 22 Oct. 1656, grad. at H. C. 1675, ordained the successor of President Oakes, 15 Nov. 1682, d. 7 Aug. 1692, æ. 36. His son, Rev. Nathaniel Gookin, H. C. 1703, was b. at Cambridge, 15 April, 1687, ordained at Hampton, 1710, d. 25 Aug., 1734, æ. 48. He had a son, Rev. Nathaniel, who grad. at H. C.

C. 1731, was ordained the first minister of North-Hampton, N. H.
31 Oct. 1739, d. 22 Oct. 1766, æ. 54. The last Nathaniel was
father of Hon. Daniel Gookin, state counsellor of N. H. 1808, and
judge of probate from Dec. 1815 to 1827. SAMUEL, Cambridge,
sheriff of the county of Middlesex, was one of the youngest children
of Major-General Gookin, and was born 21 April, 1652. He was
sheriff in 1689. See Revo. in N. E. justified. His sons Samuel
and Nathaniel were b. 11 Nov. 1681, and 16 Feb. 1686.

GOOSE, WILLIAM, Salem, was admitted to the church, 6 Aug.
1637.

GORDON, JOHN, Bridgewater 1682. 2 Coll. Mass. Hist. Soc.
vii. 149. Nine of the name had grad. at the N. E. colleges in 1828.

GORE, ||JOHN, Roxbury, was admitted freeman 1637, member
of the ar. co. 1638, d. 4 June, 1657. John Gore, perhaps a son, d.
at Roxbury, 26 June, 1705. John Gore, a descendant, grad. at
H. C. 1702. The late Governour Gore is believed to have been of
this family.

GORGES, ROBERT, son of Sir Ferdinando Gorges, came to
N. E. in Sept. 1623, with sundry passengers and families to begin
a plantation. They settled at Weymouth, but soon left the place.
Prince, i. Annals 141. THOMAS, a cousin of Sir Ferdinando
Gorges, came to N. E. in the summer of 1640, and went to York,
where he was the first mayor. He returned to England in 1643.
Hutchinson, i. Hist. Mass. 163. Savage, ii. Winthrop, 9.

GORNHILL, JOHN, Dorchester 1636, was an early member of
the church. Dr. Harris.

GORTON, JOHN, Roxbury, d. 1636. John, probably his son,
was freeman in 1669, and his son John was b. in 1655. SAMUEL,
came to N. E. 1636, remained a short time at Boston, and from
thence went to Plymouth, and in June, 1638, went to Rhode-Island,
laid the foundation of Warwick, a. 1643; went to England in 1644,
arrived at Boston on his return in 1648, and proceded to Shawomet,
to which place he gave the name of Warwick, in honour of Robert
Rich, the earl of Warwick; officiated as a minister, and d. after
the year 1676, at an advanced age. Allen, Biog. Dict. 314-316.

GOSNOLD, BARTHOLOMEW, the Englishman, who first dis-
covered Cape Cod, 14 May, 1602, and who resided on the Elizabeth
Islands some time, is, perhaps, entitled to a place in this Register.
He d. in Virginia in 1607.

GOSS, JOHN, Watertown 1631. Rev. Thomas Goss, H. C.
1737, was the minister of Bolton, Mass.

GOTT, *CHARLES, Salem, arrived there in Sept. 1628, [Prince,
i. Annals, 174] with Governour Endicott; was a deacon of the
church; representative 1635, removed to Wenham, which he represented in 1654. He d. 1667 or 8. His son Charles was baptized in June, 1639.

GOUCH, JOHN, Kittery, freeman 1652. Perhaps this name
should be spelled *Gooch*, which has had three, Joseph, Joseph, and
James, who grad. at Harvard and Bowdoin in 1720, 1747, and 1823.

GOULD, JOHN, Charlestown, freeman 1638, had sons John, b. 1646; John 2d b. 1648. His first wife d. 1647. Sixteen persons of the name of Gould had grad. at the N. E. colleges in 1826. *JOHN, Topsfield, freeman 1664, was probably the same who was prosecuted under Andros' administration, and the representative in 1690. Hutchinson, i. Hist. Mass. 356. JARVICE, Hingham 1635, died at Boston, 27 May, 1656. NATHAN, Connecticut, was a magistrate or assistant in 1657, and named in the charter of Conn. granted in 1662. THOMAS, Boston, perhaps the freeman of 1641, d. 26 Oct. 1662. *THOMAS*, Charlestown, was one of the founders of the Baptist church, which was gathered at Charlestown, in May, 1665, and now the first Baptist church in Boston, and the first who officiated as minister. He d. in Boston in Oct. 1675. Shaw, Hist. Boston, 243. Benedict, i. Hist. Baptists, 385—391. ZACCHEUS, Lynn 1640, had a son Daniel. Lewis.

GOULDER, FRANCIS, Plymouth 1644. 2 Coll. Mass. Hist. Soc. iii. 184.

GOVE, JOHN, Cambridge 1657, had children Mary, John, Aspinwall, Nathaniel, and James. From him probably descended Jonathan Gove, H. C. 1768, of New-Boston, N. H. a physician of some eminence in that region.

GOWING, ROBERT, Dedham, freeman 1644, whose son John was b. 1645.

GOYT, JOHN, Marblehead 1648. Dana, Historical Discourse.

GRAFFORT, JARVIS, Salem 1637, who may be the same with Jervas Garford, which see. ‡THOMAS, Portsmouth, was a counsellor of the province of New-Hampshire in 1692. He m. Bridget Daniel, a widow, 11 Dec. 1684, and perhaps removed to Boston, where Mr. Thomas Graffort died 6 August, 1697.

GRAFTON, JOSEPH, Salem 1637, died in Barbadoes, in Feb. 1670. Savage, i. Winthrop, 332.

GRANGER, LANCELOT, Ipswich 1648, from thence to Newbury, where he died. From him descended the Hon. Gideon Granger, P. M. General of the U. S. Coffin. JOHN, Scituate 1640.

GRANNIS, EDWARD, Hadley 1671.

GRANT, CHRISTOPHER, Watertown 1634, had sons, Joshua, b. 1637; Caleb, 1639; Benjamin, b. 1641. EDWARD, Boston, died, according to an inscription copied into the Dorchester Sexton's Memorial, p. 29, 12 June, 1630, and was interred in the north burying ground. Mrs. Jane Grant was of Rowley 1643. JOHN, arrived at Salem 10 Oct. 1633, with Thomas Wiggin. Winthrop, i. Hist. N. E. 115. MATTHEW, Dorchester, came over in 1630, with Maverick and Warham, and was admitted freeman in 1631. SAMUEL, Boston 1640. SETH, Cambridge 1634, from whence he removed.

GRANTHAM, ANDREW, Newbury, d. 15 Dec. 1667.

GRAVES, JOHN, Roxbury, freeman 1637, d. 15 Nov. 1644. JOHN, Concord 1643, had sons, Benjamin, who married Mary Hoar 1668; John, who married Mary Chamberlain 1671; and Abraham. Shattuck. JOSEPH, Sudbury, aged a. 46 in 1689, [See Revo. in

N. E. Justified, 30] may have been son of Thomas Greaves, below. RICHARD, a pewterer, was a grantee of Salem in 1637, was of Lynn in 1638, and an inhabitant of Salem in 1655, and perhaps as early as 1640. SAMUEL, Lynn 1635, had a son Samuel, and his descendants remain. There was a Thomas Graves of Lynn in 1638, who d. 24 Jan. 1697. Lewis. THOMAS, Dorchester, perhaps the freeman in 1640, removed to Virginia, where he, and his wife, and divers of his children died. Winthrop, ii. Hist. N. E. 342.

GREAVES, THOMAS, Salem, arrived there in June, 1629, and went the same year to Charlestown, where he died 31 July, 1653. His son Joseph was b. 1645. There was a Thomas Graves who requested to be made free 19 October, 1630, who, Prince says, was afterwards a rear-admiral in England. Prince, i. Annals, 188. ii. 4. 2 Coll. Mass. Hist. Soc. ii. 164, 165. *THOMAS, Charlestown, perhaps son of the preceding, grad. at H. C. 1656, was representative in 1677 and 1678, a fellow of H. C., died 30 May, 1697, æ. 59. Hon. Thomas Greaves, of this family, grad. at H. C. 1703, was a judge of the supreme court of Mass. and died 19 June, 1747, æ. 63.

GRAY, ROBERT, Andover, b. about 1634, d. in 1718, æ. 84, leaving a son Robert, the ancestor of Rev. Robert Gray, H. C. 1786. Twenty-five of the name had grad. at the N. E. colleges in 1826. THOMAS, Marblehead 1631, where he was living in 1648. Savage, i. Winthrop, 85. Dana, Historical Discourse.

GREGSON, THOMAS, New-Haven. (See GRIGSON.)

GREELEY, ANDREW, was an early inhabitant of Salisbury. Samuel and Augustus Greele, brothers, from Wilton, N. H., grad. at Harv. and Dart. Coll. in 1802 and 1813. The former resides in Boston.

GREEN, BARTHOLOMEW, Cambridge, freeman 1634. His wife was Elizabeth. Many persons of this name have spelled it *Greene*, particularly the Rhode-Island family. The whole number of graduates (written both ways) at the N. E. colleges in 1826, was 56, eleven of whom had been ministers. *HENRY*, the first minister of Reading, resided some time in Watertown; was admitted freeman, 1640, ordained 5 Nov. 1645, and d. 11 Oct. 1648, [Rev. S. Danforth] though Governour Winthrop assigns the 3d mo. for his death, but some mistake may have been made in a numeral so much resembling the 8th. ‡HENRY, New-Hampshire, was one of the counsellors of that province in 1685. *HENRY, Malden, was representative in 1689. JAMES, Massachusetts, freeman 1647. ‖*JACOB, Charlestown, freeman 1650, member of the ar. co. 1650, representative in 1677, was son of the following. JOHN, Charlestown, was born in London, and came to N. E. in 1632, with his wife Perseverance, and 3 children, John, Jacob, and Mary. He was admitted freeman in 1642, was an elder of the church, and d. 22 April, 1658. Alden, Coll. of Epitaphs. 2 Coll. Mass. Hist. Soc. ii. 179. JOHN, Providence 1637, afterwards of Warwick, and it is supposed ancestor of General Nathaniel Greene, the distinguished revolutionary officer. Savage, i. Winthrop, 256, 286. ||JOHN, Cambridge, member of the ar. co. 1639. JOHN, freeman 1654, was probably of Salem. JOHN, Kittèry 1652. ‡JOHN, Rhode-Island, one of Sir Edmund Andros' council 1687. NATHANIEL, Cambridge, freeman 1645, was, with his wife, member of the church in 1658. PERCIVAL, Cambridge, freeman 1636, d. before 1658, leaving a widow, Ellen, who m. Thomas Fox, and two children, John and Elizabeth. Percival Greene, H. C. 1680, the first of the name at that institution, was his descendant according to W. Winthrop, and d. 10 July, 168–, æ. 25. RALPH, Boston, had a son John, b. in 1642. A John Green d. in Boston 1703, æ. 54. RICHARD, brother in-law of Thomas Weston, and one of the managers of his plantation at Weymouth, d. at Plymouth in 1622. Prince, i. Annals, 123. 2 Coll. Mass. Hist. Soc. ix. 82. ||RICHARD, member of the ar. co. 1638. SAMUEL, Cambridge, of Boston in 1686, [2 Coll. Mass. Hist. Soc. ii. 103] and perhaps the freeman 1635, was a printer and the great ancestor of many of the name, who have been known in this country for their devotion to the typographic art. He d. 1 Jan. 1702, æ. 87. His children were Elizabeth, Sarah, Samuel, Joseph, Deborah, Lydia, Jonas, and Bartholomew. His son Samuel was b. 6 March, 1648, lived in Boston, and d. in July, 1690, whose son Timothy was one of the first printers in Connecticut, and d. 5 May, 1757, æ. 78. Timothy had a son Samuel, who d. in May, 1752, æ. 40, and was the father of Timothy of New-London, who d, 10 March, 1796, æ. 59, and grandfather of Rev. William Green, D. C. 1791, an episcopal minister who settled at Fredericksburg, Va. SERGEANT, freeman 1636. THOMAS, Ipswich 1648. THOMAS, sen. died at Malden, 19 Dec. 1667. WILLIAM, Charlestown, freeman 1644.

GREENFIELD, SAMUEL, freeman 1635, was of Exeter 1645.

GREENHILL, SAMUEL, Cambridge 1635.

GREENLEAF, EDMUND, Newbury, freeman 1638, is mentioned by Johnson [Hist. N. E. 193] as " an ancient and experienced lieutenant," under captain Gerrish in 1644. He removed to Boston and d. there. *STEPHEN, son of the preceding was born a. 1630, may have been of Boston in 1657, but resided in Newbury, was admitted freeman 1677, elected representative in 1676 and 1686, was a captain of the militia, and d. 1 Dec. 1690. [Coffin.] His sons were, Stephen, b. 15 Aug. 1652; John, b. 21 June, 1662, d. 24 May, 1734; Samuel, b. 30 Oct. 1665; Tristram, b. 11 Feb. 1668; Edmund, b. 10 May, 1670. He had 3 daughters, who with the sons, all married.

GREENLAND, JOHN, Charlestown 1644, had a son John, b. 1644, and admitted freeman 1679. There was a Doctor Greenland of Newbury in 1665, whose name might be Henry.

GREENOUGH, WILLIAM, Boston 1656, a captain, d. 6 Aug. 1693. Eight of the name had grad. at college in N. E. in 1828.

GREENSMITH, ||STEPHEN, member of the ar. co. 1638. Winthrop, i. Hist. N. E. 214, 234.

GREENWAY, JOHN, an inhabitant of Dorchester in 1636, was perhaps the John Grinoway admitted freeman in 1631.

GRICE, CHARLES, Braintree, freeman 1651, d. 14 Nov. 1663. Josiah Grice d. at Boston in 1691.

GRIDLEY, ||RICHARD, Boston, freeman 1634, member of the ar. co. 1658, was a captain. See Savage, ii. Winthrop, 216. Snow, Hist. Boston 119. He had sons, Joseph, Believe, a member of the ar. co. in 1662 ; and Tremble, b. in 1642. Ten persons of the name had grad. at Yale, and two at Harvard, in 1826. THOMAS, was one of the first proprietors of Northampton in 1653.

GRIFFIN, HUGH, Sudbury, freeman 1645, d. 27 June, 1656. His son Shemuel was b. 1644. Four of the name had grad. at Y. C. in 1828, of whom was Rev. Edward D. Griffin, D. D., president of Williams College. JOHN, Connecticut 1646. I. Mather, Ind. Wars from 1614 to 1675, p. 63. *RICHARD, Concord 1635, admitted freeman 1638, representative 1639, 1640, was an elder of the church, and d. 5 Aug. 1661. He gave his property to Christopher Woolly. Shattuck. RICHARD, Massachusetts, was admitted freeman 1657.

GRIGGS, GEORGE, Boston 1636, d. 23 June, 1660. *JOSEPH, Roxbury, freeman 1653, was m. in 1654, representative 1680, d. 10 Feb. 1716, æ. 90. John Griggs, perhaps a brother d. at Roxbury, 23 Jan. 1692. THOMAS, Roxbury, 1639, d. 23 May, 1646.

GRIGSON ‡THOMAS, New-Haven, was one of the principal men, and an assistant of New-Haven colony, and the first settler of what now forms the town of East-Haven, at a place called Solitary Grove. He was lost at sea in Mr. Lamberton's vessel, which sailed from New-Haven in Jan. 1646. Jane, his widow, lived to a great age. His son Richard lived in London. His daughters were Mary, Anna, Susan, Sarah, Phebe, and 3 others. Dodd, East-Haven Register, 123.

GRIMES, SAMUEL, Boston, freeman 1642. A Mr. Grimes was of Plymouth in 1643.

GRINOWAY, JOHN, admitted freeman 1631. (See GREENWAY.)

GRISWOLD, FRANCIS, Cambridge 1637, freeman 1645. His wife was Mary, and their daughter Hannah was b. 1 March, 1644. The name on the Cambridge records is spelled Greshold, Greshould, and Grissell. Twenty-one of the name had in 1828 received the honours of Yale College. EDWARD, came from England in 1639. with Rev. E. Hewett and settled in Windsor. M'Clure.

GROSSE, ISAAC, Boston, admitted member of the church 1635. Savage, i. Winthrop, 248 ii. 216. EDMUND, Boston, d. 1 May, 1654, having a son Isaac, b. 1642, and probably others. Rev Thomas Gross grad. at D. C. 1784 and Nahum H. Groce grad. at H. C. in 1808.

GROSVENOR, JOHN, Roxbury, d. 26 Sept. 1691. William Grosvenor grad. at H. C. 1693. Twelve others of the name had grad. in N. E. in 1828.

GROUT, JOHN, Sudbury 1646, was born a. 1619, and was selectman 30 years, town clerk 7 years, d. 25 July, 1697, æ. 78. Shattuck. A John Grout of Watertown had a son, John born in 1641, who was probably admitted freeman 1680.

GROVER, ANDREW, Malden, d. 24 April, 1674. EDMUND, Salem 1637, d. June, 1683, æ. 82. Edward and Nehemiah Grover, of Beverly, were admitted freeman in 1678. Joseph and Stephen Grover, clergymen, grad. at D. C. in 1773 and 1786. JOHN, Charlestown 1634, had a son John, b. in 1640. A John Grover d. at Malden, 19 Feb. 1674. THOMAS, Charlestown 1640, whose son Lazarus was b. in 1642.

GRUBB, THOMAS, Boston, freeman 1634, had sons, John, b. 1638; Samuel, b. 1641; John, 1644; Herman, b. 1645. A Thomas Grubb d. at Boston, 15 July, 1692.

GUILD, SAMUEL, freeman 1642, was perhaps of Dedham. One of the same name was a grantee of Newbury, and d. at Haverhill, 21 Feb. 1683. Six of the name of Guild had grad. at H. C. in 1827.

GUILE, JOHN, Boston, was admitted freeman 1643. The name of *Gile* exists in Massachusetts.

GUNN, JOSEPH, was admitted freeman by the Mass. colony in 1636. Moses and Frederick Gunn grad. at Y. C. 1748, and 1810. THOMAS, Massachusetts, freeman 1635. John Gunn was a proprietor of Westfield in 1678.

GUNNISON, ‖*HUGH, Boston, admitted to the church 1634; member of the ar. co. 1646, perhaps was of Kittery in 1652, and the representative of Wells in 1654. He had sons Joseph and Elihu, born in Boston in 1640 and 1649.

GUPPIE, JOHN, Weymouth, freeman 1653. This name, written Guppy, is found in Dover, N. H. and its vicinity.

GURNELL, JOHN, Massachusetts, freeman 1643. Mr. Whitman in his Hist. of the Anc. and Hon. Art. Co., p. 153, gives the name of John Gumall, a member of the Co. in 1640, who may be the same as the preceding.

GURNEY, EDWARD, Cambridge 1636. John Gurney was an early inhabitant of Braintree, where his wife d. in 1661. The name exists in Plymouth county. Rev. David Gurney, H. C. 1785, was the minister of Middleborough, Ms.

GUTCH, ROBERT, Salem, was admitted to the church, 21 March, 1641, freeman 1642. He removed from Salem.

GUTTERIDGE, ‖JOHN, Boston, a tailor, was admitted member of the church 1642, member of the ar. co. 1640. His son Joseph was b. 1642. He is probably the same whom Mr. Savage from the colony records of Massachusetts, calls John Guttering, admitted freeman in 1642. RICHARD, Guilford 1650. WILLIAM, Watertown, 1636, had sons, Jeremiah, James, and Benjamin who were born in 1637, 1639, and 1642.

GUTTERSON, WILLIAM, Ipswich 1648, d. 26 June 1666.

GUY, NICHOLAS, Watertown, a deacon, was admitted freeman in 1639.

131

HACKBURNE, ABRAHAM, Boston, freeman 1639, had sons, Isaac, b. 1642; Joseph, b. 1652. SAMUEL, Massachusetts, was admitted freeman 1638.

HACKER, WILLIAM, Lynn 1643. Lewis. Possibly the same as Hagar below.

HADDEN, JERAD, or GARRAD, Cambridge 1632, [Holmes] freeman 1634, was one of the proprietors of Salisbury in 1640, where he was living in 1663. Andrew Hadden, an aged man, died in Rowley, 1701. GEORGE, perhaps a son of the early resident at Cambridge, grad. at H. C. in 1647.

HADLOCK, NATHANIEL, Charlestown, freeman 1646, went to Lancaster. Nathaniel, his son, was b. 1643. John Hadlock, of Concord, died 1675.

HAGAR, WILLIAM, Watertown, d. 10 Jan. 1685. Uriah Hagar, M. D., grad. at H. C. in 1798.

HAGGETT, HENRY, Massachusetts, was admitted freeman in 1670. The name of *Hackett* exists in Mass. and N. H.

HALE, JOHN, the first minister of Beverly, was son of Deacon Robert Hale, and was born at Charlestown, 3 June, 1636, grad. at H. C. 1657, was ordained 20 Sept. 1667, was chaplain in the expedition to Canada from 4 June to 20 Nov. 1690; d. 15 May, 1700, æ. 64. He m. (1) Rebecca Byles or Byley, 15 Dec. 1664; (2) Sarah Noyes, 31 March, 1684; (3) widow Elizabeth Clark, 8 August, 1698. He had sons, 1. Robert, born 3 Nov. 1668, grad. at H. C. 1686, was many years a magistrate in Beverly, and died 24 June, 1719, æ. 50; 2. James, b. 14 Oct. 1685, grad. at H. C. 1703, ordained the minister of Ashford, Conn., 26 Nov. 1718, died in Oct. 1742, æ. 57; 3. Samuel, b. 13 Aug. 1687, m. Apphia Moody, 29 May, 1714, settled in Newbury, and had sons, Samuel Hale, A. A. S., of Portsmouth, who grad. at H. C. 1740, and d. 10 July, 1807, æ. 89; Richard, of Coventry, Conn., the father of Nathan Hale, who was executed as a spy in the revolution; and John, of Gloucester; 4. John, b. 24 Aug. 1692. A daughter of Rev. John Hale m. Rev. John Chipman, of the 2d church, Beverly. Samuel Hale, of Portsmouth, had sons, Hon Samuel, of Barrington, N. H., who died 28 April, 1828; John, H. C. 1779, who d. 13 July, 1791, æ. 33; Hon. William, of Dover, and Thomas W. of Barrington. JOHN, Newbury, son of Thomas, of Newbury, was born a. 1636, and was admitted freeman 1678, and by 3 wives had sons, John, born 1661; Samuel, b. 1664; Thomas, b. 1668; Joseph, b. 1674; Benjamin, and Moses. Moses was b. 10 July, 1678, grad. at H. C. 1699, was the minister of Byfield parish, Ms. and d. Jan. 1743, æ. 65. Coffin. ||ROBERT, a deacon of Charlestown, and one of the founders of the church in 1632, was admitted freeman in 1634, member of the ar. co. 1644, an ensign of the military company, died 19 July, 1659. Two of his sons were, John, minister of Beverly, and Samuel, b. in 1644. THOMAS, Masssachusetts, was admitted freeman in 1634. THOMAS, a glover, born in 1604, came with his wife Tamosin, and settled in Newbury 1635, admitted freeman 1638, lived in Haverhill in 1646, afterwards in Salem, but d. in Newbury,

Dec. 1682.   He had 3 sons, who settled in Newbury, 1. Thomas, b. 1633, m. Mary Hutchinson, 26 May, 1657, d. 22 Oct. 1688, leaving sons *Thomas*, b. 11 Feb. 1659, was a magistrate, and d. 8 Jan. 1746, having had sons, Ezekiel, b. 1689; Ebenezer, b. 1695; Nathan, b. 1691; David, b. 1697; and *Samuel*, b. 6 June, 1674; 2. John, b. 1636, who is already noticed; 3. Samuel, who m. Sarah Ilsley in 1673.   Coffin.

HALL, EDWARD, Cambridge 1636, freeman 1638, perhaps the son of John Hall, of Lynn, and the one who d. there in 1669, whose wife was Sarah, and children were Joseph, Ephraim, Sarah, Elizabeth, Rebecca, and Martha.   Sixty-three persons of the name of Hall had grad. at the N. E. colleges in 1826.   Edward was one of the proprietors of Bridgewater in 1645.   There was an Edward Hall, of Braintree, whose son John was b. in 1651.   JOHN, Lynn, was admitted freeman 1634.   JOHN, freeman 1635, was perhaps of Salisbury 1640.   JOHN, Charlestown, perhaps the freeman in 1640, had a son John born in 1645.   RALPH, Exeter 1639.   Kingsley Hall, of Exeter, was appointed a provincial counsellor of N. H. in 1698.   RICHARD, Dorchester 1644, had son Jonathan born in 1659.   ROBERT, a blacksmith of Boston, was a member of the church in 1634. ||SAMUEL, a member of the ar. co. 1638, may have been the same who d. in Malden 1680.   Hutchinson, i. Hist. Mass. 46.   1 Coll. Mass. Hist. Soc. ix. 152.   *SAMUEL, Salisbury 1640, was representative 1655.   *STEPHEN, Stow, was the representative in 1689.   THOMAS, Cambridge 1648, had wife, Elizabeth, and three daughters in 1658.

HALLET, ANDREW, Lynn, removed to Sandwich 1637. Lewis.   One of the name is on the catalogue of Brown College.

HALLOWELL, GABRIEL, Plymouth colony, came to N. E. before 1631, and d. 1664, æ. 83.   WILLIAM, Boston, 1653, had sons, William and Benjamin, born in 1654 and 1656.

HALSALL, GEORGE, Boston, freeman 1645, had sons, Joseph, b. 1644; Benjamin b. 1654.

HALSEY, ||GEORGE, was member of the ar. co. 1650.   James Halsey, H. C. 1737, of Dedham, died April 1789, æ. 82.   Twelve others of the name had grad. at N. E., N. J., and Union colleges in 1828.   THOMAS, Lynn 1637.   Lewis.

HALSTEED, NATHANIEL, Dedham, freeman 1641, d. 3 Feb. 1644.   NATHAN, Concord 1642.   Shattuck.   WILLIAM, Concord, d. 27 July, 1645.

HAM, WILLIAM, Exeter 1646.   John Ham was of Dover in 1668.   John Ham grad. at D. C. in 1797.

HAMBDEN, JOHN, who came from London to N. E. in 1623, and "wintered with the Plymouth colonists," is supposed by Dr. Belknap to be the same person, who afterwards distinguished himself by his opposition to the arbitrary demands of Charles I. [Belknap, ii. Biog. 229.]   The illustrious patriot, John Hampden, was mortally wounded in Chalgrove field, Oxfordshire, while fighting against Prince Rupert, and d. 18 June, 1643.   He had contemplated a removal to America, but is said to have been prevented by express orders from the King.

HAMILTON, WILLIAM, Boston 1654, had a son Gustavus, b. in 1654. Sixteen of the name had received the honours of the N. E. and N. J. colleges in 1828.

HAMLET, JOHN, Boston, was admitted a member of the church in 1634. WILLIAM, Cambridge and Watertown, freeman 1651, removed to Billerica, and was one of the first Baptists there. His children were, Jacob, Rebecca, Sarah, and Thomas.

HAMLIN, ‡GILES, Connecticut, was an assistant in 1685. EZEKIEL, Boston 1655, had sons Ezekiel and Joseph.

HAMMERSTON, EDWARD, Cambridge, d. 24 Aug. 1646.

HAMMETT, THOMAS, Casco Bay 1658. Benjamin and William Hammett grad. at H. C. in 1766 and 1816.

HAMMOND, BENJAMIN, son of William and Elizabeth Hammond, a sister of William Penn, came from London to Sandwich, m. there in 1650, and removed to Rochester. His 2d son, John, m. Mary, daughter of Rev. Samuel Arnold. ‖*LAWRENCE, Charlestown and Boston, freeman 1666, was member of the ar. co. 1666; its lieutenant 1672; captain of the militia; representative of Charlestown 1672, six years, died at Boston, 29 July 1699. THOMAS, Hingham 1636, freeman 1637, perhaps the same who d. at Watertown 1655. Nathaniel Hammond d. at Newton 29 May, 1691. WILLIAM, freeman 1636, d. 8 Oct. 1662, æ. 94. Elizabeth Hammond, probably his widow, d. at Watertown 1669, æ. 90. Mr. Lewis names a William Hammond of Lynn 1636, who d. 1637.

HANCOCK, NATHANIEL, Cambridge 1635, d. before 1652. His son Nathaniel m. Mary Prentice, 8 March, 1664, and had Nathaniel, b. and d. 1655; Mary; Sarah; Nathaniel, 2d, b. 29 Oct. 1668; Abigail; Samuel, b. 2 Jan. 1673; Abigail; Elizabeth; Ebenezer, and Joseph. Rev. John Hancock, b. in 1671, was probably another son, although his birth is not found. He was father to Rev. John Hancock, of Braintree, whose son JOHN, b. 12 January 1737, was president of the congress which declared the colonies of America free and independent States on the memorable 4 July, 1776.

HANDFORTH, NATHANIEL, was b. 1608, was a haberdasher from London; settled in Lynn 1637, d. Sept. 1687, æ. 79.

HANDY, JOHN, Massachusetts, was admitted freeman in 1638. Perhaps this name should be *Hardy*, John, who was of Salem in 1638.

HANNUM, WILLIAM, was one of the first proprietors of Northampton, 1653.

HANFORD, THOMAS, first minister of Norwalk, came to N. E. as early as 1650, was probably the freeman in May, 1650, was ordained in 1654, and officiated, according to Mather, almost 40 years. His descendants are still in Norwalk, and are respectable.

HANMORE, JOHN, Scituate, between 1633 and 1657.

HANNIFORD, JOHN, Boston 1645, had sons, Samuel and John b. in 1645 and 1652.

HANSETT, ‖JOHN, Braintree 1644, was member of the ar. co. 1647. His son John b. 1641, d. at Roxbury 1654.

HARBOUR, JOHN, Braintree, a. 1654. By Jael, his wife, he
had several children.

HARCHER, WILLIAM, Lynn, 1636, removed to South-Hampton, L. I. a. 1640, but perhaps returned and died at Lynn in 1661.
Lewis.

HARDIER, ||JOHN, was member of the ar. co. 1641, perhaps
of Braintree. RICHARD, freeman 1648, d. at Braintree, 27 December 1657.

HARDING, ABRAHAM, Medfield, freeman 1645, d. 22 March,
1655. Son Abraham was born 1655. JOHN, Massachusetts, freeman 1640, may have been the representative of Medfield in 1689.
‡ROBERT, a captain, and one of the selectmen of Boston, was
admitted freeman in 1631, went to Rhode-Island, where he was an
assistant in 1641.

HARDMAN, JOHN, Lynn 1647. Lewis.

HARDY, JOHN, Salem 1637. Joseph Hardy was of Salem in
1648. RICHARD, Concord 1639. Shatuck. THOMAS, was
one of the 12 first settlers of Ipswich in 1633. Perry, in his Hist.
Sermon, at Bradford, p. 68, speaks of John and William Hardy,
brothers, who came to N. E. in the family of Gov. Winthrop as la-
bourers, to whom the governour gave land in Ipswich. Eight of
the name had grad. at D. C. in 1828.

HARKER, ANTHONY, Boston, was admitted freeman 1636.
JOHN, written also *Hurker*, was of Kittery, and admitted freeman
1652.

HARLAKENDEN, RICHARD, is mentioned by Dr. Holmes
in his Hist. Cambridge, as one of the proprietors of that town in
1632. ‡ROGER, a lieutenant-colonel, came from Earl's-Colne, in
Essex, in 1635, in the same ship with Sir Henry Vane, settled at
Cambridge ; was admitted freeman 1636, elected assistant 1636 to
1638, 3 years ; d. of the small pox, 17 Nov. 1638, leaving a widow
and two daughters. Savage, i. Winthrop, 277.

HARLOW, WILLIAM, Lynn 1637. Lewis. Rev. William
Harlow, Y. C. 1826, was ordained at Canton, 18 March, 1829.

HARMAN, NATHANIEL. (See HERMAN.) One of the name
grad. at D. C. in 1793.

HARNDALE, BENJAMIN, Lynn 1647.

HARNETT, EDWARD, Salem 1643. Edward, his son, was
admitted to Salem church in 1646.

HARPER, JOSEPH, was of Braintree at an early period.

HARRADEN, EDWARD, Gloucester 1664.

HARRIMAN, LEONARD, Rowley, was admitted freeman
1647. JOHN, a graduate at Harvard College in 1667, was a clergyman, and perhaps his son.

HARRINGTON, RICHARD, Charlestown 1643, freeman 1647.
ROBERT, Watertown 1642. Five of the name have grad. at H.
C. and 3 at Yale, Brown, and Vermont colleges.

HARRIS, ||ANDREW, was a member of the ar. co. 1639.
Twenty-eight of the name had grad. at the N. E. and N. J. colleges
in 1828. ||ANTHONY, member of the ar. co. 1644, belonged to

Ipswich in 1648. ARTHUR, one of the first settlers of Bridgewater 1645, removed to Boston, according to Mr. Mitchell, and died there. GEORGE, Salem 1637. Joseph, of Salem 1652, was probably his son. JOHN, Rowley, cousin of Rev. N. Rogers, was admitted freeman in 1647, and had children Ezekiel, Nathaniel, John, and Mary. Felt. William and Thomas Harris were of Rowley a. 1650. RICHARD, Cambridge, d. 29 August, 1644. ROBERT, Roxbury, admitted to the church, 8 Aug. 1647, freeman 1650. ‡THOMAS, Providence 1637, was an assistant under the first charter 1654, and under the second, from Charles II, from 1666 to 1669, four years, died 1685. His son Thomas d. 22 Feb. 1711, whose son Thomas was b. 19 Oct. 1665, d. 1 Nov. 1741, leaving sons, Henry, Thomas, Charles, Gideon, and Wait. He had also a son Nicholas. THOMAS, Boston, a. 1680, from Patuxet, R. I., and probably a descendant from the R. I. stock, d. 5 Jan. 1679, leaving a son Benjamin, b. 1694, d. 1722, whose son Cary, b. 10 Feb. 1720, d. 20 Jan. 1750, was father of Captain William Harris, b. 7 July, 1744, for several years an instructer of youth in Boston and Charlestown, and in 1776, an officer in the revolution. He d. at Sterling, Ms., 30 Oct. 1778, æ. 34. Rev. Thaddeus Mason Harris, D. D., of Dorchester, H. C. 1787, is a son of Captain Harris. THOMAS, Ipswich 1648, perhaps also of Rowley. WALTER, Massachusetts, freeman 1641. WILLIAM, Salem 1635, removed to R. I. 1636, with Roger Williams; in 1678, sailed for England, and was taken by a Barbary corsair, 24 Jan. 1679, carried to Algiers and sold in the market, and remained in captivity more than a year; was redeemed at the cost of $1200; travelled through Spain and France, and arrived at London, 1680, and d. before Feb. 1681. His children were, 1. Andrew, b. 1634 or 1635, m. Mary Tew, of Newport 1670, d. 5 May, 1686, leaving Mary and Toleration; 2. Toleration, b. 1645, killed by the Indians, 1675; 3. Mary; 4. Howlong, who m. Arthur Fenner, in 1684. Rev. T. M. Harris, D. D. Ms. letter.

HARRISON, ‖EDWARD, Boston, member of the ar. co. 1638. JOHN, Boston, freeman 1641, had a son John b. in 1652. Mark, signed the application 1654, in Hutchinson's Coll. 255. ‖RICHARD, was member of the ar. co. 1646. *THOMAS*, who according to Calamy [ii. Account, 122] was bred in N. E., went to England, and was a celebrated preacher in London, became a doctor of divinity, and succeeded Dr. Thomas Goodwin. There is a note by Mr. Savage, [ii. Winthrop, 336] respecting a Mr. Harrison, perhaps the same.

HART, JOHN, Salem, admited to the church, 30 Sept. 1638; was of Marblehead in 1648, and d. 1656. Twenty of the name had grad. at the N. E. colleges in 1828. ISAAC, Lynn 1640, removed to Reading 1647. EDMUND, Weymouth, was admitted freeman 1634. NATHANIEL, Ipswich 1636. Thomas Hart, of Ipswich 1648, d. there, 8 March, 1674. SAMUEL, Lynn 1640. Lewis. STEPHEN, Cambridge 1632, freeeman 1634.

HARTSHORN, THOMAS, Reading, was admitted freeman 1648. Descendants are in Amherst, N. H. The late Rev. Levi

Hartshorn, one of them, grad. at D. C. 1813, was the minister of the first church in Gloucester, Ms., and d. 27 Sept. 1819, æ. 30.

HARTWELL, WILLIAM, Concord, freeman 1642, a petitioner for the grant of Chelmsford, died 12 March, 1690. He had sons, John, b. 1640; Samuel, b. 1645, m. Ruth Wheeler 1665; William; Martha. His descendants are numerous in Lincoln, Bedford, Ms., and New-Ipswich, N. H. Shattuck, MS Hist. Concord.

HARVARD, JOHN, a minister of Charlestown, was educated at Emmanuel College, Cambridge; came to N. E. a. 1636; was admitted freeman, 2 Nov. 1637; d. at Charlestown, 14 Sept. 1638, leaving £779. 17. 2. for the college which perpetuates his name. He left a wife, but probably no children.

HARVEY, *THOMAS, Amesbury, a captain of the militia, was representative at the Dec. session 1690, and Feb. session 1691. Four of this name had grad. in 1826 at Yale and Dartmouth, viz : Rufus, Y. C. 1783; Joseph, D. C. 1794; Matthew, D. C. 1806, a member of congress, and Rev. Joseph, Y. C. 1808. WILLIAM, Boston, freeman 1647, d. 15 August, 1658. He had sons, Thomas, b. 1641; William, b. 1651; Thomas, 2d, b. 1652; Increase, b. 1654.

HARWOOD, GEORGE, Boston, had a son John born in 1639. George Harwood, of London, was treasurer of Mass. company in 1629. HENRY, Boston, came to N. E. as early as 1630, and was admitted freeman 1633. Winthrop, [i. Hist. N. E. 40.] mentions one Harwood, "a godly man," who, Mr. Savage supposes, was Henry Harwood of Boston. HENRY, Salem, was admitted freeman 1643. JOHN, Boston, was admitted freeman 1649.

HASKELL, ROGER, Salem 1637, died in 1667. TOBIAS, Lynn 1645. Lewis. *WILLIAM, representative of Gloucester 1672, 1679, 1681, to 1683, and 1685, and a lieutenant. Six of the name had grad. at the N. E. colleges in 1828.

HASSARD, THOMAS, was a ship-carpenter, and lived in Boston, and was a member of the church, and admitted freeman 1636. Of the name of *Hazard* there have been six graduates at Brown, and two at N. Jersey, College.

HASSELL, JOHN, Ipswich 1636, was admitted freeman 1637. RICHARD, Cambridge, freeman 1647, had, by Joanna, his wife, Joseph and Hester, b. in 1645 and 1648.

HASTINGS, JOHN, Braintree, freeman 1645, removed to Cambridge in 1656, and was a deacon of the church. His children were Walter and Samuel, born in England, and John, Seaborn, and Elizabeth, baptized at Braintree. He is the ancestor of the graduates of this name at Harvard College. THOMAS, freeman 1635, was deacon of the church in Watertown, and perhaps the representative of that town in 1673. WALTER, Cambridge 1659, son of Deacon John Hastings, had children, John, b. 2 Dec. 1660, grad. at H. C. 1681; Walter, b. 1662; Nathaniel, b. and d. 1669, Hannah, Sarah, and Elizabeth.

HATCH, PHILIP, Kittery, was admitted freeman 1652. THOMAS, Massachusetts, freeman 1634. WILLIAM, Scituate 1633, died in 1652.

HATHAWAY, EPHRAIM, came to N. E. a. 1670, with his brothers Isaac and Jacob, and settled first at Taunton, that part now Dighton, where his male posterity remain. John Hathaway, esq., of that place, the oldest now living, has sons, John ; Ephraim ; Ephraim A. ; Francis ; and Rev. George W. Hathaway, an Episcopal clergyman. Isaac and Jacob, brothers of Ephraim, settled in Freetown, and their descendants are very numerous in Bristol county. Thirteen of the name had grad. at the N. E. colleges in 1826. MS letter of G. W. Hathaway.

HATHERLY, TIMOTHY, an assistant of Plymouth colony 1636, 21 years, came to N. E. in the ship Ann, which arrived at Plymouth in July, 1623. He d. in 1666, leaving no children. 2 Coll. Mass. Hist. Soc. iv. 241.

HATHORNE, *‡WILLIAM, Dorchester, freeman 1634, representative May, 1635, and Dec. 1636 ; removed to Salem, and admitted to the church, 12 June, 1637, representative Sept. 1637, and 20 years afterwards, speaker of the house 1644, 7 years ; captain of the militia 1645 ; major 1656 ; assistant 1662 to 1679, 18 years ; d. about 1681, æ. 74. His sons were, Eleazar, b. 6 August, 1637 ; Nathaniel, born 28 August, 1639 ; John, and perhaps others, whose descendants remain in Salem. JOHN, Salem, probably brother of the preceding, was admitted to the church 1 Oct. 1643, and d. 12 Dec. 1676. ‡*JOHN, Salem, son of the Hon. William Hathorne, was born 4 August, 1641, admitted freeman 1677 ; elected representative 1683 ; assistant 1684 to 1686 ; one of the first counsellors under the charter of William and Mary, 1692 ; died 10 May, 1717, æ. 76. NATHANIEL, probably brother of William and John, was of Lynn in 1634. Lewis.

HAUGHTON, HENRY, was an elder of the church in Salem, and d. in 1629. Felt, Annals Salem.

HAULEY, *JOSEPH, was representative of Northampton in 1683, 1685, 1691 and onward, was probably the graduate at H. C. in 1674, and the ancestor of Col. Joseph Hawley, an estimable character of Northampton, born in 1724, educated at Yale College, and d. in 1788, æ. 64. See Tudor's life of Otis, and Hutchinson, iii. Hist. Mass. 295. ROBERT, whose name in the colony records is spelled *Haule*, was admitted freeman in 1644. THOMAS, Roxbury, was slain by the Indians with Capt. Wadsworth and others, 27 April, 1676. His wife d. 1651. He had a son Joshua born in 1654.

HAVEN, RICHARD, came from the west of England, and settled at Lynn 1645, had a wife Susanna, who died 7 Feb. 1682, and 12 children. The sons were, Joseph, b. 22 Feb. 1650 ; Richard, b. 25 March, 1651 ; John, b. 1656 ; Samuel, b. 1660 ; Jonathan, b. 1662 ; Nathaniel, b. 1664 ; and Moses, b. 1667. [Lewis.] Joseph was one of the first settlers of Framingham, Mass., and was grandfather of Rev. Samuel Haven, D. D. of Portsmouth, who was born 4 August, 1727, grad. at H. C. 1749, was ordained 6 May, 1752, d. 3 March, 1806, æ. 79. The late excellent and esteemed Nathaniel Appleton Haven, born 14 Jan. 1790, grad. at H. C. 1807, died at

Portsmouth, 3 June, 1826, was grandson of Dr. Haven, being son of Hon. N. A. Haven, H. C. 1779, and member of congress from N. H. from 1809 to 1811.

HAWCHETT, JOHN, Massachusetts, freeman 1637. The name of Hanchet was in Roxbury, and John Hanchet, d. there in Feb. 1684.

HAWES, BARNABAS, Dorchester 1637. RICHARD, Dorchester, was admitted freeman 1638. ROBERT, Salem, a. 1645. WILLIAM, Boston 1652.

HAWKE, ADAM, Lynn 1637. Lewis. JOHN, Lynn, came over in 1630, and was admitted freeman 1634. Mr. Lewis says he died 5 August, 1694. MATTHEW, came from Cambridge, England, and settled at Hingham 1638, where he was the second town clerk. He was admitted freeman 1642. Lincoln, Hist. Hingham, 46.

HAWKESWORTH, THOMAS, Salisbury 1640, d. 8 October, 1651. Coffin.

HAWKINS, ABRAHAM, was admitted freeman 1645, and d. 6 Jan. 1648. ‡ANTHONY, one of the associates named in the charter of Connecticut, 20 April, 1662, was elected assistant in 1668. JAMES, Boston 1648, had a number of sons. William Hawkins d. at Boston in 1693. ROBERT, Massachusetts, came to N. E. in 1630, and was admitted freeman 1636. ‖*THOMAS, a captain, and representative in 1639, lived in Dorchester and Boston, was admitted freeman 1639; member of the ar. co. 1644, and died abroad about the year 1654. Savage, ii. Winthrop, Index. He had sons Abraham and Job, who were born in 1636 and 1640. TIMOTHY, Watertown 1638, had a son Timothy born there in 1639.

HAWLEY, ROBERT, and others. (See HAULEY.)

HAYBORNE, SAMUEL, Roxbury 1639, d. 27 Dec. 1642. His son John was born 1640.

HAYDEN, JAMES, Charlestown, freeman 1637, had sons, James, b. 1637; John, born 1639, d. 1675. WILLIAM, Windsor 1640. JOHN, freeman 1634, was of Braintree 1640, and had sons, Jonathan, b. 1640; Ebenezer, b. 1645; Nehemiah, b. 1647.

HAYES, ROBERT, Ipswich 1638. Felt. Eight of the name had grad at the N. E. colleges in 1828.

HAYNES, ‡JOHN, Cambridge, came to N. E. 1633, from Copford-Hall in Essex, in company with Rev. Thomas Hooker, was admitted freeman in 1634, elected an assistant in 1634 and 1636, and governour in 1635. He removed to Connecticut in 1636, settled at Hartford, was elected the first governour of that colony in April, 1639, and every second year afterwards, until his death in 1654. By two wives he had 8 children, Robert, Hezekiah, John, Roger, Mary, Joseph, Ruth, and Mabel, the last three by the second wife. Hezekiah enjoyed Copford-Hall, which descended to his heirs. Robert d. in England without issue. Roger came to N. E. but returned. Trumbull, i. Hist. Conn. 216, 217. *JOHN*, son of the preceding, came to N. E. with his father, grad. at H. C. 1656, returned, and was admitted to the degree of Master of Arts at Cambridge, England, and was settled in the ministry at, or near, Colchester, in Essex, where he left issue. Ibid 216. *JOSEPH*, brother of the preceding, grad. at H. C. 1658, became the minister of Hartford, and d. 24 May, 1679, leaving one son, John, a magistrate, and judge of the superiour court of Conn., who grad. at H. C. 1689, and had sons who d. without issue. JOHN, Sudbury 1640, freeman 1646, was representative 1669. He may be the John Haynes who was one of the selectmen 18 years, and deacon of the church, who died 11 Dec. 1710. JAMES, Massachusetts, freeman 1638. SAMUEL, Portsmouth, a deacon and one of the founders of the church 1671, m. Mary Fifield, 9 Jan. 1673, and had sons, Matthias, b. 7 March, 1677; William, b. 7 Jan. 1679; Samuel, b. 5 July, and 3 daughters. His descendants, of which there are many in N. H., write the name *Haines*. Mr. Coffin gives me the name of Samuel Haines, born in 1611, who came from London and was wrecked at Pemaquid in August, 1635. THOMAS, Sudbury, d. 28 July, 1640. *WALTER, Sudbury, freeman 1640, representative 1641, 1644, 1648, 1651, one of the selectmen 10 years, died 14 Feb. 1665. WILLIAM, Salem, was admitted to the church 1648.

HAYWARD, GEORGE. (See HEYWOOD.) JAMES, Woburn, d. 20 Nov. 1642. *JOHN, Watertown 1640, perhaps also at Dedham, and the representative in 1645. A John Hayward died at Charlestown, 29 Dec. 1672. JOHN, spelled also Hayward and Howard, was brought up in the family of Captain Myles Standish, was a carpenter, and lived in Bridgewater; represented that town at Plymouth court 1678. He was the ancestor of Rev. Simeon Howard, of Boston, H. C. 1758, who d. 13 Aug. 1804, æ. 71, Rev. Zechariah Howard, of Canton, Mass., H. C. 1784, and of Rev. Bezaleel Howard, D. D.. of Springfield, Mass., who grad. at H. C. 1781. ROBERT, Northampton 1659. SAMUEL, Charlestown, was admitted freeman 1649; perhaps also of Boston, where Samuel, son of Samuel Hayward, was born 1646. THOMAS, Cambridge 1635, Bridgewater 1651, d. in 1681. *WILLIAM, Hampton, freeman 1640, was representative from 1641 to 1645, five years.

HAYWOOD, JOHN, was made postmaster of the whole colony of Massachusetts in 1678. Felt, Annals, 260.

HAZELTINE, JOHN, Rowley, was admitted freeman 1640, removed to Bradford. ROBERT, Rowley, freeman 1640, m. Ann, his wife, in Oct. 1639, and his was the first marriage in Rowley.

HAZEN, EDWARD, was of Rowley 1650. Richard Hazzen was a constable of Haverhill in 1702. Richard Hazzen, perhaps his son, grad. at H. C. 1717, and d. at Hampstead, N. H.

HEALD, JOHN, Concord, freeman 1641, according to tradition, came from Berwick, England. He d. 24 May, 1662. By Dorothy, his wife, he had 4 sons and 4 daughters. John and Gershom were two of the sons. Shattuck.

HEALEY, WILLIAM, Cambridge 1645, had children, Hannah, Elizabeth, Sarah, William, Grace, Nathaniel, Martha, Samuel, Paul, and Mary. THOMAS, Cambridge 1635.

HEARD, JOHN, Dover, had children, Benjamin, born 20 Feb. 1644; Mary; Abigail; Elizabeth; Hannah; John, b. 24 Feb. 1659; Joseph, b. 4 Jan. 1661; Samuel, b. 4 Aug. 1663; Catharine; Tristram, b. 4 March, 1667. His wife was Elizabeth, who escaped destruction when Major Waldron and many others were killed in 1689. See the 1st vol. of Belknap's Hist. N. H. , sub anno 1689. JOSEPH, Massachusetts, was admitted 1657. LUKE, Newbury, was admitted freeman 1639, went to Salisbury, thence to Ipswich, and died a. 1647, leaving two sons, John and Edward, and a widow Sarah, who was a Wyatt, from Assington, Essex. THOMAS, Pascataqua 1631. WILLIAM, Plymouth 1623.

HEATH, BARTHOLOMEW, was born a. 1600, settled in Newbury, where his son John was b. 15 Aug. 1653. Coffin. *ISAAC, Roxbury, freeman 1636, was representative in 1637 and 1638, perhaps d. 29 Dec. 1694. ISAAC, Roxbury, freeman 1652, had a son Isaac, b. in 1655, and d. 12 Nov. 1684. *ISRAEL, Roxbury, appears to have been representative in 1636, 1637. PELEG, Roxbury, was admitted freeman 1652. *WILLIAM, Roxbury, freeman 1634, was representative at the first general court at Boston, 14 May 1634, and in 1637, 1639 to 1642, six years, and in 1645 for Dover. He d. 30 May, 1652.

HEATON, NATHANIEL, Massachusetts, freeman 1636. Samuel and Rev. Stephen Heaton grad. at Y. C. in 1728 and 1733.

HEDGE, JOHN, born a. 1610, came to N. E. and settled at Lynn, 1634. WILLIAM, Lynn, freeman 1634, perhaps to Sandwich 1637. One of this name was one of the first settlers of East-Hampton, L. I. 1650.

HEMAN, FRANCIS, Massachusetts, freeman 1646.

HEMINGWAY, RALPH, Roxbury, freeman 1634, d. 12 June, 1699. He had sons, John b. 1641; Joshua, b. 1643. His descendants write the name *Hemenway* and *Hemmenway*, two of whom, Rev. Phinehas and Rev. Moses, D. D. grad. at H. C. in 1730 and 1755. SAMUEL, New-Haven 1662, d. 20 Sept. 1711, æ. 75. Rev. James Heminway grad. at Y. C. in 1704.

HENCHMAN, ||DANIEL, Boston, a member of the ar. co. 1675, was a distinguished captain in Philip's war. THOMAS, Chelmsford. (See HINCHMAN.) WILLIAM, Boston 1653.

HENING, RICHARD, Newbury 1674. The name of *Hennen* exists in New-England.

HENDRICK, *DANIEL, Haverhill, was born a. 1610, representative in 1681, and was living in 1700.

HENRICKSON, PETER, Boston, had a son John, b. in 1642.

HEPBURN, GEORGE, Massachusetts, was admitted freeman 1636. Samuel Hepburn grad. at N. J. College in 1803.

HERBERT, JOHN, Salem 1637, freeman 1641, went to South-Old, L. I. SYLVESTER, Boston 1652.

HERMAN, NATHANIEL, Braintree 1640, freeman 1643, had a son Nathaniel, b. in 1640.

HERRICK, HENRY, Salem 1629, was admitted freeman 1631, was one of the founders of the church in Beverly 1667, d. in 1670.

WILLIAM, was one of the grantees named in the Indian deed of South-Hampton, L. I. 1640.

HERRING, THOMAS, Massachusetts, freeman 1654. This name has existed in the state of N. J.

HERSEY, ||WILLIAM, Hingham 1635, freeman 1638, member of the ar. co. 1652, had a son William, who was m. in 1656. Lincoln says the name is written in the Hingham records *Hersie, Harsie,* and *Hearsey.*

HETHERSAY, ROBERT, Charlestown, 1641. Coffin.

HETT, THOMAS, Hingham 1637, was admitted freeman 1642. Winthrop, ii. Hist. N. E. 129. A Thomas Hett, sen., d. at Charlestown 6 June, 1668.

HEWENS, JACOB, Dorchester, was admitted to the church 1658 ; freeman 1660. Son Samuel was b. 1658. James Hewins grad. at H. C. in 1804.

HEWES, EDWARD, Massachusetts, freeman 1636. JOHN, Scituate 1639, Plymouth 1643. ||*JOSHUA, Roxbury, freeman 1634, was representative in 1641 ; member of the ar. co. 1643, (spelled *Hughes* by Whitman) had sons, Joshua, b. 1639 ; Joshua, 2d, b. 1639, and perhaps d. at Boston 1706. ||Joseph, member of the ar. co. 1637, probably belonged to Lynn. RICHARD, Dorchester 1637. ROBERT, Lynn 1642.

HEWETT, EPHRAIM, minister of Windsor, d. 4 Sept. 1644. Johnson, [Hist. N. E. 222] in some elegiac verses on several of the ministers who had died before 1650, says,

" And *Huet* had his arguings strong and bright,"

but the name is erroneously printed *Hest,* in the copy of his work published in ii. Coll. Mass. Hist. Soc. viii 25. NICHOLAS, Boston. had a son Zebadiah, b. in 1644.

HEYDEN, JOHN. (See HAYDEN.)

HEYMAN, JOHN, Charlestown, 1677. Spelled also *Heman* and *Hayman.* *SAMUEL, Watertown, representative 1690, was one of the counsellors named under the charter of William and Mary, granted in 1691.

HEYWOOD, GEORGE, Concord, one of the earliest settlers, d. 14 April, 1671 ; had sons, John, b. 1640, m. Anna White 1671 ; Joseph, b. 1643, m. Hannah Hosmer 1665 ; Simon ; George, b. 1654. Shattuck, MS Hist. Concord. JOHN, Concord, m. Susanna Atkinson 1656, who d. 1665 ; m. Sarah Symonds in 1665, by whom he had John, b. 1662 ; Benone, b. 1666 ; William, b. 1674, and several daughters. He d. 11 Jan. 1707. Ibid. Five of the name had grad. at Harv. and Dart. in 1828.

HIBBERT, ROBERT, Salem 1646, afterwards of Beverly, and d. there, 7 May, 1684, æ. 72. Joseph Hibbert d. there 1701, æ. 53. Rev. Thomas Hibbert, of Amesbury, grad. at H. C. 1748, and d. Sept. 1793, æ. 60. This name is also spelled *Hebard* and *Hibbard.* Rev. Augustine Hibbard grad. at D. C. in 1772.

HIBBINS, ‡*WILLIAM, a merchant of Boston, freeman 1640, representative 1640, 1641, was elected assistant 1643 to 1654, twelve years, d. 23 July, 1654. His widow Anne was executed in June, 1656, for the supposed crime of witchcraft. Hutchinson, i. Hist. Mass. 173.

HICHBORN, DAVID, Boston 1654. Benjamin, Benja. A., and Doddridge C. Hichborn grad. at H. C. in 1768, 1802, and 1816.

HICKS, RICHARD, Boston 1649, had sons Timothy, b. 1649, and Richard, b. 1656. ROBERT, Plymouth 1623. ZECHARI-AH, Cambridge 1657, had sons, Zechariah, b. 1657; John, b. 1660; Thomas.

HIDE, EDMUND. (See HYDE.)

HIGGINS, ABRAHAM, Salem 1637. JOHN, Boston, 1655. RICHARD, Eastham 1644.

HIGGINSON, FRANCIS, one of the first ministers of Salem, was educated at Emmanuel College in Cambridge ; came to N. E. in June, 1629, was ordained at Salem, 6 August, 1629, and d. in August, 1630, leaving a wife and eight children. His son Francis, was admitted a member of the church in Salem, 14 April, 1639 ; went to England, and was settled the minister of Kirkby-Steven, in Westmoreland, where he died a. 1670, in his 55th year. *JOHN,* the sixth minister of Salem, son of the preceding, was b. 6 Aug. 1616, came to N. E. with his father, was a preacher in 1637, and officiated some time as chaplain at Saybrook fort; removed in 1641 to Guilford ; in 1659 to Salem, where he was ordained in August, 1660, d. 9 Dec. 1708, æ. 92, having been a minister of the gospel 72 years. *JOHN, Salem, son of the preceding, was admitted freeman 1677, was representative in 1689. His son John was born in August, 1675, and m. Hannah Gardner, 11 Sept. 1695, and had a son John, b. 10 Jan. 1698, grad. at H. C. 1717, was register of deeds, and d. in July, 1746.

HIGGS, JOHN, perhaps Hicks, d. at Boston, 22 Oct. 1693.

HILDRETH, RICHARD, Cambridge, freeman 1642, was a petitioner for the grant of Chelmsford in 1653, where many of his descendants have resided. Sarah, his wife, d. 15 June, 1644, and by another, Elizabeth, he had Sarah, b. 8 Aug. 1648.

HILL, ABRAHAM, Charlestown, freeman 1640, d. at Malden, 13 Feb. 1670. Two of his sons were, Isaac, b. 29 Oct. 1641, who m. Hannah Hayward in 1666; and Abraham, b. Oct. 1643, who had a son Abraham, b. in Aug. 1670. He is the ancestor of the Hills of Cambridge, and of several families in New-Hampshire. Thirty persons of the name of Hill had grad. at the N. E. colleges in 1826. ||JOHN, Dorchester, freeman 1642, member of the ar. co. 1643, had a son Samuel, b. in 1640. Jonathan Hill of Dorchester went early to Dorchester. John Hill was of Medfield in 1658. JOHN, Boston, a blacksmith, was a member of the church in 1640. There was a John Hill of Rowley before 1652, and a John Hill of Beverly in 1659. ||JOHN, a merchant, was admitted to the church in Boston 1645, freeman 1646; member of the ar. co. 1647, was a captain of the militia. Snow, Hist. Boston 124. *JOSEPH, Malden. (See HILLS.) PETER, Saco 1652. RALPH, one of the first settlers of Billerica, in 1653, d. 29 Nov. 1663, leaving sons, Ralph, Jonathan, and Nathaniel, who all settled in Billerica. *RALPH, Billerica, son of the preceding, was representative in 1689, 1692, 1693, and 1694 ; was a captain of the militia, and a selectman 11 years ; d. 2 May, 1695. RICHARD, New-Haven 1639. THOMAS Plymouth 1638. WILLIAM, Concord, freeman 1633, removed to Fairfield Sept. 1644, with Rev. John Jones. Shattuck. WILLIAM, Massachusetts, freeman 1634. WILLIAM, Windsor 1640. ||*VALENTINE, Boston 1638, freeman 1640, member of the ar. co. 1638, representative 1652 to 1655 and 1657, d. 1662. He m. Mary, daughter of Governour Eaton, of New-Haven.

HILLIARD, ANTHONY, Hingham 1638.   Lincoln, Hist. Hingham. EMANUEL, Hampton, was lost with six others in a boat going from Hampton, 20 Oct. 1657. Timothy Hilliard, perhaps his son, was of Hampton, in 1686, and was probably the ancestor of Rev. Timothy Hilliard H. C. 1764, of Barnstable and Cambridge, who was born in Kensington, N. H., and d. 9 May, 1790, æ. 43. HUGH, Massachusetts, freeman 1644. JOB, Salem 1653, is styled a fisherman. WILLIAM, Boston 1642.

HILLYER, JOHN, Windsor, 1640.

HILTON, EDWARD, the father of the settlement of New-Hampshire, came from London, and settled at Dover in the spring of 1624, where he resided from 15 to 20 years, and then removed to Squamscot Patent, or Exeter, and d. a. 1671, leaving an estate apprised at £2204. His sons, Edward, William, Samuel, and Charles were his administrators. EDWARD, the eldest son of the preceding, m. ˙Ann, the daughter of Rev. Samuel Dudley, and grand-daughter of Governours, Dudley and Winthrop, and had children, Winthrop, Dudley, Joseph, Jane, Ann, Mary, and Sobriety, and d. in 1699. Winthrop, the eldest son, born a. 1671, was appointed a counsellor of N. H., but did not serve ; was a distinguished officer in the wars with the Indians, by whom he was killed in June 1710. Farmer and Moore, i. Hist. Coll. 241—251. *WILLIAM, brother of Edward Hilton, with whom he settled at Dover in 1623, appears to have been at Plymouth in 1621. He was representative in 1644, when he lived in Newbury, where he had children born ; Sarah, 1641 ; Charles, b. July, 1643 ; Ann, b. 1649 ; Elizabeth 1650, and William, b. 1653. He may have been also of Charlestown, where William Hilton, d. 7 Sept. 1675, having had sons, Nowell and Edward born there, 4 May, 1663, and 3 March, 1665. John Hilton d. in Boston in 1705.

HILLS, HERCULES, Scituate, returned to England. 2 Coll. Mass. Hist. Soc. iv. *JOSEPH, was born a. 1602, came to N. E. and was admitted freeman 1645, first resided at Charlestown, then at Malden, and last at Newbury, where he d. 5 Feb. 1688, æ. 86. He was representative of Malden in 1647 and from 1650 to 1656, and speaker in 1647, and represented Newbury in 1667. He wrote his name *Hills*. He had sons, Joseph, who d. 1674 ; Gershom, b. 27 July, 1639, and other children. His 2d wife, Anne, widow of Henry Lunt, he m. 8 March, 1664.

HINCHMAN, EDMUND, Chelmsford, died 27 Oct. 1668, and his widow, Elizabeth, m. Rev. John Fiske. Allen, Hist. Chelmsford. *THOMAS, Chelmsford, freeman 1654, was a magistrate, and a major of the Middlesex regiment; a representative in 1666, 1667, 1671, and 1676; d. 18 July, 1703. He wrote his name as above, which was pronounced as if spelled *Hinksman.*

HINCKLEY, SAMUEL, was an inhabitant of Scituate in 1638. ‡§THOMAS, Plymouth, son of the preceding, was an assistant of Plymouth colony, one of Sir Edmund Andros' council 1687, was elected governour from 1680 to 1689, excepting the time Andros exercised his power. He died in 1706, æ. 88.

HINCKS, ‡JOHN, Portsmouth, was a counsellor in 1683. This name is frequently written *Hinks* and *Hinckes.* Samuel Hinks grad. at H. C. 1701.

HINDS, JAMES, Salem 1637. Four of the name have received the honours of Harvard and Williams colleges.

HINSDALE, ROBERT, Dedham, freeman 1638, was one of the founders of the church, 9 Nov. 1638; removed to Deerfield. [Worthington, Hist. Dedham.] Two of his sons were, Barnabas, b. in 1639, and settled in Hadley; and Gamaliel, born in 1642. The town of Hinsdale, in N. H. derives its name from Colonel Ebenezer Hinsdale, one of his descendants. Rev. Ebenezer Hinsdell, another of them, grad. at H. C. 1727.

HINSON, RALPH, Boston, woollen-draper, was a member of the church a. 1634.

HITCHCOCK, MATTHIAS, New-Haven 1639, had sons, Eliakim, Nathaniel, and John. Sixteen of this name had grad. at the N. E. colleges in 1826. *RICHARD, Saco 1652, was a representative in 1660.

HITCHEN, EDWARD, Massachusetts, freeman 1635.

HOADLEY, JOHN, Guilford 1648, was one of the seven pillars of the church. 1 Coll. Mass. Hist. Soc. x.

HOAG, JOHN, Newbury 1669, had sons, John, b. 1670; Jonathan, b. 1671; Nathan; Benjamin; and probably others, whose descendants abound in N. H. Samuel W. Hoag grad. at Union College in 1821.

HOAR, JOHN, Concord 1660, had brothers, Daniel, who d. in London, and the following. He was the deliverer of Mrs. Rowlandson in 1676. He died 2 April, 1701. Daniel, his only son, was great-grandfather of the Hon. Samuel Hoar, of Lincoln, Ms. Shattuck. *LEONARD*, the third president of Harvard College, at which he grad. in 1650, went to England, was a physician and clergyman, and settled as the latter, at Wensted, in Essex. He was ejected from office for non-conformity, and returned to N. E. 1672, and in July, was elected president, but resigned 15 March, 1675, and d. at Braintree, 28 Nov. same year. He had no sons, but two daughters, Bridget and Tryphena. His widow, a daughter of Lord Lisle, m. Mr. Usher, of Boston, and d. 25 May, 1723. Mrs. Joanna Hoar, probably his mother, d. at Braintree, 21 Dec. 1661. A William Hoare was of Beverly in 1659.

HOBART, CALEB, Braintree, who d. 4 Sept. 1711, æ. 89, was probably son of Thomas Hobart, of Hingham. *EDMUND, freeman 1634, came from Hingham, in England, in 1633, and settled at Charlestown, from thence to Hingham, in 1635, which he represented from 1639 to 1642, four years. He d. 8 March, 1646, leaving sons, Edmund, Thomas, Peter, Joshua, and two daughters. EDMUND, Hingham 1635, son of the preceding, d. in 1686, æ. 82. His children were Daniel, Samuel, and John. *GERSHOM*, son of Rev. Peter Hobart, grad. at H. C. 1667, was admitted freeman 1673, was ordained at Groton, Mass., 26 Nov. 1679; dismissed by the town, Dec. 1685, d. 19 Dec. 1707, æ. 62. *JEREMIAH*, brother of the preceding, grad. at H. C. 1650, was ordained at Topsfield, 2 Oct. 1672, dismissed 21 Sept. 1680; went to Hempstead, L. I., was there settled 1682, removed to Haddam, Conn., and reinstalled there 14 Nov. 1700; died in March 1717, æ. 87. He m. Dorothy, daughter of Rev. Samuel Whiting, of Lynn. *JAPHET*, brother of the preceding, was born in April, 1647, grad. at H. C. 1667, went to England before 1670 in the capacity of surgeon of a ship, with a design to go from thence to the East-Indies, but was never heard of afterwards. Lincoln, Hist. Hingham, 115. *JOSH-UA*, the minister of South-Old, L. I., brother of the preceding, was born in England, grad. at H. C. 1650, d. in Feb. or March, 1717 æ. 89, having been settled there 45 years. Savage, ii. Winthrop, 222. Wood, Hist. Sketch. ‖*JOSHUA, a captain, son of Edmund Hobart, lived in Hingham, was admitted freeman 1634, member of the ar. co. 1641, representative 1643, twenty-five years, speaker of the house 1674, d. 28 July, 1682. His children were, Joshua; Enoch, b. 1654; and probably Solomon, and two daughters. Lincoln, Hist. Hingham. *NEHEMIAH*, second minister of Newton, Ms., was son of Rev. Peter Hobart, was born 21 Nov. 1648, grad. 1667, at H. C. of which he was fellow from 1707 to 1712; was ordained 23 Dec. 1674; freeman 1675, d. 12 Aug 1712, æ. 64. His wife was Sarah, daughter of Edward Jackson, sen. *PETER*, the first minister of Hingham, was the son of Edmund Hobart, and b. at Hingham, England, in 1604, was educated at the university of Cambridge, came to N. E. 8 June, 1635, and admitted freeman same year. He settled at Hingham in Sept. 1635 and there died 20 Jan. 1679, in his 75th year. Lincoln gives the names of his children, Joshua, Jeremiah, Gershom, Japhet, Nehemiah, David, Josiah, Israel, and 3 daughters. SAMUEL, Massachusetts, whose name is spelled *Hubbert*, was admitted freeman 1635. THOMAS, son of Edmund Hobart was admitted freeman 1634, settled in Hingham 1635, and had sons, Caleb, Joshua, and Thomas. Lincoln, Hist. Hingham, 156.

HOBBS, CHRISTOPHER, Saco 1652. Maurice Hobbs was of Newbury. Richard Hobbs, of Newbury, was drowned 1665. Humphrey Hobbs was one of the founders of the church at Amherst, N. H. 1741. Thomas Hobbs d. at Boston 1690.

HOBSON, HUMPHREY, Rowley 1665, was admitted freeman 1665, and probably ancestor of Humphrey Hobson, a magistrate of Mass. 1747. WILLIAM, Rowley, died a. 1659.

HODGKINS, WILLIAM, Ipswich 1665, died 26 Dec. 1693. Felt.

HODGKINSON, WILLIAM, Plymouth 1623.

HODSON, GEORGE, Cambridge 1641, came over, it is supposed, in 1630. His son Abiah was b. 1648. Nathaniel Hodson grad. at H. C. 1693.

HOFFARD, WILLIAM, Windsor 1640.

HOGG, RICHARD, Boston, a tailor, freeman 1640, had sons, Joseph, b. 1636, and John, b. 1643.

HOLBROOK, *JOHN, Weymouth, freeman 1640, representative 1651, 1664, 1669, 1671 to 1673, 1680, 1681, 1685, 1686, and 1692; was a captain of the militia. A John Holbrook died in Roxbury, 25 Dec. 1678. RICHARD, freeman 1648, might be one of the first settlers of Huntington, L. I. THOMAS, Braintree, freeman 1645, had sons, John and Peter, b. in 1653, and 1655. WILLIAM, Weymouth, freeman 1647, had a son William born in 1657.

HOLCOMB, THOMAS, came from England in 1639 with Rev. E. Hewett. M'Clure.

HOLCOMBE, THOMAS, Massachusetts, freeman 1634. Rev. Reuben and Rev. Frederick Holcombe grad. at Yale and Williams in 1774, and 1809.

HOLDEN, JUSTINIAN, a proprietor of Watertown, was admitted freeman 1657, was of Cambridge 1672, and appears to have been of Groton in 1677. RANDALL, Massachusetts, came to N. E. in a London ship 1646, went to Rhode-Island. Savage, ii. Winthrop, Index. 1 Coll. Mass. Hist. Soc. vii. 93. RICHARD, Watertown, had a son Stephen, b. in 1642.

HOLGRAVE, *JOHN, Salem, freeman 1633, was representative at the first general court at Boston, 14 May, 1634. JOSEPH, Salem 1637. JOSHUA, Salem, was admitted to the church, 12 Nov. 1637.

HOLLEY, SAMUEL, Cambridge 1636. His will, dated 22 Oct. 1643, is on the Suffolk co. records. Eight of the name had grad. at the N. E. colleges in 1828.

HOLLIGE, RICHARD, Boston, was admitted to the church and freeman in 1639.

HOLLIMAN, EZEKIEL, Salem, of Dedham in 1635, went to R. I., and was one of the founders of the first Baptist church in America. Savage, i. Winthrop, 293. Benedict, Hist. Baptists.

HOLLINGWORTH, RICHARD, Salem 1637, d. 1654. His son Richard was made freeman 1665. Savage, ii. Winthrop, 24.

HOLLISTER, *JOHN, Weymouth, freeman 1643, was representative 1644. There appears to be two of this name admitted freemen in 1643. The name exists in Vermont.

HOLLOWAY, JOSEPH, Lynn 1636, removed to Sandwich 1637. JOSEPH, Lynn 1656, d. 29 Nov. 1693. Lewis.

HOLMAN, EDWARD, Plymouth 1623. ||JOHN, Dorchester, was member of the ar. co. 1637; had sons, John and Thomas, b.

1637 and 1641. John Holman grad. at H. C. 1700. WILLIAM, Cambridge 1636.

HOLMES, GEORGE, Roxbury, freeman 1639, d. 18 Dec. 1645. *JOHN*, minister of Duxbury, was a student under President Chauncy in 1658, and succeeded Rev. Ralph Partridge, but was the minister there only a few years. JOHN, Plymouth 1638. *NATHANIEL, Roxbury, son of George Holmes, was b. in 1639, and was representative in 1689. *OBADIAH*, Salem, was admitted 24 March, 1639, to the church, from which he was excommunicated; went to Rehoboth, became a Baptist; removed to Newport, R. I., and was the minister there in 1652, d. 1682, æ. 76. He had 8 children, and his descendants in 1790, were estimated at 5000. His son Obadiah was a judge and preacher in New-Jersey. John, another son, was a magistrate in Philadelphia. One of Obadiah's sons was living in Newport in 1770 at the age of 95. Benedict, i. Hist. Baptists, 371—375. RICHARD, Rowley 1643, was born in 1610. ROBERT, Cambridge 1636, freeman 1641, had a wife Jane, and sons, John, Joseph, and Ephraim. A Robert Holmes d. at Newbury, 18 Sept. 1673. WILLIAM, a major, of Plymouth colony 1638, d. in Boston 1649, without any family. Holmes, i. Annals, 578, where there are some interesting notes of him.

HOLT, NICHOLAS, Newbury 1635, removed to Andover, and was one of the founders of the church there 1645, died in 1685, æ. 78. He had sons, Samuel, b. at Newbury, 6 Nov. 1641; Henry; Nicholas; James; and John. He had two daughters b. at Newbury in 1636 and 1638. WILLIAM, New-Haven 1643, had sons, John, b. 1645; Nathaniel, b. 1647; Eleazar, b. 1651; Thomas, b. 1653; Joseph, b. 1655; Benjamin, b. 1658.

HOLTON, ROBERT, slater, a member of the church in Boston, was admitted freeman 1634. *WILLIAM, Northampton 1654, was representative 1665 to 1667, 1669 to 1671, one year for Hadley.

HOLYOKE, *EDWARD, Lynn 1630, [Lewis] came from Tamworth, in the county of Stafford, and on the borders of Warwickshire; [Brazer, Sermon of Dr. E. A. Holyoke, 10] was admitted freeman in 1638; representative 1639 to 1643, and 1647 and 1648; removed to Springfield, which he represented in 1650 and part of 1660. He d. 4 May, 1660, leaving a son Elizur, and a daughter, who m. George Keysar. *ELIZUR, Springfield, son of the preceding, was admitted freeman in 1648, was a captain, and representative in 1656, 1661, 1667, 1670, and 1673 to 1675, 7 years, and d. 6 Feb. 1676. He m. 20 Nov. 1640, Mary, daughter of Hon. William Pynchon. She d. 26 Oct. 1657. He had a son who was chosen captain in Philip's war 1676, and died in Sept. following. [Hubbard, 86.] JOHN, Springfield, probably another son, grad. at H. C. 1662, was admitted freeman in 1677, representative in 1691. Elizur Holyoke, of Boston, the representative in 1704, 1705, 1706, and 1707, was probably father of Rev. Edward Holyoke, H. C. 1705, and president of the college, who was a native of Boston, and father of the venerable centenarian, Edward Augustus Holyoke, born at Marblehead, 1 Aug. 1728, grad. at H. C. 1746, and died at Salem, 31 March, 1829.

HOMWOOD, or HONIWOOD, WILLIAM, was of Cambridge 1641, had a wife Winifred, and daughter Elizabeth. St. John Honeywood grad. at Y. C. in 1782.

HOOD, JOHN, Lynn 1650, Kittery 1652. RICHARD, Lynn 1650, came from Lynn, England, and d. 12 Sept. 1695, having sons Joseph and Benjamin.

HOOKE, FRANCIS, Kittery, was a magistrate there 1688. *WILLIAM*, a preacher at Taunton, and settled the minister of New-Haven, in 1644, returned to England 1656, and became chaplain to Oliver Cromwell. He died, says Calamy, in March, 1677, æ. 77. Mather says, 21 March, 1677, Trumbull, 1667, and Savage, 1668. *WILLIAM, Salisbury, freeman 1640, mentioned by Winthrop [ii. Hist. N. E. 125] as a godly gentleman, was representative in 1643 and 1647. He d. in 1654, leaving a widow Eleanor.

HOOKER, THOMAS, one of the first ministers of Cambridge and Hartford, was born at Marfield, in Leicestershire, about 1586; was educated at Emmanuel College, Cambridge, came to N. E. in company with Rev. John Cotton and Samuel Stone, and arrived at Boston, 3 Sept. 1633; was settled over the church at Cambridge, 11 Oct. 1633, admitted freeman 14 May, 1634, went to Connecticut in July, 1636, and settled at Hartford, where he d. 7 July, 1647, æ. 61, leaving a widow Susan, and several children. Three of his daughters m. Rev. Thomas Shepherd, Rev. Roger Newton, and Rev. John Wilson. Twenty-two persons of the name of Hooker, most of whom his descendants, had grad. at the N. E. colleges in 1828. *SAMUEL*, minister of Farmington, was son of the preceding and grad. at H. C. 1653, was ordained 1661, and d. 6 Nov. 1697, aged a. 64. Rev. John Hooker, Y. C. 1751, the minister of Northampton, who died 6 Feb. 1777, æ. 48, was from this family.

HOOPER, JOHN and ROBERT, were of Marblehead in 1674, where the name continues to the present time, having furnished many enterprising men. Eleven of the name had grad. at H. C. in 1828. WILLIAM, Reading, was admitted freeman 1648, d. 5 Dec. 1678.

HOPKINS, ‡§EDWARD, came to N. E. with Rev. John Davenport, and settled at Hartford 1638, was elected magistrate 1639, and frequently governour between 1640 and 1654. He returned to England, and d. in London, March, 1657, in his 58th year. His widow, who was aunt of Gov. Yale, founder of Yale Coll., died 17 Dec. 1698. Savage, i. Winth. 230. Twenty-seven persons of the name of Hopkins had grad. at the N. E. Colleges in 1826. JOHN, Cambridge, was admitted freeman 1635. STEPHEN, Plymouth, one of the first Pilgrims, came over 1620; was an assistant from 1633 to 1636, four years. THOMAS Providence 1641. 3 Coll. Mass. Hist Soc. i. 4. WILLIAM, was an assistant of Connecticut in 1642. WILLIAM, Roxbury, d. 28 April, 1688.

HOPKINSON, MICHAEL, Boston, member of the church, freeman 1640, dismissed to Rowley, and there d. 1657. John, who d.

at Rowley, 29 May, 1704, and Jonathan, who d. 11 Feb. 1719, æ. 76, were probably his sons.

HORNE, JOHN, freeman 1631, was of Salem in 1637, was a carpenter by profession, and a deacon of the church 54 years; d. 1685, æ. 82, leaving children, John, Symond, Joseph, Benjamin, Elizabeth Gardner, Jehoadan Harvey, Mary Smith, and Ann Felton. Felt, Annals, 279. This name has now become Orne, and has furnished a number of enterprising and useful men. William Horne was of New-Hampshire in 1665, and had sons, John and William, whose descendants remain.

HORSLEY, JOSEPH, Rowley, d. 1699. John Hosley grad. at H. C. 1779.

HORTON, BARNABAS, was of South-Old, L. I. about 1640. THOMAS, Springfield 1639. WILLIAM, Charlestown, d. 21 Jan. 1655. Six of the name had grad. at Yale, Harv., Union, and N. J. coll. in 1828.

HOSFORD, WILLIAM, was admitted freeman 1634. Spelled Horseford in colony records. Isaac Hosford grad. at D. C. 1826.

HOSIER, SAMUEL, came to N. E. in 1630, and settled in Watertown; was admitted freeman 1631.

HOSKINS, JOHN, Massachusetts, was admitted freeman 1631. The name of *Haskins*, perhaps the same, exists in Massachusetts. JOHN, was admitted freeman 1634. THOMAS, freeman 1635. There were families of this name in Beverly, where Roger Hoskins d. in 1694, æ. 50.

HOSMER, JAMES, Concord, freeman 1637, came according to tradition from Hockhurst, in the county of Kent, England, and d. 7 Feb. 1685. His wife in 1665. His sons were, James, who m. Sarah White in 1658, had 4 children, and was killed in Sudbury fight 1676; John, a petitioner for the grant of Chelmsford 1653; Stephen, b. 1642, m. Abigail Wood 1667. Shattuck, MS Hist. Concord. THOMAS, came with his brother James to N. E. and settled at Cambridge as early as 1632, and was admitted freeman 1635. Rev. Stephen Hosmer, H. C. 1699, was of East-Haddam, Conn. and d. 16 June, 1749. Hon. Titus Hosmer and Hon. Stephen Titus Hosmer grad at Y. C. 1757 and 1782.

HOUCHIN, ||*JEREMY, a tanner of Boston, was admitted freeman 1640, member of ar. co. 1641, was representative for Hingham from 1651 to 1659, excepting 1656; for Salisbury in 1663. He was admitted a member of Dorchester church in 1639. His sons, Jeremy and John, were born in Boston in 1652 and 1655. His name is spelled *Howchenes* in the colony records.

HOUGH, *‡ATHERTON, son, it is supposed, of Atherton Hough, mayor of Boston, in Lincolnshire, England, 1628, [See Thompson's Hist. of Boston, England] came to N. E. in 1633, with Rev. John Cotton, and settled at Boston. He was chosen assistant 1635, and representative in 1637, d. 11 Sept. 1650. His daughter Elizabeth d. 14 Oct. 1643. *SAMUEL*, the second minister of Reading, probably son of the preceding, was educated at H. C.,

150

although he did not graduate; succeeded Rev. Henry Green, and d. at Boston, 30 March, 1662. Savage, ii. Winthrop. Index.

HOUGHTON, HENRY. (See HAUGHTON.) *JOHN, Watertown, thence to Lancaster as early as 1652, and was representative 1690, and perhaps for 13 years afterwards. *RALPH, Lancaster, freeman 1668, was town clerk, and the 2d representative of that town in 1673, and again elected in 1689. He was cousin to the preceding. Willard, Hist. Lancaster.

HOULDEN, RANDALL. (See HOLDEN.)

HOULDER, NATHANIEL, Dorchester, was member of the church 1636. Dr. Harris.

HOUSE, JOHN, Cambridge, d. 22 April, 1644. SAMUEL, a ship-carpenter, of Scituate 1633, removed to Cambridge. 2 Coll. Mass. Hist. Soc. x. Index.

HOVEY, DANIEL, Ipswich 1637, d. 29 April, 1695. John Hovey is mentioned in the Revolution in N. E. Justified, 39. Joseph Hovey was of Hadley in 1677.

HOWARD, JOHN, Dedham 1636. JOHN, Bridgewater. (See HAWARD.) ||NATHANIEL, member of the ar. co. 1641, freeman 1643, belonged to Dorchester. Samuel Howard was of Boston in 1658. William Howard was a member of the ar. co. in 1661. ROBERT, Lynn 1650, was admitted freeman 1652, and had a son Edward. Lewis.

HOWE, ABRAHAM, Roxbury, freeman 1638, died 20 Nov. 1683. His sons were, Abraham, who died 1684; Isaac, b. 1639; Israel, b. 1644. Twenty-two persons of the name of Howe had grad. at the N. E. colleges in 1826. ||*DANIEL, Lynn, the first lieutenant of the ar. co. 1637, was admitted freeman 1634, representative 1636 and 1637, removed to South-Hampton, L. I. of which he was a grantee and one of the first settlers. Mr. Lewis says he had a son Edward, who was master of a vessel, and was wrecked in 1676, as mentioned by Hubbard, 644. Whitman [Sketch of ar. co. 147] spells the name *Haugh*. *EDWARD, Lynn 1630, [Lewis] was admitted freeman 1636, was representative at 7 courts in 1638, 1642, and 1643; died in April, 1639. *EDWARD, Watertown, freeman 1634, was a ruling elder of the church, and representative in 1635; d. in 1644. JAMES, freeman 1637, was of Ipswich 1648, and d. in May, 1702, æ. 104. Sewall, MS. He gave testimony relating to the line between Ipswich and Rowley a short time before he died. JEREMIAH, Lynn 1647. Lewis. JOHN, Watertown, freeman 1640, was son of John Howe, of Hodinhull, Warwickshire, said to be related to Lord Charles Howe, earl of Lancaster in 1641. Worcester Magazine. JOHN, Sudbury, freeman 1640, had sons, John, b. 1640; Samuel, b. 1642, and removed to Marlborough, and d. 10 July, 1678. He might be the John Howe killed by the Indians, 20 April, 1675. JOSEPH, Lynn 1640, died a. 1651. Lewis. WILLIAM, Dorchester 1641, probably went to Chelmsford a. 1656.

HOWELL, EDWARD, Lynn, freeman 1638, owned 500 acres at Lynn, was one of the grantees named in the Indian deed of South-

Hampton, L. I. 1640. Twelve of the name had grad. in N. E., N. Y., and N. J. in 1826. ‡JOHN, was elected a magistrate of Connecticut in 1647. John Howell grad. at Y. C. 1721.

HOWEN, ROBERT, Boston, freeman 1642, had a son Israel, b. in 1642.

HOWES, ABEL, perhaps Hewes or Huse, (See Huse) was admitted freeman in 1642. One of the name of Howes grad. at Williams College in 1809.

HOWLAND, JOHN, one of the first pilgrims, was elected an assistant of Plymouth colony from 1633 to 1635, 3 years, d. 23 Feb. 1673, æ. about 80, being the "last of those in the town of Plymouth who came in the May-Flower 1620." Henry Howland was one of the proprietors of Bridgewater in 1645, and might be a son. Rev. John Howland, H. C. 1741, of Carver, who d. 4 Nov. 1804, æ. 84, was a descendant.

HOWLETT, *THOMAS, was b. 1599, and was one of the first settlers of Ipswich, freeman 1634, representative 1635, d. 22 Dec. 1667. William Howlett grad. at H. C. 1727.

HOWMAN, JOHN, requested to be made freeman, 19 Oct. 1630.

HOYT, JOHN, one of the first settlers of Salisbury 1640. SIMON, Massachusetts, was admitted freeman, 18 May, 1631. Eight had in 1828 received honours at the N. E. colleges.

HUBBARD, BENJAMIN, Charlestown, freeman 1634, had sons, Benjamin, Thomas, and James. Fifty-three persons of the name of Hubbard, 11 of them ministers, had grad. at the N. E. colleges in 1826. GEORGE, a deputy at the first general assembly of Conn. 1639, was of Guilford 1650. JAMES, Lynn 1637, perhaps d. at Watertown 1638, leaving a son Thomas b. that year. JOSEPH, Newbury 1637. JOHN, Hadley 1660. RICHARD, Ipswich, son of William Hubbard, grad. at H. C. 1653, was representative in 1660, d. 3 May, 1681. He wrote his name *Hubberd*. ROBERT, Boston 1652, had sons Daniel and John b. before 1657. *WILLIAM, came to N. E. as early as 1630, when he requested to be made free, and was probably admitted in 1638, unless the William Hubbard of Lynn was a different person. He settled in Ipswich, which he represented in 1638, six years, until 1646. He removed to Boston and died a. 1670, leaving sons, William, Richard, and Nathaniel. *WILLIAM*, minister of Ipswich, and the historian of New-England, was son of the preceding, and was b. in England 1621, grad. at H. C. 1642, ordained probably as a colleague, and d. 14 Sept. 1704, æ. 83. He m. Margaret, daughter of Rev. Nathaniel Rogers. THOMAS, Billerica 1656, d. Nov. 1663.

HUCKIN, ‖THOMAS, member of the ar. co. 1637, its ensign 1639. James Huckins was of Durham, N. H., and a constable in 1683.

HUDSON, FRANCIS, Boston 1640, was son of William Hudson, of Chatham, in Kent, and d. 3 Nov. 1700, æ. 82. Judge Sewall says that he was one of the first who set foot on the peninsula of Boston. His son Samuel was b. 1650. JAMES, Boston 1642, had

sons, James, born 1646; John, born 1654. JOHN, Lynn 1637.
Winthrop, ii. Hist. N. E. 48. NICHOLAS, Massachusetts, was
admitted freeman 1637. RALPH, Cambridge 1635, thence to
Boston, freeman 1636. THOMAS, Lynn 1637, had a son Jonathan. WILLIAM, Lynn, freeman 1631 ; afterwards of Boston.
Snow, Hist. Boston, 108. Shaw, Hist. Boston, 67. ||WILLIAM,
was born a. 1619, freeman 1640, member of the ar. co. 1640; captain 1661.

HUET, EPHRAIM, Windsor. (See HEWETT.) Johnson
spells this name as above ; but Trumbull writes it *Hewett*.

HUGGINS, JOHN, Hampton, d. 1670, leaving son John, and
perhaps James.

HUGHES, JOSHUA, Roxbury. (See HEWES.) The name of
Hughes has furnished several graduates at N. J. College, and one
at Harvard.

HULBERT, WILLIAM, freeman 1632, may have been one of
the proprietors of Northampton as early as 1658.

HULL, EDWARD, Braintree 1650. Six persons of the name
of Hull had grad. at Y. C. in 1828, of whom was General William
Hull, governour of Michigan. *‡GEORGE, Dorchester, freeman
1633, was representative at the first general court, 14 May, 1634 ;
removed to Connecticut, and was elected an assistant in 1637.
There was a George Hull of Beverly in 1674. *ISAAC*, was a
minister of the first Baptist church before 1679. ||JOHN, Boston,
freeman 1632, was member of the ar. co. 1638 ; its captain 1671.
‡||*JOHN, Boston, grandson of Robert Hull, was probably admitted
freeman 1649, member of the ar. co. 1660 ; its captain 1678,
treasurer of Massachusetts 1676, assistant from 1680 to 1683. He
d. 29 Sept. 1683, leaving an only child, Hannah, b. 14 Feb. 1658,
who m. Judge Samuel Sewall. He left a large estate. He or the
preceding was representative for Wenham in 1668; for Westfield
from 1671 to 1674, and for Salisbury 1679. There was a John
Hull who died at Newbury, 1 Feb. 1670. *JOSEPH, Hingham,
freeman 1635, was representative at two courts in 1638 and 1639.
Mr. Savage [ii. Winthrop, 175] supposes that the town of Hull, in
Massachusetts, was "so called in honour of Joseph Hull, of Hingham." If so, it is believed to be a solitary instance of the name
of an individual, however distinguished, being given to a town at
so early a period. May not this small maritime town derive its
name from a seaport, in Yorkshire, England, whence some of the
early settlers embarked for the shores of New-England ? REUBEN,
a merchant of Portsmouth, m. Mary Farmside, and had sons, Joseph, b. 1677 ; Reuben, b. 1684, and several daughters. RICH-
ARD, Massachusetts, freeman 1634. ROBERT, Boston, blacksmith, was admitted freeman 1637, and d. 28 July, 1663, æ. 73.
S. Sewall, MS Diary makes him the grand-father of John Hull, the
assistant. [———,] a minister, whose name of baptism has not
been ascertained, preached some time at Weymouth; appears to
have at Bass River, [Beverly] and at the Isles of Shoals. He came
to N. E. as early as 1635. Savage, i. Winthrop, 162.

HU LLING, ——, Massachusetts, was admitted freeman 1639.

HUMFREY, ‡†JOHN, who was chosen deputy-governour at the second meeting of the Mass. company in England, came to N. E. 1632, and was elected an assistant from 1632 to 1641. He settled in Lynn 1634 [Lewis]; was admitted member of the church in Salem, 16 Jan. 1638 [Felt], and returned to England 26 Oct. 1641. [Winthrop, ii. Hist. N. E. 46.] He m. Lady Susan, daughter of the Earl of Lincoln, and she, with their children, came to N. E. His children were, John, who was probably member of the ar. co. 1641; Joseph; Theophilus; Ann; Dorcas, and Sarah, who were all dead in 1681, excepting Ann, who having been the widow of William Palmes, m. Rev. John Miles, of Swanzey. Hutchinson, i. Hist. Mass. 21. Felt. Lewis.

HUMPHREY, JAMES, an elder of the church in Dorchester, was admitted freeman 1645, and d. 12 May, 1686, æ. 78. Eleven persons of the name of Humphrey and Humphreys had grad. in N. E. in 1826. JONAS, Dorchester, was admitted to the church 1639, freeman 1640. Jonas, perhaps his son, was admitted freeman 1654, and had a son Jonas b. in 1661.

HUNKING, JOHN, Portsmouth 1650, had children, John, born 2 March, 1651, died in England; Hercules, b. 11 July, 1656; John, [?] b. 6 April, 1660; Peter, b. 20 March, 1663; William, b. 6 Jan. 1667, and Mark, b. 17 May, 1670, and was a counsellor of N. H. in 1710.

HUNKINGS, WILLIAM, Providence 1641.

HUNN, GEORGE, a tanner, of Boston, was admitted freeman in 1637, and d. in June, 1640. Nathaniel, probably his son, was of Boston, and a member of the ar. co. 1662.

HUNT, EDMUND, Cambridge 1634, was an early settler of Duxbury, and one of the proprietors of Bridgewater 1645. Forty-one persons of this name had been educated at the colleges in N. E. and N. J. in 1826. ENOCH, Weymouth 1640. *EPHRAIM, Weymouth 1655, freeman 1671, representative 1689 to 1691, and a captain of the militia. *JONATHAN, was representative of Northampton in 1691. WILLIAM, Concord 1641, died at Marlborough in Oct. 1667, leaving sons, Samuel, freeman 1654; Nehemiah; Isaac, and William. Shattuck. [——,] a minister, who had been settled in Wroxall, in Warwickshire, came to N. E. according to Calamy, but at what time is uncertain.

HUNTER, ROBERT, Rowley, was admitted freeman 1640. Sixteen of this name are on the catalogues of the N. E. colleges.

HUNTING, JOHN, Dedham, freeman 1638, was an elder of the church, and one of its founders in 1638. His sons, Samuel and Nathaniel, were b. in 1640 and 1643. Rev. Nathaniel Hunting, H. C. 1693, who was ordained in Sept. 1699, at East-Hampton, L. I. and d. in 1753, was his grandson. Six others of the name had grad. at Harvard and Yale in 1826.

HUNTINGTON, ——, was one of the first settlers of Saybrook in 1637, from thence went to Norwich, where the family have ever enjoyed high distinction. Thirty-four of the name have grad. at Yale College, besides 10 at the other N. E. colleges, several of whom have been much distinguished in publick life. WILLIAM, Salisbury 1661.

HUNTLEY, JOHN, Boston 1652, had sons, Moses and Aaron.

HURD, ||JOHN, Boston, tailor, freeman and member of the ar. co. 1640, had sons, Benjamin and Samuel, and d. 23 Sept. 1690. Isaac Hurd was admitted freeman in 1670.

HURLBERT, WILLIAM, Windsor 1640.

HUSE, ABEL, was b. a. 1602, came from London, and settled at Newbury, a. 1639; d. 29 March, 1690. He had 12 children, all by his 3d wife, and born after he was 60 years old. The sons were, Abel, Thomas, William, John, and Ebenezer. Coffin. Stephen, the son of Abel Huse, was b. 16 Nov. 1702, and grad. at H. C. 1726. Jonathan and Nathaniel Huse, clergymen, grad. at D. C. in 1788 and 1802.

HUSSEY, *‡CHRISTOPHER, one of the first settlers of Newbury and Hampton, was born at Darking, in Surry, in England, [Lewis] was admitted freeman 1634, was at Hampton 1639, and the representative in 1658, 1659, and 1660; was a provincial counsellor of New-Hampshire, and d. 1685. He m. Theodate, daughter of Rev. Stephen Bachelor, and left two sons, Stephen and John, and several daughters. Stephen lived in Nantucket, and there d. in 1718, æ. 88. John became a preacher to the Quakers, and lived in Newcastle, Delaware. *JOSEPH, a captain of Hampton, and the representative in 1672.

HUTCHINS, GEORGE, Cambridge, freeman 1638, had a son Luke, b. 6 April, 1644. JOHN, Newbury 1640, had sons, Joseph, b. 15 Nov. 1640, and Benjamin, b. 15 May, 1641. He went to Haverhill as early as 1657. RICHARD, Massachusetts, admitted freeman 18 May, 1631.

HUTCHINSON, EDWARD, son of Richard, admitted freeman 4 March, 1634, was of Boston, and removed to Rhode-Island, as early as 1638, but returned to Massachusetts. Benedict. Twenty-two of the name had grad. at the N. E. colleges in 1826. ||*EDWARD, Boston, son of William and the famous Ann Hutchinson, was admitted freeman 3 Sept. 1634, member of the ar. co. 1638, captain in 1657, representative in 1658, went in 1675 on an expedition to the Nipmug country, and was wounded in an engagement with the Indians, 4 or 5 miles from Brookfield, on 2d August, and d. of his wounds at Marlborough, 19 August, 1675, æ. 67. He had sons, Elisha; Edward, b. 1651; Benjamin, b. 1656, and perhaps others. To his honour, he entered his dissent against the sanguinary law in 1658, for punishing the quakers with death on their return to the colony after banishment. ‡||*ELISHA, Boston, son of the preceding, was admitted freeman 1668; member of the ar. co. 1660, captain 1676, representative 1680 to 1683, assistant 1684, 1685, and 1686, and one of the first council under the charter of William and Mary 1692. He d. 10 Dec. 1717, æ. 77. His son, the Hon. Thomas Hutchinson, b. 30 Jan. 1674, d. 3 Dec. 1739, æ.

65, was father of Governour Thomas Hutchinson, the historian of Massachusetts, who was b. 9 Sept. 1711, grad. at H. C. 1727, and d. in England, 3 June, 1780, in his 69th year. Three of the governours sons, Thomas, Elisha, and William Sanford grad. at H. C. 1758, 1762, and 1770. FRANCIS, Boston, son of William Hutchinson, a member of the church, was admitted freeman 1635, and d. it is presumed, 17 Nov. 1661. GEORGE, is named by Prince [ii. Annals, 69] as a member of the church of Charlestown in 1632. ||JOHN, was member of the ar. co. 1645. RALPH, Northampton 1660. RICHARD, Boston, freeman 1635, was one of the disarmed in 1637, returned to England, and was a member of the corporation for propagating the gospel among the Indians, 1649. Hutchinson, i. Hist. Mass. 154. RICHARD, Salem 1637. Felt. SAMUEL, Lynn 1637. Lewis. THOMAS, Boston 1632, [Prince, ii. Annals, 69] Lynn 1637. Lewis. *WILLIAM, came to N. E. 1634, and settled at Boston which he represented in 1635, having been admitted freeman the same year. He went to Rhode-Island, and d. a. 1642. His widow, Ann, the celebrated female theologian, removed to the Dutch country, and in 1643, she, with all her family, excepting one daughter, being 16 persons, was killed by the Indians. Savage, ii. Winthrop, Index. Hutchinson, i. Hist. Mass. 55—57, 66, 70—74.

HYLAND, THOMAS, Scituate 1637

HYDE, EDMUND, Massachusetts, freeman 1649. Thirteen of the name of Hyde have grad. at the N. E. colleges. GEORGE, Boston 1642, had a son Timothy b. in 1644. JONATHAN, Cambridge 1650, that part now Newton, was admitted freeman 1663, and d. 5 Oct. 1711. He had sons, Jonathan, b. 1651; Samuel, b. 1652; Joshua, b. 1654; John, b. 1656; Abraham, b. 1658; Daniel, b. 1661; William, b. 1662; Eleazar, b. 1664. His name was frequently written and pronounced *Hides*. SAMUEL, Cambridge Village, now Newton, 1647, was a deacon of the church, and d. 12 Sept. 1689. His wife was Temperance. A daughter Sarah was b. 1644.

IBROOK, RICHARD, Hingham 1635. Lincoln, Hist. Hingham, 43.

ILSLEY, JOHN, Salisbury, was admitted freeman 1639. His name is spelled *Ellsley* in the colony records. WILLIAM, Newbury, was born a. 1608, came from Newbury, England, and d. in 1681. He had sons, John, b. 1641; William, b. 1647; Joseph, b. 1649; Isaac, b. 1652.

INCE, JONATHAN, distinguished as a mathematician, and perhaps the surveyor mentioned by Belknap, in his Hist. N. H. p. 87, grad. at H. C. 1650, and was lost at sea with John Davis and Nathaniel Pelham.

INES, MATTHIAS, was admitted freeman 1646. Mr. Savage, among the disarmed men in 1637 [i. Winthrop, 248] gives the name of Mathewe Iyans.

INGALLS, EDMUND, came from Lincolnshire, England, and settled at Lynn in 1629; d. in 1648, having a wife Ann, and nine children : Robert ; Elizabeth ; Faith, who m. Andrew Allen ; John, who lived at Lynn and Ipswich ; Sarah ; Henry, b. 1627, admitted freeman 1673, lived in Andover, and d. there in 1719, æ. 92, whose descendant, Captain Henry Ingalls, d. in 1803, æ. 84 ; Samuel ; Mary, and Joseph. His descendants have been numerous and respectable. Among them, may be named, Rev. Calvin Ingalls, Rev. Jedidiah Ingalls, Charles Ingalls, esq., and William Ingalls, M. D. A. Lewis and A. Abbot, MS letters. FRANCIS, brother of the preceding, b. a. 1601, was a tanner, and settled in Lynn in 1629. His tannery is said to have been the first in Massachusetts. Lewis. ROBERT, Lynn, son of Edmund, was born in England, and was buried 3 Jan. 1698. His wife, Sarah, d. 8 April, 1696. His children were Robert, Sarah, and Nathaniel. *SAMUEL, Ipswich 1665, freeman 1681, was representative 1690.

INGERFIELD, GEORGE, was a lieutenant at Kittery in 1668.

INGERSOLL, JOHN, Northampton 1658, perhaps of Westfield in 1668. Thirteen óf the name of Ingersoll had grad. at the N. E. colleges in 1826. RICHARD, Salem 1637, d. a. 1644, leaving sons, George, of Gloucester, and a selectman in 1652 ; and Nathaniel, and sons-in-law, Richard Pettingell, and William Haines. There was a John Ingersoll, a mariner of Salem in 1657, and freeman 1668. George and John Ingersoll were of Casco in 1665.

INGERSON, JOHN, Salem 1665. 2 Coll. Mass. Hist. Soc. viii. 106.

INGHAM, THOMAS, Scituate 1657. 2 Coll. Mass. Hist. Soc. iv.

INGLISH, WILLIAM, Boston 1652.

INGRAHAM, EDWARD, Salem 1638. Four of the name had grad. at the N. E. colleges in 1828. JOHN, Hadley 1666, was admitted freeman 1683. WILLIAM, Boston 1653, had sons, William, b. 1656, and Edward, b. 1657. Francis Ingraham d. in Boston in 1699.

INGOLDSBY, JOHN, Boston, admitted freeman 1642, had sons, John and Ebenezer, b. in 1649 and 1650.

IRELAND, PHILIP, Ipswich, whose wife, Grace, d. 13 May, 1692.

IRESON, EDMUND, Lynn 1650, d. Dec. 1675, æ. 74. He had a son Benjamin, whose descendants remain. Lewis. RICHARD, Lynn 1643. Judge Sewall records the death of a Capt. Ireson, 3 Feb. 1691, who was between 86 and 90 years of age.

ISAACS, *JOSEPH, Cambridge 1636, freeman 1637, was representative in 1638. Isaac, Ralph, Benjamin, and Ralph, grad. at Y. C. in 1750, '61, '81, and '84.

ISABELL, ROBERT, Salem 1637. Felt.

ISLIN, THOMAS, Sudbury, freeman 1640, d. 21 Feb. 1664.

IVES, MILES, Watertown 1639. Michael Ives, was of Boston in 1651. Eleven of the name had grad. at Y. C. 1828.

IVORY, THOMAS, Lynn 1640, d. 1664. Lewis. THOMAS, son of the preceding, was of Lynn 1642, and d. 18 July, 1690. WILLIAM, a carpenter, lived at Lynn, and other places, and d. at Boston, 3 Oct. 1652.

JACKLING, EDMUND, a glazier of Boston, was a member of the church and admitted freeman 1635. He had a son Samuel, b. in 1640.

JACKMAN, JAMES, was born a. 1618, and came from Exeter, in England, and settled at Newbury as early as 1648; d. 30 Dec. 1694. His sons were, James, b. 22 June, 1654; Richard, b. 1659, and several daughters. His name is erroneously *Jackson* in 2 Coll. Mass. Hist. Soc. viii. 106.

JACKSON, ABRAHAM, the ancestor of the Plymouth Jacksons, came over in the second ship at the age of 13, with secretary Morton; was his apprentice, and m. Remember, his daughter, 18 Nov. 1657. His sons were Eleazer, Abraham, John, and Nathaniel. The name of Jackson has prevailed in all the N. E. states, and 24 had grad. at the different colleges in 1828, fifteen having received degrees at H. C. ||EDMUND, Boston, freeman 1636, member of the ar. co. 1646, was a shoemaker and constable. His sons by three wives, were, John, b. 20 Oct. 1638; Thomas, b. 1 March, 1640; Samuel, b. 24 June, 1642; Jeremiah, b. July, 1645; Isaac, b. 22 Nov. 1651; Edmund, b. 30 Oct. 1654. *EDWARD, born in 1602, came from the parish of White-Chapel in London, a. 1640, was admitted freeman 1645, purchased a farm of Governour Bradstreet, of 500 acres at Cambridge, for £140, recently possessed by Jonathan Hunnewell, esq., and there settled. He was elected representative in 1647, and continued in that office 16 years and was much engaged in publick life. Johnson [Hist. N. E. 110] mentions him among the worthy men of the colony. He belonged to Newton after the separation of that town from Cambridge, and there d. 17 July, 1681, æ. 79, leaving an estate of £2477. 19, of which he gave 400 acres of land at Billerica, some books and manuscripts, and all the debts due to him in England to Harvard College. His children by his 1st wife were. Hannah, who m. John Ward, of Newton; (which see) Francis, who d. 5 Oct. 1648, and Rebecca, who m. Thomas Prentiss of Newton. His last wife, whom he m. 14 March, 1649, was Elizabeth, widow of John Oliver, and daughter of John Newgate, of Boston. His children were, 1. Sarah, b. 5 Jan. 1650, m. Rev. Nehemiah Hobart, of Newton, 21 March, 1678, d. 23 Feb. 1712; 2. Edward, b. 15 Dec. 1652, a deacon of the church at Newton, and representative 1702, d. 30 Sept. 1727, æ. 75, having had Edward, Abigail, Samuel, Elizabeth, and Hannah; 3. Jonathan, who probably m. and had issue; 4. Sebas, who m. Sarah Baker 1671, d. 6 Nov. 1690, having had Edward, b. 1672; John; John, 2d; Mary; Jonathan; Sarah; Elizabeth; Joseph, born 6 March, 1691; 5. Lydia, b. 1656, m. Joseph Fuller 1680, d. 12 January, 1726; 6. Elizabeth, b. 28 April, 1658, m. John Prentiss and a Bond, and d. 25 Jan. 1741; 7. Hannah, who m. Nathaniel Wilson, and d. 26 Sept. 1690; 8. Ruth, b. 16 Jan. 1664, d. 1692 unmarried. Joseph, above, the youngest son of Sebas, m. Patience Hyde, 28 Nov. 1717, and was grandfather of Timothy Jackson, esq., (the only son of Timothy, who d. 1774) who represented Newton in the general court 15 years in succession, from 1797, and who d. 22 Nov. 1814, æ. 58. The oldest son of the last named was one of the representatives of Boston in 1819 and 1820, but now resides on the ancient estate at Newton. Four other sons are inhabitants of Boston. Two of the sons, viz. William, of Newton, and Francis, of Boston, are representatives in the general court the present year. GEORGE, a surgeon of Marblehead, accompained the expedition to Canada 1690 in that capacity; purchased a farm in Scituate Aug. 1702. Samuel and Edmund, of Abington, 1716, were probably his sons. JOHN, Salem, had 50 acres of land allotted him in 1636. His house was burnt same year. He was member of the church 1648, and d. a. 1656. His son John m. in 1659, and his grandson, John, was b. 1660. He may be the "godly man" mentioned in ii. Winthrop, 19. JOHN, Cambridge Village, [Newton] brother of Edward, of Cambridge, was admitted freeman 1641, was deacon of the church, and d. 30 Jan. 1674. His sons were, John, who d. 18 Oct. 1675, æ. 36; Edward, b. 1650; Abraham, b. 1655, d. 1739, leaving an only son John, whose only son John left an only son Thomas; Joshua, b. 1659, and 6 daughters. JOHN, Boston, freeman 1643, was a carpenter, and d. a. 1673. His wife was Martha, and his son John was b. 26 June, 1643. JOHN and RICHARD, were of Portsmouth, a. 1650, where, in 1730, there were 9 ratable persons of the name. MARCUS, Charlestown 1645. NICHOLAS, Rowley 1650, d. 1698, leaving three sons, Samuel, b. 1649; Jonathan, b. 1650; Caleb, b. 1652. The two last lived in Rowley. Jonathan had sons, Jonathan, Joshua, Daniel, and 3 daughters. Caleb, had a son Caleb, b. in 1687, and one daughter. *RICHARD, Cambridge 1636, representative 1637, 1638, 1641, 1648, 1653, 1661, d. 22 June, 1672, æ. a. 90, leaving no children. He m. the widow of Richard Brown, of Watertown, 1662. ROBERT, Hempstead, L. I. 1665. Wood, Hist. Long-Island. SAMUEL, Scituate 1633, m. Esther Sillis, Nov. 1639, made free in 1644, d. in 1682, æ. 72. He had an only son Jonathan, b. 1647, d. 1725, whose only son Jonathan, b. 1685, had an only son Jonathan, b. 1633, whose two sons, Ward Jackson and Samuel Jackson, are of Boston and Scituate. WILLIAM, Rowley, one of the first settlers, d. 5 May, 1687, leaving daughters, Mary and Deborah, 1640 b. and 1640, and no male issue.

JACOB, *NICHOLAS, came from Hingham, England, in 1633, resided a short time at Watertown, was admitted freeman 1636, went to Hingham, which he represented in 1648 and 1649, and d. 5 Jan. 1657. Lincoln, Hist. Hingham, 22. RICHARD, Ipswich, freeman 1635, d. 1676, leaving an estate of £1067. 2. 3. He, or his son Richard, m. a daughter of Samuel Appleton. Samuel Jacob, of Newbury, d. 16 July, 1672.

JAFFREY, GEORGE, was b. a. 1637, lived sometime at Newbury, where he m. Elizabeth Walker, 7 Dec. 1665; went to Great Island, [New-Castle, N. H.] and was speaker of the N. H. assembly. His son George, b. a. 1683, grad. at H. C. 1702, was appointed a mandamus counsellor in 1716, and d. 8 May, 1749, æ. 66. George Jaffrey, son of the last, grad. at H. C. 1736, was a counsel-

lor of N. H. 1766, and d. 25 Dec. 1801, æ. 85. Descendants of
this family remain at Portsmouth.

JAMES, EDWARD, requested to be made freeman 19 Oct.
1630. Twelve of the name had, in 1828, received the honours of
the N. E. and N. J. colleges. ERASMUS, Marblehead 1648.
FRANCIS, Hingham 1638. Lincoln, Hist. Hingham, 46.

JAMES, GAWDY, Massachusetts, was admitted freeman 1642.
HUGH, Pascataqua 1631. Adams, Annals Portsmouth. *JOHN*,
minister of Derby, Conn. prior to 1697, was educated, according to
Mather, at Harvard College. It is not improbable that he was son
of Rev. Thomas James of Charlestown. PHILIP, Hi..gham 1638.
Lincoln, Hist. Hingham, 46. THOMAS, Dedham 1641, had a son
John born that year. A Thomas James was one of the founders of
the first Baptist church in Rhode-Island and a Thomas James died
at Lancaster, 13 March, 1660. *THOMAS*, the first minister of
the church in Charlestown, formed in Nov. 1632, was a native of
Lincolnshire, England, arrived in this country, 5 June, 1632, was
admitted freeman 1632, ordained 2 Nov 1632 ; went as a missionary to Virginia with Messrs. Knowles and Thompson 1643 ; removed
to New-Haven, and afterwards returned to England, and was in the
ministry at Needham until 1678, being then about 86 years of age.
He was buried at Needham. Hubbard, Hist. N. E. 191. Calamy,
ii. Account, Index. Prince ii. Annals, 77. *THOMAS*, the first
minister of East-Hampton, L. I. was probably son of the preceding,
and alluded to by Johnson, when speaking of the departure of Mr.
James of Charlestown, as follows:

"Thy son young student may rich blessing be ;
"Thy loss repayre ;"

unless the " young student" was John James, son of the Charlestown minister, and b. at Charlestown in 1632, and perhaps the minister of Derby. The East-Hampton minister was settled, according
to Mr. Wood, in 1650 and d. in 1696, [Hist. Sketch, 32, 40—42]
leaving, it is inferred, no posterity. If he was the son of Rev.
Thomas James, Mr. Savage [i. Winthrop, 94] mistakes in giving
to the father the station at L. I., occupied by the son in 1665.
WILLIAM, was among those requesting to be made freemen 19
Oct. 1630, and appears to have lived in Salem in 1639, and may
have removed to the county of Middlesex.

JAMESON, ROBERT, Watertown 1643. Coffin. Thomas,
counsellor at law, Thomas, a clergyman, and John Jameson grad. at
D. C. in 1797, 1818, and 1821.

JANES, JOSEPH, and WILLIAM, were of Northampton in
1658.

JAQUES, HENRY, a carpenter of Newbury 1640, d. 24 Feb.
1687, æ. 67. His children were, Henry, born 1649, went to Woodbridge, N. J. ; Daniel ; Mary, who m. Richard Brown ; Hannah,
wife of Ephraim Plumer ; Sarah, wife of John Hale ; Ruth, Abigail.
Stephen, Richard, and Abiel Jaques grad. at H. C. in 1707, 1720,
and 1807.

JAQUITH, ABRAHAM, Charlestown 1644, was admitted freeman in 1655.   His son Abraham was b. 1644.   This name is sometimes spelled as the preceding.

JARRATT, JOHN, Massachusetts, freeman 1640; d. 1648.

JARVIS, JOHN, was a merchant, and d. at Boston, 24 Sept.
1656.   Seven of the name had grad. at Harv. and Yale in 1828, of
whom at Y. C. were Rev. Abraham Jarvis, D. D. 1761, and Rev.
Samuel Farmar Jarvis, D. D. in 1805.

JEFFREY, THOMAS, Massachusetts, was admitted freeman
1634.   WILLIAM, Weymouth, whose name is frequently spelled
Jeffries, was admitted freeman 18 May, 1631, having come to N.
E. several years before the arrival of Governour Winthrop.   Savage,
i. Winthrop, 44, 138.

JEFTS, HENRY, was one of the first settlers of Billerica, and
d. there 24 May, 1700, æ. 94.   His descendants are in Boston and
various parts of Massachusetts.

JELLETT, JONATHAN, Massachusetts, freeman 1635.

JEMPSON, JAMES, Boston, had a son James, b. in 1651.

JENKINS, EDWARD, Scituate 1647.   Seven of the name had
grad. in 1828 at the N. E. and N. J. colleges.   JOEL, Braintree
1640, freeman 1646, had a son Theophilus, born in 1642.   REY-
NOLD, Kittery 1652, perhaps the same who removed from Dorchester to Cape Porpus in 1632.

JENKS, JOSEPH, Lynn 1645, came from Hammersmith, England, was a blacksmith, and lived at the iron works.   He d. March,
1683.   He was a very ingenious man, and his descendants throughout N. E. have been respectable.   He had 3 sons, Joseph; John,
who d. 1698, and Samuel.   Joseph removed to Pawtucket, R. I.
where he built the first house erected there.   His sons were, Joseph,
b. at Pawtucket 1656, governour of R. I. 5 years from 1727, and d.
15 June, 1740, æ. 84; William, a judge, who d. 1765, æ. 91;
Nathaniel, a major, who d. 1723, æ. 61, and Ebenezer, a minister
at Providence.   Lewis.   Lord's Lempriere.   Benedict, Hist. Baptists.   Eight of the name had grad. in 1828 at Harv. and Brown
colleges.

JENNER, *THOMAS, a minister, who preached at Weymouth and other places, was admitted freeman 1636, and representative in 1640.   Savage, i. Winthrop, 250.

JENNINGS, RICHARD, b. at Ipswich in England, and came
over with Rev. Nathaniel Rogers in 1636, but returned home in 1639.

JENNISON, ROBERT, Watertown 1637, freeman 1645, had a
son Samuel, b. in 1645.   Five of the name in 1828 had grad. at
H. C. and two at D. C.   *WILLIAM, Watertown, freeman 1631,
member of the ar. co. in 1637, representative 1637 to 1642, and
1645, seven years; captain of the military band in 1638.   Johnson
[Hist. N. E. 192] calls him *Ienings*, and supposes he was in England in 1651.

JENNY, ‡JOHN, Plymouth, came over in the ship James in
1623, and was elected an assistant of Plymouth colony in 1637,
1638, and 1639.

JEPSON, JOHN, Boston, admitted townsman 1647, had a son John, b. in 1657, who m. Apphia Rolfe, of Newbury 1696.

JEWELL, THOMAS, Braintree 1642, had sons, Joseph, born 24 April, 1642; Nathaniel, b. 15 April, 1648, and several other children.

JEWETT, *EZEKIEL, Rowley, freeman 1669, a deacon of the church; representative 1690, d. 2 Sept. 1723, æ.80. Faith, his wife, d. 15 Oct. 1715, æ. 74. Sixteen of the name had grad. at Harv. and Dart. in 1828. *JOSEPH, Rowley, freeman 1639, was representative 1651 to 1654, and 1660, d. a. 1661. His last wife, whom he m. 13 May, 1653, was widow of Bozoun Allen. He had seven children. JEREMIAH, the eldest son of the preceding, lived in Ipswich in 1666; [2 Coll. Mass. Hist. Soc. x. Index] afterwards of Rowley, and d. there 20 May, 1714, æ. 77. *MAXI-MILIAN, Rowley, brother of Joseph Jewett, was admitted freeman 1640, representative 1641 and 16 years afterwards, and was living in 1682. *NEHEMIAH, Ipswich, freeman 1668, representative 1689 to 1694, and probably later, speaker of the house in 1694.

JIGGLES, WILLIAM, Salem 1637, was a shipwright, and died a. 1659.

JOHNSON, DAVY, Massachusetts, requested to be made free-man 19 Oct. 1630. Fifty two persons of the name of Johnson had grad. at the N. E. and N. J. colleges in 1828. EDMUND, Hampton, d. 10 March, 1651, leaving children, Peter, John, James, and Dorcas. His widow m. Thomas Coleman, 11 July 1651. *ED-WARD, the author of " A History of New-England," called the Wonder Working Providence, came from Herne-Hill, a parish in Kent, to N. E. in 1630; was admitted freeman 18 May, 1631; member of the ar. co. 1637; lived sometime at Charlestown, was one of the founders of the town and church at Woburn, which town he represented 28 years from 1643 to 1671, excepting 1648, and was speaker a short time in 1655. He was a captain; town clerk a. 30 years, and sustained various other offices. He d. 23 April, 1672, leaving a widow, Susan, 5 sons, Edward, George, William, Matthew, John, and 2 daughters. EDWARD, Mass., freeman 1638. EDWARD, Kittery, freeman 1652, perhaps the same who was of York, and mentioned by Winthrop, i. Hist. N. E. 210, and perhaps ii. 210. STEPHEN, Andover, had sons, Francis, b. 1666; Stephen; Joseph, and Benjamin. EDWARD, Woburn, son of Captain Edward Johnson, m. Catharine Baker, 10 Jan. 1649, and his son Edward, b. 5 Nov. 1650, m. Sarah Walker, 12 Jan. 1687, and had a son Edward, b. 4 May, 1689. FRANCIS, a lieutenant, of Salem, was admitted freeman 1631, and by Joane, his wife, had children, Naomi, Ruth, Elizabeth, and Francis. A Francis John-son d. in Boston in 1691. HUMPHREY, Roxbury, where his son Mehitophel was born 16 Sept. 1644; of Scituate in 1655, when his son Joseph was born. ISAAC, Boston, one of the founders of the Massachusetts colony, and one of its most distinguished and useful members. He was of Clipsham, in Rutlandshire, the son of Abraham Johnson, esq., and grandson of Robert Johnson. His wife was Arabella, daughter of the Earl of Lincoln, who "left an earthly paradise in the family of an earldom to encounter the sorrows of a wilderness, for the entertainments of a pure worship in the house of God." She d. at Salem soon after her arrival, in 1630, and tradition says was buried in the Potter's field, although Judge Lynde makes the place of her interment near the site of St. Peter's church. Her husband survived her but a few weeks, and d. 30 Sept. 1630. ||*ISAAC, a captain of Roxbury, freeman 1635, was member of the ar. co. 1645, and its captain in 1667, representative in 1671, was one of the six captains slain by the Indians in taking Narraganset Fort, 19 Dec. 1675. [Hubbard. Mather. Hutchinson, i. Hist. Mass. 273.] His sons were, John, b. 3 Nov. 1639; Isaac, b. 2 Jan. 1644; Joseph, b. and d. 1645; Nathaniel, b. 1 May, 1647. JAMES, Pascataqua 1631, and was there in 1647. ||JAMES, a captain, was a glover, member of the church, admitted freeman 1636, member of the ar. co. and its lieutenant in 1658. He m. a daughter of Elder Thomas Oliver, and had sons, Joseph, b. 1644; James, and John, b. 1653, and probably others. ||*JOHN, Roxbury, freeman 1631, representative at the first general court 1634, and 15 years afterwards, member of the ar. co. 1638, surveyor general of the Massachusetts colony, d. 29 Sept. 1659, leaving 5 children, of whom John d. 1661. Savage, ii. Winthrop, Index. JOHN, Rowley 1652. JOHN, was a proprietor of Lancaster 1654. *JOHN, Haverhill, representative 1690. MARMADUKE, one of the early printers in N. E. lived in Cambridge. *MATTHEW, Woburn, son of Captain Edward Johnson, was representative 1686, 1689 to 1692, 5 years, and probably afterwards. He m. Hannah Palfrey, 12 Nov. 1658, and a 2d wife, Rebecca Wiswall, 23 Nov. 1666. RICHARD, Lynn 1637, perhaps also of Salem, had children, Daniel, Samuel, Elizabeth, and Abigail. He d. 1666. Lewis. ROBERT, grad. at H. C. 1645. He may have been related to Captain Edward Johnson, but the supposition of the late W. Winthrop, esq., that he was his son and is alluded to in his Hist. N. E. p. 165, is altogether improbable. SOLOMON, Sudbury 1639, freeman 1651, had sons Joshua and Nathaniel, b. 3 Feb. 1640; Caleb, b. 1 Feb. 1646. There was a deacon of this name in Marlborough. THOMAS, Hingham 1635, is probably the one named by Winthrop, [ii. Hist. N. E. 305] who met with difficulty in conducting a raft to Boston in 1646. It appears from Boston records that he was drowned at or near Boston, 29 May, 1656. THOMAS, one of the early settlers of Andover, perhaps son of James, of Boston, d. 1719, æ. 88, leaving sons, John, who d. 1741, æ. 74; Thomas; James; Peter, and Josiah. THOMAS,ᶻ grad. at H. C. 1661. WILLIAM, Charlestown, perhaps brother of Capt. Edward Johnson, d. 9 Dec. 1677. Son James was b. in 1643. *‡WILLIAM, Woburn, son of Capt. Edward Johnson, was admitted freeman 1651, was b. in England, probably at Herne-Hill. He was elected representative 9 years, from 1674 to 1683, excepting 1675; assistant in 1684 and 1685, one of the committee of safety in 1689; a military officer of the various grades from ensign to major. He

d. 22 May, 1704. Of his children, were, William, born 26 Feb. 1656; Edward b. 19 March, 1657; Ebenezer, b. 29 March, 1659.

JOLLIFE, JOHN, Boston 1665, freeman 1673, was for many years a leading man in town affairs [Hutchinson, i. Hist. Mass. 334]; one of the council of safety in 1689, and one of the first council under the charter of William and Mary, 1692; d. 23 Nov. 1701. Several of this name have been members of the British Parliament. The name is spelled by Hutchinson, *Joyliffe*.

JONES, *ABRAHAM, Hull, freeman 1673, was representative 1689. Fifty-eight persons of the name had grad. at the N. E. and N. J. colleges in 1825. ALEXANDER, Pascataqua 1631. EDWARD, Mass., and probably Charlestown, was admitted freeman 1631. *ELIPHALET*, settled the minister of Huntington, L. I. in 1677, was son of Rev. John Jones, and was born at Concord, 11 Jan. 1641. He was living in April, 1731. Wood, Hist. Sketch, 45. GRIFFITH, Springfield 1646. HENRY, Lynn 1642. ISAAC, Dorchester, freeman 1654. JAMES, Massachusetts, was admitted freeman 1644. *JOHN*, one of the first ministers of Concord came to N. E. in the ship Defence, with Rev. Thomas Shepard, and arrived 3 Oct. 1635. [MS Birth and Life of Rev. Thomas Shepard.] JOHN, son of the preceding, grad. at H. C. 1643, and was admitted freeman in 1645. Johnson, in noticing some of the early graduates of Harvard, says, "Mr. Jones, another of the first fruits of this college, is employed in these Western parts, in Mevis, one of the Summer Islands." Hist. N. E. 165. JOHN, Cambridge 1648, freeman 1650, after which year he appears to have resided in Concord, and d. there, 22 June, 1673. His children were, Samuel, b. 8 Oct. 1648; Ephraim, b. 1650; Elizabeth; Joseph, b. 1654; John, b. 1656; Rebecca, and William. Dorcas, his widow, m. William Buss, of Concord. JOHN, Portsmouth 1640, was b. about 1615, and was living in 1665. Belknap, i. Hist. N. H. 47. MATTHIAS, Boston 1637, had sons, John and Thomas, b. in 1638 and 1643. RICE, Boston, d. 3 Jan. 1663. His son Matthew was b. in 1651. THOMAS, Newbury, as early as 1639, went to Exeter, and may have afterwards removed to Kittery, where was a Thomas Jones in 1652. There was a Thomas Jones, of Gloucester, who d. in 1671. *THOMAS, Dorchester, freeman 1638, representative at the March session 1638. Thomas, b. 1635; Isaac, freeman 1654, and David, of Dorchester, were probably his sons. THOMAS, Concord, went to Fairfield, Conn., in Sept. 1644. Shattuck. THOMAS, Charlestown, freeman 1646, d. 24 Oct. 1666. THOMAS, Guilford, Conn., was an inhabitant in 1650. WILLIAM, Cambridge 1635. WILLIAM, Portsmouth 1640; Bloody-Point 1644. Belknap, i. Hist. N. H. 47. ‡†WILLIAM, New-Haven, was an assistant and depùty-governour of New-Haven colony, and also of Connecticut. He d. 17 Oct. 1706, æ. 82. His wife was a daughter of Governour Eaton.

JORDAN, FRANCIS, Ipswich 1634. ROBERT, Casco-Bay 1658, was born in 1611. STEPHEN, Ipswich 1648, removed to

Newbury, and d. 8 Feb. 1670. THOMAS, freeman of Massachusetts 1647. THOMAS, Guilford 1650.

JOSE, RICHARD, Portsmouth 1659, had sons Richard, b. 10 Nov. 1660, who was sheriff of the province of New-Hampshire; Thomas, b. 27 June, 1662; John, b. 27 May, 1668; Samuel, b. 6 May, 1672, and 4 daughters.

JOSSELYN, *HENRY, Scarborough, came to N. E. as early as 1631, was representative to the general court at Boston 1660, and a counsellor under the government of Gorges. The name is spelled in most of our histories Jocelyn and Jocelin. JOHN, brother of the preceding, visited New-England in 1638, and again in 1663. In his last visit, he arrived at Boston, 28 July, 1663, tarried there a few weeks, and then visited his brother at Scarborough, where he remained eight years, and made it his " business to discover all along the natural and chyrurgical rarities of this New-found-world." His work, which he called " New-England's Rarities," &c., was published in 1672. THOMAS, Hingham 1637, Lancaster 1654, died 3 Feb. 1661. His widow m. in 1664, Henry Kerly. Nathaniel, perhaps his son, admitted freeman in 1673, had a son Nathaniel, b. in 1658. Three of the name, spelled Josselyn, Joslen, and Joslin, grad. at Harv. Brown, and Union colleges in 1765, 1814, and 1821.

JOY, ||THOMAS, Boston 1638, member of the ar. co. 1658, freeman 1665, removed to Hingham, and d. in 1677 or 1678. His sons born in Boston, were, Samuel, in 1639; Thomas, in 1642; Joseph, in 1645; Ephraim, in 1646. Snow, Hist. Boston, 106. Savage, ii. Winthrop, 294. Lincoln, Hist. Hingham, 52.

JOYCE, JOHN, Lynn, removed to Sandwich 1637. Lewis.

JOYLIFFE, JOHN, Boston 1665, (See JOLLIFFE.)

JUDD, THOMAS, Cambridge 1634, freeman 1636. Thomas Judd, one of the first settlers of Waterbury, Conn. was great-grandfather of Rev Jonathan Judd, first minister of Southampton, Ms. who d. 28 July, 1803 in his 84 year. Eleven of the name had grad. at the N. E. colleges in 1826.

JUDKINS, JOB, Boston 1638, had sons, Samuel, b. 1638, and Joel, b. 1643. THOMAS, Gloucester 1664.

JUDSON, WILLIAM, Concord 1635, came from England in 1634, with his sons Joseph, Jeremiah, and Joshua. He removed to Hartford in 1639. Nineteen persons of this name had grad. at Yale and Brown colleges in 1828.

KALDER, AUSTIN, Dedham 1639, had a son Lot, b. in 1640.

KATHARICK, MICHAEL, Massachusetts, was admitted freeman in 1641. Savage, ii. Winthrop, 371.

KEAIS, SAMUEL, Portsmouth, a deacon, m. Mary Hody in 1696, and had a son Samuel, b. in 1697. Alden, in i. Coll. Mass. Hist. Soc. x.

KEAYNE, BENJAMIN, a merchant of Boston, and the only son of Capt. Robert, was admitted freeman 1639, was a major; m. a daughter of Gov. Thomas Dudley, whom he repudiated, and d. as Mr. Savage supposes, in 1668. i. Winthrop, 314. ii. 4. CHRIS-

TOPHER, Cambridge, spelled also *Cayne, Cane*, and *Kene*, was a member of the church, with his wife Margery, and d. as early as 1658, leaving children, Jonathan, Nathaniel, Deborah, Ruth, and Esther. HUMPHREY, Massachusetts, was admitted freeman, 1642. JAMES, (See KEENE.) ||*ROBERT, a merchant of Boston, a captain, and one of the founders of the artillery company, was admitted freeman in 1636, represented Boston in 1638 and 1639, and d. 23 March, 1656. Savage, ii. Winthrop, Index. Whitman, Hist. Ar. Co. 10, 29—37.

KEENE, JAMES, Braintree, was the first captain of that place, as appears by a scrap found in the town records. John Keene grad. at H. C. 1709.

KEEP, JOHN, Long-Meadow (Springfield) 1644. Sprague, Hist. Disc. 83.

KEITH, JAMES, the first minister of Bridgewater, came from Scotland, a. 1662, having been educated at the university of Aberdeen. He was ordained in the spring of 1664, and d. 23 July, 1719, æ. 76. His first wife was Susanna Edson, his 2d, widow Mary Williams, of Taunton. His sons were, James, Joseph, Samuel, Timothy, John, and Josiah, whose posterity are scattered throughout the U. S. There was in Bridgewater alone, in 1810, 200 persons bearing the name of Keith. 2 Coll. Mass. Hist. Soc. vii. 161, 162.

KELLOGG, JOSEPH, a lieutenant of Hadley 1662. SAMUEL, was of Hadley in 1669.

KELLOND, THOMAS, Boston 1665. 2 Coll. Mass. Hist. Soc. viii. 68, 105. See i. Hutch. Hist. Mass. 223.

KELLY, ABEL, Salem, from whence he removed, was member of the church in 1641. ||DAVID, Boston, member of the ar. co. 1644, had sons, David, b. 1647; Samuel, b. 1653. JOHN, Newbury, one of the first settlers, d. 28 Dec. 1644, leaving several children, of whom John, b. 2 July, 1642, lived in Newbury, was admitted freeman 1669, and d. 21 March, 1718, æ. 75, leaving among other children, a son John, b. 17 June, 1668, and who d. 29 Nov. 1735, leaving two sons, 1. John, b. 8 Oct. 1697, d. in Atkinson, N. H. 27 April, 1783, æ. 85, and was father of Moses, a colonel, and the sheriff of Hillsborough county, who d. 2 Aug. 1824, æ. 86, and William, H. C. 1767, the first minister of Warner, N. H. ordained 5 Feb. 1772, dismissed 1801, and d. 18 May, 1813, æ. 66, whose son John, D. C. 1804, is a counsellor at law, and was one of the founders of the N. H. Hist. Society, and its recording secretary ; 2. Richard, b. 8 May, 1704, who d. in 1774, the grand-father of John, D. C. 1791, ordained the 2d minister of Hampstead, N. H. 5 Dec. 1792. *ROGER, representative for the Isles of Shoals, at the first general court of Mass. under the new charter 1692.

KELSEY, WILLIAM, Cambridge, was admitted freeman in 1635. This name exists in N. H. and is sometimes spelled *Kelso*.

KEMP, EDWARD, Dedham, freeman 1638, perhaps the same person who d. at Chelmsford, 17 Dec. 1668. SAMUEL, Billerica 1659, probably afterwards of Andover and Groton.

KEMPSTER, DANIEL, Cambridge, was admitted freeman 1647.

KEMPTON, EPHRAIM, Scituate 1645. MANASSEH, Plymouth, came to N. E. before 1631. Julian, his widow, d. in 1664, æ. 81. Davis, Morton's Memo. 226.

KENDAL, FRANCIS, Woburn, freeman 1647, is ancestor to most of the name (now generally written *Kendall*) in N. E. Eleven had grad. at the N. E. colleges in 1828, of whom are Samuel, H. C. 1731, was minister of New-Salem, and d. 31 Jan. 1792, æ. 85; Samuel, D. D., H. C. 1782, was ordained at Weston, Mass. 5 Nov. 1785, d. 15 Feb. 1815, æ. 61; David, H. C. 1794, ordained at Hubbardston, Mass. 20 Oct. 1802; and James, D. D., who grad. at H. C. 1796, and was ordained over the 1st church in Plymouth, Mass., 1 Jan. 1800. JOHN, Cambridge 1647, perhaps the freeman of Woburn admitted in 1679. THOMAS, Lynn, freeman 1648, removed to Reading.

KENNEY, RICHARD, New-Hampshire 1680. THOMAS, Gloucester 1664. Gibbs.

KENNET, RICHARD, Boston, d. 1 April, 1693.

KENNICUT, ROGER, Malden 1670. Thomas grad. at Brown College in 1822.

KENNISTON, ALLEN, Salem, freeman 1642, died a. 1668. JOHN, Greenland, N. H. 1676, had his house burnt, and was himself killed by the Indians, 16 April 1677. i. Belknap. Hist. N. H. 127.

KENRICK, GEORGE, Plymouth and Scituate, freeman 1635 by Plymouth colony, went to Rehoboth 1645. 2 Coll. Mass. Hist. Soc. iv. 239. JOHN, Boston 1639, and member of the church, was admitted freeman 1654, removed to Muddy-River, now Brookline, where Anna, his wife, d. 15 Nov. 1656, from thence to Newton, where d. 29 Aug. 1686, aged 82. Judith, probably his widow, d. at Roxbury, 23 August, 1687. Of his children, were Joseph, b. 18 Feb. 1640; John, the ancestor of John, esq. of Newton, 3 Oct. 1641; Elisha, b. 18 Oct. 1645, and 3 daughters. Many of his descendants write the name *Kendrick*, of whom are Daniel and William Poole, brothers, graduates at Brown and Harvard. JOHN, Ipswich and Rowley, m. Lydia Cheney, 12 Nov. 1657.

KENT, JAMES, Newbury, freeman 1669, d. Dec. 1681, leaving, besides other children, a son John, to whom was given, by his uncle Richard, Kents Island in Parker River, during the life of said John, and at his death to descend to the son of John, Colonel Richard Kent, who entailed it to his son Captain Richard, and thence to descend to the eldest male heir, *in perpetuum*. Coffin. JOHN, Massachusetts, was admitted freeman in 1654. JOHN, Newbury, d. 30 Jan. 1718, aged 78. JOHN, who settled in Suffield, Conn., as early as 1686, d. 1721, leaving a son Elisha, Y. C. 1729, a clergyman, whose son Moss, Y. C. 1752, was father of the Hon. James, LL. D. the distinguished jurist and late the chancellor of the State of New-York. JOSHUA, Dedham, freeman 1646. One of this name d. at Boston, 5 Jan. 1703. From one of the early families of this name in Massachusetts, it is supposed Ebenezer Kent of Charlestown descended, who was master of a vessel near 50 years, and who after having his property destroyed by the British in the conflagration of Charlestown, retired to Reading, and d. in 1776, æ. 72. Ebenezer, his son, b. at Charlestown in 1730, d. in London in 1766, leaving two sons, Ebenezer, an officer in the American revolution, and William Austin, of Concord, N. H., a Senator of the N. Hampshire legislature in 1809, 1813, and 1814, whose sons are, Colonel William; George, D. C. 1814; John, who d. at Boston 1826, and Edward, H. C. 1821. RICHARD, Ipswich, received a grant of land in 1635, near Chebacco River; was admitted freeman 1635, went with the first settlers to Newbury, where he d. 11 June, 1654. He left several daughters and an only son John, perhaps the freeman of 1654, whose son John was father of Richard and John. Coffin. Felt. RICHARD, Newbury as early as 1636, was brother of James, the first named in this article. He d. 25 Nov. 1689, without issue. Coffin. STEPHEN, Newbury, brother of the first Richard, freeman 1639, removed to Haverhill and from thence to Woodbridge, N. J. Coffin. SAMUEL, Springfield, d. 2 Feb. 1691. ||WILLIAM, Boston, member of the ar. co. d. 9 June, 1691.

KERLEY, HENRY, born a. 1632, was a captain and lived in Lancaster in 1653, from thence went to Marlborough after 1676. [Revo. in N. E. Just. 35.] His wife, a sister of Mary Rowlandson, was killed by the Indians in 1676. Sons Henry and William were b. in 1658 and 1659. WILLIAM, Sudbury a. 1641, removed to Lancaster and d. 14 July, 1670, leaving a son William, of Sudbury in 1646, and of Lancaster in 1653.

KETCHAM, EDWARD, Massachusetts, freeman 1637. JOHN, whose name is spelled *Catcham*, was of Ipswich in 1648. Edward, John, and Samuel were of Huntington, L. I. in 1672, and John as early as 1665.

KETTLE, RICHARD, Charlestown, freeman 1635, had sons, John, b. 1639, perhaps of Portsmouth in 1663; Joseph, b. 1640, freeman 1670, Samuel, b. 1642, freeman 1670, d. in 1676; Nathaniel, b. 1644, and perhaps William who d. in 1679. Richard d. 28 June, 1680. Edward, of Boston, d. 1704, æ. 50.

KEYES, ROBERT, Watertown 1633, had a son Elias and several daughters, b. there. He may have removed to Newbury and d. there, 16 July, 1647, having a daughter b. in 1645. SOLOMON, Newbury 1654. JOHN, Springfield 1669. Five of the name had grad. in 1826.

KEYSER, GEORGE, Lynn, born a. 1617, was a tanner, freeman 1638, removed to Salem and d. Sept. 1690, aged 73. He m. Elizabeth Holyoke. Lewis. THOMAS, Lynn 1638, had a son Timothy, b. in Boston 1645.

KIBBY, ||HENRY, Dorchester, freeman 1642, member of the ar. co. 1644, d. 10 July, 1661.

KIDDER, JAMES, Cambridge 1653, Billerica 1663, had 9 sons, of whom James, b. 3 Jan. 1654, Enoch, and Ephraim settled in Billerica, from whence two of his descendants, Jonathan and Joseph, grad. at Harv. and Yale in 1751 and 1764. The latter, minister of Dunstable, N. H., d. Sept. 1818, æ. 77. THADDEUS, Lynn, freeman 1672.

KILBURN, GEORGE, Rowley, freeman 1644.

KILCUP, ||ROGER, Boston, member of the ar. co. d. 1 Oct. 1702, æ. 52.

KILHAM, AUSTIN, freeman 1641. DANIEL, spelled *Kilhen*, by Whitman, was member of the ar. co. 1645. Daniel, his son, was freeman 1680. JOHN, Wenham 1654.

KIMBALL, HENRY, Watertown, freeman 1638, had sons John and Richard, born in 1637 and 1643. The last was probably admitted freeman in 1685. This name which had in 1825 furnished 28 graduates at the N. E. colleges, is written in the ancient records *Kembal*, and *Kemble*, and, it is probable, was formerly the same as Kemble, a name common in England, whereas it is said that Kimball is seldom or never found there. RICHARD, freeman 1635, was one of the early proprietors of Watertown, and received the grant of a house-lot, 23 Feb. 1637, in Ipswich, to which place he probably removed. RICHARD, Ipswich, d. in 1675, leaving a wife, and sons, Henry, Richard, Thomas, Benjamim, and Caleb, most of them young, and daughters, Elizabeth, Mary, Sarah, and the wife of John Severns. Felt. THOMAS, of Ipswich in 1665, was one of the first settlers of Bradford, where he was killed by the Indians, 3 May, 1676, and his wife and 5 children, viz. Joanna, Thomas, Joseph, Priscilla, and John, were taken prisoners, carried 40 miles into the wilderness, but returned on the 13 June, the same year. Hubbard, Indian Wars, 84. Perry, Hist. Discourse.

KIND, ARTHUR, Boston 1646, had son James, b. in 1655.

KING, DANIEL, a merchant, was born a. 1601, came to N. E. and settled at Lynn as early as 1648, d. 27 May, 1672. His son Daniel was also of Lynn in 1648. Lewis. GEORGE, Newbury, freeman 1637, removed from thence. JOHN, Cambridge 1635. *JOHN, Northampton, a. 1654, was representative in 1679. *PETER, Sudbury 1654, a deacon of the church, was representative 1689 and 1690, d. 27 Aug. 1704. RALPH, a captain, resided in Lynn 1648, and d. 1689. Lewis. THOMAS, Sudbury, d. 3 Jan. 1644. Shattuck. THOMAS, Watertown 1641, Sudbury 1656, was one of the petitioners for the grant of Marlborough. THOMAS, an elder of the church, Scituate 1638. Coffin. WILLIAM, admitted freeman 1636, appears to have lived in Salem and Lynn. A William King d. in Boston in 1690.

KINGMAN, *HENRY, Weymouth, freeman 1636, was a representative in 1652, and d. in May, 1660, leaving sons, Edward; Thomas, perhaps freeman 1681, and John, freeman 1666, and 3 daughters. JOHN, of Weymouth, probably his son, removed quite early to Bridgewater. 2 Coll. Mass. Hist. Soc. vii. 148.

KINGSBURY, HENRY, came to N. E. in 1630, and was living at Ipswich in 1648. Savage, i. Winthrop, 368, 375. *JOHN, Dedham, freeman 1636, representative 1647. John Kingsbury, a proprietor of Watertown, was probably the same. JOSEPH, Dedham, freeman 1641, had sons, Joseph, b. 1640; John, b. 1643; Eleazar, b. 1645, and very probably others. Some account of him may be found in Worthington's Hist. Dedham, p. 100. THOMAS, perhaps a brother of Henry, came over, it is believed, at the same time with him. See Winthrop, ii. Hist. N. E. 340.

KINGSWORTH, HENRY, Guilford 1650.

KINGSTON, THOMAS, Rowley, freeman 1672.

KINSLEY, JOHN, Dorchester 1636, had a son Eldad, b. in 1638. SAMUEL, one of the early settlers of Billerica, was admitted freeman 1651, d. 21 May, 1662. Spelled also *Kingsley*. STEPHEN, one of the first ruling elders of the church, in Braintree, settled at Dorchester, but soon removed to Braintree, was admitted freeman 1640, ordained ruling elder 12 Oct. 1653. Whitney, Hist. Quincy, 37.

KINSMAN, ROBERT, Ipswich, received a grant of land in 1637, and d. in January 1665. Robert, his son, was admitted freeman 1674, and was probably the representative from Ipswich in 1692. Revolution in N. E. Justified, 14.

KIRK, THOMAS, sent in 1665 to arrest Messrs. Whalley and Goffe. Hutch.

KIRBY, RICHARD, Lynn, went to Sandwich in 1637. Lewis. WILLIAM, Boston 1640.

KIRMAN, *JOHN, Cambridge 1632, representative in March 1635. He may have removed to Weymouth.

KIRTLAND, JOHN, Lynn 1641. NATHANIEL, Lynn 1638, went to South-Old, L. I., was one of the first settlers there, but returned to Lynn and d. in Dec. 1686. PHILIP, a shoemaker, of Lynn 1636, and probably the first in a place which is now celebrated for its numbers of this occupation, went with the preceding to South-Old. His son Philip remained at Lynn. This name is often spelled *Kertland*. Lewis.

KITCHELL, ROBERT, Guilford 1650. 1 Coll. Mass. Hist. Soc. x.

KITCHEN, JOHN, Salem, admitted to the church 1643, freeman 1642, is styled a shoemaker in deeds of conveyance.

KITTREDGE, JOHN, the ancestor of all of the name in this country, came when a young man from England, without any relations, excepting his mother, and settled at Billerica as a farmer, [Mr. N. Kittredge] and there d. 18 Oct. 1676. His children were, 1. John, b. 24 Jan. 1666, m. Hannah French, 3 Aug. 1685, had 11 children, six being sons, and d. 27 April, 1614, being the first of the name in America styled Dr., a prefix so common among his descendants; (Rev. Mr. Abbot [Hist. Andover, 150] mistakes in saying he came from Germany ;) 2. James, b. 21 March, 1668; 3. Daniel, b. 23 July, 1670, who had 7 children; 4. Jonathan, born 1674, d. 1696; 5. Benoni, b. 1677. Descendants are very numerous.

KNAP, NICHOLAS, Watertown 1631, had sons, Timothy, b. 1632; Joshua, b. 1634; Caleb, b. 1636. WILLIAM, Watertown

1640, d. 30 August, 1658, æ. 80. His son William was of Watertown in 1640. Fr. Knapp, an Englishman, and the author of one of the recommendatory poems addressed to Pope, which he wrote in N. E. lived in Watertown, and might be of this family.

KNEELAND, PHILIP, Lynn 1637. Samuel, William, and William Kneeland grad. at H. C. 1743, 1744, and 1751. The last William was a physician, and d. 2 Nov. 1788, æ. 56.

KNIGHT, ALEXANDER, Ipswich 1635. EZEKIEL, Salem 1637, Braintree 1640, where his son Ezekiel was born. There was an Ezekiel Knight of Wells in 1653. GEORGE, Hingham 1638. Lincoln, Hist. Hingham, 46. JOHN, Newbury 1635, had sons, John, b. 1648; Joseph, b. 1652. JOHN, Watertown, freeman 1636, was a proprietor of Sudbury. JOHN, Woburn 1653, [3 Coll. Mass. Hist. Soc. i. 44] was perhaps the freeman of 1643. MICHAEL, Massachusetts, freeman 1654. PHILIP, Wenham 1669. RICHARD, Weymouth 1638, [Winthrop, ii. Hist. N. E. 348] and perhaps the same who was admitted a townsman of Boston, 31 Jan. 1642, and member of the church. RICHARD, a deacon, was brother of the first named John, was born a. 1602, lived in Newbury; was admitted freeman 1636. ROBERT, Boston 1642, had sons, Samuel and James, b. in 1642 and 1653. ROBERT, Marblehead 1648. ROBERT, Kittery 1652. ROGER, Pascataqua 1631. Belknap, i. Hist. N. H. Appx. WALTER, Salem 1627. WILLIAM, Salem, was admitted an inhabitant, 2 Jan. 1637, probably removed to Lynn, and d. 5 Jan. 1656. The children of the one at Lynn were, Jacob, who d. 1695; Ann; Francis; Hannah; Daniel; Elizabeth, and Mary. Lewis. [*WILLIAM*,] the first minister of Topsfield, was admitted freeman 1638, received a grant of 200 acres of land at Ipswich in 1639, began to preach at Topsfield in July, 1641, and died, it is supposed, in 1655. He is mentioned in Mather's First Classis of ministers, but without a christian name, which I have supplied as above on the authority of Rev. Mr. Felt, and Mr. Coffin.

KNOLLYS, HANSERD, one of the early preachers at Dover, from whence he soon went to Long-Island, and is said to have returned to England, and there d. 19 Sept. 1691, æ. 93. Belknap, i. Hist. N. H. 41. Savage, i. Winthrop, 291, ii. 5.

KNOTT, GEORGE, settled in Sandwich 1637, whither he went, it is supposed, from Lynn. Lewis.

KNOWER, THOMAS, Massachusetts 1631. Winthrop, i. Hist. N. E. 72. GEORGE, d. at Malden, 13 Feb. 1675.

KNOWLES, ‡ALEXANDER, Massachusetts, freeman 1636, went to Connecticut, and was elected a magistrate in 1657. *JOHN*, the second minister of Watertown, was b. in Lincolnshire; was educated at Magdalen College, in Cambridge, was chosen fellow of Catharine-Hall in 1625; came to N. E. in 1639, and the same year was admitted member of the church in Boston. He was ordained, 9 Dec. 1640, as colleague with Rev. George Phillips; went as a missionary to Virginia in 1642, returned to Watertown the next year, and in 1650, sailed for England, and was a preacher in the cathedral of Bristol, but was silenced in 1662. He then went to London, and was there during the plague in 1665. This worthy man, who should have been commemorated by Eliot and Allen, and whose death should have been marked by Savage, died 10 Nov. 1685, at an advanced age. Calamy [ii. Account, 605—608] gives a good account of his character. One of his children was born at Watertown in 1641. RICHARD, Cambridge 1638, whose son James was b. 17 Nov. 1648.

KNOWLTON, JOHN, Ipswich, freeman 1641, died a. 1654, leaving children, John, freeman 1680; Abraham, and Elizabeth. THOMAS, a deacon of Ipswich 1648, brother of John, d. 3 April, 1692. WILLIAM, Ipswich, a bricklayer, d. 1644. Felt. WILLIAM, Hingham 1635, whom Lincoln [Hist. Hingham, 43] calls *Nolton*.

KOLDOM, ||CLEMENT, member of the ar. co. 1645. (See COLDHAM.)

LACY, LAURENCE, Andover, had a son Laurence, b. 1683. Abbot, Hist. Andover, 39.

LADD, DANIEL, a lieutenant, came over as early as 1639, and settled at Ipswich. William Ladd, esq. grad. at H. C. in 1797.

LAIGHTON, *THOMAS, Lynn, freeman 1638, representative 1646, 1648 to 1653, 1656 to 1658, 1660 and 1661, 12 years, died 8 August, 1697. His children were, Thomas, freeman 1672; Margaret; Samuel; Rebecca, and Elizabeth. Lewis. The name is spelled *Laughton* and *Layton* in old records.

LAKE, JOHN, admitted to the church in Boston and freeman in 1644, was a tailor, and had a son Caleb, b. 1655. THOMAS, Boston, admitted freeman 1641, may have been the merchant mentioned by Hutchinson and Hubbard, or the merchant may have been the Thomas Lake, who was admitted freeman in 1671. Stephen and Thomas, sons of Thomas Lake were born in Boston in 1649 and 1656. William Lake was of Salem in 1665. A Capt. Lake was killed in Maine in 1676, by the Indians. See Hubbard's Indian Wars.

LAKEMAN, *WILLIAM, was representative of the Isles of Shoals in 1692.

LAKIN, JOHN, was one of the first proprietors of Groton, where was a Lieut. Lakin in 1677. THOMAS, admitted freeman 1670. WILLIAM, Groton, d. 10 Dec. 1672, æ. 91.

LAMB, EDWARD, was one of the proprietors of Watertown in 1633. His son Samuel was b. 1637. Joshua Lamb is named in 1 Coll. Mass. Hist. Soc. v. 236. THOMAS, came over in 1630 in the fleet with Gov. Winthrop and settled at Roxbury, where he d. 3 April, 1645. His wife d. in 1639. Winthrop, ii. Hist. N. E. 340. WILLIAM, Boston, d. in 1685. John and Daniel Lamb d. at Springfield in 1690 and 1692.

LAMBERT, FRANCIS, Rowley, d. 1648. JONATHAN, Rowley in 1664. Four persons of this name had grad. at the N. E. colleges in 1826. MIGHILL, Lynn 1644, lived on Nahant, and d. 18 Aug., 1676. Lewis. RICHARD, Salem 1637. ROBERT, came from Dartmouth, England, and was one of the founders of the first Baptist church in Boston 1665.

LAMBERTON, ――――, New-Haven 1643, was one of the principal inhabitants, and one of the owners of the ship in which he and a number of worthy persons were lost at sea, the beginning of the year 1646. Johnson, Hist. N. E. 214. Winthrop, ii. Hist. N. E. 266. Mather, i. Magnalia, 76—78.

LAMPREY, HENRY, Boston 1653. This name exists in New-Hampshire.

LAMPSON, BARNABAS, Cambridge 1635. WILLIAM, Ipswich, freeman 1637, died 1 Feb. 1659.

LANDEN, JOHN, Portsmouth 1640. 1 Belknap, 47. Adams [Annals 395] gives this name Lander. THOMAS, Lynn, removed to Sandwich 1637. Lewis.

LANE, ANDREW, Hingham 1635, perhaps went to Portsmouth, where Andrew Lane purchased in 1650, houses, &c. valued at £1000 sterling. Lincoln, Hist. Hingham, 43. *JOB, Malden, freeman 1656, removed to Billerica, (that part which is now Bedford) which he represented in 1676 and 1679 ; was the representative of Malden in 1685, to which place he may have returned. His son, Major John Lane, was representative of Billerica in 1702, and d. 17 Jan. 1715. Ten persons of the name in N. E. had received a publick education in 1826. SAMSON, Pascataqua 1631, belonged to Teignmouth, Devonshire. WILLIAM, Boston 1651, freeman 1657, had sons Samuel and John, b. in 1651 and 1653. Henry Lane d. at Boston in 1690.

LANGDON, BENJAMIN, Boston 1678, where were also David, John, and Philip Langdon, who had children born as early as 1685. Philip, who d. 11 Dec. 1697, had a son Samuel, b. 22 Dec. 1687, the father of Rev. Samuel Langdon, D. D., born 12 Jan. 1723, grad. 1740 at H. C. of which he was president from 1774 to 1780, having previously been the minister of the first church in Portsmouth. He was afterwards settled at Hampton-Falls, in N. H., where he d. 29 Nov. 1797, æ. 75. TOBIAS, Portsmouth, m. Mary Hubbard, 17 Nov. 1636, and had 6 sons, of whom, John, the youngest, b. 28 May, 1704, was father of Hon. John Langdon, of Portsmouth, senator in Congress from N. H. 12 years, chief magistrate of the State 8 years, two of which were with the title of *President*. Governour Langdon was b. 1740, d. 18 Sept. 1819, æ. 79. Fourteen persons of the name had grad. at the N. E. colleges in 1826.

LANGER, RICHARD, Hingham 1636. Lincoln, Hist. Hingham, 44.

LANGFORD, JOHN, Salem, freeman 1645, was living there in 1689, as appears from the Revolution in New-England Justified, p. 41.

LANGHORNE, RICHARD, Rowley, d. 1669. Spelled also *Longhorne*. THOMAS, spelled also *Longhorn*, was of Cambridge in 1647, and had children, Samuel, Mercy, Sarah, Elizabeth, Mary, and Patince.

LANGLEY, ABEL, Rowley before 1652. WILLIAM, Lynn, was admitted freeman 1638. (See LONGLEY.)

LANGSTAFF, HENRY, Pascataqua 1631, was one of grand jury in 1643.

LANKTON, GEORGE, Northampton, a. 1658. Rev. Levi Lankton, Y. C. 1777, was the minister of Alstead, N. H. This name is probably the same which is often spelled *Langton*, which may be the true orthography. JOSEPH, Ipswich 1648. ROGER, Ipswich, freeman 1635. SAMUEL, freeman 1681. Rev. Samuel Langton was ordained minister of the 2d parish in York, 3 July, 1754, and d. in Dec. 1794.

LAPHAM, THOMAS, Scituate 1668.

LARGE, WILLIAM, Hingham 1635, removed to Province-Town, Cape Cod. Lincoln, Hist. Hingham, 43.

LARKHAM, THOMAS, a minister at Dover, came from Not-ham, in England, which name, probably in compliment to him, was given to Cocheco, or Dover, a. 1642. He began preaching at Dover, a. 1640, left the place in 1642, returned to England, and died 1669, æ. 68. Winthrop. Calamy. Belknap. Mordecai and Cornelius Larkham were inhabitants of Beverly in 1681 and 1697.

LARKIN, ||EDWARD, Charlestown, freeman 1640, member of the ar. co. 1644, had sons, John, b. 1640, d. 27 Dec. 1677; Thomas, b. 1644, d. 20 May, 1676. Descendants are numerous in Massachusetts.

LARNIT, ISAAC, Woburn 1653 [3 Coll. Mass. Hist. Soc. i. 45]; removed to Chelmsford and was one of the first settlers, and d. there 4 Dec. 1657. This name is probably the same with *Larned* or *Lerned*.

LASKIN, HUGH, Salem 1637, freeman 1639, d. a. 1659.

LATHAM, CARY, Cambridge 1642. ROBERT, Cambridge, lived two or more years with Rev. Thomas Shepard, removed to Bridgewater; had two sons, James and Chilton. 2 Coll. Mass. Hist. Soc. vii. MS Diary of Rev. Thomas Shepard. WILLIAM, Plymouth 1623. This name exists in Massachusetts and New-Hampshire.

LATIMORE, CHRISTOPHER, Marblehead 1648. John Latimer grad. at H. C. 1703.

LAURIE, GILBERT, Boston, from whence he went to Portsmouth, where he was a preacher in the absence of Mr. Moodey, in 1686. 1 Coll. Mass. Hist. Soc. x. 45. Adams, Annals Portsmouth, 86.

LAW, ANDREW, Hingham 1654, had sons, Joshua, Josiah, and Caleb. John and George Law were also of Hingham in 1652. JOHN, Concord, m. Lydia Draper, and had sons, John, b. 1661; Thomas, b. 1663; Stephen, born 1665, and Samuel. Shattuck. RICHARD, a principal gentleman of Stamford 1664. Trumbull.

LAWES, FRANCIS, Salem, freeman 1637, died a. 1666, leaving a daughter Mary, the wife of John Neal.

LAWRENCE, JOHN, Watertown, freeman 1637, whose wife was Elizabeth, had children, John, b. 14 March, 1636; Nathaniel,

b. 1639, of Groton, and freeman 1671 ; Joseph, b. 1643 ; Mary, b. 1645; Peleg, b. 11 Jan. 1648 ; Enoch, b. 5 May, 1649, m. Ruth Shattuck. THOMAS, was admitted freeman 1638, and died at Hingham, 5 Nov. 1655.

LAWSON, CHRISTOPHER, Boston 1643, was born a. 1616. He appears to have been in N. H. in 1644. His son Thomas was born in Boston, 1643. *DEODATE*, a preacher at Danvers in 1688, was admitted freeman 1680, and was settled the third minister of the 2d church in Scituate, from which he was dismissed in 1698.

LAY, ROBERT, Lynn 1638. John Lay grad. at Y. C. in 1780.

LAYLAND, HENRY, Dorchester 1653.

LAYTON, THOMAS, Dover, d. 22 Jan. 1672, leaving a son Thomas, whose descendants remain in Dover, where the name is now written, as perhaps it might have been formerly, *Leighton*.

LAZELL, ISAAC, Hingham 1649, removed to Bridgewater. Rev. Ebenezer Lazell grad. at Y. C. 1788.

LEACH, JOHN, Salem 1637, died a. 1659. LAWRENCE, Salem, was admitted freeman in 1631, d. 1662, æ. 83, leaving a widow Elizabeth and son, Clement, who lived in England. Richard, another son, died in 1647, and left a son John. Felt, Annals Salem, 119, 215. ROBERT, Salem 1637, was freeman 1644. RICHARD, Salem, member of the church 1648, d. 1687, leaving several children.

LEADBETTER, HENRY, Dorchester, was admitted freeman 1671.

LEADER, GEORGE, Kittery 1654. JOHN, Boston 1652, had a son Thomas, born there in 1654. RICHARD, Pascataqua, was in possession of Capt. John Mason's lands at Newichawannock in 1652. Belknap, i. Hist. N. H. 86. Winthrop, in a letter to his son [ii. Hist. N. E. 356] speaks of a Mr. Leader, as does Felt in his Annals of Salem, and Lewis in his Annals of Lynn. THOMAS, Boston 1647, d. 28 Oct. 1663.

LEAGER, JACOB, Boston, was admitted freeman in 1641, and d. 24 Feb. 1664.

LEAKE, THOMAS, Dorchester, was admitted to the church 1640, d. 27 Oct. 1678. Davenport's Sexton's Monitor. It is possible that this was the Thomas Lake admitted freeman in 1641.

LEARNED, ISAAC. (See LARNIT.) William, Woburn, probably son of the preceding.

LEAVITT, *JOHN, Hingham, freeman 1636, representative 1644, 1656, 1664, and perhaps at the Oct. session in 1690, was a deacon, and d. 20 Nov. 1691, æ. 83. His children were, John, who d. before 1690; Samuel; Israel, b. 14 Sept. 1637; Moses; Josiah, b. 4 May, 1653; Nehemiah, b. 21 Jan. 1656; Mary ; Sarah ; Hannah, and Abigail. Samuel and Moses probably settled in Exeter, where two of these names were living in 1683. [Belknap, i. Hist. N. H. Appx.] Israel had a son John, who died 29 July, 1748, leaving a son John, who d. 13 April, 1797, æ. 88. Lincoln. Hist. Hingham, 44, 175. JOHN, Bloody-Point, N. H. 1645.

THOMAS, Exeter 1639. Aratus Leavitt, had a son Thomas, b. in N. H. in 1686.

LECHFORD, ||THOMAS, one of the earliest lawyers in N. E., was of Boston in 1638, and a member of the ar. co. in 1640. He is author of a tract, entitled, " Plain-Dealing : or Nevves from New-England," which was published in London in 1642.

LEE, ABRAHAM, was a chymist, and lived in Dover in 1680, and was killed by the Indians 27 June 1689. The name of Lee had furnished 24 graduates at the N. E. colleges in 1826, of whom the first at H. C. was Thomas Lee, 1722, a merchant of Salem, who d. 14 July, 1747, æ. 45. Joseph Lee, H. C. 1729, was a judge of the court of common pleas, and d. 5 Dec. 1782. JOHN, Ipswich 1648, d. 1671. John his eldest son was a surgeon in the navy; Joseph, another son, m. Mary Woodhouse, and settled in Concord as early as 1696. Shattuck. *SAMUEL*, minister of Bristol, was born in London in 1623 ; was educated at Oxford ; came to N. E. 24 June, 1686, and was settled at Bristol, (now R. I.) 8 May, 1687. He sailed for England in 1691 ; was captured by a French privateer, and carried into St. Maloes, in France, where he d. in 1691, in his 64th year. Holmes, i. Annals, 435. SAMUEL, Malden, was admitted freeman in 1671. [———] Plymouth 1644. 2 Coll. Mass. Hist. Soc. iii. 184. THOMAS, Ipswich 1648, brother of John Lee, d. in 1662, aged a. 82. WALTER, Northampton 1659, Westfield 1676.

LEEDS, BENJAMIN, Dorchester, member of the church 1658, freeman 1670. Joseph Leeds lived in Dorchester in 1658, and perhaps in Westfield in 1666. Two of the name of Daniel Leeds grad. at H. C. in 1761 and 1783. RICHARD, Salem 1637.

LEET, ‡ANDREW, eldest son of Governour William Leet, was chosen magistrate in 1678. He m. a daughter of Thomas Jordan. JOHN, brother of Andrew, was, it is said, the first male child born in Guilford. †‡§WILLIAM, came to N. E. in 1637, and settled at Guilford as early as 1643; removed to Hartford, where he d. 16 April, 1683. He was an assistant of New-Haven colony from 1643 to 1657; deputy-governour in 1658; governour in 1661; assistant of Conn. after its union with New-Haven 1665 ; deputy-governour 1669 to 1675 ; governour 1676.

LEFFINGWELL, MICHAEL, Woburn 1642. Yale College has four of the name of Leffingwell on its catalogue. THOMAS, Saybrook 1637, was one of the original purchasers of the town of Norwich, from Uncas and his two sons, Owaneco and Attawanhood in 1659. Pease and Niles. Gazetteer of Conn.

LEGAT, JOHN, Exeter 1646. Thomas Legate, esq. was a member of the first provincial congress of Mass. 1774. Boston Mag. i. 606.

LEGGE, JOHN, was born a. 1610, freeman 1635, Marblehead 1648. A John Legge was admitted freeman 1680, and a John Legge grad. at H. C. 1701.

LEIGH, THOMAS, Roxbury, d. 19 July, 1694.

LEIGHTON, THOMAS. (See Laighton and Layton.)

LEISTER, EDWARD, Plymouth 1620.   Eliphalet Lester was a Baptist minister at Saybrook, a few years since.

LELAND, HENRY, Medfield, had sons, Hopestill, born 1655; Ebenezer, b. 1657, and Eleazar, b. 1660.

LEMMON, ROBERT, Salem 1637, was admitted to the church, 7 Feb. 1641, and probably freeman in 1642, instead of Robert Looman, which doubtless should be Lemmon.   Dr. Joseph Lemmon, of Marblehead, grad. at H. C. 1735.

LEONARD, HENRY, Lynn, was admitted freeman 1668. JAMES, Raynham, Massachusetts, with his brother Henry, set up a forge iron manufacture there. [Fobes, in 1 Coll. Mass. Hist. Soc. iii. 170.]   His son Thomas was a judge and d. in 1713; being grandfather of Hon. George Leonard, LL. D. who grad. at H. C. 1748, and d. in 1819, æ. 90.   Twenty-eight of this name had grad. at the N. E. colleges in 1826, of whom, at Harvard, have been Rev. Nathaniel Leonard, of Plymouth, 1719, Rev. Abiel Leonard, D. D., of Woodstock, 1759, Hon. Daniel Leonard, chief justice of the superior court of Bermuda, 1760, and several others.   JOHN, Springfield 1639.   Josiah and Abel Leonard of Springfield died in 1688 and 1690.   SOLOMON, was one of the proprietors of Bridgewater in 1645.

LETHERMORE, JOHN, Massachusetts, freeman 1635.   Savage, ii. Winthrop.

LETTICE, THOMAS, Plymouth 1638.   Davis, Morton's Memo. 384.

LETTIN, RICHARD, Concord before 1650.   Shattuck.

LEVENS, JOHN, Roxbury, freeman 1634, whose 1st wife died 10 Oct. 1638, had sons, John, b. 1640 ; Peter and Caleb, (twins) b. 1644.

LEVERETT, ||HUDSON, Boston, son of the following, was born in 1640, was member of the ar. co. in 1656.   Hon. John, the 8th president of H. C. was his son.   §‡†||*JOHN, son of Elder Thomas Leverett, came with his father to N. E. ; was admitted freeman 1640 ; member of the ar. co. 1639 ; its captain in 1654 ; representative 1651 to 1653, 1663, and 1664, 5 years ; speaker of the house 1663 and 1664 ; major-general 1664 ; assistant 1665 to 1670, 6 years ; deputy-governour 1671 and 1672 ; governour 1673 to 1678, 6 years ; received the order of Knighthood from Charles II in 1676; d. 16 March, 1679.   Church, in his Memoirs of Philip's war, makes Governour Leverett to have died in 1676, which is evidently a mistake for the death of Governour Winthrop, of Conn. who d. at Boston, 5 April, 1676.   THOMAS, Boston, was admitted member of the church in Oct. 1633, was its ruling elder a number of years.   He was admitted freeman, 4 March, 1634. Savage, i. Winthrop, 114.

LEVERIDGE, WILLIAM, came to N. E. in the ship James, and arrived at Salem, 10 Oct. 1633 ; went to Dover, and preached there until 1635, when he seems to have been in Boston, being admitted a member of the church there 9 August that year. He was in Sandwich in 1640, and in 1657 was employed as a missionary by the commissioners of the united colonies. He accompained the first settlers of Huntington, L. I., where he remained until 1670, when he removed to Newtown, on the same island, and d. there. Hon. Silas Wood informs me that some of his posterity reside at Newtown, and are among the most respectable people of that town.

LEWIS, EDMUND, freeman 1636, one of the first settlers of Watertown, where his sons, James and Nathaniel, were born; removed to Lynn, a. 1640, where he d. in 1651. His wife was Mary, and his children were, John, Thomas, James, Nathaniel, and two others, whose descendants are numerous, some of them still remaining at Lynn. Thirty-eight persons of this name had been educated at the various colleges in N. E. in 1826. GEORGE, Scituate 1636, came from East-Greenwich, in Kent, England, and was admitted a member of the church in Plymouth; dismissed 23 Nov. 1634, and settled in Scituate, from whence he removed to Barnstable, and was killed by the Indians at Blackstone's farm, 26 March, 1676. His wife was Sarah Jenkins, whom he m. in England, and his children were, 1. George; 2. Thomas; 3. Edward; 4. James, who m. Sarah Lane, and had 10 children, of whom John, the eldest, was b. 29 Sept. 1656, m. Hannah Lincoln, of Hingham, where he resided, and had 9 children, the 2d of whom was Rev. Daniel Lewis, of Pembroke, Mass., b. 29 Sept. 1685, grad. at H. C. 1707, ordained 3 Dec. 1712, d. 29 June, 1753, æ. 68, 5. John; 6. Jabez; 7. Mary; 8. Sarah. Daniel Lewis, H. C. 1734, was son of Rev. Daniel. Hon. John Lewis, of North-Yarmouth, Me. a senator of Mass. was son to a brother of Rev. Daniel, and d. 4 March, 1803, æ. 85. A. Lewis, MS Letter. GEORGE, Casco-Bay 1658, and probably 1676. Hubbard, Eastern Ind. Wars, 33. JOHN, Casco-Bay 1665. Hutch. Coll. 398. JOHN, Scituate 1637. 2 Coll. Mass. Hist. Soc. iv. 239. JOHN, Lynn 1640, freeman 1646, had one son, John, whose descendants reside in Lynn. Lewis. JOHN, Boston 1637, had 3 children, John, b. 12 Sept. 1638; Samuel, b. 24 June, 1641; Elizabeth, b. 10 Sept. 1642. Ibid. JOHN, Roxbury, had Peter and Andrew, (twins) born 11 Sept. 1644 Ibid. He probably d. 16 Nov. 1647. Roxbury records. JOHN, Charlestown 1638, probably d. at Malden, in Sept. 1657. He had sons, John, b. 1638; Samuel, b. 1641. Perhaps he was the John of Boston. *PHILIP, of Portsmouth, that part which is now Greenland, 1665, was one of the first representatives in the N. H. assembly under the provincial government, 1680. ROBERT, Salem, removed to Newbury, and d. 4 May, 1643. Felt. Coffin. THOMAS, Dorchester 1636. Dr. Harris. THOMAS, New-Hampshire 163–. [Belknap, i. Hist. N. H. 20.] Perhaps the same who was at Saco in 1636, is styled gent. and died a. 1640. WILLIAM, a proprietor of Cambridge, was brother of Edmund, came from England 1630, and was admitted freeman 6 November 1632. He returned to England where he married; came over again and settled at Roxbury. He had five children, 1. John, b. 1 Nov. 1635; 2. Christopher, b. 1636; 3. Lydia, b. 25 Dec. 1639; 4. Josiah, b. 28 July, 1641; 5.

Isaac, born 15 April, 1644, m. Mary, lived in Boston; d. there, 6
April 1693, having had five children, of whom Isaac, the eldest son,
b. 31 Aug. 1683, m. Hannah Hallet, and had 8 children b. in Boston.
Nathan, the 7th child, b. 6 Dec. 1721, was grandfather to Alonzo
Lewis, the poet and historian of Lynn.   There was a William Lew-
is, a proprietor of Lancaster 1654, who died there, 3 Dec. 1671.
John Lewis was also an early proprietor there.   *WILLIAM, was
representative of Hadley in 1662, and of Northampton in 1664.
    LIDGET, ||CHARLES, Boston, member of ar. co. 1679.   PE-
TER, Boston, admitted freeman 1673.   He or the preceding, was
the Colonel Lidget named by Hutchinson, i. Hist. Mass. 334.
Judge Sewall mentions in his diary the death of a Mr. Lidget, 26
April, 1675.
    LIGHTFOOT, FRANCIS, came from London and settled at
Lynn; freeman 1636, d. 1646.
    LINCOLN, ROBERT, Boston, d. 6 May, 1663.   Records.
SAMUEL, came from Hingham, in England, 1637; lived a short
time at Salem, and removed to Hingham, Mass.   His children were,
Samuel; Daniel, b. 1652; Mordecai, b. 1657; Mary; Thomas;
Martha; Sarah; Rebecca.   The Hon. Levi Lincoln, lieutenant-
governour of Massachusetts, was a descendant from this family.
Lincoln, Hist. Hingham, 126, 148.   STEPHEN, Hingham, came
from Windham, in England, and arrived in this country in 1638,
with his wife, and son Stephen, who had but one son and three
grandsons, viz.: Stephen, (a bachelor) David, and James.   David
had sons, David, Matthew, and Isaac.   Isaac grad. at H. C. 1722,
and had sons, Isaac, James, Nathaniel, and Heman.   The second
David d. 1 Feb. 1814, æ. 79.   He was father of Rev. Perez Lincoln of Gloucester, who d. 20 June, 1811.   Ibid. 151.   THOMAS,
a weaver, brother of Samuel, came from Hingham, England, in
1633, and settled at Hingham, Mass. a. 1636.   His 1st wife was
Susanna, who d. 1641; his 2d, whom he m. 1663, was Mary Chubbuck.   He d. 2 Sept. 1675, leaving no issue.   Ibid. 148.   THO-
MAS, a cooper, of Hingham 1636, may be the one admitted freeman in 1637.   He had a son Benjamin, admitted freeman 1677,
and a grandson Benjamin, who was father to Col. Benjamin Lincoln,
whose son Benjamin was the celebrated revolutionary general, who
d. 9 May, 1810.   Bela Lincoln, H. C. 1754, and M. D. at Aberdeen,
was brother of the general.   Benjamin and Theodore Lincoln, H.
C. 1777 and 1785, were sons of the general.   Benjamin married a
daughter of James Otis, and d. 18 Jan. 1788, æ. 32, leaving two
sons, Benjamin, H. C. 1806, who d. at Demarara, and James Otis,
H. C. 1807, who d. at Hingham, 12 Aug. 1818.   Ibid.   THO-
MAS, a husbandman, settled in Hingham as early as 1638.   Ibid.
THOMAS, Hingham 1636, was a miller, removed to Taunton before 1652; was living in 1683 at the age of 80 years.   Of the four
persons of the name of Thomas Lincoln, above, two were admitted
freemen in 1637 and 1642, but it is not easy to designate them.
Twenty-two persons of the name had graduated in N. E. in 1826,

among whom may be found divines, lawyers, physicians, and statesmen, who may trace to the above as their common ancestors. Ibid.

LINDALL, JAMES, Duxbury, was one of the proprietors of Bridgewater in 1645. *TIMOTHY, son of the preceding was b. in Duxbury; admitted freeman 1678, settled in Salem, which he represented in 1692, and probably afterwards. He d. 6 Jan. 1699, æ. 58. His wife, Mary Veren, he m. in 1672 and had 9 children, of whom Timothy was baptized 4 Nov. 1677, grad. at H. C. 1695, was representative of Salem, speaker of the house, counsellor, judge of the court of common pleas, and d. 1760, æ. 83.

LINDON, AUGUSTINE, Boston 1652. Savage, MS note. JOHN, New-Haven, d. 1667.

LINDSAY, CHRISTOPHER, Lynn, d. 1668, leaving sons John and Eleazar. Lewis.

LINE, THOMAS. (See LYNDE.)

LINGE, BENJAMIN, New-Haven 1651, a first settler at Stony River, d. 27 April 1673, died without issue, and his widow m. Col. John Dixwell.

LINNET, ROBERT, Scituate 1639, removed to Barnstable.

LINTON, RICHARD, came over as early as 1630, and settled at Watertown; was one of the first settlers of Lancaster, and d. 30 March, 1665. Willard, Hist. Lancaster, 27.

LIPPINCOT, RICHARD, Boston, freeman 1640, had a son John, b. in 1644.

LISLE, THOMAS, a barber-surgeon of Boston. (See LYALL.)

LITCHFIELD, LAWRENCE, Scituate 1646. There was a Litchfield whose christian name is not given, who was a member of the ar. co. in 1640. Rev. Joseph Litchfield, a grad. of Brown University 1773, d. at Kittery, 28 Jan. 1828, æ. 78. Rev. Paul Litchfield, H. C. 1775, d. at Carlisle, Mass. 5 Nov. 1827, æ. 76.

LITTLE, GEORGE, Newbury 1640, a tailor, came from Unicorn-street, in London. His 1st wife was Alice Poor. His children were, Joseph, b. 22 Sept. 1653; John, b. 28 July 1655; Moses, born 11 March 1657; Sarah, born 1661. His 2d wife was Eleanor Barnard. Descendants are numerous, and some of them have been distinguished in publick and private life. He was the first of Baptist sentiments in Newbury. Coffin. THOMAS, Plymouth 1644, removed to Marshfield. 2 Coll. Mass. Hist. Soc. iii. 184. Rev. Ephraim Little, 1695, minister of Plymouth, and Thomas, H. C. 1695, were probably descendants.

LITTLEFIELD, *FRANCIS, Wells, representative 1660. JOHN, was admitted freeman in 1671.

LITTLEHALE, RICHARD, Newbury 1638, thence to Haverhill, where he d. 18 Feb. 1684.

LIVERMORE, JOHN, Watertown as early as 1642, was the great ancestor of Matthew Livermore, esq., b. at Watertown, 14 Jan. 1703, grad. H. C. 1722, d. at Portsmouth, 14 Feb. 1776, and probably of the Hon. Samuel Livermore, Nassau 1752, a senator in congress from N. H. 8 years from 1793, judge of the superiour court from 1782 to 1790, and several years its chief justice, two of whose sons, Edward St. Loe Livermore and Arthur Livermore have been judges of the same court, and the latter, chief justice, and also representative in congress, 6 years. A Samuel Livermore was admitted freeman in 1671. Ten persons of the name had grad. at the N. E. and Princeton colleges in 1826.

LLOYD, JAMES, came from Somersetshire, a. 1670, resided a short time at Rhode-Island, but finally settled at Boston, where he d. in July, 1693. His son Henry, who lived at Queen's county, L. I., was father of James Lloyd, a celebrated physician of Boston, whose son, Hon. James Lloyd, H. C. 1787, has been distinguished as a statesman and member of the U. S. Senate.

LOBDELL, ISAAC, freeman 1673. JOHN, freeman 1673.

LOCKE, WILLIAM, Woburn 1659. Rev. Samuel Locke, D. D., minister of Sherburne, Mass., was a native of Lancaster, and grad. in 1775 at H. C., of which he was president from 1770 to 1773.

LOCKWOOD, EDMUND, freeman 18 May, 1631, was of Cambridge in 1632, and probably removed to Connecticut with Messrs. Hooker and Stone. Rev. Samuel Lockwood, D. D., of Andover, Conn., who grad. Y. C. 1745, and d. 18 June, 1791, might be a descendant of him or the following. Seven others of the name had grad. at Yale in 1826. ROBERT, Watertown 1634, had sons, Jonathan, b. 1634; Joshua, b. 1638; Daniel, b. 1640; Ephraim, b. 1641; Gershom, b. 1643.

LOMBARD, BERNARD, Scituate 1633, freeman 1634, removed from thence to Barnstable. Solomon Lombard, H. C. 1723, minister of Gorham, Me., was a native of Truro, and probably his descendant. THOMAS, Massachusetts, whose name as well as the preceding, is frequently spelled *Lumbert,* was admitted freeman in 1631.

LONG, JOSHUA, said by Mr. W. Winthrop to have been of Charlestown, grad. at H. C. in 1653. PHILIP, Ipswich 1648, had a son Joseph, b. in Boston in 1652. ROBERT, Plymouth 1623, Davis, Morton's Memo. ROBERT, Charlestown, was admitted freeman in 1635, and perhaps was the father of Joshua above. ROBERT, seaman, probably the freeman in 1636, settled in Newbury, was deacon of the church, and died of the small pox, 27 Dec. 1690. Alice, his wife, d. 17 Jan. 1691. He had several children. Coffin. SAMUEL, Ipswich 1648.

LONGFELLOW, WILLIAM, Newbury, was born a. 1653, m. Anne, a daughter of Henry Sewall, 10 Nov. 1678, and according to Mr. Coffin was drowned at Cape Breton in 1690. His son Stephen was b. at Newbury, 10 Jan. 1682, and had a son Stephen, b. at Newbury, 7 Feb. 1723, grad. at H. C. 1742, moved to Portland 1745, where he was a schoolmaster, town clerk from 1750 to 1772; register of probate from 1761 to 1776, and clerk of the court. He d. 1 May, 1790, æ. 67.

LONGHORN, THOMAS. (See LANGHORNE.)

LONGLEY, RICHARD, Lynn 1640, had sons William and Jonathan. Lewis. WILLIAM, son of the preceding (perhaps the freeman under 1638, named *Langley*) was clerk of the writs in Lynn 1655. It is believed he went to Groton, and there d. 29 Nov. 1680.

LOOKER, HENRY, Sudbury, was admitted freeman in 1643. JOHN, Sudbury, freeman 1646, d. 18 June, 1653.

LOOMAN, ROBERT, [Savage, ii. Winthrop 372] should be LEMMON, which see.

LOOMIS, JOHN and JOSEPH, Windsor 1640. Samuel and William Loomis were of Westfield in 1685.

LORD, JOHN, Watertown, d. 23 April, 1669. NATHANIEL, Kittery, freeman 1652, was probably father of captain Samuel Lord, mentioned in Sullivan's Hist. of Maine, and the ancestor of many families of the name in that State. The late Hon. John Lord, of South-Berwick, was a descendant, whose son Rev. Nathan Lord, D. D. a graduate at Bowd. college, 1809, and the minister of Amherst, N. H. from 22 May, 1816 to Oct. 1828, is the president of Dartmouth college. RICHARD, Cambridge 1632, freeman 1635, removed with the emigrants from that town to Connecticut, where the name of Lord has existed from its earliest settlement. Of the 24 persons of this name who had grad. in N. E. in 1826, 18 were educated at Yale college. Rev. Benjamin Lord, D. D. for 60 years the minister of Norwich, grad. there in 1714, and d. in April, 1784, æ. 90. *ROBERT, Ipswich, was born a. 1612, admitted freeman 1636, was elected representative 1638, was clerk of probate, marshal, town clerk, and recorder of deeds. [Coffin.] He had a son Robert, born a. 1634, who was probably the one who d. 11 Nov. 1696. Catharine Lord, a widow, had a grant of land in Ipswich in 1641. ROBERT, of Boston in 1651, probably d. in Charlestown, 13 July, 1678. Two Joseph Lords d. in Charlestown in 1678 and 1679, and Joseph Lord, from that town grad. at H. C. in 1691, and was minister of Charlestown, S. C. Joseph Lord, his son, grad. at H. C. 1726, was a preacher and physician, and d. at Westmoreland, N. H. 1789, æ. 86, leaving descendants, of whom is Hon. Jotham Lord, late a member of the council of N. H., who is a grandson. WILLIAM, a cutler by profession, was admitted member of the church in Salem, 18 Aug. 1639, freeman 6th Sept. following, and was sworn constable of Salem, 14 Sept. 1640. He d. 14 Jan. 1673, aged a. 89. Felt, Annals, 242.

LORING, THOMAS, Hingham, freeman 1636. Savage, ii. Winthrop, 255. Lincoln, Hist. Hingham, 43. Benjamin, John and Thomas Loring were admitted freeman in 1673. Fifteen of the name had grad. at the N. E. colleges in 1826.

LOTHROP, ‡BARNABAS, son of the following, was b. at Scituate in 1636, and settled in Barnstable. He m. Susanna Clark in 1658. He was an assistant of Plymouth, and one of the first counsellors of Massachusetts after its union with Plymouth under the charter of William and Mary 1692. He d. at Barnstable in

1715, æ. 79. *JOHN*, the first minister of Scituate and Barnstable, was educated at Oxford, and was a clergyman in Kent county and in London, arrived at Plymouth from England in 1634, and soon settled at Scituate, from whence he removed, 11 Oct. 1639, to Barnstable, and d. 8 Nov. 1653. His sons were, Thomas, who settled in Barnstable; Samuel, in New-London 1648; Joseph, in Barnstable; Benjamin, in Charlestown; Barnabas and John, both at Barnstable. Of his daughters were Jane and Barbara. Many of Rev. John Lothrop's descendants have written the name *Lathrop*, of whom there appear 15 on the catalogues of the different N. E. colleges, whose names have this orthography. The true spelling of the name of the minister, as written by himself, appears to be *Lothropp*. See 2 Coll. Mass. Hist. Soc. i. 173. ||*THOMAS, Salem, freeman 1634, member of the ar. co. 1645, representative 1647, 1653, and 1664, was one of the founders of the church in Beverly 1667, representative of Beverly 1672 to 1675, 4 years; was many years captain, and sustained that office in Philip's war, when with more than 60 of his men he was killed in battle, near Deerfield, 18 Sept. 1675. Increase Mather calls him " a godly and courageous commander." He left a widow, Bethiah, but no children.

LOUDER, RICHARD, Charlestown 1641, had sons John and Jeremy.

LOVE, JOHN, Boston, d. 1 Dec. 1653, JOHN was appointed one of the mandamus counsellors of N. H. as early as 1692. Belknap.

LOVEJOY, JOHN, Andover, freeman 1673, d. Nov. 1690, having had 5 sons, who settled in Andover, viz: John; William, who d. 1748, æ. 91; Christopher, who d. 1737, æ. 78; Joseph, who d. 1737, aged 76; Nathaniel, who d. 1758, aged 84; Ebenezer, who d. 1759, æ. 86. Abbot, Hist. Andover, 27.

LOVELAND, ROBERT, Massachusetts 1645. Savage, ii. Winthrop, 262.

LOVELL, ROBERT, was admitted freeman 1635. THOMAS, Ipswich in 1665. Hutchinson [i. Hist. Mass. 385] memtions a Captain Lovell without date or residence. This name in N. E. has furnished 10 graduates at the N. E. colleges, 7 of whom grad. at H. C. John Lovell, H. C. 1728, was the celebrated master of the South Grammar School in Boston. He d. at Halifax in 1778. WILLIAM, Dorchester 1635. Winthrop, i. Hist. N. E. 174.

LOVERING, JOHN, freeman 1636, might be the same who lived at Dover in 1665.

LOVETT, DANIEL, Braintree, had a son James, b. in 1648, and daughters Martha, Mary, and Hannah. JOHN, Mendon, d. 26 July, 1668. JOHN, sen. of Beverly, d. 5 Nov. 1686, æ. 76.

LOW, ANDREW, was an inhabitant of New-Haven in 1639. JOHN, Boston 1637. Snow, Hist. Boston, 60. JOHN, Sudbury 1641. THOMAS, Ipswich 1644, probably that part now Essex, died 8 Sept. 1677, leaving sons, Thomas and John, and several daughters. Among his descendants are the late William Low, representative of Amherst, who d. in 1826, aged 74, his brother deacon John Low, of Beverly, who d. 18 March, 1829, æ. 74, [of whom is a biographical memoir in Boston recorder of 28 May 1829] Gen. Solomon Low, of Boxford, Ms., and Joseph Low, esq. of Concord, the adjutant and inspector general of N. H..

LOWDEN, AUGUSTINE, freeman 1660. JOHN, Charlestown, freeman 1668.

LOWELL, or LOWLE, JOHN, Newbury, freeman 1641, was son of Percival Lowle, and d. 10 July, 1647. His children were Joseph, b. 28 Nov. 1639; Benjamin, b. 12 Sept. 1642; Thomas, b. 4 June, 1644; Elizabeth, b. 1646, m. Philip Nelson of Rowley. Coffin. JOHN, Boston, 1655, who probably d. 7 June, 1694, had a son John, b. 26 Aug. 1655. JOHN, Weymouth 1658, had a son John, b. in 1658. PERCIVAL, a merchant, came from Bristol, England, with his sons, Richard and John, also merchants, and settled at Newbury, where he d. 8 Jan. 1665. Coffin. RICHARD, son of the preceding, was b. a. 1602, and lived in Newbury, and d. 5 August, 1682. WILLIAM, Massachusetts, was admitted freeman 1642.

LUCE, THOMAS, Charlestown, had a son Samuel, b. there in 1644. This name is very common at Martha's Vineyard.

LUCKIS, WILLIAM, Marblehead 1648. Dana, Hist. Discourse.

LUDDEN, JAMES, Weymouth 1636.

LUDDINGTON, WILLIAM, Charlestown 1642, removed to New-Haven, and d. 1662. He had William; Henry, who d. in 1676;. Hannah; John, and Thomas. See an account of his descendants in Dodd's East-Haven Register, 132—134.

LUDKIN, GEORGE, came from Norwich in England, and settled at Hingham 1635 ; admitted freeman 1636, removed to Braintree, and d. there 22 Feb. 1648. ||WILLIAM, Hingham 1637, freeman 1638, member of the ar. co. 1651, was drowned near Boston, 27 March, 1652.

LUDLOW, ‡†ROGER, Dorchester, came to N. E. in 1630, was an assistant 4 years, until 1634, when he was elected deputy-governour. He removed with the first emigrants to Windsor, where he was an assistant in 1636, and was also deputy-governour; removed to Fairfield, in 1639, and in 1654, went to Virginia, where he is supposed to have died. The first code of laws of the colony of Connecticut was compiled by him. WILLIAM, Connecticut, of which colony he was an assistant from 1640, probably several years. Mather, i. Magnalia. Descendants of one or both of the above probably remain, as the catalogues of New-Jersey and Schenectady colleges contained in 1826, seven persons of the name of Ludlow.

LUFF, JOHN, a weaver, was of Salem in 1637.

LUFKIN, HUGH, Salem 1654.

LUIN, HENRY, Boston 1636, had a son Ephraim, b. 1639.

LUKAR, MARK, was one of the founders of the first Baptist church in Newport, R. I. 1644. ||[———] member of the ar. co. 1640.

LUKER, HENRY, Sudbury. (See LOOKER.)

LUMBARD, JOHN, Springfield, d. 15 May, 1672.

LUMBERT, BERNARD. (See LOMBARD.)

LUMKINS, *RICHARD, Ipswich, was admitted freeman in 1638, and representative the same year. Of the name of Lumkin, two had grad. in N. E. in 1827.

LUMMUS, EDWARD, formerly written *Lomas* and *Lumax*, came from Wales and settled in Ipswich as early as 1648. He had 4 sons, Jonathan, who lived in Ipswich; Edward, who settled in New-Jersey; Samuel, in Hamilton, and Nathaniel, in Dover. Life of Aaron Lummus, p. 6.

LUNT, HENRY, Newbury, freeman 1638, d. 10 July, 1662. His children were, Sarah; Daniel, b. 1641; John, b. 1643, d. 1678; Priscilla; Mary; Elizabeth; Henry, b. 1652. His widow, Anne, m. Joseph Hills in 1665.

LUSHER, *‡ELEAZAR, Dedham, freeman 1638, was elected representative 1640, 12 years, assistant from 1662 to 1672, 11 years; was the captain of a military band in 1644, and afterwards major. He d. 13 Nov. 1672. Johnson [Hist. N. E. 192] describes him as " one of a nimble and active spirit, and strongly affected to the way of the truth." Worthington [Hist. Dedham, 50] says the following couplet was repeated by the generation which immediately succeeded Major Lusher.

" When Lusher was in office, all things went well,
" But how they go since, it shames us to tell."

There was a Samuel Lusher of Dedham, who d. 28 Dec. 1638.

LUTHER, SAMUEL, the second Baptist minister of Swanzey, Mass. was ordained 1685, d. in 1717. His posterity are numerous in that vicinity. Benedict, i. Hist. Baptists, 426.

LUXFORD, REUBEN, Massachusetts, was admitted freeman in 1634, and another Reuben Luxford was admitted freeman in 1674. This name was in Lancaster in 1668.

LYALL, ||FRANCIS, Boston 1638, was member of the ar. co. 1640. His son Joseph was b. in 1642, member ar. co. 1668. Probably the same with Francis Lisle, a barber-surgeon, [see Snow's Hist. Boston, 118] who Mr. Savage says, went to England and served in the Parliament's army.

LYE, ROBERT, Lynn 1638. Descendants remain. Lewis.

LYFORD, JOHN, came to N. E. in 1624, preached at Plymouth, from whence he went to Nantasket, [Hull] and from thence to Cape Ann in 1625. For mutinous conduct he was banished from Plymouth colony. He sailed in 1627, with some of his people to Virginia, and d. soon after his arrival there. Prince, i. Annals, 148, 152, 154, 169. The name of Lyford exists in New-Hampshire, where are two magistrates bearing it. MORDICAI, was of Hingham in 1642.

LYMAN, RICHARD, was of Massachusetts, and was admitted freeman in 1633. He might be father to the three brothers, Richard, John, and Robert Lyman, who were among the first settlers of Northampton, where the name has continued with reputation to the present time. Robert Lyman was admitted freeman in 1682.

Thirty-nine persons of the name had grad. at the N. E. colleges in 1826, the greater part of whom were educated at Yale College.

LYNDE, ‖‡*JOSEPH, son of Thomas Lynde, was b. at Charlestown, 3 June, 1636, admitted freeman 1671, represented Charlestown in 1674, 1679, and 1680; member of the ar. co. 1681; one of the committee of safety 1689; and counsellor under the charter of William and Mary 1692. Of the 12 persons of the name of Lynde, who had grad. in N. E. in 1826, the most distinguished were the Hon. Benjamin Lynde, H. C. 1686, chief justice of the superior court of Massachusetts, who d. 28 Jan. 1743, æ. 79, and his son, [Lord, ii. Lempriere's Univ. Biog. 245] Hon. Benjamin Lynde, who grad. at H. C. 1718, and filled the same office with his father. ‖SIMON, member of the ar. co. 1658, m. Hannah, daughter of John Newgate, and had 9 sons and 2 daughters. *THOMAS, Charlestown, freeman 1635, was elected representative 1636, 1637, 1645, and 1657, was perhaps the deacon of Charlestown, who d. 30 Dec. 1676. Ancient records name Thomas, Joseph, Hannah, and Sarah as children of Thomas Lynde. THOMAS, Charlestown, freeman 1645, was probably father of the Thomas Lynde, b. in 1647.

LYNN, HENRY, Boston 1631, came to N. E. in 1630. Savage, i. Winthrop, 61.

LYON, GEORGE, freeman 1669. JOHN, Marblehead 1648. PETER, Massachusetts, was admitted freeman 1649. RICHARD, was the coadjutor of President Dunster in improving the New-England version of the Psalms. ‖WILLIAM, Roxbury, member of the ar. co. 1645, freeman 1666, d. in 1692. His son Joseph was b. 1654. WILLIAM, Roxbury, d. there in 1714.

LYSCOM, ‖HUMPHREY, member of the ar. co. 1678.

LYTHERLAND, WILLIAM, Boston, was living in 1684, at the age of 74. Shaw, Hist. Boston, 32.

MACCARTY, ‖THADDEUS, Roxbury, member of the ar. co. 1681. Thomas Maccarty grad. at H. C. and died before 1699. Rev. Thaddeus Maccarty, H. C. 1739, was minister of Worcester.

MACLOAD, MORDECAI, Lancaster 1658, was killed with his wife and two children, 22 August, 1675, by the Indians. Willard, Hist. Lancaster, 26, 28.

MACY, *THOMAS, admitted freeman 1639, resided in Newbury, from thence to Salisbury, which he represented in 1654; removed to Nantucket in 1659, and was one of the first settlers. Holmes, i. Annals 313.

MADDOX, JAMES, came from Bristol, England, and settled early in Newbury. JOHN, brother of James, lived in Lynn and Salem, whence he went to Newbury, and there died a. 1644.

MADER, ROBERT, Massachusetts, freeman 1643.

MAGOON, JOHN, Scituate 1657. 2 Coll. Mass. Hist. Soc. iv. 241. This name is in New-Hampshire.

MAIES, DANIEL, Massachusetts, freeman 1660. Those under this name havé their surname variously written in old records. JOHN, Roxbury, was admitted freeman 1641, d. 28 April, 1670.

John May or Mayo, sen., d. at Roxbury. 28 April, 1688, and a John May or Maies was admitted freeman 1660.

MAIN, JOHN, Boston, d. 27 March, 1699. Rev Amos Main, H. C. 1729, was minister of Rochester, N. H.

MAJOR, JOHN, Boston, d. 15 July, 1692.

MAKEPEACE, ||THOMAS, was a member of the ar. co. 1638. Hutchinson, i. Hist. Mass. 98. Savage, i. Winthrop, 289.

MAKOON, JOHN, was of Cambridge in 1663, perhaps Magoon, above.

MALBON, ‡RICHARD, was an assistant of New-Haven colony in 1637. Winthrop, ii. Hist. N. E. 95. Thomas Malbone grad. at H. C. 1752.

MALLARD, ||THOMAS, member of the ar. co. 1685.

MALLORY, PETER, New-Haven 1644, had sons Peter, b. 1653. Thomas, b. 1659; Daniel; John; Joseph, two Samuels, and William. Dodd, East-Haven Register, 134, 135.

MANLEY, RALPH, Charlestown, d. in Sept. 1630. There was a John Manley of Braintree, at an early period.

MAN, SAMUEL, minister of Wrentham, grad. at H. C. 1665, admitted freeman 1679; ordained 13 April, 1692; d. 22 May, 1719, æ. 72. RICHARD, Scituate 1646.

MANN, WILLIAM, Providence 1641.

MANNING, ||JOHN, Boston, was member of the ar. co. 1640; ensign of the same in 1648. He had sons, John, b. 1643; Ephraim, b. 1655. There was a John Manning of Ipswich as early as 1640; and a John Manning was sheriff of Yorkshire, L. I. in 1672. The name in the 14th century was written *Mannyng*; the Rev. William Mannyng being the minister of Charlecote, in Warwickshire, A. D. 1378. THOMAS, was an inhabitant of Ipswich in 1636, and d. a. 1668, æ. 74. WILLIAM, Cambridge, was admitted freeman 1640. Susanna his wife, d. 16 Oct. 1650. WILLIAM, Cambridge, freeman 1643, was probably the person, sent a. 1670, as a messenger to England to invite Urian Oakes to come to N. E. and settled in that place. See Holmes, Hist. Cambridge. His wife was Dorothy, and his children were, Samuel, b. 21 July, 1644; John, b. 31 March, 1650; Hannah; Sarah, and Mary. Samuel settled in Billerica, where he was representative in 1695 and 1696, and town clerk 6 years, and d. 22 Feb. 1711, æ. 66.

MANSFIELD, *ANDREW, Lynn 1637, was town clerk in 1666, representative from 1680 to 1683. He had a son Andrew. The first graduate of the name in N. E. was Samuel Mansfield, H. C. 1690. JOHN, Lynn, freeman 1643, was probably a proprietor of Lancaster in 1654. ROBERT, Lynn 1642. *SAMUEL, Springfield, representative 1680, 1683, and 1684. THOMAS, Lynn 1642.

MANTON, EDWARD, one of the first proprietors of Providence. Coffin.

MANWARING, ||NATHANIEL, member of the ar. co. 1644. David Manwaring grad. at Y. C. 1759.

MAPES, THOMAS, South-Old, L. I. 1640. Wood, Hist. L. Island, 34.

MARBLE, JOHN, Boston 1646. WILLIAM, Charlestown, was admitted freeman 1654. Joseph and Samuel Marble lived in Andover, a. 1670.

MARCH, JOHN, Salem, admitted to the church, 12 May, 1639, took the oath of freeman in 1642. HUGH, Newbury 1656, was b. a. 1622. He had a son HUGH, who was b. 1656.

MARCY, JOHN, Chalestown, d. 4 Oct. 1638. His son John d. 2 May, 1641. GEORGE, freeman 1666.

MARGESON, EDMUND, one of the Plymouth pilgrims, d. in 1621.

MARION, JOHN, Watertown 1643, freeman 1652, had sons, John, b. 1643, Isaac, b. 1652; Samuel, b. 1655, member of the ar. co. 1691, and probably d. in Boston, 7 Jan, 1705, æ. 86.

MARKHAM, NATHANIEL, Charlestown, d. 26 Sept. 1673. DANIEL, freeman 1674.

MARKLEY, JOHN, Casco 1665. Hutchinson, Coll. of Papers, 398.

MARRETT, JOHN, a proprietor of Watertown 1642, perhaps freeman in 1665. THOMAS, Cambridge, freeman 1636, was a deacon of the church there, had two sons, John, who d. in 1663, and Thomas, both born in England. He d. 30 June, 1664. This name is spelled *Marryott* in the colony records.

MARSH, ALEXANDER, Massachusetts, freeman 1654. Thirty-three persons of this name had grad. at the N. E. colleges in 1826. GEORGE, Hingham 1635. ONESIPHORUS, Hingham 1654, freeman 1672. THOMAS, of Hingham, was admitted freeman 1654. JOHN, Charlestown, d. 1 Jan. 1666.

MARSHALL, CHRISTOPHER, was admitted freeman in 1635. Calamy notices one of this name, who was partly educated under Rev. John Cotton, and was the minister of Wood-Kirk in Yorkshire, England, and d. in Feb. 1673, æ. 59. EDMUND, Salem, admitted to the church, 8 Jan. 1637, took the oath of freeman the same year. He removed from Salem. JAMES, Windsor, 1640. JOHN, Boston, had sons, John, b. 1645; Thomas, b. 1656. There was a John Manshall of Billerica in 1659. Samuel and John Marshall, d. at Boston 1690 and 1694. ROBERT, Salem 1637. THOMAS, Boston, was a shoemaker and ferryman. His son Eliakim was born in 1637. Snow, Hist. Boston, 79, 119. Savage, i. Winthrop, 248. ii. 213, 216. THOMAS, Boston, a tailor, was admitted to the church in 1643, and perhaps freeman in 1644. Thomas Marshall d. at Andover in Jan. 1708, æ. nearly 100. Joanna Marshall, d. there in May, 1708, aged about 100. ||*THOMAS, Lynn 1634, was a captain, and probably the member of the ar. co. in 1640 and the freeman of 1641. He was representative 6 years, 1659 to 1668 excepting 1661, 1662, 1665, and 1666. He died 23 Dec. 1689. Dunton [2 Coll Mass. Hist. Soc. ii. 117] says that he was one of Cromwell's soldiers. Rebecca, his wife, d. in August, 1693. He had sons, John, who might have been at Billerica, and Thomas, who was admitted freeman in 1653, and settled in Reading. Lewis.

MARSHFIELD, SAMUEL, was a proprietor of Westfield in 1666, d. in Springfield in 1692.

MARRYOTT, NICHOLAS, Salem 1636, Marblehead 1648, was born a. 1613. Coffin. THOMAS, Cambridge 1636. (See MARRETT.)

MARSTON, JOHN, Salem, born about 1616, admitted to the church, 9 Aug. 1640, freeman 1641, had a son John, baptized 12 Sept. 1641, perhaps of Andover. ROBERT, spelled *Marstin* in Hutchinson's Coll. of Papers, 255. THOMAS, Salem 1637; went to Hampton; admitted freeman 1641, and d. 1672. *THOMAS, Hampton, was representative in 1677. WILLIAM, Salem 1637, d. 30 June, 1672.

MARTIN, ABRAHAM, Hingham 1635. AMBROSE, Concord 1638, had a son Joseph, b. in 1640. Savage, i. Winthrop, 289. CHRISTOPHER, Plymouth, one of the first pilgrims, d. 8 Jan. 1621. Prince, i. Annals, 96. JOHN, Charlestown, was admitted freeman in 1640. JOHN, freeman 1665. RICHARD, Casco 1665. Hutchinson Coll. 398. (See MARTYN.) ROBERT, Massachusetts, freeman 1640. SOLOMON, Massachusetts, freeman 1652. THOMAS, Massachusetts, freeman 1639. WILLIAM, Groton, d. 26 March, 1672, æ. 76. WILLIAM, Reading, one of the first selectmen, was admitted freeman in 1653.

MARTYN, *‡RICHARD, Portsmouth, one of the founders of the first church 1671, representative in 1672 and 1679; counsellor of the province of New-Hampshire 1680, speaker of the N. H. assembly, d. in 1693. His children were, Richard, b. 10 Jan. 1660, grad. at H. C. 1680, was sometime a preacher; Michael, b. 3 Feb. 1667; John, b. 9 June 1668; Elias, b. 18 April, 1670, and daughters, Mary, Sarah, Elizabeth, and Hannah, born in 1655, 1657, 1662, and 1665.

MASON, ARTHUR, Boston 1656, was a constable, and is mentioned by Hutchinson, i. Hist. Mass. 232. Twenty-four persons of the name of Mason had grad. in N. E. in 1826. EDMUND, was a proprietor of Watertown in 1642. HENRY, Massachusetts, freeman 1650. HENRY, Scituate 1650. *HUGH, Watertown, freeman 1635, representative 1644 and 1645, 1660, 1661, 1664, 1672, 1674 to 1677, 10 years; was a captain of the militia, and d. 10 Oct. 1678. His wife d. 21 May, 1692. Mr. Shattuck gives me the names of his children, viz.: Hannah, b. 23 Sept. 1636, m. Capt. Joshua Brooks, of Concord; Mary, who m. Rev. Joseph Estabrook; John, b. 1 Jan. 1644, m. Hannah Ramsden, and settled in Concord; Joseph, b. 10 Aug. 1646, d. 22 July 1702; Daniel, b. 19 Feb. 1649, who according to W. Winthrop, grad. at H. C. in 1666; and Sarah, b. 25 Sept. 1651. ‡†*JOHN, the distinguished Pequot warrior, came early to N. E. and settled at Dorchester, which he represented in 1635 and 1636, having been admitted a freeman in 1635. He removed with Mr. Warham to Windsor, in 1636, was elected a magistrate from 1642 to 1659; removed to Saybrook 1647; to Norwich in 1659; was elected deputy-governour in 1660, and the 9 succeeding years; was major-general, and d. at Norwich in

1672 or 1673, æ. 72. He left three sons, Samuel, John, and Daniel, whose posterity have ever remained in Connecticut, and are spread over the country. Jeremiah Mason, LL. D., of Portsmouth, is a descendant. 1 Coll. Mass. Hist. Soc. yiii. 122—125. JOHN, the proprietor of New-Hampshire, towards the settlement of which he expended a considerable estate. He d. in England, 26 Nov. 1637, having never come to N. E. His only child, Jane, m. John Tufton, esq., and had John, who d. without issue, and Robert, who took the name of Mason. ‡ROBERT, grandson of the preceding, was declared proprietor of New-Hampshire, by Charles II, 1677, and by mandamus in 1680. He was a counsellor in 1682, at which time he resided in Portsmouth. He was named as one of Sir Edmund Andros' council, but died in 1686, leaving two sons, John Tufton Mason, who d. in Virginia, without issue ; and Robert Tufton Mason, who m. Catharine Wiggin, and was lost at sea in 1696, leaving two children, John Tufton, who d. at Havanna in 1718, and Elizabeth, who was living in 1738. The last John Tufton Mason had two sons, John Tufton and Thomas Tufton. ROBERT, Roxbury 1637. His wife d. that year. RALPH, Boston 1637, had sons, Zuriel, [?] b. 1637 ; John, b. 1640 ; Jacob, born 1644. ‡SAMUEL, Connecticut, son of Major-General John Mason, was elected an assistant in 1683. ‡STEPHEN, Massachusetts, was one of the first council under the charter of William and Mary, 1692. Douglas, Summary.

MASSEY, JEFFREY, Salem, one of the earliest members of the church, was b. in England 1592 ; freeman 1634, d. 1677, aged about 84. His son John, b. 1631, is said by Dr. Bentley to have been the first male child born in Salem, but he probably mistakes. See Felt's Annals, 256. The cradle in which he was rocked is in the cabinet of the Mass. Historical Society.

MASTERS, JOHN, Watertown, was admitted freeman in 1631; was a proprietor, and perhaps a resident, at Cambridge. He d. 21 Dec. 1639, and his wife died five days after him. Prince, ii. Annals, 30, 31, 60. Savage, i. Winthrop, 69, 76, 81. Nicholas S. Masters, Y. C. 1779, Josiah Masters, Y. C. 1783, a member of Congress, and W. Masters, of Vermont, are probably his descendants. NATHANIEL, Beverly 1659.

MATHER, COTTON, minister of the North church in Boston, was son of Rev. Increase Mather, D. D., and was b. 12 Feb. 1663; grad. at H. C. 1678, admitted freeman 1680, ordained a colleague with his father, 13 May, 1685, and d. 13 Feb. 1728, æ. 65. He m. (1) Abigail, daughter of Colonel John Philips ; (2) widow Elizabeth Hubbard, daughter of Dr. John Clark ; (3) widow George, a daughter of Samuel Lee. By the 1st and 2d, he had 15 children, of whom Rev. Samuel Mather, D. D., b. 30 Oct. 1706, grad. at H. C. 1723, and was ordained as colleague with Rev. Joshua Gee, of Boston, 21 June, 1732, and d. 27 June, 1785, æ. 78.

ELEAZAR, minister of Northampton, was son of Rev. Richard Mather, and was b. at Dorchester, 13 May, 1637, grad. at H. C. 1656, ordained 23 June, 1661, and d. 24 July, 1669, æ. 32. His wife was daughter of Rev. John Warham, and by her, who afterwards m. Rev. Solomon Stoddard, he had an only daughter, who became the wife of Rev. John Williams. *INCREASE*, minister of the North church in Boston, a brother of the preceding, was b. at Dorchester, 21 June, 1639, grad. at H. C. 1656, ordained 27 May, 1669, appointed president of H. C. 1685, from which he received the degree of D. D., resigned the presidency 1701, was an agent in England for procuring a new charter, which he obtained in 1691 from King William and Queen Mary. He m. Maria, a daughter of Rev. John Cotton. She d. in 1714. He d. 23 Aug. 1723, æ. 85. His children were, 1. Maria; 2. Elizabeth, who m. Capt. Greenough and Mr. Byles; 3. Sarah, who m. Rev. Mr. Walter, of Roxbury; 4. Abigail, who m. Newcomb Blake and Rev. John White; 5. Hannah; 6. Jerusha; 7. Cotton, already mentioned; 8. Nathaniel, b. 6 July, 1669, grad. at H. C. 1685, d. 17 Oct. 1688 at Salem; and Samuel, H. C. 1690. *NATHANIEL*, a minister in London, was brother of the preceding, and was b. at Lancaster, England, 20 March, 1630, grad. at H. C. 1647, went to England, and was presented to a living at Barnstaple, by Oliver Cromwell in 1656, from which he was ejected after the restoration. He d. in London, 26 July, 1697, æ. 67, having preached 47 years in England, Ireland, and Holland. *RICHARD*, the third minister of Dorchester, was son of Thomas and Margaret Mather, and was b. at Lowton, in the parish of Winwick, in Lancashire, in 1596, was sometime a student at Oxford, became a preacher, and came to N. E. in 1635, settled over the church at Dorchester, 23 Aug. 1636, and d. 22 April, 1669, æ. 73. He m. 29 Sept. 1624, Catharine, daughter of Edmund Hoult. She d. in 1655, and he m. Sarah, the widow of Rev. John Cotton, 26 Aug. 1656. His children, all by the first wife, were, Samuel, Timothy, Nathaniel, and Joseph, born in England, and Eleazar, and Increase, b. in Dorchester. *SAMUEL*, a minister in Dublin, son of the preceding, was b. in Lancashire, 13 May, 1626, grad. at H. C. 1643, admitted freeman 1648, went to England, from thence to Scotland and Ireland, and finally settled in Dublin, where he d. 29 Oct. 1671, æ. 45. *SAMUEL*, minister of Windsor, was son of Timothy Mather, and grad. at H. C. 1671, was ordained 1682, and d. 18 March, 1726, æ. 77. TIMOTHY, father of the preceding, was son of Rev. Richard Mather, and lived in Dorchester. His sons were, Samuel; Nathaniel, b. 2 Sept. 1658; Joseph, b. 25 May, 1661, and probably others.

MATHIS, MARMADUKE, is mentioned in Snow's Hist. of Boston, and may possibly be the minister of the name of *Matthews*. The name of *Mathes* prevails in some parts of Mass. and N. H.

MATSON, JOHN, Boston, was admitted freeman in 1633. THOMAS, Boston, freeman in 1634, was also of Braintree, and a military officer there. His son Joshua was b. 1640. THOMAS, freeman 1666, d. at Boston in 1690.

MATTHEWS, FRANCIS, Pascataqua 1631. JOHN, Roxbury, freeman 1641, may have removed to Springfield, and d. 25 April, 1684. His son Gershom was b. 1641. *MARMADUKE*, a minis-

ter, who preached at Hull, Malden, Lynn, and other places, returned to England, and, according to Calamy, died in 1683. MOR-
DECAI, graduated at H. C. in 1655.

MATTOCKS, DAVID, Massachusetts, freeman 1650. Those
under this head have their names spelled *Mattock, Mattucks, Mad-
dock,* and *Maddox,* so that it is difficult to fix on the true orthography of each. HENRY, Saco 1652. JAMES, a cooper of Boston,
was member of the church, and admitted freeman in 1638. JOHN,
Lynn. (See MADDOX.)

MATTOON, HERBERT, Kittery 1652, Ebenezer, M. C. from
Massachusetts and Noah D. Mattoon grad. at D. C. in 1776, and
1803.

MAUD, DANIEL, a schoolmaster in Boston, was admitted
freeman in 1636, and became the first permanently established minister of Dover in 1642, and remained in office until his death in
1655.

MAUDSLEY, JOHN, Dorchester, a member of the church, was
admitted freeman in 1638. One of this name was in Westfield in
1670. His son Joseph was b. 1638. Thomas, perhaps another
son, was admitted to the church in 1658. This name is said to be
the same as *Mosely.* ||HENRY, Braintree 1638, member of the
ar. co. 1643, freeman 1646, had a son Samuel, b. 1641.

MAULE, THOMAS, shop-keeper of Salem, was brought before
the council, 19 Dec. 1695, to answer for printing and publishing
a pamphlet of 260 pages, entitled, " Truth held forth and maintained."

MAVERICK, ANTIPAS, Kittery 1652. ||ELIAS, freeman
1633, was of Charlestown 1643, member of the ar. co 1654. He
had sons, John, b. 1635 ; Elias, b. 1643 ; Paul, b. 1657. ||JAMES,
member of the ar. co. 1658. *JOHN,* one of the first ministers of
Dorchester, came to N. E. in 1630 ; d. at Boston, 3 Feb. 1636, æ.
60. John Maverick, perhaps his son, was of Boston in 1652, and
had a son John, born in 1653. MOSES, Salem, admitted freeman
1634, became a member of the church, 12 June, 1637 ; was settled in Marblehead as early as 1648, one of the founders of the
church there, 24 May, 1684 ; died 28 January 1686, aged 76.
Dana, in his Hist. Discourse, p. 13, mistakes the time of his death.
SAMUEL, freeman 1632, lived at Noddle's Island, the settlement
of which he commenced in 1628 or 1629. He d. 10 March, 1664.
His son Samuel was one of the commissioners by Charles II in 1664
to subjugate the Dutch, and settle controversies in the New-England colonies. Hutchinson, i. Hist. Mass. 26.

MAURY, ROGER, freeman 1631, was member of the church in
Salem, in the records of which, the name is spelled *Maurice,* or
Maurie. He probably went to Providence.

MAXFIELD, CLEMENT, Dorchester 1658.

MAXWELL, JOHN, freeman 1669.

MAY, ||GEORGE, was member of the ar. co. 1661, freeman
1665. JOHN, Roxbury, probably the John Maies in colony records, admitted freeman in 1641, d. 28 April, 1670.

MAYHEW, *THOMAS, Watertown, freeman 1637, representative 1636 to 1644, excepting 1642 ; removed to Martha's Vineyard, of which he was governour, and where he was a preacher to the Indians in the neighbourhood of the Vineyard, 23 years. He d. in 1681, æ. 92. His son Thomas, who was lost at sea in 1657, had 3 sons, Matthew, a preacher, who d. in 1710 ; Thomas, a judge ; John, a preacher to the Indians at Tisbury and other places, who d. at Chilmark, 3 Feb. 1689, æ. 37. Experience, the son of John, was a minister, and began to preach in 1694, d. 1756 æ. 84. He was the father of Joseph, H. C. 1730 ; Nathan, H. C. 1731 ; Jonathan, the celebrated Boston divine, H. C. 1744, who was ordained 17 June, 1747, d. 9 July, 1766, æ. 44, and Zechariah, a missionary among the Indians, who d. 6 March, 1806, æ. 89. Davis, Morton's Memo. 275.

MAYNARD, JOHN, Cambridge 1634, freeman 1644, perhaps of Sudbury, and one of the proprietors of Marlborough. He or the following, d. at Sudbury, 10 Dec. 1672. JOHN, was admitted freeman in 1649.

MAYO, JOHN, minister of Barnstable, and the first settled over the old North church in Boston, was installed 9 Nov. 1655, dismissed 1672, and d. in May, 1676. Judge Davis says that " there are many of the name of Mayo in the Cape towns, probably descended from the Rev. Mr. Mayo." Morton's Memo. 216. Joseph Mayo was of Newbury 1679. Nathaniel Mayo, of Eastham, m. Hannah, daughter of Gov. Prence.

MEAD, GABRIEL, Dorchester, freeman 1638. HENRY, Massachusetts, freeman 1665. WILLIAM, Gloucester, was one of the selectmen in 1647. William and Richard Mead d. at Roxbury in 1683 and 1690. Fifteen of the name had grad. at the N. E. colleges in 1826.

MEADER, JOHN, Oyster-River (Durham, N. H.) 1669. This name continues in New-Hampshire, and is now written *Meder*. ||JOHN, ar. co. 1676.

MEADOWS, PHILIP, Roxbury 1642.

MEAKINS, THOMAS, Massachusetts, freeman 1637. *THOMAS, jun., Braintree, freeman 1636, was representative in 1644, had a son Thomas, b. 8 June, 1643, who, or the father, was probably the same who settled at Hadley as early as 1666.

MEANE, JOHN, Cambridge, was buried 19 March, 1646. His wife was Ann, by whom he had several children. John, his son, d. Oct. 1646.

MEARS, JOHN, Boston, d. 12 Nov. 1663. ROBERT, Boston 1638.

MEGAPOLENSIS, JOHN, was a Dutch minister of Long-Island before 1668. Wood, Hist. Sketch, 29.

MEGGOT, JOSEPH, whose name is spelled in the colony records *Maggott*, and in the Cambridge records *Mygate*, was admitted freeman in 1635, and probably lived in Cambridge.

MEIGS, JOHN, Weymouth, had a son John, b. in 1641. This name exists in Connecticut, where five, Timothy, President Josiah,

Return J., a senator in congress and governour of Ohio, Henry M. C., and Rev. Benjamin C. Meigs have grad. at Y. C.

MELLEN, RICHARD, Weymouth, was admitted freeman in 1639. Rev. John Mellen, H. C. 1741, was ordained at Sterling, Mass. 19 Dec. 1744, and d. at Reading, 4 July, 1807, æ. 85. Three of his sons grad. at H. C.; 1. John, b. 8 July, 1752, grad. 1770, minister of Barnstable, where he was ordained 12 Nov. 1783; d. at Cambridge, 19 Sept. 1828; 2. Henry, counsellor at law, Dover, N. H. grad. 1784, d. 31 July, 1809, æ. 52; 3. Prentiss, a senator in Congress, and chief justice of the Superior court in Maine, was b. in 1764, and grad. in 1784.

MELLOWS, ABRAHAM, Massachusetts, freeman 1634. ED-WARD, Charlestown, freeman 1634, was sworn constable, 13 April 1637, [Winthrop, ii. Hist. N. E. 347] d. 5 May, 1650. His son Abraham was b. 1645. OLIVER, Boston, freeman 1634, perhaps the father of John, whose son John was b. in 1649. Winthrop, ii. Hist. N. E. 347. RICHARD, Charlestown, had a son James, b. 1642.

MERCER, THOMAS, Boston, d. 28 May, 1699.

MERCHANT, JOHN, Braintree 1638. His wife Sarah d. 3 Dec. 1638. WILLIAM, Watertown 1641, probably went to Ipswich, and d. 4 Sept. 1668.

MERIAM, GEORGE, Concord, freeman 1641, d. 29 Dec. 1675, Susanna, his wife, d. 8 Oct. 1675. His children were, Elizabeth, b. 1641; Samuel, b. 1642; Hannah; Abigail; Sarah, and Susanna. Shattuck, MS Hist. Concord. JOHN, admitted freeman in 1647, might have been of Hampton. JOSEPH, Concord, brother of George Meriam, was admitted freeman in 1638, d. 1 Jan. 1641, leaving sons, Joseph, who m. Sarah Stone, 1653; John, b. 1640—1; m. Mary Cooper, and had a large family. Shattuck. JOSEPH, Cambridge, freeman 1650, had a son Joseph, b. in 1658. *ROB-ERT, Concord, brother of George, was a merchant, and admitted freeman 1638, town clerk from 1654 to 1676, representative from 1655 to 1658, four years, and deacon of the church d. 15 Feb. 1681, æ. 72, leaving no issue. His wife d. 22 July, 1693, æ. 72. Shattuck, MS Hist. Concord. WILLIAM, Lynn, freeman 1649, d. 1689. His wife was Sarah; and sons, Joseph, William, and John. Lewis, MS Annals Lynn.

MERRICK, HENRY, Scituate 1638. THOMAS, came from Wales in 1630, and settled in Roxbury, from whence he went to Springfield in 1636. [Sprague, Hist. Discourse.] Seven of the name had grad. at Harv. and Yale in 1828.

MERRILL, JOHN, Newbury, freeman 1640, d. 12 Sept. 1673, without issue. Coffin. NATHANIEL, Newbury, brother of the preceding, d. 16 March, 1655, leaving wife Susanna, and children, Nathaniel, who d. in 1682; John; Abraham; Daniel, b. 20 Aug. 1640, freeman 1684; and Abel, b. 20 Feb. 1644.

MERRITT, NICHOLAS, Marblehead 1648. (See MARRYOTT.) HENRY, Scituate 1638. Coffin.

MERRYFIELD, HENRY, Dorchester 1658, had a son Benjamin. James Merrifield d. in Boston in 1690.

MESSINGER, HENRY, Boston, freeman 1665, had a son John, b. there in 1641. Three, Henry, James, and Roswell, all clergymen, have grad. at H. C.

METCALF, JOHN, Medfield, freeman 1647. His son Joseph, b. 1658. *JOSEPH, Ipswich, freeman 1635, was elected representative 2 Sept. 1635, and several years afterwards, d. in 1665, æ. 60. MICHAEL, Dedham, freeman 1640. MICHAEL, Dedham, freeman 1645, had a son Michael, born that year. *THOMAS, Dedham, 1652, representative in 1691. THOMAS, Ipswich 1648, freeman 1674.

MIDDLEBROOK, JOHN, went with Rev. John Jones to Fairfield, in Sept. 1644. Shattuck.

MIDDLECOTT, ‡RICHARD, Massachusetts, was, according to Douglass, one of the first counsellors under the new charter 1692.

MIDDLEWAITE, ||——— was admitted member of the ar. co. 1639.

MIGHILL, *THOMAS, Rowley, freeman 1640, was representative in 1648. His children were Samuel, Thomas, John, Ezekiel, Nathaniel, Stephen, and Mary. *THOMAS*, minister of Scituate, was son of the preceding, and was b. at Rowley, 29 Oct. 1639; [J. Coffin] grad. at H. C. 1663, ordained over the 2d church in March, 1684, d. in Feb. 1689.

MILBOURNE, WILLIAM, Boston, d. in Aug. 1699.

MILDMAY, WILLIAM, son of Sir William Mildmay, of Graces, in Essex, grad. at H. C. in 1647, and probably returned home. Sir Walter Mildmay was the founder of Emmanuel College, in Cambridge, England, 1584;—a college which supplied New-England in its early days, with some of the greatest lights which illuminated its churches.

MILES, JOHN, Concord, whose 1st wife, Sarah, d. 18 July, 1678, m. Sarah Rediat, and had, 1. John, b. 20 May, 1680, father of Jonathan Miles, H. C. 1727, and great-grandfather of Rev. Noah Miles, D. C. 1780; 2. Samuel, b. 19 Feb. 1682. A John Miles was admitted freeman in 1638, who is supposed to be the preceding. Shattuck, MS Hist. Concord. *JOHN*, minister of Swanzey, came from South Wales to N. E. about 1662, formed a Baptist church in Rehoboth, 1663, went to Swanzey, a. 1667, and d. 3 Feb. 1683, leaving a widow Ann, the daughter of John Humphrey, and children, John, Susanna, and Samuel, "then at college," as expressed in his last will. Shattuck. Felt. SAMUEL, freeman 1645, perhaps of Boston, where Samuel, son of Samuel and Elizabeth Miles, was b. 27 April, 1662. *SAMUEL*, minister of King's chapel, Boston, probably the son of Rev. John Miles, grad. at H. C. 1684, went to England; was admitted to the degree of Master of Arts at Oxford; received holy orders; returned to N. E. and became rector of King's chapel, 29 June, 1689; d. 4 March, 1729.

MILLER, ALEXANDER, Dorchester, freeman 1638. Forty-four persons of the name of Miller were on the catalogue of the N. E., N. Y, and N. J. colleges in 1826. *ANTHONY, Dover, was representative from 1674 to 1676, three years. JAMES, Charlestown, d. 2 Aug. 1676. *JOHN*, one of the first ministers of Rowley, where he resided from 1639 to 1641, came to N. E. as early as 1638, lived a short time at Roxbury, admitted freeman 1639, went to Yarmouth in 1641, remained there several years, and died at Groton, 12 June, 1663. He was the first town clerk of Rowley. JOHN, Newbury, whose wife Mary d. 1663. THOMAS, Dorchester had sons, John and Jonathan. A Thomas Miller was of Rowley, a. 1648, and a Thomas Miller d. at Springfield in 1690. WILLIAM, Ipswich 1648, perhaps went to Northampton, where William Miller was one of the first settlers.

MILLERD, or MILWARD, THOMAS, Newbury 1641, had several daughters born in that place. He d. at Boston, 1 Sept. 1653. He may be the mate of the Hector, noticed by Winthrop, i. Hist. N. E. 187, and by Mr. Savage, in a note, p. 188. The name still exists in Massachusetts. A Mr. Milward was of Gloucester in 1642.

MILLET, RICHARD, requested to be made freeman, 19 Oct. 1630, and probably the same, who took the oath, 11 June, 1633. THOMAS, Dorchester, was admitted freeman 1637. THOMAS, Gloucester 1660, had sons John, Nathaniel, and Thomas, of age in 1664.

MILLS, JOHN, requested freedom, 19 Oct. 1630, and admitted freeman in 1632. Joy and Recompence, daughters of John Mills, were baptized in Boston church, Oct. 1630, and are the first recorded as baptized there. Prince, ii. Annals, 5. JOHN, freeman 1633, might be the father of Joy and Recompence, and the town clerk of Braintree in 1653. Twenty-one of the name had grad. in N. E. at the different colleges in 1828.

MILNER, MICHAEL, Lynn 1638, went to Long-Island 1640. Lewis.

MINARD, THOMAS, Hingham 1636. Lincoln, Hist. Hingham. JOHN, Boston, d. 4 Oct. 1658.

MINGAY, *JEFFREY, Hampton, freeman 1640, was representative 1650, d. 1658.

MINOR, THOMAS, Massachusetts, was admitted freeman in 1634, and perhaps went to Conn., where the name exists, and where eight had grad. at H. C. in 1828.

MINOT, *GEORGE, Dorchester, freeman 1634, representative in 1635 and 1636, was ruling elder of the church, 30 years, and d. 24 Dec. 1671, æ. 78. He had sons, John ; James ; Stephen ; Samuel, b. 6 Dec. 1635, d. 18 Dec. 1690. JAMES, Dorchester, son of the preceding, was b. 31 Dec. 1628 ; m. Hannah, daughter of Israel Stoughton, and d. 30 March, 1676. His children were, Israel, b. 18 Oct. 1654 ; George, b. 14 Nov. 1655 ; James, b. 2 April, 1659 ; William, b. 18 Sept. 1662. Rev. T. M. Harris, MS Letter. JAMES, Dorchester 1634, Boston 1645, was son of Thomas Minot, esq. of Saffron-Welden, England. W. Gibbs, MS letter. JOHN, Dorchester, son of George Minot, was b. in England, in 1626. His sons were, 1. James, b. 18 Sept. 1653 ; grad. at H. C. 1675, settled in Concord ; 2. John, who d. of small pox, 6 April, 1690, leaving

several sons; 3. Stephen, b. 10 Aug. 1662, settled in Boston, was
grandfather of Stephen, H. C. 1730, who d. 14 Jan. 1787, æ. 75,
whose son George Richards Minot, H. C. 1778, is the well known
historian of Massachusetts; 4. Samuel, b. 3 July, 1665. Rev. T.
M. Harris, MS letter. STEPHEN, Dorchester, brother of the preceding, was b. 6 May, 1631, and d. 13 Feb. 1671, leaving issue.
Ibid. THOMAS, one of the first settlers of New-London 1648.
Trumbull, i. 169.
    MIPHAM, JOHN, Guilford 1643. Ibid. 285.
    MIRECK, JAMES, Newbury 1656, was born a. 1612. Judge
Sewall records the burning of his house in 1686. JOHN, Charlestown 1642, had a son Benjamin, b. in 1644.
    MITCHELL, EDWARD, Hingham 1638, was probably a son
of the following. EXPERIENCE, came to N. E. in the third ship,
named the Ann, in 1623; was one of the company of pilgrims at
Leyden, in Holland, where he left a brother (who permanently
settled and d. there); was one of the first proprietors of Plymouth;
removed to Duxbury as early as 1645; from thence to Bridgewater,
where he died a. 1689, aged nearly 90 years. He had 4 sons,
Thomas, Jacob, John, and Edward. Edward had a son Edward,
b. 7 Feb. 1716, who was a colonel and magistrate many years, and
d. 23 Dec. 1801, æ. 85, whose son Cushing Mitchell, esq. was father of Nahum Mitchell, H. C. 1789, a member of the Mass. Hist.
Society, late treasurer of the Commonwealth of Massachusetts, and
one of its members in Congress. The descendants of Experience
Mitchell are numerous and respectable, and several have grad. at
H. C. Twenty-six of the name in N. E. had grad. at the N. E.
colleges in 1826. JONATHAN, came early to N. E., and resided at Charlestown, at Concord in 1635, at Saybrook, at Weathersfield, and at Stamford. He d. in 1645, æ. 54. Mather, ii. Magnalia 66. *JONATHAN*, the fourth minister of Cambridge, was
son of the preceding, and was b. in 1624, came to N. E. in 1635,
grad. at H. C. 1647, was ordained 21 Aug. 1650, d. 9 July, 1668,
æ. 42. He m. Margaret, daughter of Rev. Thomas Shepard, his
predecessor. His children were, Nathaniel, b. 1 March, 1659;
John; Samuel, b. 14 Oct. 1660, grad. at H. C. 1681; Jonathan
who grad. at H. C. 1687, and d. 14 March, 1695, and perhaps others. ‡MATTHEW, Springfield 1636, perhaps the same who was
elected magistrate of Connecticut 1637. Matthew Mitchell went
with Rev. Mr. Denton to Hempstead, L. I. in 1643. WILLIAM,
Charlestown, d. 23 Jan. 1678. WILLIAM, Newbury, had several
children, and d. 16 July, 1654.
    MITCHELSON, ‖EDWARD, Cambridge 1636, bought Simon
Willard's farm. He was member of the ar. co. 1639. His wife was
Ruth Bushell, his children were Ruth, Bethiah, Edward, b. 1644,
grad. at H. C. 1665, and Elizabeth. WILLIAM, Cambridge 1658.
    MIX, STEPHEN, minister of Weathersfield, grad. at H. C.
1690, ordained 1694, d. 22 or 28 August, 1738, æ. 66.
    MIXER, ISAAC, Watertown, was admitted freeman in 1638.

MODESTY, JOHN, Dorchester, d. 27 Oct. 1661, [MS copy of Records.] The race has probably become extinct.

MONK, GEORGE, Boston, d. 7 Sept. 1698. Dunton [2 Coll. Mass. Hist. Soc ii. 103] gives some account of him. William Monk d. at Boston in 1690.

MONTAGUE, RICHARD, Boston 1646, perhaps freeman 1680.

MOODY, *CALEB, son of William Moody, was born a. 1637, settled in Newbury, which he represented in 1677 and 1678. He d. 25 August, 1698 æ. 61. He had several children, of whom were Daniel and Samuel. Samuel, was b. 4 Jan. 1676, grad. at H. C. 1697, was ordained the minister of York, 20 Dec. 1700, d. 13 Nov. 1747. His son Joseph, b. 1700, grad. at H. C. 1718, was ordained over the 2d church in York 1732, dismissed 1741, d. 20 March, 1753, æ. 53. The celebrated master, Samuel Moody, H. C. 1746, for thirty years the preceptor of Dummer Academy, was son of Joseph, and d. at Exeter, 17 Dec. 1795, æ. 70, having never married. DEBORAH, whom Winthrop calls "a wise and anciently religious woman," lived at Lynn in 1640, having purchased Mr. Humphrey's plantation. Mr. Savage [ii. Winthrop, 123] has more acquaintance with this lady, however *slight* it may be, than any one else. Mr. Coffin informs me that Sir Henry Moody, knight, is named in Salem records as her son. JOHN, Roxbury, was admitted freeman 1633. Winthrop, i. Hist. N. E. 106. Prince, ii. Annals, 96. *JOSHUA*, first minister of the first church in Portsmouth, was son of William Moody, and was b. in England, in 1633, grad. at H. C. 1653, commenced preaching at Portsmouth 1658; was ordained 1671; was at Boston, the assistant minister of the first church, from 23 May, 1684 to 1692; was invited to the presidency of H. C. which he declined; returned to his charge at Portsmouth, but d. while on a visit at Boston, 4 July, [Boston records say the 6] 1697, æ. 64. His son Samuel, H. C. 1689, was a preacher at New-Castle, N. H.; m. Esther Green, of Boston, 4 April, 1695, and had sons, Joshua, b. and d. 1696; Joshua, 2d, b. 31 Oct. 1697, probably grad. at H. C. 1716; Samuel, b. 29 Oct. 1699, was a magistrate, and d. at Brunswick, Me., Sept. 1758, æ. 59, and one daughter, Mary, all born at New-Castle. Both the Rev. Joshua Moody and his son Samuel wrote the name *Moodey*. SAMUEL, came to N. E. in 1635, went to Hartford, thence to Hadley with the first settlers. He had three sons, John, Samuel, and Ebenezer, and 3 daughters. John had five children, and d. in Hartford. Samuel d. at 80 years and Ebenezer at 83. Coffin. WILLIAM, came from Wales, [Tradition] as early as 1634, was admitted freeman 1635, and after a short residence in Ipswich, settled in Newbury, where he d. 25 Oct. 1673. He had three sons, Joshua and Caleb, already noticed, and Samuel, who m. Mary Cutting, 30 November, 1657, had sons, William, b. in 1661; John, b. in 1663; Samuel, b. 1671; Cutting, and probably others, one of whom was ancestor of Rev. Silas Moody, H. C. 1761, the minister of Arundel, Me., who d. in April, 1816. Twenty-five of the name of Moody had grad. at the N. E. colleges in 1826, most of whom have descended from William Moody.

MOORE, FRANCIS, Cambridge, freeman 1639, had a son John, b. 20 March, 1645. Catharine, his wife, d. 28 Dec. 1648. He m. Elizabeth, 2d wife, before 1658. FRANCIS, Cambridge, son of the preceding, was admitted freeman 1652, and m. before 1658. GEORGE, Scituate 1636, kept a ferry at Jones River, Kingston, Mass., 1633. 2 Coll. Mass. Hist. Soc. iv. 224. GOLD-EN, Cambridge 1636, freeman 1641, was one of the first settlers of what now constitutes Lexington, in 1642 ; removed to Billerica, and there d. 3 Sept. 1698, æ. 89. His wife was Joan, and his children were, Hannah, Lydia, and Ruth. JAMES, Salem, was admitted freeman 1637; d. 1659. JEREMY, Hingham 1638, was admitted freeman 1644. JOHN, Dorchester, came to N. E. in 1630, was a deacon of the church, and removed to Windsor with Rev. John Warham, a. 1636. There were three of the name of John Moore among the early freemen, and they were admitted to the oath in 1631, 1633, and 1636. JOHN, Cambridge 1636. There also appears to have been a John Moore at Salem in 1637 ; one at Lynn in 1641, and one at Braintree, whose wife d. in 1643. JOHN, Sudbury 1643, d. 6 June, 1674. His son Jacob was born in 1645. See Revo. in N. E. Justified. *JOHN, Lancaster, was representative at the Dec. session in 1689 and Feb. session in 1690. *JOHN, jun., Lancaster was representative at the June session, 1689. RICH-ARD, Plymouth 1623. Davis, Morton's Memo, 382. RICHARD. (See MOWER.) SAMUEL, Salem, freeman 1632, had a family of 7 persons in 1637. Felt. THOMAS, Massachusetts, freeman 1631. THOMAS, Pascataqua 1631. Adams, Annals Portsmouth, 18. THOMAS, Salem, admitted member of the church 1639, freeman 1642 ; dismissed from the church, and probably removed. A Thomas Moor d. in Boston in 1690. WILLIAM, Exeter 1645, was a representative from that town in the provincial assembly of N. H. WILLIAM, Kittery 1652. WILLIAM, Ipswich, 1665, d. 1671, [2 Coll. Mass. Hist. Soc. viii. 107] where the name is Mover.

MOORES, EDMUND, Newbury 1640, was born a. 1614, and had sons, Jonathan, b. 1646 ; Richard, b. 1653, and several daughters. Ann, his wife, d. in 1670.

MORELL, WILLIAM, an episcopal minister, came to N. E. in Sept. 1623, with Capt. Robert Gorges, and resided at Weymouth, but left the country in a short time.

MORGAN, BENNET, Plymouth 1623. Davis, Morton's Memo. 378. JAMES, Roxbury, freeman 1643. MILES, Springfield 1645, d. 28 May, 1699. Sprague, Hist. Discourse. ROBERT, Salem 1637, b. in 1600, was one of the founders of the church in Beverly in 1667. ROGER, Charlestown, d. 23 Dec. 1675.

MORLEY, JOHN, Massachusetts, was admitted freeman 1645.

MORRILL, ||ABRAHAM, Cambridge 1632, member of the ar. co. 1638, removed to Salisbury, and there died a. 1662. Jacob Morrill, probably his son, was representative in 1689. Rev. Isaac Morrill, H. C. 1737, was born in Salisbury, 20 May, 1718, ordained at Wilmington, 20 May, 1741, and died 17 August, 1793, æ. 75. His son Samuel, H. C. 1766, who d. 21 Sept. 1785, æ. 41, was father of Governour David, L. Morril and Judge Samuel Morril, of New-Hampshire. ISAAC, Roxbury, freeman 1633, was b. in England in 1588, came to N. E. as early as 1632, and d. 18 Oct. 1662, aged 74. Isaac and Abraham, sons of Isaac Morrill, were b. in 1633 and 1640 at Roxbury.

MORRIS, *EDWARD, Roxbury, was representative from 1678 to 1686, 9 years. Grace, his widow, d. 6 June, 1705. *‖RICHARD, Roxbury, was representative 1635, member of the ar. co. 1637, probably went to Exeter, a. 1638. Dr. Belknap, [i. Hist. N. H.] calls him *Merrys*. RICE, Charlestown, d. 1647. SARGENT, Massachusetts, was admitted freeman 1633. THOMAS, New-Haven, d. 21 July, 1673. WILLIAM, New-Haven 1639, had sons, John, Eleazar, Ephraim, Thomas, b. 1651, Joseph, b. 1656. Dodd, East-Haven Register 135—137.

MORSE, ANTHONY, Newbury, was admitted freeman 1636, d. 12 Oct. 1686. He had 5 sons and 4 daughters. Three of the sons were Anthony, Benjamin, a deacon, and Joshua. Two of his sons went to Woodstock, Conn. [Coffin.] one of whom was the ancestor of Rev. Jedidiah Morse., D. D., the well known geographer, who died at New-Haven, in June, 1826, aged 65. Twenty-one of the name of Morse had grad. at the N. E. colleges in 1826. DANIEL, Dedham, freeman 1635, had sons, Obadiah, b. 1639, freeman 1677, Daniel, b. 1640; Jonathan, b. 1643, freeman 1672. He lived also in Medfield, and had sons, Nathaniel and Samuel, b. there. JOHN, Dedham, one of the early settlers, had sons, John, b. 1639; Joseph, b. 1640, Ezra, b. 1643. JOSEPH, Dedham, one of the early settlers, had a son Samuel, born in 1639, who lived in Medfield, and whose house was the first *fired* by the Indians, when that town was destroyed, 21 Feb. 1676. Hubbard, Ind. Wars, 62. JOSEPH, Ipswich 1646, had sons, John admitted freeman in 1654, and Joseph. Coffin. ROBERT, Newbury 1657, removed to Elizabeth-Town, New-Jersey. Coffin. SAMUEL, Dedham, freeman 1640, d. 5 Dec. 1654 at Medfield. WILLIAM, one of the proprietors and first settlers of Newbury, was b. a. 1614, and died Nov. 1683. His son Timothy was b. 10 June, 1648. He had several daughters. Mather [ii. Magnalia, 391] gives a marvellous account of his house being the scene of demoniacal operations, which Mr. Coffin says were performed by a vicious boy in his family.

MORTON, CHARLES, minister of Charlestown, the eldest son of Nicholas Morton, who was descended from an ancient family at Morton, in Nottinghamshire, the seat of Thomas Morton, the secretary of Edward III, was educated at Wadham College, Oxford, settled as the minister of Blisland in Cornwall, from whence he was ejected after the restoration of Charles II; came to N. E. in July 1686, and soon settled over the church at Charlestown, 5 Nov. 1686, d. 11 April, 1698, aged 72. Penhallow [2 Coll. Mass. Hist. Soc. i. 162] says, he d. in 1696, and Bartlett, [2 Coll. Mass. Hist. Soc. ii. 176] 1706, at the age of 80, but they both mistake. Nicholas Morton,

H. C. 1686, who d. 3 Nov. 1689, was probably his son. GEORGE, came to N. E. in July, 1623, in the ship Ann; settled at Plymouth, and d. in June, 1624, leaving a widow and four children, Nathaniel; John; Patience, and Ephraim, who was representative of Plymouth in 1692. Davis, Morton's Memo. Preface. NATHANIEL, Plymouth, son of the preceding, was b. in England, a. 1612, came with his father to N. E. 1623, was admitted freeman in 1635, m. Lydia Cooper the same year, and had 8 children. She died in 1673, and he m. Ann Templar, a widow, of Charlestown. He d. 28 June, 1685. Ibid. THOMAS, one of the first settlers at Mount Wollaston [Braintree, now Quincy] in 1625, was a lawyer, and gave much trouble to the early colonists. He was seized by Capt. Standish in 1628, and in 1630, by order of the court of assistants of Massachusetts, was sent to England, but returned; was imprisoned for writing his New English Canaan;—went to Agamenticus, Maine, and d. in 1644 or 1645. Prince. Hutchinson. Whitney, Hist. Quincy, 9—17. THOMAS, sen. and jun., were of Plymouth, in 1623. Davis, Morton's Memo. 378, 379, 382.

MOSE, JOHN, Massachusetts, was admitted freeman in 1640.

MOSELY, SAMUEL, a captain in Philip's war 1675. See Hubbard.

MOSS, JOHN, Boston, freeman 1636, d. 26 May, 1657. Rev. Joseph Moss grad. at H. C. 1699, and Rev. Reuben Moss, at Y. C. in 1787. JOSEPH, Watertown 1637, had sons, Joseph, b. 1637; John, b. 1638. and Jonathan, b. 1643.

MOTT, ADAM, Hingham, was admitted freeman 1637. NATHANIEL, Braintree, married Hannah Shooter 1656. His son Nathaniel, b. 1657.

MOULTHROP, MATTHEW, New-Haven 1639, m. Jane, and had Matthew, Elizabeth, Mary. Dodd, East-Haven Register, 137—139. He d. 22 Dec. 1668.

MOULTON, JAMES, was born in 1602, came to N. E. and settled at Salem; was admitted to the church, 31 Dec. 1637, freeman 1638, was living at Wenham in 1667. Felt. *JOHN, Newbury 1637, removed to Hampton 1638, was admitted freeman, and represented that town in 1639, died a. 1660. Henry and William Moulton d. at Hampton in 1664. *ROBERT, a ship-builder, was of Salem as early as 1629, admitted freeman, 18 May, 1631, representative of Charlestown at the first court in 1634, died in 1655, leaving son Robert, and a daughter who m. an Edwards. Felt, Annals, 226, 320. ROBERT, Salem, son of the preceding, was admitted to the church 1640, and there died in the fall of 1665, leaving children, Robert, Abigail, Samuel, Hannah, John, Joseph, Miriam, and Mary. He was admitted freeman in 1631. Ibid. 226, 320. THOMAS, Newbury 1637, went to Hampton; was admitted freeman in 1638. Belknap, i. Hist. N. H. 36. This name has been a distinguished one in the county of York, Me. Hon. Jeremiah d. at York, 22 Oct. 1727, æ. 77.

MOUNTFORT, ||BENJAMIN, was member of the ar. co. 1679. JOHN, ar. co. 1697.

MOUNTJOY, BENJAMIN, Salem, died 1659. GEORGE, Boston, freeman 1647, Casco 1665. (See Munjoy.) JOHN, Maine 1675. Hubbard, Ind. Wars.

MOURT, GEORGE, author of Mourt's Relation of the Beginning of Plymouth.

MOUSALL, *||JOHN, born a. 1596, came to N. E. and settled at Charlestown, was admitted freeman 1634, representative in 1635; member of the ar. co. 1641, probably removed to Woburn. John Mousall, admitted freeman in 1651, might be his son. *RALPH, Charlestown, came to N. E. as early as 1630, admitted freeman 1631, representative 1636 to 1638, 3 years, a deacon of the church, d. 30 April, 1657. This name is *Mushell* in the colony records.

MOWER, RICHARD, a mariner of Salem, was b. in 1612, admitted to the church in 1642 and freeman 1643. Richard, captain of a merchant vessel, and Thomas Gardner Mower, M. D., grad. at H. C. in 1738 and 1810.

MOXON, GEORGE, the first minister of Springfield, was a native of Yorkshire; was educated at Cambridge University, came to N. E. and was admitted freeman, 7 Sept. 1637, became the minister of Springfield the same year, remained there until 1653, when he returned to England, and d. 15 Sept. 1687, æ. 85. He had several children born at Springfield. George, one of his eldest sons, was among the ejected ministers after the restoration. Calamy, ii. Account, 313.

MULFORD, JOHN, was one the first settlers of East-Hampton, L. I., 1650. Wood. One of the name of Mulford was an assistant in 1658 of Connecticut.

MULLINS, WILLIAM, Plymouth 1620, one of the first pilgrims, d. 21 Feb. 1621. Prince, i. Annals, 98.

MUNDAY, HENRY, Salisbury, admitted freeman 1640. His wife d. 22 July, 1654.

MUNINGS, GEORGE, Watertown, freeman 1635, d. at Boston, 24 Aug. 1658. His son George was b. in 1655. This name is probably misspelled *Manings* in Christian Examiner for 1828, page 501.

MUNJOY, GEORGE, Boston, freeman 1647, had sons, John, b. 1653; George, b. 1656. He probably removed to Casco before 1665. Hutchinson, Coll. 398. (See Mountjoy.)

MUSSELWHITE, JOHN, Newbury 1635, came from Beaverstock, in Wiltshire, was admitted freeman 1639, and died 30 Jan. 1670. This name, written *Mussellwhit* in the colony records, and *Mussiloway* in the Newbury records, has now become *Siloway*, and is thus spelled by his descendants, who are in the vicinity of Newbury. Coffin.

MUSHELL, RALPH, freeman 1631. (See Mousall.)

MUSSEY, JOHN, Ipswich 1635, removed to Salisbury, and d. 12 April, 1690. ROBERT, one of the first settlers of Ipswich, was admitted freeman 1634. His eldest son, Joseph, settled in Newbury. A Hester Mussey was a proprietor in 1632 of Cam-

bridge, [Holmes, Hist. Cambridge] in the vicinity of which the
name has been common. A widow Mussey was of Hampton in
1638. Belknap, i. Hist. N. H. 37. Three of the name, Benjamin,
William, and Artemas Bowers, natives of Lexington, Mass., grad.
at H. C. in 1774, 1793, and 1824. Reuben D. Mussey, M. D., the
professor at Dartmouth, grad. at that institution in 1803. The
name besides written as above, is also spelled *Muzzey* and *Muzzy*.

MUST, EDWARD, Massachusetts, was admitted freeman in
1634.

MYCALL, JAMES, Braintree 1657, had a son James, b. in 1658.

MYGATE, JOSEPH, Cambridge 1634. (See MEGGOT.)

MYLAM, ||JOHN, a cooper, was admitted a member of the
church in Boston 1635, freeman 1636, member of the ar. co. 1641.
He had sons, Benjamin, b. 1639; John, b. 1640; Eliasaph, b. 1642;
Samuel, b. 1644; Ebenezer, b. 1646, and Joseph, b. 1651. John
Maylem, possibly of this family, grad. at H. C. 1715.

NASH, GREGORY, Charlestown 1630, with his wife, d. in
Feb. 1631. Eleven persons of this name, six of them clergymen,
had grad. at the N. E. colleges in 1828, of whom Rev. William
Nash, Y. C. 1791, was of West-Boylston, Mass., and d. in March,
1829, æ. 60. *JACOB, Weymouth, freeman 1666, was representative in 1689 and 1690. *JAMES, Weymouth, freeman 1645,
was representative in 1655, 1662, 1667; was a captain of the militia, and probably father of Jacob, the preceding, and James, both
of whom were admitted freeman in 1666. ‡JOHN, Connecticut,
was an assistant in 1672. ROBERT, Boston 1643. Snow, Hist.
Boston, 120. SAMUEL, Duxbury 1645, was a representative in
1653. *TIMOTHY, Hadley 1663, freeman 1678, was a representative in 1692. WILLIAM, Massachusetts, was admitted freeman
in 1634.

NASON, RICHARD, Kittery 1652. Reuben Nason, H. C.
1802, was minister of Freeport, Me.

NEAL, ALEXANDER, Braintree m. Mary Belcher in 1655.
EDWARD, Weymouth 1662, perhaps of Westfield in 1686.
*FRANCIS, Falmouth 1658, representaive 1670. FRANCIS,
Salem, was admitted freeman in 1675. HENRY, Braintree 1642,
had sons, Samuel, b. 1647; Henry, b. 1649; Joseph, by 2d wife,
b. 1660. JOHN, Massachusetts, was admitted freeman in 1642.
WALTER, Pascataqua 1631, one of the stewards of Captain John
Mason, was a captain, and was styled the governour of Pascataqua
in 1631. He left N. E. in August, 1633. See Belknap, i. Hist.
N. H. and Savage, ii. Winthrop, Index. Walter Neal, perhaps his
son, was of N. H. in 1660, and in 1673 was appointed a lieutenant
under James Pendleton. He had a son Samuel, by Mary, his wife,
born 14 June, 1661. Three of the name of Neal had grad. at H.
C. in 1828.

NEEDHAM, EDWARD, Lynn, 1639 was one of the grantees
of South-Hampton, L. I. 1640, d. 16 May, 1677. Lewis. JONAS,
Lynn 1650, d. 24 Oct. 1674, æ. 64. Ibid. NICHOLAS, Exeter
1639, was one of the witnesses of the genuine deed of the Indian

sachems to Rev. John Wheelwright, 1638. WILLIAM, Braintree, freeman 1648, perhaps d. in Boston, 30 Dec. 1690. A John Needham d. in Boston in 1690.

NEGUS, BENJAMIN, Boston, was admitted to the church 1642, freeman in 1648; had sons, Benjamin, b. 1641; Samuel, b. 1645. JONATHAN, of Lynn and Boston, was b. in 1601, admitted freeman in 1634. Snow, in his Hist. Boston, spells this name *Negoose.*

NELSON, ‖JOHN, a captain, and member of the ar. co. 1680, was one of the council of safety, upon the seizure and imprisonment of Sir Edmund Andros in 1689. Hutchinson, i. Hist. Mass. 340. PHILIP, Rowley, the eldest son of Thomas Nelson, came to N. E. with his father in 1638, grad. at H. C. in 1654, admitted freeman in 1667. He caused some trouble in the church at Rowley by pretending to cure a deaf and dumb boy in imitation of our Saviour, by saying Ephphatha. The ministers of the neighbouring churches were called together, and the boy was brought before them to see whether he could speak or not. He was interrogated, but "there he stood," say the records, "like a deaf and dumb boy as he was." They could not make him hear, nor could he speak. Coffin, MS Letter. Nelson died, according to Mr. Coffin, 20 Aug. 1691, which is doubtless correct, yet Mr. Winthrop, who makes him a military officer, says he d. 4 Dec. 1721. *THOMAS, Rowley, freeman 1639, was representative in 1640. He brought from England two sons, Philip, the preceding, and Thomas, who lived in Rowley, and d. 5 April, 1712, æ. 77, leaving issue, which sons, when he returned to England, where he d. in Aug. 1648, he left in care of their great uncle, Richard Dummer. Thirteen of the name had received the honours of the N. E. colleges in 1828.

NETHERLAND, WILLIAM, Massachusetts, was admitted freeman in 1635.

NEWBURY, ‡BENJAMIN, was an assistant of Connecticut in 1685. A Captain Newbury was an officer in Philip's war 1676. RICHARD, Weymouth 1655. *THOMAS, Lynn, was representative in 1635. Savage, i. Winthrop, 398. ‡WALTER, Rhode-Island, was one of Sir Edmund Andros' council in 1687. Hutchinson, i. Hist. Mass. 317.

NEWCOMB, FRANCIS, Braintree 1640, d. 27 May, 1692, æ. upwards of 100 years. He had sons, John; Peter, of Braintree, b. 16 May, 1640; Abijah. Three of the name had grad. at H. C. in 1828, and the same number at Dart. College.

NEWELL, ABRAHAM, Roxbury, freeman 1635, d. 13 June, 1672, æ. 92. Sixteen of the name of Newell had grad. at Harvard and Yale colleges in 1828. ABRAHAM, Roxbury, freeman 1653, d. 17 August, 1692. His son Abraham was b. in 1654.

NEWGATE, *JOHN, a merchant, selectman, and constable of Boston, was admitted freeman in 1635, and elected representative at the March and Sept. sessions 1638. He d in 1665, leaving several children. One of his daughters m. Simon Lynde, one m. Peter Oliver, and Elizabeth, a third, m. John Oliver, and afterwards, Edward Jackson. A Joshua Newgate died at Boston, 12 Nov.

1658. ||NATHANIEL, Boston, son of the preceding, was member of the ar. co. in 1646. He had one son, Nathaniel, whose children were, Isabel; Lewis, b. 1697; John, b. 1703, some of whom wrote the name *Newdigate*.

NEWHALL, ANTHONY, an inhabitant of Lynn 1636, was also of Salem, and died a. 1657. Dr. Horace and Rev. Ebenezer Newhall grad. at H. C. 1817 and 1818. THOMAS, Lynn 1630, had sons, John, who m. Sarah Lewis, 10 April, 1646; Thomas, who was the first child born in Lynn, m. Elizabeth, daughter of Robert Potter, 29 Sept. 1652, and was buried 1 April, 1687, æ. 57. Lewis.

NEWLAND, WILLIAM, Lynn, removed to Sandwich 1637. Ibid.

NEWMAN, ANTIPAS, the second minister of Wenham, where he began to preach in 1657, was ordained in Dec. 1663, d. 15 Oct. 1672. He was one of those ministers who signed the petition or address to the general court of Mass. 1670. [See Hutchinson's Hist. Mass. i. 249, 250.] He m. Elizabeth, daughter of Gov. John Winthrop, in 1658. She afterwards m. Zerubbabel Endecott, of Salem. Mr. Felt gives me the names of Mr. Newman's children, viz. : John, Samuel, Waitstill, Elizabeth, and Sybil. ‡FRANCIS, New-Haven, was an assistant in 1653, and governour of the colony from 1658 to 1661. He was also an agent to Gov. Stuyvesant at Manhadoes, and a commissioner of the United Colonies. He died in 1661. JOHN, Ipswich 1634. *NOAH*, Rehoboth probably son of Rev. Samuel Newman, whom he succeeded as minister, d. 16 April, 1676. He m. Joanna, daughter of Rev. Henry Flint, 3 Dec. 1669. ROBERT, New-Haven 1669. *SAMUEL*, was born at Banbury, in England, [Lord, ii. Lempriere's Univ. Biog. 381, says *Bombay*] in 1600 or 1691, was educated at Oxford, and came to N. E., according to Judge Davis, in 1636, was admitted freeman in 1638, lived in Dorchester one year and a half, in Weymouth about 5 years, and in Rehoboth from 1644 to his death, 5 July, 1663. Samuel, probably his eldest son, lived in Rehoboth, and had several children. Antipas and Noah, above, were probably his sons. Hope, his daughter, was born at Weymouth, 29 Nov. 1641. THOMAS, Ipswich 1665, d. in 1676, leaving sons, Thomas, John, and Benjamin.

NEWMARCH, JOHN, Rowley 1643. John Newmarch, minister of Kittery, Joseph Newmarch, of Newcastle, a counsellor of New-Hampshire 1754, grad. at H. C. in 1690 and 1728.

NEWT, JAMES, Pascataqua 1632, was one of the grand jury in 1643. This name exists in New-Hampshire, and is spelled *Nute*.

NEWTON, ANTHONY, Lancaster 1652, freeman 1671. JOHN, Massachusetts, was admitted freeman 1633. JOHN, the freeman of 1643, was probably of Marlborough. RICHARD, Sudbury 1640, freeman 1645, had sons, John, Moses, and Ezekiel. Moses had 8 sons and 2 daughters. *ROGER*, the first minister of Farmington, was ordained 13 Oct. 1652, was dismissed 1657; removed to Milford, where he was installed 22 August, 1660. He d.

7 June, 1683. He m. Mary, the eldest daughter of Rev. Thomas Hooker. Rev. Roger Newton, D. D., who grad. at Y. C. 1758, was probably a descendant. Twelve persons of the name had grad. in N. E. in 1827.

NICHOLAS, WALTER, Massachusetts, was admitted freeman 1636. Savage, ii. Winthrop, 366.

NICHOLET, CHARLES, came from Virginia, and was invited to preach at Salem, with Rev. John Higginson, in 1671, and two years after, by a vote of the town, was chosen to continue for life; but the church did not give their concurrence. He afterwards received a call from a new church in Salem, which was gathered at Lynn in 1674, but left the place soon after and went to England in 1672. Judge Sewall. J. Coffin. Spirit of the Pilgrims, ii. 176. Felt, Annals.

NICHOLS, ADAM, Massachusetts, was admitted freeman in 1670. DANIEL, Charlestown, d. 2 July, 1659. DAVID, Boston, d. 13 March, 1653. JAMES, Malden, freeman 1668, d. 30 May, 1695. RANDALL, Charlestown 1642. RICHARD, Ipswich 1648, perhaps afterwards of Reading, where a Richard Nichols d. 22 Nov. 1674. THOMAS, Scituate 1645, Hingham 1653. Eighteen persons of the name had grad. at the N. E. colleges in 1828.

NICHOLSON, EDMUND and FRANCIS, were of Marblehead in 1648.

NICKERSON, WILLIAM, Massachusetts, freeman 1638.

NIGHTENGALE, BENJAMIN and WILLIAM, Braintree before 1690. John Nightengale, of Hull, d. in Boston 1706. Samuel Nightengale, H. C. 1734, was from Braintree.

NILES, JOHN, Braintree 1639, freeman 1647, d. in Feb. 1694, æ. 94. He had sons, John b. 4 March, 1639; Joseph, b. 1640; Nathaniel, b. 1642; Samuel, b. 1644; Increase, b. 1646; Benjamin, b. 1650; Isaac, b. 1658. Samuel Niles, H. C. 1699, was minister of Braintree. Nine persons of the name had grad. at the N. E. colleges in 1828.

NOBLE, THOMAS, Massachusetts, freeman 1681.

NOCK, THOMAS, New-Hampshire, and probably of Dover, d. 29 Oct. 1666. One of his descendants, James Nock, an elder of the church at Durham, was killed by the Indians in 1724. Belknap, ii. Hist. N. H.

NODDLE, WILLIAM, from whom Noddle's Island takes its name, was admitted freeman in 1633. Savage, i. Winthrop, 39, 80.

NORCROSS, JEREMIAH, Watertown 1642, d. in 1657, leaving sons, Nathaniel and Richard. JOHN, Cambridge 1642. *NATHANIEL*, freeman 1643, was educated at one of the universities in England, and was a preacher, and received a call to be the minister at Nashaway, in 1644; but probably returned to England, and may have been the one ejected from his living at Walshingham, in Norfolk, after the restoration. Calamy. Winthrop. RICHARD, Watertown, son of Jeremiah, m. Mary Brooks, 24 June, 1650. THOMAS, Watertown, was admitted freeman 1652.

NORDEN, *NATHANIEL, Marblehead, a captain, was representative in 1689 and 1690. SAMUEL, Boston, was admitted freeman in 1666.

NORMAN, JOHN, Salem 1637, Marblehead 1648, d. in 1673, æ. about 60. He left a wife, Arabella, and children. Felt. Dana. RICHARD, Salem, came to N. E. as early as 1627, and died in 1683. His sons were, probably, John, above named ; Richard, b. in 1623, and living in Marblehead in 1672, and William, of Marblehead in 1648.

NORRIS, EDWARD, the fourth minister of the first church in Salem, was admitted to the church in Boston 1639 [Records of First Church] ; went the same year to Salem, where he was ordained 18 March, 1640 ; was admitted freeman 13 May following ; d. 10 April, 1659, about 70 years old. Felt, Annals Salem, 200—202. Upham, Ded. Sermon, 55, 61. EDWARD, Salem, son of the preceding, member of the church 1639, was a schoolmaster from 1640 to 1671, died in 1684, æ. 70. He left two children, Edward, baptized 18 Oct. 1657, and Elizabeth. Descendants remain.

NORTH, RICHARD, one of the first proprietors of Salisbury 1640, was admitted freeman 1641.

NORTHEND, EZEKIEL, was born a. 1622, and lived in Rowley in 1652.

NORTHUP, STEPHEN, one of the early proprietors of Providence. Coffin.

NORTHY, JOHN, an inhabitant of Marblehead in 1648, was born a. 1607, and of Scituate 1670. Sometimes *Nothey*.

NORTON, ||*FRANCIS, Pascataqua 1631, where he was an agent of Captain John Mason, until about the year 1641, when he removed to Charlestown ; was admitted freeman 1642, elected member of the ar. co. 1643 ; captain of the militia ; representative 11 years, 1647, 1650, 1652 to 1661, excepting 1656 and 1657, d. 27 July, 1667. Johnson commemorates him as " a man of a bold and cheerful spirit, being well disciplined, and an able man." FREE-GRACE, early of Saco, probably of Ipswich 1665. 2 Coll. Mass. Hist. Soc. viii. *GEORGE, Salem, was admitted freeman in 1634, removed to Gloucester, which he represented in 1642, 1643, and 1644. He died about 1659. George Norton, perhaps a son, was admitted freeman 1631. *JOHN*, the second minister of Ipswich, and the third of the First church in Boston, was b. at Starford, in the county of Hertford, 6 May, 1606, was educated at the University of Cambridge ; came to N. E. in 1635, and settled at Ipswich 1636, removed to Boston, a. 1653, where he was installed 23 July, 1656 ; was appointed an agent by the Massachusetts colony after the restoration, to address Charles II. He sailed for England in Feb. 1662, returned in September, and d. 5 April, 1663, æ. 57, leaving a wife, Mary, but probably no children. Mather. Allen. Holmes. *JOHN*, the second minister of Hingham, was nephew to the preceding, and son of William Norton, of Ipswich. He grad. at H. C. 1671, was ordained 27 Nov. 1678, d. 3 Oct. 1716, aged 66. Lincoln, History Hingham, 24. Felt, MS Letter

JOHN, Springfield, died 24 August, 1687. Rev. W. B. Sprague.
NICHOLAS, Weymouth, had sons, Isaac, b. 3 May, 1641, and
Jacob, b. 1 March, 1644. RICHARD, Boston, had a son Richard,
b. in 1649. Samuel Norton, probably a relation, d. at Boston, 28
June, 1654. WALTER, a captain, [Prince, ii. 4] was admitted
freeman, 18 May, 1631, and perhaps the Captain Norton, who was
killed by the Indians in 1634, at the same time with Capt. John
Stone. But Mr. Savage in the Index to his Winthrop makes the
name of the captain, *John*. WILLIAM, Ipswich, brother of the
Rev. John Norton, of Boston, was admitted freeman in 1636, and
probably d. 30 April, 1694. He had a brother Thomas, who lived
in London. Felt, MS Letter. Twenty persons of the name of Norton had grad. at the N. E. colleges in 1828.

NORWICK, JOHN, Massachusetts, was admitted freeman 1640.
NORWOOD, RICHARD, Cambridge, d. 13 May, 1644.
FRANCIS, Gloucester 1664. John and Francis Norwood grad. at
H. C. and D. C. in 1771 and 1818; the latter a clergyman in Mere-
dith, N. H.

NOTT, GEORGE, was an inhabitant of Sandwich in 1637.
(See KNOTT.) Ten of the name of Nott had grad. at Yale and
Union colleges in 1828, one of whom, Rev Eliphalet Nott, D. D.,
presides over the last named institution.

NOWELL, ‡INCREASE, Charlestown, one of the assistants
from 1630 to 1655; one of the founders of the church at Charlestown 1632, secretary of the colony from 1644 to 1649, six years; d.
1 Nov. 1655. The name of his wife was Parnell, to whom 1000
acres of land on the east side of Cochecho River, in N. H. was granted, probably after her husband's death. [Plan of the land by surveyor Danforth.] His children were, Increase, b. 1630, d. 1633;
Samuel, the following; Eleazar, b. and d. 1636; Increase, 2d, b.
23 May, 1640; Alexander, who grad. at H. C. 1664, freeman 1671,
and was the author of several almanacks, and d. in 1672, and perhaps George, a member of the ar. co. in 1662. ‡SAMUEL, son of
the preceding, was born at Charlestown, 12 Nov. 1634, grad. at H.
C. 1653, became a preacher; was elected an assistant from 1680 to
1686; went to England, and was in London in 1688. He owned
a considerable tract of land in New-Hampshire, near his mother's,
and bounded on Newichewannock River, and Dover line. This
name is found in Mass. and N. H.

NOYE, BENJAMIN, Lynn, removed to Sandwich 1637. [Lew-
is.] This name should probably be *Nye*, which is common in Sandwich, and its neighbourhood. Seven had grad. at the N. E. colleges in 1828.

NOYES, JAMES, one of the first ministers of Newbury, was
born at Choulderton, in Wiltshire, in 1608, came to N. E. in 1634,
with Rev. Thomas Parker, with whom, after having preached nearly one year at Medford, he settled at Newbury in 1635, where he
d. 22 Oct. 1656, æ. 48. He m. Sarah, eldest daughter of Joseph
Brown, of Southampton, England, by whom (who d. 13 Sept. 1691,)
he had a large family. He left six sons, 1. James, the following, b.

1640; 2. Moses, b. 1643; 3. Joseph, b. 14 Oct. 1644; 4. *Thomas, b. 10 August, 1648, m. Martha Pierce 1669, was a captain and magistrate, and representative in 1689, 1690, and 1692; 5. John, b. 4 June, 1649, freeman 1675, member of the ar. co. d. at Boston 1678, and perhaps father to Dr. Oliver Noyes, H. C. 1695; 6. William, b. 22 Sept. 1653, and 2 daughters. *JAMES*, minister of Stonington, son of the preceding, was born 11 March, 1640, grad. at H. C. 1659, began to preach at Stonington in 1664, was ordained 10 Sept. 1674, and having imparted religious instruction to his people, above 50 years, d. 30 Dec. 1719, in his 80th year. *MOSES*, brother of the preceding, was born at Newbury, 6 Dec. 1643, grad. at H. C. 1659, was ordained the first minister of Lym, Conn., where he d. 10 Nov. 1726, æ. 83, having spent 60 years with his people. JOSEPH, Sudbury, one of the selectmen 28 years from 1662, d. 16 Nov. 1717. He m. for 2d wife, Mary, widow of Major Simon Willard, 14 July, 1680. She d. 28 Dec. 1715. Shattuck. *NICHOLAS, brother of Rev. James Noyes, of Newbury, was b. about 1616, and came from Wiltshire to N. E. in 1634, and was admitted freeman 1637, settled in Newbury, which he represented in 1660, 1679, and 1680. He d. 9 Nov. 1701, æ. 85. He had sons, John, b. 20 Jan. 1646, m. Mary Poor, 1668; Nicholas, born 1647; Cutting, born 1649; Timothy, born 1655; James, b. 1657; Thomas, b. 1663, and 7 daughters. *NICHOLAS*, the seventh minister of the first church in Salem, was son of the preceding, and was b. at Newbury, 22 Dec. 1647, grad. at H. C. 1667, preached 13 years at Haddam, was ordained 14 Nov. 1683, and d. 13 Dec. 1717, æ. 70, having never married. 1 Coll. Mass. Hist. Soc. x. Index. *PETER, Sudbury, was admitted freeman 1640, representative 1640, 1641, and 1650, a selectman 21 years, and deacon of the church, d. 23 Sept. 1657. Shattuck. *PETER, Sudbury, freeman 1673, was elected representative in 1679, 1690, and 1691. *THOMAS, Sudbury 1640, was a selectman 12 years, and representative at the 2d session in 1664. He died 7 Dec. 1666. Thirty-four of the name had grad. at the N. E. colleges in 1828.

NURSE, FRANCIS, Salem-Village, had children, John, Sarah, Rebecca, Samuel, Francis, Mary, Elizabeth, and Benjamin. Their mother, Rebecca, was hung in the witchcraft delusion, 19 July, 1692.

NUTT, MILES, freeman in 1637, might be of Woburn in 1653 [See 3 Coll. Mass. Hist. Soc. i.]; died at Malden, 2 July, 1671.

NUTTER, ‡ANTHONY, an elder of the church at Dover 1662, was admitted freeman 1666, and was appointed a counsellor of N. H. in 1682. HATEVIL, an inhabitant of Dover in 1649.

NUTTING, JOHN, freeman 1660, was a petitioner for the grant of Chelmsford in 1653. NATHANIEL, Groton, a. 1677.

OAKES, *EDWARD, Cambridge, freeman 1642, was elected representative 15 years, between 1659 and 1682, and, in 1684, represented Concord, where he d. 13 Oct. 1689. He had sons, Urian, the president of H. C., Edward, and Thomas. His daughter Hannah m. deacon James Blood in 1657. GEORGE, Lynn, 1654, d.

July, 1688. He had sons, George ; John, perhaps member of the ar. co. 1682, and Richard. Lewis. SIMON, is named by Dr. Holmes in his Hist. of Cambridge, as one of the proprietors in 1632. THOMAS, Cambridge, freeman 1642, brother of Edward, d. before 1659. His children were, Thomas, b. and d. in 1648 ; Elizabeth ; Hannah ; Thomas, 2d, baptized 20 March, 1659. *‡THOMAS, son of Edward Oakes, was b. at Cambridge, 18 June, 1644, grad. at H. C. 1662, settled as a physician in Boston ; representative in 1689, and the same year was elected an assistant. He went to England as agent for Massachusetts soon after, and assisted in procuring the new charter. He d. at Welfleet, 15 July, 1719, æ. 75. Dunton's account of his character may be found in 2 Coll. Mass. Hist Soc. ii. *URIAN*, the fifth minister of Cambridge and the fourth president of Harvard College, was the son of Edward Oakes, [Holmes, i. Annals, 425] and was b. in England. He grad. at H. C. 1649 ; soon went to England, and was the minister of Tichfield, in Hampshire. He was silenced in 1662 ; returned to America, a. 1671, and was installed at Cambridge, 8 Nov. 1671 ; freeman 1672, entered upon his duties as president of H. C., 7 April, 1675 ; d. 25 July, 1681, in his 50th year. Urian Oakes, H. C. 1678, who d. 3 Nov. 1679, was probably his son, as might be, perhaps, Laurence Oakes, a bachelor of arts, who d. at Cambridge, 13 June, 1679, æ. 18. Edward Oakes grad. at H. C. in the class of 1679, and died young.

OAKMAN, SAMUEL, Casco-Bay 1658. Mebzar Turner Oakman grad. at H. C. 1771.

OBER, RICHARD, Beverly 1679, had sons, Hezekiah, b. 1681 ; Richard, b. 1684 ; Nicholas, b. 1686. This name, written sometimes *Obear*, still prevails in the neighbourhood of Beverly, and is found in New-Hampshire.

ODELL, WILLIAM, Concord 1639, had a son James, b. in 1639. JOHN, of Fairfield, Conn., in 1668. This name exists in several parts of New-Hampshire.

ODIORNE, JOHN, Portsmouth 1660, was one of the grand jury in 1686. Jotham Odiorne, a counsellor of N. H., who d. 16 Aug. 1748, æ. 73, was probably his son. Thomas Odiorne, D. C. 1791, author of poems, was from this family.

ODLIN, ||JOHN, one of the first settlers of Boston, was probably member of the ar. co. in 1638, whose name is spelled by Whitman, *Audlin*. He d. 18 Dec. 1685, æ. 83 years, leaving sons, Elisha, John, and Peter. Elisha was b. 1 July, 1640, freeman 1675, lived in Boston, and was father of Rev. John Odlin, of Exeter, N. H., who was b. 18 Nov. 1681, grad. at H. C. 1702, d. 1754, æ. 72, whose sons Elisha and Woodbridge grad. at H. C. 1731 and 1738 and were ministers of Amesbury and Exeter. Peter, the youngest son of the first John, was b. 2 August, 1646, and lived in Boston. This name is still found at Exeter, and some other parts of New-Hampshire.

OFFLEY, ||DAVID, member of the ar. co. 1638. Thomas Offley was collector of Salem in 1689. Felt, Annals, 291.

OGDEN, ‡JOHN, Connecticut, was elected an assistant of the colony in 1656. There was an Ogden of Fairfield, Conn., in 1668. Hon. David Ogden, a judge of the superiour court of Conn. grad. at Y. C. in 1728.

OLDAGE, RICHARD, Windsor 1640. 1 Coll. Mass. Hist. Soc. v. 168.

OLCOTT, or ALCOTT, ‡JOHN, is named as one of the council of Mass. in 1692. More than ten of the name of Olcott have received the honours of the N. E. colleges.

OLDHAM, *JOHN, arrived at Plymouth, in the ship Ann, in July, 1623, where he lived a short time; went to Nantasket, now Hull, and from thence to Cape Ann. He was admitted freeman, 18 May, 1631, when he probably resided in Watertown, which town he represented in the first general court of Mass. in 1634. He was killed in his bark at Rhode-Island, by the Indians, in August, 1636. It is said his posterity still remain in Massachusetts, and one of the name of John Oldham died at Danvers in 1827. 2 Coll. Mass. Hist. Soc. x. Index. RICHARD, Cambridge, d. before 1658, leaving a widow, Martha (whom. Thomas Brown, of Cambridge) and sons, Samuel, freeman in 1673, and John. THOMAS, Scituate 1650. Coffin.

OLIVER, ‖JAMES, Boston, son of elder Thomas Oliver, [Prince, ii. Annals, 70] was admitted freeman 1640, member of the ar. co. 1637, and its captain from 1656 to 1666. JOHN, Boston, brother of the preceding, and according to Mr. Savage, [i. Winthrop, 96] was the graduate at H. C. in 1645. He was admitted freeman in 1640, and d. 12 April, 1646 [Interleaved Almanack, 1646]; a worthy and excellent character. See Winthrop, ii. Hist. N. E. 257. His wife was Elizabeth, daughter of John Newgate, and she afterwards m. Edward Jackson. (See JACKSON.) His children were, 1. John, b. 1638, d. 1639; 2. Elizabeth, b. 28 Feb. 1640, m. Enoch Wiswall; 3. Hannah, b. 1642, d. 1653; 4. John, 2d, b. 15 April, 1644, lived in Boston; was a member of the ar. co. 1680, and had sons, Sweet, b. 1668; John, b. 1688; William, b. 1694; Samuel, b. 1698; Hammond, b. 1699; Ebenezer, b. 1703, and 4 daughters; 5. Thomas, b. 10 Feb. 1646, lived in Newton, where he d. 2 Nov. 1715, having been a representative, counsellor, and deacon. He m. Grace Prentice, 1667, and Mary Wilson in 1682, and had children, Grace; Elizabeth; John; Hannah; Thomas; Samuel, b. 1679, John, 2d; Nathaniel, b. 1 Feb. 1685, perhaps the graduate 1701, and Mary, most of whom d. in infancy. ‖*JOHN, Boston, freeman 1634, was member of the ar. co. 1637, and representative at the May session in 1638. It is supposed that he was brother to Elder Thomas Oliver. He removed to Newbury, and d. in 1642. Joanna, his widow, m. Capt. William Gerrish. His only daughter, Mary, b. 7 June, 1640, m. Samuel Appleton, of Ipswich, in 1656. ‖PETER, son of Elder Thomas, was an eminent merchant in Boston, admitted freeman 1640, member of the ar. co. 1643, its captain in 1669, d. in 1670. His sons were Nathaniel, b. 8 March, 1652, who was one of the council of safety in 1689, and d. in Boston, 5 April, 1704; Peter, b. 3 March, 1655, grad. at H. C. 1675; James, b. 19 March,

1658, grad. at H. C. 1680, settled as a physician at Cambridge, and
d. 8 April, 1703, æ. 45; Daniel, b. 28 Feb. 1664, d. 23 July, 1732,
æ. 69, whose sons, Daniel, b. 14 Jan. 1704 ; Andrew, b. 28 March,
1706, and Peter, b. 26 March, 1713, grad. at H. C. in 1722, 1724,
and 1730. Andrew was the lieutenant-governour, and Peter, the
chief justice of Massachusetts. RICHARD, is mentioned several
times in Hubbard's Indian Wars, and a Lieutenant Oliver was em-
ployed in the commencement of Philip's war, 1675. ||SAMUEL,
Boston, brother of the preceding, was member of the church 1642,
of the ar. co. 1648, and was drowned 27 March, 1652, leaving a
widow by the name of Lydia. THOMAS, an elder of the church
in Boston, and a worthy and useful man, came to N. E. in 1631,
was admitted freeman in 1632, and died in 1657. Ann, his wife,
d. in June, 1637. His sons were the four above named; Nathaniel, who was killed 9 Jan. 1633, æ. 15, and Daniel, who d. in May,
1635. Twenty-five of the name of Oliver, and the greater part, if
not all, descendants from Elder Thomas Oliver, had grad. at Harv.
College in 1828.

OLMSTEAD, JAMES, Cambridge, admitted freeman, in 1632,
served as constable several years. NICHOLAS, one of the Pequot
soldiers in 1637. Five of the name had grad. at Yale College in
1828.

OLNEY, THOMAS, Salem, was admitted freeman 1637, went
to Rhode-Island with Roger Williams, and was one of the founders
of the first Baptist church in this country. [Hutchinson, i. Hist.
Mass. 371.] Two of his descendants had grad. at Brown Coll. in 1827,
and the name has been common in Rhode-Island. *THOMAS*,
probably son of the preceding, born in Hertford, England, a. 1631,
was minister of the Baptist church in Providence, and d. 11 June,
1722. Benedict, i. Hist. Baptists, 478.

ONG, ———, came to N. E. in the ship Lyon, and arrived at
Nantasket, 5 Feb. 1631. Frances Ong, probably his widow, was
buried at Watertown, Nov. 1638. Savage, i. Winthrop, 42. Simon and Isaac Ong were of Watertown in 1646 and 1669. Jacob
Ong was of Groton in 1678.

ONION, ROBERT, Roxbury, was admitted freeman in 1646.
Mary, his wife, d. in 1643. Savage, ii. Winthrop, 95.

ONTHANK, CHRISTOPHER, one of the early proprietors of
Providence, and probably an inhabitant. This name still exists in
N. England.

ORDWAY, ABNER, Watertown 1643. JAMES, Newbury
1649, freeman 1668, had sons, Ephraim, b. 1650; James, b. 1651;
John, b. 1658, and 4 or 5 daughters. Judge Sewall mentions him
in his Diary as an aged man.

ORNE, JOHN, formerly written *Horne*, was a deacon of Salem
54 years. (See HORNE.) There have been a number of graduates
of the name of Orne at H. C.

ORRICE, GEORGE, Boston, had sons, John, b. 1646, d. at
Boston, 19 Dec. 1699 ; Jonathan, b. 1656. Sometimes spelled
Orris.

ORTON, THOMAS, Charlestown 1642. Samuel, James, Azariah, a clergyman, and Milton P. Orton grad. at colleges in 1765, 1787, 1813, and 1824.

ORY, ||RALPH, was member of the ar. co. 1640. Whitman, Hist. Sketch, 150.

OSBORN, JOHN, Weymouth, had sons, John and Ephraim, b. in 1639 and 1657. John, a proprietor of Westfield, was probably freeman 1673. RICHARD, Hingham 1635. THOMAS, Charlestown, freeman 1648, was one of the founders of the Baptist church in May, 1665. THOMAS, East-Hampton, L. I. 1650. WILLIAM, Salem, was admitted to the church, 24 March, 1639, freeman 22 May, 1639. There was a William Osborn at Dorchester, soon after, whose son Recompence was b. on Sunday, 26 May, either in 1639 or 1644, [Records illegible] and grad. at H. C. 1661. William Osborn, of Braintree in 1650, had a son Bezaleel, b. that year. Seventeen of the name had grad. at the N. E. colleges in 1828.

OSGOOD, CHRISTOPHER, Ipswich, was admitted freeman in 1635, died in 1650, leaving a wife, Margery, and children, Mary, Abigail, Elizabeth, and Christopher. Felt. *CHRISTOPHER, son of the following, born a. 1643, lived in Andover, a captain, admitted freeman in 1675, representative at the Dec. session 1690, d. 1723, æ. 80. He was probably the one imprisoned 9 or 10 days, in the time of Sir Edmund Andros, without "a mittimus, or any thing laid to his charge." [See Revo. in N. E. Justified, p. 39.] His sons were, Christopher, who settled in Billerica, and built the first mills on Concord River, where intersected by the Middlesex canal, and Ezekiel, whose son Capt. Samuel d. in 1748, aged 46. *JOHN, born 23 July, 1595, came from Andover, England, [Coffin] and settled at Newbury, was admitted freeman 1639, went to Andover, was one of the founders of the church, Oct. 1645, and elected the first representative in 1651, in Oct. of which year he d. æ. 56. His sons were, 1. John; 2. Stephen, freeman in 1669, who had sons Stephen and Hooker; 3. Christopher, above; 4. Thomas, who settled in Andover, and had sons Thomas and Josiah. A number of his descendants, who are very numerous, have grad. at Harvard and Dartmouth. *JOHN, Andover, son of the preceding, was a captain, often a selectman, and representative in 1666, 1669, 1689, and 1690. In the time of Sir Edmund Andros, he was one of those who suffered imprisonment illegally. [See Revo. in N. E. Just. 39.] He d. in 1693. His sons were, John, who d. 1725, æ. 71; Timothy; Peter, and Samuel. Mary, his wife, was one among those accused, in 1692, of witchraft, and who, by confessing the alleged crime, saved her life. After the delusion had subsided, she made a recantation. See Hutchinson, Calef, and Abbot. WILLIAM, a mill-wright, was born a. 1609, and was one of the proprietors of Salisbury 1640. [Coffin.] Twenty-five of the name had grad. at the N. E. colleges in 1828.

OTIS, JOHN, Hingham, was admitted freeman 1636. He or his son John settled at Scituate, a. 1662, and d. 1684, leaving several sons, of whom John, who settled in Barnstable, is the common ancestor of civilians, statesmen, and orators of celebrity. 2 Coll. Mass. Hist. Soc. iv. 248. Sixteen of the name had grad. at H. C. in 1828. RICHARD, Dover 1662, killed 27 June, 1689, at the same time with Major Waldron. He had sons, Richard; Stephen, who m. Mary Pitman, 16 April, 1674 ; Solomon, b. 1663, d. 1664; Experience, b. 1666, and perhaps others. Descendants remain in New-Hampshire.

OTLEY, ABRAHAM, Lynn 1641. ||ADAM, Lynn 1641, member of the ar. co. 1641, married a daughter of John Humfrey. Lewis.

OWEN, JOHN, New-Haven 1642. Rev. John Owen, H. C. 1723, was minister of Groton, Conn., and John Owen, perhaps his son, grad. at Y. C. in 1756. THOMAS, Massachusetts 1641. Savage, ii. Winthrop, 51. WILLIAM, Braintree 1651, had a son Daniel, b. 1 Aug. 1651.

OXENBRIDGE, JOHN, the sixth minister of the first church in Boston, was b. in Daventry, Northamptonshire, England, 30 Jan. 1609, was educated at Oxford, where he was sometime a tutor. In 1634 he went to Bermuda and took charge of a church; returned to England; in 1662 went to Surrinam, and from thence to Barbadoes. He came to N. E. in 1669, was admitted freeman 1670, and on the 10th April was installed as colleague with Rev. James Allen. He d. 28 Dec. 1674, æ. 65. His daughter, Theodora, m. Rev. Peter Thatcher. Mather. Calamy. Allen.

PACKARD, SAMUEL, Weymouth, where his son John was b. 1655, removed to Bridgewater, and is the great ancestor of Rev. Asa Packard, of Marlborough, Harv. Coll. 1783, his brother, Rev. Hezekiah Packard, D. D. of Wiscasset, H. C. 1787 ; Rev. Theophilus Packard, D. D., of Shelburne, Mass., D. C. 1796, and of several others who have grad. at Harvard and Bowdoin colleges.

PADDLEFOOT, JONATHAN, Cambridge 1658, had children, Mary, Jonathan, Zechariah, and Edward. The name of *Paddleford* exists in New-England, and two have grad. at Yale College.

PADDOCK, ROBERT, Plymouth, d. 25 July, 1650. He had sons, Robert, b. 1634 ; Zechariah, b. 1636; John, b. 1643, m. Anna Jones, Swanzey, 1673.

PADDY, JOHN, Boston, d. 8 Jan. 1663. WILLIAM Plymouth 1636, a deacon of the church, removed to Boston 1651, and there d. 24 August, 1653. He m. Alice, daughter of Edmund Freeman in 1639. He had two sons, born in Plymouth, Thomas and Samuel. Davis, Morton's N. E. Memo. 279. ||WILLIAM, Boston, member of the ar. co. 1652, d. 11 Nov. 1653. Records of Boston.

PAGE, EDWARD, member of the ar. co. in 1661. JOHN, came from Dedham, England, with Gov. Winthrop, in 1630, was admitted freeman in 1631, and d. 18 Dec. 1676, æ. 90. His wife was Phebe, and he had sons, Samuel, b. 1633, and Daniel, born 10 August, 1634. Savage, i. Winthrop, 47, 54. JOHN, Dedham, was admitted freeman in 1640. *ROBERT, Salem 1637, went to Hampton, admitted freeman 1642, representative 1668. *ROGER,

Hampton, representative 1657. WILLIAM, Watertown, a. 1642, d. 19 Feb. 1665. He had a son John, who d. 1642.

PAGET, THOMAS, Massachusetts, was admitted freeman 1647.

PAIGE, ABRAHAM, Boston 1665. ||NICHOLAS, was a witness to certain articles of peace, dated 15 July, 1675, in Hubbard's Indian Wars p. 21—23, and probably the captain named p. 26, and afterwards a colonel, and member of the ar. co. 1693, and its captain 1695.

PAINE, ARTHUR, a tailor of Boston, was admitted to the church in 1639. This name is sometimes spelled *Payne*, and thus written it has 12 graduates on the different catalogues of the N. E. colleges, besides 25 spelled Paine. EDWARD, Lynn 1637, probably removed to Exeter or Dover a. 1643. JOHN, Ipswich, from whence he went to Nantucket, and there d. 13 July, 1677. ||*MOSES, Braintree, was member of the ar. co. 1644, freeman 1647, a lieutenant, representative 1666 and 1668. He had Moses, b. 1646; Moses, 2d, b. 1652; William, b. 1 April, 1657, and several daughters. A Moses Paine, sen., of Boston, d. 15 Dec. 1690. *ROBERT, Ipswich, was born a. 1601, freeman 1641, representative 1647 to 1649, three years. Dorcas, his wife, d. 23 Feb. 1681. Johnson [Hist. N. E. 110] calls him " a right godly man, and one whose estate hath holpe on well with the work of this little commonwealth." ROBERT, perhaps son of the preceding graduated at Harvard College in 1656, and was living in 1698. *STEPHEN, Hingham, freeman 1639, was representative 1641. ||STEPHEN, Braintree, freeman 1653, member of the ar. co. 1649, m. Hannah Bass in 1651, and had sons, Stephen, b. 8 March, 1653; Samuel, b. 10 June, 1654; and others. THOMAS, Salem, Lynn 1637, Salem, freeman 1641, died a. 1644. THOMAS, Dedham 1642, had a son Thomas, b. 1644. WILLIAM, Ipswich, freeman 1640, removed to Boston, and d. 10 Oct. 1660, leaving an only son John, who died at sea. His daughter Hannah, was the wife of Samuel Appleton, and died before her father. WILLIAM, a shoemaker by profession, was of Salem, and died a. 1660. There was a William Paine, a proprietor of Watertown in 1642, who might be the freeman of 1650.

PAINTER, THOMAS, Boston, a joiner, came to N. E. in 1630, was member of the church and freeman in 1640, lived also in Charlestown, Rowley, New-Haven, and Hingham. He came to N. E. in 1630. Hutchinson, i. Mass. 208. WILLIAM, a captain, lived in Cambridge in 1635, and d. at Charlestown, 28 August, 1666.

PALFREY, JOHN, Cambridge 1658, was a constable in 1674. His children were Rebecca, John, and Elizabeth. *PETER, Salem 1626, one of the first inhabitants of that ancient town, and its representative in 1636. His children were, Jonathan, baptized 1636; Jehodan, b. 1636; Remember, b. 1638; Mary, b. 1639, and perhaps others. He removed to Reading, and there d. 15 Sept. 1663. Descendants remain in the same place settled by him 200 years, and one of them, Warwick Palfray, esq., now fills the same station in the government occupied by his ancestor.

PALGRAVE, RICHARD, Charlestown 1630, was admitted freeman 1631, had a son Increase, b. in 1634.

PALMER, ||*ABRAHAM, Charlestown, freeman 1631, was representative at the first general court 1634, and 4 years afterwards, and a member of the ar. co. in 1638. EDWARD, Massachusetts 1639. Savage, ii. Winthrop, 71. Hutch. i. Mass. 385. An Edward Palmer is named in a commission granted by Charles II. See i. Coll. Mass. Hist. Soc. v. 232. ||GEORGE, was a member of the ar. co. in 1641. *HENRY, Newbury, a. 1635, freeman 1642, went to Haverhill, which he represented 1667, 1674, 1676, to 1679, six years. He d. 1680. JOHN, Hingham, perhaps also at Scituate, was admitted freeman in 1637. Winthrop, i. Hist. N. E. 331. JOHN, Charlestown, d. in Aug. 1676. JOHN, Boston, a carpenter, was received as a townsman 30 March, 1640, and probably the freeman, 2 June, 1641. ‡JOHN, one of Sir Edmund Andros' council, both in N. E. and New-York, went to England, and returned in 1688, with a commission or appointment for chief judge of the Supreme court under Andros. He wrote an answer to the Declaration of the Inhabitants of Boston in 1689, to which a reply was made. NICHOLAS, Windsor 1640. 1 Coll. Mass. Hist. Soc. v. 168. THOMAS, Rowley 1643, d. in 1669. WALTER, constable of Charlestown 1636, was admitted freeman 1638. His son Benjamin was b. in 1642. Winthrop, i. Hist N. E. 76. ii. 345. WILLIAM, Newbury 1637, freeman 1638, removed to Pascataqua before 1643, when he was one of the grand jury, and may be the same who was at Kittery in 1652. WILLIAM, and his son William, were of Plymouth in 1623. Davis, Morton's Memo. 383.

PANTRY, WILLIAM, Cambridge 1634, was admitted freeman in 1635.

PARDEE, GEORGE, New-Haven, m. Martha Miles, 20 Oct. 1650, and d. 1700, æ. 71, leaving sons John, George, and Joseph. The East-Haven and North-Haven Pardees are descended from him. Dodd, East-Haven Register, 140—142.

PARDON, WILLIAM, Massachusetts, admitted freeman 1645.

PARIS, ||THOMAS, Cambridge, freeman 1637, was member of the ar. co. 1641, and it is said was a physician. His son Thomas, born at Cambridge, 21 July, 1641, grad. at H. C. 1659, was living in 1698, and perhaps d. 12 Sept. 1707.

PARK, JACOB, Massachusetts, freeman 1657. JOSEPH, was one of the proprietors of Salisbury 1640. Felt. RICHARD, one of the first proprietors of Cambridge Farms, [Lexington] 1642. Boston News-Letter, i. 266.

PARKER, ABRAHAM, came from England before 1645, when he was admitted freeman; settled in Woburn, and from thence removed to Chelmsford, where he d. 12 August, 1685. His children were, Anna, b. 1645; John, b. 1647, who settled in Chelmsford; Abraham, freeman 1682; Isaac; Moses, who was born in Chelmsford, and the father of Aaron Parker, one of whose grandsons is the Hon. Abel Parker, of Jaffrey, N. H., was more than 20 years judge of probate for the county of Cheshire, being appointed to that office, 17 May, 1802. Two of the sons of Judge Parker, Edmund, judge of probate, in Hillsborough county, and Joel, a counsellor at Law, are alumni of Dart. College, and have been members of the N. H. legislature, and another has been a member of the state senate, and is now register of probate for Cheshire county. *AMARIAH, was representative of Reading in 1684. EDMUND, was one of the proprietors of Lancaster in 1654. Willard, Hist. Lancaster. GEORGE, Kittery, was admitted freeman in 1652. ||HENRY, was a member of the ar. co. in 1645. JACOB, of Chelmsford in 1655, had a son Thomas, b. 28 March, 1657. JOHN, carpenter, Boston 1635, had sons, Thomas, b. 1635; Noah, b 1638. JOHN, of Woburn, and one of the petitioners for the grant of Chelmsford 1653. Allen, Hist. Chelmsford. 3 Coll. Mass. Hist. Soc. i. 45. JOHN, Billerica, the first clerk of the writs, and an active man in the early affairs of that town, d. at Charlestown, 14 June, 1669. It is uncertain which of the John Parkers was the freeman in 1652. JOHN, Cambridge-Village 1650, died 23 Oct. 1713. He had sons, John, b. 15 Feb. 1652; Jeremiah, b. 16 Jan. 1654 ; Thomas, b. 1 Feb. 1658; Isaac, b. 15 March, 1662; Jonathan, b. 6 Nov. 1665, who was father of Rev. Thomas Parker, of Dracut, H. C. 1718, whose son, Dr. Jonathan Parker, of Litchfield, N. H., grad. at H. C. 1762, and was father of Rev. Edward L. Parker, of Derry, N. H., who grad. at D. C. 1807. JOHN, Kittery, was admitted freeman 1652. JOHN, Hingham 1636. Lincoln, Hist. Hingham, 45. JOHN, who grad. at Harvard College in 1661, might have been son of Robert Parker, of Cambridge. *JAMES, a preacher, was admitted freeman in 1634, lived in Weymouth, and was the representative from 1639 to 1643. He received a call to settle as the minister of Portsmouth in Dec. 1642, which he declined. He left N. E. and went to Barbadoes, from whence he wrote, in 1646, a letter to Gov. Winthrop, which is in Hutch. Coll. 155—158. JAMES, Woburn, freeman 1644, was one of the grantees of Billerica but does not appear to have resided there. He may be the Captain James Parker, one of the early settlers of Groton, a deacon of the church, and town clerk 20 years. James Parker was one of the committee of safety, who assumed the government when Andros was deposed. Hutchinson i. Hist. Mass., 340. Joseph, John, James, Josiah, and Samuel Parker were residents or proprietors of Groton, a. 1678. [Shattuck.] JOSEPH, Newbury, (where his son Joseph was b. 15 May, 1642,) went to Andover, and was one of the founders of the church in Oct. 1645. He died in 1678, leaving besides Joseph, sons, Stephen, b. 1651, and Samuel. MATTHEW, Boston, d. 19 Sept. 1652. NATHAN, Newbury, d. 6 April, 1679. NATHAN, one of the founders of the church in Andover 1645, d. 1685, leaving sons, John, b. 1653, d. 1738, æ. 85 ; James ; Robert ; and Peter. John had sons, John, Nathan, Benjamin and James ; the last three, proprietors of Concord, N. H. in

1726. NICHOLAS, Boston, freeman 1634, had sons, Jonathan, b. 1640; Abiel, b. 1641; Joseph, b. 1643. ||RICHARD, a merchant of Boston, was admitted freeman in 1641, member of the ar. co. 1638. ROBERT, butcher, Boston and Roxbury, was admitted a member of Boston church 1634, and freeman in 1635, removed to Cambridge. He had sons, Benjamin, John, Richard, Nathaniel, b. 28 July, 1643. Benjamin, settled in Billerica. *THOMAS*, the first minister of Newbury, the only son of Rev. Robert Parker, was b. in 1596; was sometime a student at Oxford, and afterwards pursued his studies in Ireland under Dr. Usher, and in Holland, under Dr. Ames. He came to N. E. with "several devout christians out of Wiltshire," and arrived here in May, 1634; settled the next year at Newbury, and died there, 24 April, 1677, in his 82d year. Mather, [i. Magnalia, 435] says he " lived all his days a *single man*," and that after having spent a great part of his life in " *apocalyptical studies*, he went unto the *apocalyptical virgins*." THOMAS, Lynn, freeman 1637, removed to Reading, where he had sons, Joseph, b. 1642, and d. 1644; Nathaniel, b. 16 May, 1651; Jonathan, b. 18 May, 1656. WILLIAM, Scituate 1640, removed to Barnstable. WILLIAM, Watertown, freeman 1641, had a son Ephraim, b. in 1640, and may have removed to Sudbury. The ancestor of Judge William Parker, of Portsmouth, Hon. A. M. at H. C. under 1722, who d. 29 April, 1781, æ. 77, and of Bishop Samuel Parker, H. C. 1763, who d. at Boston, 6 Dec. 1804, æ. 59, was William Parker, of Portsmouth, who m. 26 Feb. 1703, Zurviah Stanley, who, the annalist of Portsmouth [MS Letter] says, was a daughter to the earl of Derby. Fifty-nine persons of the name of Parker had grad. at the N. E. colleges in 1826.

PARKHURST, GEORGE, Watertown, was admitted freeman 1643. Joseph, perhaps his son, was of Chelmsford as early as 1666, and his descendants have remained there ever since. Rev. John Parkhurst, one of them, grad. at H. C. 1811. The earliest graduate of the name in the U. S., was Rev. Samuel Parkhurst, New-Jersey College 1757.

PARKMAN, ELIAS, Dorchester 1635, removed to Windsor 1636. ELIAS, of Boston, had a son Elias, b. in 1651. Rev. Ebenezer Parkman, a native of Boston, grad. at H. C. 1721, ordained at Westborough, Mass., 28 Oct. 1724, d. 9 Dec. 1782, æ. 80. Samuel Parkman, esq., of Boston, had 4 sons educated at Harvard, Francis, grad. 1807, minister of the New North church, Boston; George, 1809, physician, Samuel, 1810, and Daniel, 1813, a merchant of Boston.

PARKS, *||WILLIAM, Roxbury, freeman 1631, was representative in 1635, and 32 years afterwards until 1679; member of the ar. co. 1638, deacon of the church, d. 11 May, 1685. Johnson, [Hist. N. E. 110, where the name, as well as in the 2 Coll. Mass. Hist. Soc. iv. 25, is erroneously printed *Parker*] who acted with him as a representative 21 years, says, " he was a man of a pregnant understanding, and very useful in his place." Widow Ann Parks d. in 1708, æ. 93. RICHARD, Cambridge 1647. (See PARK.)

THOMAS, Cambridge-Village, had sons, Thomas, b. 1654; John, b. 1656 ; Edward, b. 1661, and died 11 Aug. 1690.

PARMELIN, JOHN, Guilford 1650. 1 Coll. Mass. Hist. Soc. x. JOHN, jun., Guilford 1650. Ibid. The name of *Parmelee* has been common in some parts of Connecticut, and may be the same with the preceeding. Ebenezer Parmelee grad. at Y. C. 1758, and Rev. Elisha Parmelee, H. C. 1778, was the minister of Lee, Mass.

PARMENTER, BENJAMIN, Salem 1637, b. a. 1610, was of Gloucester in 1680. JAMES, d. at Sudbury, 21 Nov. 1678. JOHN, Sudbury, was admitted freeman in 1640. JOHN, Sudbury 1640, son of the preceding, d. 12 April, 1666. His son Joseph was born in 1642. ROBERT, Braintree, freeman 1650, a deacon of the church, d. 27 June, 1696, æ. 74. Sons, John, b. 23 Oct. 1653 ; Joseph, b. 20 Dec. 1655. This name is sometimes written *Parmiter*.

PARR, ABEL, Massachusetts, was admitted freeman 1641.

PARRIS, *JOHN, Groton 1677, which he represented in May, 1689, and is the first representative on record. A John Parris, of Braintree, m. Mary Jewell, 30 Sept. 1664. *ROBERT, Dunstable, representative 1689. *SAMUEL*, the first minister of Danvers, Ms., was son of Thomas Parris, of London, [Judge Samuel Parris] and was born 1653 [Coffin] ; was educated at H. C., but did not graduate, was ordained 15 Nov. 1689, and left the ministry in June, 1696 ; removed to Concord, where he lived in 1705, and in 1711 preached six months in Dunstable. In his society, and it has been said, in his family, commenced the witchcraft infatuation in 1692. He had two sons, Samuel, who settled in Sudbury, and Noyes, who grad. at H. C. 1721. THOMAS, came to N. E. in June, 1683, settled at Newbury as early as 1685, thence went to Pembroke, Mass. He is the ancestor of Judge Samuel Parris, of Hebron, Me., whose only son, Hon. Albion Keith Parris, D. C. 1806, late gover- nour of Maine, is judge of the supreme court in that state.

PARROT, *FRANCIS, Rowley, town clerk, was admitted freeman 1640, representative 1640 and 1642, returned to England and died a. 1656. JOHN, Rowley 1643.

PARSONS, HUGH, Springfield 1649, had a son Samuel, b. in 1649. See Hutchinson, i. Hist. Mass. 165. JEFFREY, Glouces- ter 1664. JOSEPH, Springfield 1646, a colonel, d. 9 Oct. 1683. His son Benjamin, born in 1649. SAMUEL, East-Hampton, L. I. 1650. THOMAS, Dedham and Medfield. Worthington, Hist. Dedham, 23. ||WILLIAM, Boston, a joiner, was admitted to the church in 1643, freeman 1645, member of the ar. co 1646, d. 29 Jan. 1702, æ. 87.

PARTRIDGE, ALEXANDER, came over with his wife and family in 1645, was banished from Massachusetts, and went to Rhode-Island. Winthrop, Hist. N. E. 251. Hutchinson, Coll. 226. GEORGE, Duxbury 1636, was one of the proprietors of Bridgewater in 1645. JOHN, Portsmouth 1660, m. Mary Fernald, 11 Dec. 1660, and had son John, and 7 daughters. JOHN, Medfield 1654. NATHANIEL, tailor of Boston, member of the church, was admitted freeman 1644. *RALPH*, the first minister of Duxbury, arrived at Boston, from England, 14 Nov. 1636, soon settled at Duxbury, where he died a. 1658, having been a preacher 40 years. Davis, Morton's Memo. Allen, Biog. Dict. *SAMUEL, Hadley, son of William Partridge, who came from Berwick, on Tweed, to N. E. and died in Hadley, [Alden] in 1668, was representative 1685 and 1686. He had sons, William and Samuel, b. in 1669 and 1671. WILLIAM, Salisbury 1640, came from Olney, in Buckinghamshire, England, and died in 1654, leaving a widow Ann. His children were, John ; Hannah ; Elizabeth ; Nehemiah ; who lived in Portsmouth, and Sarah. Coffin. WILLIAM, Medfield, freeman 1653, m. Sarah Pierce, 23 Nov., who d. 1656. By another wife he had sons, Nathaniel, John, and Elisha. †‡WILLIAM, a counsellor, and the lieutenant-governour of New-Hampshire, was b. in 1655 ; lived in Portsmouth and Newbury, and'd. 3 Jan. 1729, in his 75th year, and was buried at Newbury. He m. Mary Brown, 8 Dec. 1680, and had children, 1. Richard, born at Portsmouth, 9 Dec. 1681, was an agent in England, and was living in London in 1749 ; 2. Nehemiah, b. 9 March, 1683 ; 3. Mary, b. 19 Oct. 1685, m. Governour Belcher, and d. 1736 ; 4. William, b. 1 May, 1687 ; 5. Elizabeth, b. 23 Sept. 1692.

PARY, WILLIAM, Massachusetts, was admitted freeman 1646.

PASMORE, JAMES, Concord 1644.

PATCH, JAMES, Salem, died a. 1658. JOHN, Salem, about 1648, had children born there. W. Gibbs. NICHOLAS and EDMUND, were admitted inhabitants of Salem in 1639. Elizabeth Patch, who d. 14 Jan. 1716, æ. 87, was the first female born in Salem. Hutchinson, Hist. Mass. *THOMAS, Wenham, freeman 1670, was representative in 1689.

PATESHALL, RICHARD, Boston 1665, freeman 1673, perhaps the captain named in Hubbard. Richard Pateshall, Harvard College 1735, of Boston, d. 25 Aug. 1768, æ. 55.

PATRICK, DANIEL, came to N. E. as early as 1630, was admitted freeman 1631, resided at Watertown and Cambridge ; removed to Connecticut, and was killed by a Dutchman at Stamford in 1643. Winthrop, ii. Hist. N. E. 151.

PATTEN, WILLIAM, Cambridge, freeman 1645, d. 10 Dec. 1668. His son Thomas settled in Billerica, and d. there in Jan. 1689, æ. 54, leaving 4 sons. His other children were, William, b. and d. 1646 ; Nathaniel ; Mary, and Sarah.

PATTERSON, EDWARD, New-Haven 1639, perhaps the Pequot soldier 1637, named in 2 Coll. Mass. Hist. Soc. viii. 139, and the one who d. in 1669. EDWARD, Hingham 1655. JAMES, Billerica 1659.

PAUL, DANIEL, Kittery 1652.

PAYBODY, WILLIAM. (See PEABODY.)

PAYSON, EDWARD, Roxbury, freeman 1640, whose first wife d. in 1641, had by a second, sons, John, b. 1643, freeman 1680 ; Jonathan, b. 1644, a deacon of the church at Roxbury, amd d. 15

Nov. 1719, and probably others. *EDWARD*, the fifth minister of Rowley, was son of Edward Payson, and was b. at Roxbury, 20 June, 1657 ; grad. at H. C. 1677, freeman 1680, was ordained 25 Oct. 1682, d. 22 Aug. 1732, æ. 75. Elizabeth, his wife, d. 1 Oct. 1724, æ. 60. He afterwards m. Elizabeth, widow of Hon. S. Appleton. His sons, Samuel, H. C. 1716; Eliot; Stephen; Jonathan ; David, and Phillips. Phillips, H. C. 1724, the minister of Walpole, was ancestor of the several distinguished clergymen of the name. The late Rev. Edward Payson, D. D., of Portland, was of the fifth descent, the whole line being clergymen from the Rowley minister. Edward, son of Dr. Payson, is an under-graduate at Bowdoin. GILES, Roxbury, freeman 1631, a deacon of the church, d. 28 Jan. 1689, æ. 78. His son Samuel was b. 1641, and d. 1697.

PAYTON, BEZALEEL, Boston 1643, died about 1651. His daughters, Mary and Sarah were b. in 1643 and 1646. Savage, ii. Winthrop, 336. ROBERT, Lynn 1639. Lewis.

PEABODY, FRANCIS, perhaps of Salisbury or Hampton, was admitted freeman 1642. JOHN, was one of the proprietors of Bridgewater 1645. *JOHN, Boxford, freeman 1674, representative 1689 to 1691, was perhaps father to Rev. Oliver Peabody, of Natick, a native of Boxford, and born in 1698, grad. at H. C. 1721, d. 2 Feb. 1752. Hon. Oliver Peabody, of Exeter, H. C. 1773, b. at Andover, 2 Sept. 1752 is probably of this family. His sons, twins, grad. at H. C. in 1816, and are settled at Exeter and Springfield. WILLIAM, Duxbury, a. 1645, was representative at Plymouth, 1659. He m. Elizabeth, daughter of John Alden, and she d. at Little-Compton, 31 May, 1717, æ. 92. Sewall, New Heaven and New Earth, 64. Bradford, Notes on Duxbury.

PEACH, ARTHUR, a soldier in the Pequot war 1636. See a story of him in I. Mather's Indian Wars from 1614 to 1675, p. 55. Winthrop, i. Hist. N. E. 269. JOHN, Marblehead 1648, born a. 1612, had a son John, admitted freeman 1683.

PEACOCK, RICHARD, Roxbury 1638, had a son Samuel, b. in 1639, d. at Boston 1691. William Peacock was of Dorchester 1655.

PEAKE, CHROSTOPHER, Roxbury, freeman 1635, d. 22 May, 1666. His sons were, Joseph, b. 1644 ; probably Jonathan, who d. in 1700, and others. WILLIAM, Scituate between 1633 and 1657. PEARSE, WILLIAM, Boston 1665.

PEARSON, *JOHN, born 1615, was perhaps at Lynn 1639; was at Rowley 1647, when he was admitted freeman ; representative 1678, 9 years ; was ordained deacon at Rowley, 24 October, 1686 ; d. 2 Nov. 1697. His widow d. 12 Jan. 1703. He is the ancestor of Joseph Pearson, H. C. 1758 ; Rev. Eliphalet Pearson, LL. D., and Dr. Abiel Pearson, D. C. 1779.

PEASE, HENRY, Mass., freeman 1634. JOHN, Salem, was freeman 1637, perhaps one of the first four settlers of Martin's Vineyard. ||JOHN, was a member of the ar. co. 1661, a captain, and probably removed to Enfield before 1684. ROBERT, Salem 1637, member of the church 1643, d. in 1644.

PEASLEE, JOSEPH, Newbury, freeman 1642, removed to Haverhill, supplied the place of a minister in Amesbury as a lay preacher, or " gifted brother," as the church calls him. He died in 1661, leaving children Joseph and Elizabeth. Coffin.

PECK, JEREMIAH, minister of Waterbury, was educated at H. C. according to Mather [i. Magnalia 82]; was ordained 26 Aug. 1669, d. 7 June, 1699. *JOSEPH, Hingham, was admitted freeman 1638, representative 1639 to 1642, four years; removed to Rehoboth, and there d. 22 Dec. 1663. Savage, ii. Winthrop, Index. Lincoln, Hist. Hingham, 45. NATHANIEL, Hingham 1635. Lincoln, Hist. Hingham, 43. *ROBERT*, one of the first ministers of Hingham, admitted freeman 1638, was ordained 28 Nov. 1638, sailed for England, with his wife and son Joseph, 27 Oct. 1641. Mr. Savage supposes that he was brother to Joseph of Hingham. Lincoln, Hist. Hingham, 23. THOMAS, Boston, 1652, had a son Joseph b. in 1656.

PECKER, JAMES, Boston, was born in 1622. This name exists in Mass. and N. H. James and Jeremiah Pecker grad. at H. C. 1743 and 1757.

PECKHAM, JOSEPH, Newport 1644, was one of the founders of the first Baptist church.

PIERCY, MARMADUKE, Salem 1637. Felt. Mr. Savage, [i. Winthrop, 318] calls his name *Perry*, but corrects it in his errata, vol. ii. 398.

PELHAM, ‡||HERBERT, came to N. E. 1639, and settled at Cambridge, was member of the ar. co. 1639, freeman 1645, elected assistant from 1645 to 1649, five years; returned to England, resided at Brewer's Hamlet in Essex, where it is supposed he died a. 1676, had sons, Herbert, b. 3 Oct. 1645, and d. soon after; Edward, who grad. at H. C. 1673, and probably others. Davis, Morton's Memo. 467. Boston News-Letter, ii. 77. NATHANIEL, who grad. at H. C. 1651, was probably son of the preceding, or of the following. He was lost at sea, in 1657, with John Davis and Jonathan Ince. *WILLIAM, was admitted freeman in 1631, and settled as early as 1640 in Sudbury, which he represented in 1647, and where he was the first captain of the military band in 1644. Johnson speaks of his being in England when he wrote. See Hist. N. E. 192.

PELL, JOSEPH, Lynn, was admitted freeman 1638. WILLIAM, Boston freeman 1635, was disarmed in 1637, was a tallow-chandler. Edward, son of Edward Pell, of Boston, grad. at H. C. 1730, and was the minister of Harwich, Mass.

PEMBERTON, JAMES, came over as early as 1630 and requested to be made freeman, 19 Oct. that year. JAMES, Newbury and Boston, was admitted freeman 1648. His sons were John, b. at Newbury, 16 Feb. 1648; Thomas, b. 1652, d. 1693; Joseph, b. 1655, the two last at Boston, where he probably d. 11 Oct. 1696. JOHN, Boston, was admitted freeman 18 May, 1631. JOHN, Boston, was admitted freeman 1634, was a member of the church, from which he was dismissed to Newbury in 1640.

PENDLETON, *‖BRYAN, was born a. 1599, came early to N. E. and settled at Watertown; was admitted freeman 1634, was selectman of Sudbury, where he also resided, two years [Shattuck]; representative of Watertown 1636 to 1639, 1647 and 1648, six years; member of the ar. co. 1646; a captain of the militia; removed to Portsmouth, which he represented in 1654, 1658, 1660, 1661, 1663; was a major of the military forces, purchased a neck of land at the mouth of Saco River, 1658, removed thither 1665, returned to Portsmouth 1676; appointed a counsellor under President Danforth in 1680, in which, or the following year, he died, (Folsom) leaving one son, James, and a daughter, who married Seth Fletcher, minister of Saco. JAMES, son of the preceding, one of the founders of the first church in Portsmouth 1671, had, by Hannah, his wife, Bryan, b. 27 Sept. 1659; Joseph, b. Dec. 1661; Edmund, b. 24 June, 166– ; Ann, b. 1667 ; Caleb, b. 8 August, 1669. Some of this family probably migrated southward. He removed to Stonington, Conn. before 1681, where he has numerous descendants at the present day. James Pendleton, Gent. was of the Narraganset country in 1686.

PENHALLOW, SAMUEL, author of a Narrative of the Indian Wars, was born at St. Mabon, in Cornwall, England, 2 July, 1665, came to N. E. with Rev. Charles Morton in 1686; went to Portsmouth, and there m. Mary, daughter of President Cutt, 1 July, 1687; was a counsellor 1702; judge of the superior court 1714; chief justice, 1717, which office he sustained until his death, 2 Dec. 1726, æ. 61. His son John, a captain, d. before 1736. Elizabeth, Joseph, Richard, and Susanna received legacies from his estate and were probably his children. Benjamin, grad. at H. C. in 1723, but died young.

PENN, *JAMES, Boston, requested to be made freeman, 19 Oct. 1630; was a ruling elder of the church, representative 1648, 1649; marshall of the colony, and d. 30 Sept. 1671. Prince, ii. Annals, 69. Hutchinson, i. Mass. 246. Felt, Annals, Salem, 77.

PENNIMAN, JAMES, Boston, freeman 1632, Braintree 1639, d. 26 Dec. 1664. He had sons, James, ar. co. 1673; Samuel, b. 1645, freeman 1678; John, freeman 1671, perhaps Joseph, freeman 1678, and others. Joseph Penniman, H. C. 1765, minister of Bedford, Ms.

PENTICUS, JOHN, appears in the colony records as admitted freeman in 1640, but there is probably some error in the name. Savage, ii. Winthrop. 370.

PEPPER, ‖MICHAEL, was member of the ar. co. 1642. ROBERT, Roxbury, freeman 1643, was in Springfield as early as 1645. A Robert Pepper d. at Roxbury in 1684.

PEPPERELL, WILLIAM, Kittery, was a native of Cornwall, England, came to N. E. as early as 1676, m. a daughter of John Bray, of Kittery, became a wealthy merchant, was a magistrate, and d. 15 Feb. 1734, æ. 86. He was father of Sir William Pepperell, Bart. who d. 6 July, 1759, æ. 63, whose only son Andrew, H. C. 1743, d. 1 March, 1751, æ. 26.

PERCY, MARMADUKE. (See Piercy.)

PERHAM, JOHN, Chelmsford 1666. Benoni Perham, H. C. 1800, was born in Chelmsford, 14 Dec. 1777, was a lawyer, and d. in Baltimore, 14 May, 1804, æ. 26. Jonathan, another descendant, was many years representative of Chelmsford.

PERKINS, ABRAHAM, Massachusetts, was admitted freeman 1640. ISAAC, Massachusetts, freeman 1642. *JOHN, Ipswich, was born a. 1590, came to N. E. and was admitted freeman in 1633, settled in Ipswich 1633, representative 1636, d. 1654. He might be the same person who arrived with Mr. Williams, 5 Feb. 1631. See Winthrop's Hist. N. E. 42. JOHN, Ipswich 1634, son of the preceding, was admitted freeman in 1637. WILLIAM, Ipswich 1633, [Prince, ii. Annals, 86] freeman 1634, is supposed to have been the same who preached at Gloucester 1651—1655, and became the second minister of Topsfield, and d. 21 May, 1682, æ. 75, leaving sons, Tobijah, John, Timothy, probably William, who d. at Topsfield in 1696, and five daughters who all married. ||*WILLIAM, Weymouth, was member of the ar. co. 1638, representative 1644, and leader of the military band, according to Johnson, Hist. N. E. 191. There was a William Perkins, of Roxbury, whose son William d. in 1639. Forty-two persons of the name had grad. in N. E. in 1826.

PERLEY, ALLEN, came from Wales, and landed at Charlestown, 12 July, 1634, settled in Ipswich in 1636, and was admitted freeman 1642. Coffin. *JOHN, Boxford, was representative from 1689 to 1691.

||PERRY, ARTHUR, Boston, freeman 1640, was the town drummer, [Snow, Hist. Boston, 116] member of the ar. co. 1638, and d. 9 Oct. 1652. Two of his sons were, Seth, b. 1639. admitted member of the ar. co. 1662, and John, born 1642. FRANCIS, Salem, 1637, born a. 1608, was a wheelwright, and removed from Salem. JOHN, Roxbury, freeman 1633, d. 27 Sept. 1642. His son John was b. 1639. Samuel Perry d. at Roxbury in 1706. Obadiah Perry, freeman 1678, was one of the founders of the church at Dunstable. WILLIAM, Scituate 1638. WILLIAM, a proprietor of Watertown in 1642, might be the William Pary freeman in ——.

PESTER, WILLIAM, Salem 1637. Felt.

PETERS, ANDREW, Ipswich 1665, perhaps the same who d. at Andover 1713, æ. 77, having had sons, Andrew, William, John, and Samuel. Abbot, Hist. Andover, 37. Rev. Andrew Peters, of Middleton, who d. in 1756, was a descendant. *HUGH*, the fourth minister of Salem, was born at Fowey in Cornwall 1599, was educated at Trinity College, came to N. E. 6 Oct. 1635, took charge of the church at Salem, 21 Dec. 1636, sailed for England as an agent of the colony, 3 August, 1641, and was executed for high treason, 16 Oct. 1660, aged 61. John Winthrop of Conn., m. one of his daughters. Another was baptized at Salem 1640. His widow, a second wife, came to N. E. after his execution. *THOMAS*, minister of Saybrook, brother of the preceding, was a minister in Cornwall, England, from whence he was driven by Sir Ralph Hopton in

the time of the civil wars ; came to N. E. and commenced a settlement at Pequot River with John Winthrop in 1646.   He remained
here but a short time, being called back to his people, to which he
returned in 1647.   Winslow, N. E. Salamander Discovered.   WIL-
LIAM, Boston, is said in the life of Hugh Peters, a work which it is
hazardous to quote, to have been a brother of the preceding, and to
have had sons, John, Andrew, Thomas, William, Samuel, and Joseph.   Samuel Peters, Hist. of Hugh Peters.

PETTINGILL, RICHARD, came from Wales, [Coffin] settled
in Salem, admitted to the church and freeman 1641, removed to
Newbury, and there died.

PETTITT, THOMAS, Exeter 1639.

PETTY, JOHN, Springfield, d. 18 March, 1680.   The name of
Pattee exists in N. H.

PEVERLY, JOHN, Pascataqua 1631.   Descendants probably
remain.   Thomas Peverly, D. C. 1818, a lawyer in Northumberland, N. H., d. 18 April, 1829, æ. 32.

PHELPS, GEORGE, Dorchester, freeman 1635, went to Windsor with Mr. Warham.   SAMUEL, Dorchester, a. 1630, removed to
Windsor with the preceding.   ‡*WILLIAM, Dorchester, freeman
1631, came to N. E. 1630, was representative at the first court
1634 ; removed to Windsor, and was elected a magistrate in 1636.
Twenty-five of the name had grad. at the N. E. colleges in 1826.

PHESE, WILLIAM, Massachusetts, freeman 1643.   Savage,
ii. Winthrop, 373.

PHILBRICK, JOHN, Hampton 1650, was lost with his wife in
a boat going from Hampton in 1657.   Thomas Philbrick, ofHamp-
ton, admitted freeman 1668, was constable in 1684, when there
were James, Jonathan, and Samuel Philbrick residing in that town.
THOMAS, Watertown, a proprietor in 1641, was probably afterwards of Hampton, and died there in 1667.   ROBERT, Ipswich,
was one of the Pequot soldiers..

PHILLIPS, GEORGE, the first minister of Watertown, born
at Raymond in Norfolk, came over with Gov. Winthrop, and arrived
here, 2 June, 1630, admitted freeman 1631 ; d. 1 July, 1644, having been the minister there 14 years.   His wife d. at Salem, soon
after he landed, and by another wife, who d. 27 Jan. 1681, he had
Zorobabel, b. 5 April, 1632 ; Jonathan, b. 16 Nov. 1633 ; Theophilus, b. 28 June, 1636 ; Awbett, [?] who d. 1638 ; Obadiah, b. 1642.
SAMUEL, minister of Rowley, son of the preceding, was born in
Boxford, England in 1625, grad. at H. C. 1651, was ordained colleague with Rev. Ezekiel Rogers, and d. 22 April, 1696, æ. 71.
He m. Sarah, daughter of Samuel Appleton, of Ipswich.   She died
15 July, 1713, æ. 86.   His children were, Sarah, Samuel, George,
Elizabeth, Dorcas, Mary, and John.   George grad. at H. C. 1686,
and was minister of Brookhaven, L. I. 42 years, d. 1739, æ. 75.
Samuel, b. 23 March, 1658, was a goldsmith in Salem, and m. Mary, daughter of Rev. John Emerson, of Gloucester, had two sons and
four daughters.   The eldest son was Rev. Samuel Phillips, of Andover, b. 28 Feb. 1690, grad. at H. C. 1708, was ord. 17 Oct. 1711,

d. 5 June, 1771, having had 5 children, of whom were *Samuel*, b. 13 Feb. 1713, grad. at H. C. 1734, a counsellor of Mass. d. 21 August, 1790, æ. 76; *John*, b. 27 Dec. 1719, grad. at H. C. 1735, a counsellor of N. H. and the founder of Exeter Academy, d. in April, 1795, æ. 76, and *William*, b. 25 June, 1722, who was father of the late munificent patron of our charitable and religious institutions, Lieut. Gov. William Phillips, who d. at Boston, 26 May, 1827, æ. 77. Lieut. Gov. Samuel Phillips, H. C. 1771, who d. 10 Feb. 1802, aged 50, was son of Samuel, the eldest son of Rev. Samuel Phillips. John Phillips, H. C. 1788, the first mayor of the city of Boston, who d. 29 May, 1823, was, it is believed, from this family. GEORGE, Windsor 1640. 1 Coll. Mass. Hist. Soc. v. 168. ||HENRY, Dedham, was admitted freeman in 1638, member of the ar. co. 1640, was solicited to become a candidate for the ministry; was an ensign, and in 1657 resided in Boston, perhaps the representative of Hadley in 1672. Savage, ii. Winthrop, 86. Worthington, Hist. Dedham, 19, 42. Whitman, Hist. Ar. Co. Coll. N. H. Hist. Soc. ii. JOHN, Dorchester, requested to be made freeman, 19 Oct. 1630, and admitted to the oath 1632, perhaps the following. JOHN, Boston, one of the founders of the 2d church, bought of George Cleaves, his house, lands, &c. at Falmouth in 1659. [Folsom.] His son John was b. in Boston 1635. ‡||*JOHN, Charlestown, freeman 1673, member of the ar. co. 1680; its captain 1685, representative from 1683 to 1686, 4 years, one of the council of safety 1689, colonel of the militia, treasurer of the province; one of the first counsellors under the new charter 1691, and continued in office until 1716; and judge of the inferior court, d. 20 March, 1725, aged 94. JOHN, Marshfield, was killed by lightning, 31 July, 1658. Davis, Morton's Memo. 279. NICHOLAS, Weymouth 1640, d. Sept. 1672 aged 61, leaving, children, Richard, Joshua, Benjamin, Albie, Experience, and Hannah. He had a brother Henry. NICHOLAS, Boston died in 1656. ||THOMAS, was a member of the ar. co. 1644. WALTER, Wiscasset, a. 1661. 1 Coll. Mass. Hist. Soc. vii. 169. WILLIAM, Saco 1659, was appointed a magistrate in 1665, by King Charles' Commissioners, was a major in 1675. His habitation was assaulted by the Indians, 18 Sept. 1675, and soon after burnt by them. WILLIAM, Charlestown 1640, had children, Phebe, b. 1640; Nathaniel, b. 1642; Mary, b. 1644. His wife d. 1646 ||ZECHARIAH, Boston, member ar. co. 1660, was killed by the Indians at Brookfield in August, 1675. His son Zechariah was b. 1656. Wheeler's Narrative in Coll. N. H. Hist. Soc. ii. 9.

PHILPOT, WILLIAM, Boston, member of the church 1643.

PHINNEY, ISAAC, Medfield 1657. Elias Phinney, counsellor at law, Charlestown, grad. H. C. in 1801.

PHIPPEN, DAVID, Boston, freeman 1636, afterwards of Hingham. David Phippen d. at Boston, 24 Dec. 1702. JOSEPH, Hingham 1637, Boston, freeman 1644.

PHIPPS, JAMES, came from Bristol, England, and settled at, or near Pemaquid, [Bristol, Me.] before 1649, had 26 children by the same wife, 21 of them being sons. C. Mather. SOLO-

MON, Charlestown, freeman 1642, d. 25 July, 1671. Samuel, perhaps his son, grad. at H. C. 1671, was register of deeds and clerk of the court common pleas Middx., d. in 1725. §‡WILLIAM, son of the preceding, was born at Pemaquid, 2 Feb. 1650, was made a knight by James II, a. 1687, was one of the assistants in 1690, was appointed the first governour under the charter of William and Mary, in 1691, arrived in N. E. 14 May, 1692, was removed from the government; went to England in 1694, and d. in London, 18 Feb. 1695, æ. 45. His nephew Spencer Bennet, who adopted the name of Phips, grad. at H. C. in 1703, was lieutenant governour of Mass. and d. 4 April, 1757, æ. 73, whose son William grad. H. C. 1728.

PICKARD, *JOHN, Rowley, a. 1646, representative 1660, d. 1697, æ. 75. Jane, his widow, d. 20 Feb. 1716, æ. 89. He had sons John and Samuel, and 6 daughters. His descendants still remain at Rowley, and Samuel Pickard, esq., has been a representative. There was an Edmund Pickard of Pascataqua, a. 1661, who came from Northam, England.

PICKERAM, JOHN, Watertown, d. 10 Dec. 1630. Shattuck.

PICKERING, JOHN, a carpenter, probably came to N. E. in 1630, was of Ipswich in 1634, was admitted an inhabitant of Salem, 7 Feb. 1637, and died in 1657. John, perhaps his son, d. in Salem, 5 May, 1694, æ. 57, leaving sons, John, Benjamin, and William. He was the ancestor of the late Hon. Timothy Pickering, several of whose sons have grad. at H. C. JOHN, Cambridge, where his daughter Lydia was b. 5 Nov. 1638, probably went to Portsmouth, as early as 1640, and died there, 18 Jan. 1669. *JOHN, Portsmouth, son of the preceding, was a captain, representative 1691 at Boston, and speaker of the N. H. assembly. He m. Mary Stanyan, 10 Jan. 1665, and had 1. John, b. 1 Dec. 1666, m. Elizabeth Munden, 17 July, 1688; 2. Mary, b. 1668; Thomas; Sarah; Sarah 2d, and perhaps others. He was the ancestor of the Hon. John Pickering, of Portsmouth, who grad. at H. C. 1761, and probably of William Pickering, esq. of Concord, N. H. who grad. at H. C. 1797.

PICKETT, JOHN, Salem 1648. Two of the name of John Pickett grad. at Yale College 1705 and 1732.

PICKLES, JONAS, Scituate 1657. This name has existed in N. E. within a few years.

PICKMAN, BENJAMIN, Salem 1661, m. Elizabeth, daughter of Captain Joseph Hardy 1667, had 4 sons and 3 daughters and d. in 1708. His wife d. in 1727, æ. 77. His son Benjamin was b. in 1673, m. Abigail Lindall in 1704. Felt, MS Letter. NATHANIEL, of Salem, as early as 1639, died 10 Sept. 1668. His wife was Tabitha, and his children were Nathaniel, John, Benjamin, William, Samuel, and Bethiah. Felt, Annals, 233.

PICKTON, THOMAS, Beverly 1687. Ann, his widow, d. in 1683, æ. 84.

PICKWORTH, JOHN, Salem 1637. Elias Pickworth was of Beverly in 1687.

PID, RICHARD, Massachusetts, freeman 1642.

PIDCOCK, GEORGE, Scituate 1657.   2 Coll. Mass. Hist. Soc. iv. 241.

PIERCE, ABRAHAM, Plymouth 1623, one of the proprietors of Bridgewater. Davis, Morton's N. E. Memo. 382. 2 Coll. Mass. Hist. Soc. vii. 138.   ANTHONY, Watertown, freeman 1638, had sons, Jacob, b. 1637; Daniel, b. 1639, perhaps of Groton, a. 1678. DAVID, Massachusetts, freeman 1636. DANIEL, Watertown, freeman 1638, removed to Newbury, and there d. 27 Nov. 1677, leaving sons Daniel and Joshua. Joshua was b. 15 May, 1642. He m (probably a 2d wife) Ann Milward, 26 Dec. 1654, who survived him. His estate amounted to £1837. 10. *DANIEL, son of the preceding, [Coffin] settled in Newbury, which he represented in 1682 and 1683; was a captain; one of the council of safety 1689; colonel of one of the Essex regiments of militia. He d. 22 Jan. 1704. He had sons, Joshua, b. 1671, George, b. 5 March, 1682, and Daniel, who d. 2 Sept. 1690. His epitaph, still legible, is,

> " Here lies interr'd a soul indeed,
> Whom few or none excel ;
> In grace if any him exceed,
> He'll be unparallel'd."

GEORGE, Boston, died 7 Dec. 1661. ISAAC, Massachusetts, admitted freeman 1632. JOHN, Dorchester, freeman 1631, had sons, Joseph, b. in 1631; Nehemiah, b. 1639. His wife d. in 1639. JOHN, Watertown, freeman 1638, was probably one of the proprietors of Lancaster, d. at Watertown, 19 Aug. 1661. JOHN, Hingham 1646. JOHN, Boston, received as a townsman, 28 Feb. 1642, perhaps freeman in 1648. JOHN, was admitted an inhabitant of Boston in 1657, [Snow, Hist. Boston, 60] and perhaps d. 17 Sept. 1661. James Pierce, a young man belonging to Boston, was killed by lightning, in Plymouth harbour, in 1660. Davis, Morton's Memo. 284. JOHN, Gloucester 1664. Spelled *Pearse*. *JOHN, was the representative of Woburn at two sessions in May, 1689. MARK, Cambridge 1642. MICHAEL, Scituate 1647, a captain, was slain with 50 English and 20 Cape Cod Indians, in Philip's war, March, 1676. He was killed near a small brook, called Abbot's Run, which empties into Patuxet, near Providence. Hubbard, Ind. Wars, 64. 2 Coll. Mass. Hist. Soc. iv. 245. ||NEHEMIAH, Boston, member of the ar. co. 1671, d. in 1691. ROBERT, Dorchester 1640. His widow Ann, died 31 Dec. 1695, aged about 104 years. ROBERT, Woburn, freeman 1650. 3 Coll. Mass. Hist. Soc. 1. 45. The Chelmsford Pierces being from Woburn, he may be the ancestor of Gov. Benjamin Pierce, of N. H., a native of Chelmsford, THOMAS, Charlestown, freeman 1635, died 7 Oct. 1666. There was a Thomas Pierce (perhaps the same) in Woburn, in 1643. WILLIAM, the captain of the ship Lyon, who wrote his name *Peirse*, was the author of the first almanack [for 1639] published in North-America. He was killed at Providence, one of the Bahama Islands, in 1641. Savage, ii. Winthrop, Index. Prince, [ii. Annals, 69] who erroneously regards him as a member of the Boston church, says he was ancestor of Rev. James Pierce, a well known writer and English divine, who d. 1730. WILLIAM, a gentleman of high repute in Boston, arrived there in the ship Griffin, 4 Sept. 1633, was admitted freeman 1634, was one of the selectmen, and d. a. 1661 or 1669. Savage, i. Winthrop, 109. There was one of this name in Boston in 1665, who wrote his name *Pearse*. Deed of Conveyance.

PIERPONT, JAMES, came from England, and d. at Ipswich, leaving two sons, John and Robert. Sarah Pierpont's deposition, 1724. *JAMES*, minister of New-Haven, son of John Pierpont, of Roxbury, and was born a. 1661, grad. at H. C. 1681, was ordained 2 July, 1685, d. 22 Nov. 1714. *JONATHAN*, the fourth minister of Reading, was born at Roxbury, 10 June, 1665, grad. at H. C. 1685, was ordained 26 June, 1689, d. 2 June, 1709, æ. 44. He m Eliz. Angier, 29 Oct. 1691. Two of his sons were, Jonathan, b. 14 Sept. 1695, grad. at H. C. 1714, and Joseph, b. 13 Oct. 1706. *JOHN, Roxbury, son of James Pierpont, of Ipswich, was admitted freeman 1652, representative 1672, d. 30 Dec. 1690. He had sons, John b. 22 Oct. 1652; James, of New-Haven; Ebenezer, who d. 17 December, 1696; Joseph; Benjamin, H. C. 1689, a minister in Charleston, S. C., who d. a. 1697. ROBERT, Roxbury, brother of the preceding, was admitted freeman 1675, and d. 16 May, 1694, leaving a widow Sarah, living in 1724, at the age of 83. ROBERT, was of Ipswich in 1648. Felt, MS Letter.

PIERSON, ABRAHAM, came from Yorkshire, a. 1639, became the first minister of South-Hampton, L. I. 1640; went to Branford, with a part of his church, and from thence, in 1667, to Newark, N.J., [Rev. Mr. Gillit] where he is said to have d. *about* 1681. [Thomas Day, .esq., MS letter.] His descendants reside in New-York, New-Jersey and Connecticut, twelve of whom have grad. at the colleges in those states. *ABRAHAM*, son of the preceding, grad. at H. C. 1668, was ordained 4 March, 1672, at Newark, as colleague to his father, removed to Connecticut in 1692, settled at Killingworth in 1694, was appointed the first rector of Yale College in 1701, and sustained the office until his death, 5 May, 1707. His son, Rev. John Pierson, Y. C. 1711, was the minister of Woodbridge, N. J., where his descendants still remain. BARTHOLOMEW, whose name is spelled *Person*, and perhaps *Porsune*, in the list of freeman [Savage, ii. Winthrop, 375] under 1648, was of Watertown in 1640, and of Woburn in 1653. His son Bartholomew was b. in 1641. ||GILES, member of the ar co. 1647. JOHN, Rowley. (See PEARSON.)

PIGG, THOMAS, Roxbury, freeman 1634, d. 39 Dec. 1643. The singular cognomen of *Pighogg* is found in the Boston records, one of this name, dignified with the title of *Mr.*, being received as a townsman, 28 Feb. 1653.

PIGGDEN, THOMAS, Lynn 1647. Lewis.

PIKE, JOHN, Newbury 1635, removed to Salisbury, and d. 29 May, 1654, leaving sons, John, of Newbury, and Robert, of Salisbury. *JOHN, Newbury, son of the preceding, was perhaps the freeman of 1647, whose name is entered James; was the representative in 1657 and 1658. He went to Woodbridge, N. J., 1669, and was one of the first and most active settlers of that town, [Analectic Magazine, Nov. 1814] was several years a magistrate. His children, b. at Newbury, were, Joseph, b. 1638; John, 12 Jan. 1641; Hannah, 1647; Mary; Ruth; Samuel, 1655; Thomas, 1657. The late General Z. M. Pike, was one of his descendants. *JOSEPH, Newbury, son of the preceding, was b. 26 Dec. 1638, was representative from 1960 to 1692, 3 years, and a deputy-sheriff. He was killed by the Indians, 4 Sept. 1694. His sons were, John, Thomas, Joseph, and Benjamin. Rev. James Pike, H. C. 1725, the father of the distinguished Nicholas Pike, A. A. S., was a grandson. *JOHN*, minister of Dover, was son of the following, and b. 15 May, 1653, at Salisbury, grad. at H. C. 1675, was ordained successor to the second Rev. John Rayner, 31 August, 1681, and d. 10 March, 1710, æ. 57. *‡ROBERT, son of the first named John Pike, was born a. 1616, came with his father to N. E. before 1735, settled at Newbury, was admitted freeman 1637, went to Salisbury, which he represented in 1648, and 7 years afterwards. He was a lieutenant in 1647, captain 1663, major in 1788; elected assistant from 1682 to 1686, one of the council of safety 1689, and one of the first council under the charter of William and Mary 1692. This useful and respectable man d. 12 Dec. 1706, æ. 90. Sarah, his wife, d. 1 Nov. 1679, and his widow, Martha, d. 26 Feb. 1713. His children were, Sarah, b. 1641; Mary, 1643; Dorothy, 1645; Mary, 2d, 1647; Elizabeth, 1650; John, 1653, and Robert, 1655.

PILSBURY, WILLIAM, was born a. 1615, came from Staffordshire, and settled at Dorchester as early as 1642, from thence went to Newbury 1651, perhaps admitted freeman 1668, and d. 21 June, 1686, æ. 71. His sons were, Job, b. at Dorchester 1643, freeman 1670; Caleb, b. at Newbury, 28 Jan. 1654, d. 24 July, 1680; William, b. 27 July, 1656; Increase, b. 1660. Descendants are very numerous.

PINCHIN, THOMAS, Scituate. (See Pynchon.)

PINDAR, JOHN, Watertown, d. 14 April, 1662. Spelled also *Pinter*. JOHN, Ipswich 1648.

PINGRY, *MOSES, Ipswich 1648, was born a. 1610; representative 1665, deacon of the church, d. in Jan. 1695. AARON, perhaps a brother, was of Ipswich in 1648.

PINION, NICHOLAS and ROBERT, were of Lynn in 1647. THOMAS, Sudbury 1661. Thomas and Nicholas Pinion were of New-Haven after 1670.

PINNEY, HUMPHREY, Dorchester, freeman 1634, went to Windsor with Rev. John Warham. Norman Pinney grad. at Y. C. 1823.

PIPER, NATHANIEL, Ipswich 1666. Asa Piper, H. C. 1778, b. at Concord, Ms., 31 Dec. 1762, was ordained at Wakefield, N. H. 1785.

PITCHER, ANDREW, Dorchester, admitted to the church 1641, was freeman same year. Rev. Nathaniel Pitcher, H. C. 1703, was minister of the 1st church in Scituate, and d. 27 Sept. 1723.

PITFORD, PETER, Marblehead 1648.

PITKIN, WILLIAM, Connecticut, was sent by that colony in 1693, to Gov. Fletcher of New-York to negociate terms respecting the militia. See Trumbull, i. Hist. Conn. 390—393.

PITMAN, JOSEPH, Charlestown, died 27 Oct. 1658. THO-MAS, Marblehead 1648.

PITNEY, JAMES, Boston 1652. Savage, MS note.

PITT, WILLIAM, Plymouth 1623. Davis, Morton's N. E. Memo. 378. It appears that he was b. about 1592. Perhaps the one of Hingham under Pitts.

PITTS, EDMUND, Hingham, came over 1639, with his brother Leonard Pitts, and was admitted freeman the next year. His son John was b. 1653. Mr. Coffin [MSS] says a John Pitts d. at Ips-wich, 20 May, 1653. WILLIAM, Hingham 1638. Winthrop [ii. Hist. N. E. 305] mentions a Pitt, who, with [Thomas] Johnson, was endangered in a tempest, while towing a "great raft of masts and planks" to Boston, the day before a fast in 1646.

PLACE, PETER, Boston 1642, freeman 1646, had a son Jo-seph, born in 1646. THOMAS, Massachusetts, freeman 1640. WILLIAM, a gunsmith of Salem 1637, d. 15 April, 1646.

PLAISTED, JOHN, New-Hampshire, a. 1679, was speaker of the house of representatives. *ROGER, Kittery, brother of John was representative 1663, 1664, and 1673, was a military officer. See Hubbard and Sullivan.

PLASTOW, JOSIAH, Boston 1632. Savage, i. Winthrop, 62.

PLATT, *SAMUEL, Rowley, representative 1681. The name of *Platts* has existed in N. H.

PLIMPTON, ||JOHN, Dedham, was member of the ar. co. 1643, and was probably the John *Plunton*, admitted freeman 1643. Savage, ii. Winthrop, 373. He had sons, Joseph, Eleazar, and Jonathan, b. in Medfield. THOMAS, Sudbury. (See PLYMPTON.)

PLOWDEN, SIR EDMUND, came to N. E. from Virginia in 1648, and soon returned to England. Winthrop, ii. Hist. N. E. 325.

PLUMB, JOHN, Dorchester, had a son Samuel, b. in 1659.

PLUMMER, FRANCIS, came from Wales a. 1633 to N. E. and was admitted freeman, 14 May, 1634, settled in Newbury, and d. 17 Jan. 1672. Ruth, his wife, d. 17 July, 1647, and he m. 21 March, 1648, widow Ann Palmer, who d. 18 Oct. 1665; m. again Beatrice Cantlebury, 29 Nov. 1665. His sons were the following. JOSEPH, Newbury, was born a. 1630, m. Sarah Cheney, 23 Dec. 1652, and had, 1. Joseph, born 11 Sept. 1654, m. Hannah Sweet, 1685; 2. Benjamin, b. 23 Oct. 1656; 3. Sarah, b. 1660; 4. Fran-cis, b. 1662, d. 1663; 5. Francis, b. 25 Feb. 1664; 6. Deborah, born 1665; 7. Nathaniel, b. 31 Jan. 1666; 8. Jonathan, 13 May, 1668. *SAMUEL, Newbury, brother of the preceding, was born a. 1619, admitted freeman 1641, and was representative in 1676. His children were, Samuel, b. 20 April, 1647, m. Joanna Woodbury 1670; Mary, b. 1649; John, b. 11 May, 1652; Ephraim, born 16 Sept. 1654, m. Hannah Jaques, 1680; Sylvanus, born 22 Feb. 1659, m. Sarah Moody, 1682; Richard, b. 16 August 1660; Hannah, born 1666, and Lydia, b. 1668. Hon. William Plumer, M. C., and governour of N. H. in 1812, and from 1816 to 1818, four years, is a descendant.

PLYMPTON, THOMAS, Sudbury 1643, was killed in Sudbury fight in 1675. Shattuck. Two of the name of Sylvanus Plympton grad. Harv. Coll. in 1780 and 1818.

POCHER, GEORGE, Braintree, d. 29 Sept. 1639.

POLLARD, GEORGE, Salem, died about 1646. WILLIAM, Boston 1644, had sons, William, member of the ar. co. 1679, who d. 1690; John, b. 1644, and Samuel, b. 1645. A great number of the name in N. E. are descended from Thomas Pollard, the son of William Pollard, of the city of Coventry, England, and who came over at the close of the 17th century, m. Sarah, daughter of Edward Farmer, and d. 4 April, 1724, leaving 10 sons and 4 daughters.

POLLY, JOHN, Roxbury, d. 2 April, 1690, æ. 71.

POMEROY, ELTWEED, freeman 1633, went from Massachusetts and settled in Windsor. See Increase Mather's Relation of Troubles in N. E. with the Indians, p. 19, where the name is *Eltwood Pomeryes.* Fourteen of the name had grad. in 1825, at the N. E. colleges. *MEDAD, Northampton 1660, freeman 1671, representative 1684, 1686, and 1690. JOSEPH, of Westfield in 1678.

POMFRET, WILLIAM, a lieutenant, and the town clerk of Dover, 1665, d. 7 Aug. 1680.

POND, ROBERT, Massachusetts, freeman 1642. WILLIAM, Dorchester in 1659. Nine of the name had graduated in N. E. in 1826.

POOLE, ELIZABETH, Taunton 1639, " the virgin mother of that town," one of its greatest proprietors, and a chief promoter of its settlement, d. 21 May, 1654, æ. 65. Savage, i. Winthrop, 253. HENRY, Boston, d. 14 Sept. 1643. JOHN, Cambridge 1632, perhaps of Lynn in 1639, and afterwards of Reading. *JONA-THAN, Reading, was representative in 1677, perhaps freeman 1673. SAMUEL, a merchant of Boston, was member of the church 1640. WILLIAM, Dorchester, town clerk about 40 years, and often a schoolmaster, d. 24 Feb. 1672. Harris, Hist. Dorchester. Mr. Savage [i. Winthrop, 252] names a Mr. William Pool, who had a son Timothy, drowned at, or near, Taunton, 15 Dec. 1667.

POOR, DANIEL, Andover 1647, d. 1713, æ. 85, leaving sons, 1. Daniel, who d. 1735, æ. 79, and having sons, Daniel, John, Samuel, Joseph, and Thomas; 2. John. Brig. Gen. Enoch Poor, who died in New-Jersey, 8 Sept. 1780, aged 43, was from this family. JOHN, Newbury, born a. 1613, d. 23 Nov. 1684, had sons, John, b. 1642; Joseph; Henry, b. 1650; Jonathan; Edward, b. 1661, and 7 daughters. NICHOLAS, Lynn 1637. Lewis. SAMUEL,

Newbury 1648, d. 21 Dec. 1683, had sons, Samuel, b. 1653; Edward, b. 1656; Joseph, b. 1666, and several daughters.

POPE, JOHN, Dorchester, freeman 1634, had sons, John, b. 1635; Nathan, b. 1641. JOSEPH, Salem, member of the church before 1636, was admitted freeman 1637, d. about 1667, leaving sons, Joseph, Benjamin, Enos, and Samuel. RICHARD, brother of the preceding, may be the freeman of 1635, whose name is *Popp* in colony records under that year.

PORMONT, PHILEMON, a member of Boston church 1638, was a schoolmaster, and admitted freeman in 1635. He was an adherent to Rev. John Wheelright, and went with him to Exeter. He had a son Pedaiah, b. in 1640, and Joseph Pormont, perhaps another son, lived at Great Island in 1685.

PORSUNE, BARTH. Savage, ii. Winthrop, 375. (See PIERSON.)

PORTER, ABEL, Boston 1643, had a son John, b. 1643. Sixty-four persons of the name of Porter, 16 of them clergymen, had grad. at the N. E. colleges in 1825. EDMUND, Roxbury, freeman 1637. Perhaps this name should be *Edward* Porter, whose son Joseph was b. at Roxbury, 1644. *JOHN, freeman 1633, was of Salem 1637, probably representative for Hingham 1644, [Lincoln, Hist. Hingham, 163] united with the church at Salem in 1649, representative in 1668, and d. in 1676, æ. about 80, leaving children. Felt, Annals, 256. JOHN, Windsor 1640. 1 Coll. Mass. Hist. Soc. v. 168. ‡JOHN, Rhode-Island, was an assistant from 1641 to 1644. Savage, i. Winthrop, 296. JONATHAN, Salem, admitted to the church, 5 April, 1640, freeman 1641, afterwards of Beverly. NATHANIEL, Massachusetts, freeman 1637. RICHARD, Weymouth, freeman 1653. ROGER, Massachusetts, was admitted freeman 1639. SAMUEL, Salem, died a. 1659.

POTTER, ANTHONY, Ipswich 1648. JOHN, New-Haven 1639, had sons, John and Samuel. Dodd, East-Haven Register 142—144. JOHN, Warwick, was a deputy in 1672. LUKE, Concord, freeman 1638, was a deacon of the church, and d. 13 Oct. 1697. His children were Eunice; Luke, b. 1646, d. 1661; Samuel, b. 1648; Dorothy; Judah, and Bethia. Shattuck, MS Hist. Concord. NICHOLAS, Lynn 1634. ROBERT, Lynn, 1630, was admitted freeman 1634. Savage, ii. Winthrop, 147. Lewis. A Robert Potter d. at Roxbury, 17 June, 1653. Matthias Potter was of Braintree in 1661. VINCENT, Massachusetts 1639. Winthrop, ii. Hist. N. E. 346. WILLIAM, New-Haven 1639, had Nathaniel, Joseph, Hope, and Rebecca. WILLIAM, was admitted freeman in 1640. See 1. Coll. Mass. Hist. Soc. 249.

POTTS, RICHARD, Maine 1676. Hubbard.

POULTER, JOHN, Billerica and Cambridge as early as 1657, came from Raleigh in the county of Essex, England; was of Cambridge in 1698.

POWELL, *MICHAEL, Dedham freeman 1641, representative 1641 and 1648, removed to Boston, and taught, without ordination, in the second church of Boston, previous to the settlement of its first minister, Increase Mather. His son Michael was b. at Dedham in 1645. WILLIAM, Charlestown 1637, whose wife d. 1644, had a son Joshua, b. in 1644. A William Powell, of Salem, d. 1670.

POWER, JOHN, Charlestown 1643, had a son Peter, b. in 1643. Those of the name of *Powers* will probably find in him a common ancestor. NICHOLAS, named by Mr. Savage, ii. Winthrop, 148, was probably of Providence.

POWNING, HENRY, Boston, freeman 1644, had a son Henry, b. in 1654, who was member of the ar. co in 1677.

PRATT, ANTHONY, Charlestown, requested to be made free 19 Oct. 1630. His wife died 1645. JOHN, an "experienced surgeon," and member of Mr. Hooker's church, at Cambridge, was admitted 1634, and, with his wife, sailed for England on their return, and was lost in Dec. 1644, on the coast of Spain. He was above 60 years of age, and left no issue. His apology may be found in 2 Coll. Mass. Hist. Soc. vii. 126—128. Winthrop, ii. Hist. N. E. 239. JOHN, Connecticut, was a deputy at the first general assembly 1639. Trumbull, i. Hist. Conn. 103. JOHN, Dorchester, admitted to the church 1642, freeman 1643. JOHN, of Hingham, had his house burnt 15 March, 1646. Savage, ii. Winthrop, 255. JOSHUA, Plymouth 1628. His grandson Ephraim Pratt, b. in East-Sudbury, Nov. 1687, lived to be 116 years of age, and d. in Shutesbury, Ms., in May, 1804. Michael Pratt, a son of Ephraim, d. in 1826, æ. 103. MATTHEW, Weymouth, freeman 1651, had a son Joseph, b. in 1639, and perhaps Samuel, freeman 1666. PHINEAS, Plymouth 1628, removed to Charlestown, and there d. 19 April, 1680. Prince, i. Annals, 131. Records of Charlestown. RICHARD, Charlestown 1643, had a son Thomas, b. in 1646. THOMAS, Weymouth, freeman 1647. WILLIAM, Massachusetts, freeman 1651.

PRAY, JOHN, Braintree, m. Joanna Dowman, May, 1657. QUENTIN and RICHARD, were of Lynn 1645. Lewis.

PREBLE, ABRAHAM, Scituate 1637, m. a daughter of Nathaniel Tilden; removed to Kittery, and was admitted freeman 1652. Abraham Preble, esq. of York, probably a descendant, d. 14 March, 1723, in his 50th year. William Pitt Preble, H. C. 1806, of Portland, Me., as well as the late Commodore Preble, is of this descent.

PRENCE, §‡THOMAS, governour of Plymouth colony, came from Lechlade, in Gloucester, to N. E. in 1621 in the ship Ann; settled at Plymouth, was chosen assistant 1635, and 20 years afterwards; removed to Eastham, a. 1644, of which place he was one of the first settlers; elected governour 1634, 1638, 1657 to 1672, 18 years. He d. 29 March, 1673, in his 73d year. His 1st wife d. 1634. By his 2d wife, he had 7 daughters, whose names are given by Judge Davis. His son Thomas went to England, and d. young, leaving a widow and daughter, named Susanna. Davis, Morton's Memo. 421—425.

PRENTICE, HENRY, Cambridge 1640, freeman 1650, died before 1658. Elizabeth, his 1st wife, d. 13 May, 1643. By Joan, his 2d wife, he had, Mary; Solomon, born 23 Sept. 1646; Abiah;

Samuel, b. 3 Aug. 1650; Sarah, and Henry. Solomon had sons, Thomas, Stephen, Nathaniel, and others. His descendants are numerous in Massachusetts. Some of them write the name *Prentiss*. Written in this way, and as above, 25 had grad. at the N. E. colleges in 1826, ten of whom had been clergymen. VALENTINE, Massachusetts, was admitted freeman in 1636.

PRENTISS, *THOMAS, Cambridge-Village, [Newton] whose name is usually spelled *Prentice*, although he wrote it *Prentis*, was admitted freeman in 1652, had children by Grace, his wife, Grace, Thomas, Elizabeth, Mary, and John. He was representative in 1672, 1673, and 1674, commanded a company of troop, which rendered very essential service in Phillip's war. He d. 7 July, 1710, æ.89. His son Thomas m. a daughter of Edward Jackson, senr., and died 1730, æ. 55; his son John also m. ***** and died 1689, æ. 35. The epitaph on the grave-stone of Captain Prentiss is as follows:

" He that's here interr'd needs no versifying,
" A virtuous life will keep the name from dying;
" He 'll live though poets cease their scribbling rhyme,
" When that this stone shall moulder'd be by time."

Homer, History of Newton, in 1 Collection Mass. Hist. Soc. v. 271.

PRESCOTT, JOHN, Watertown 1641, and perhaps the same who was at Lancaster 1647, and the freeman in 1669, was ancestor of the Hon. Benjamin Prescott, a counsellor of Massachusetts, who d. 3 Aug. 1738, æ. 42, whose sons were, Hon. Oliver, M. D., born 27 April, 1731, grad. at H. C. 1750, d. at Groton, 17 Nov. 1804; Hon. James, a senator, counsellor, and high-sheriff of the county of Middlesex, who d. 15 Feb. 1795, and Colonel William, a distinguished officer at Bunker Hill, who died 13 Oct. 1795, aged 70. JAMES, of Hampton, whose descendants are numerous in N. H., had a son James, born in 1671. [JONAS,] Sudbury 1646. Winthrop, ii. Hist. N. E. 306. John and a Jonas Prescott were admitted freemen 1679. *JONATHAN, Concord, freeman 1679, was representative at the first general court under the new charter, 1692. His son Benjamin, born 16 Sept. 1687 [Shattuck]; grad. at H. C. 1709, was ordained at Danvers, 23 Sept. 1713, resigned 1758, died 20 May, 1777. Benjamin, his son, grad. at H. C. 1736. Seventeen of the name of Prescott graduated at the N. E. colleges before 1827.

PRESTON, ||EDWARD, was member of the ar. co. 1646. JOHN, died at Boston, 6 June, 1663. ROGER, Ipswich 1648.

PRICE, *JOHN, a captain, of Salem, son of Walter Price, was baptized 11 Jan. 1645, elected representative 1679. He m. Sarah, daughter of Henry Wolcott, of Connecticut, in 1674, and died 13 May, 1691, aged 46. He left one son Walter. Felt, Annals, 301. ||RICHARD, Boston, member of the ar. co. 1658, freeman 1665. *WALTER, a merchant, and captain, came from Bristol, England, where he m. his wife, Elizabeth, and settled at Salem, where he was admitted to the church, 6 March, 1642; freeman same year; was representative 1665. He d. 5 June, 1674, æ. 61. His wife d.

in 1674, aged 73. His children were, Theodore; John; William; Walter, H. C. 1695; Elizabeth, who m. Rev. Thomas Barnard, and Hannah. The 1st, 3d, and 4th sons were lost at sea. Felt, Annals, 246.

PRICHARD, ||*HUGH, Roxbury, freeman 1642, member of the ar. co. 1643; representative 1643, 1644, 1649, a captain, according to Johnson, [Hist. N. E. 191] in 1644. He appears to have been of Gloucester in 1645, and one of the selectmen that year. His son, Zebadiah, was b. in 1643. Joseph, one of the principal inhabitants of Brookfield, was killed by the Indians, 2 August, 1675. RICHARD, Charlestown, d. 8 March, 1670. ROGER, Springfield, freeman 1648. WILLIAM, sometimes spelled *Pritchett*, was of Ipswich in 1648, and probably one of the first settlers of Brookfield. One of the name was of Lynn in 1645.

PRIDE, JOHN, Salem 1637, died a. 1647. This name exists in Vermont.

PRIEST, DEGORY, Plymouth, one of the first pilgrims, d. 1 Jan. 1621. JAMES, Salem, admitted freeman 1643, d. 1664. JAMES, Weymouth, had a son James, b. 1640, and d. at Salem. JOHN, of Weymouth in 1657.

PRIME, MARK, Rowley 1648. Rev. Ebenezer Prime, Y. C. in 1718, was minister of Huntington, L. I., and d. 1779, aged 79. Wood, Hist. L. I. 43.

PRINCE, JOHN, Cambridge 1634, freeman 1635, perhaps afterwards of Hingham. JOHN, came from England 1638, and d. at Hull, 1676. His son, Samuel Prince, esquire, was the first representative of Rochester, under Massachusetts 1692, and was father of Rev. Thomas Prince, the distinguished annalist of N. E. who grad. at H. C. 1707, and d. at Boston, 22 October, 1758, æ. 71. RICHARD, a tailor of Salem, admitted to the church, 16 January, 1642, of which he was a deacon; became freeman the same year, d. 1675, æ. 61. Felt, Annals, 249. §‡THOMAS, governour of Plymouth colony, wrote his name *Prence*, which see. THOMAS, Gloucester 1664. Fourteen of the name had grad. at the N. E. colleges in 1825.

PRIOR, MATTHEW, Brookhaven, L. I. 1665. Wood, Hist. L. I. 48. THOMAS, Scituate 1638, d. 1639.

PROCTOR, GEORGE, Dorchester, freeman 1637, had a son Samuel, b. in 1640. JOHN, Ipswich 1635. ROBERT, Concord, freeman 1643, was one of the petitioners for Chelmsford 1653, had children, Sarah; Gershom, b. 1648; Mary, and Peter.

PROUT, *EBENEZER, Concord, son of the following, was b. at Boston; was a captain and representative in 1689 and 1690. Timothy Prout grad. at H. C. 1741, and two of the name of John Prout grad. at Y. C. 1708 and 1732. *TIMOTHY, a ship-carpenter of Boston, was admitted member of the church 1643, freeman 1644, elected representative 1685, 1689, 1689—1692, six years, died 3 Nov. 1702, æ. more than 80 years. His sons were, Timothy, born 1645, William, b. 1653; Benjamin, b. 1655, and Ebenezer, born 1656.

PRUDDEN, PETER, the first minister of Milford, arrived in N. E. 26 June, 1637, in company with Rev. John Davenport; resided some time at Dedham ; removed to Milford, where he was installed 18 April, 1640, and died in 1656, æ. 56. *JOHN*, probably son of the preceding, grad. at H. C. 1668, was settled in 1670 the minister of Jamaica, L. I., from whence he removed to Newark, N. J. in 1692; and was there settled. He resigned his charge, 9 June, 1699, and d. 11 Dec. 1725, æ. 80. Job and Jeremiah Prudden, clergymen, grad. at Y. C. 1743 and 1775. Alden. W. Winthrop. Wood.

PUDINGTON, ROBERT, Portsmouth 1640. Belknap, i. Hist. N. H. 47.

PUFFER, JAMES, Braintree 1655. Matthew Puffer was also of Braintree. The only person of the name who had grad. in N. E. in 1828 was Rev. Reuben Puffer, D. D., of Berlin, who grad. at H. C. 1778, and d. in April, 1829, aged 73.

PULCIFER, BENEDICT, probably of Maine, is named by Mather, ii. Magnalia, 509.

PUNDERSON, JOHN, New-Haven 1639. Six of the name had grad. at Y. C. in 1826, of whom Ebenezer and Thomas were clergymen.

PURCHIS, JOHN, Boston, had a son John b. in 1656. *OLIVER, Dorchester, was born 1613, came to N. E. as early as 1635, was admitted freeman 1636, and settled at Dorchester, from thence went to Lynn, which he represented 13 years from 1660, the last time in 1689; was elected an assistant in 1685, but declined taking the oath. He removed, it is believed, to Concord, in 1691, where, Mr. Shattuck [MS Letter] says he d. 20 Nov. 1701. His age was 88. This name is often written *Purchase*. THOMAS, Lynn 1644. Lewis.

PURINGTON, ROBERT, born about 1634, was of N. H. in 1665, and his posterity are still there.

PUTNAM, JOHN, Salem, came from England and was admitted freeman 1647, and d. 1663. Thirty-four of the name had grad. at the N. E. colleges in 1828, many of whom were his descendants. *JOHN, Salem, son of the preceding, was born a. 1630, admitted freeman 1665; was a military officer, and representative 1680, 1686, 1691, and 1692. *NATHANIEL, Salem 1648, was born 1621; representative 5 sessions in 1690 and 1691. THOMAS, freeman 1642, was of Lynn, and was admitted to the church in Salem, 3 April, 1643. Felt. Lewis.

PYNCHON, ‡WILLIAM, one of the founders of the church and town of Roxbury, was elected an assistant in 1628, came to N. E. in 1630; was treasurer of the Mass. colony; removed to Springfield and was the principal person in settling that town, which he left in Sept. 1652, on his return to England with Rev. George Moxon. He d. at Wraisbury, on the Thames, in Buckinghamshire in Oct. 1662, æ. 72 or 74. His 1st wife died in N. E.; his 2d at Wraisbury, 10 Oct. 1657. His children were, John ; Anna, who m. Henry Smith ; Margaret, who m. Captain William Davis, and Ma-

ry, who died 26 Oct. 1657, the wife of Capt. Edward Holyoke.
‡*JOHN, son of the preceding, was b. in England in 1625, came to
N. E. and was admitted freeman in 1648, settled at Springfield,
which he represented in 1659, 1662, and 1663. He was elected
an assistant from 1665 to 1686, 22 years; was one of Sir Edmund
Andros' council 1687, was a colonel of the Hampshire regiment; d.
17 Jan. 1703, æ. 77. He m. Amy, daughter of Gov. George Wyllys
of Hartford. She d. 9 Jan. 1699, æ. 74. His children were, Joseph; John; Mary, b. 28 Oct. 1650, d. at Hartford; William, b.
1653, d. 1654; Mehetabel, b. 1661, d. 1663. The tale of the "Cath-
olic," in the Atlantick Souvenir for 1829, p. 210 to 228, has refer-
ence to this gentleman as one of the principal characters. JOHN,
son of the preceding, was born at Springfield, 17 Oct. 1647, was
two years at H. C. was clerk of the court of sessions and of common pleas, and register of deeds. He d. 25 April, 1721. His wife,
Margaret, a daughter of Rev. William Hubbard, d. 11 Nov. 1716.
His children were, 1. John, b. at Ipswich, and had children, William, b. 11 Nov. 1703, Mehetabel; Eliza; Joseph and John, twins,
b. 7 Feb. 1705; Mary; Bathsheba; Edward; George, and Charles;
2. Margaret, who m. Nathaniel Downing, of Ipswich, and had Nathaniel, John, Margaret, Jane, Lucy, and Anne; 3. William, b. at
Ipswich 1689, m. Catharine, daughter of Rev. Daniel Brewer, and
d. 1 Jan. 1741, having had children, Sarah, William, Margaret,
Daniel, John, and Joseph. Felt, MS Letter. *JOSEPH, brother
of the preceding, was b. at Springfield, 26 July, 1646; grad. at H.
C. 1664, represented Springfield in 1681 and 1682, was a physician,
and died in Boston unmarried. THOMAS, Scituate 1638. This
name is *Pinchin* in the 2 Coll. Mass. Hist. Soc. iv. 240.

PYNE, THOMAS, Massachusetts, was admitted freeman 1635.
It is not improbable that this should be *Pinney,* a name which exists in New-England.

QUICK, WILLIAM, Charlestown 1650. Coffin.

QUILTER, MARK, came to N. E. with Rev. Nathaniel Rogers
and settled in Ipswich before 1648. Joseph Quilter is mentioned
in the Revo. in N. E. Justified, p. 38.

QUIMBY, ROBERT, was an inhabitant of Salisbury in 1663.
This name exists in various parts of New-Hampshire.

QUINCY, *EDMUND, the ancestor of the most distinguished
Quincy family in N. E., came over with Rev. John Cotton in 1633,
was admitted freeman 1634, and was deputy at the first general
court, 14 May, 1634; received a grant of land in Braintree [now
Quincy] in 1635. He died soon after, aged 33. *EDMUND,
Braintree, son of the preceding, was born in England 1627, admitted freeman 1665; was the first major and Lieut. colonel in Braintree, representative in 1670, 1673, 1675, 1679, and d. 7 Jan. 1698,
æ. 70. Joanna, his wife, d. 16 May, 1680, aged 55. His children
were, 1. Mary, b. 1650; 2. Daiel, b. 7 Feb. 1651, member of the
ar. co. 1675; 3. John, b. 5 April, 1652; 4. Joanna, b. 1654; 5.
Judith, b. 1655; 6. Elizabeth, b. 1656; 7. Edmund, b. 1657; d.
1661; and 8. Edmund, probably by a 2d wife, b. in Oct. 1681, who,

with Daniel, left male issue. Daniel, had but one son, John Quincy, (the great-grandfather of John Quincy Adams, who derives his name from him) born in 1689, was speaker of the house of representatives and member of the council 40 successive years, and d. 13 July, 1767, aged 78.' Edmund grad. at H. C. 1699, was judge of the supreme court of the province, and agent at the court of Great-Britain, d. at London of the small pox, 23 Feb. 1738, aged 56, leaving Edmund, who grad. at H. C. 1722, and d. June, 1788, aged 85, and Josiah, who was born 1709, grad. at H. C. 1728, a distinguished character, and d. at Braintree 1784, having had 3 sons, of much distinction; 1. Edmund, b. Oct. 1733, grad. at H. C. 1752, was an eminent merchant in Boston, d at sea, in March, 1768, aged 34; 2. Samuel, who grad. at H. C. 1754, was solicitor general, became a loyalist, went to Antigua, W. I. and d. in 1789; 3. Josiah, b. in Boston, Feb. 1734, grad. at H. C. 1763, was eminent for his patriotism and eloquence, went to England, and d. on his return to America, 26 April, 1775, aged 33. The Hon. Josiah Quincy, the late mayor of Boston, now president of Harvard College, is a son of the last named.

RADCLIFFE, PHILIP, Massachusetts, was sentenced 14 June, 1631, to be whipped, have his ears cropped, and then banished. Felt, Annals of Salem, 54. *ROBERT*, the first minister of King's Chapel, Boston, came over in 1686, and conmenced his ministry the succeeding summer. Dunton's Journal in 2 Coll. Mass. Hist. Soc. ii. 106. There have been several graduates in this country of the name of Radcliff.

RAINSBOROW, ||——— member of the ar. co. 1639, returned to England, and was an officer in Cromwell's army, and attained the rank of colonel. Savage, Winthrop, ii. Hist. N. E. 245, 351, 354.

RAINSFORD, EDWARD, Boston, brother of Lord Chief Justice Rainsford, was admitted freeman 1637, and was an elder of the church. He had sons, Joshua, b. 1632; John, 1634, d. at Boston 1698; Jonathan, 1636; Nathan 1641; David, b. 1644, d. 1691.

RAMSDELL, JOHN, Lynn, 1638, d. 27 Oct. 1688, aged 86, leaving sons, John and Aquila. A John Ramsdell was of Boxford in 1673.

RAND, FRANCIS, Pascataqua 1631. JAMES, Plymouth 1623. JOHN, Charlestown, d. 19 Dec. 1659. Nathan Rand, of Charlestown, was freeman 1668. John Rand, H. C. 1748, the first minister of Lyndeborough, N. H., was born in Charlestown. Eight others of the name have grad. at H. C. ROBERT, Lynn 1649, d. 8 Nov. 1694. He had 2 sons, Robert and Zachary. Lewis. THOMAS, Massachusetts, freeman 1660.

RANDALL, ABRAHAM, Dorchester, removed to Windsor, Conn. 1636. PHILIP, Massachusetts, freeman 1634. (See RENDALL.) WILLIAM, Scituate 1640. Twelve of the name had grad. at the N. E. colleges in 1828.

RANDLET, CHARLES, Exeter, was taken captive by the Indians 1675, but soon after escaped. Hubbard, Wars Eastern Indians, 20.

RANDOLPH, ‡EDWARD, called the "evil genius of New-England," was one of Sir Edmund Andros' council 1687, and his secretary of the council. Eliot, Biog. Dictionary. Farmer and Moore, iii. Coll. 29—32.

RANGER, EDMUND, Massachusetts, freeman 1671.

RASHLEY, THOMAS, member of the church in Boston in 1640, is called a student and probably the member of the ar. co. 1645. He was of Exeter 1646.

RAVENSCROFT, ||SAMUEL, was member of the ar. co. 1679, m. Dyonisia, daughter of Major Thomas Savage.

RAVENSDALE, JOHN, Massachusetts, was admitted freeman 1635. Thomas Ravensdale suffered martyrdom in Sussex, England in 1656.

RAWLING, RICHARD, Boston, member, of the church 1642.

RAWLINS, JAMES, Newbury, was admitted freeman 1634. JASPER, whose name is spelled *Rawlen,* was freeman 1633. JOSEPH, Massachusetts, freeman 1634. ||THOMAS, Boston, freeman 1631, member of the ar. co. 1642, d. 15 March, 1660. His sons were, Caleb, b. 1645 ; Samuel, b. 1655. THOMAS, Weymouth, freeman 1636, had son Joshua, b. 1642.

RAWSON, *EDWARD, born in Gillingham, in Dorsetshire, about 1615, [Coffin] came to N. E. as early as 1637, and settled in Newbury, where he was town clerk, and representative in 1638, and 8 years afterwards, having been admitted freeman in 1637. He went to Boston, a. 1650, and was Secretary of the Mass. colony from 1650 to 1686. He m. Rachel Perne, and his children were Edward, H. C. 1653, who, it is said, went to England and was settled as a preacher at Horsmanden, in Kent, from whence he was ejected after the restoration [Calamy] ; Rachel, who m. William Aubrey in 1653 ; David, b. 6 May, 1644 ; Susan, who d. at Roxbury 1654 ; Pernal, b. 1646 ; Grindall, b. 1649 ; William, b. in Boston, 21 May, 1651, settled in Dorchester, and had sons, Nathaniel, Ebenezer, Edward, Pelatiah, and Grindall ; Rebecca, who m. Thomas Rumsey in 1679, and GRINDALL, 2d, b. 1658, grad. at H. C. 1678, ordained the 2d minister of Mendon 1680, and d. 6 Feb. 1715, in his 57th year, who was father [Coffin,] *perhaps* grandfather of Grindall Rawson, H. C. 1728, minister of Hadlyme, who d. 29 March, 1777, aged 69. A third Grindall Rawson, H. C. 1741, was also a clergyman, and settled at Ware and at Yarmouth, Mass.

RAY, DAVID. (See WRAY.) SAMUEL, Salem 1637.

RAYMOND, RICHARD, Salem, freeman 1634. JOHN, Beverly, d. 18 Jan. 1703, aged 87. JOHN, jun. Beverly, freeman 1683. WILLIAM, Portsmouth 1631. *WILLIAM, Salem 1648, afterwards of Beverly, a captain, and representative in 1685 and 1686. This name is often spelled *Rayment* in Beverly records.

RAYN, JOSEPH, was attorney general of New-Hampshire, a. the time of Cranfield. Rayn or Raynes was a name at York, in 1668.

RAYNER, *HUMPHREY, Rowley, was representative 1649, and d. in 1660. Jachin Rayner, d. at Rowley 1708, and a Mrs. Rayner d. there 1698. *JOHN*, minister of Plymouth and Dover, brother of the preceding, came to N. E. about 1635, and settled at Plymouth, where he was the minister 18 years; went to Dover in 1655, and d. there in April, 1669. His sons were, John; Joseph, b. 1650, d. 1652, and probably others. The name is often spelled *Reyner*. JOHN, minister of Dover, son of the preceding, grad. at H. C. 1663; was ordained in 1671, and d. at Braintree, 21 Dec. 1676, æ. about 34. THOMAS, one of the first settlers of Hempstead, L. I. 1643. Wood's Hist. L. I. ‡THURSTON, Watertown, removed to Connecticut, and was elected a magistrate 1643 —1661. Mather, Magnalia. Trumbull. WILLIAM, freeman 1670.

READ, *ESDRAS, Salem, admitted to the church, 10 May, 1640, freeman 1641, dismissed to Wenham, which he represented in 1648 and 1651, and from thence went to Chelmsford with Rev. John Fiske in 1655. ||JOHN, Braintree, freeman 1640, member of the ar. co. 1644, had sons, John, b. 29 Aug. 1640; Thomas, b. 20 Nov. 1641. PHILIP, Weymouth 1641, freeman 1660, had a son Philip, b. in 1641, who was probably of Concord in 1670. ROBERT, Exeter 1638, d. at Hampton 1658. There was a Robert Read of Boston in 1646. THOMAS, Salem, came to N. E. 1630, settled in Salem, was admitted freeman 1634, and died abroad before 1663, having been a colonel. THOMAS, Lynn 1637. Felt, Annals, 218. THOMAS, Sudbury, perhaps the freeman admitted 1656, d. 13 Sept. 1701. Shattuck. His son Thomas, freeman 1679. *WILLIAM, Weymouth, freeman 1635, representative 1636, 1638, had a son William, b. in 1639. WILLIAM, Dorchester, member of the church 1636, freeman 1638, perhaps was of Boston 1646. WILLIAM, Weymouth, was admitted freeman 1653. Some of those under this name wrote it *Reed*, but they cannot be distinguished. Of the 60 graduates at the N. E., N. J., and Union colleges, 33 are entered *Read* and 27, *Reed*.

REDDING, JOSEPH, Cambridge 1632, freeman 1634, of Ipswich 1648. MYLES, Massachusetts, freeman 1634, was one of the proprietors of Billerica in 1665. THOMAS, Saco, 1652. This name exists in New-Hampshire.

REDDINGTON, *ABRAHAM, was representative in 1686, perhaps for Topsfield. DANIEL, freeman 1685.

REDFORD, CHARLES, Salem, was a merchant and d. 1692. Felt, Annals, 302.

REDIAT, JOHN, Sudbury, freeman 1645, was one of the proprietors of Marlborough. His son John, was b. 1644.

REDMAN, JOHN, Hampton, one of the early settlers, and living in 1685, at the age of 70. Adams, Annals Portsmouth, 397. Robert Redman was of Dorchester in 1658.

REDNAP, JOSEPH, was a wine-cooper, came from London, was admitted freeman in 1634, and d. in Boston in 1686, æ. 110. Hutchinson, i. Hist. Mass. 306.

REED, ESDRAS, Salem. (See READ.) Twenty-seven of the name, spelled *Reed*, had grad. at the N. E. colleges in 1828.

REEVE, JOHN, Salem 1659. Spelled also *Reeves*. Hon. Tapping Reeve, LL. D., judge of the supreme court of Conn. grad. at N. J. College in 1763. Several others of the name have grad. at Yale.

REMICK, CHRISTIAN, Kittery 1652.

REMINGTON, JOHN, Newbury 1637, freeman 1639, removed to Andover, and thence to Rowley and to Roxbury. He had Joseph, b. 1650, and Thomas. JONATHAN, who was b. in Rowley 1639, may have lived in Cambridge, where was a Jonathan Remington before 1670. Five have grad. at H. C.

RENDALL, PHILIP, was admitted freeman in 1634. Edward and James Rendall were of New-Hampshire in 1686. ROBERT, Weymouth, was admitted freeman in 1647.

REVELL, ‡JOHN, was chosen assistant, 20 Oct. 1629, came over 1630, and returned to England in the ship Lyon, with William Vassall the same year. Savage, i. Winthrop, N. E. 20. THOMAS, one of the judges of Charles I, king of England, came to N. E., and died in Braintree. Whitney, Hist. Quincy, 36.

REVERDY, PETER, a French protestant wrote memoirs concerning Sir Edmund Andros as early as 1689. Revo. in N. E. Just. 40.

REYNER, JOHN. (See RAYNER.)

REYNOLDS, HENRY, Lynn 1647, Salem 1650. Lewis. JOHN, Weymouth, freeman 1635. A John Reynolds was early at the Isles of Shoals. See 1. Coll. Mass. Hist. Soc. vii. 250. ||NATHANIEL, member of the ar. co. 1658, freeman, 1665. ROBERT, Boston, freeman 1634, d. 27 April, 1659. Snow, Hist. Boston, 118. WILLIAM, Salem, admitted to the church 1640, removed to Providence as early as 1641.

RHODES, HENRY, Lynn 1643, was born a. 1608. [Lewis.] JOSEPH, Lynn, freeman 1677. Simon Rhodes grad. at Y. C. in 1736.

RICE, *EDMUND, Sudbury, freeman 1640, representative 1640, was one of the petitioners for the grant of Marlborough, to which place he probably removed. His son Benjamin was b. in 1640. EDWARD, a deacon of Marlborough, was admitted freeman in 1651. His descendants are numerous and have been remarkable for longevity. Worcester Magazine, ii. 185. HENRY, Sudbury 1640, was admitted freeman 1648, and was one of the proprietors of Marlborough. PHILIP, Boston 1640. was a member of the church. RICHARD, Concord 1635, admitted freeman 1641, died 9 June, 1709, æ., according to the records, " more than 100 years," but Mr. Shattuck makes him but 97. It is said that he left 8 sons, who lived to great ages. ROBERT, Boston, disarmed in 1637, had sons, Joshua, b. 1637, Nathaniel, b. 1639. THOMAS, Sudbury, perhaps son of Richard, was admitted freeman 1660, and d. 16 Nov. 1691.

RICHARDS, EDWARD, Dedham 1639, freeman 1641, had a son John, b. in 1641. There was an Edward Richards of Lynn, who d. 26 Jan. 1690, æ. 74, leaving a son John. Lewis. JAMES, Massachusetts, admitted freeman 1652. ‡JAMES, Connecticut, was elected magistrate in 1665. ‡||JOHN, Dorchester, member of the ar. co. 1644, its lieutenant in 1667 ; a captain and major ; representative for Newbury from 1671 to 1673, 3 years, for Hadley 1675, of Boston 1679 and 1680; speaker Feb. 1680, was elected assistant 1680 to 1686; and one of the first counsellors under the charter of William and Mary 1692. He d. at Boston, 2 April, 1694. He m. Elizabeth, widow of Adam Winthrop, 3 May, 1654. NATHANIEL, Cambridge, freeman 1632. Holmes, Hist. Cambridge. THOMAS, Massachusetts, was admitted freeman 1640. ||THOMAS, freeman 1645, member of the ar. co. 1648. WILLIAM, Weymouth 1658. Of the name of Richards, 18 had grad. at the N. E. colleges in 1828.

RICHARDSON, AMOS, a tailor, lived in Boston, was admitted freeman 1665, and had sons, John, baptized 3 Jan. 1648 ; Stephen, b. 14 June 1652; Samuel, b. 18 Feb. 1660. Of the name of Richardson, 19 had grad. at the various colleges in New-England in 1826. EDWARD, Newbury, was born a. 1619. His sons were, Edward, b. 21 Dec. 1649 ; Caleb, b. 18 Aug. 1652 ; Moses, b. 4 April, 1658. Coffin. *EZEKIEL, Charlestown, came to N. E. in 1630, and with his wife was admitted to the church in Boston, from which they were dismissed 11 Oct. 1632. He was admitted freeman 18 May, 1631, was representative at the Sept. court 1635 ; removed to Woburn, and there died 28 Oct. 1647. His son John d. 7 Jan. 1643, and his daughter Ruth d. the same year. JAMES, went from Woburn to Chelmsford as early as 1659. He m. Bridget Hinchman, 28 Nov. 1660, and had several children. His son James was b. 26 Oct. 1661. *JOHN*, the third minister of Newbury, grad. in 1666, at H. C., of which he was a fellow ; admitted freeman 1675, ordained 20 Oct. 1675, and d. 27 April, 1696, in his 50th year. He m. Mary Pierson of Woburn, 28 Oct. 1673, and his children were, Sarah, b. 19 Sept. 1674 ; John, b. 15 July, 1676 ; Mary, b. 1677 ; Elizabeth, b. 1680 ; Catharine, b. 15 Sept. 1681. Coffin. *JOSIAH, Chelmsford 1659, was admitted freeman 1674, town clerk 3 years, selectman 14 years, representative 1689 and 1690, captain of the military company, and d. 22 July, 1695, aged a. 60. He m. Remembrance, daughter of William Underwood, 6 June, 1659, and his children were, 1. Sarah, b. 1660, m. William Fletcher of Chelmsford ; 2. Mary, b. 1662, m. Moses Barron, of Chelmsford ; 3. Josiah, b. 18 May, 1665, was a lieutenant, and by Marcy, his wife, had sons, Josiah, Robert, Zachariah, and William, of whom the last is ancestor of William M. Richardson, LL. D., chief justice of New-Hampshire ; 4. Jonathan, b. 8 Oct. 1667, m. Elizabeth Bates, and d. 21 Feb. 1753 ; 5. John, b. 14 Feb. 1669 ; 6. Samuel, b. 21 Feb. 1672. d. April, 1754 ; 7. Remembrance, b. 20 April, 1684. The descendants in the several branches of this family are scattered in various parts of the U. States. RICHARD, Boston 1654. SAMUEL, was admitted freeman in 1638, and settled in Woburn 1642, d. 23 March, 1658. His sons were, John or

Joseph, [Boston and Midd'x. co. records differ in the name] b. 23 July, 1643 ; Samuel, b. 22 April, 1646 ; Stephen, b. 15 Aug. 1649 ; Thomas, b. 1651, d. 1657. Joanna, his widow, d. 1666. THO-MAS, brother of the preceding, freeman 1638, was one of the first settlers of Woburn, where he d. 28 Aug. 1651. His children were Thomas, b. 4 Oct. 1645, who settled in Billerica, d. 25 Feb. 1721, the ancestor of the many families who have lived in that town, and of Hon. Joseph Richardson, of Hingham, M. C.; Isaac, b. 24 May, 1643 ; Nathaniel, b. 2 Jan. 1650. WILLIAM, Newbury 1655, d. 25 March, 1658, leaving sons, Joseph, b. 1655; Benjamin, b. 13 May, 1658. Coffin.

RICHMOND, EDWARD, Rhode-Island, one of the purchasers of land in the Narraganset country with Major Humphrey Atherton.

RIDGDALE, JOHN, Plymouth 1620, one of the first pilgrims, who d. before March, 1621.

RIDGE, JOHN, Newbury, d. 1666.

RIGBY, EDWARD, Lancaster 1654. Some of the early Rig-bys in N. E. came from Rigby in Lancashire. JOHN, Dorchester, was admitted freeman 1642.

RIGGS, EDWARD, Roxbury was admitted freeman and d. in 1634. THOMAS, Gloucester 1664. Elias Riggs, a graduate and tutor of N. J. College, was settled in the ministry.

RILEY, JOHN, Springfield, freeman 1671, d. 24 Oct. 1684. HENRY, Rowley, d. 1710, æ. 82.

RINDGE, DANIEL, Ipswich 1648. Daniel Rindge, H. C. 1709, is the only graduate of the name in N. E.

RING ROBERT, one of the first proprietors of Salisbury, was admitted freeman in 1640. THOMAS, Exeter, d. in 1667. WIL-LIAM, Salem, a. 1632.

RIPLEY, ABRAHAM, Hingham, son of William Ripley, was admitted freeman in 1655. JOHN, Hingham, brother of the pre-ceding, was admitted freeman in 1655, m. daughter of Rev. Peter Hobart, and had six sons, John, Joshua, Jeremiah, Josiah, Peter, and Hezekiah. WILLIAM, father of the preceding, came from Hingham, England, with his wife, sons Abraham and John, and 2 daughters, and settled at Hingham, Ms., in 1638, was admitted free-man 1641, and d. 20 July, 1656. His descendants are very re-spectable, of whom is Rev. Ezra Ripley, D. D., of Concord, Ms., a native of Woodstock, who grad. at H. C. 1776.

RISHWORTH, *EDWARD, Wells 1643, Kittery 1652, repre-sentative of York 1653, and the 12 succeeding years; was a magis-trate, and living in 1683. His name is frequently *Rushworth* in old records, but he wrote it as above, which has been a baptismal name in Maine, probably from him. His wife was daughter of Rev. John Wheelwright.

RIX, WILLIAM, Boston, d. 13 Nov. 1657. His sons were, Eli-sha, b. 1645 ; John, 1648 ; Thomas, 1654 ; Ezekiel, 1656. The name exists in N. H.

ROAKE, ||JOSEPH, member of the ar. co. 1658. (See ROCK.)

ROBBINS, JOHN, was a proprieter of Bridgewater in 1645.
RICHARD, Cambridge, had sons, John; Samuel, b. 1643, and
Nathaniel. He and his wife Rebecca were members of the church.
William Robbins d. in Boston in 1693. Robert Robbins was of
Concord in 1678.

ROBERTS, JOHN, Ipswich, freeman 1639. JOHN, was one
of the selectmen of Dover in 1665. ROBERT, Boston 1646, Ipswich 1648, and d. in 1663, leaving a widow and 8 children. SI-
MON, Boston 1655, had sons, John and Simon. ||THOMAS,
member of the ar. co. 1644, freeman 1645, may have been the
principal landholder in Exeter, named by Savage, ii. Winthrop,
Hist. N. E. 327. WILLIAM, Oyster-River, now Durham, N. H.,
was killed by the Indians 1675.

ROBERTSON, WILLIAM, Concord 1670. Shattuck. A
John Robertson was killed by the Indians at Salisbury, 21 Oct.
1676. Coffin.

ROBINSON, ISAAC, Scituate 1633, son of that celebrated puritan, the Rev. John Robinson, who died at Leyden, in Holland, 19
Feb. 1625, [i. Prince, 159] in his 50th year, [Dr. Holmes, i. Annals, 191, erroneously makes his death in 1625—6] is mentioned
by Prince as a venerable man, whom he had seen, and who died
over 90 years of age. Prince, i. Annals, 160. Mr. Lewis informs me that an Isaac Robinson lived in Lynn in 1637. JOHN,
Ipswich, probably the freeman in 1641, died 1 March, 1657. JOHN,
brother of Isaac, settled at, or near Cape Ann. The late Professor
James F. Dana, M. D., informed me, that Abraham, his son, and
grandson of Rev. John Robinson, died at the age of 102 years,
and that it was engraved on his tombstone that he was the first child
born of English parents on that side of Massachusetts-Bay. JOHN,
freeman 1685. WILLIAM, Salem 1637, was admitted member of
the church, 16 Sept. 1638. WILLIAM, Dorchester 1636, two of
whose sons were, probably, Nathaniel, freeman in 1673, and Thomas, who were of Boston in 1650. A Robinson of Exeter was
killed by the Indians in 1675.

ROBY, HENY, Dorchester 1639, and it is likely, went the same
year to Exeter, in the vicinity of which the name has continued to
the present time.

ROCK, JOSEPH, Boston, freeman 1652, had sons, John and
Joseph. Snow, Hist. Boston, 136.

ROCKETT, RICHARD, Braintree, whose son John was born
1641, and wife Agnes, d. in 1643.

ROCKWELL, WILLIAM, Dorchester, requested to be made
freeman in 1630, and was admitted 18 May, 1631. Ten of the
name had grad. at Y. C. and one at Dart. in 1828.

ROCKWOOD, NICHOLAS, Medfield 1651, had a son Benjamin. SAMUEL, admitted freeman in 1682. Two of the name
had grad. in 1828 at each of the colleges at Harv. Dart. and Midd.

RODGERS, —— came to N. E. in 1628, as a minister for
Plymouth, but "proving craz'd in his brain," he was sent back by
the colonists the next year. Prince, i. Annals, 193.

ROGERS, DAVID, Braintree, d. 24 Sept. 1642. Of this name there was a number of families among the early emigrants to N. E., and it is not improbable that several besides the ministers of Ipswich and Rowley, were descended from that distinguished martyr, the *first* "of that blessed company who suffered in the reign of Mary." There have been many literary men of the name, no less than 48 having grad. in N. E., 13 of whom have been clergymen. *EZEKIEL*, the first minister of Rowley, was the son of Richard Rogers, of Weathersfield, England, and a cousin of Rev. Nathaniel Rogers, of Ipswich, was born in 1590. He came to N. E. in 1638, was admitted freeman, 23 May, 1639, settled at Rowley, where he d. 23 Jan. 1661, æ. 70. His 3d wife was daughter of Rev. John Wilson, of Boston. His children d. young, and he left no issue. EZEKIEL, son of Rev. Nathaniel, was born in N. E., grad. at H. C. in 1659, was living in Ipswich, 1666, [2 Coll. Mass. Hist. Soc. viii. 107] and d. 5 July, 1674, leaving issue. JOHN, the fifth president of H. C., brother of the preceding, was born in England, and probably at Assington, came with his father to N. E. 1636, grad. at H. C. 1649, was a physician, and succeeded President Oakes in 1682, and d. 2 July, 1684. He m. Elizabeth Denison, and his children were, 1. Elizabeth, b. 26 Feb. 1661; 2. Margaret, 18 Feb. 1664; 3. John, 1666; 4. Daniel, b. 25 Sept. grad. at H. C. 1686, was a physician in Ipswich, and perished on Hampton Beach in a violent snow storm, 1 Dec. 1722, leaving Daniel, who grad. at H. C. 1725, ordained the minister of Littleton, 15 March, 1732, d. Nov. 1782, æ. 76; 5. Nathaniel, b. 22 Feb. 1670, grad. at H. C. 1687, was ord. the 2d minister of the 1st church in Portsmouth, 3 May, 1699, d. 3 Oct. 1723, æ. 54, leaving Nathaniel, a physician and magistrate, who grad. at H. C. 1717, and d. 15 Nov. 1746; 6. Patience, b. 25 May, 1676. *JOHN*, the seventh minister of Ipswich, was son of the preceding, was born 7 July, 1666, and grad. at H. C. 1684. He was ordained 12 Oct. 1692, and died 28 Dec. 1745, æ. 79. He m. Martha, daughter of John Whittingham, 4 March, 1691, by whom [who d. 9 March, 1759, æ. 89] he had, 1. John, b. 19 Jan. 1692, grad. at H. C. 1711, the minister of Eliot, Me., and d. 1773; 2. Martha; 3. William, b. 19 June, 1699, settled in Maryland; 4. Nathaniel, b. 4 March, 1702, grad. at H. C. 1721, settled colleague with his father, and d. 1775, æ. 73; 5. Richard, b. 2 Dec. 1703, a merchant of Ipswich; 6. Elizabeth; 7. Daniel, b. 28 July, 1707, grad. at H. C. 1725, installed the first minister of the 2d church in Exeter, 1748, died Dec. 1785, in his 80th year; 8. Elizabeth, 2d, a twin with Daniel; 9. Samuel, b. 31 Aug. 1709, grad. at H. C. 1725, was a physician, and d. at Ipswich, 21 Dec. 1772. *JOHN, a deacon in Weymouth, was admitted freeman 1637, representative 1659, died 11 Feb. 1661. There was a John Rogers in Dedham in 1636, and one of this name was of Scituate in 1648, and perhaps one of the proprietors of Bridgewater in 1645. JOHN, Watertown, was admitted freeman 1638, d. 22 Dec. 1673, aged 80. JOHN, an early inhabitant of Billerica, d. there, 25 Jan. 1686, leaving 4 sons, 1. John, born a. 1641, settled in Billerica, and was killed by the Indians, 5 August, 1695, of whose descendants, three have grad. at H. C., viz: in 1802, Timothy Foster, minister of Bernardstown, Ms. in 1809; Artemas, esq., of Henniker, N. H., and in 1817, Micajah, an instructer of youth; 2. Thomas, who settled in Billerica, and was killed, with his son Thomas, aged 11 years, 5 Aug. 1695; 3. Daniel; 4. Nathaniel, who also settled in Billerica. *NATHANIEL*, the third minister of Ipswich, was the second son of Rev. John Rogers, of Dedham, England, who d. 18 Oct. 1639, aged 67, a descendant from the prebendary of St. Paul's, and the first who suffered martyrdom under the bigoted Queen Mary. He was b. in 1598, was educated at Emmanuel College, and came to N. E. in 1636, and was ordained as colleague with Rev. John Norton, 20 Feb. 1638, admitted freeman 1639, and d. 3 July, 1655, aged 57. He m. Margaret, daughter of Robert Crane, of Coggeshall, England. She died 23 Jan. 1676. Their children were, John; Nathaniel, who died 14 June, 1680; Samuel, who d. 21 Dec. 1693; Timothy; Ezekiel, and one daughter, who m. Rev. William Hubbard. These were living at the time of their father's death. ROBERT, one of the early inhabitants of Newbury, d. 1664, leaving children, Robert, Thomas, John, and Elizabeth. His widow m. William Thomas. SIMON, Concord, freeman 1640, whose wife d. 1 Aug. 1640, was perhaps of Boston in 1642, where Nathaniel, Simon, Gamaliel, and Joseph, sons of Simon Rogers, were born from 1642 to 1662. THOMAS, one of the first pilgrims of Plymouth, 1620, died the first winter. Joseph Rogers, of Plymouth, 1623, might be his son. Davis, Morton's Memo. 376. THOMAS, Massachusetts, was admitted freeman in 1637. THOMAS, Saco 1652, had his house burned by the Indians in Oct. 1676. WILLIAM, Kittery, freeman 1652. WILLIAM, Boston, had several children born there and died 13 July, 1664.

ROISE, ROBERT, Massachusetts, was admitted freeman 1634. The name of *Royce* exists in N. E.

ROLFE, BENJAMIN, Newbury, where he was born a. 1641. *BENJAMIN*, the second minister of Haverhill, was son of Benjamin Rolfe, and was born 13 Sept. 1662 [Coffin]; grad. at H. C. 1684, ordained in Jan. 1694, and was slain by the Indians in an attack on Haverhill, 29 August, 1708, aged 46. DANIEL, EZRA, and THOMAS, were of Ipswich in 1648, and David Rolfe died in Salem, a. 1654. HENRY, one of the proprietors of Newbury in 1635. JOHN, one of the first settlers of Newbury, and a proprietor of Salisbury, was admitted freeman 1639, and died 8 Feb. 1663. His last wife, Mary Scullard, he m. in 1656.

ROMAN, JOHN, Cambridge, d. 19 Dec. 1638. The name of *Romeyn* has furnished 5 clergymen in our country, two of whom were distinguished for their rank and talents.

ROOT, JOSHUA, Salem 1637. JOHN, admitted freeman in 1669. JOSIAH, (Root or Roots,) was one of the founders of the church in Beverly 1667. RICHARD, Massachusetts, freeman

1637. THOMAS, Salem 1637, perhaps went to Northampton, where Thomas Root was one of the earliest proprietors.

ROPER, JOHN, Dedham, freeman 1641, Lancaster 1656, killed by the Indians 1676. He had sons, Ephraim and Benjamin, b. at Dedham in 1644. Ephraim, and his 2d wife, and a daughter, were killed by the Indians in 1697. His first wife was killed by them in 1675. WALTER, was born a. 1612, admitted freeman in 1642, lived in Ipswich in 1666, and afterwards in Andover, but d. in Ipswich in 1680.

ROPES, GEORGE, Salem 1637, died a. 1670, leaving a wife Mary, and sons, John and George. He is the ancestor of a numerous and respectable line of descendants.

ROSE, GEORGE, Concord, freeman 1640, died 20 May, 1649. This name is *Rowes* in the colony records. ROBERT, one of the first settlers of East-Hampton, L. I., 1650. Wood. Several of the name have grad. at N. J. and Union colleges.

ROSS, JOHN, Cambridge, d. 1640. Thomas Ross was of Cambridge in 1659. He had several sons, one or two of whom settled in Billerica, where Seeth, his widow, was killed by the Indians, 5 August, 1695.

ROSSETER, BRAY, was admitted freeman 18 May, 1631, and removed to Windsor before 1640. Bryan Rosseter, possibly the same, was one of the early physicians of N. E. and was living in Guilford, Conn., 1650. He had a son Josiah, and one of his daughters m. Rev. John Cotton, of Plymouth. Nine of the name had grad. in N. E. in 1826. ‡EDWARD, Boston, was chosen one of the asssistants, 20 Oct. 1629; came to N. E. 1630, and d. 23 Oct. that year. Prince, ii. Annals.

ROWE, JOHN, Gloucester 1664. Gibbs. MATTHEW, New-Haven 1650, had sons, John, Joseph, and Stephen. NICHOLAS, Portsmouth 1640. His wife was Elizabeth. Belknap, i. Hist. N. H. 47.

ROWELL, THOMAS, Salem 1649, d. about 1662. Felt, Annals Salem, 180. THOMAS, Boston, died 29 Dec. 1658. VALENTINE, Salisbury, resided there at an early period.

ROWLAND, HENRY, Fairfield, Conn. 1668. Several of the name, probably his descendants, have been clergymen. Eight have grad. at the N. E. colleges.

ROWLANDSON, JOSEPH, the first minister of Lancaster, son of Thomas Rowlandson, grad. at H. C. 1652, being the only graduate that year. He went to Lancaster in 1654; was ordained a. 1660; went to Weathersfield when Lancaster was destroyed by the Indians, 10 Feb. 1676, and there d. 24 Nov. 1678. Mary, his wife, a daughter of John White, published a narrative of her captivity and various removes while a prisoner. His children were, two Marys, the last b. 1665; Joseph, b. 2 March, 1661; Sarah, b. 1669. See Willard's Hist. Lancaster and his preface to the 5th edition of Mrs. Rowlandson's captivity. There is on the Essex co. files of a. 1651, a piece of satirical poetry written by him, (for which he was prosecuted) also his submission to the court for his offence of writing the same. They are printed at length in the sixth edition of Mrs. Rowlandson's Captivity. THOMAS, Ipswich, [?] whose name is *Rawlinson* in the colony records, was admitted freeman 1638, d. at Lancaster, 17 Nov. 1657, leaving several sons, of whom were the preceding, and Thomas, who was killed at Lancaster, by the Indians, 10 Feb. 1676. Willard, Hist. Lancaster.

ROWLEY, HENRY, Scituate 1634. 2 Coll. Mass. Hist Soc. iv. 239. One of the name grad. at Union College in 1823.

ROUSE, FAITHFUL, Massachusetts, freeman 1644. William Rouse d. at Boston in 1705, æ. 65. Peter P. Rouse grad. at Union College in 1818.

ROYAL, WILLIAM, North-Yarmouth, Me., was born 1640, d. 7 Nov. 1724, in his 85th year. Hon. Isaac Royal, his son, resided at Antigua, W. I., near 40 years, returned to N. E. in 1737, and d. 7 June, 1739, æ. 67. A Mr. Royal, or Ryall was a patentee of some part of Maine. See Winthrop, i. 304.

RUCK, *JOHN, Salem, son of Thomas, was admitted freeman 1665, representative 1685. Peter Ruck, perhaps a son, grad. at H. C. 1685. SAMUEL, Boston 1657. THOMAS, Salem, freeman and member of the church 1640, died in 1670, leaving a widow and children. Felt, Annals, 239.

RUDDOCK, JOHN, Sudbury, freeman 1640, was one of the first settlers of Marlborough, one of the selectmen, town clerk 1669, and deacon of the church. Worcester Magazine, ii. 185. JOLLIFF, or JOYLIFFE, d. at Boston 1649.

RUGG, JOHN, Lancaster 1654, freeman 1669, whose widow was killed by the Indians, 1697. Joseph, (probably a son) his wife, and 3 children were killed at the same time. Amos Willard Rugg, a descendant, grad. at H. C. 1805.

RUGGLES, GEORGE, was admitted freeman 1634. His son Samuel was born at Braintree, 1648. JEFFREY, came from Sudbury to N. E. in 1630, and died the same year. Winthrop, i. Hist. N. E. 47, 379. JOHN, Boston, came to N. E. 1630, admitted freeman 1632, had a daughter, who d. in Jan. 1631. Prince, ii. Annals, 17, 69. ||JOHN, Roxbury freeman 1637, member of the ar. co. 1646, died about 1658, leaving sons, John, freeman 1663; Thomas; Samuel, a captain, who died 15 Aug. 1692, and who had sons, Samuel, Joseph, Thomas, and others. *JOHN, Roxbury, freeman 1656, representative 1658, 1660, and 1661, had sons, John, b. 1651; John, 2d, 1653; Thomas, 1655; Samuel, 1657. SAMUEL, Charlestown 1647. THOMAS, Roxbury, freeman 1639, d. 16 Nov. 1644.

RUMBALL, DANIEL, was born in 1600, and was of Salem in 1665. 2 Coll. Mass. Hist. Soc. viii. 106.

RUSH, JASPER, Dorchester, admitted to the church and freeman in 1644.

RUSS, JOHN, Newbury 1635, [Coffin] went to Andover, and d. 1692. [Abbot.] His sons were, John, b. 24 June, 1642; Jonathan; Thomas; Josiah; and Joseph.

RUSSELL, DANIEL, a preacher, and a native of Charlestown, grad. in1669 at H. C., of which he was a fellow, and was invited in 1678 to settle as the minister of Charlestown, [See 3 Coll. Mass. Hist. Soc. i. 261] but he died 4 Jan. 1679. The name of Russell has ever been distinguished in the annals of Massachusetts, and has prevailed in all the N. E. states. Forty-seven had grad. at the N. E. colleges, in 1826, of whom 13 have been clergymen. GEORGE, Hingham 1636; Scituate between 1636 and 1657. 2 Coll. Mass. Hist. Soc. iv. 240. The George Russel who was at Boston in 1680, is supposed by Hutchinson to have been a younger brother of the celebrated Lord William Russel, who was beheaded in Lincoln's Inn Fields, 21 July, 1683, æ. 42. ‡*JAMES, Charlestown, son of the Hon. Richard Russell, was born 4 Oct. 1640, admitted freeman 1668, elected representative 1679, assistant from 1680 to 1686, counsellor under the new charter 1692, was a judge, and treasurer of Massachusetts, d. 28 April, 1709, æ. 68. His wife was Maybel, daughter of Gov. Haynes. JOHN, Charlestown and Boston, finally settled in Boston, where he became the first minister of the Baptist church, 28 July, 1679. He d. 24 Dec. 1680. According to Benedict, the Russells of Providence and its vicinity are descended from him. JOHN, Woburn, may be the one admitted freeman in 1644. He is styled in Woburn records, "the Anabaptist," and d. 1 June, 1676. JOHN, Cambridge 1636, may be the one called sen., and admitted freeman in 1681. JOHN, Roxbury, was admitted freeman 1654. JOHN, New-Haven, died 1681. Dodd, 146, 162. JOHN, minister of Weathersfield, Conn., grad. at H. C. 1645, [W. Winthrop] removed to Hadley in 1659, and was there installed, and d. 10 Nov. 1692. It was in his house in Hadley that Whalley and Goffe, two of the judges who sentenced Charles I to death, were for a long time concealed, and where they are supposed to have died. A Philip Russell was of Hadley in 1664. JONATHAN, minister of Barnstable, son of the preceding, grad. at H. C. 1675, was ordained 19 Sept. 1683, d. 21 Feb. 1711, æ. 56. His son Jonathan, who grad. at Y. C. 1708, succeeded his father in the ministry, 29 Oct. 1712. John Russell, H. C. 1704, a physician of Barnstable, was probably another son. Lothrop and John Russell, graduates of H. C. in 1743 and 1751, were of Barnstable. NOADIAH, minister of Middletown, Conn., grad. at H. C. in 1681, was ordained 24 Oct. 1688, and died 3 Dec. 1713, aged 55. He was a schoolmaster in Ipswich before he settled at Middletown. RALPH, New-Haven, d. 1679. Dodd, 146, 162. ‡‖*RICHARD, Charlestown, came from Herefordshire, England, with Maud, his wife, a. 1640. He was elected representative 1642, 12 years, and speaker of the house in 1654, 1656, and 1658; member of the ar. co. 1644; assistant from 1659 to 1675, 16 years, and many years treasurer of the colony. He d. 14 May, 1676, æ. 65. Hon. Chambers Russell, judge of the supreme court of Massachusetts, son of Hon. Daniel Russell, was one of his descendants. He grad. at H. C. 1731, and d. 24 Nov. 1767, æ. 54. Hon. Thomas Russell, of Boston, who d. 1796, was also a descendant. ROBERT Andover, d. 1710, æ. 80, having five sons. *SAMUEL*, minister of Branford, Conn., son of Rev. John Russell, of Hadley, grad. at H. C. 1681, was ordained in March, 1687, and d. 25 June, 1731, æ. 71. WILLIAM, Cambridge 1645, who, with his wife Martha, was member of the church in 1658. His sons were, Joseph, b. in England ; Benjamin ; John, b. 1645 ; Philip ; William ; Jason, b. 1658 ; Jesse, b. 1660.

RUST, HENRY, Hingham 1635, was admitted freeman in 1638. [Lincoln, Hist. Hingham, 51.] Rev. Henry Rust, H. C. 1707, was ordained the first minister of Stratham, N. H., in 1718, and died 20 March, 1749, æ. 63. *NATHANIEL, Ipswich, freeman 1674. was representative in 1690 and 1691. There was a Dr. Rust of Ipswich about the middle of the last century.

RUTH, VINCENT, Massachusetts, was admitted freeman in 1645. Savage, ii. Winthrop, 374.

RUTTER, JOHN, Sudbury 1642, whose son John, born about 1649, is probably the same who was of Marlborough in 1689, and mentioned in the Revo. in N. E. Justified, p. 30. Micah M. Rutter, of East-Sudbury, general of the 2d brigade, 3d division of Mass. militia, is probably a descendant.

RYDEAT, JOHN. (See REDIAT.)

SABIN, BENJAMIN, Rehoboth, 1673, had a son Benjamin, b. 1673. Rev. *John Sabin*, Brown College 1797, was ordained minister of Fitzwilliam, N. H., 6 March, 1805.

SACKETT, SIMON, Cambridge 1632, where it is supposed he died, as a widow Sackett is afterwards mentioned. SIMON, was of Springfield, a. 1654. JOHN, an early proprietor of Westfield. John Sackett was of Northampton in 1660. Rev. Richard Sacket grad. at Y. C. 1709.

SADLER, ANTHONY, Salisbury, freeman 1639, was drowned 23 April, 1650. An Anthony Sadler, who m. a daughter of John Cheney, had a son Abiel, b. 2 Nov. 1650. JOHN, admitted freeman 1642, was probably of Gloucester, and one of the earliest proprietors of that town. RICHARD, Lynn, freeman 1638, came from Worcester, in England, settled at Lynn 1636, where he was appointed clerk of the writs in 1641. Richard Sadler, perhaps his son, came also to N. E. but returned home in 1647, and was ordained at Whixal Chapel, 16 May, 1648, from whence he removed to Ludlow, in Shropshire, where he was ejected after the restoration, and died at Whixal, 1675, æ. 55. Calamy. E. Winslow.

SAFFERY, SOLOMON, was a land surveyor as early as 1642. Hutchinson, i. Hist. Mass. 191.

SAFFORD, THOMAS, Ipswich 1648, d. 1667, leaving a widow, son Joseph, and three daughters. JOHN, was of Ipswich 1665.

SAFFYN, ‡*JOHN, Scituate 1650, [Coffin] Boston, freeman 1671, representative 1684 to 1686, 3 years, counsellor under the charter of William and Mary in 1692 ; d. at Bristol, R. I., 29 July, 1701. 3 Coll. Mass. Hist. Soc. i. 137.

SALE, EDWARD, Marblehead, freeman 1637. Winthrop, ii. Hist. N. E. 349, where the name is *Seale*. MANUS, Charlestown,

whose name is *Sally* in colony records, was admitted freeman **1647.**
Ephraim Sale was member of ar. co. **1674.**

SALISBURY, JOHN, Swanzey, one of the first victims in Philip's war, was killed, 24 June, 1675. Swanzey Records.

SALLOWS, MICHAEL, Salem 1635. Thomas, perhaps his son, died a. 1663.

SALMON, DANIEL, Lynn 1634, was born a. 1610, was a Pequot soldier. He had a son Daniel. Lewis. THOMAS, Northampton 1659.

SALTER, WILLIAM, Boston, admitted member of the church 1635, freeman 1636, had sons, Peleg, b. 1635; Jabez, born 1647, member of the ar. co. 1674; Elisha, b. 1653. Savage, i. Winth. N. E. 248. ii. 216. THEOPHILUS, Ipswich 1648, Salem 1654. Felt, Annals Salem, 189. Rev. Richard Salter, D. D. grad. at H. C. 1739.

SALTONSTALL, ⟨GURDON, minister of New-London and governour of Connecticut, was son of Col. Nathaniel, and great-grandson of Sir Richard Saltonstall, and was born at Haverhill, 27 March, 1666, grad. at H. C. 1684, ordained 25 Nov. 1691 ; elected governour in Jan. 1708; died 20 Sept. 1724, æ. 59. His wife, Jerusha, who d. at Boston, 25 July, 1697, was daughter of William Whittingham of Boston, and their descendants still remain in New-London, and are also in New-York. Allen, Biog. Dict. ‖HENRY, son of Sir Richard Saltonstall, grad. at H. C. 1642, was member of the ar. co. 1639, went to England, and from thence to Holland in 1644 ; received the degree of M. D. from the University of Padua, in Italy, Oct. 1649, and a degree at Oxford, 24 June, 1652. Wood, ii. Fasti Oxon, 100. Whitman. ‡*NATHANIEL, Haverhill, son of Richard, and grandson of Sir Richard, was born a. 1639, grad. at H. C. 1659, took the oath of freeman 1665, was representative 1666, 1669 to 1671, four years, captain 1670, elected assistant 1679 to 1682, and again from 1689 to 1692 ; colonel of the Essex regiment, counsellor under the charter of William and Mary, died 21 May, 1707. His wife was a daughter of Rev. John Ward, by whom he left 3 sons, Gurdon, already noticed, Richard, and Nathaniel, both H. C. 1695, and one daughter, Elizabeth, wife of Mr. Denison and Rev. Roland Cotton. (See COTTON.) Richard, the 2d son, resided in Haverhill; had 2 sons, who were educated at H. C., 1. Richard, b. 14 June, 1703, grad. 1722, a judge of the superiour court, who died 20 Oct. 1756, æ. 53, leaving 3 sons and 2 daughters, and 2. Nathaniel, a merchant, who grad. in 1727, and d. young. Richard, one of the 3 sons of Judge Richard, was born 5 April, 1732, grad. at H. C. 1754, was a colonel in the old French war ; became a loyalist in the time of the revolution, went to England and d. at Kensington, 6 Oct. 1785, aged 53. Nathaniel, his brother, a physician of Haverhill, was b. 10 Feb. 1746, grad. at H. C. 1766, d. 10 Feb. 1796, aged 50, [Winthrop, MS Catalogue] leaving 3 sons, one of whom is the Hon. Leverett Saltonstall, an eminent counsellor at law of Salem, Mass., who graduated at H. C.

1802. 2 Coll. Mass. Hist. Soc. iv. 159—167. ||PETER, probably a son of Sir Richard, was a member of the ar. co. in 1644. Whitman. ‡SIR RICHARD, son of Samuel, and grandson of Gilbert Saltonstall, esq., of Halifax, in Yorkshire, came to N. E. in 1630, and resided a short time at Watertown, from whence he returned to England in 1631. He was the first named associate to the six original patentees of Massachusetts, and one of the first assistants, and present at their first court, 23 Aug. 1630. He lived until 1658, when his will was made, and probably some time afterwards. 2 Coll. Mass. Hist. Soc. iv. 154. He had sons, Richard, Henry, Samuel, Robert, Peter. He had also two daughters, who, in 1644, resided in the family of the Earl of Warwick, and Lady Manchester. MS Letter of Rosamond Saltonstall, 1644. ‡*RICHARD, son of the preceding, was born in 1610, came to N. E. 1630, and settled at Ipswich. He was admitted freeman 1631, representative in 1635 and 1636, elected assistant 1637 to 1649, and 1664; went to England 1672, returned in 1680, and again elected assistant 1680, 1681, and 1682, went to England in 1683, and remained there. He d. at Hulme, 29 April, 1694, aged 84. He left an estate in Yorkshire. Ibid., 137. ||ROBERT, son of Sir Richard, and probably the same named by Hutchinson, [i. Hist. Mass. 22, 98] was a member of the ar. co. in 1638. SAMUEL, Watertown 1642, son of Sir Richard, d. 21 Jan. 1696. In the archives of the Amer. Antiquarian Soc. at Worcester, is a letter from his sister, Rosamond Saltonstall, dated at Warwick-house, 26 April, 1644, in which she speaks of his being "likely to be a *constant settler*" at Watertown.

SAMS, JOHN, received his education in N. E. and went to England, and was the successor of Rev. John Owen, D. D., at Coggeshall, in Essex, from whence he was ejected, and died a 1675. Calamy, ii. Account, 303. THOMAS, Salem 1638, Marblehead 1648. One of the name of Sams graduated at Brown College in 1806.

✗ SAMPSON, ||ROBERT, member of the ar. co. 1639. HENRY, Plymouth 1623, married Ann Plumer, and settled in Duxbury. Davis, Morton's Memo. 377. RICHARD, Boston, freeman 1674. Seven of the name had grad. at the N. E. colleges in 1828.

SANBORN, JOHN, STEPHEN, and WILLIAM, were of Hampton in 1643. Their descendants are numerous in N. Hampshire, where is a large and flourishing township, settled principally by the name, and which is called Sanbornton.

SANDERBANK, JOHN, Massachusetts, freeman 1643.

SANDERSON, ROBERT, Watertown 1642, had son Joseph, b. 1642. A Deacon Robert Sanderson d. at Boston, 7 Oct. 1696.

SANDEN, ARTHUR, Marblehead 1648.

SANDYS, HENRY, a merchant of Boston, admitted freeman 1640, had a son John, b. in 1646. A Henry Sands is mentioned as of Rowley in 1643.

SANFORD, JOHN, Boston, admitted freeman in 1632, under the name of *Sampeford* in colony records, and in Prince, ii. Annals, 69; was disarmed 1637 [Savage, ii. Winth. N. E. 248]; went to R.

I., and was secretary and treasurer of that colony. Sixteen of the name had grad. at the N. E. colleges in 1828. JOHN, freeman 1670. JAMES, Boston, d. 2 Nov. 1661. ◊PELEG, Rhode-Island, was governour of the colony 1680, 1681, and 1682. RICHARD, Boston, member of the church 1640, freeman 1641. ||ROBERT, Boston 1650, freeman 1652, member of the ar. co. 1661. THOMAS, whose name is spelled *Samford*, was admitted freeman in 1637. ||THOMAS, member of the ar. co. 1666.

SARGENT, WILLIAM, Ipswich 1634, afterwards of Newbury, Salisbury, and of Amesbury, where Mr. Coffin says he died. Twenty-one of the name of Sargeant and Sargent had grad. in N. E. in 1828. *WILLIAM, Gloucester, representative 1671, 1690, and 1691. WILLIAM, Charlestown 1642. (See SERGEANT.)

SAUNDERS, DANIEL, Cambridge, d. 27 Feb. 1640. This name, which is also written *Sanders*, has furnished 8 graduates at the N. E. colleges. JOHN, Weymouth, was the overseer of Weston's plantation in 1623. Prince, i. Annals, 127. I. Mather, Ind. Wars from 1614 to 1675, 12. Morton's Memo., 41. JOHN, Ipswich 1634, probably the freeman under 1636. There were two others of the name of John Saunders admitted freemen in 1640 and 1650, one of whom was of Braintree, and m. Mary Munjoy in 1657. *JOHN, Newbury 1645, born a. 1625 [Coffin] ; representative in 1685, had daughters, Sarah and Mary, b. in 1646 and 1649. MARTIN, Braintree, freeman 1640, whose wife, Rachel, d. Sept. 1651 ; m. in 1654, Elizabeth Bancroft, and in 1655, Lydia Hardier. ||ROBERT, Cambridge 1636, member of the ar. co. 1638, freeman 1639. WILLIAM, a carpenter of Massachusetts 1636. Winthrop, ii. Hist. N. E. 347.

SARTELL, RICHARD, Watertown. (See SAWTELL.)

SAVAGE, *||EPHRAIM, Boston, son of Major Thomas Savage, was b. 20 July, 1645, grad. at H. C. 1662, admitted freeman 1672, member of the ar. co. 1674, captain of the same in 1683. He served in the expedition to Canada in 1690, was representative of Boston, 1703 to 1708, and 1710, seven years. He d. in the winter of 1730—1, leaving daughters, Sarah, Mary, and Hannah, who all married. John, his son, was born 30 Nov. 1674, and grad. at H. C. 1694. ||HABIJAH, Boston, eldest brother of the preceding, was born 1 August, 1638, graduated at Harvard College 1659, admitted freeman 1665, member of the ar. co. 1665, and was a captain of the militia, and d. in 1668 or 1669. He m. Hannah, a daughter of Hon. Edward Tyng, 8 May, 1661, and his children were, 1. Joseph, b. 15 Aug. 1662 ; 2. Thomas, b. 17 Aug. 1664 ; 3. and 4. Hannah and Mary, (gemini) b. 27 Aug. 1667. HENRY, Haverhill 1644. [Coffin.] John Savage was of Portsmouth 1732. ‡||*THOMAS, Boston, came to N. E. as early as 1635, admitted freeman 1636, member of ar. co. 1637, and its captain in 1651. He represented Boston in 1654, and the 8 succeeding years ; Hingham in 1663; Andover in 1671, 1677, and 1678, and was speaker of the house in 1659 and 1671. He was a major, and at one time was commander-in-chief of the forces in the early part of Philip's War 1675 ; was elected assistant in 1680 and 1681, and died 14 Feb. 1682, æ. 75. By his 1st wife, Faith, (who d. 20 Feb. 1652) daughter of William and the celebrated Ann Hutchinson, he had seven children ; and by his 2d, Mary, (whom he m. 15 Sept. 1652) daughter of Rev. Z. Symmes, he had eleven. His 18 children were, 1. Habijah, already noticed ; 2. Thomas (in next section) ; 3. Hannah, b. 1643 ; 4. Ephraim, above noticed ; 5. Mary, b. 1647 ; 6. Dyonisia, b. 1649 ; 7. Perez, born 17 Feb. 1652, a lieutenant in Philip's War, and honourably named by Hubbard, pp. 19, 40, and who died unmarried, in Mackanosse, in Barbary, 1694 ; 8. Sarah, b. 1653 ; 9. Richard, b. 1654 ; 10. Samuel, b. 1656 ; 11. Samuel, 2d, b. 1657 ; 12. Zechariah, b. 1658 ; 13. Ebenezer, born 22 May, 1660, member of the ar. co. 1682, m. Martha Allen ; 14. John, b. 1661 ; 15. Benjamin, b. October, 1662, member of the ar. co. 1682 ; 16. Arthur, b. 1664 ; 17. Elizabeth, b. 1667 ; 18. Elizabeth, 2d, b. 1669. The 9, 10, 12, 14, 17, and 18 died in infancy or young. Eleven of the name, and all of them descendants of Major Savage, had grad. at H. C. in 1828. See Whitman, Hist. Ar. Co. 40. Savage, i. Winthrop, 248. ii. 53, 216. Hubbard. Hutchinson. Alden. ||THOMAS, Boston, second son of the preceding, was b. 28 May, 1640, became member of the ar. co. in 1665, was an officer in Sir William Phipps' expedition to Canada, 1691, and a lieutenant-colonel of the Suffolk regiment. He d. 2 July, 1705, æ. 65. He m. Elizabeth, daughter of Joshua Scottow, of Boston, by whom he had, 1. Thomas, b. 20 July, 1665 ; 2. Thomas, 2d, b. 2 August, 1668 ; 3. Scottow, b. 4 Feb. 1671 ; 4. Habijah, b. 10 Sept. 1674 ; 5. Elizabeth, b. 4 Aug. 1677 ; 6. Arthur, b. 29 March, 1680 ; 7. Faith, b. 11 Aug. 1682 ; 8. Faith, 2d, b. 3 Oct. 1683 ; 9. Lydia, b. 6 Sept. 1686. Habijah, his 4th son, grad. at H. C. 1695, was a lieutenant-colonel, and was representative of Boston three years, and d. 16 Sept. 1746, æ. 72. Thomas, 2d son of lieut. col. Habijah, was born 5 Jan. 1711, died 19 Dec. 1760, and was grandfather of the learned and distinguished antiquary of New-England, whose valuable notes in his edition of Winthrop's Hist. N. E. have been so often cited in this work.

SAVILL, EDWARD, Weymouth, whose son Obadiah was b. in 1640. WILLIAM, Braintree 1640, had sons, John, born 22 April, 1642, freeman 1684 ; Samuel, b. 30 Oct. 1643 ; Benjamin, b. 28 Oct. 1645 ; William, b. 17 July, 1652.

SAVORY, ANTHONY and THOMAS, came from Slade, in Devonshire, before 1640. Anthony settled near Merrimack River. There was a Robert Savory of Newbury 1657.

SAWIN, THOMAS, was admitted freeman 1652.

SAWTELL, RICHARD, Watertown 1639, had a son Jonathan born in 1639, freeman 1671, one of the early settlers of Groton, as were also Obadiah, Richard, and Zechariah Sawtell, who might be sons of Richard. THOMAS, Massachusetts, was admitted freeman in 1649.

SAWYER, EDWARD, Rowley 1643. Coffin. HENRY, York 1675. Hubbard. THOMAS, Lancaster, 1647, whose wife was Mary, had sons, Thomas, Ephraim, Joshua, James, Caleb, Nathaniel, and several daughters. WILLIAM, Salem and Newbury, had sons, John, b. 24 August, 1645, freeman 1681 ; Samuel, b. 22 Sept. 1648, freeman 1673 ; and several daughters. Twelve of the name are on the catalogues of Harvard and Yale.

SAXTON, GILES, came to N. E. as early as 1630, was admitted freeman 18 May, 1631. If he was the minister of Scituate, he came from Yorkshire, and according to Mather returned to England in his old age.

SAYLE, WILLIAM, a captain, and sometime governour of Bermuda, was in Boston in 1646, and the same year sailed for England, where he was in 1647, but came over again in 1648. Winslow, N. E. Salamander Discovered, 17. Winthrop, ii. 334.

SAYRE, JOB, Lynn 1635, went to Long-Island. Lewis. THOMAS, Lynn, 1635, was one of the grantees of South-Hampton, L. I. 1640. This name exists in N. J., where several have grad. at its college. Ebenezer Sayer grad. at H. C. 1768.

SAYS, THOMAS, Massachusetts, freeman 1639. Perhaps *Sayre*, above.

SAYWARD, HENRY, Hampton 1646. Coffin.

SAYWELL, DAVID, Massachusetts, freeman 1666.

SCADLOCK, WILLIAM, Saco, whose name is put *Chaddock* in Sullivan, p. 218, 219, died in 1662. Geo. Folsom.

SCALES, JOHN, Rowley 1648, was a member of the church before 1667. THOMAS, Massachusetts, was admitted freeman 1640. WILLIAM, Rowley 1640. Coffin. Four of the name, viz : James ; his son Stephen, William, and Abraham, grad. at H. C. in 1733, 1763, 1771, and 1800.

SCAMMON, RICHARD, Portsmouth 1642, m. Prudence, only daughter of William Waldron, had son William, b. in 1664. WILLIAM, Boston 1640.

SCARBOROUGH, ||JOHN, Roxbury, freeman 1640 ; member of ar. co. 1643, was killed by the discharge of a gun, 9 June, 1645. Samuel Scarborough died at Roxbury, of the small pox, in 1721.

SCARLET, JOHN, Boston 1653, had a son John born in 1657. Samuel Scarlet was of Boston in 1665.

SCOFIELD, RICHARD, Ipswich 1648. Frederick, Azariah, and Jared Scofield grad. at Y. C. in 1801. Several of the name *Scovel, Scovell,* and *Scovil,* have grad. at the N. E. colleges.

SCOTCHFORD, JOHN, Concord 1635, was town clerk, m. Susanna Meriam, and d. 10 June, 1696, without issue. Shattuck.

SCOTT, BENJAMIN, Cambridge and Braintree, had sons, b. in the last place, John, b. 1640 ; Joseph, b. 1644 ; Benjamin, born 1646 ; John, 2d, b. 1648. A Benjamin Scott d. at Rowley in 1671. EDWARD, Hadley 1662. Coffin. JOHN, Massachusetts, was admitted freeman in 1643. JOHN, whose name is spelled *Skot* in the colony records, was admitted freeman in 1639. RICHARD, Boston, a shoemaker, was admitted member of the church 28 Aug. 1634. Savage, i. Winth. N. E. 151, 293. ||ROBERT, Boston, freeman 1637, member of the ar. co. 1637, had sons, Nathaniel, b. 1638 ; Redemption, b. 1652 ; Eleazar, b. 1654. ROGER, Lynn

1642. Lewis. THOMAS, Cambridge 1635, probably removed to Ipswich and d. 1654. His son Thomas, of Ipswich in 1648, and of Stamford in 1654, d. 1657. Coffin. Felt.

SCOTTOW, ||JOSHUA, Boston, freeman 1639, member of ar. co. 1645; its ensign in 1657, a captain, and the author of two tracts published in Boston 1691 and 1694. He d. in 1698. Of his seven children noted in the records, 4 are named in his will, viz.: Thomas, b. 30 June, 1659, grad. at H. C. 1677 ; Elizabeth, wife of Lieut.-col. Thomas Savage ; Rebecca, who m. B. Blackman, and Mary, wife of Capt. Samuel Checkley. *Scotts* is the name of a place in Norfolk co., England. 2 Coll. Mass. Hist. Soc. iv. 101. Mr. Felt gives the name of Sarah as the one who m. Mr. Blackman. THOMAS, brother of the preceding, was a joiner, lived in Boston ; was admitted freeman 1639, and member of the church. Ibid. Snow, Hist. Boston, 116.

SCRANTON, JOHN, Guilford 1650. 1 Coll. Mass. Hist. Soc. x., where the name is *Scrantom*. DENNIS, who is mentioned in Hutchinson's Coll. p. 335, was probably of Connecticut.

SCRUGGS, *THOMAS, Salem, freeman and representative in 1635 ; soon after banished from Massachusetts. Felt, MS Annals. WILLIAM, Salem, died a. 1654. Ibid.

SCUDDER, JOHN, Salem 1647. THOMAS, Salem, died a. 1658. This has been a common name in N. J.

SCULLARD, SAMUEL, Newbury 1637, d. April, 1647, leaving issue.

SEABURY, JOHN, Boston, had a son Samuel, born 1640. SAMUEL, Duxbury, one of the early settlers, and a chirurgeon, might have lived in Weymouth in 1660. He died in 1680. Rev. Samuel Seabury grad. at H. C. 1724.

SEAGAR, THOMAS, Newbury 1637.

SEARCH, JOHN, Boston, freeman 1642. Anna, his wife, d. 11 May, 1674, æ. 85.

SEARLE, ANDREW, Massachusetts, was born in England, a. 1616. William Searle was of Ipswich in 1667. Ephraim Searle was admitted freeman 1671.

SEARS, RICHARD, Salem 1638. THOMAS, Newbury, m. Mary Hilton 1656, and d. 26 May, 1661.

SEAVER, ROBERT, Roxbury, freeman 1637, had sons, Shubael, b. 1639, who was living in 1724 ; Caleb, b. 1641, d. at Boston, 6 March, 1714. Nicholas Sever, of this family, grad. at H. C. 1701, was the minister of Dover, N. H., from 1711 to 1715, removed to Plymouth co. and was judge of the court of common pleas ; died 7 April, 1764, aged 84. His son, Hon. William Sever, A. A. S., who grad. at H. C. 1745, was judge of probate in Plymouth co., and d. in June, 1809, æ. 81.

SEAVEY, WILLIAM, Portsmouth 1631 ; selectman in 1657. Capt. William Seavey a patriot of the revolution, d. at Rye, N. H., March, 1829, æ. 84.

SECCOMBE, RICHARD, came from the west of England, and settled at Lynn as early as 1660, and d. 1694. His children were,

Noah, Richard, and Susanna. He is the ancestor of Rev. John, of Harvard, Ms., H. C. 1728, Rev. Joseph, of Kingston, N. H., H. C. 1731, and of John Secombe, esq., of Amherst, N. H. Seccombe is the name of a place in the Isle of Purbeck, on the coast of Dorsetshire.

SEDGWICK, ||*ROBERT, Charlestown, freeman 1637, representative and member of the ar. co. 1637, captain of the ar. co. 1640, and the 4th major-general of Massachusetts. He went to England, where, it is said, some of his descendants reside, and was employed by Cromwell in 1654. He was engaged in the great expedition against the Spanish West-Indies, when Jamaica was taken. There he d. 24 May, 1656, having, as appears from Thurloe's State Papers, v. 138, 154, just been advanced to the rank of major-general by the protector. William and Robert Sedgwick, probably his sons, were members of the ar. co. in 1666 and 1674. One of them on returning from Jamaica, which place he had visited, died on his passage, and was buried at Boston. Benjamin, one of his descendants, was father to Hon. Theodore Sedgwick, judge of the superior court of Mass., a native of Hartford, b. in May, 1746, and died at Boston, 24 Jan. 1813. He left a son, Theodore Sedgwick, esq., and a daughter, who is the lady of so much literary celebrity. Hutchinson, i. Hist. Mass. 169. Savage, ii. Winthrop, 247. Lord, ii. Lempriere, 612. Edwards Hist. West-Indies.

SEDLEY, JAMES, Weymouth, at an early period.

SEELEY, ROBERT, Watertown, freeman 1631, was perhaps the Lieut. Siely, or Seeley, in the Pequot war. I. Mather, 42. Capt. Sieley of Stratford was killed in battle with the Indians, 19 Dec. 1675. Hutchinson, i. Hist. Mass. 271. The name of *Seele* is common in Bristol co. Mass.

SEERS, JOHN, Woburn, was b. 1613, admitted freeman 1641.

SELLICK, DAVID, Boston, had sons, David, Jonathan, and John, b. in 1638, 1641, and 1643.

SELWYN, HENRY, minister of Brooklyn, L. I. was installed 1660, resided at New-Amsterdam ; went to Holland, it is said, in 1664, but probably returned.

SENDALL, SAMUEL, Boston, freeman 1645,'lived in Newbury in 1653.

SENSION, MATTHIAS, Massachusetts, freeman 1634. Savage, ii. Winthrop, 364.

SERGEANT, WILLIAM, Charlestown, freeman 1638, perhaps the preacher at Malden, mentioned by Johnson, Hist. N. E. 211. He had several children born at Charlestown as early as 1644. ‡PETER, one of the council of safety 1689, and one of the first counsellors under the new charter 1692. Madam Sergeant, perhaps his wife, d. 10 Nov. 1700. Interleaved Almanack.

SESSIONS, ALEXANDER, Andover, freeman 1677, had sons, John, born 1674 ; Alexander ; Timothy ; Samuel ; Nehemiah ; Josiah, and Joseph. Abbot, Hist. Andover, 36. Hon. Darius Sessions, Y. C. 1737, was lieutenant-governour of R. I.

SEVER, ROBERT, Roxbury. (See SEAVER.)

SEVERANCE, JOHN, Ipswich 1636, was a proprietor and inhabitant of Salisbury in 1640, where he d. 9 April, 1682.

SEVERENE, ||JOHN, Boston, freeman 1637, member of ar. co. 1642.

SEWALL, ||DAVID, member of the ar. co. 1664. Whitman, 158. HENRY, Newbury and Rowley, son of Henry Sewall, the mayor of Coventry, in England, 1606, [Dugdale, Antiq. Warw.] was baptized 8 April, 1576, came to N. E. and settled first at Newbury, thence removed to Rowley, and d. there in March, 1656. *HENRY, son of the preceding, came to N. E. in 1634, freeman 1637, settled at Newbury, returned to England, a. 1647, resided at Warwick, Bishop-Stoke, and at Baddesly, of which place he was the minister [Hutchinson, i. Hist. Mass. 455]; returned to N. E. in 1659, sent for his family which came over in 1661, was representative 1661, 1663, 1668, and 1670. He died at Newbury, 16 May, 1700, æ. 86. He m. Jane, daughter of Stephen and Alice Dummer, 25 March, 1646, by whom, (who d. 13 Jan. 1701) he had, 1. Hannah, b. at Tunworth, England, 10 May, 1649, m. Jacob Tappan, of Newbury, and d. 12 Nov. 1699; 2. Samuel (see next article); 3. John, b. 10 Oct. 1654, m. 27 Oct. 1674, Hannah Fessenden, and d. 8 Aug. 1699; 4. Stephen, b. 19 Aug. 1657, m. 13 June, 1682, Margaret, daughter of Rev. Jonathan Mitchel, and d. 17 Oct. 1725; 5. Jane, b. 25 Oct. 1659, m. 24 Sept. 1677, Moses Gerrish, and d. 29 Jan. 1717; 6. Ann, b. 3 Sept. 1662, m. in 1676, William Longfellow; 7. Mehitabel, b. 8 May, 1665, m. William Moody, and d. 8 Aug. 1702; 8. Dorothy, b. 29 Oct. 1668, m. Ezekiel Northend, of Rowley, 10 Sept. 1691. The 3, 4, and 5, were b. in Baddesly, the 6, 7, and 8, in Newbury. From John, the 2d son, descended Hon. David Sewall, LL. D., H. C. 1755, Professor Stephen Sewall, H. C. 1761, and William B. Sewall, H. C. 1803. From Stephen, the 3d son, Mitchel Sewall, H. C. 1718, Chief Justice Stephen Sewall, H. C. 1721, Jonathan Sewall, H. C. 1748, and the late Jonathan Mitchel Sewall, of Portsmouth, derived their descent. ‡||SAMUEL, Boston, son of the preceding, was born at Bishop-Stoke, in England, 28 March, 1652, came to N. E. in 1661, grad. at H. C. 1671, was admitted freeman 1678, became a member of the ar. co. 1679, of which he was captain in 1701. He was elected an assistant 1684 to 1686, and again from 1689 to 1691, six years; was one of the first counsellors under the new charter 1692, and continued in office until 1725, and was the last survivor of the first named counsellors. He was appointed judge of the superiour court 1692; chief justice in 1718; judge of prob. in 1715, and d. at Boston, 30 Jan. 1730, in his 78th year. He m. 28 Feb. 1676, Hannah, only child of Hon. John Hull, with whom he received, it is said, £30,000 in N. E. shillings. He had 14 children, of whom 6 arrived to adult age, viz.: 1. Samuel, b. 11 June, 1678, m. Rebecca, daughter of Gov. Joseph Dudley, and settled in Brookline, d. 27 Feb. 1751, æ. 72; 2. Hannah, b. 1680, d. unmarried; 3. Elizabeth, b. 29 Dec. 1681, m. Grove Hirst, esq., 17 Oct. 1700, and d. 10 July, 1716; 4. Joseph, D. D., b. 15 Aug. 1688, grad. at H. C. 1707, ordained as colleague pastor with Rev. E. Pemberton, of the Old South, Boston, 16 Sept. 1713, d. 27 June, 1769, in his 81st year, leaving son Samuel, b. 2 May, 1715, grad. at H. C. 1733, d. 19 Jan. 1771, the father of the late Samuel Sewall, LL. D., the third chief justice of the supreme court of Massachusetts, of the name of Sewall, who was b. at Boston, 11 Dec. 1757, grad. at H. C. 1776, d. at Wiscasset, Me., 7 June, 1814, whose sons, Rev. Samuel Sewall, of Burlington, and Rev Edmund Quincy Sewall, of Boston, grad. at H. C. 1804 and 1815 ; 5. Mary, born 28 Oct. 1691, m. Samuel Gerrish, of Boston, and d. 16 Nov. 1710 ; 6. Judith, b. 2 Jan. 1702, m. Rev. William Cooper, of Boston, 12 May, 1720, and d. 23 Dec. 1720.

SEWARD, EDWARD, Ipswich 1637, whose name is also spelled *Sayward.* ROBERT, Portsmouth 1649.

SEWELL, THOMAS, Massachusetts 1649. Winthrop [ii. Hist. N. E. 184] gives an account of a Nathaniel Sewell who was murdered. There appears to have been an Edward Sewell living in Exeter in 1683.

SEXTON, GILES, came from Yorkshire and was minister of Scituate. (See SAXTON.) THOMAS, Boston, had sons, Thomas, b. 1647 ; Samuel, b. 1653, d. at Boston 1693 ; Joseph, born 1656. James Sexton was of Westfield in 1686.

SEYLE, or SAYLE, FRANCIS, Massachuestts, admitted freeman 1640. WILLIAM. (See SAYLE.)

SHAFFLIN, MICHAEL, Salem. (See CHAFFLIN.)

SHAPLEIGH, ALEXANDER, Kittery, a. 1660. Only one of this name, Samuel, H. C. 1789, has grad. in N. E. NICHOLAS, Boston 1645, who had a son Benjamin b. that year. He may have removed to Kittery as early as 1652, and have been the Major Shapleigh, mentioned by Hubbard, Ind. Wars.

SHARP, ROBERT, Braintree 1642, d. at Roxbury, July, 1653. His son John, b. 12 March, 1643, was probably the lieutenant killed by Indians, with Capt. Wadsworth and others, 27 April, 1676. SAMUEL, was chosen in London, 30 April, 1629, to be one of John Endicott's council at Salem, and the same year came to N. E., and was admitted freeman in 1632. He succeeded Mr. Haughton as ruling elder of Salem church, and d., according to Dr. Bentley, in 1658, but Mr. Felt says, 1656 or 7. His children were, Elias, baptized 1 Jan. 1637 ; Edward, bap. 14 April, 1639 ; Mary, 1640 ; Experience, (daughter) 1641 ; Nathaniel, 10 Nov. 1644. Alice, his widow, d. 1667. Felt, Annals, 194, 231. ‡THOMAS, Boston, was chosen assistant in England, 20 Oct. 1629, and came to N. E. in 1630 and was one of the founders of the first church in Boston. His house was burnt in 1631, and he returned to England the same year. Prince, i. Annals, 195, 247. ii. 22.

SHATSWELL, JOHN, Ipswich 1634, was deacon of the church. RICHARD, Ipswich 1648, d. 13 July, 1694, æ. about 64. THEOPHILUS, Haverhill, d. 1663. Coffin.

SHATTUCK, SAMUEL, a felt-maker, of Salem, was admitted member of the church, 15 May, 1642, from which he was ex-communicated, having embraced the sentiments of the Quakers. He

went to England but returned,* and was living in 1692. Calef,
More Wonders. His children were, Samuel, b. 1649; Retire, b.
1664, and six daughters. WILLIAM, Watertown 1642, died 14
Aug. 1672, æ. 50. By his wife, Susanna, who, after his death, m.,
18 Nov. 1673, Richard Norcross, and d. 11 Dec. 1686, he had 10
children, 1. Susanna, b. 1643, m. Joseph Morse, 1661; 2. Mary, b.
25 Aug. 1645, m. Jonathan Brown, 1661; 3. John, born 11 Feb.
1646, m. Ruth Whitney, 20 June, 1664, lived in Watertown, and
was drowned as he was passing over Charlestown ferry, 14 Sept.
1675, leaving John, b. 4 June, 1666; Ruth, b. 1668; William, b.
11 Sept. 1670, and Samuel, of whom John had 7 children, lived in
Groton, and according to tradition was killed by the Indians, 8
May, 1709, and left an only son Jonathan, b. 29 April, 1693,
the grandfather to Dr. Caleb Shattuck, of Oakham, Mass., who
grad. at D. C. 1794, and great-grandfather of the historian of Concord, Mass.; 4. Philip, father of Rev. Benjamin Shattuck, of Littleton, Mass., b. 15 March, 1685, grad. at H. C. 1709, ordained 25
Dec. 1717, whose son Stephen, b. 10 Feb. 1710, was father of Dr.
Benjamin, of Templeton, Mass., b. 11 Nov. 1742, grad. H. C. 1765,
died 14 Jan. 1794, æ. 52, leaving sons, Benjamin, H. C. 1797, and
George Cheyne, M. D., of Boston; 5. Rebecca, who m. Samuel
Church; 6. Joanna, who d. 1672; 7. William, of Watertown, who
had 8 children; 8. Benjamin; 9. Abigail, who m. Jona. Morse; 10.
Samuel. L. Shattuck, MS Letter.

SHAW, ABRAHAM, Dedham, freeman 1637. ANTHONY,
Boston, whose son William was b. 1654. JOHN, Plymouth 1638.
Davis, Morton's Memo. 384. ||JOHN, Boston, member of the ar.
co. 1646, had sons, John, b. 1648, freeman 1681; Samuel, b. 1651;
Joseph, b. 1657. He d. 23 July, 1687. JOSEPH, Hingham, removed to Bridgewater, and was among the settlers of that place.
JOSEPH, Dedham 1636, freeman 1639, and probably of Weymouth
in 1643. *ROGER, Cambridge 1636, freeman 1638; removed to
Hampton, which he represented in 1651 and 1652. He d. 1660,
leaving sons, Joseph and Benjamin, and 4 daughters. THOMAS,
Charlestown, whose son John was b. in 1647. Twenty-three of the
name had grad. in N. E. in 1828.

SHAVE, THOMAS, Hingham 1637. Lincoln, Hist. Hingham,
45.

SHEAFE, JACOB, Guilford 1643, one of the seven pillars of
the church. 1 Coll. Mass. Hist. Soc. x. 92. He may be the fol-
lowing. ||JACOB, Boston, member of ar. co. 1648, came from
Cambrock, in Kent, and died 22 March, 1658, æ. 58. [Alden, iii.
Coll. Epitaphs, 164.] He m. Margaret, daughter of Henry Webb,
and left two daughters, Elizabeth, b. 1644, who m. Robert Gibbs,
and Mehetabel, the wife of Sampson Sheafe, who settled at New-
Castle, N. H., and was a provincial counsellor in 1698, whose son
Sampson, b. at Newcastle in 1681, grad. at H. C. 1702, died 1772,
aged 91, was father of Jacob Sheafe, esquire, a merchant of Portsmouth, who d. 26 June, 1791, æ. 75. Hon. James Sheafe, H. C.

1774, is son of the last, as was also Jacob Sheafe, esquire, who d. at Portsmouth, 25 Jan. 1829, æ. 81.

SHED, DANIEL, Braintree 1647, removed to Billerica before 1675. Sons, Daniel, b. 3 Aug. 1647; John, b. 2 March, 1655, both of whom settled in Billerica; Zechariah, born 17 June, 1656. His daughters were Mary, Hannah, Elizabeth.

SHEDER, JOHN, Guilford 1650. 1 Coll. Mass. Hist. Soc. x. 92.

SHEFFIELD, EDMUND, Braintree, freeman 1644, d. 13 Oct. 1705, æ. 90. He had sons, Edmund, b. 15 Dec. 1646; Isaac, b. 15 March, 1652; Matthew, b. 14 June, 1653; Samuel, born Nov. 1657.

SHELDON, ISAAC, Dorchester 1634, removed to Windsor as early as 1640, and perhaps to Northampton, a. 1658. The one at Northampton had 15 children. JOHN, freeman 1680. WILLIAM, Billerica 1659. Sixteen of the name had grad. in N. E. in 1828.

SHELLEY, ROBERT, Scituate 1638, removed to Barnstable.

SHEPARD, EDWARD, Cambridge, freeman 1643. His first wife, Violet, died 9 Jan. 1649. His second wife was Mary. His children were, John, Abigail, and Deborah, born in England; and Sarah, who was baptized in Braintree. JOHN, Massachusets, freeman 1640. *JEREMIAH*, minister of Lynn, son of Rev. Thomas Shepard, of Cambridge, was b. 11 Aug. 1648, grad. at H. C. 1669, admitted freeman 1680, d. 2 June, 1720, æ. 72. Before his settlement at Lynn, he preached at Rowley. Mary, his wife, died 28 March, 1710, æ. 53. His children were, Hannah, born 1676, m. John Downing, of Boston; Jeremiah, b. 1677, d. 1700; Mehetabel, who d. 1688; Nathaniel, b. 16 June, 1681; Margaret, who d. 1683; Thomas, b. 1687, d. 1709; Francis, who d. 1692; John, who m. Alice Tucker, 1722; Mehetabel, 2d, who m. Rev. James Allin, of Brookline. Lewis. *JOHN, Lynn, representative 1689, may have been brother of the preceding. JOHN, Cambridge, son of Edward Shepard, was admitted freeman in 1650. His children were, John; Sarah; Violet; Elizabeth; Edward, b. 1662; Samuel, born 1664; and Thomas, b. 1666. RALPH, Dedham 1636, Weymouth 1639. ‖*SAMUEL, Cambridge, brother of Rev. Thomas Shepard, arrived in N. E. 2 Oct. 1635, freeman 1636, representative 1639, 1640, 1644, and 1645, member of ar. co. 1640, returned to Europe, and in 1658 was a major, and living in Ireland. His wife was Hannah, and his children were, Thomas, born 1638; Samuel, b. 1639, died 1646; Jane, b. 1645, who remained in N. E. *SAMUEL*, minister of Rowley, son of Rev. Thomas Shepard, of Cambridge, was b. Oct. 1641, grad. at H. C. 1658, admitted member of the church at Cambridge, 19 July, 1663, ordained 15 Nov. 1665, and d. 7 April, 1668, æ. 26. His son Samuel, baptized 25 August, 1667, grad. at H. C. 1685. His wife, it is supposed, was daughter of Rev. Henry Flint. *THOMAS*, third minister of Cambridge, was son of William Shepard, and was born in Towcester, in Northamptonshire, England, 5. Nov. 1605 [his MS diary]; was educated at Emmanuel

College; came to N. E., on his second attempt to come thither, 3
Oct. 1635, freeman 1636, and settled at Cambridge, over a new
church, 1 Feb. 1636. He d. 25 Aug. 1649, æ. 44. He had three
wives : (1) Margaret Touteville, who d. in N. E. ; (2) Joanna
Hooker, daughter of Rev. Thomas, who d. 28 April, 1646, and (3)
Margaret Boradile, whom he m. 8 Sept. 1647. His children were,
Thomas; Samuel; John, b. 2 April, 1646; and Jeremiah, b. 1648.
THOMAS, minister of Charlestown, son of the preceding, was b.
in London, 5 April, 1635, grad. at H. C. 1653, was ordained as colleague pastor with Rev. Z. Symmes, 13 April, 1659, and d. of small
pox, 22 Dec. 1777, in his 43d year. His wife was Hannah Tyng,
whom he m. 3 Nov. 1656. *THOMAS*, minister of Charlestown,
only son of the preceding, was born 5 July, 1658; grad. at H. C.
1676, preached his first Sermon, 19 May, 1678, succeeded his father, 5 May, 1680, and died 8 June, 1685, æ. 27, leaving no male
issue. ||WILLIAM, admitted member of the ar. co. 1642.

SHEPLEY, JOHN, Salem 1637. Ether Shepley, of Saco, Me.,
district attorney U. S. court, grad. at D. C. in 1811.

SHERBURNE, *HENRY, born a. 1612, and settled at Portsmouth as early as 1631, was probably the representative of Portsmouth at the general court of Mass. in 1660, and the ancestor of
many families in the eastern part of N. H. Henry Sherburne, born
a. 1674, was appointed a provincial counsellor of N. H., and d. 29
Dec. 1757. Samuel Sherburne, a merchant of Portsmouth, grad.
at H. C. 1719. Henry Sherburne, who grad. at H. C. 1728, was
appointed a counsellor of N. H. in 1766, was speaker of the house
of representatives, and d. 30 March, 1767, æ. 58. Joseph and John
Sherburne were also mandamus counsellors in 1733 and 1734.
JOHN, Portsmouth 1653, was probably a son of the preceding.
WILLIAM, Portsmouth 1644. Coffin.

SHERLOCK, ‡JAMES, New-Hampshire, was a mandamus
counsellor in 1684, perhaps the sheriff of Sir Edmund Andros 1688.

SHERMAN, BEZALEEL, a graduate of H. C. in 1661, d. before the year 1698. Mather, ii. Magnalia, 24. EDMUND, Massachusetts, admitted freeman in 1636. *JAMES*, the second minister
of Sudbury, began to preach there in 1677, and in July, 1705, was
"deposed from his pastoral office." He died 1718. 1 Coll. Mass.
Hist. Soc. x. 87. *JOHN*, the third minister of Watertown, was b.
in Dedham, Essex, England, 26 Dec. 1613, came to N. E., Mather
says, in 1634 ; Dr. Eliot says 1635, and settled at Watertown, from
whence he went to New-Haven colony, and sustained some civil
office, although it is believed not that of a magistrate, as stated by
Mather. He returned to Watertown, and succeded Phillips and
Knowles, and d. 8 Aug. 1685, in his 72d year. By his first wife he
had 6 children ; by his second, Mary, (who d. 9 March, 1710) who,
according to Mather, was a daughter of Mr. Launce, and grand-
daughter of Thomas Darcy, the Earl of Rivers, he had 20 children.
See Magnalia. *JOHN, Watertown, freeman 1637, a captain, town
clerk, and representative 1651, 1653, and 1663, whose wife Martha
died 7 Feb. 1701, had children, John, born 2 Nov. 1638 ; Martha ;

Mary; Sarah; Elizabeth; Joseph, born 14 May, 1650; Grace; Grace, 2d, and perhaps others. L. Shattuck, MS letter. PHILIP, Massachusetts, was admitted freeman in 1634. RICHARD, Boston 1635, was a merchant. and d. 30 May, 1660. SAMUEL, Boston 1637, had sons, Philip, b. in 1637, and Nathaniel, b. in 1642, who was probably of Lynn 1697. He was admitted freeman 1640, and may have removed to Connecticut, where Samuel Sherman was a magistrate from 1662 to 1664, and again in 1665, after the union of New-Haven with Connecticut. THOMAS, Ipswich 1636.

SHERRIT, HUGH, Ipswich, freeman 1635, d. at Haverhill, 5 Sept. 1678, aged a. 100. His name appears as witness to a deed in 2 Coll. Mass. Hist. Soc. iv. 170.

SHIPPEN, ||EDWARD, member of the ar. co. 1669.

SHORE, SAMSON, a tailor, and member of the Boston church 1641.

SHORT, ABRAHAM, Pemaquid. (See SHURD.) ANTHO-NY, one of the grantees of Newbury, 1634, d. 4 April, 1671. Coffin. *HENRY, Ipswich, freeman 1634, was elected representative in March 1635, but did not hold his seat. He removed to Newbury, which he represented in March, 1644. Elizabeth, his wife, d. 22 March, 1647. He m. Sarah Glover, 9 Oct. 1648, and died 5 May, 1673, leaving Henry and Sarah, his children. Ibid. Henry d. 23 Oct. 1706.

SHOTTON, SAMSON, one of the purchasers of land with Gorton, in 1643. Winthrop, ii. Hist. 121.

SHOVE, GEORGE, minister of Taunton, was ordained 19 Nov, 1665, according to Dr. Harris, who, in his Hist. of Dorchester, calls him *Shore*. He m. Hopestill Newman, 12 July, 1664, and had sons, Nathaniel, who d. 20 April, 1693; Samuel; Seth. He m. again in 1674, to Mrs. Walley, and d. 21 April, 1687. Mrs. Margaret Shove was of Rowley 1643. *SETH*, minister of Danbury, Conn., son of the preceding, grad. at H. C. 1687, ord. 13 Oct. 1697, d. 3 Dec. 1735, æ. about 68.

SHRIMPTON, HENRY, a brazier, was son of Edward Shrimpton, of Bednall-Green, near London; was admitted to the church in Boston, 1639. He had sons, Samuel, b. 1643; Henry b. 1653, and Jonathan, b. 1656. ‡||SAMUEL, Boston, son of the preceding, was b. 1643, was member of the ar. co. 1670; its captain 1694, freeman 1673, one of Sir Edmund Andros' council 1687, one of the council of safety 1689, and colonel of the Suffolk regiment. He d. 5 Feb. 1698, æ. 55. His son Samuel was member of the ar. co. 1695.

SHURD, ABRAHAM, Pemaquid 1640. Savage, i. Winth. Hist. N. E. 61, 79.

SHURTLEFF, WILLIAM, Marshfield, was killed by lightning in June, 1666. Rev. William Shurtleff, H. C. 1707, was born at Plymouth, 4 April, 1689, was minister of New-Castle and Portsmouth, and d. May, 1747, æ. 58. S. Davis, esq.

SHUTE, JAMES, Ipswich. (See CHUTE.) Three of the name of Daniel Shute, grad. at H. C. in 1743, 1775, and 1812. RICHARD, Boston, d. 2 October, 1703, æ. 72.

SHUTER, PETER, Braintree, d. 15 July, 1654. Spelled also *Shooter*.

SIBLEY, JOHN, Salem, admitted freeman 1634. Three of the name of Sibley have grad. at Brown, and one at Harvard. JOHN, Massachusetts, freeman 1635.

SIELEY, ROBERT, Watertown. (See SEELEY.)

SILL, JOHN, Cambridge, freeman 1638, d. before 1658. His wife was Joanna ; his children, Joseph and Elizabeth, were born in England. Joseph lived in Cambridge and had several children, and might be the Captain Joseph Sill who was a conspicuous officer in Philip's War.

SILLIS, RICHARD, Scituate 1638. 2 Coll. Mass. Hist. Soc. iv. 239. His daughter Esther, m. Samuel Jackson in 1639.

SILSBEE, HENRY, Lynn 1658, had sons, Henry, John, and Samuel. Lewis.

SILVER, THOMAS, Ipswich 1637, removed to Newbury, and d. 6 Sept. 1682.

SILVESTER, RICHARD, Weymouth. (See SYLVESTER.)

SIMMONS, MOSES, Plymouth 1623, Duxbury a. 1640. Formerly written *Simonson*. THOMAS, Scituate 1646.

SIMPKINS, ||NICHOLAS, a captain, was member of ar. co. 1650. Rev. John Simpkins grad. at H. C. in 1784.

SIMPSON, JOHN, Watertown, whose son John was born 1638. This name prevails in Mass., N. H., and N. J.

SINGLETARY, RICHARD, Salem 1637, Newbury 1638, removed to Haverhill, and d. 25 Oct. 1687, æ. 102. Nathaniel Singletary was killed at Haverhill by the Indians 13 Aug. 1689, and Richard Singletary was killed at Lancaster in 1707.

SISTER, GIDEON, Massachusetts, freeman 1643. Savage, ii. Winthrop, 373.

SKATE, JOHN, Weymouth 1658. The name of Scates exists in New-Hampshire.

SKELTON, SAMUEL, one of the first ministers of Salem, came from Lincolnshire, and arrived in N. E. 29 June, 1629, and was ordained with Rev. Francis Higginson, teacher of the church, 6 August, 1629 ; d. 2 August, 1634, leaving several children. His wife d. 15 March, 1631. BENJAMIN, of Salem, had a son John, baptized in 1639 ; and NATHANIEL, of Salem, had a son John, b. 1648. The name exists in Mass., N. H., and Vermont.

SKERRY, HENRY, Salem, freeman 1637, was born a. 1605, and was living 1675. FRANCIS, Salem, freeman 1637, was born in 1608, and died a. 1692. Land which he bought of Peter Palfrey is still occupied by his descendants.

SKIDMORE, THOMAS, Cambridge 1643, where his son Joseph was born ; of Lancaster in 1653. There was a Thomas Skidmore of Huntington, L. I., 1672.

SKINNER, THOMAS, Malden 1653—a name common in N. E., and which has furnished 14 graduates at the different colleges.

SKIPP, JAMES, Lynn 1637, removed to Sandwich. Lewis.

SLAWSON, GEORGE, Lynn 1637, removed to Sandwich. Lewis.

SLEEPER, THOMAS, Hampton 1646. Descendants are in New-Hampshire.

SMALL, FRANCIS, Casco-Bay 1658; Portsmouth 1685, at the age of 65. Adams, Annals, 396. EDWARD, Kittery 1640.

SMALLEY, JOHN, Plymouth; thence to Eastham 1644. Rev. John Smalley, D. D., grad. at Yale in 1756.

SMALLIDGE, WILLIAM, Boston 1653.

SMART, JOHN, Hingham 1635, Exeter 1647, in the vicinity of which, and in other parts of N. H., the name exists.

SMEAD, WILLIAM, Dorchester 1658. One of this name was freeman in 1680.

SMEDLEY, BAPTIST, Concord 1639, freeman 1644, died 16 Aug. 1675, æ. 68. His children were, Samuel, b. 1646, killed by Indians at Brookfield, 2 Aug. 1675; Mary; James. Shattuck, MS Hist. Concord. *JOHN, Concord, brother of the preceding, freeman 1644, representative 1667 and 1670. His son John, freeman in 1677, m. Sarah Wheeler 1669.

SMITH, ARTHUR, Connecticut 1636. This name is the most frequent of any in N. E., and perhaps in the United States. It had furnished 214 graduates at the different colleges in N. E. and N. J. in 1825, one fourth of whom have been settled clergymen. ||BEN-JAMIN, freeman 1641, member of the ar. co. 1643, was probably of Lynn, and born a. 1612. Coffin. ‡BENJAMIN, was an assistant of R. I. in 1672. CHRISTOPHER, freeman 1643, was probably the settler at Northampton in 1658. DANIEL, Watertown, whose son Daniel was b. in 1642, d. 14 July, 1660. ‡DANIEL, Plymouth, assistant, and one of Sir Edmund Andros' council in 1687. Hutchinson, i. Mass. 317. EDWARD, Weymouth 1642. FRANCIS, Roxbury, freeman 1631, came to N. E. 1630, and probably from Buxall. Winthrop, i. Hist. N. E. 379. FRANCIS, Hingham 1635, freeman 1637, removed to Taunton. Lincoln, Hist. Hingham. FRANCIS, Boston, freeman 1640, had sons, John and Joseph, b. in 1644 and 1646. He may have been the Francis Smith of Reading in 1647. GEORGE, Dover 1645, was town clerk, and a prominent man in that place. GEORGE, Ipswich 1648. *HENRY, Hingham, admitted freeman 1638, was representative in 1641. HENRY, minister of Weathersfield, Conn., died in 1641, or, according to Mr. Savage [ii. Winth. N. E. 390], in 1648. HENRY, Dedham 1639, had sons, Daniel, Samuel, Joseph, and John, born from 1639 to 1644. *HENRY, Springfield, a captain, and one of the first settlers, was represensative in 1651. He married Anna, daughter of William Pynchon, and had children, Mary, Elizabeth, Rebecca, Elisha, and Martha. He returned to England, with his father-in-law and Rev. George Moxon, in 1652. Breck, Century Discourse. HUGH, Rowley, admitted freeman 1642, died 1656. JAMES, Salem 1637; Marblehead 1648, died a. 1661, leaving a widow Mary and son James. JAMES, Weymouth, whose son Nathaniel was b. 1639. JAMES, Boston, a ship-master, was member of the church 1644. Winthrop [i. Hist. N. E. 243, 379] notices a Capt. James Smith. JAMES, admitted freeman 1654. JOHN,

Dedham, d. 14 Aug. 1645. Of the name of John Smith or Smythe, admitted freemen by the Massachusetts colony before 1660, there are six, viz : one in 1633, two in 1636, one in 1639, one in 1647, and one in 1654. It would therefore be difficult to assign to each his respective residence. JOHN, Plymouth 1643, was one of the early settlers of Eastham. JOHN, Weymouth, 1638. Savage, i. Winth. Hist. N. E. 289. JOHN, Salem 1635, went to Rhode-Island with Roger Williams, and was president of the colony 1649. Ibid, ii. 262. Rev. Dr. Harris. Two others of the name of John Smith were early proprietors of Providence. JOHN, Boston, a tailor,, admitted member of the church 1638, and perhaps the member of the ar. co. 1644. *JOHN, Lynn 1638 ; Reading 1647, representative 1669. Lewis. JOHN, Watertown 1639, whose wife d. in 1639, probably was the one who removed to Lancaster, and d. July, 1669. Willard, Hist. Lancaster. JOHN, Boston, came from Ireland, and was admitted to the church in 1640. JOHN, Sudbury 1646. JOHN, Saco, freeman 1653. Folsom. JOHN, Charlestown, a ship-carpenter, d. 26 March, 1673. ‡*JOHN, Hingham, probably freeman 1654, was representative from 1683 to 1686; elected assistant in 1686; d. in May, 1695. His son John was b. 1653. JOHN, Rowley 1643, died 1661, leaving one daughter, Sarah. JOHN, Dorchester, whose son Samuel was b. 1659. A John Smith was of Hadley in 1665. JOHN, Salem 1660. Hutchinson, i. Hist. Mass. 187. JOSEPH, Hampton, had a son John, b. 9 Jan. 1669, who m. 1694, Susanna Chesley, and had sons, John, born 1695, of Durham ; Joseph, b. 1701, a colonel, who d. 29 March, 1781, aged 80 ; Samuel ; Benjamin ; Ebenezer ; and Winthrop. ||LAW-RENCE, Dorchester, freeman 1643, member of the ar. co. 1642. MATTHIAS, Massachusetts, freeman 1645. MATTHEW, Watertown, was drowned at Noddle's Island, 21 May, 1658. MIG-HILL, Charlestown, freeman 1647, had a son Samuel, b. in 1648. NATHANIEL, freeman 1668. NEHEMIAH, Exeter, d. in 1673. OBADIAH, Dorchester 1661. *PHILIP, Hadley 1660, representative 1677, 1680 to 1684, 6 years, was a deacon of the church, selectman, and lieutenant of the troop. He d. in the winter of 1684. Mather says he was " murdered with an hideous witchcraft." See ii. Magnalia, 394, 395. *RALPH*, minister of Plymouth, and a preacher at several places, came to N. E. with Rev. Francis Higginson, in 1629. He died at Boston, 1 March, 1661–2. RALPH, came to this country in 1633, from Hingham, England, and settled at Hingham, Mass., as early as 1635. Lincoln. RICHARD, Rhode-Island, purchased, in 1641, of the sachems, a tract of land in the Narraganset country. His son Richard purchased Hog-Island in 1658. RICHARD, Sudbury 1646. ROBERT, Exeter 1638, where are now living several families of the name of Smith, some of whom may be his descendants : but the late chief-justice and governour, the Hon. Jeremiah Smith, LL. D., of that town, is descended from the late William Smith, esquire, of Peterborough, who was of Scotch ancestry. ROBERT, Ipswich 1648. ROW-LAND, Marblehead 1648. SAMUEL, Salem or Lynn, freeman

1634, d. 1642. Lewis. *SAMUEL, Hadley, was born a. 1598, and was representative 1661, six years. He was living in 1678. *THOMAS, Weymouth, freeman 1633, representative 1635. THOMAS, Salem 1637, perhaps of Lynn 1649. THOMAS, Watertown, freeman 1637, had sons, James, b. 1637; John, 1639; Thomas, b. 1640, perhaps the child whose remarkable preservation is recorded in ii. Winthrop, 267; Joseph, b. 1643. THOMAS, Ipswich and Newbury 1638, had sons, John; James, who was drowned at Cape Breton, 1690; and Matthias; and a number of daughters. He d. 26 April, 1666. *WILLIAM, Weymouth, freeman 1635, representative 1636 and 1637, had a son Nehemiah, b. in 1641, perhaps settled in Exeter. WILLIAM, Charlestown, probably the one admitted freeman 1644. Son Nathaniel, b. 1640.

SNAWSELL, ||THOMAS, Boston 1665, was a member of the ar. co.

SNELL, THOMAS, Bridgewater in 1682. Eight of the name of Snell had grad. in N. E. in 1825.

SNELLING, JOHN, Boston 1657. JOHN, Saco, freeman 1653. Folsom. THOMAS, from Dartmouth, d. 16 Oct. 1661. Coffin. WILLIAM, Newbury, a physician, son of Thomas Snelling, esq., of Chaddlewood, in Devonshire, m. Margaret, daughter of Giles Stagge, 5 July 1648. He removed to Boston, before 1655, and d. there, leaving two children.

SNOW, NICHOLAS, Plymouth 1623, removed to Eastham, a. 1644. RICHARD, Woburn 1653. 3 Coll. Mass. Hist. Soc. i. 45. THOMAS, Boston, freeman 1642. WILLIAM, Bridgewater, 1682, had sons, William and Joseph.

SOMERBY, ANTHONY, Newbury, son of Richard, and grandson of Henry Somerby, came from Little-Bytham, in Lincolnshire, in 1639, in the ship Jonathan, and was admitted freeman 1642. He was the first schoolmaster in Newbury, and the town clerk 38 years from 1648. He died July "the last," 1686. HENRY, Newbury, brother of the preceding, came with him to N. E. in 1639, and was admitted freeman 1642, and d. 2 Oct. 1652. His children were, Sarah, b. 1644; John, b. 24 Dec. 1648; Elizabeth, b. 1646; Daniel, b. 18 Nov. 1650.

SOMES, MORRIS, Gloucester 1664. Gibbs.

SOULE, GEORGE, Plymouth 1620, one of the first pilgrims, removed, as early as 1644, to Duxbury, where the name still exists.

SOUTHARD, JOSEPH, Massachusetts, freeman 1683. This name exists in N. H. and in Massachusetts.

SOUTHCOT, RICHARD, appears among those desiring to be made freemen, 18 Oct. 1630. THOMAS, one of the patentees of Massachusetts, was admitted freeman 1631. [Prince i. Annals, 180. ii. 32.] Mr. Savage [i. Winth. Hist. N. E. 57] says, "he probably never came over;" but this was conjectured before he had prepared the list of freemen for his ii. volume, in which the name of Thomas Southcot appears among those desiring "to be made freemen," 19 Oct. 1630. He was admitted the 18 May, following, and probably soon returned to England, or left the colony, as he had this liberty granted in July, 1631.

SOUTHGATE, RICHARD, was b. in Coombs, in Suffolk, Eng. in 1673, came to N. E. in 1715, returned and brought over his family in 1717, and settled at Leicester, and died in 1758, æ. 88. He had sons, Stuart and Richard. Worcester Mag. i. 100.

SOUTHMAYD, WILLIAM, Middletown, Conn., 1665, died 1702, æ. 57, leaving 8 sons, William, b. 1674; John, b. 1676, grad. at H. C. 1697, was ordained the minister of Waterbury, Conn., and d. 1755; William, b. 1679; Giles, 1680, died 1738; Allen, 1685; Daniel, 1687; and Joseph, b. 1695, d. 1772. William, son of Rev. John, grad. at Y. C. in 1761, and died in 1777. Rev. Daniel S. Southmayd, MS note to Mr. Shattuck.

SOUTHWICK, LAWRENCE, Salem, member of the church 1639, from which he was excommunicated on account of joining the quakers. His wife was Cassandra, and his sons were, John, Josiah, Daniel, and Provided. He and his wife were sent to the east end of Long-Island, where they died about 1660, within three days of each other. Felt, Annals Salem, 196—203.

SOUTHWORTH, ‡CONSTANT,, Plymouth, an assistant, was admitted freeman of that colony 1637, died 1678, leaving 3 sons, Edward, Nathaniel, and William. Descendants are in Mass. and N. H. ‡THOMAS, Plymouth, brother of the preceding, was elected an assistant of Plymouth colony in 1652, and 10 years afterwards, until 1667; was a captain, and a worthy character. He died 1669, æ. 53. His wife was Elizabeth, daughter of Rev. John Rayner, and their only child m. Lieut. John Howland.

SOWTHER, NATHANIEL, Plymouth, was clerk of the court 1643. This name is distinct from Southworth. [2 Coll. Mass. Hist. Soc. iii. 184.] There was a Nathaniel Souther admitted freeman by Mass. in 1653, who may be the preceding, and the one mentioned by Lincoln as of Hingham in 1653, and then 62 years of age.

SPARHAWK, JOHN, was of Cambridge, and, from an interleaved almanack, it appears that he d. 21 Sept. 1644. *NATHANIEL, a deacon of Cambridge, was admitted freeman in 1639, was elected representative from 1642 to 1647, six years, one of which, it appears, was for Wenham. He d. 28 June, 1647. Mary, his wife, d. 25 Jan. 1644, and Catherine, a 2d wife, survived him but 7 days. His children were, Anna, who m. Dea. John Cooper; Mary; Esther; Samuel, who d. 1639; Elizabeth, who died 1692; Nathaniel, of Cambridge, who m. 31 Oct. 1649, Patience, daughter of Rev. Samuel Newman, and had, 1. Mary; 2. Sybil; 3. Esther; 4. Samuel, who m. a Whiting, and d. 1719, æ. 49, leaving, John, who grad. at H. C. 1723, and was a merchant in Plymouth; 5. Nathaniel, b. 1664, a deacon of Cambridge, who d. 1734, æ. 69, whose son Nathaniel, H. C. 1715, was minister of Lynnfield, Mass., and d. 1732, æ. 38, and father of Edward P. Sparhawk, H. C. 1753, and John Sparhawk, a physician of Philadelphia; 6. John, minister of Bristol, who grad. at H. C. 1689, d. 1718, æ. 46, leaving two sons, 1. John, minister of Salem, who was b. in Aug. or Sept. 1713, grad.

at H. C. 1731, ordained 1736, died 30 April, 1755, æ. 42; and 2. Nathaniel, of Kittery, born 4 March, 1715, a judge and counsellor, who m. Elizabeth, daughter of Sir William Pepperell, and three of whose sons grad. at H. C., viz : Nathaniel, in 1665 ; William, who took the name and title of Sir William Pepperell, 1766 ; and Samuel, in 1771. Rev. John, of Salem, m. a Porter, and had 13 children. Three of the sons who lived to mature age, were, 1. Nathaniel ; 2. John, of Portsmouth, N. H., speaker of the house of representatives, who d. 5 September, 1787, æ. 45, the father of Samuel Sparhawk, esq., of Concord, N. H., late secretary of state ; 3. Samuel, a merchant.

SPARKS, JOHN, Ipswich 1665 [2 Coll. Mass. Hist. Soc. viii. 107], perhaps previously of Saco. The name of Sparks was also in Rowley soon after this period. Rev. Jared Sparks, distinguished for his historical researches in this country and in Europe, grad. at H. C. 1815, and was sometime minister of Baltimore.

SPAULDING, EDWARD, Braintree, where Margaret, his wife, d. in Aug. 1640. He removed to Chelmsford, having been admitted freeman in 1640, and there d. 26 Feb. 1670. His sons were, Edward , Benjamin, b. at Braintree, 7 April, 1643 ; Andrew, b. 19 Nov. 1653, a deacon of the church in Chelmsford, and died 5 May, 1713 ; and perhaps some others. His descendants are numerous in several parts of N. E. and some have been distinguished. Rev. Samson Spaulding, H. C. 1732, was the minister of Tewksbury, Mass., almost 60 years, and died 15 Dec. 1796. Asa Spalding, of Connecticut, grad. at Y. C. 1752, and perhaps was the father of Asa Spalding, an eminent lawyer of Norwich, in that state, who grad. at Y. C. 1778, and d. in Aug. 1811, æ. 54. Lyman Spalding, M. D., of Portsmouth and New-York, who d. 30 Oct. 1821, æ. 46, Matthias Spalding, M. D., of Amherst, born at Chelmsford, 25 June, 1769, a graduate of H. C. 1798; Noah, M. B., at D. C. 1800 ; James, M. D., 1814 ; Phineas, M. D., 1823, and Jason C., M. D, 1828, are probably descendants from him. Joseph Spaulding, a soldier of the revolution, who d. at Chelmsford in 1820, æ. 64, fired the first gun in the battle of Bunker Hill, and was supposed to be the one who killed Major Pitcairn, as he always asserted that he took aim at him. *EDWARD, Chelmsford, son of the preceding, was representative in 1691.

SPEAR, GEORGE, Dorchester and Braintree, was admitted freeman in 1644. He had children, George ; Sarah, born 1647 ; Samuel, b. 18 Oct. 1651 ; and Hannah, born 1653. Rev. Samuel Spear, of Province-town, Mass., who grad. at H. C. 1715, was a descendant, as are the several families in and around Boston.

SPENCER, GARRETT, Cambridge 1634, Lynn 1637, admitted freeman 1637. *JOHN, Ipswich and Newbury, freeman 1634, represented Ipswich 1635, Newbury 1636, returned to England 1638, and d. 1648. Coffin. MICHAEL, Cambridge 1634, Lynn 1637. Lewis. ROGER, Saco 1653. THOMAS, Cambridge 1632, brother of John Spencer, was admitted freeman in 1634. THOMAS, Concord 1666, was probably the freeman 1681. THO-

MAS, Pascataqua 1631, Kittery 1652. *WILLIAM, Cambridge 1632, freeman 1633, representative 1635, and one of the founders of the ar. co. 1637.

SPERRY, ———, Connecticut 1661. Hutch. i. Hist. Mass. 199.

SPOFFORD, JOHN, sen., Rowley 1643, died 22 April, 1696. This name is often spelled *Spafford.*

SPOOER, JOHN, Boston, freeman 1639, had a son John, born in 1650. Snow [Hist. Boston] spells this name *Spore.* JOHN, Marlborough, freeman 1653.

SPOONER, THOMAS, Salem, admitted freeman 1638. Six of the name had grad. at the N. E. colleges in 1828.

SPRAGUE, FRANCIS, Plymouth 1623 [Davis, Morton's Memo. 379]; of Duxbury afterwards. The Sprague genealogy, published by Hosea Sprague, 1828, says he had no sons. JOHN, Plymouth, one of Sir Edmund Andros' council 1687. Hutchinson, i. Hist. Mass. 317. *JOHN, Malden, freeman 1653, a captain, and representative at the Nov. session 1689, 1690, and 1691. *PHINEHAS, Malden, representative Dec. session, 1689, and February and May, 1690. ||*RALPH, arrived at Salem 1628, and settled at Charlestown 1629, freeman 1631, representative 1635, 9 years, member of ar. co. 1638, was the first constable of Charlestown, 1630, and a military officer. ||*RICHARD, Charlestown, brother of the preceding came to N. E. 1628, freeman 1631, member of the ar. co. 1638, its lieutenant 1665, captain of the Charlestown militia, representative 1644, 1659, to 1666, 9 years. He died 25 Nov. 1668. *RICHARD, Charlestown, probably son of the preceding, was representative from 1681 to 1686 (excepting 1684), and 1689, 7 years. WILLIAM, arrived at Salem with his brothers, Ralph and Richard, in 1628, and with Governour Endecott's consent, went with them to Mishawum [Charlestown] in 1629. He went to Hingham, about 1635; had sons, Anthony, b. before 1636; John, b. 1638; Samuel, b. 1640; Jonathan, b. 1643, d. 1647; Jonathan, 2d, b. 1648, settled in Rhode-Island; William, b. 1650, and went to Bridgewater. His daughters were, Elizabeth Persis, Mary, and Hannah. The genealogy of this branch of the Sprague family, to the fourth generation, may be found in a pamphlet of 48 pages, published in 1828, by Hosea Sprague, of Hingham.

SPRING, HENRY, Massachusetts, was admitted freeman 1660. Descendants are in Mass. Six of the name had grad. at Harv. and Yale in 1828.

SPUR, JOHN, Boston, whose son Ebenezer was b. 1642. (See SPOOER.) ROBERT, Dorchester 1658, freeman 1666.

SQUIRE, GEORGE, Concord 1643. JOHN, one of the early town clerks of Reading. ||THOMAS, freeman 1634, member of the ar. co. 1646.

STACKHOUSE, RICHARD, Salem 1638, Beverly 1659. Felt, Annals Salem, 188.

STACY, HENRY, Marblehead 1648. HUGH, Dedham 1640; Lynn, freeman 1643, was, with his wife, received member of the church at Salem in 1659. JOHN, Lynn 1641, Marblehead 1648.

*SIMON, Ipswich, freeman 1668, a captain, and representative 1685, 1686, 1689, and 1690, d. 27 Oct. 1699. THOMAS, who was of Ipswich in 1648.

STAINWOOD, PHILIP, Gloucester 1664.

STANBURY, JOSIAH, Lynn 1639. Lewis. THOMAS, Boston, d. 27 Sept. 1652. His sons were, Thomas, b. 1642; John, b. 1645; and Nathan, b. 1646.

STANDISH, JAMES, Salem, admitted member of the church, 23 June, 1639, freeman 1640, had 20 acres of land granted to him in 1636. His name is given *Standige* by Mr. Savage in his list of freemen, in ii. Winth. Hist. N. E. 370. ‡MYLES, the brave captain of the Plymouth pilgrims 1620, and their defender from the hostile movements of the Indians, d. at Duxbury, in 1656. He was elected assistant of the colony 19 years, and at the head of the military forces. His will, made 7 March, 1655 [Coll. N. H. Hist. Soc. i. 259—261], names 4 sons, Alexander, Myles, Josiah, and Charles. Myles removed to Boston, and was living there in 1662. Alexander and Josiah (who m. a daughter of John Alden) were several times representatives from Duxbury.

STANHOPE, JONATHAN, Sudbury 1664, was born a. 1632, and d. 25 Oct. 1702, æ. 70. He is mentioned in the Revo. in N. E. Justified, 31, 32.

STANDLAKE, DANIEL, Scituate 1636, died in 1638. 2 Coll. Mass. Hist. Soc. iv.

STANIFORTH, THOMAS, Concord 1644. Shattuck. Three of the name of Daniel Staniford grad. at H. C. in 1738, 1772, and 1790.

STANLEY, CHRISTOPHER, Boston, a captain, and by occupation a tailor, was admitted freeman 1641. Snow, Hist. Boston, 119. Nine of the name had grad. at Y. C. in 1828. MATTHEW, Lynn 1646. Lewis. ||*THOMAS, Lynn, freeman and representative in 1635, and member of the ar. co. 1640. TIMOTHY, Cambridge, admitted freeman 1635.

STANTON, ROBERT, Dorchester 1659. Rev. Robert Stanton grad. at H. C. 1712. THOMAS, was an interpreter in the Pequot war, 1637. He had a son Robert, who, with his father, is noticed in a postscript to Hubbard's Indian Wars, p. 6.

STANYAN, *ANTHONY, Boston 1641; Exeter, where he was town clerk in 1647; of Hampton, which he represented in 1654, had a son John, b. in Boston 1642, who settled in Hampton. Descendants still remain in N. Hampshire.

STAPLES, ABRAHAM, Dorchester 1658. ABNER, Mendon, freeman 1673. EDWARD, and SAMUEL, Braintree, at an early period. JOHN, Weymouth, freeman 1648, had sons Increase and Joseph, b. about 1641.

STAR, COMFORT, Cambridge, was a physician at Ashford in Kent, came to N. E. as early as 1634, settled in Cambridge, removed to Duxbury; thence to Boston, where he d. 2 Jan. 1659 or 60. *COMFORT*, son of the preceding, was born at Ashford, in Kent, a. 1624, grad. 1647, at H. C., in the catalogue of which, his name is put *Consolantius*; returned to England, and settled, at Carlisle, in Cumberland, from whence he was ejected; was afterwards pastor of a church in Lewes, Sussex, where he d. in Oct. 1711, æ. 86. Calamy. JOHN, one of the proprietors of Bridgewater 1645. THOMAS, Yarmouth 1640, is styled a chirurgeon, and was living there in 1670. Thacher, i. Med. Biog. 18.

STARBUCK, *EDWARD, an elder of the church at Dover, was representative in 1643 and 1646. He came from Derbyshire. His wife was Eunice Reynolds, from Wales. Coffin.

STARK, WILLIAM, Lynn 1641. Lewis. Eight of the name of Stark had received the honours of the colleges of N. E. and N. J. in 1828. The late General John Stark, who d. 8 May, 1822, was of Scotch ancestry, and was b. at Londonderry, N. H., 17 Aug. 1728.

STARKWEATHER, ROBERT, Roxbury 1643. This name exists in Mass. and Conn., where several have been publickly educated.

STEARNS, CHARLES, Watertown, freeman 1646, was probably the same who m. Rebecca Gibson, of Cambridge in 1654. Eighteen of the name had grad. at Harv. and Yale in 1828. ISAAC, Watertown 1630, probably the great ancestor of the Stearnses in Massachusetts, was admitted freeman 18 May, 1631. The name is written Sterné and Starne in the earliest records. He d. 29 Aug. 1676. He had sons, Isaac, b. 6 Jan. 1632, freeman 1665; Samuel, b. 24 April, 1638, and very probably others, who were b. before he came to N. E. JOHN, one of the first settlers of Billerica, d. 5 March, 1669. His 1st wife was Mary Lathrop, of Plymouth colony. John, his eldest son, by the 2d wife, and the first child born in Billerica on record, was b. the 2d week in May, 1654, was a man of influence in his native town, and d. 26 Oct. 1728, æ. 74. From him descended Hon. Isaac Stearns, Rev. Josiah Stearns, of Epping, N. H., whose son Rev. Samuel Stearns is minister of Bedford, Mass. *NATHANIEL, Dedham, a lieutenant, and representative in 1684.

STEBBINS, EDMUND, Cambridge, freeman 1634, removed to Connecticut as early as 1636. See I. Mather's Relation of Troubles in N. E. with the Indians, 43. JOHN, Roxbury, freeman 1647, d. 4 Dec. 1681, æ. 70. His wife d. 1686. JOHN, Watertown, where his son John was b. 1640, was perhaps the one who settled at Northampton as early as 1658. MARTIN, Roxbury 1640. ROWLAND, was of Springfield in 1641, as were also Increase in 1650, and Benjamin, who d. in 1698. THOMAS, Springfield 1641, a lieutenant, d. 25 Sept. 1683.

STEDMAN, ISAAC, Scituate 1648. 2 Coll. Mass. Hist. Soc. iv. 239. JOHN, Cambridge, freeman 1640, died of the small pox, 24 Nov. 1678. Alice, his wife d. 6 March, 1691, æ. 80. His daughters were Elizabeth, Sarah, and Martha. ROBERT, Cambridge, freeman 1638, d. 20 Jan. 1667. He had two sons, John, b. 27 Dec. 1642, and Thomas, who d. 2 April, 1659. From John descended John Stedman, H. C. 1712, who d. 5 Sept. 1719.

STEELE, GEORGE, Cambridge 1632, was admitted freeman 1634. Nineteen of the name of Steele had been educated at the N. E. colleges in 1828, ten of whom grad. at Yale. HENRY, Cambridge 1632. ‡*JOHN, Dorchester 1630, a proprietor of Cambridge 1632, freeman 1635, representative of Cambridge 1635, removed to Hartford, and was a magistrate or assistant in 1636. Savage, i. Winthrop, 285.

STEPHENS, JOHN, Hingham 1638. Lincoln.

STEPHENSON, ANDREW, Cambridge, freeman 1643, had children, Deborah, Sarah, Rebecca, John, b. 1644, Mary, Lydia, Andrew, and Hannah. JOHN, Boston, had sons, John, b. in 1645, and James, b. in 1653. MARMADUKE, was tried for being a Quaker, i. Hutch. 183, was a day-labourer in Skipton, Yorkshire, when he had a call to go to America. Life of John Richardson, p. 25. THOMAS, Portsmouth, d. 7 Dec. 1663. Margaret, his wife, d. 26 Nov. same year.

STETSON, ROBERT, Scituate 1636. WILLIAM, Charlestown. (See STITSON.) Four of the name of Stetson had grad. in N. E. in 1828.

STEVENS, HENRY, Boston 1637, freeman 1652, d. 5 Oct. 1689. He had sons, John, b. 1637; James, 1640; Joseph, 1642; Onesesimus, 1643. There was a Henry Stevens of Lynn in 1634. *JAMES, Gloucester 1664, freeman 1671, representative 1680. JOHN, Newbury 1639, removed to Salisbury and perhaps the freeman of 1641, had sons, John, b. 20 June, 1639, and Timothy, b. 22 Sept. 1641, both at Newbury. Coffin. JOHN, Andover, 1644, was probably admitted freeman 1642. He d. in April, 1662, having had 5 sons, John, Nathan, said to have been the first child born in Andover, Joseph, Ephraim, and Benjamin. David, the son of deacon Joseph, was father of Rev. Joseph Stevens, of Charlestown, who grad. at H. C. 1703, and d. of small pox in Nov. 1721, whose son, Rev. Benjamin Stevens, D. D., grad. at H. C. 1740, and was the minister of Kittery, Me., and d. 18 May, 1791, æ. 71. JOHN, Guilford 1650. Abbot, Hist. Andover, 21. NICHOLAS, Charlestown, d. 17 May, 1646. TIMOTHY, a captain and deacon of Roxbury, d. 31 Jan. 1708. Rev. Timothy Stevens, H. C. 1687, was minister of Glastonbury, Conn. and d. 16 April, 1725. THOMAS, Guilford 1650. THOMAS, Sudbury 1654, was town clerk 15 years. Shattuck. *WILLIAM, Gloucester, freeman 1640, representative 1644. WILLIAM, Salem, admitted member of the church 29 Dec. 1639, freeman 1642, removed to Newbury, and d. 19 May, 1653. Sons, John, b. 19 Nov. 1650; Samuel, b. 1652.

STEWART, DUNCAN, one of the early settlers of Newbury, d. in Rowley, in 1717, æ. 100 years. Coffin. JOHN, Springfield, a. 1654, d. 21 April, 1690. (See STUART.) ‖RICHARD, member of the ar. co. 1652.

STICKNEY, WILLIAM, came from Hull in England, was admitted a member of Boston church, from which he was dismissed to Rowley; was admitted freeman 1640, and d. in 1664 or 5. His children were Samuel, who settled in Bradford, which he represented 1689 and 1690; John; Andrew, of Rowley; Amos, of Newbury, who d. 1678; Mary; Faith, and Mercy. Descendants are in Vt., Mass. Maine, and New-Hampshire. William Stickney, esq. a worthy magistrate of Billerica, who d. 27 August, 1781, æ. 76, was from the Bradford branch of the family.

STILEMAN, ELIAS, Salem, a member of the church, came to N. E. as early as 1629, and was admitted freeman 1632; chosen clerk of the court of Essex county 1653, and d. it appears in 1662, aged not less than 70. The name of his wife was Judith. Felt, MS letter. Ibid, Annals, 216. *ELIAS, Salem, son of the preceding, was admitted to the church 18 Aug. 1639, removed to Portsmouth, as early as 1659, which he represented in 1667, and 5 years afterwards, and once as late as 1690, was appointed one of the counsellors under President Cutt 1680, was secretary of N. H. and captain of the militia. He may be the member of the ar. co. 1645. His wife was Ruth Maynard, whom he m. 10 April, 1667. His residence was sometime at Great-Island, now New-Castle. He died in 1695. RICHARD, Cambridge 1643; went to Salem as early as 1646, and from thence to Portsmouth. His wife was Hannah. His children were, Samuel, b. at Cambridge, 23 May, 1644; Mary, Elizabeth, Sarah, and Richard, born at Portsmouth from 1657 to 1668, the four last by his wife Mary.

STILES, JOHN, came from Milbroke in Bedfordshire, England, in 1634, and settled in Windsor, Conn. in 1635. His son John was father of Rev. Isaac Stiles, of North-Haven, Conn. whose son Rev. Ezra Stiles, D. D., LL. D., was the learned president of Yale College, and d. 12 May, 1795, æ. 67. Holmes, Life Pres. Stiles. HENRY, Windsor 1640. ROBERT, Boxford 1673. Nine of the name have grad. at Yale and one at Harvard.

STILWELL, JASPER, Guilford, Conn. 1650.

STIMPSON, or STIMSON, JOHN, freeman 1645. Joseph and Daniel Stimpson, clergymen, grad. at H. C. in 1720 and 1759.

STIRK, GEORGE, grad. at H. C. 1646, and is said in a MS of Rev. Andrew Eliot, D. D., to have been an eminent chymist, and one who wrote several Latin treatises.

STITSON *||WILLIAM, a deacon of the church in Charlestown, was admitted freeman 1633; member of the ar. co. 1648, representative from 1667 to 1671, five years. 3 Coll. Mass. Hist. Soc. i. 261.

STOCKBRIDGE, JOHN, Scituate 1638; [2 Coll. Mass. Hist. Soc. iv. 239] perhaps the same who d. at Boston, 13 Oct. 1657.

STOCKER, EBENEZER, Lynn 1674, m. Sarah Marshall, had sons, Thomas, Ebenezer, Samuel, John, and d. 2 Nov. 1704.

STOCKING, GEORGE, Cambridge, freeman 1635. This name exists in the county of Berkshire.

STODDARD, *||ANTHONY, Boston 1639, admitted freeman 1640, member of the ar. co. 1639, representative 1650, 1659, 1660, and 20 years in succession from 1665 to 1684. By his 1st wife, a daughter of Emanuel Downing, he had Solomon, b. 1643, Samson,

b. 3 Dec. 1645, d. at Boston, 4 Nov. 1698 ; and probably Simeon ; by his 2d, Barbary, the widow of Capt. Joseph Weld, whom he m. in 1648, and who d. 15 April, 1655, he had Stephen, b. 6 Jan. 1654 ; by the 3d, Christiana, he had, Anthony b. 16 June, 1656 ; Joseph, b. 1 Dec. 1663 ; John, b. and d. in 166– ; Ebenezer, b. 1 July, 1664. Seventeen of the name, and most of them his descendants, had grad. at Harv. and Yale in 1828. *SOLOMON*, second minister of Northampton, son of the preceding, was born 4 Oct. 1643, grad. at H. C. 1662, was ordained, 11 Sept. 1672, and d. 11 Feb. 1729, æ. 85. He married the widow of Rev. Eleazar Mather, his predecessor. (See MATHER.) Esther, his widow, d. 10 Feb. 1736, æ. 92. Two of his sons were, Rev. Anthony, H. C. 1697, who was ordained the minister of Woodbury, Conn. 27 May, 1702, and d. 6 Sept. 1760, æ. 82, and Hon. John, b. 11 Feb. 1681, H. C. 1701, a counseller, of Massachusetts, who d. at Boston, 19 June, 1748, æ. 66. ‖SIMEON, Boston, brother of the preceding, was member of the ar. co. 1675, and was living in 1729. He was father of the Hon. Anthony Stoddard, H. C. 1697, who was b. 24 Sept. 1678, d. 11 March, 1748, whose son Simeon, H. C. 1726, was a merchant of Boston ; of David, b. 5 Dec. 1685 ; Jonathan, b. 5 Feb. 1688.

STODDER, JOHN, Hingham 1640, was admitted freeman in 1642. His descendants are probably in Mass., where the name continues.

STONE, DANIEL, Cambridge, son of deacon Gregory Stone, was admitted freeman 1643. DAVID, Cambridge, brother of the preceding, freeman 1647, m. Dorcas, and had children David, Daniel, b. 1646, Dorcas, John, Samuel, and Nathaniel. *GREGORY, a dea. of Cambridge, freeman 1636, representative 1638, one of the proprietors of Watertown, d. 30 Nov. 1672, æ. 80. His wife was Lydia, and his children were John ; Daniel ; David ; Elizabeth, who m. a Potter of Ipswich ; Samuel, who had sons Samuel, Isaac, John, and several daughters ; Sarah, who m. a Meriam, of Concord, and Lydia, who m. a Fiske, all of whom were members of the church in 1658. JOHN, Roxbury, d. 26 Oct. 1643. JOHN, a captain, was killed by the Pequot Indians in his bark on Connecticut river in 1634. Hutchinson, i. Hist. Mass. 385. Winthrop, i. Hist. N. E. iii. 122. 2 Coll. Mass. Hist. Soc. x. Index. JOHN, Guilford 1650. JOHN, Sudbury 1640, son of deacon Gregory Stone, had a son Daniel, b. in 1644. *JOHN, Cambridge, freeman 1665, representative 1682 and 1683. JOHN, Beverly, 1659, was one of the founders of the church in 1667. He had a son John of Beverly in 1659, and probably Nathaniel. JOHN, grad. at H. C. 1653, went to England and was admitted to the degree of Master of Arts in the university of Cambridge. He was a classmate with Rev. Samuel Hooker, and might be son of the following, who was the colleague of Mr. Hooker's father. *SAMUEL*, one of the first ministers of Cambridge and Hartford, was born in Hartford, England, and was educated at Emanuel College, came to N. E. in 1633, and settled at

Cambridge with Rev. Thomas Hooker, 11 Oct. 1633, admitted freeman 1634, removed to Hartford with Mr. Hooker in 1636, and there d. 20 July, 1663. SIMON, a deacon of Watertown, was admitted freeman 1636, and was probably the representative in 1678 and 1679. His son John was b. in 1635. WILLIAM, Guilford, Conn. 1658. 1 Coll. Mass. Hist. Soc. x. Index. Twenty-seven of the name had grad. at the N. E. colleges in 1828, twelve of whom grad. at Harvard.

STORY, ANDREW, Ipswich, was one of the Pequot soldiers. AUGUSTINE, Massachusetts a. 1638. Savage, i. Winth. N. E. 26, 409, 411. GEORGE, Boston, called a young merchant from London. Winthrop, ii. Hist. N. E. 69. A George Story was of Maine in 1643. ISAAC, Watertown 1635. Shattuck. WILLIAM, Ipswich 1648. A William Story was admitted freeman 1671.

STOUGHTON, ‡‖*ISRAEL, Dorchester, freeman 1633, representative from 1634 to 1636, member of the ar. co. 1637, its captain in 1642, elected assistant in 1637 and the seven succeeding years. He returned to England, was a lieutenant-colonel to Rainsborow, and d. in the time of the civil wars, at Lincoln, in England. Whitman [Hist. Sketch. of Ar. Co. 14, 147] erroneously calls him *Ezekiel.* Winthrop, ii. Hist. N. E. 245. THOMAS, Dorchester, admitted freeman 1631, removed to Connecticut in 1635 or 1636. John Stoughton grad. at Y. C. in 1755. †‡WILLIAM, lieutenant governour of Massachusetts, was son of the Hon. Israel Stoughton, and grad. at H. C. 1650; went to England, and had a fellowship at New College, Oxford, was a preacher in the county of Sussex, and is placed by Calamy among the ejected ministers after the restoration. He returned to N. E. and was elected an assistant 1671 and until 1686; was an agent for Massachusetts colony in England in 1677; one of Sir Edmund Andros' council in 1687; one of the first counsellors under the new charter 1692; chief-justice of the province; lieutenant-governour 1692, 9 years, and commander-in-chief from 1694 to 1699. He d. a bachelor, at Dorchester, his residence, 7 July, 1701, æ. 70.

STOVER, SYLVESTER, Kittery 1652.

STOW, ‖*JOHN, Roxbury, freeman 1634, member of the ar. co. 1638; representative 1639. His wife d. 1638. JOHN, Concord, freeman 1636, had a son Nathaniel. RICHARD, Massachusetts, came over as early as 1630. SAMUEL, son of John Stow, of Roxbury, grad. at H. C. in 1645, and was living, according to Mather, in 1698. There was a Samuel Stow admitted freeman in 1644, who may be the same. ‖THOMAS, Braintree, member of the ar. co. 1638, had a son John, b. 3 Feb. 1641. THOMAS, Concord, freeman 1653. *WILLIAM, Hampton, was representative in 1644, 1648, and 1649. (See EASTOW.]

STOWELL, SAMUEL, Hingham 1649, had a son Samuel, born in 1655.

STOWERS, JOHN, Watertown, freeman 1636. NICHOLAS, Charlestown, freeman 1631, had sons, Joseph, b. in 1632, died 29

Dec. 1672; John, b. 1638. RICHARD, Charlestown, was on a jury 28 Sept. 1630. He may be the person admitted freeman in 1650.

STRANGE, GEORGE, Hingham, freeman 1635. JOHN, Boston 1651.

STRATTON, JOHN, Salem 1637. A John Stretton was one of the first settlers of East-Hampton, L. I. 1650. Wood. RICHARD, Watertown, d. 25 July, 1658, æ. 30.

STRAWBRIDGE, ‖THOMAS, member of the ar. co. 1638. John and George Strawbridge grad. at N. J. College in 1797 and 1802.

STREET, NICHOLAS, minister of Taunton and New-Haven, came from England, preached some time at the former place, and was settled at New-Haven in 1659, where he d. 22 April, 1674. His children were Samuel, Susannah, Sarah, Abiah, and Hannah, all of whom married. Dodd, East-Haven Register. *SAMUEL*, Minister of Wallingford, son of the preceding, grad. at H. C. 1664, was ordained 1674, died 16 Jan. 1717. He m. (1st) Anna Miles, 3 Nov. 1664, and had, 1. Anna, born 1665; 2. Samuel, b. 1667; 3. Mary, b. 1670; 4. Nicholas, b. 14 July, 1677; 5. Sarah, b. 1681; (2d)Mardline Daniels, by whom he had, 6. Samuel, 2d, b. 1685; 7. James, b. 1686; 8. Anna; (3d) Hannah Glover, by whom were born, 9. Eleanor, in 1691; 10. Nathaniel, in 1693; 11. Elnathan, born 2 Sept. 1695, who was father of Rev. Nicholas Street, Y. C. 1751, the minister of East-Haven, Conn., who was b. 21 Feb. 1730; 12. Mary, b. 1698; 13. John, b. 1703. Ibid.

STREETER, STEPHEN, Charlestown 1644, probably the freeman admitted that year, whose name is spelled *Streete* in ii. Winthrop, 373.

STRICKLAND, JOHN, Massachusetts, freeman 1631, perhaps one of the first settlers of Huntington, L. I. a. 1650. The name is *Stickland* in the colony records.

STRONG, JOHN, Hingham 1635, removed to Taunton, and from thence to Northampton as early as 1659. [Lincoln, Hist. Hingham.] He had 17 children. His son Thomas had 15, son Jedidiah 12, son Samuel 12, and his grandson Jonathan 17. Sixty-one of the name, 17 of them clergymen, had grad. at the N. E. colleges in 1828. RETURN, Windsor 1640. 1 Coll. Mass. Hist. Soc. v. 168.

STUART, JOHN, Springfield a. 1654. (See STEWART.) Eight of the name of Stuart had grad. in N. E. in 1828, of whom is the learned professor at the Andover Theological Institution.

STUBBS, JOSHUA, Massachusetts, was admitted freeman 1649.

STYCH, HENRY, Lynn, was living in 1653, at the age of 102. Lewis.

STUDSON, ROBERT, Scituate a. 1638.

SUMNER, GEORGE, freeman 1657, was of Northampton in 1659. ROGER, Dorchester, freeman 1657, removed to Lancaster, was a deacon of the church, and d. at Milton, 26 May, 1691, æ. 66. His son Samuel was b. in 1658. THOMAS, Rowley 1643. *WILLIAM, Dorchester, freeman 1637, representative 1658, 1666—

1670, 1672, 1678—1681, and 1685 and 1686, 13 years. He had sons, Samuel, b. 1638; Increase, b. 1642; and perhaps William, of Boston in 1656. Increase Sumner, H. C. 1767, governour of Massachusetts, born at Roxbury, 27 Nov. 1746, and who d. 7 June, 1799, in the third year of his office, was descended from this family. William H. Sumner, adjutant-general of Massachusetts, who grad. at H. C. 1799, is son of Governour Sumner. Thirteen others had grad. in N. E. in 1828.

SUNDERLAND, JOHN, Boston, had sons, John and James, b. in 1640 and 1646.

SUTTON, JOHN, Hingham 1638, Scituate 1650. LAMBERT, Woburn, freeman 1644, d. 27 Nov. 1649. RICHARD, was a proprietor of Lancaster 1653. WILLIAM, Newbury 1679.

SWAIN, FRANCIS, Exeter 1645. JEREMY, Charlestown, had sons, Jeremy, b. 1638; and John, born 1644. ‡*JEREMY, Reading, probably son of the preceding, representative 1689, and was elected assistant in 1690. NICHOLAS, Exeter 1643. RICHARD, Rowley, admitted freeman 1638, removed to Hampton. *ROBERT, Haverhill, representative 1684. ‡WILLIAM, Weathersfield, was an assistant or magistrate in 1637, and was one of the first and principal settlers of Branford, Conn., in 1644. WILLIAM, Hampton, d. about 1658.

SWAN, HENRY, Salem, was admitted to the church, 19 May, 1639, and on the 22 May, same year, freeman of the colony. *RICHARD, member of the church in Boston, was admitted freeman 1640; dismissed to the church in Rowley; was representative 1666 to 1673, and 1675, ten years. This name is written *Swain* in some old records. *WILLIAM, was a representative at the general court, and probably from Watertown, 25 May, 1636.

SWEETE, JOHN, a ship-carpenter of Boston, and member of the church, was admitted freeman 1641. His son John was born 1651.

SWEETING, ‖JOHN, member of the ar. co. 1673. Whitman, 160.

SWEETMAN, THOMAS, Cambridge, freeman 1638, whose wife was Isabella, had children, Elizabeth; Rebecca; Ruhamah; Samuel, b. 16 April, 1659, grad. at H. C. 1677; Bethiah; and Hepsibah.

SWEETSER, SETH, Charlestown, freeman 1638. Seth Sweetser, one of his descendants, grad. at H. C. 1722, and died 15 Jan. 1778, æ. 74.

SWETT, BENJAMIN, Newbury as early as 1657, removed to Hampton, was a captain, and was killed by the Indians, at Black-Point, Maine, 29 June, 1677. [Hubbard, Hist. N. E. Belknap.] His wife was Hester, daughter of Nathaniel Weare. He had sons, Joseph and Moses, b. in Newbury, in 1658 and 1661. JOHN, one of the grantees of Newbury, and admitted freeman 1642, was probably father of the preceding.

SWIFT, THOMAS, Dorchester, freeman 1635, had sons, Thomas, b. 1635, freeman 1666; Obadiah, b. 1638, m. in 1661, Rest,

daughter of Humphrey Atherton.   The first graduate of the name
was Rev. John Swift, H. C. 1697, minister of Framingham, who was
ord. 8 Oct. 1701, and d. at the age of 67.   Rev. John Swift, of Ac-
ton, H. C. 1733, d. 7 Nov. 1775, æ. 63.

SWINERTON, JOB, Salem, admitted to the church and freeman in 1639.   JOHN, a physician of Salem, d. 6 Jan. 1691, leaving a widow Hannah,who d. in 1713, æ. 71.   Felt, 300.

SYCKES, RICHARD, Dorchester, was admitted to the church
1639, and freeman 1640, probably removed to Springfield, and there
d. in March, 1676.

SYLVESTER, RICHARD, Weymouth, requested to be made
freeman, 19 Oct. 1630, and was admitted 1634, unless there were
two of the name.   His sons, Increase and Joseph, were b. in 1634
and 1638.   Savage, i. Winthrop's N. E. 289, ii. 77.

SYMMES, ZECHARIAH, the second minister of Charles-
town, after the church was gathered in 1632, was son of William
Symmes, and was born at Canterbury, 5 April, 1599.   He came to
N. E. in August, 1634, and settled at Charlestown the same year.
He was admitted freeman 1635, and d. 4 Feb. 1671, æ. 72.   By
Sarah, his wife, with whom he lived almost 50 years, he had Ruth,
b. 1635; Zechariah; Timothy, b. 1640, d. 1641; Deborah, b. 1642;
Elizabeth, who m. Hezekiah Usher; Mary, who m. Thomas Savage; William, and several others, in all, according to Mather, 13,
of whom 5 were sons.   Johnson mentions the number of his children as being ten, when he wrote, and as " following the example of
their father and grandfather," both of whom he probably knew before he left England, Canterbury being but 4 miles from Herne-Hill,
the residence of Johnson.   *ZECHARIAH*, first minister of Bradford, was son of the preceding, and was born at Charlestown, 9 Jan.
1638, grad. at H. C. 1657, was ordained 27 Dec. 1682, d. 22 March,
1708, æ. 70.   His son Thomas was born at Bradford, 1 Feb. 1678,
grad. at H. C. 1698, and was the first minister of Boxford, where
he was ordained 20 Dec. 1702, dismissed 1708, and afterwards succeeded his father at Bradford, where he d. 6 Oct. 1725, in his 48th
year, having had 3 wives—(1st) Elizabeth, daughter of Rev. Thomas Blowers, by whom he had, Thomas, Andrew, John, Elizabeth,
Anna, Abigail, and Sarah; (2d) Hannah, who d. 1718, daughter
of Rev. John Pike, of Dover; and (3d) Eleanor Moody, a widow,
the daughter of Dr. Benjamin Tompson, of Roxbury.

SYMONDS, HENRY, Boston, freeman 1643.   Snow, Hist.
Boston, 124.   JOHN, Braintree, freeman 1638, might have been
the one of the same name at Salem, who died a. 1671.   JOHN,
Pascataqua 1631, Kittery 1652.   MARK, Ipswich, was born in
1584, was admitted freeman 1638, and d. a. 1659.   ††*SAMUEL,
Ipswich, descended from an ancient and honourable family in Yield-
ham, in Essex, where he had a good estate [Hutch. Coll. 287],
came to N. E., and was admitted freeman in 1638.   He was chosen
representative from 1638, 5 years, assistant from 1643 to 1672, 30
years, deputy-governour from 1673 to 1678, six years.   He died in
Oct. 1678.   He m. the widow of Daniel Epes.   [Epes, MS Gene-

alogy.] He had a large family. The sons were, Samuel, who died
a. 1655; William, who lived at Wells; and Harlakenden, admitted
freeman in 1665. The daughters were, Elizabeth, who m. Capt.
Daniel Epes in 1644, Ruth, who m. Rev. John Emerson, of Gloucester; Priscilla, who m. Thomas Baker, of Topsfield; Susanna;
Dorothy, who m. Joseph Jacob; Martha, who m. John Denison;
and Mary, who m. Peter Duncan. Rebecca, the widow of Deputy-
governour S. d. 21 July, 1695. [Felt.] A letter written by him is
preserved in Hutch. Coll. of Papers, p. 227. SAMUEL, Lynn
1634, d. 26 July, 1675. Lewis. THOMAS, Braintree 1638, had
daughters Joan and Abigail. WILLIAM, Concord 1636, was a
constable in 1645, and removed from town, perhaps to East-Hampton, L. I., where was a William Symonds in 1650. WILLIAM,
Ipswich 1637. *WILLIAM, Wells, son of Deputy-governour Symonds, was admitted freeman 1670, was the representative of Wells,
Me. in 1676. He died 22 May, 1679. Some notice of him may
be found in Hubbard's Wars with the Eastern Indians, p. 26.

SYNDERLAND, ||JOHN, Boston 1644. Coffin. Member of
the ar. co. 1658. (See SUNDERLAND.)

TABOR, PHILIP, Massachusetts, was admitted freeman 1634.

TAINTER, JOSEPH, was a proprietor of Watertown and Sudbury, about 1640.

TALBOT, WILLIAM, sailmaker, Boston 1651. One of the
name has grad. in N. E.

TALBY, JOHN, Salem 1639, died a. 1644. Hutchinson, i. Hist.
Mass. 371. Dorothy Talby was executed in 1638. Winthrop, i.
Hist. N. E. 279.

TALCOTT, ‡*JOHN, Cambridge, freeman 1632, was representative at the first general court 1634; removed to Connecticut and
was an assistant there in 1654. ‡SAMUEL, probably son of the
preceding, grad. at H. C. in 1658; and was elected a magistrate in
1685, and d. before 1698. Two Samuel Talcotts grad. at Y. C. in
1733 and 1757.

TALMAGE, THOMAS, Boston, freeman 1634, of Lynn in
1637, may have removed to East-Hampton, L. I. THOMAS, Jr.
East-Hampton, L. I. 1650. WILLIAM, Boston, was admitted freeman 1634. Savage, ii. Winth. 216.

TANNER, NICHOLAS, Swanzey, 1663.

TAPLEY, CLEMENT, Massachusetts, where the name exists,
was admitted freeman 1640.

TAPP, EDMUND, one of the pillars of Milford 1639, [i. Trumbull, 107] and perhaps the assistant of New-Haven colony in 1643,
unless the name of the assistant was Edward.

TAPPAN, JOSEPH, Massachusetts, was admitted freeman 1634.
The name of Tappan has prevailed in some parts of Massachusetts,
and some of them were descendants from Abraham Toppan, which
see. Rev. Dr. Tappan, it is said, altered the name from Toppan to
Tappan.

TAPPING, ‡JOHN, was elected one of the magistrates of Connecticut in 1662. JOHN, of Boston in 1665. RICHARD, Bos-

ton 1632, was admitted freeman 1634, and had sons, Timothy, b. 1633; Joseph, b. 1645. ‡THOMAS, Connecticut, a captain, was elected magistrate 1651. This name is sometimes *Topping*, in ancient records.

TARBELL, THOMAS, sen. and jun. were of Groton in 1677. Thomas Tarbell, jun. d. at Charlestown in 1678.

TARBOX, JOHN, Lynn 1630, had two sons, Samuel, who had 18 children, and John. His descendants remain at Lynn. Lewis.

TARLETON, RICHARD, came from England and settled at Portsmouth, where his son Elias, by Ruth, his wife, was b. 13 August, 1693. Elias had a son Elias, b. in 1720, and died at the age of 91, who was father of Hon. William Tarleton, of Piermont, a counsellor of N. H., and sheriff of Grafton county, who d. 19 March, 1819, æ. 67, leaving a large family.

TARNEY, BENJAMIN, Concord, was admitted freeman 1641. MILES,, Boston 1638, freeman 1643.

TATMAN, JOHN, Roxbury, freeman 1638, d. 28 Oct. 1670. His son Jabez was b. 1641.

TAY, HENRY, Ipswich, died a. 1655. WILLIAM, Boston, 1642, freeman 1650, and had sons, Isaiah, b. 1649, Abiel in 1652, Nathaniel in 1654, Jeremiah in 1657. He appears to have lived in Billerica in 1659, where he was town clerk one year. William Tay, probably a son, was admitted freeman 1663. Widow Grace Tay d. at Roxbury, 1712, æ. 91.

TAYLOR, ANTHONY, Hampton 1638. Fifty-three of the name of Taylor had grad. at the N. E., N. J., and Union colleges in 1828. CLEMENT, Dorchester 1639. Harris. EDWARD, Lynn 1639, removed to Reading, and was admitted freeman 1648. *ED-WARD*, the first minister of Westfield, Mass. was born in the village of Sketelby, near Hinkley, in Leicestershire, and came to N. E. in 1668, grad. at H. C. 1671; commenced preaching at Westfield in Dec. 1671, was ord. June, 1679; admitted freeman 1680. He d. 29 June, 1729, æ. about 83. He m. in 1674, Elizabeth Fitch, who d. in 1689. His 2d wife d. in 1729. One of his daughters was mother of president Stiles. He left 14 quarto volumes closely written of about 400 pages each. Holmes, Life of Pres. Stiles, 381. E. Davis, Hist. Westfield, 28, 29. GEORGE, freeman in 1638, was of Lynn, in 1637. Lewis. Winthrop, ii. Hist. N. E. 21. GREGORY, Watertown, freeman 1634. HENRY, Portsmouth 1640, died 1649. Belknap, i. Hist. N. H. 47. JAMES, Concord, m. Isabel Tompkins 1641, and d. 22 Jan. 1690. Shattuck. *JO-SEPH*, the third minister of South-Hampton, L. I. grad. 1669 at H. C., of which he was a fellow; was ordained the successor of Rev. Robert Fordham, March, 1680, d. in April, 1682, æ. 31. JOHN, probably of Lynn, came from Haverhill, in England, in company with Governour Winthrop, arrived in 1630, and was admitted freeman 1631. His wife and child d. soon after they arrived in 1630. JOHN, Windsor 1640. JOHN, the freeman of 1651, was of Cambridge, where he d. 7 Sept. 1683, æ. 73. His wife was Catharine. His son Joseph was perhaps the graduate at H. C. 1669, and the

minister of South-Hampton, L. I.   *JAMES, Boston, freeman
1683; representative 1689 and 1693.   JONATHAN, Springfield
1649.   PHILIP, Massachusetts, freeman 1642.   RICHARD, Boston, freeman 1642, had a son John, b. 1646.   SAMUEL, Ipswich
1648.   THOMAS, Watertown, had a son Sinbred, b. in 1642, admitted freeman 1677, and lived in Reading.   THOMAS, Springfield d. 1691.   WILLIAM, Lynn 1642.   WILLIAM, Concord
1654, d. 6 Dec. 1696, having had sons, John, b. 1654; Abraham
1656; Isaac 1659; Jacob 1662; Joseph 1665.   Shattuck, MS.
Hist. Concord.

TEMPLE, ABRAHAM, Salem 1636, had a son of the same
name.   RICHARD, Charlestown 1647, perhaps also of Concord,
where a Richard Temple d. 15 March, 1689, leaving sons, Isaac,
Abraham, and Richard, the last two probably admitted freeman in
1671 and 1672.   SIR THOMAS, came to N. E. in 1657, and remained in Boston a short time, was admitted member of 2d church
in Boston 24 June, 1670, and d. 27 March, 1674.   Hutchinson, i.
Hist. Mass. 190.

TENNEY, THOMAS, Rowley, 1640.   Fifteen of the name had
grad. in N. E. in 1828.   WILLIAM, Rowley 1640.   William
Tenney was b. at Rowley 1640.   Sixteen of the name had grad. at
the N. E. colleges in 1828.

TERRY, STEPHEN, Massachusetts, freeman, 18 May, 1631,
removed to Windsor as early as 1640.   SAMUEL, Springfield, a.
1654.   Sprague, Hist. Disc. 24.   Samuel Terry, H. C. 1710, was
minister of Barrington and Uxbridge.

TEWKSBURY, HENRY, Newbury, 1663, whose son Henry
was b. 15 Dec. 1664.

THACHER, ANTHONY, Marblehead 1635; Marshfield,
Yarmouth 1664, was brother of Rev. Peter Thacher, of Sarum, England, and came to N. E. in 1635, with 9 children.   In attempting
to go from Ipswich bay to Marblehead with his family, and Rev.
John Avery and others, the vessel on board which they all were
was cast away on Thacher's Island, and all perished excepting Mr.
Thacher and his wife.   He d. at Yarmouth, aged a. 80.   He had
two sons born after this accident and before 1640, viz. Judah, who
settled in Connecticut, and John in Plymouth colony.   Alden, i.
Coll. Epitaphs, 120—123.   ‡JOHN, Yarmouth, son of the preceding, was a colonel and many years counsellor of Massachusetts, and
d. 8 May, 1713, in his 75th year.   His first wife was Rebecca
Winslow; his 2d, Lydia Gorham, who d. 2 Aug. 1744, æ. 83.
His children were 18, of whom 8 were by the first wife.   1. Peter,
who m. Thankful Sturges; 2. Josiah, who m. Mary Hedge; 3. Rebecca; 4. John, who m. Desire Dimmock; 5. Bethiah; 6. Elizabeth; 7. Hannah; 8. Mary; 9. Lydia; 10. Desire; 11. Hannah;
12. Mercy; 13. Judah, who m. Sarah Crosby; 14. Mary-Anna;
15. Joseph, who m. Ruth Hawes; 16. Benjamin, who m. Hannah
Lombard; 17. Mary; 18. Thomas, who m. Thankful Baxter.   His
children all married excepting the 7th and 8th.   Ibid. 122, 123.
PETER, minister of Milton, son of Rev. Thomas Thacher, of

Boston, was b. at Salem, 18 July, 1651, grad. at H. C. 1671, ordained 1 June, 1681; d. 27 Dec. [Allen, Biog. Dict. says the 17th] 1727, in his 77th year. By his wife, Theodora, daughter of Rev. John Oxenbridge, whom he m. 21 Nov. 1677, he had, 1. Theodora; 2. Bathsheba; 3. Oxenbridge, b. 17 May, 1681, grad. at H. C. 1698, d. at Milton, 29 Oct. 1772, æ. 91; 4. Elizabeth; 5. Mary; 6. Peter, born 6 Oct. 1688, grad. at H. C. 1706, was ordained at Middleborough, Mass., 2 November, 1709, and d. 22 April, 1744, æ. 56; 7. John; 8. Thomas; 9. John, 2d. He had two other wives, the widow of Rev. John Bailey, of Boston, and Elizabeth, widow of Rev. Joshua Gee, of Boston. *RALPH*, son of Rev. Thomas Thacher, of Boston, was a minister at Martha's Vineyard in 1697. Mather, i. Magnalia, 80. *SAMUEL, a deacon of Watertown, was admitted freeman 1642, elected representative 1665, 1666, 1668, and 1669, and d. 30 Nov. 1669. His wife Hannah was member of the church in Cambridge in 1658. *THOMAS*, first minister of the Old South Church in Boston, was son of Rev. Peter Thacher, of Old Sarum, England, and was b. 1 May, 1620. He arrived at Boston 4 June, 1635, and received his education under President Chauncy. He was ordained at Weymouth, 2 Jan. 1645, as the successor of Mr. Newman, removed to Boston, where he was installed 16 Feb. 1670, and d. 16 Oct. 1678, æ. 58. He m. a daughter of Rev. Ralph Partridge, 11 May, 1643, by whom (who d. 2 June, 1664) he had 3 sons and one daughter. Rev. T. M. Harris, D. D. Eccl. Memoranda in MS. Thomas Thacher, probably his son, d. at Boston, 2 April, 1686.

THALE, NICHOLAS, was an inhabitant of Watertown in 1645. Coffin.

THAXTER, *JOHN, son of the following, resided in Hingham, which he represented in 1666. He d. March, 1687, having had 12 children, of whom Samuel was a colonel, representative, and counsellor, and had 4 children, two of whom were, Elizabeth, who m. Capt. John Norton, and afterwards Colonel Benjamin Lincoln, the father of the distinguished revolutionary general, and Samuel, who was b. 8 Oct. 1695, grad. at H. C. 1714, and d. 4 Dec. 1732. Samuel, son of the last, was b. 15 Nov. 1723, grad. at H C. 1743, and was an officer in the old French war, and present at the masacre of Fort William Henry, 1757. He d. at Bridgewater, 6 Aug. 1771. Lincoln, Hist. Hingham, 47, 116, 123. THOMAS, Hingham 1638, was admitted freeman in 1642, and d. 14 Feb. 1654, his wife, Elizabeth, surviving him. He is the common ancestor of all of the name in Hingham and its vicinity. He left sons John and Samuel. The first five graduates of the name at H. C. are his descendants, and perhaps all the others are. Ibid, 47.

THAYER, NATHANIEL, Taunton 1665. NATHANIEL, Boston, had a son Cornelius, b. 14 Nov. 1684, a deacon of the church, on whose death, in 1745, Dr. Colman preached a funeral sermon, whose son, Nathaniel Thayer, was b. 17 July, 1710, the father, probably, of Rev. Ebenezer Thayer, of Hampton, N. H., b. at Boston, 16 July, 1734, grad. at H. C. 1753, died 6 Sept. 1792. Rev. Nathaniel Thayer, D. D., of Lancaster, Mass., son of the last, grad. at H. C. 1789, and was ordained 9 Oct. 1793. RICHARD, Boston 1640. RICHARD, son of the preceding, lived in Braintree, where he m. Dorothy Pray, 24 Dec. 1651, and had, Richard, b. 31 Aug. 1655 ; Nathaniel, b. 1 Jan. 1658. THOMAS, Braintree, freeman 1647, died in 1665, leaving a wife, Margery, and 3 sons, 1. Thomas, died 1692, æ. 70, who had sons, Isaac, b. 1654, d. 1690 ; John, b. 1656 ; Isaac, b. 1661 ; Ebenezer, b. 1665, and 2 daughters ; 2. Shadrach, who had sons, Trial, b. 1657 ; Timothy, 1666 ; Ephraim, b. 1669, who m. in 1692, Sarah, daughter of John Bass, and the ancestor of between 2000 and 3000 descendants; William, b. 1675 ; Samuel, b. 1667, and 4 daughters ; 3. Ferdinando, who had sons, David, b. 1660 ; Jonathan ; David, 2d, and several daughters.

THOM, WILLIAM, Lynn 1638, went to Long-Island 1640. Lewis.

THOMAS, ‖EVAN, a vintner of Boston, was admitted freeman 1641, member of the ar. co. 1653, died 25 Aug. 1661. Savage, i. Winth. N. E. 25. DAVID, Marblehead 1648. FRANCIS, Boston, had a son John b. in 1665. GEORGE, Boston, whose wife was Rebecca, had sons, Peter, born 6 Feb. 1682 ; George, born 16 March, 1685 ; Maverick, born 19 March, 1694. Peter, had sons, George, Elias, Peter, William, and Moses. From Moses descended Isaiah Thomas, LL. D. of Worcester, Joshua, M. D., Alexander, D. C. 1792, Isaiah, H. C. 1825, and Rev. Moses George Thomas, of Concord, N. H., who grad. at Brown in 1825, and was ord. 25 Feb. 1829. HUGH, Roxbury, freeman 1651, d. 6 May, 1683, æ. 76. NATHANIEL, Marshfield, 1643. ROWLAND, Springfield 1650, Westfield 1670, d. 21 Feb. 1697, at Springfield. WILLIAM, born a. 1599, came to N. E. and settled at Newbury, where he d. 1 Jan. 1680, æ. 80. Susannah, his wife, d. 27 March, 1677. ‡WILLIAM, an assistant of Plymouth colony seven years, from 1642 to 1650, came to N. E. a. the year 1630, and d. in Aug. 1651, æ. 77. His son Nathaniel served in Philip's war, 1675. Davis, Morton's Memo. 250. Twenty-seven of the name had received the honours of college in N. E. in 1828.

THOMPSON, Anthony, New-Haven 1639, who had a son John. Dodd, 154—156. EDMUMD, Salem 1637, was admitted to the church 29 Dec. 1639. JAMES, Charlestown, d, a. 1682. JAMES, Woburn, was born a. 1593, admitted freeman 1634, when he probably resided in Charlestown. Eliza, his wife, d. Nov. 1639, and he m. Susanna Blodget in Feb. 1644. His son James was born 24 Jan. 1646. JOHN, New-Haven 1639, was a brother of Anthony Thompson, d. 11 Dec. 1674. Dodd, 154—156. JOHN, Watertown, freeman 1635, d. in Feb. 1639. JOHN, Concord 1640, freeman 1653, had a son John, b. in 1642. JOHN, Plymouth 1649, had a son John, born that year. JONATHAN, Woburn 1659, was probably the son of James or Simon, of that place. His sons were, Jonathan, James, Simon, and Ebenezer, of whom Jonathan, b. 28 Sept. 1663, was the great-grandfather of Sir Benjamin Thompson, the distinguished philosopher, known by the name of Count Rumford, who was b. at Woburn, 26 March, 1753. The late President Adams and others have conjectured that the count was descended from Rev. William Tompson, of Braintree, but Mr. Jackson, of Boston, by a careful examination of the Woburn town records, has traced his descent to the early Thompsons of Woburn, and thus settled all conjectures respecting his ancestry. MAURICE, Cape-Ann 1639. Felt, Annals Salem, 121. ||ROBERT, a major, and some time an inhabitant of Boston, was a member of the ar. co. 1639. His name often occurs in ancient records in connexion with grants and titles of land. SIMON, Ipswich 1636, d. in 1675, leaving a wife Rachel, and Thomas, Samuel, and Hannah Woods, grandchildren, and sons-in-law Abraham Fitts and Josiah Woods. Felt. SIMON, Woburn 1643, perhaps the freeman in 1648, and one of the first settlers of Chelmsford. A Simon Thompson died in 1658. SIMON, Woburn 1644, probably son of the preceding, had sons, John, b. 4 April, 1645 ; James, b. 20 March, 1649. THOMAS, one of the first settlers of East-Hampton, L. I. 1650. Wood. WILLIAM, New-Haven 1647. Dodd, 154. *WILLIAM*, Braintree. (See TOMPSON.) Forty-six had grad. at the N. E. and N. J. colleges in 1828.

THORNDIKE, JOHN, settled in Ipswich in 1633, returned to England in 1668, and there d. in 1670, leaving six daughters and one son, *PAUL, a lieutenant, and representative of Beverly in 1680, where he resided, who m. Mary Patch in April, 1668, and had sons, John born 22 Jan. 1674 ; Paul, and Herbert. John m. Joanna Dodge, 1696, and had six sons. Paul m. and had 10 sons, of whom Andrew, born 12 Nov. 1719, was father of Hon. Israel Thorndike, a wealthy merchant of Boston.

THORLAYE, RICHARD, one of the first settlers of Rowley, removed to Newbury, where his son Francis also resided, had a numerous family, and d. 26 Nov. 1703. This name is now written *Thurlo* and *Thorla*.

THORNDON, JOHN, one of the founders of the first Baptist church in Newport, 1644.

THORNE, WILLIAM, Massachusetts, was admitted freeman 1638. Union College presents one graduate of this name in 1811.

THORNTON, PETER, Boston 1637, had a son Joseph born that year. THOMAS, Massachusetts, freeman 1634, probably removed to Windsor. 1 Coll. Mass. Hist. Soc. v. 168. *THOMAS*, minister of Yarmouth, came to N. E., according to Mather, after the general ejectment of ministers following the restoration of Charles II. He removed to Boston, and d. there, 15 Feb. 1700, æ. near 93 years. Calef, More Wonders, 62. Sewall, MS. Mather [ii. Magnalia, 418] gives an account of his daughter Priscilla. Timothy Thornton was a representative of Boston in 1693, 1694, and 1695.

THORPE, HENRY, Massachusetts, freeman 1645. THOMAS, of Ipswich, died a. 1677.

THORWELL, THOMAS, Boston, is styled captain, and d. 11 March, 1661.

THROCKMORTON, GEORGE, probably the one who arrived at Nantasket 5 Feb. 1631, although Mr. Savage, in a note in i. Winthrop, Hist. N. E. 42, considers *John* as the one who arrived in the ship Lyon at this time; yet the list of freemen admitted 18 May following, gives the name of *George*. JOHN, Salem 1639, became a Baptist, and went to Rhode-Island. Hutchinson, i. Hist. Mass. 371. 3 Coll. Mass. Hist. Soc. i. 172. Savage, i. Winth. 42. Felt, Annals Salem.

THURSTON, DANIEL, Newbury, d. 16 Feb. 1666, leaving no family. Coffin. DANIEL, Newbury 1637, whose 1st wife d. in 1648, m. the same year to Anna Lightfoot, and left posterity. JOHN, Newbury 1641. JOHN, Dedham freeman 1643, had a son Benjamin born 1640, freeman 1665. John Thurston, of Medfield, freeman 1663, was probably a son. Thomas Thurston, also of Medfield, had sons, John, b. 1656, Thomas, Nathaniel, and others. RICHARD, Salem, 1637, perhaps of Boston 1652. Edward Thurston was of Newport, R. I., in 1672.

THWING, BENJAMIN, joiner, Boston, member of the church 1642, freeman 1645, had sons Edward and John, and was a proprietor of Watertown, and probably of Concord.

TIBBETTS, JEREMIAH, Dover 1656, by Mary, his wife, had, Jeremiah, b. 5 June, 1656; Mary, 1658; Thomas, born 24 Feb. 1660; Hannah, 1662; Joseph, 7 Aug. 1663. HENRY, who was of Dover in 1665. WALTER, Salem, died a. 1651. This name is also spelled *Tebbets*, *Tibbits*, *Tibbets*, and *Tibbitts*.

TICKNER, WILLIAM, Scituate 1646.

TIDD, JOHN, Woburn, died 24 April, 1657. JOHN, Charlestown 1644, had sons John and James. ROBERT, freeman 1643.

TIFT, WILLIAM, Massachusetts, was admitted freeman 1641.

TILDEN, NATHANIEL, Plymouth and Scituate, came from the county of Kent, and perhaps from Tentenden, before 1628, and died in 1641. Lydia, his widow, m. Timothy Hatherly. Thomas, who arrived at Plymouth in the ship Ann, in 1623, was probably his son. Joseph, another son, and the eldest, lived in Scituate, and d. in 1670. 2 Coll. Mass. Hist. Soc. iv. 242.

TILESTONE, THOMAS, Massachusetts, was admitted freeman in 1637. One of the name had grad. in N. E. in 1828. The venerable John Tileston, the master of the north writing school in Boston, d. in 1826, æ. 92. *TIMOTHY, Dorchester, freeman 1666, representative in 1689. Cornelius Tilestone d. at Dorchester in June, 1659.

TILLINGHAST, PARDON, was b. at Seven-Cliffe, near Beachy-Head, England, a. 1622, came to N. E. and was settled the Baptist minister of Providence in 1645. Benedict, i Hist. Baptists, 478.

TILLOTSON, JOHN, Rowley, thence to Newbury, m. Dorcas Coleman 1648, and had children, Mary; John, b. 1651; James, 1652; Philadelphia, 1656; Joseph, 1657; Jonathan, 1659, and others.

TILLEY, EDWARD and JOHN, two of the pilgrims of Plymouth, came to N. E. in 1620, and both d. the next year. JOHN, Massachusetts, admitted freeman 1635.

TILTON, JOHN, Lynn 1642, had a son John of Lynn in 1642. PETER, Windsor 1640. 1 Coll. Mass. Hist. Soc. 168. ‡*PETER, representative of Hadley from 1665 to 1676, excepting 1667, 1669, and 1671, was a deacon of the church, and elected assistant from 1680 to 1686, seven years. WILLIAM, Lynn 1645, died a. 1653.

TINGLEY, PALMER, Ipswich 1639, was one of the Pequot soldiers. SAMUEL, d. at Malden in Dec. 1666. Rev. Pelatiah Tingley grad. at Y. C. 1761.

TINKER, JOHN, Boston 1651, freeman 1654, Lancaster 1657, where he was town clerk. He went to " Pequid" 1659. Willard, Hist. Lancaster. THOMAS, one of the Plymouth pilgrims, arrived in 1620, and d. before March, 1621.

TINKHAM, EPHRAIM, Plymouth, had sons, Ephraim, b. 1649, Ebenezer, b. 1651 ; Samuel, b. 1656 ; John, b. 1656; Isaac, b. 1666.

TITCOMB, *WILLIAM, came from Newbury, England, and settled at Newbury, admitted freeman 1642, representative 1655, d. 24 Sept. 1676. His children were, sons, Peniel, b. 1650 ; Benaiah, b. 1653 ; William, 1659 ; Thomas, b. 1661 ; and John, and 7 daughters. Col. Titcomb, who was killed in the French war 1755, was a descendant.

TITTERTON, ||SAMUEL, member of the ar. co. 1643.

TITUS, ROBERT, Weymouth, freeman 1640. Abiel, b. 1640, Content and Samuel Titus were of Long-Island in 1672.

TODD, *JOHN, Rowley 1650, representative 1686. His widow d. 1710. Twelve of the name had grad. at Y. C. in 1828, of whom several were clergymen. ||JOSHUA, freeman 1639, member of the ar. co. 1644. WALTER, Rhode-Island 1664. 2 Coll. Mass. Hist. Soc. vii. 93.

TOLL, JOHN, Sudbury freeman 1645. John C. Toll, the only graduate of the name, received his degree at Union College in 1799.

TOLMAN, THOMAS, Dorchester, was admitted freeman 1640. Thomas and John Tolman, probably his sons, were admitted freeman 1678.

TOMLYNS, ||*EDWARD, Lynn 1630, was representative at the first general court 1634, again in 1635 and 1644, member of the ar. co. 1638, clerk of the writs in 1643. He went to Long-Island in 1640, but returned to Lynn; went to England in 1644, resided in London, and appears to have been at Dublin in Ireland in 1679. Lewis, MS Annals of Lynn. *TIMOTHY, Lynn 1630, brother of the preceding, was admitted freeman 1633, was representative 6 years, from 1635 to 1640. Savage, ii. Winth. Hist. N. E. 5. Ibid.

TOMPKINS, JOHN, Concord, removed to Fairfield, Sept. 1644. Shattuck. JOHN, jun. Salem 1637, freeman 1642. RALPH,

Dorchester, freeman 1638. SAMUEL, one of the proprietors of Bridgewater 1645. Rev. Isaac Tompkins, d. at Haverhill in 1826.
TOMPSON, ARCHIBALD, Marblehead 1637, was drowned in 1641. Winthrop, ii. Hist. N. E. 43. BENJAMIN, Braintree, son of Rev. William Tompson, was born 14 July, 1642, grad. at H. C. 1662, was famed as a poet, physician, and schoolmaster, and d. 13 April, 1714, æ. 72, leaving 8 children and 28 grand-children. Specimens of his poetry may be found in the first edition of Hubbard's Indian Wars, and in the Magnalia. *EDWARD*, minister of Marshfield, was probably son of the preceding. He grad. at H. C. 1684, instructed a school several years at Newbury, was ordained at Marshfield, 14 Oct. 1696, and d. 16 March, 1705, æ. 40. His son Samuel, born at Newbury, 1 Sept. 1691, grad. at H. C. 1710, and was the minister of Gloucester. William, another son, H. C. 1718, was ordained the minister of Scarborough, Me. 1727, and d. Feb. 1759, aged a. 60. Rev. John Tompson, of Standish and Berwick, Me. who grad. at H. C. 1765, was son of Rev. William, of Scarborough, and d. 21 Dec. 1828, æ. 88. GEORGE, Reading, d. 7 Sept. 1674. *JOSEPH, Billerica, son of Rev. William Tompson, was b. at Braintree, 1 May, 1640, m. Mary Brackett, 24 July, 1662, and soon after settled in Billerica, where he was a schoolmaster, captain, selectman, town clerk, deacon of the church, many years, and in 1699, 1700, and 1701, a representative to the general court. He d. 13 Oct. 1732, æ. 92. Mary, his 2d wife, d. 9 Oct. 1743, æ. 91. Benjamin Tompson. esq. and Colonel William Tompson, magistrates and representatives of Billerica, were his descendants. *SAMUEL, brother of the preceding, was born in England, a. 1631, came to N. E. with his father in 1637, lived in Braintree, which he represented 14 years, from 1676 to 1679 and 1682 to 1691, and where he was ordained deacon 2 Nov. 1679. He d. 18 June, 1695, æ. 64. He m. Sarah Shepard, 14 Sept. 1656. His son Samuel was b. 6 Nov. 1662. He m. a 2d wife, Elizabeth Billings, in 1680. *WILLIAM*, one of the first ministers of Braintree, now Quincy, came from Lancashire, where he had been a preacher, to N. E. in 1637, and was installed 24 Sept. 1639. He was admitted freeman, 13 May, 1640; went to Virginia as a missionary in 1642, returned in 1643. While absent, his wife, Abigail, d. in Jan. 1643. He d. 10 Dec. 1666, aged 68. Anna, a second wife, survived him. His children were William, Samuel, Joseph, Benjamin, and a daughter, who m. William Very. This family has been uniform in omitting the *h* in the name, which is erroneously retained throughout the History of Quincy. WILLIAM, graduated at H. C. 1653, and was probably son of the preceding. He became a preacher and was invited to settle at Springfield. He m. 19 Nov. 1655, Catharine, daughter of Richard Treat, of Weathersfield, and appears to have been living in 1698.

TOOLLY, EDWARD, New-Haven 1665. Dodd. E. Haven Reg.

TOOTHACHER, ROGER, Billerica, admitted an inhabitant 1660, had a son, grandson, and great-grandson, all physicians, of the name of Roger.

TOPLIFF, CLEMENT, Dorchester 1637, had a son Jonathan, b. that year. Samuel Topliff grad. at H. C. 1795.

TOPPAN, ABRAHAM, Newbury, was admitted freeman in 1638, m. Susanna Goodale of Yarmouth, Eng. and had sons, Abraham; Isaac; Jacob, admitted freeman 1677; Peter; John, b. 23 April, 1651. Peter m. Jane, daughter of Christopher Batt, 3 April, 1661; was a physician, and killed by a fall, 10 Nov. 1707, and was father of Rev. Christopher Toppan, of Newbury, b. 15 Dec. 1671, grad. at H. C. 1691, ordained 9 Sept. 1696, d. 23 July, 1747, æ. 75, whose wife was Sarah Angier, of Waltham, Ms., and two of whose sons were educated at H. C., Edmund, a physician of Hampton, who grad. 1720, and Bezaleel, who grad. 1722, and d. 1762, æ. 58. Edmund was father of the Hon. Christopher Toppan, of Hampton, whose son Edmund grad. at H. C. 1796.

TOPPING, ‡THOMAS. (See TAPPING.)

TORREY, JAMES, was a lieutenant of Scituate in 1640. PHILIP, Roxbury, was admitted freeman in 1644, d. May, 1686. *SAMUEL*, minister of Weymouth, succeeded Rev. Thomas Thacher in 1656, and d. 21 April, 1707, æ. 75, having been a faithful minister 51 years. He m. Mrs. Mary Symmes, 30 July, 1695. ||*WILLIAM, Weymouth, freeman 1642, member of the ar. co. 1641, representative from 1642 to 1649, excepting 1646 and 1647, and perhaps the representative again from 1679 to 1683. Johnson [Hist. N. E. 110] says that he was " a good penman and skilled in the Latin tongue," and was "usually Clarke of the deputies." Sixteen of the name had received the honours of the N. E. colleges in 1828.

TOTENHAM, HENRY, Woburn 1653. 3 Coll. Mass. Hist. Soc. i. 45.

TOUTON, JOHN, a physician from Rochelle, in France, settled in Massachusetts as early as 1662.

TOWER, JOHN, Hingham 1637, freeman 1638, Lancaster 1654. Savage, ii. Winth. N. E. 234. Willard, Hist. Lancaster.

TOWLE, ROGER, was admitted freeman 1644

TOWNE, WILLIAM, Cambridge, freeman 1637, with his wife Martha, belonged to the church in 1658. He had a son Peter, who was b. in England.

TOWNSEND, ||JOHN, was a member of the ar. co. 1641. Twenty persons of the name of Townsend had grad. at the N. E. colleges in 1826. ROBERT, Portsmouth 1665. THOMAS, Lynn, freeman 1638, d. 22 Dec. 1677. Lewis. Thomas, Henry, and John Townsend, probably his sons, were among the first settlers of Oyster-Bay, Long-Island. WILLIAM, Boston, freeman 1636, had sons, Peter, b. 1642, d. 14 May, 1696; James, b. 1646; Penn, b. 1651; John, b. 3 Sept. 1653. ||*PENN, Boston, son of the preceding, was b. 20 Dec. 1651, member of the ar. co. 1674, representative 1686, 11 years; d. 21 Aug. 1727, æ. 75.

TOZER, RICHARD, Boston 1657, probably went to Maine, and was killed by the Indians in October, 1675. Hubbard. Sullivan.

TRACY, STEPHEN, Plymouth 1623, Duxbury 1645. A. Bradford. STEPHEN, Saybrook 1637, probably ancestor of the distinguished families of this name in Connecticut. Hon. Uriah Tracy, of this state, d. 9 July, 1807, æ. 53. THOMAS, Salem 1637. Seventeen of the name had grad. at the N. E. colleges in 1828.

TRAIN, JOHN, Watertown 1640. Rev. Charles Train, of Framingham, grad. at H. C. 1805.

TRAPP, THOMAS, was one of the first four settlers at Martin's Vineyard. Coffin.

TRASK, *WILLIAM, came to N. E. with Governour Endecott, and arrived at Salem, Sept. 1628, requested to be made freeman 19 Oct. 1630, was a captain, and represented Salem 5 years, from 1635 to 1639. He d. in 1666, and was buried under arms, leaving children, Mary, b. 1637; William, baptized 19 Sept. 1640, Susan, Mary, and John. Prince, i. Annals, 174. Felt, Annals Salem, 227.

TRAVERS, DANIEL, Boston 1652, had sons Daniel, Jeremiah, and Timothy. HENRY, Newbury 1644, had a son James, b. 28 April, 1645. RICHARD, Boston, a. 1652.

TREADWELL, EDWARD, Ipswich 1637. Felt, MS Letter. THOMAS, Ipswich, freeman 1638, d. 8 June, 1670. Winthrop, ii. Hist. N. E. 346. Felt, MS letter.

TREADWAY, NATHANIEL, Sudbury 1640, whose son Jonathan was b. 1640. Rev. James Treadway grad. at Y. C. 1759.

TREAT, ‡RICHARD, Weathersfield, was elected an assistant of Connecticut in 1658. §†‡ROBERT, New-Haven colony, was elected assistant in 1659, of Connecticut colony 1673, one of Sir Edmund Andros' council 1687, governour 1683 to 1697, fifteen years; d. 12 July, 1710, in his 89th year. Dr. Holmes [i. Annals, 504] says he had been governour or deputy-governour of Connecticut 32 years. SAMUEL, minister of Eastham, was son of the preceding, and grad. at H. C. 1669, was ordained 1672, d. 18 March, 1717, in his 69th year. His wife was Abigail, widow of Rev. Benj. Estabrook, and daughter of Rev. Samuel Willard. Eight at Yale and two at Harvard of this name had grad. in 1828.

TREFETHEN, HENRY, New-Hampshire 1687, where the name continues. He was one of the grand-jury of New-Hampshire, 1687. This name is spelt *Trevethan* in England.

TRELAWNY, ROBERT, the owner of Richmond's Island, Maine, about 1643.

TRESCOTT, WILLIAM, Dorchester, freeman 1643. John Trescott d. at Dorchester in 1740, æ. 90. Col. Lemuel Trescott, probably a descendant, d. at Lubec, Me., in 1826.

TRERICE, NICHOLAS, Charlestown, where his son John was b. in 1639, of Woburn in 1643, where his son Samuel was b. that year.

TRESLER, THOMAS, Salem, admitted to the church 15 Dec. 1639, freeman 1642, died a. 1654. This name in the Salem records is *Trusler*.

TRICKEY, THOMAS, Exeter 1644. Persons of this name, probably his descendants, are in New-Hampshire.

TRIMMINGS, OLIVER, Exeter 1644.

TRIPP, JOHN, Portsmouth, R. I., deputy in 1672.

TRISTRAM, RALPH, Saco 1652. Samuel, Saco about the same time. This name is frequently *Trustrum*, and by mistake is *Trentrum* in Sullivan.

TROTT, THOMAS, Dorchester, freeman 1644. Bernard Trott was of Boston in 1665. Lemuel Trott grad. at H. C. 1733.

TROTMAN, JOHN, Boston 1645.

TROTTER, WILLIAM, Newbury, one of the early settlers, m. Cutbury Gibbs in 1652, and had several children.

TROWBRIDGE, JAMES, Dorchester 1658, married 1659 to Margaret, and had sons, James, Jonathan, and William, b. in Dorchester, and John and Thomas, and perhaps Caleb, b. in Newton, to which place he removed. Hon. Edmund Trowbridge, H. C. 1728, who d. 2 April, 1793, æ. 84, was a descendant. Holmes, ii. Annals, 396.

TRUE, *HENRY, Salisbury, freeman 1675, representative 1689, was probably the ancestor of Rev. Henry True, the first minister of Hampstead, N. H., who grad. at H. C. 1750, was ordained 24 June, 1752, and d. 22 May, 1782.

TRUESDALE, RICHARD, Massachusetts, freeman 1635, perhaps brother-in-law of Gov. Winthrop. [ii. Winth. 353.] JOHN, sen. and jun., were of Kittery in 1652. SAMUEL, admitted freeman in 1685, settled at Cambridge Village, and m. Abigail, daughter of Dea. Jno. Jackson.

TRULL, JOHN and SAMUEL, of Billerica 1675. John d. 15 June, 1704, æ. 70. The name is probably derived from Trull in Somersetshire.

TRUMBULL, DANIEL, Lynn 1647. Lewis. JOHN, Cambridge 1636, freeman 1640, had sons, John, b. 4 August, 1641, and James, born 1647. JOHN, Rowley as early as 1643, and perhaps earlier, and the *second* John Trumbull admitted freeman in 1640. He was probably the deacon of Rowley church, ordained 24 Dec. 1686. This name has been much distinguished in Connecticut.

TUCKE, ROBERT, Watertown, freeman 1639, probably the same who went to Hampton, and d. 1665. EDWARD, Hampton, died a. 1653.

TUCKER, JOHN, Hingham at an early period. John Tucker m. Mary Richardson, of Newbury in 1676. Ephraim and Manasseh Tucker were admitted freemen in 1678. ROBERT, Weymouth 1639. *ROBERT, Milton, was representative in 1680 and 1681. ROGER, Salem, died a. 1661.

TUCKERMAN, JOHN, Boston 1655. Rev. Joseph Tuckerman, D. D., formerly the minister of Chelsea, grad. at H. C. 1798.

TUDOR, OWEN, came from Wales, and was one of the early settlers of Windsor. His son Samuel began the settlement on the east side of Conn. River, at Windsor, about 1677. Rev. Samuel Tudor, of Windsor, was a descendant, and father of Dr. Elihu Tudor, who d. at East-Windsor, 6 March, 1826, æ. 93. Boston News-Letter of March, 1826.

TUFTS, PETER, was b. in 1617, came from England as early as 1654, admitted freeman 1665, settled in that part of Charlestown now Malden, and died 13 May, 1700, æ. 83, leaving a wife, Mary, who d. Jan. 1703, sons, Peter, Jonathan, and John, and daughters, Mary Edes, Elizabeth Lynde, Mercy Waite, and Sarah Oakes. *PETER, Medford, freeman 1679, a captain, and representative in 1689, m. Elizabeth Lynde, 26 August, 1670, and d. a. 1721, leaving 11 children. His son Peter probably removed to Quaboag, Brookfield. His son Thomas grad. at H. C. 1701, was a merchant of Charlestown, and d. a. 1734. Simon Tufts, who grad. at H. C. 1724, a physician of Medford, was son or grandson of Capt. Peter. He d. 30 Jan. 1747, æ. 47, leaving two sons educated at Harvard, Simon, a physician of Medford, who grad. in 1744, and d. in Dec. 1786, and Cotton, a physician of Weymouth, and president of the M. M. S., and often a senator and counsellor of the commonwealth. Cotton Tufts. H. C. 1767, was son of the last named, and Cotton Tufts, H. C. 1789, was son of the 2d Simon Tufts. Rev. John Tufts, H. C. 1708, minister of the 2d church in Newbury, Rev. Joshua Tufts, H. C. 1736, the first minister of Litchfield, N. H., Thomas, Abijah, Hall, and Joseph Tufts, all graduates of Harvard College, were descended from the first Peter.

TUPPER, THOMAS, Lynn, removed to Sandwich 1637, and d. in 1676, æ. 97. Ann, his wife, died 1675, æ. 97. One of this name, and probably his son, was a preacher to the Indians in Plymouth colony, a. 1692. Mather, i. Magnalia, 517.

TURELL, ||DANIEL, a captain of Boston in 1646, member of the ar. co. in 1656, d. 23 Jan. 1699. WILLIAM, of Boston, had a son William b. in 1657. Rev. Ebenezer Turell of Medford, H. C. 1721, was, it is believed, of this family.

TURIN, ||DANIEL, member of the ar. co. 1660. Whitman.

TURNER, Humphrey, Scituate 1633, died a. 1673, leaving a numerous descent, John being the eldest son. 2 Coll. Mass. Hist. Soc. iv. 243. JEFFREY, Dorchester, freeman 1643, had sons, Praisever, born in 1640 and settled in Northampton; Increase, b. in 1642. JOHN, Plymouth, one of the first pilgrims 1620, died in 1621. JOHN, Salem, son of John Turner, who d. at Barbadoes in 1668, d. at Salem, 1680, leaving an estate of £6788. His children were, John, Elizabeth, Eunice, Freestone, and Abiel. Felt. JOHN, Lynn 1647. Lewis. JOHN, Medfield, freeman 1649, had sons, John, b. 1651; Isaac, and Samuel. MICHAEL, Lynn 1637, went to Sandwich same year. Lewis. ||*NATHANIEL, a captain in the Pequot war, was of Lynn in 1630, admitted freeman 1632, representative at the first court in 1634, again in 1635. He removed to New-Haven in 1638, and was one of the purchasers of Stamford from the Indians in 1640. He was lost at sea in the same ship with Thomas Gregson, Mr. Lamberton, and others, who sailed from New-Haven in Jan. 1646. There was a Captain Turner who was killed by the Indians in Philip's war, 1675. ||ROBERT, Boston, freeman 1634, member of the ar. co. 1640, a lieutenant 1662, had 7 sons born in Boston, of whom Ephraim was admitted freeman in

1666. WILLIAM, Dorchester 1642. A William Turner was one of the founders of the first Baptist church in Boston, and came from Dartmouth, England. Benedict.

TUTHILL, JOHN, New-Haven 1644, perhaps of South-Old in 1640. JOHN, Massachusetts, was admitted freeman in 1671.

TUTTLE, HENRY, Hingham, came over in 1637, and was admitted freeman 1638. Lincoln, Hist. Hingham, 43, where the name is spelled *Tuttil.* ||*JOHN, Ipswich 1637, member of the ar. co. 1643, was representative at the March session 1644. JOHN, Boston 1653. RICHARD, husbandman, Boston, freeman 1636, d. 8 May, 1640. Savage, ii Winthrop, 216. ||SIMON, Ipswich, d. in Jan. 1692, may have been the member of the ar. co. 1651. WILLIAM, Charlestown 1637. Winthrop, ii. Hist. N. E. 348. WILLIAM, New-Haven 1645. had sons, Thomas, Jonathan, Joseph, Simon, and Nathaniel. Dodd, East-Haven Register, 156.

TWELLS, ROBERT, Braintree, freeman 1663, was a lieutenant, m. Martha Brackett 1651. Name spelled Twellers and Twelves. Mr. Whitney [Hist. Quincy, 47] might have found his name in the Braintree records.

TWISDEN, JOHN, Scituate 1639, removed to Georgiana, Me. 2 Coll. Mass. Hist. Soc. iv.

TWITCHELL, BENJAMIN, was one of the proprietors of Lancaster 1654. JOSEPH, Massachusetts, was admitted freeman 1634.

TYBBOT, WILLIAM, Gloucester, freeman 1642, perhaps Tibbetts.

TYLER, ABRAHAM, Haverhill 1650, d. 6 May, 1673. Saltonstall, Hist. Haverhill. JOB, Andover a. 1653, had a son Moses, who died 1727, æ. 85, having had 10 sons. NATHANIEL, Lynn 1642.

TYLLEY, JOHN. (See TILLEY.) Samuel Tyley grad. at H. C. 1733.

TYNG, ‡||*EDWARD, a merchant of Boston 1639, was admitted to the church, and to the oath of freeman in 1641, member of the ar. co. 1642, representative 1661 and 1662, assistant from 1668 to 1681, 14 years, and colonel of the Suffolk regiment. It appears that he was elected major-general after Leverett, but it is not known that he served in that office. He removed to Dunstable, and there d. 28 Dec. 1681, æ. 81. He had two wives, the last Mary by name, and his children were, Jonathan ; Edward ; Hannah, who m. Habijah Savage ; Eunice, the 2d wife of Rev. Samuel Willard ; Rebecca, who m. Governour Joseph Dudley, and another daughter, who m. a Searle. Alden, Coll. Epitaphs. ‡EDWARD, second son of the preceding, was one of Sir Edmund Andros' council 1687, and was appointed governour of Annapolis, and was taken prisoner on his passage to that place, carried into France, where he d. His wife was a daughter of Thaddeus Clarke, of Portland, and his children were, 1. Edward, a brave naval commander, b. 1683, and d. at Boston, 8 Sept. 1755 ; 2. Jonathan, who d. at an early age ; 3. Mary, who m. Rev. John Fox, of Woburn ; 4. Elizabeth, who m. a brother of Dr. Franklin.   Ibid, ii. 98.   ‡JONATHAN, Woburn, son of the preceding, was b. 15 Dec. 1642; was one of Sir Edmund Andros' council 1687, a magistrate, and a man of influence.   He d. 19 Jan. 1724, æ. 82.   He m. Sarah, daughter of Hezekiah Usher, and she probably d. in March 1714.   Judith, his widow, d. 5 June, 1736, in her 99th year.   Two of his sons were, 1. John, who grad. at H. C. 1691, lived in Chelmsford, and was a major, and killed by the Indians, in Aug. 1710, leaving son John, who grad. at H. C. 1725, the eccentrick Judge Tyng, of Tyngsborough, Ms., who d. 7 April, 1797, æ. 93; 2. Eleazar, who grad. at H. C. 1712, for many years a magistrate and colonel of the Middlesex regiment, who d. in 1782, aged 92.   ‖*WILLIAM, a merchant of Boston, and brother of the first Edward Tyng, was admitted freeman 1638, became member of the ar. co. 1638, its ensign in 1640, captain of the military company of Braintree 1644, representative of Boston 1639, and the eight succeeding years, and treasurer of the colony from 1640 to 1644.   He d. 18 Jan. 1653, leaving an estate of £2774. 14. 4.   His wife Jane d. 3 Oct. 1652.   Five daughters are named in the records.   Mather, in the Magnalia, i. 129, gives his name as an assistant in 1643, but it appears that he never sustained that office.   Savage, ii. Winth. Hist. N. E. 99.

UFFORD, THOMAS, Roxbury, was admitted freeman 1633, went to Springfield, and was among the earliest settlers.   This name is *Uffot* in the colony records, but Sprague [Hist. discourse, 1825, p. 14] spells it Ufford.   His descendants are in Trumbull, and other towns in Connecticut.   Ufford is the name of a place in Suffolk, Eng., which was the seat of Robert de Ufford, the earl of Suffolk.

UNDERHILL, ‖*JOHN, a captain, came to N. E. in 1630, was admitted freeman in 1631, and resided first at Boston, from whence he went to Dover.   He was a representative from Boston at the first general court in 1634, and a member of the ar. co. in 1637, and was engaged in the Pequot war.   He went to Connecticut, and settled at Stamford, which he represented in the general court at New-Haven, in 1643; removed to Flushing, on L. I., in 1646, from thence to Oyster-Bay, and was a delegate from that place to the assembly held at Hempstead by Gov. Nicolls.   Captain Underhill died, it is supposed, in 1672, at Oyster-Bay.   His descendants still remain on Long-Island, and are respectable.   Most of them, says Mr. Wood, have " exchanged the warlike habiliments of their ancestor for the Quaker habit."   His posterity may also be in New-Hampshire, where the name exists.   Wood, Hist. Long-Island, 76.

UNDERWOOD, JOSEPH, Hingham 1637.   JOSEPH, Watertown, perhaps the preceding was admitted freeman 1645, d. 16 Feb. 1677.   His wife d. 21 March, 1668.   MARTIN, Watertown, was admitted freeman 1634.   *THOMAS, Hingham, freeman 1637, was representative in 1637 and 1648.   WILLIAM, Concord 1639, freeman 1650, was one of the first settlers of Chelmsford.

UPHAM, *JOHN, Weymouth, freeman 1635, was a representative in 1636.   His son John was b. 5 June, 1640.   NATHANIEL, Malden, freeman 1653.   Rev. Edward Upham, H. C. 1734, a native of Malden, was probably a descendant. A lieutenant Upham died in Boston of wounds he received in the capture of Narraganset Fort, 19 Dec. 1675. [Hubbard, Indian Wars.] John Upham, of Charlestown, d. 25 Nov. 1677, and another John Upham d. there of small Pox in 1678. Phinehas Upham d. at Malden, in Oct. 1676. Twelve of the name had grad. at Harv. and Dart. in 1828, of whom five have been clergymen.

UPSALL, ||NICHOLAS, Boston, member of the church, was admitted freeman 1631 ; member of the ar. co. 1637. He was apprehended Oct. 1656 for reproaching the magistrates and espousing the cause of the Quakers, fined £20, and banished the colony. He went to Plymouth, but returned, and d. 20 Aug. 1666. His son Experience was b. 1640. He had several daughters. Hutchinson, i. Hist. Mass. 183. Snow, Hist. Boston. Whitman, Sketch Ar. Co. 13. The name is sometimes spelled *Upshall*. RICHARD, was on a jury, 28 Sept. 1630, to view the body of Austin Bratcher.

URAN, JOHN, was of New-Hampshire in 1686.

USHER, ||*HEZEKIAH, Cambridge, freeman 1639, removed to Boston, a. 1646, was a member of the ar. co. 1638, representative for Billerica 1671, 1672, and 1673, and d. in May, 1676. Two sons were b. at Cambridge, Hezekiah, in June, 1639, d. at Lynn, 11 July, 1697 ; buried in Boston ; and John, who d. an infant, in Sept. 1643. John, 2d, of the name, was born in Boston in 1648. By a 2d wife, Elizabeth, daughter of Rev. Z. Symmes, he had Zachariah, b. in 1654. His 3d wife, Mary, survived him. ‡†||JOHN, lieutenant-governour of New-Hampshire, son of the preceding, was b. in Boston, 27 April, 1648, was admitted freeman in 1673, and was a bookseller and stationer. He was a member of the ar. co. 1673; afterwards a colonel, and in 1687 one of Sir Edmund Andros' council. He was appointed lieutenant-governour of N. H. 1692, was in office a. five years, re-appointed in 1702 under Governour Dudley. He removed from Portsmouth to Medford, and there d. 5 Sept. 1726, æ. 78. His son John grad. at H. C. in 1719 ; was a minister and d. 30 April, 1775, aged 76 [Winthrop], leaving a son John, who grad. at H. C. 1743, was the Episcopal minister of Bristol, R. I. where he d. July, 1804, aged a. 81.

UTLEY, SAMUEL, Scituate 1657. 2 Coll. Mass. Hist. Soc. iv. 241. This name is in Massachusetts.

VALENTINE, JOHN, Boston, was admitted freeman 1675.

VANE, ‡*HENRY, the eldest son of Sir Henry Vane, was born in 1612, was educated at Westminster school and Magdalen-Hall, Oxford. He came to N. E. after having been to Geneva, and arrived at Boston, in 1635 ; was admitted freeman 1636, and elected assistant and governour the same year. In 1637, he was chosen representative for Boston, and soon after returned to England, and joined the party against King Charles the I. After the restoration he was tried for high treason, and was beheaded on Tower-hill, 14 June, 1662, aged 50, leaving an only son Christopher, who was created baron Barnard by king William, and who is ancestor of the present Darlington family.

VAN-ZUREN, CASPER, was a Dutch minister on Long-Island prior to 1677. Wood, Hist. L. I. 29.

VARNEY, HUMPHREY, Dover 1664, m. Sarah Storer,. 2 March, 1664, and had, Peter, b. 29 March 1665; John, b. 14 Aug. 1666; Joseph, b. 8 Oct. 1667; Abigail, b. 1669. WILLIAM, Salem, died a. 1654.

VARNUM, GEORGE, Ipswich 1635, died a. 1649. SAMUEL, came, it is said, from Wales, or the west part of England, and settled in Ipswich before 1649, removed to Dracutt, where he had two sons killed by the Indians in 1676. Hubbard. He m. Sarah Langton, and had 5 sons, three of whom had families : 1. Thomas, b. in Ipswich, m. a Jewett, and had sons, Samuel and Thomas, and one daughter ; 2. John, who m. Dolly Prescott, of Groton, and left sons, John, Abraham, Jonas, and James, and 3 daughters ; 3. Joseph, who had sons, Joseph, Samuel, and John. The late Hon. Joseph Bradley Varnum, many years in Congress from Massachusetts, and speaker of the house of representatives, was descended from Joseph.

VASSALL, ‡WILLIAM, came to N. E. as early as 1630, and soon returned, but came back, says Hubbard, in 1635, and settled at Scituate, from whence he went to Barbadoes in the West Indies, and there died in 1655. 2 Coll. Mass. Hist. Soc. iv. 240. Savage, ii. Winthrop, 260. The historian of Quincy supposes the Major Vassall, who came from the West Indies and settled in that town, to have been a son of the assistant above named. Lewis, John and William Vassall, H. C. 1728, 1732, and 1733, were sons of Major Vassall. JOHN, Scituate, a lieutenant in 1657, was probably the son of the preceding. 2 Coll. Mass. Hist. Soc. iv. 244.

VAUGHAN, GEORGE, Portsmouth 1631, left the country in August, 1634. Savage, i. Winthrop, 423. GEORGE, Scituate 1656. Coffin. WILLIAM, one of the founders of the Baptist church in Newport 1644. ‡WILLIAM, one of the principal men in Portsmouth and one of the first counsellors of the province of N. H., was admitted freeman 1669. Much may be found of him in the first vol. of Belknap's Hist. N. H. He d. in 1719. He m. Margaret, daughter of Richard Cutt, 8 Dec. 1668, and had, 1. Eleanor, b. 1670; 2. Mary, b. 1672; 3. Cutt, b. 9 March, 1674 ; 4. George, b. 13 April, 1676, grad. at H. C. 1696, was lieutenant-gov. of N. H. ; m. Elizabeth Eliot, 9 Jan. 1701, and had Sarah ; William, H. C. 1722, the projector of the Louisburg expedition ; Margaret ; George ; Elizabeth ; and Eliot, who d. at Portsmouth, 1 July, 1758 ; 5. Bridget ; b. 1678 ; 6. Margaret, b. 1680 ; 7. Abigail, 1683 ; 8. Elizabeth, b. 1686. Margaret, wife of Major Vaughan, d. 22 Jan. 1691.

VEAZEY, ROBERT, was an early proprietor of Watertown. There was a Veazey or Vesey at Pascataqua in 1632, named by Prince, ii. Annals, 70. The name continues in the vicinity of Portsmouth. WILLIAM, Braintree 1646, had sons, William, b. 1647; Solomon, b. 1650 ; Samuel, b. 1656.

VENNER, ‡ARTHUR, Rhode-Island, a captain, and assistant in 1672. (See FENNER.) ‖THOMAS, a wine-cooper, Salem, was admitted to the church, 25 Feb. 1637, freeman 1638, member

of the ar. co. 1645, when he probably lived in Boston. He returned to England, and became a preacher to a sect, called fifth mon-
archy men, who raised an insurrection, which was suppressed by the
civil power, when Venner, with twelve of his followers, who declared themselves invulnerable, was executed in Jan. 1661. His son
Thomas was baptized in Salem, 16 May, 1641. Lempriere, Felt.

VEREIN, JOSHUA, accompanied Roger Williams to Rhode-
Island in 1636. HILLIARD, Salem, d. 20 Dec. 1683, aged 63.
His wife was Mary Conant. Felt, Annals, 275. PHILIP, came
from Salisbury, England, settled in Salem; freeman 1635; became
a quaker, was tried and imprisoned. Hutchinson, i. Mass. 187.
Savage, i. Winthrop, 283. PHILIP, Salem, son of the preceding,
was admitted to the church, 3 Jan. 1641, freeman same year.
Felt.

VERMAES, BENJAMIN, Massachusetts, freeman 1642. Savage, ii. Winthrop, 372.

VERY, THOMAS, Gloucester 1647, was born a. 1626. This
name is found in several parts of Essex county.

VIALL, or VYALL, JOHN, weaver, Boston 1639, freeman
1641, had a son Joseph, b. in 1654. This name still exists in Massachusetts.

VICKERY, SETH, Hull, was admitted freeman in 1680. This
name has been in New-Hampshire within a few years.

VINALL, JOHN, and STEPHEN, were of Scituate, a. 1640.
2 Coll. Mass. Hist. Soc. iv. 240. Coffin.

VINCENT, HUMPHREY, Cambridge 1634, removed to Ipswich, and received a grant of land in 1638; d. 5 Dec. 1664. JOHN,
Lynn, removed to Sandwich 1637. Lewis. WILLIAM, Salem
1637, freeman 1643, was, with his wife, member of the church
1650; removed to Gloucester and was one of the selectmen.

VINES, RICHARD, came to N. E. before 1615, [Belknap, i.
Biog. 354] under Gorges, but failed in effecting a settlement at that
time. He was appointed governour of the plantation at Saco, 2
Sept. 1639. Savage, ii. Winthrop, Index. He went to Barbadoes.
Two of his letters to Gov. Winthrop, dated there in 1648, are in
Hutchinson, Coll. 222—224.

VINSON, THOMAS, one of the first four settlers of Martin's
Vineyard. Coffin.

VOSE, RICHARD, Dorchester 1635, removed to Windsor, a.
1636. Thomas Vose was of Dorchester in 1661. ROBERT, freeman 1666, may be the Robert Vose, whom the family tradition reports to have come from Lancashire, England, and settled on a farm
in that part of Dorchester, now Milton, which is still in possession
of the name and family. Several of his descendants have been distinguished for their merit as military officers, and 7 of the name
have grad. at the N. E. colleges. Hon. Roger Vose, H. C. 1790,
of Walpole, N. H. was a senator of the N. H. legislature, and represented the State 4 years in Congress, from 1813 to 1817. Hon.
John Vose, D. C. 1795, senator in the N. H. legislature, and an
eminent instructor, is a descendant from this family.

WADDELL, WILLIAM, was one of Samuel Gorton's company 1643. Savage, ii. Winthrop, 148.

WADE, *JONATHAN, Ipswich, freeman 1634, one of the first settlers; representative 1669 and probably 1681 and 1682; d. 1684. Susanna, his wife, d. 29 Nov. 1678. His sons were, Jonathan, who d. 1688; Nathaniel, and Thomas. Thomas, a colonel, m. Elizabeth Cogswell 1670, lived in Ipswich, and d. 4 Oct. 1696, whose sons were, Jonathan, Thomas, Nathaniel, and William. William was killed at sea, 3 April, 1697. NATHANIEL, Ipswich, son of the preceding, was a major, and resided also in Medford. He m. Mercy, daughter of Gov. Bradstreet, in 1672, and had children, Nathaniel, Mercy, Jonathan, Samuel, Ann, Dorothy, and Dudley. He d. 28 Nov. 1707. NICHOLAS, Scituate 1638. 2 Coll. Mass. Hist. Soc. iv. 240. RICHARD, Lynn, freeman 1637, removed to Sandwich 1637. Lewis.

WADLEIGH, ‡ROBERT, Exeter, was one of the provincial counsellors in 1684. ii. Belknap, App'x. Joseph, John, and Robert Wadleigh, three brothers, of Exeter, were presented by the grand jury in a bill charging them, with several others, with high treason in 1683. i. Belknap, 158. This name is sometimes spelled *Wadley*.

WADSWORTH, CHRISTOPHER, was one of the early settlers of Duxbury. 2 Coll. Mass. Hist. Soc. vii. 138. x. 58, 67, 69. Thirteen of the name had grad. at Harv. and Yale in 1828. ‡JOHN, Connecticut, elected magistrate or assistant in 1679, perhaps was the decided and resolute captain, mentioned by Trumbull, i. 390—393 and Holmes, ii. 449. SAMUEL, a captain, of Milton, freeman 1668, was killed by the Indians, 18 April, 1676, with Lieut. Sharp and 26 soldiers, and, with his companions, was buried at Sudbury, where there is a monument to his memory, placed there by his son, Rev. Benjamin Wadsworth, H. C. 1690, minister of the first church in Boston, and president of H. C., who died 17 March, 1737, æ. 68. Alden, i. Coll. Ep. 46. WILLIAM, Cambridge 1632, went to Connecticut, and probably settled at Hartford. I. Mather, Relation, &c. 43. Hubbard. Trumbull.

WAINWRIGHT, FRANCIS, Ipswich 1648, freeman 1671, d. at Salem, 19 May, 1692. Francis Wainwright, perhaps his son, grad. at H. C. 1686, was a merchant in Ipswich, a magistrate, and colonel of the militia, and d. 3 Aug. 1711. A Francis Wainwright graduated at Harvard College in 1707, and four John Wainwrights grad. there in 1709, 1711, 1734, and 1742. THOMAS, was an inhabitant of Dorchester in 1659.

WAITE, GAMALIEL, Boston 1637, d. 9 Dec. 1685, aged 87. He had a son Samuel, b. 1641. *JOHN, Malden, freeman 1665, representative from 1666 to 1684, was speaker of the house in 1684. ‖RETURN, member of the ar. co. in 1662. ‖RICHARD, a tailor, of Boston, was a member of the church in 1633; freeman 1637, member of the ar. co. 1638; probably went to Watertown, where John and Thomas, sons of Richard Waite, were b. in 1639 and 1641.

WAKE, WILLIAM, Salem, died a. 1654. Felt.

WAKEFIELD, WILLIAM, Hampton, was admitted freeman 1638. JOHN, d. in Boston 1703, æ. 63. ‖SAMUEL, member of ar. co. 1676.

WAKELEY, THOMAS, Hingham 1635, freeman 1636, probably at Casco-Bay 1665, and the same, who, with his wife, son, daughter-in-law, and two grandchildren, was there murdered by the Indians in 1675. I. Mather, Hist. Phillip's War, 13.

WAKEMAN, JOHN, was treasurer of New-Haven colony 1656. Trumbull, i. Hist. Conn. 227. *SAMUEL, Cambridge, freeman 1632, representative 1635, was a proprietor of Dorchester, removed to Hartford, was a member of the church, and was probably killed at Providence, one of the Bahama Islands, in 1641. Winthrop, ii. Hist. N. E. 33. Rev. Jabez Wakeman, H. C. 1697, was minister of Newark, N. J., and d. 8 Oct. 1705, æ. 26.

WAKING, THOMAS, Massachusetts, freeman 1660.

WALCOT, WILLIAM, Salem 1637, appears to have removed to Providence. This name appears to be different from Wolcott, formerly pronounced Woolcott, and still retaining this pronunciation in some parts of N. E. The graduates of this name at H. C. are, Samuel Walcot 1698; Robert Folger Walcutt, and Samuel Baker Walcott. Thomas Walcut, of Boston, was one of the earliest students at D. C., and one of the founders of the Mass. Historical Society.

WALDERNE, EDWARD, Ipswich 1648. Felt.

WALDO, CORNELIUS, Ipswich 1654, removed to Chelmsford, was a deacon of the church, and d. 3 June, 1701. CORNELIUS, son of the preceding, was probably one of the founders of the church at Dunstable, 16 Dec. 1685, and a representative in 1689. Cornelius Waldo, perhaps his son, was a merchant, of Boston, and was the grandfather of Hon. Daniel Waldo, of Worcester. One of the Waldo family went to North-Bridgewater, Mass., and from thence to Pomfret, Conn. Nine of the name had grad. at the N. E. colleges in 1826. *JOHN, Chelmsford 1675, son of Deacon Waldo, was representative at the May session 1689 for Dunstable.

WALDRON, ALEXANDER, Dover, a relation of Major Waldron, d. 7 June, 1676. Those under this name have it often spelled *Waldren* and *Waldern*. RALPH, Boston, d. in Barbadoes, 29 Nov. 1653. ‡*RICHARD, came from Somersetshire, England, a. 1635, and settled at Dover, which he represented in the general court at Boston 22 years, commencing with 1654; was speaker of the house from 1666 to 1668, 1673, 1679, and part of 1674. He was a captain, and afterwards major of the military forces; was one of the first counsellors of the province of N. H. 1680, and president in 1681, on the death of John Cutt. He was killed by the Indians 27 June, 1689, in their attack on Dover, when he was a. 80 years old. His children, by two wives, one of whom was Ann, were, 1. Paul, who d. in Algiers. a. 1669; 2. Timothy, who died while a student at H. C.; 3. Richard (see next article); 4. Eleazar, b. 1665; 5. Elizabeth, b. 1666; 6. Mary, 1668; 7. Esther; 8. Mary. The sons, excepting Richard, d. without issue. Two of the daughters m. Rev. Joseph Gerrish and his brother John Gerrish. The Waldron family is supposed, in a letter from Rev. John Walrond, of Ottery, in England, to Rev. William Waldron, of Boston, *penes me*, to be desended from an ancient famlly in Devonshire, the seat of which was granted by the crown of England to Richard Walerand, a. the year 1130, and to prove the identity of the names, the writer cites Skinner's Ætymologicon Linguæ Anglicanæ as follows : " Walarand, olim Prænomen, nunc Cognomen, ab Anglo-Sax. *Walpian*, volvere, et *Rand*, et Scutum, volvere scutum, i. e. Clypeum huc illuc circumagit. *Waldron* autem Cognomen contractum est, a *Walarand*." ‡*RICHARD, son of the preceding, was born in 1650, lived in Portsmouth, which he represented at Boston in 1691. He was appointed a counsellor of N. H. in 1681 ; was chief justice of the court of common pleas ; judge of probate ; chief military officer of N. H. many years, and died 30 Nov. 1730, aged 80. By his first wife, who died 1682, a daughter of President Cutt, he had one child, Samuel, who died an infant ; by his 2d, Eleanor (born 5 March, 1669, d. Sept. 1727), daughter of Major William Vaughan, he had, 1. Richard, b. 21 Feb. 1694, grad. at H. C. 1712, m. Elizabeth Westbrook, was a judge, counsellor, secretary of the province, father of Thomas Westbrook Waldron, also a counsellor, and colonel, who was grandfather of Maj. Richard Russel Waldron, of Portsmouth ; 2. Margaret, b. 1695 ; 3. William, b. 4 August, 1697, grad. at H. C. 1717, was ordained over the brick church in Middle Street, Boston, 23 May, 1722 ; and d. 20 Sept. 1727, æ. 30, leaving issue ; 4. Anna, born 27 Aug. 1698, m. Rev. Henry Rust, of Stratham, a. 1719, d. 1734 . 5. Abigail, b. 28 July, 1704, m. Judge Nathaniel Saltonstall, about 1726, died 1735, aged 31 ; 6. Eleanor, b. 1706. *WILLIAM, brother of Major Richard Waldron, was admitted freeman 1640, lived in Dover, which he represented in 1646, and was drowned at Kennebunk, in Sept. 1647. Winthrop, ii. Hist. N. E. 278.

WALES, NATHANIEL, Dorchester, 1636, perhaps the same who d. in Boston, 4 Dec. 1661, leaving a son Nathaniel, who died there 10 May, 1662.

WALFORD, JEREMIAH, Pascataqua 1631. Adams, Annals Portsmouth. He, or perhaps a son of the same name, was living in 1688. ‡JOHN, was a counsellor of New-Hampshire in 1692. THOMAS, Charlestown 1628 [Hutch. i. Hist. Mass. 17], went to Portsmouth, a. 1631, was one of the grand jury in 1654, died about 1667, leaving an estate of £1433. 3. 8. His wife Jane, b. in 1597, was accused of, and prosecuted for, witchcraft. Belknap, i. N. H. 47. Savage, i. Winthrop, 53. Coll. N. H. Hist. Soc. i.

WALKER, AUGUSTINE, Charlestown, was admitted freeman in 1641, and d. before 1655, leaving sons, Samuel, b. 11 Oct. 1642 ; Augustine, b. 14 Dec. 1646 ; James, b. 25 July, 1648, and perhaps others. He was the ancestor of Rev. Timothy Walker, H. C. 1725, the first minister of Concord, N. H., whose son Hon. Timothy Walker, b. in Concord, 26 June, 1737, grad. at H. C. 1756, was father of Charles Walker, esq. b. 25 Sept. 1765, grad. at H. C. 1789.

the eldest son of whom is Charles Walker, esq. of the city of New-York, who grad. at H. C. 1818. HENRY, Gloucester 1664. ‖ISAAC, a merchant, of Boston, member of the ar. co. 1644, was admitted freeman 1646, had sons, Nicholas, Stephen, and perhaps Isaac member of ar. co. 1676. JOHN, Boston, freeman 1634, may have been the one who removed early to Rhode-Island. *JOSEPH, Billerica, freeman 1678, was representative at the two sessions in May, 1689. *RICHARD, Lynn 1630, freeman 1634, was representative in 1640 and 1641; was an ensign in 1631, afterwards a lieut. and captain. His children were Richard and Samuel who settled in Reading, and Tabitha and Elizabeth. He died in May, 1687, æ. 95. [Lewis.] He or his son Richard represented Reading in 1648, 1649, 1650, and 1660, and was the *leader* of the military band in that town in 1644, mentioned by Johnson, [Hist. N. E. 192] without any Christan name, which Whitman [Hist. Sketch of Ar. Co.] erroneously supplies with *Robert*. There was a Richard Walker in Boston in 1638. ROBERT, Boston, freeman 1634, was living 10 June, 1684, at the age of 78. [Snow.] He had sons, born in Boston, Zechariah, 1637; John, 1639; Jacob, 1644; Joseph, b. 1646; Eliakim, 1652; John, 2d, b. 1656. SAMUEL, Exeter 1639. *SAMUEL, Woburn, probably the son of Augustine, b. in 1642, was admitted freeman 1674, and elected representative at the two sessions in May, 1689. SHUBAEL, a captain, of Lynn 1650, d. Jan. 1689. THOMAS, Boston, d. 11 Aug. 1659, leaving sons, John, b. 1652, and Samuel, b. 1656. WILLIAM, Hingham 1636. Lincoln, Hist. Hingham, 45. *ZECHARIAH*, perhaps the son of Robert Walker, and born at Boston 1637, was, according to Mather, aducated at H. C. but died not graduate; was the minister of Jamaica, L. I. from 1663 to 1668; removed to Stratford, Conn. and settled over the 2d church; from thence to Woodbury, where he was settled 3 May, 1670.

WALL, JAMES, Pascataqua 1631, was one of the witnesses to the Indian deed to Wheelwright, April, 1638. This name is erroneously printed *Cornall*, in Coll. of N. H. Hist. Socciety i. 148. JOHN, Exeter 1639, Portsmouth 1640. Belknap, i. Hist. N. H. 47.

WALLEN, RALPH, Plymouth 1638. Davis, Morton's Memo. 380, 385.

WALLER, CHRISTOPHER, Ipswich, was born a. 1620. Coffin. MATTHEW, Salem 1637, removed to Providence.

WALLEY, ‖‡JOHN, was member of the ar. co. 1671, its captain in 1679, one of Sir Edmund Andros' council 1687; one of the council under the charter of William and Mary 1692, a judge of the supreme court of Mass.; commander of the expedition against Canada, 1690, the journal of which by him may be found in Hutchinson, i. Hist. Mass. 470. He d. 11 Jan. 1712, æ. 68. *THOMAS*, minister of Barnstable, was ejected for his nonconformity, and came from London in 1663, and died at Barnstable, 24 March, 1679, æ. 61.

WALLINGFORD, JOHN, Dover 1687. Hon. Thomas Wallingford, a judge of the Superiour court of New-Hampshire, who d.

4 August, 1771, æ. 75, was probably a descendant. George W. Wallingford, H. C. 1795, d. in 1823.

WALLINGTON, NICHOLAS, Newbury 1655, was admitted freeman 1670.

WALLIS, *NICHOLAS, Ipswich, representative 1691. NATHANIEL, Casco 1665. Hutch. Coll. 398. ROBERT, Ipswich 1638. THOMAS, Massachusetts, freeman 1643.

WALSINGHAM, FRANCIS JOHNSON, Marblehead 1648. Dana, Hist. Discourse, 7.

WALTER, NEHEMIAH, the fourth minister of Roxbury, was b. in Ireland, Dec. 1663 ; came with his father to N. E. about 1680 ; grad. at H. C. 1684, was ordained as colleague with Rev. John Eliot, 17 Oct. 1688, d. 17 Sept. 1750, in his 87th year. His son Thomas, H. C. 1713, was his colleague from 19 Oct. 1718 to his death, 10 Jan. 1725.

WALTHAM, HENRY, Weymouth, a merchant, d. 29 January, 1659. He had a brother Thomas. WILLIAM, Weymouth, d. about 1641.

WALTON, GEORGE, Exeter 1639, was living at Great-Island [New-Castle, N. H.] in Dec. 1685, at the age of 70. Mather, ii. Magnalia, 393. Adams, Annals Portsmouth, 398. Col. Shadrach Walton, of New-Castle, probably his descendant, was appointed a counsellor in 1716, and d. 3 Oct. 1741, æ. 83. Benjamin Walton, H. C. 1729, was, according to W. Winthrop, son of Col. Walton. HENRY, Boston, aad sons, Job and Adam, b. there in 1639 and 1643. He was probably one of the grantees named in the Indian deed of South-Hampton, L. I. 1640. JOHN, spelled also *Wolten* and *Wotten*, was of Portsmouth 1640. (See WOTTEN.) *THOMAS, Weymouth, was represeutative in 1636. *WILLIAM*, minister at Marblehead, came from Seaton, in Devonshire, England, settled in Hingham 1635, was admitted freeman 1636, went to Marblehead as early as 1639, where he was the minister nearly thirty years, though not ordained. He d. in Aug. or Sept. 1668. [Dana.] Mather [i. Magnalia, 215] calls him William Waltham, and the errour is adopted where we should hardly expect to find it [Winthrop, ii. Hist. N. E. 390] ; but where so many errours are corrected, and omissions are supplied, the perpetuating the mistake can be readily excused. Mr. Walton's children, b. at Seaton, were, John, born 6 April, 1627 ; Elizabeth, b. 1629 ; Martha, b. 1632 ; in Hingham, Nathaniel was b. 3 March, 1636 ; in Marblehead, Samuel, born 5 June, 1639 ; Josiah, 20 Dec. 1641 ; Mary, b. 14 May, 1644.

WALVER, ABRAHAM, received his degree at H. C. 1647, went to England, and was settled in the ministry in the county where his friends resided. Hutchinson, i. Hist. Mass. 108.

WANNERTON, THOMAS, Pascataqua and Maine, was a captain, and was killed in 1644, as may be seen in ii. Winthrop, p. 177.

WANTON, EDWARD, Scituate 1640.

WARD, ‡ANDREW, Watertown, freeman 1634, accompanied the first settlers to Connecticut, and was elected a magistrate in 1636. He may be the same who was early in Springfield, and who went with Rev. Richard Denton, to Hempstead, L. I., in 1643. Trumbull. Wood, Hist. Sketch L. I. 40. Twenty-four persons of the name of Ward, had grad. at the N. E. colleges in 1826. BENJAMIN, a ship-carpenter of Boston, was member of the church there 1640, and admitted freeman 1641. HENRY, was a proprietor of Lancaster in 1654. Willard. JAMES, a graduate of H. C. 1645, went to England ; had a fellowship at Maudlin College, Oxford, and received the degree of M. B. from that University. *JOHN*, the first minister of Haverhill, was son of Rev. Nathaniel Ward, of Ipswich, and was b., as Dr. Cotton Mather supposes, at Haverhill, England, 5 Nov. 1606 ; came to N. E. as early as 1639, admitted freeman 1643, settled at Haverhill 1645, and d. there, 27 Dec. 1693, æ. 88. His daughters were, Elizabeth, b. 7 April, 1647, m. Hon. Nathaniel Saltonstall, and Mary, b. 24 June, 1649, who, Mr. Coffin says, m. Rev. Benjamin Woodbridge, the clergyman who d. at Medford. JOHN, Salem, died a. 1656. Felt. *JOHN, Cambridge, that part now Newton, was probably the freeman in 1649. He was representative in 1689, and about 15 years afterwards. He m. Hannah, daughter of Edward Jackson, and had 8 sons and 5 daughters. She d. 21 April, 1704, æ. 73. The sons were, John, b. and d. 1654 ; John, 2d, b. 1659 ; William, b. 1664 ; Richard, b. 1667, who was a representative and deacon, and d. 1739 ; Edward, b. 1672 ; Eleazar, b. 1673 ; Jonathan, b. 1674 ; Joseph, b. 1677. The late Col. Joseph Ward, of Newton, was grandson of Eleazar, and was Muster Master General and Acting Aid to General Washington, in the Revolutionary War. MILES, of the county of Essex, and probably Salem, was admitted freeman 1641, and died a. 1650. *NATHANIEL*, the first minister of Ipswich, and author of the " Simple Cobler of Aggawam," was son of Rev. John Ward, and was b. at Haverhill, England, in 1570 ; was educated at Cambridge University, and came to N. E. in June, 1634. He was soon settled at Ipswich, but returned to England in 1647, and d. at Shenfield, in Essex, in 1653, aged 83. His son John is noticed above. One of his daughters married the celebrated Giles Firmin. *OBADIAH, Sudbury 1654, Marlborough 1662, was a representative in 1689. ROGER, Massachusetts, was admitted freeman in 1637. *SAMUEL, Sudbury, freeman 1637, was representative in 1637 and 1638. A Samuel Ward d. at Charlestown, 30 August, 1682. THOMAS, an inhabitant of Hampton, came to N. E. as early as 1630, and was admitted freeman 1635. *WILLIAM, Sudbury, freeman 1643, was representative in 1644, removed to Marlborough, where he was one of the first deacons of the church d. a. 1686. His sons were, John, William, Increase, b. 1644, Richard, Eleazar, and Samuel.

WARDHALL, THOMAS, shoemaker, Boston, member of the church 1633, was admitted freeman 1635, went to Exeter with Rev. John Wheelwright in 1638. Belknap, i. Hist. N. H. 36. Savage, i. Winthrop, 248. WILLIAM, Boston, was b. in 1604, went to Exeter with the preceding, but probably returned to Boston, as he had sons Eliakim, Urall, [?] Elihu, Benjamin, and Samuel, born there after 1635. This name is sometimes spelled *Wardwell.*

WARDWELL, SAMUEL, Andover, probably son of the preceding, was executed for supposed witchcraft in 1692. Margaret, his widow, d. 1695. Sons, William, Samuel, and Eliakim.

WARE, ||ROBERT, member of the ar. co., was admitted freeman in 1647. *JOHN, Wrentham, freeman 1677, was representative in 1689. SAMUEL, Boston, freeman 1675. ||WILLIAM, freeman and member of the ar. co. 1643, admitted as townsman of Boston, 31 Jan. 1653, d. 11 Feb. 1658.

WARHAM, JOHN, one of the first ministers of Dorchester, came to N. E. 1630, having been a minister in Exeter, England, and, with Mr. Maverick, settled at Dorchester in June, 1630, from whence in 1635, he went with the most of his church to Windsor, and formed the first settlement of that place, where he d. 1 April, 1670. WILLIAM, Newbury, m. Hannah Adams in 1681.

WARNER, ANDREW, Cambridge 1632, freeman 1634, removed to Hartford. Hutchinson, i. Mass. 97. DANIEL, Ipswich 1648, perhaps of Hadley in 1662. DAVID, Hatfield, freeman 1673. JOHN, born a. 1616, was an inhabitant of Ipswich in 1648, and probably went early to Brookfield. Foot, Hist. Serm. 29. JOHN, Warwick, R. I. was one of Gorton's company 1643, Savage, ii. Winthrop, 147. Nine of the name of Warner had grad. at Y. C. in 1826.

WARRANT, JOHN, Newbury, d. 1666.

WARREN, ABRAHAM, Salem 1637, perhaps also of Ipswich in 1648, and died a. 1654. Felt. ARTHUR, Weymouth, had sons, Arthur, b. 1639, and Jacob, b. 26 Oct. 1642. JACOB, Chelmsford 1666. JOHN, Watertown, came to N. E. 1630, freeman 1631, d. 13 Dec. 1667. JOHN, Massachusetts, freeman 1645. JOSEPH, Plymouth 1623. NATHANIEL, Plymouth 1644. PETER, Boston, had sons, John and Benjamin, b. in 1661 and 1665. RICHARD, one of the first pilgrims at Plymouth 1620, d. 1628. Elizabeth, his widow, d. 1673, aged a. 90.

WARRINER, WILLIAM, freeman 1638, was of Springfield. Sprague, Hist. Discourse. He d. 2 June, 1676.

WASHBURN, JOHN, son of John, was one of the proprietors of Bridgewater, 1645, d. before 1670. His sons were, John, Samuel, Joseph, Thomas, and Jonathan, whose descendants have extended to the remotest parts of the country. 2 Coll. Mass. Hist. Soc. vii. 149, 153. Mr. Wood [MS Letter] names William, John, and Daniel Washburn among the first settlers of Oyster-Bay.

WASS, THOMAS, Newbury, d. 18 Aug. 1691.

WATERHOUSE, ||DAVID, Boston, was member of the ar. co. 1679, and one of the council of safety 1689. Hutchinson, i. Hist. N. H. 337. RICHARD, Portsmouth 1674, had sons, by his wife Sarah, Richard, b. 19 April, 1674 ; Samuel, b. 9 May, 1676, and perhaps others. He is the ancestor of the distinguished philanthropist, B. Waterhouse, M. D., of Cambridge, the father of vaccina-

42   305

tion in this country. THOMAS, Dorchester, admitted member of the church 1639, and freeman 1640.

WATERMAN, RICHARD, Salem 1637, removed to Rhode-Island, and was one of the founders of the first Baptist church in America. Benedict. Savage, ii. Winthrop, 148. Felt. THOMAS, Roxbury 1641, d. 22 Jan. 1676. His wife d. 1641.

WATERS, GEORGE, Salem, was admitted to the church, 23 May, 1641. LAWRENCE, Watertown 1635; Lancaster 1647, freeman 1666, had sons, Lawrence, b. 1635, died at Boston 1693; Stephen, born 1642; Daniel; Joseph, and Ephraim. Willard. RICHARD, a gunsmith, of Salem, was admitted freeman 1639. MERRY, ship-carpenter, Boston, member of church 1632.

WATKINS, ||THOMAS, Boston 1652, member of the ar. co. 1666, d. 16 Dec. 1689.

WATSON, CALEB, son of John, was b. at Roxbury in June, 1641, grad. at H. C. 1661, admitted freeman 1666, was a schoolmaster at Hartford, Conn. GEORGE, Plymouth colony, came over before 1631, and d. 1689, aged a. 89. JOHN, Roxbury, freeman 1645, may have removed to Cambridge, where John, Abraham, and Isaac, sons of John and Rebecca Watson, were b. in 1653, 1661, and 1669. ROBERT, Windsor 1640. 1 Coll. Mass. Hist. Soc. v. 168. THOMAS, Salem, was admitted to the church 1639, and freeman 1640.

WATTLES, WILLIAM, Ipswich 1648.

WATTS, HENRY, Casco-Bay 1658; d. after 1684. [Geo. Folsom, MS letter.] There was a Judge Watts of Chelsea, whose son Samuel grad. at H. C. in 1738, and d. in Dec. 1791, æ. 76.

WAY, AARON, Massachusetts, freeman 1651. Calef, More Wonders, 123. GEORGE, Boston 1651, perhaps also of Providence. HENRY, one of the principal inhabitants of Dorchester, d. in 1667, æ. 84. Savage, i. Winthrop, 43, 59, 79. ii. 177. ||RICHARD, Dorchester, was a member of the ar. co. 1642, its lieutenant in 1671. RICHARD, was of Scituate in 1651.

WEARE, ‡*NATHANIEL, Newbury 1656, where several of his children were born; removed to Hampton, where he was one of the principal men; admitted freeman 1666, representative of Hampton; agent for the province of N. H. to England in the time of Cranfield; was a counsellor of N. H. 1692, d. 13 May, 1718, æ. 87. His son Peter, b. at Newbury, 15 Nov. 1660, was ancestor of Hon. Meshech Weare, H. C. 1735, the first president of N. H. in 1784; chief justice, and one of the most valuable men in the State, who d. 1786, æ. 72. *PETER, Kittery, freeman 1652, was representative at the 2d session 1660. PETER, Newbury, died 12 Oct. 1653.

WEBB, CHRISTOPHER, Braintree, freeman 1645, was town clerk; removed to Billerica, where several of his children were b. His sons, John and Peter were born in Braintree in 1655 and 1657. GEORGE, New-Hampshire, and probably Dover, a. 1649. HENRY, a mercer, came from Salisbury, England, with his wife Dowsabel, and settled at Boston, where he was a member of the church, and admitted freeman in 1638. His daughter Margaret m. Jacob Sheafe. ‖*JOHN, freeman 1636, member of the ar. co. 1643, removed to Chelmsford, which he represented in 1663, 1664, and 1665; was a captain, and a man of wealth; died 16 Oct. 1668. His name appears in records, John Webb, alias Evered. He sold his seat in Chelmsford to Edward Colburn. See Hubbard's Indian Wars. JOHN, was one of the first proprietors of Northampton 1653. JOSEPH, Boston 1675. *JOSEPH*, minister of Fairfield, grad. at H. C. 1684, was ordained 15 August, 1694, over the 1st church, d. 19 Sept. 1732. Rev. Joseph Webb, Y. C. 1715, was probably his son. RICHARD, Cambridge, freeman 1632, d. at Boston, 2 July, 1659. WILLIAM, Boston, freeman 1636, d. Dec. 1644. There was a William Webb early at Weymouth.

WEBBER, THOMAS, Boston, was a mariner, and a member of the church in 1643. Two persons of this name, brothers, Samuel and John, grad. at Harv. and Dart. in 1784 and 1792. The first, born at Byfield, 13 Jan. 1760, was president of H. C. from 1806 to his death, 17 July, 1810; the last born 11 May, 1762, grad. at D. C. 1792, and was the minister of Sandown and Campton, N. H. Samuel Webber, M. D., of Charlestown, N. H·, son of President Webber, grad. at H. C. 1815.

WEBSTER, §‡JOHN, was a magistrate of Connecticut in 1639, and elected governour in 1656. Within about four years afterwards, he, with three others of the name, Mr. Russell, the minister of Weathersfield, and other associates, purchased the territory included in the towns of Hadley, Hatfield, Granby, and Amherst, Mass., and removed thither. He died at Hadley 1665. See Lord's Lempriere, Holmes' and Trumbull. The great lexicographer of our country is one of his descendants. JOHN, came from Ipswich, England, as early as 1634, and settled at Ipswich; was probably the one admitted freeman 1635, and died before 1647, leaving a widow, who m. John Emery, and 4 sons : John, b. 1632, m. Anna Batt 1653 ; Stephen, Nathan, Israel, and 4 daughters. The sons of Nathan were, John, Nathan, and Samuel, of whom Samuel was father of Rev. Samuel Webster, D. D., of Salisbury, b. 1718, grad. 1737, died 18 Jan. 1796. It is sufficient honour for this family that it includes among its descendants one of the greatest orators and statesmen of this or any other country. JOHN, who is styled a brewer, was of Portsmouth, and a constable. He d. in 1662. There was a John Webster, a blacksmith, early at Haverhill. JOHN, a baker, was admitted inhabitant of Salem, 29 Jan. 1638. THOMAS, an early inhabitant of Hartford, is mentioned by Trumbull, i. Hist. Conn. 69. Perhaps he was of Hadley in 1665. THOMAS, Massachusetts, was admitted freeman 1644. WILLIAM, of Hadley, was born in 1617.

WEDGEWOOD, JOHN, Ipswich 1637, was a soldier in the Pequot war, in which he was wounded. Hubbard, Ind. Wars, 130.

WEED, JONAS, Massachusetts, was admitted freeman in 1631.

WEEDEN, EDWARD, Boston, had a son Samuel born 1644.

SAMUEL and WILLIAM, were among the founders of the first Baptist church in Newport 1644. Benedict.

WEEKS, AMMIEL, Dorchester admitted to the church 1656, and freeman 1657. GEORGE, Dorchester, admitted to the church 1639, freeman 1640, d. 27 Oct. 1659. JOHN, Plymouth 1637. Davis, Morton's Memo. LEONARD, Portsmouth 1667, had sons, John, b. 14 June, 1668 ; S.muel, b. 1670 ; Joseph, b. 1671 ; Joshua, born 1674 ; and daughters Mary and Margaret. Rev. Joshua Wingate Weeks, H. C. 1758, Clement Weeks, H. C. 1772, and William Weeks, H. C. 1775, were of this family. THOMAS, Oyster-Bay, L. I. 1654.

WELBYE, GEORGE, Lynn 1638. Lewis.

WELCH, THOMAS, is named by Trumbull, i. 107, as one of the pillars of Milford, 1639.

WELD, DANIEL, Roxbury, freeman 1641, had sons, Benjamin, b. 1655 ; Daniel, b. 1659, and perhaps others ; d. 22 July, 1666, æ. 81. A Daniel Weld, of Braintree, had a daughter, b. in 1643, and his wife Alice d. in 1647. *EDMUND*, son of Rev. Thomas Weld, grad. at H. C. 1650 ; went to Ireland, and was the minister of Inniskean, and d. 2 March, 1668, æ. 50. Alden. *JOSEPH, a captain, and five years representative of Roxbury from 1636, was brother of Rev. Thomas Weld. He was admitted freeman 1636, and died 7 Oct. 1646, leaving a widow Barbary, who m. Anthony Stoddard, of Boston. Capt. Weld's children were, Edmund, b. 14 July, 1636 ; Sarah, b. 31 Dec. 1640 ; Daniel, b. 18 Sept. 1642, grad. at H. C. 1661, and was a physician in Salem ; Joseph, bap. and died 1645 ; Thomas, who died 1649. JOHN, Roxbury, was b. in England, 28 Oct. 1623, came to N. E., says a family MS, in 1638, admitted freeman 1650, d. 20 Sept. 1691, æ. 68. His wife was Margaret, b. 2 April, 1629, d. 13 Sept. 1692, æ. 63. Their children were, John, b. 1649 ; Joseph, b. and d. 1650 ; Joseph, 2d, b. 1653 ; Margaret Elizabeth, Abigail, Esther, and Hannah. *THOMAS*, one of the first Ministers of Roxbury, arrived in N. E. 5 June, 1632, and soon after admitted freeman, and settled at Roxbury. He returned to England with Rev. Hugh Peters in 1641, and is stated in the Roxbury church records to have d. in London in 1661 [see Alden] ; but as his name appears in Calamy among the ejected ministers in 1662, he may have lived to a later period, and certainly so if he wrote the verses in the Magnalia on Rev. Samuel Danforth, 1674, which have frequently been ascribed to him. The writer of those verses, however, is conjectured to have been his grandson, Rev. Thomas Weld, of Dunstable. The children of Mr. Weld were, John, a minister of Riton, in the county of Durham [Calamy, ii. Account, 291] ; Edmund, H. C. 1650 ; Thomas, the following, and perhaps some born in England. *THOMAS, Roxbury, son of the preceding, was admitted freeman 1654, was representative 1676 and 1677, d. 17 Jan. 1683. His children were, Samuel ; Thomas, b. 1653 ; Samuel, 2d, b. 1655 ; John, b. 1657, d. 1686 ; Edmund, born 1659 ; Daniel ; Dorothy ; Joseph, born 1666 ; and Margaret. *THOMAS*, the first minister of Dunstable, N. H., son of

the preceding, was baptized at Roxbury, 12 June, 1653; grad. at
H. C. 1671; freeman 1675, was ordained 1685; d. 9 June, 1702,
in his 50th year. His 1st wife, Elizabeth, died 19 July, 1687, and
their son Thomas grad. at H. C. 1701, and d. at Roxbury, 21 July,
1704, æ. 20. His 2d wife, Mary Savage, d. at Attleborough, Mass.,
2 June, 1731, æ, 64, and their son Habijah, b. 2 Sept. 1702, grad.
at H. C. 1723, was ordained at Attleborough, 1 Oct. 1727, died 14
May, 1782, in his 80th year. Samuel, another son of Rev. Thomas
Weld, d. at Roxbury, 17 Jan. 1717.

WELDEN, ROBERT, Charlestown, whom Gov. Winthrop calls
"a hopeful young gentleman and experienced soldier," d. 16 Feb.
1631. Christopher Welden, sen. d. at Charlestown, 29 April, 1668.
See Dudley's Letter to Countess of Lincoln.

WELLINGTON, ROGER, Watertown 1642, had sons, John,
b. 1638; Joseph, b. 1643. Descendants are in Mass. and N. H.

WELLMAN, THOMAS, Lynn 1650, who d. 1672, had a son
Isaac and 4 daughters. Two of the name have been clergymen in
New-Hampshire.

WELLS, EDWARD, Boston 1645. Those under this name are
sometimes written *Welles*. GEORGE, Lynn, removed to South-
Hampton, L. I., a. 1640. ISAAC, Scituate 1638 [2 Coll. Mass.
Hist. Soc. iv. 240]; removed to Barnstable. Coffin. ‡JOHN,
Connecticut, was elected magistrate in 1658. One of this name
was of Hadley in 1665. RICHARD, born a. 1607, was of Lynn
1637, and probably one of the proprietors of Salisbury 1640.
§‡†THOMAS, Connecticut, magistrate 1637, deputy-governour
1656, governour 1658 and 1659, d. 1660. THOMAS, Ipswich,
freeman 1637, perhaps the member of the ar. co. 1644, d. in Oct.
1666, leaving a widow, and sons, John and Thomas, the latter b.
11 Jan. 1646. Felt. *THOMAS*, the first minister of Amesbury,
received a degree from H. C., in the catalogue of which, his name
is placed under 1669; was ordained in 1672, and d. 10 July, 1734,
æ. 86. WILLIAM, Lynn 1644, perhaps one of the first settlers of
South-Old, L. I. See Wood's Sketch, 34.

WELSH, THOMAS, Cambridge 1645, perhaps d. at Charlestown, 31 Dec. 1680. Rev. Nathaniel Welsh, as spelled by Mather,
although recent catalogues have it *Welch*, grad. at H. C. 1687, was
the minister of Enfield, Conn. and d. before 1699.

WENBOURN, WILLIAM, Boston 1638, freeman 1644, had a
son John, b. in 1638. Snow, Hist. Boston, 137. He removed to
Exeter, and was chosen clerk of the writs there in 1643.

WENDELL, THOMAS, Boston, d. 10 Dec. 1646. THOMAS,
was of Ipswich in 1648. Jacob Wendell, the first graduate of the
name at H. C., d. 7 Sept. 1761, æ 71.

WENSLEY, *SAMUEL, Salisbury, freeman 1639, rep. 1642,
1645, and 1653, d. 2 June, 1663. His wife d. 2 June, 1649.
RICHARD, grad. at H. C, 1684, and d. before 1699.

WENTWORTH, PAUL, Rowley, had sons, William, Sylvanus, Paul, Ebenezer, Aaron, Moses, and 5 daughters, who were all
baptized 16 May, 1696. Two other sons, Benjamin and Edward,

were baptized in 1699 and 1701. He and his wife were dismissed from the church at Rowley to New-London in June, 1707. SAM-UEL, Portsmouth or Dover, was son of William Wentworth, and was born a. 1642, admitted freeman 1676, and by Mary, his wife, had, 1. Samuel, b. 9 April, 1666; 2. Parnel, a daughter, b. 21 Oct. 1669; 3. John, b. 16 June, 1672; 4. Mary, b. 5 Feb. 1674; 5. Ebenezer, b. 9 April, 1677; 6. Dorothy, b. 27 June, 1680; 7. Ben-ning, b. 28 June, 1682. John, the 2d son, was lieutenant-governor of the province of N. H. from 1717 to 1729, and d. 12 Dec. 1730, æ. 58, having had 16 children, one of whom was Benning Went-worth, H. C. 1715, the governour of N. H. from 1741 to 1767, and who d. 14 Oct. 1770, æ. 75. John Wentworth, H. C. 1755, was his nephew, and succeeded him as governour of N. H.; was after-wards governour of Nova-Scotia, and d. at Halifax, 8 April, 1820, æ. 84. WILLIAM, the great ancestor of the Wentworths of N. E. was of Exeter in 1639, and was a ruling elder of the church in Do-ver, and living in 1689, at more than 80 years of age. Belknap.

WERMALL, JOSEPH, Scituate between 1633 and 1657. 2 Coll. Mass. Hist. Soc. iv. 240.

WEST, EDWARD, Lynn 1637. FRANCIS, was an early set-tler of Duxbury, and a proprietor of Bridgewater 1645. 2 Coll. Mass. Hist. Soc. x. Index. *JOHN, Salem, was admitted to the church 1648, was representative of Beverly in 1677, where, and at Salem, the name has been common. Thomas West was of Salem or Bev-erly in 1665. JOHN, Saco 1652. MATTHEW, Lynn 1636, freeman 1637. NATHANIEL, Newport, was one of the found-ers of the first Baptist church 1644. ROBERT R., Providence 1641. 3 Coll. Mass. Hist. Soc. i. 4. *THOMAS, freeman 1668, representative 1686 of Hadley.

WESTBROOK, JOHN, Portsmouth 1665.

WESTCOTT, STUKELEY, Salem 1639, removed to Rhode-Island, and was one of the founders of the first Baptist church. Stukely Westcott, one of his descendants, is now a magistrate in Vermont.

WESTGATE, ‖[JOHN,] was a member of the ar. co. 1641, and perhaps the same mentioned by Hutchinson, i. Hist. Mass. 209.

WESTMORELAND, JAMES, Boston 1652.

WESTON, EDMUND, Duxbury, a. 1645. 2 Coll. Mass. Hist. Soc. x. 57. *FRANCIS, Salem, freeman 1633, representative at the first general court 1634, removed to Providence, and was one of the founders of the first Baptist church in America. Savage. Benedict. Felt. THOMAS, commenced the first settlement, in May, 1622, of Weymouth, a town, although the settlement was suspended a short time, probably the oldest in Massachusetts, out of Plymouth colony. He was a "merchant of good account in Lon-don." He returned to England, and d. at Bristol.

WESTWOOD, ‡WILLIAM, Cambridge 1632, freeman 1635, removed with Rev. Mr. Hooker and his company to Hartford, and was one of the first magistrates in 1636.

WETHERELL, JOHN, Cambridge 1635, a proprietor of Watertown, was admitted freeman in 1642. *WILLIAM*, Cambridge 1635, removed to Scituate, and was the first minister of the second church from Sept. 1645, until his death, 9 April, 1684, at the age of a. 84. He wrote several elegies, and one so late as 1679, on Mrs. Sarah Cushing, of Scituate.

WEYBORNE, THOMAS. (See WYBORNE.)

WEYMOUTH, ROBERT, came from Dartmouth in England and settled at Kittery as early as 1652. Edward Weymouth, perhaps his son, m. Hester Hodsdon in 1663.

WHALE, PHILEMON, Sudbury, freeman 1648, d. 21 Feb. 1676. ||WILLIAM, was member of the ar. co. 1645.

WHALLEY, EDWARD, one of Cromwell's lieutenant-generals, and one of the judges who sentenced to death Charles I, came to N. E. in July, 1660, and resided in various places. Stiles, Hist. of the Judges. Hutchinson. Holmes. Worcester Magazine.

WHARTON, EDWARD, Salem, 1663, was one of the early quakers. Felt. ‡RICHARD, one of Sir Edmund Andros' council in 1687, belonged to Massachusetts. Hutch. i. Mass. 317.

WHEAT, MOSES, Concord, was admitted freeman 1642. He came over with his brother Joshua in 1636 ; and d. in May, 1700, having had children, Samuel, b. 1641 ; Hannah, Joshua, Remembrance, John, and Sarah. His brother returned to England. Shattuck, MS Hist.

WHEATLEY, JOHN, whose name is spelled *Whetley* in colony records, was admitted freeman 1642. LIONEL, of Boston in 1653, freeman 1673, had a son Samuel b. there.

WHEELER, DAVID, Hampton and Newbury, had sons, John, Jonathan, and Nathan, born in Newbury in 1653, 1657, and 1659. EPHRAIM, Concord, freeman 1638, had a son Isaac b. in 1638. Thirty distinct families of the Wheelers were living in Concord between 1650 and 1680, and their descendants are scattered through N. E. Shattuck, MS letter. GEORGE, Concord 1636, freeman 1641, d. 1684, leaving issue. A George Wheeler of Newbury had a son Ephraim, b. in 1662. A John Wheeler died at Newbury in 1670. ISAAC, Charlestown, freeman 1643, may have been the same who went to Fairfield in 1644. JOHN, Concord, removed with the first settlers to Fairfield in September, 1644. Shattuck. JOSEPH, Concord, born a. 1600, freeman 1640, may be the same who died in Newbury, 13 Oct. 1659. JOSHUA, Concord 1636. OBADIAH, Concord 1638, freeman 1641, d. 27 Oct. 1671, æ. 63. His sons, John and Samuel, were b. 1641 and 1644. RICHARD, freeman 1669. ROGER, Boston, d. 7 Dec. 1661. THOMAS, Boston, freeman 1637, was a tailor, and d. 16 May, 1653. Sons, Jonathan and Joseph, were b. 1637 and 1640. THOMAS, Concord, perhaps the freeman of 1641, was a captain in Philip's war, and accompained Capt. Edward Hutchinson in his expedition into the Nipmug country in 1675, and published a narrative of its events, which has been republished in Coll. N. H. Hist. Soc. vol. ii. He d. 10 Dec. 1676. THOMAS, the freeman of 1642, was probably of Lynn. *TIMOTHY, Concord, a captain, was admitted freeman 1640, representative from 1663 to 1672, excepting 1667 and 1670, d. 30 July, 1687, æ. 86. Son Timothy, freeman 1675. Twenty-six of the name had grad. at the N. E. colleges in 1826.

WHEELOCK, *RALPH, was born in Shropshire, England, in 1600, was educated at Clare-Hall, in Cambridge [M'Clure and Parish]; came to N. E. 1637, settled in Dedham, and was one of the founders of the church 1638; admitted freeman same year; was of Medfield when that became a separate town, which he represented in 1653, 1663, 1664, 1666, and 1667, and where he d. in Nov. 1688, æ. 84. He had sons, Benjamin, b. in 1639; Samuel, in 1642, and Eleazar, who settled in Medfield and afterwards in Mendon, and who was grandfather of Rev. Eleazar Wheelock, D. D., the founder and first president of Dartmouth College. President W. was b. 1711, d. 1779. John Wheelock, LL. D., his son and successor, was b. 1754, d. 4 April, 1817, aged 63.

WHEELWRIGHT, JOHN, the founder and first minister of Exeter, came from Lincolnshire, and arrived at Boston, 26 May, 1636; preached at Boston and Braintree; was banished from the Mass. colony; went to Exeter in 1638; to Wells, about 1642; to Hampton 1647; was in England in 1658, returned after the restoration, and succeeded Rev. Wm. Worcester, at Salisbury, and there d. 15 Nov. 1679. His last will, made 25 May, 1679, names his son Samuel, son-in-law Edward Rishworth, his grandchildren Edward Lyde, Mary White, Mary Maverick, William, Thomas, and Jacob Bradbury, to whom he gave his estate in Lincolnshire, England, in Maine, and other places. *SAMUEL, Wells, son of the preceding, was representative in 1671. THOMAS, Kittery, brother of the preceding, was admitted freeman in 1652.

WHIPPLE, *JOHN, Ipswich, freeman 1640, was representative 1640, and six years afterwards; a deacon of the church, and died 30 June, 1669, leaving a widow, Jennett, a son John, and daughters, Susanna Worth, Mary Stone, Sarah Goodhue, and the wife of Anthony Potter. Sarah, his 1st wife, died 14 June, 1658. Felt. Johnson, Hist. N. E. 110. *JOHN, Ipswich, freeman 1668, a captain, was the representative of Ipswich 1674, 1679, and 1682. MATTHEW, Ipswich, brother of Deacon John Whipple, received a grant of land in 1638, and died a. 1647. His sons were, John; Matthew; Joseph, freeman 1674, d. 11 May, 1699; his daughters were, Mary, Ann, and Elizabeth. Felt.

WHITSON, JOHN, Scituate 1637. 2 Coll. Mass. Hist. Soc. iv. 241. Coffin.

WHITCOMB, JOHN, Lancaster 1654, d. 24 Sept. 1662, leaving a son John. JOHN, Scituate 1644. JAMES, Boston 1665.

WHITE, ANTHONY, Sudbury 1640. The name of White prevails in every state and nearly every county in N. E. No less than 70 had grad. at the various colleges in 1826, 22 of whom have been clergymen. DANIEL, Hadley 1662. Coffin. EDWARD, Dorchester, freeman 1636. EDWARD, Roxbury, freeman 1647, had sons, Zachary and Samuel, and perhaps John, a freeman in 1684. EMANUEL, Watertown, a. 1640. Winthrop, ii. Hist. N.

E. 346. HUMPHREY, was a grantee of Ipswich in 1640. W. Gibbs. JOHN, Cambridge 1632, was admitted freeman 1633. There was a John White at Salem in 1638, one at Lynn in 1630, and one at Kittery in 1652; one at Lancaster in 1653, who was father of Mrs. Mary Rowlandson, whose Narrative of Removes is well known. *JOHN, Hadley, freeman 1666, was the representative in 1669. *NATHANIEL*, a graduate of H. C. in 1646, was pastor of a church at Bermuda, from thence removed to Nevis, in the West-Indies, where he was living when Johnson wrote. NICHOLAS, Massachusetts, freeman 1642. PAUL, Newbury, a captain, was b. in 1581, and d. 20 July, 1670, æ. 89. RESOLVED, brother of Peregrine White, was of Scituate 1638; had sons, William, b. 1642; John, b. 1644; Samuel, b. 1646; Josiah, b. 1654. Coffin. RICHARD, Sudbury 1640. Shattuck. *SAMUEL, Weymouth, son of Thomas White, was born 1642, admitted freeman 1666, representative 1679. He m. Mary Dyer, and d. without issue. Shattuck. *THOMAS, Weymouth, was representative 1636 and 1637, died Aug. 1679, leaving children, 1. Joseph, of Mendon; 2. Samuel, above; 3. Thomas, of Braintree; 4. Hannah, who m. John Baxter; 5. Ebenezer, b. 1648, d. 24 Aug. 1703, who was father of Ebenezer White, H. C. 1692, minister of Bridge-Hampton, L. I., who d. 1756, æ. 84. Shattuck. THOMAS, Sudbury 1640. Shattuck. A Thomas White d. at Charlestown, 30 May, 1664. WILLIAM, one of the first pilgrims of Plymouth 1620, d. 21 Feb. 1621. His widow Susanna m. Edward Winslow. His son Peregrine, the first born after the arrival of the pilgrims, and, as Prince supposes, [i. Annals, 76] " the first of European extract in N. England," was born in Nov. 1620, and died at Marshfield, 22 July, 1704, aged 83. His grandson Joseph d. at Yarmouth in 1782, æ. 78. WILLIAM, b. 1610, came to N. E. and settled at Ipswich, a. 1635; from thence went to Newbury, and finally settled at Haverhill, where he d. 1690, æ. 80, leaving children, whose descendants are exceedingly numerous. WILLIAM, Boston, had a son William b. in 1646.

WHITEHAND, GEORGE, Massachusetts, freeman 1634.

WHITEHEAD, DANIEL, one of the purchasers of Huntington, L. I. 1653. Wood, 44. SAMUEL, Cambridge 1635.

WHITEHOUSE, Thomas, New-Hampshire 1688, where the name still continues.

WHITEFIELD, JOHN, Dorchester 1634, removed with the first settlers to Windsor in 1635 or 1636.

WHITFIELD, HENRY, the first minister of Guilford, was the only son of an opulent lawyer, and was born 1597, came from Okely, in Surry, to N. E. in 1639, and was one of the founders of the church and town of Guilford. He returned to England, and d. in the ministry, in the city of Winchester. He had 10 children, several of whom settled in this country.

WHITING, JOHN, son of William Whiting, of Connecticut, grad. at H. C. 1653, was a preacher several years at Salem, having previously been a member of the church at Cambridge. He removed to Hartford, and was settled over the first church, according to

Trumbull, in 1669, and died, according to Trumbull, in 1709. But Mather [ii. Magnalia, 23] marks his death before 1699. His first wife was Sybil, daughter of deacon Edward Collins, and his children were, Sybil ; John ; William. William was baptized at Cambridge, 19 Feb. 1660, lived in Connecticut, was a major. He probably had other children, who were born at Hartford, where Rev. Mr. Dodd, in East-Haven Register, says he m. Phebe, daughter of Thomas Grigson, the gentleman lost at sea in 1646. *JOHN*, the graduate at H. C. of 1657, was son of Rev. Samuel Whiting, of Lynn, and probably went to England before 1661, where he was settled in the ministry at Leverton, in Lincolnshire. He d. before 1699, as Mather says, " a godly conformist." *JOHN*, the second minister of Lancaster, was son of Rev. Samuel Whiting, of Billerica, in which place he was b. 1 Aug. 1664, grad. at H. C. 1685 ; was ord. 3 Dec. 1691, and was " shot and scalped about noon," 11 Sept. 1697, by the Indians [S. Sewall], æ. 33, leaving a widow, Alice. *JOSEPH*, minister of Lynn and South-Hampton, was son of Rev. Samuel Whiting, of Lynn, where he was born 1641 ; grad. at H. C. 1661 ; was assistant to his father several years, and ordained his successor in 1680 ; was admitted freeman 1671 ; went to South-Hampton, L. I., about 1682, and was the minister there until his death, 7 April, 1723, æ. 82. His first wife was Sarah, daughter of Hon. Thomas Danforth, dep. gov. ; his last was Rebecca, who d. 21 April, 1723, æ. 63. Samuel, his eldest son was b. 3 July, 1674, and John, his 6th son (the intermediate ones dying in infancy), was b. at Lynn, 20 June, 1681, grad. at H. C. 1700, was ordained at Concord, 14 May, 1712, d. 4 May, 1752, æ. 71. His wife was Mary, daughter of Rev. John Cotton, of Hampton, and his children were, as furnished by Mr. Shattuck, 1. Mary, b. 13 August, 1713, m. Rev. Daniel Rogers, of Lyttleton ; 2. John, b. 1714, d. 1716 ; 3. John, 2d, born 25 June, 1716, d. at Royalston, Ms., leaving a numerous family ; 4. Thomas, b. 25 June, 1717, was a merchant in Boston, and father of Thomas Whiting, H. C. 1775, who d. at Concord, 28 Sept. 1820, æ. 72 ; 5. Anne, b. 1718, d. 1719 ; 6. Sarah, b. 7 Sept. 1719 ; 7. Stephen, b. 6 Aug. 1720 ; 8. Elizabeth, who m. Rev. Samuel Webster, D. D., of Salisbury. ‡JOSEPH, Connecticut, believed to be a son of Captain William Whiting, was elected an assistant in 1683. NATHANIEL, Dedham, freeman 1642, had a son Nathaniel, born 26 Sept. 1644. He was the ancestor of Rev. Samuel Whiting, H. C. 1769, the first minister of Rockingham, Vermont, who was b. at Wrentham, Ms., 28 Jan. 1750, d. May, 1819. *SAMUEL*, minister of Lynn, was son of John Whiting, Mayor of Boston, in Lincolnshire, where he was b. 20 Nov. 1597 ; was a minister at Skirbick and other places. He arrived at Boston, 26 May, 1636, was soon admitted freeman, and the same year settled at Lynn, where he d. 11 Dec. 1679, æ. 82. By his first wife he had two sons, who, with their mother, d. in England, and one daughter, who m. Mr. Weld, probably Thomas, the son of Rev. Thomas Weld. By his 2d wife, Elizabeth (who d. 3 March, 1678), a daughter of the Right Hon. Oliver St. John, he had, Samuel, John, Joseph, and two daughters, one of whom m. Rev. Jeremiah Hobart. *SAMUEL*, the first minister of Billerica, was son of the preceding, and was b. in Eng. a. 1633, grad. at H. C. 1653, admitted freeman 1656; settled in Billerica 1658, was ordained there 11 Nov. 1663, d. 28 Feb. 1713. He m. Dorcas Chester, 12 Nov. 1656. She d. 15 Feb. 1713. Their children were, 1. Elizabeth, b. 1660, m. Rev. Thomas Clark; 2. Samuel, b. 19 Jan. 1662, d. 14 March, 1715, æ. 51, leaving issue; 3. John, before noticed; 4. Oliver, b. 8 Nov. 1665, m. Anna, daughter of Capt. Jonathan Danforth, 22 Jan. 1690, had 9 children, and d. 22 Dec. 1736, æ. 71, having been many years a magistrate; 5. Dorothy; 6. Joseph, b. 7 Feb. 1669, perhaps the graduate at H C. 1690, d. 6 Sept. 1701, æ. 32; 7. James; 8. Eunice; 9. Benjamin; 10. Benjamin; the four last dying in infancy. Samuel, the fourth son of Oliver, was b. 6 Sept. 1702, was a deacon in Billerica, and died 4 Nov. 1772, being grandfather of the present Deacon Samuel Whiting, who has sustained the offices of magistrate and representative of Billerica many years. ‡WILLIAM, Hartford, one of the most respectable of the early settlers, was elected a magistrate in 1642, and the next year was chosen treasurer of the Conn. colony. Hutchinson, i. Hist. Mass. 98, gives one of this name. See Trumbull, and I. Mather, Indian Wars, from 1614 to 1675.

WHITMAN, JOHN, the common ancestor of a large posterity in Massachusetts, came to N. E. as early as 1638, when he was admitted freeman; abode a short time at Charlestown, from whence he went to Weymouth, where he d. quite advanced, a. 1692. His children were Thomas; John, freeman 1681; Abiah, freeman 1681; Zechariah, and Sarah Jones, Mary wife of John Pratt, Elizabeth, who m. John Green, Hannah, who m. Stephen French, and Judith King. MS Communication of Hon. Nahum Mitchell. ROBERT, Ipswich 1666. 2 Coll. Mass. Hist. Soc. viii. 107. THOMAS, Weymouth, son of John Whitman, was admitted freeman in May, 1653, m. Abigail, daughter of Nicholas Byram, 22 Nov. 1656, and had sons, John, Ebenezer, Nicholas. VALENTINE, an interpretor 1654. Hutch. Coll. 267. He was probably of Providence. ZECHARIAH, one of the pillars of Milford 1639. Trumbull, Hist. Conn. 107. *ZECHARIAH*, minister of Hull, is supposed [MS Genealogy] to have been son of John Whitman, of Weymouth. He grad. at H. C. 1668, was ordained 13 Sept. 1670, freeman 1673; d. 5 Nov. 1726. His age has been variously stated by different authorities, at 78, 82, and 85.

WHITMARSH, JOHN, Weymouth, had sons, Increase and Simon, b. in 1655 and 1661. NICHOLAS, an inhabitant of Weymouth in 1659, was freeman 1681. Ezra Whitmarsh grad. at H. C. 1723.

WHITNEY, JOHN, Watertown, freeman 1636, d. 1 June, 1673, æ. 84. Eleanor, his wife, d. 11 May, 1659. His sons were, John, Thomas, Jonathan, Richard, Benjamin, and Joshua, all of whom settled in Watertown, and had families. Shattuck, MS letter. JOHN, Watertown, son of the preceding, was admitted freeman 1647, and had sons John, b. 1635; Caleb, b. 1640; Benjamin, b.

1643; John, 2d, b 1644. RICHARD, brother of the preceding, was admitted freeman 1651. STEPHEN, was one of the first settlers of Huntington, L. I. Wood.

WHITON, JAMES, Hingham 1647; Lancaster 1644, freeman 1660, had sons, James and Matthew, b. in 1649 and 1659.

WHITRED, THOMAS and WILLIAM, inhabitants of Ipswich in 1648. Felt.

WHITTIMORE, LAWRENCE, Roxbury, freeman 1637, d. 24 Nov. 1644. His wife d. 1642. FRANCIS, Cambridge 1653, had sons, Francis; John, b. 1 Oct. 1654; Samuel, b. 1 May, 1658.

WHITTIER, THOMAS, Haverhill, was admitted freeman 1666. John G. Whittier, the poet of Haverhill, is perhaps a descendant.

WHITTINGHAM, ||JOHN, Ipswich 1637, member of the ar. co. 1638, a son of Baruch, and grandson of Rev. William Whittingham, the famous puritan minister in the reign of Queen Mary, who, it is said, m. a daughter of John Calvin, came to N. E. with his mother from Lincolnshire. He m. a daughter of William Hubbard, and d. between 1644 and 1651, [Johnson] and probably in 1648, leaving sons, Richard, and William, and 3 daughters. WILLIAM, son of the preceding, grad. at H. C. 1660, m. a daughter of J. Lawrence, and d. of small pox in London, leaving children, 1. Richard, H. C. 1689, who went to London, and enjoyed the family estate in Lincolnshire; 2. William, who d. in the West Indies; 3 Mary, who m. Gov. Saltonstall; 4. Elizabeth, who m. Samuel Appleton and afterwards Rev. Edward Payson; 5. Martha, who m. Rev. John Rogers. Alden, Coll. Epitaphs.

WHITTINGTON, ||RICHARD, member of the ar. co. 1646. EDWARD, who had a grant of land in Andover in 1673. Abbot.

WHITTREDGE, NATHANIEL, Lynn 1637.

WHITWELL, SAMUEL, Boston 1652, had a son Samuel, b. in 1653.

WICKENDEN, WILLIAM, Salem, removed to Providence 1639, became a Baptist minister, and d. 23 Feb. 1669. Benedict, Hist. of Baptists, i. 477.

WICKS, FRANCIS, sometimes Weeks, Salem 1635, went to Rhode-Island with Roger Williams. John Wicks is mentioned by Savage, ii. Winthrop, 148. Rev. Thomas S. Wickes grad. at Y. C. in 1814.

WICOM, *DANIEL, a captain, was of Rowley, and representative in 1689 and 1690, and d. 15 April, 1700, æ. 65.

WIGGIN, ‡*THOMAS, an active and useful man in the first settlement of N. H., came to N. E. as early as 1631, was agent or governour of the upper plantation; a captain; resided some time in Hampton, which he represented in 1645; was elected an assistant from 1650 to 1664. Mr. Coffin gives the year 1667 for the time of his death. His son Andrew resided in Exeter, m. Ann, daughter of Gov. Bradstreet in 1659, and had, Thomas, b. 5 March, 1661; Simon, b. 17 April, 1664; Hannah, b. 10 Aug. 1666; Mary, b. 1668, and probably others.

WIGGLESWORTH, MICHAEL, minister of Malden, and a writer of verses of some note, graduated in 1651, at H. C. of which he was a fellow. He was probably admitted freeman 1680, d. 9 June, 1704, æ. 74. Allen puts the time of his death in 1705. His son Edward, H. C. 1710, and grandson Edward, H. C. 1749, both D. D's. were the first and second professors of divinity at H. C. at which nine of the name had grad. in 1828.

WIGHT, HENRY, Medfield, freeman 1647. Of the six graduates of this name at H. C. four were clergymen. THOMAS, Dedham, had sons, Samuel and Ephraim, b. in 1639 and 1645.

WIGLEY, EDWARD, Concord 1666. Shattuck.

WIGNAL, ALEXANDER, Massachusetts, freeman 1631.

WILBORNE, MICHAEL, Boston 1657.

WILCOMB, or WELCOME, RICHARD, was ale-house keeper at the Isles of Shoals 1683.

WILCOCKSON, WILLIAM, Massachusetts, freeman 1638. David and David B. Wilcockson grad. at Y. C. in 1744 and 1798.

WILCOX, ||WILLIAM, freeman 1636, member of the ar. co. 1638, d. at Cambridge, 28 Nov. 1653. Nine of the name had grad. at the N. E. colleges in 1828.

WILDBORE, SAMUEL, Boston, freeman 1634, d. 29 Sept. 1656. This name is probably the same with *Wilbur.*

WILDE, WILLIAM, Rowley 1643, afterwards of Ipswich, died a. 1662. The name of *Wild, Wilde,* and *Wildes* has had 9 graduates at the N. E. colleges.

WILDER, EDWARD, came as early as 1638 to N. E. with his mother, a widow, who d. 20 April, 1652, and settled at Hingham, and was admitted freeman 1644. He m. Elizabeth Ames, of Marshfield, before 1654, and had sons, John, Ephraim, Isaac, and Jabez, and 4 daughters. He d. 18 Oct. 1690. His widow d. 9 June, 1692. THOMAS, Charlestown, [Benedict, i. Hist. Baptists, 388] was admitted freeman 1641, became an inhabitant of Lancaster, 1 July, 1659 ; was one of the selectmen, and d. 23 Oct. 1667, leaving 3 sons, 1. Thomas, b. at Charlestown 1644, d. Aug. 1717, leaving sons, *James,* a colonel, who m. a daughter of Capt. Andrew Gardner, and had sons James and Gardner ; *Joseph,* who also m. a daughter of Capt. Gardner, and had sons, Thomas, of Leominster ; Andrew ; Joseph, a judge, who d. 20 April, 1776, æ. 59 ; and Caleb, a colonel ; 2. John, who had sons, John, Thomas, and Ebenezer; 3. Nathaniel, of Lancaster, who was killed by the Indians in July, 1704, leaving posterity. The first Joseph was a representative, chief justice of the court of common pleas 1731 to 1757, judge of probate from 1739 to 1757, and d. 29 March, 1757, æ. 74. Willard, Hist. Lancaster, 87.

WILKINS, BRAY, born a. 1610, lived in Lynn 1634, in Salem 1654, and is probably the ancestor of the Wilkins families in the county of Essex, where Rev. Daniel Wilkins was born, and who grad. at H. C. 1736, was ordained the first minister of Amherst, N. H., 23 Sept. 1741, died 11 Feb. 1784, in his 73d year, having had 10 children, of whom John, grad. at H. C. 1764, and died at Athens,

Ohio.   John H. Wilkins, H. C. 1818, of Boston, is grandson of
Rev. Mr. Wilkins, of Amherst.   There was a Wilkins, who was
admitted a member of Dorchester church in 1640.

WILKINSON, JOHN, Malden, d. in Dec. 1675.   Ann Wilkinson, d. at Billerica, 8 Feb. 1692, æ. 94.   LAWRENCE, was early
at Providence.

WILLARD, GEORGE, probably first of Cambridge, was of Scituate 1638, from whence he removed.   Deborah, and Daniel, his
children, were baptized at Scituate, 14 September 1645, by Rev.
William Wetherell, and Joshua, another child, was baptized 2 November, 1645.   ‡*SIMON, came from the county of Kent, and resided in Cambridge in 1634, from thence to Concord in 1635, to
Lancaster as early as 1660 ; was of Groton in 1672, and, on the
breaking up of that town in 1676, went to Salem, but d. at Charlestown, 24 April, 1676.   He was early a military officer, and attained
the rank of major, and commanded the forces in Ninigret's and Philip's wars.   He represented Concord 14 years, commencing with
1636, and was elected assistant 22 years, from 1654 to his death.
He m. (1) Mary Sharp, (2) Elizabeth Dunster, sister of President
Dunster, (3)Mary Dunster, and had 9 sons ; Josiah, who settled in
Weathersfield ; Samuel, minister of Groton, and Boston ; Simon, b.
23 Nov. 1649, a deacon of Salem ; Henry, b. 4 June, 1655, who
lived in Lancaster ; John, b. 15 Jan. 1657, who lived in Concord ;
Daniel, b. 29 Dec. 1650, of Boston ; Joseph, b. 4 Jan. 1660, who
went to England ; Benjamin, of Grafton ; Jonathan, born 14 Dec.
1669, who settled in Sudbury.   His daughters were two Elizabeths,
the last the wife of Robert Blood ; Mary, who m. Cyprian Stevens ;
Sarah, who m. Nathaniel Howard ; Hannah, who m. Capt. Thomas Brintnall ; Mercy, who m. Joshua Edmunds ; Abovehope, and
Dorothy, who d. unmarried.   In speaking of the loss of Major Willard and Richard Russell, Dr. Increase Mather [Indian Wars, 32]
says "the death of a few such is as much as if thousands had
fallen."   Hubbard calls him that " worthy and experienced soldier,"
and Rev. Mr. Pemberton calls him " a sage patriot in our Israel,
whose wisdom assigned him a seat at the council board, and his
military skill and martial spirit entitled him to the chief place in the
field."   A letter from him to the commissioners of the United Colonies, 1654, is presented in Hutch. Coll. 263—268.   SAMUEL,
author of the " Complete Body of Divinity," the first folio volume
printed in America, minister of Groton and Boston, son of the preceding, and was b. at Concord, 31 Jan. 1640, grad. at H. C. 1659 ;
was ordained at Groton, probably in 1663, having begun to preach
there in 1662, from whence he was driven by the Indians, when
that town was burnt, in March, 1676.   He was installed pastor of
the Old South church, 31 March, 1678, officiated as vice-president
of H. C. from 6 Sept. 1701 to his death, 12 Sept. 1707, æ. 67.   He
m. (1) Abigail Sherman, 8 Aug. 1664, whose mother was grand-
daughter of Lord Darcy, Earl of Rivers ; (2) Eunice, daughter of
Edward Tyng, a. 1679.   His children were, 1. Abigail, b. 1665 ;
2. Samuel, b. 1668 ; 3. Mary ; 4. John, b. 8 Sept. 1673, grad. at

H. C. 1690, settled in Kingston, Jamaica, was father of Rev. Samuel Willard, of Biddeford, Me., who grad. at H. C. 1723, ord. Sept.
30, 1730, d. Oct. 25, 1741, æ. 36, whose son, Rev. Joseph Willard,
D. D., LL. D., b. at Bideford, Dec. 29, 1738, grad. at H. C. 1765,
afterwards tutor and fellow, was president of H. C. from 1781, to
his death, 25 Sept. 1804 ; 5. Elizabeth ; 6. Simon, who grad at H.
C. 1695 ; 7. Edward, b. 1680 ; 8. Josiah, b. May, 1681, grad. at
H. C. 1698, where he was afterwards a tutor, and was long the secretary of the province of Mass., a counsellor and judge of probate,
and d. 6 Dec. 1756 ; 9. Eunice ; 10. Richard, who was drowned
29 June, 1697, soon after he entered Harv. College ; 11. William ;
12. Margaret ; 13. Edward, 2d ; 14. Hannah ; 15. Sarah ; 16 Eunice, 2d ; 17. Sarah, 2d ; 18. Richard, 2d ; 19. Edward, 3d ; 20. one
other ; the last fourteen by his 2d wife. Thirty-four of the name
had grad. at the N. E colleges in 1828, of whom are six of as many
generations in uninterrupted succession from Maj. Simon Willard.

WILLES, MICHAEL, Dorchester, freeman 1638, one of the
founders of the 2d church in Boston, 1650. This name is spelled
Willyes on Dorchester church records.

WILLET, HEZEKIAH, Swanzey, was killed by the Indians,
26 June, 1676. Hubbard. FRANCIS, Newbury 1672. ‡THO-
MAS, Plymouth colony, came from Leyden as early as 1630 ; was
elected an assistant from 1651 to 1664 ; was the first mayor of New-
York after its conquest by the English, died at Barrington, R. I., 4
August, 1674, æ. 64.

WILLEY, ALLEN, husbandman, was admitted member of the
Boston church in 1633.

WILLIAMS, *ABRAHAM, was representative of Marlborough
in 1679. One hundred and forty seven of the name of Williams had
grad. in 1825, at the colleges in N. E., New-Jersey, and Union in
New-York. BELSHAZZAR, Salisbury, d. 1651. Coffin. DAN-
IEL, one of the first proprietors of Providence. Coffin. ELEA-
ZAR, Salem, was admitted to the church, 6 Aug. 1637. Felt.
FRANCIS, Portsmouth, came over in 1631, as governour of the
settlement, commenced by Mason and Gorges, and was in N. H. in
1643, but soon after left, and went to Barbadoes. GEORGE, Salem, freeman 1634, died a. 1654. HENRY, Casco 1665, was
wounded in Saco, 10 Oct. 1676. Hutch. Coll. 398. Hubbard, Ind.
Wars. ||HUGH, Boston, freeman 1642, was a member of the ar.
co. *ISAAC, a captain, was son of Robert Williams, of Roxbury,
where he was b. 1 Sept. 1638, settled in Newton, which he represented in 1692, 1695, 1697, 1699, 1701, and 1705. He had children, Isaac ; Martha, b. 1663 ; William, H. C. 1683 ; Eleazar, who
settled in Stonington. The founder of Williams college descended
from this family. *JAMES*, a preacher at Plymouth, is named by
Savage, ii. Winthrop, 391. JOHN, Scituate 1639. JOHN,
Pascataqua 1631. A John Williams is mentioned by Felt, Annals
Salem, 110. A John Williams was of Newbury 1641, where he d.
1674. Another John Williams died in Mass. 1658. *JOHN*,
minister of Deerfield, was son of Deacon Samuel Williams, and was

b. at Roxbury, 10 Dec. 1664, grad. at H. C. 1683, was ordained 18 Oct. 1688, captured by the Indians, 28 Feb. 1704, when Eunice, his wife, a daughter of Rev. Eleazar Mather, was killed; returned from captivity, and d. 12 June, 1709, æ. 65. His sons were, Eleazar, H. C. 1708, minister of Mansfield; Samuel; Eliakim; Stephen, H. C. 1713, minister of Longmeadow; Warham, H. C. 1719, minister of Waltham; John, killed by the Indians; Eliakim, 2d. John, 2d, a major; Elijah, and several daughters. ||NATHANIEL, Boston, freeman 1640, member of the church and of the ar. co. 1644, had sons Joseph, b. 1641; Nathaniel, b. 1642, member of the ar. co. 1667; John, b. 1644. NICHOLAS, Roxbury, freeman 1652, d. 27 Aug. 1692. RICHARD, Dorchester, and Boston, had a son Benjamin, b. 1645. ROBERT, Roxbury, came from Norwich, in England, was admitted freeman in 1638, and is the common ancestor of the divines, civilians, and warriors of this name, who have honoured the country of their birth. His sons were, Samuel, a deacon of Roxbury, freeman 1650, who d. 28 Sept. 1698; Isaac, already noticed; Stephen, b. 8 Nov. 1640, a captain, who d. at Roxbury, 15 Feb. 1720, and Thomas, who d. without issue. The family estate at Roxbury remained in possession of his descendants until 1826. The last possessor of it was Thomas Williams, esq. counsellor at law, son of Dr. Thomas Williams, H. C. 1757. ROBERT, Boston, freeman 1643, was a member of the church, had a son Joseph, b. in 1644. He, or the preceding, was a member of the ar. co. 1644. ROBERT, Providence 1639, was a brother of Roger Williams, of Providence. A Robert Williams was one of the first settlers of Oyster-Bay, L. I. 1650. *ROGER*, was born in Wales 1599, was educated at Oxford, came to N. E. and arrived at Nantasket, 5 Feb. 1631; settled at Salem as teaching elder with Rev. Samuel Skelton, 12 April, 1631; went the same year to Plymouth, where he preached two years, and returned to Salem in 1633, and was the sole pastor after Mr. Skelton's death. He was banished the Mass. colony, in Nov. 1635, went to Rhode-Island 1636, and laid the foundation of that colony, for which he went to England in 1643 for a charter, which he obtained, and landed with it at Boston, in Sept. 1644; was in England again from 1651 to 1654, and on his return was chosen president of the colony, and remained in office until 1657. This earliest and boldest champion of the rights of all men " fully to have and enjoy their own judgements and consciences in matters of religious concernment," d. at Providence in April, 1683, æ. 84. His wife was Mary, and his children were, Mary; Freeborn; Providence, b. Sept. 1638, the first of European parentage born in Rhode-Island; Mercy; Daniel; and Joseph, whose descendants amount to several thousands. Coll. R. I. Hist. Soc. i. ii. Felt, Annals Salem. Upham, Ded. Sermon, 52. Holmes, i. Annals, 411. ROGER, Massachusetts 1630, requested to be made freeman 19 Oct. 1630. He may have been the early settler of Windsor, [1 Coll. Mass. Hist. Soc. v. 168] or the member of the ar. co. in 1647. THOMAS, one of the first pilgrims of Plymouth 1620, died before March, 1621. THOMAS, Boston, freeman

1631, died a. 1646.   He set up the first ferry between Winnisimmet
and Charlestown 1631.   Holmes, ii. Annals, 210.   WILLIAM, Salem, 1637, perhaps a proprietor of Watertown 1641.   *WILLIAM*,
minister of Hatfield, was son of Captain Isaac Williams, of Newton,
and was born a. 1664, grad. at H. C. 1683, and d. 31 August,
1741.   He m. (1) Eliza, daughter of Rev. Seaborn Cotton ; (2) a
daughter of Rev. Solomon Stoddard.   By the first he had Rev. William Williams, H. C. 1705, minister of Weston, and Rev. Elisha
Williams, H. C. 1711, the third president of Yale College; by the
2d, Rev. Solomon Williams, H. C. 1719, minister of Lebanon,
Conn. and Hon. Israel Williams, H. C. 1727.   He had also 3 daughters.

WILLIAMSON, MICHAEL, Ipswich 1638.

WILLIS, HENRY, was a volunteer in the Pequot expedition
1636.   Those under this head have the name spelled in old records,
Willis, *Willice*, *Willys*, *Willust*, &c.   The Connecticut family of
this name has usually written it *Wyllys*, which see.   GEORGE,
Hartford.   (See WYLLYS.)   JEREMY, Lynn 1637.   JOHN,
spelled *Willust* in colony records, was member of the church in
Boston, was admitted freeman in 1632.   He was cast away in a
N. E. tempest in returning from Noddle's Island, 21 Nov. 1634,
and perished.   Winthrop, i. Hist. N. E. 150, 385.   A Mr. Willis
was representative from Lynn at the first general court, 1634, who
is considered by Mr. Savage [ii. Winthrop, Index, 428, John Wil-
les] the same as the preceding.   JOHN, one of the proprietors of
Bridgewater, was a representative at the Plymouth court 1657.   He
had a brother Nathaniel, also a proprietor of Bridgewater in 1645.
NICHOLAS, Boston, spelled *Willust* in the colony records, was
admitted freeman 1634.   Savage, ii. Winthrop, 216.   RICHARD,
Plymouth 1630.   ROBERT, an inhabitant of Boston in 1642.
THOMAS, Lynn 1634, removed to Sandwich 1637.   Lewis.   WIL-
LIAM, Scituate 1640.   2 Coll. Mass. Hist. Soc. iv. 247.

WILLOUGHBY, †‡||*FRANCIS, Charlestown, member of the
ar. co. 1639, freeman 1640, was chosen representative in 1642,
1646, and 1640, assistant 1650, 1651, 1664, deputy-governour 6
years from 1665 to 1671.   He d. 4 April, 1671, leaving a wife
Margaret, who, after marrying Capt. Laurence Hammond, d. 2 Feb.
1683.   His children were, Hannah, b. 17 May, 1643 ; Nehemiah,
b. 8 June, 1644 ; Jeremiah, b. 29 July, 1647 ; Jonathan ; William,
who d. 1678.   Gov. Willoughby left an estate of £4050. 5. 4.

WILLOW, GEORGE, Cambridge, with Jane his wife, was
member of the church.   He was living in 1688, at the age of 86.
He had sons, Thomas, b. 1638 ; Stephen, b. 1644, freeman 1665.

WILLS, MICHAEL, Boston, was one of the founders of the 2d
church.   THOMAS, freeman 1638, was of Massachusetts where
the name exists.

WILMOT, NICHOLAS, Boston 1657.   A Thomas Wilmot was
of Braintree soon after this period.

WILSON, *DANIEL, was representative of Northampton 1665.
HENRY, Dedham, freeman 1641, whose son Michael was b. 1644.
    44   321

JACOB, Braintree, had a son Isaac, who was b. 1641. *JOHN,* freeman 1633, the first minister of Boston, third son of Rev. William Wilson, D. D., was b. at Windsor, in England, in 1588; was educated at King's College, Cambridge; settled at Sudbury, in Suffolk; came to N. E. with Gov. Winthrop in 1630; was installed 27 August, same year, over the first church, and d. 7 Aug. 1667, æ. 78, having had for his colleagues the celebrated Cotton and Norton. He was brother to Rev. William Wilson, who gave £1000 to New-England. Edmund, his eldest son, named for his great uncle, Edmund Grindall, archbishop of Canterbury, went to Europe, travelled in Holland, in Italy, where he received the degree of M. D., and from thence went to England, and died a. 1658. *JOHN,* son of the preceding, was b. in England, in July, 1621, grad. in the first class at H. C. 1642, was admitted member of the church in Boston 1644; freeman 1647; ordained as colleague with Rev. Richard Mather at Dorchester, and after two years, was settled in Medfield, where he was pastor 40 years, and d. 23 Aug. 1691, æ. 70. His children b. in Medfield, were Elizabeth, Increase, and Thomas. *JOHN, was a representative of Malden in 1689. JOSEPH, Dorchester, was admitted freeman 1638. LAMBERT, was an early chirurgeon in Salem. MATTHEW, New-Haven 1642. NATHANIEL, Roxbury, had sons, Joseph and Benjamin, twins, b. in 1656, both died in infancy. THEOPHILUS, received a grant of land in Ipswich 1638. THOMAS, admitted freeman 1634, was probably of Exeter in 1639. Belknap, i. Hist. N. H. 36. WILLIAM, joiner, Boston, admitted to the church 1635, freeman 1636, disarmed in 1637, had sons, Shoarborn, b. 1635; John, b. 1639: Joseph, b. 1643, settled in Andover, and d. in 1718, æ. 75; Newgrace, b. 1645.

WILTON, DAVID, or DAVIS, Dorchester, freeman 1633, perhaps of Northampton in 1660.

WINBORN, JOHN, was a preacher at Manchester before 1686, and left that place as early as 1689. Felt.

WINCHELL, NATHANIEL, Westfield 1686.

WINCHESTER, *ALEXANDER, freeman 1636, Braintree 1639, which he represented in 1641. Ebenezer and Isaac Winchester grad. at H. C. in 1744 and 1764. JOHN, Muddy-River, now Brookline, was admitted freeman 1637, d. 25 April, 1694, æ. upwards of 80, leaving sons, John, Josiah, and Jonathan. Rev. Jonathan a descendant, grad. at H. C. in 1737. ||RICHARD, according to Whitman, was a member of the ar. co. 1638, but the name should probably be *John,* the preceding.

WINCOLL, HUMPHREY, Cambridge 1634. *JOHN, a captain, was admitted freeman in 1646, and represented Kittery in 1653, 1654, 1655, 1675, 1677, and 1678. He is mentioned in Hubbard's Indian Wars. ROBERT, Massachusetts, was admitted freeman 1635. THOMAS, Watertown 1642, d. 10 June, 1657.

WINES, BARNABAS, Watertown, was admitted freeman in 1635. FAINTNOT, Massachusetts, freeman 1644.

WING, JOHN, Lynn, removed to Sandwich 1637. He m. Deborah, daughter of Stephen Batchelor. This name continues in that vicinity. ROBERT, Boston, had sons, John, b. 1637, member of the ar. co. 1671, its captain 1693, probably d. at Boston, 22 Feb. 1704; Jacob, b. 1642; Joseph, b. 1646, freeman 1679.

WINGATE, JOHN, Dover as early as 1666, was admitted freeman, died a. 1689; had children, Ann, b. 18 Feb. 1667; John, b. 13 July, 1670; Joshua; and Caleb. Joshua, m. Mary Lunt of Newbury, 1702, lived in Hampton, N. H., and, with his wife, d. over 90 years of age. He was at the conquest of Louisburg 1745, and afterwards a colonel. Two of his sons were, Rev. Paine Wingate, H. C. 1723, of Amesbury, and John Wingate, H. C. 1744, who d. a bachelor, 4 Sept. 1812, æ. 87. Hon. Paine Wingate, of Stratham, is son of the former. He was born 14 May, 1739, grad. at H. C. 1759, and now [1829] the oldest living graduate, and after being the minister of Hampton-Falls ,was one of the first Senators from N .H. in Congress 1789, four years, and Judge of the Supreme court of N. H.. Joseph Wingate, esq. of Hallowell, was also a son of Rev. Paine Wingate, of Amesbury. OLIVER, from Bridgetown, England, was cast away at the Isles of Shoals in 1664. Coffin.

WINN, EDWARD, Woburn, freeman 1643, had a son Increase b. in 1641, and probably others.

WINSHIP, ||*EDWARD, Cambridge, freeman 1635, member of the ar. co. 1638, was representative 1663, 1664, 1681 to 1686, eight years, d. 2 Dec. 1688, æ. 76. He had sons, Ephraim, b. 1643, freeman 1679; Edward, b. and d. 1648; Edward, 2d, b. 1655; Samuel, b. 1658; Joseph, b. 1661; and seven daughters. This name is also spelled *Windship*.

WINSLOW, §‡EDWARD, son of Edward Winslow, esq., was born in Worcestershire 1594; came to N. E. with the Plymouth pilgrims 1620; was chosen an assistant 13 years from 1634, and elected governour in 1633, 1636, and 1644. He d. 8 May, 1655, while a commissioner of the united colonies to superintend the expedition against the Spaniards in the West-Indies. Elizabeth, his wife, d. at Plymouth, 24 March, 1621, and on the 12 May following, he m. Susanna, widow of William White, and this was the first marriage in New-England. Gov. Winslow had 4 brothers and three sisters. *EDWARD, representative of Salisbury 1644. Coll. N. H. Hist. Soc. ii. 215. GILBERT, brother of Gov. Edward, came over in the May Flower, 1620. Davis, Morton's Memo. JOHN, brother of the preceding, came over in 1621, m. Mary Chilton, and went to Boston, and probably freeman in 1672. JOHN, of Boston, a son or grandson, was born in 1665, and brought the prince of Orange's declaration to N. E. from Nevis in Feb. 1689, for which he was imprisoned by Sir Edmund Andros' although he offered £2000 security. JOSIAH, brother of the preceding, came to N. E. before 1633, and probably a. 1621. §‡JOSIAH, Plymouth, son of Gov. Edward, was born a. 1629; was elected assistant 1657, governour from 1673 to 1679, seven years. He d. 18 Dec. 1680, æ. 51, being the first governour, a native of New-England. His wife was Penelope Pelham, daughter of Herbert Pelham. She d. in 1703, æ. 73. Isaac Winslow, his son, was counsellor of Massachusetts, and d. in 1738. His grandson, John Winslow, was captain of the expedition against Cuba in 1740, and afterwards rose to the rank of major-general in the British service, and was judge of the court of common pleas, and d. at Hingham in April, 1774, in his 72d year. Isaac Winslow, son of General Winslow, was a physician, and d. in 1819, æ. 81. The late John Winslow, esq. was son of Dr. Winslow. KENELM, brother of Gov. Edward, was of Plymouth 1633.

WINSOR, JOSEPH, Lynn, removed to Sandwich 1637. Lewis. JOSHUA, Providence 1639. ROBERT, Boston, had a son Thomas, b. in 1652.

WINTER, JOHN, Scituate 1637, from whence he removed to Cambridge, and was there in 1672. A John Winter was of Watertown, and a Timothy Winter was early at Braintree. Hon. Francis Winter, H. C. 1765, a patriot of the revolution, and chaplain, d. at Bath, Me. in 1826, æ. 82.

WINTHROP, ||ADAM, Boston, son of Gov. John Winthrop, was born in England, 7 April, 1620, was admitted freeman 1641, member of the ar. co. 1642, d. 24 August, 1652, æ. 32. His wife was Elizabeth Glover. ‡||*ADAM, Boston, son of the preceding, grad. at H. C. 1668, was elected representative in 1691 and 1692, member of the ar. co. 1692, a member of the council under the charter of 1691, d. in August, 1700. His son Adam, who grad. at H. C. 1694, d. 2 Oct. 1743, was father of Adam, H. C. 1724, and John, H. C. 1732, the learned professor at Cambridge, and a member of the Royal Society, who d. 3 May, 1779, in his 65th year. Four sons of professor Winthrop grad. at H. C., John in 1765, Adam in 1767; James, LL. D. 1769, who d. in Sept. 1821, and William, S. H. S. in 1770, who d. 5 Feb. 1825, æ. 72. ||DEANE, son of Gov. John Winthrop, of Massachusetts, was b. 16 March, 1623, was member of the ar. co. 1644, freeman 1665, was concerned in the settlement of Groton, which probably was named in honour of his father, whose paternal seat was at Groton, in Suffolk, England. He d. at Pulling Point, 16 March, 1704, æ. 81. He had a son Deane, b. 6 Sept. 1653, who m. and lived in Boston. HENRY, brother of the preceding, was drowned at Salem, 2 July, 1630, a few days after his arrival in New-England. ‡FITZ-JOHN, son of Gov. John Winthrop of Connecticut, was born at Boston, 14 March, 1639 [Records]; was one of Sir Edmund Andros' council 1687; assistant of Connecticut 1689; major-general of the land army designed against Canada; agent to Great-Britian 1694; was a member of the Royal Society; governour of Connecticut in 1698, until his death, which occurred at Boston, 27 Nov. 1707, in his 69th year. §‡†JOHN, the great ancestor of the Winthrops in this country, and the father of the Massachusetts colony, was son of Adam Winthrop, and was born at Groton, in Suffolk, England, 12 Jan. 1588. He arrived in N. E. 12 June, 1630, and soon settled at Boston; was elected assistant 4 years; deputy-governour in 1636, 1644, and

1645; was governour in 1630, and eleven years afterwards. He d. 26 March, 1649, æ. 61. Mather, [i. Magnalia, 109] gives his birth 12 June, 1587, but it will be more safe to follow his learned and accurate annotator. He m. (1) 16 April, 1605, Mary, daughter of John Forth, esq. by whom he had John, Henry, Forth, and 3 daughters; (2) the daughter of William Clopton; (3) 29 April, 1618, Margaret, daughter of Sir Tindal Knight, by whom (who d. 14 June, 1647) he had, Adam, Stephen, Deane, Samuel, Anne, and William; (4) Martha, widow of Thomas Coytmore in 1648, and had one son, Joshua, b. 12 Dec. 1648, d. 11 Jan. 1659. Savage, ii. Winthrop, Index. §‡†JOHN, son of the preceding, was b. 12 Feb. 1606; was educated at the universities of Cambridge and Dublin, came to N. E. in 1631; freeman, 3 April, 1632, settled at Ipswich, where Martha, his wife, the daughter of Henry Painter, d. soon after he went there. He was elected an assistan' from 1632 to 1649; went to Connecticut, was a magistrate in 1651; a deputy-governour; and in 1657, governour, which office he filled until his death, at Boston, 5 April, 1676, æ. 70. He was one of the founders of the Royal Society in England. His children were Gov. Fitz-John, Hon. Waitstill, and 3 daughters, all by Elizabeth, his 2d wife. Ibid, i. 64, 65, and ii. Index. Holmes, i. Annals, 387. ‖*STEPHEN, brother of the preceding, was admitted freeman 1636, member of the ar. co. 1644; representative for Portsmouth 1644; went to England, and lived in the parish of St. Margaret's, Westminster, commanded a regiment, and was member of parliament in Cromwell's time. His wife was Judith, and his children were Stephen and John, b. in Boston 1644 and 1646, who probably d. young; Margaret, who m. Henry Ward and Edmund Willie, both of London, and was living in 1699; Judith, who m. Richard Hancock, a clothmaker, of London. Ibid, i. 126. Rev. J. B. Felt, MS letter. ‡‖WAIT-STILL, son of Gov. John Winthrop, of Connecticut, was b. at Boston, 27 Feb. 1642, was one of Sir Edmund Andros' council 1687; member of the ar. co. 1691; one of the first council under the new charter 1692; d. at Boston, 7 Sept. 1717, æ. 75. He m. Mary, daughter of Hon. William Browne of Salem. She d. 14 June 1690. His son John, who grad. at H. C. 1700, was fellow of the Royal Society; m. a daughter of Gov. Joseph Dudley, and d. 1 August, 1747, leaving a son John-Still Winthrop, who was b. 15 Jan. 1720, d. 6 June, 1776, whose sons were, John, H. C. 1770; Francis-Bayard, of New-York; William, of New-York; Joseph, of Charlestown, S. C. who died 1828; Thomas-Lindall, H. C. 1780, of Boston, the lieutenant-governour of Massachusetts. Five sons of Lieut-Gov. Winthrop are on the catalogue of Harv. College, viz. James, a counsellor of Boston, who has taken the name of Bowdoin, John-Temple, Francis-William, George-Edward, and Robert-Charles.

WISE, JOHN, Cambridge, d. 9 Sept. 1644. *JOHN, minister of Chebacco parish, Ipswich, was son of the following, and was baptized at Roxbury, 15 August, 1652; grad. at H. C. 1673; was ordained in 1682. He was imprisoned in 1688, by order of Sir Edmund Andros, for remonstrating against taxes, imposed without an assembly, as a grievance. He was a representative in 1689, and in 1690 one of the chaplains in the expedition against Canada. He d. 8 April, 1725, æ. 73. Rev. Jeremiah Wise, H. C. 1700, minister of Berwick from Nov. 1707, to 20 Jan. 1756, and Henry Wise, H. C. 1717, a merchant of Ipswich, were probably his sons. JOSEPH, Roxbury, d. 12 Sept. 1684, had sons, Joseph, born 1643 ; John, b. 1652 ; Henry, b. 1654.

WISEMAN, JAMES, Boston 1655, had a son James, born at Braintree.

WISWALL, ICHABOD, from Dorchester, entered H. Coll. 1644, and left without a degree in 1647, was minister of Duxbury, about 30 years. He is characterized as a gentleman of piety and learning ; was the agent of Plymouth colony in England, in 1689, for obtaining a new charter. He d. 20 July, 1700. His only son, Peleg, [S. Davis] grad. at H. C. 1702, and died at Boston, 2 Sept. 1767, aged 84. *JOHN, Dorchester, a deacon of the church, was admitted freeman 1636, representative 1646, removed to Boston, and was an elder of the first church ; d. 17 Aug. 1687, æ. 86, leaving an only son, John. Sexton's Monitor for Dorchester, 2, 28. THOMAS, Dorchester, about 1639, freeman 1652, removed to Newton, where he was ordained the first ruling elder of the church, 20 July, 1664. He d. 6 Dec. 1683. Ebenezer Wiswall, freeman 1675, who d. at Newton 1691, Enoch, freeman 1685, Thomas, of Newton, and Capt. Noah, killed in battle, 6 July, 1690, might be his sons. His last wife was Isabella Farmer, widow, from Ansley, in Warwickshire, from whom, in a direct line, descended Rev. Richard Farmer, D. D., master of Emmanuel College, Cambridge, and author of the Essay on the Learning of Shakspeare. She d. at Billerica, 21 May, 1686.

WITCHFIELD, JOHN, Massachusetts, was admitted freeman in 1633.

WITHEREDGE, EDWARD, Boston, was a mariner ; admitted to the church in 1643, and freeman in 1644.

WITHERS, *THOMAS, Pascataqua 1631, representative of Kittery in 1656. Francis Withers grad. at H. C. 1790.

WITHINGTON, HENRY, Dorchester 1637, was a ruling elder of the church 29 years, and d. 2 Feb. 1666, æ. 79. John and Henry Withington were admitted freeman in 1673 and 1677. ||RICHARD, Dorchester, freeman 1640, member of the ar. co. 1646, was ordained deacon of the church, 1 March, 1669.

WITHMAN, JOHN, Massachusetts, freeman 1642, probably the same as Whitman.

WITT, JOHN, Lynn 1650, d. Dec. 1675. His first wife was Elizabeth ; 2d, Sarah. His sons were John and Thomas. JONATHAN, Lynn 1650, d. 1665.

WITTER, WILLIAM, Lynn 1630, Salem, d. 1659, æ. 75, leaving children Josiah and Hannah. Benedict, i. Hist. Baptist, 364. Lewis.

WOLCOTT, ‡HENRY, came from Somersetshire to N. E. 1630, freeman 1634. He settled in Dorchester, but in 1636, removed to

Windsor, and was elected a magistrate in 1643, and d. in 1655, in his 78th year. He is the great ancestor of the three governours of this name in Connecticut, of whom the *first*, Roger Wolcott, was b. at Windsor, 4 Jan. 1679, governour from 1751 to 1754, and d. 17 May, 1767, æ. 88; the *second*, Oliver Wolcott, LL. D., grad. at Y. C. 1747, was governour in 1796, and d. 1 Dec. 1797, aged 71; the *third*, the late Governour Oliver Wolcott, LL. D., who grad. at Y. C. 1778. Erastus Wolcott, a distinguished character, was brother to the second Governour Wolcott, and d. 14 Sept. 1793, aged 70. *JOHN, Cambridge, freeman 1635, was representative at the May session, 1635. There was a John Wolcott or Woolcott, of Newbury, before 1670, who was born a. 1639, and whose children were b. there. JOHN, Cambridge, 1635.

WOLFE, PETER, Salem, freeman 1634, was one of the founders of the Church in Beverly, 1667. Flint, Sermon on death Dr. Abbot.

WOLLASTON, —— who is styled a captain, came to N. E. in 1625, and was the first settler of Mount Wollaston, in Braintree, (now Quincy) but left the place for Virginia the next year. Prince, i. Annals, 152, 162.

WOOD, ANTHONY, Ipswich 1665. 2 Coll. Mass. Hist. Soc. viii. 107. The word *Wood* forms a part of more than twenty names in this Register. When it occurs as a distinct name in old records, the *s* is frequently added, and it is probable a correct designation of this difference is not in every instance preserved in the following list. DANIEL, Ipswich, 1648. EDWARD, Charlestown, freeman 1640, d. 27 Nov. 1642. Edward Wood, of Charlestown, perhaps his son, settled in Springfield as early as 1643. ||JOHN, probably at Lynn 1630, freeman 1640, member of the ar. co. 1642, may be the same who was at Salem in 1646. Felt, Annals Salem, 172. JONAS, Springfield, 1636. NICHOLAS, Dorchester, freeman 1641, may be the same who was of Medfield in 1656. Hutchinson, i. Mass. 108. MICHAEL, Concord 1642, was only son of William Wood, and d. 13 May, 1674, leaving children, Abraham, Isaac, Jacob, Thompson, John, and Abigail. Shattuck, MS. Hist. Concord. ||RICHARD, whose name is spelled *Woodde*, was a member of the ar. co. 1642, its captain in 1677. ROBERT, Dedham, d. 3 Dec. 1638. *WILLIAM, Lynn 1630, freeman 1631, representative 1636, removed to Sandwich 1637, was town clerk there until 1650, when he again removed, and was living in 1685. WILLIAM, the author of New-England's Prospect, printed at London 1634, was very early in this country. He sailed from Boston on his return to England, 15 August, 1633, but is supposed to have returned to New-England, and Mr. Shattuck [MS. Letter] conjectures that he was the William Wood who resided in Concord, and died there, 14 May, 1671, æ. 86, while Mr. Lewis contends for his being the early resident at Lynn, above named.

WOODBRIDGE, BENJAMIN, the first graduate at H. C. 1642, was son of Rev. John Woodbridge, of Wiltshire, England, and was b. at Highworth 1622. After completing his education,

he returned to England, was settled at Salisbury, 16 Nov. 1648;
afterwards succeeded Dr. Twiss at Newbury; was ejected from office in 1662, and d. at Englefield, [perhaps the summit of Cooper's
Hill] in Berkshire, 1 Nov. 1684, æ. 62. *BENJAMIN*, a nephew
of the preceding, and son of Rev. John Woodbridge, of Andover
and Newbury, was sometime minister of Bristol [Coffin], and in
1688, was minister in Kittery. He d. at Medford, 15 Jan. 1710.
His wife was Mary, a daughter of Rev. John Ward. ‡*JOHN*, the
first minister of Andover, was brother to the first named Benjamin
Woodbridge, and was born at Stanton, in Wiltshire, in 1613. He
came to N. E. in 1634, and settled at Newbury as a planter, and
was the town clerk, but becoming a preacher, he was ordained at
Andover in Oct. 1645. [Mather says 16 Sept. 1644.] He went to
England in 1647; returned in July, 1663, and took up his residence at Newbury; was elected an assistant in 1683 and 1684, and
acted as a magistrate till his death, 17 March, 1695. Mr. Savage,
[ii. Winthrop, 391 and 397] gives two dates for the time of his
death, 1696 and 1695, the last of which is confirmed by the Newbury town records. Mr. Woodbridge m. Mercy, daughter of Gov.
Thomas Dudley. She was born 27 Sept. 1621, d. 1 July, 1691.
They had 12 children, of whom were, Sarah and Lucie, b. in Newbury in 1640, and 1642; John, Benjamin, and Timothy, who were
clergymen; Thomas, a captain, born a. 1649, who m. Mary Jones
1672, had several children, and d. at Newbury, 2 March, 1681; and
Joseph, who married Martha, grand-daughter of Rev. N. Rogers,
20 May, 1686, and had sons, Joseph and Nathaniel, b. in 1687 and
1696. The other children are not known. Most of his children
were probably born while he was absent in England. He left three
sons and two sons in law in the ministry, and four grandsons preparing for it. *JOHN*, minister of Killingworth and Weathersfield,
was son of the preceding, grad. at H. C. 1664, settled at Killingworth 1666; removed in 1679 to Weathersfield, and d. in 1690.
His son John grad. at H. C. 1694, was ordained the first minister
of West Springfield, June 1698, and d. 10 June 1718, æ. 40, leaving sons, John and Benjamin. John was b. 25 Dec. 1702, grad.
at Y. C. 1726; was minister at Poquonoc, (Windsor) and South-
Hadley, and d. 10 Sept. 1783, æ. 80, being the ninth John Wood-
bridge in the ministry through as many successive generations.
Benjamin grad. at Y. C. and was minister of Amity, now Wood-
bridge, Conn. Three grandsons of Rev. John Woodbridge, of
South Hadley, were in the ministry in 1828, viz. John, D. D. of
Hadley; Benjamin R. of Norwich; and Sylvester, of Greenville,
N. Y. *TIMOTHY*, minister of Hartford, was son of Rev. John
Woodbridge, of Andover and Newbury, and grad. at H. C. 1675;
was ordained 18 Nov. 1685, and d. 30 April, 1732. He was probably born in England.

WOODBURY, HUMPHREY, son of the following, was born a.
1609, came to N. E. in 1628, and settled at Salem; was admitted to
the church in July, 1648, and was one of the founders of the church
in Beverly in 1667, and was living in 1681.

WOODBURY, *JOHN, Salem, came from Somersetshire, in Eng· and arr. in N. E. in 1624; settled at Salem in 1626; went to Eng. in 1627, returned in 1628, was a member of the church; is on the list of those desiring freedom 1630; was represen. at the courts in May and Sept. 1635, and in Sept. 1638. He died in 1641. Felt, Annals Salem, 153. Gibbs, MS letter. NICHOLAS, Salem, received a grant of land in 1638, and d. in Beverly, 19 May, 1686. æ. 70. *PETER, Beverly, supposed to be grandson of John Woodbury, was born in 1640; was admitted freeman 1668, elected representative 1689; was a deacon of the church, and died 5 July, 1704, æ. 64. His son Josiah, b. 15 June, 1682, was grandfather of Peter Woodbury, b. 28 March, 1738, d. at Francistown, N. H. in March, 1819, leaving a son Peter, who is father of Hon. Levi Woodbury, D. C. 1809, a senator in Congress from N. H. and of James Trask Woodbury, H. C. 1823, of Bath, N. H. WILLIAM, Salem, was admitted to the church, 29 Dec. 1639, freeman 1641; and one of the founders of the church in Beverly 1667; d. in 1674. Tradition makes him a brother of John Woodbury, but some facts indicate that he was a son.

WOODCOCK, NATHANIEL, Rehoboth, d. 28 April, 1676. ||RICHARD, Boston, member of the ar. co. 1658, d. 12 Nov. 1662. WILLIAM, was a physician of Salem early as 1662.

WOODFORD, THOMAS, freeman 1635, Northampton, 1658.

WOODHOUSE, *HENRY, came from London, and settled in Concord, a. 1650; was admitted freeman 1656, representative in 1685, 1690, and d. 16 June, 1700. Shattuck. ROBERT, Boston, 1640, had sons, Joseph and Nathaniel, b. in 1641 and 1642. A John Woodice or Woodhouse died in 1659, probably at Salem.

WOODHULL, RICHARD, was one of the early settlers of Brookhaven, L. I. Wood, Hist. L. I. 121.

WOODIN, JOHN, Portsmouth, an inhabitant as early as 1636, states in a deposition that he had a large family of children. Coffin, MS.

WOODLAND, JOHN, Braintree 1651, had a son John, b. in 1652. His wife was Martha.

WOODMAN, *ARCHELAUS, Newbury, freeman 1637, came from Wales, according to Mr. Coffin, and was representative in 1674 and 1675. *EDWARD, Newbury, brother of the preceding, was admitted freeman 1636, representative in 1636, 1637, 1639, 1643, 1659, 1660, 1664 and 1670. He had sons, Jonathan, Edward, and others, Joshua Woodman, who lived in Andover, died 1703, æ. 67. JOHN, was admitted freeman 1666, and was a man of some distinction at Dover. RICHARD, Lynn, 1644, d. 1647. Lewis.

WOODMANSEY, ROBERT, Boston, 1644, had a son Seth, b. 1644. JOHN, Boston, was admitted freeman 1673. JAMES, d. at Boston in Feb. 1694.

WOODROFFE, WILLIAM, one of the ejected ministers, whom Mather calls *Woodrop*, came to N. E. after 1660, preached at Lancaster, Springfield, and other places, between 1670 and 1680.

He has probably descendants in this country, the name being common to some parts of it. Seventeen had grad. in 1828 at Yale and New-Jersey colleges, of whom six have been clergymen. Ephraim T. Woodruff was a minister of Coventry, Conn. a few years since.

WOODS, JOHN, Sudbury 1643, probably admitted freeman 1645, had sons, John and Francis, born in 1641 and 1645. He was one of the petitioners for Marlborough, where he removed, and died 10 July, 1678. Twenty persons of the name had received the honours of the N. E. colleges in 1826. RICHARD, Roxbury, d. 6 Dec. 1658, " an old man." Records.

WOODWARD, EDWARD, Ipswich 1665. GEORGE, Watertown 1641, freoman 1646, d. 31 May, 1676. HENRY, Dorchester 1638, perhaps an inhabitant of Northampton in 1658. JAMES, Dover 1646. NATHANIEL, an eminent land surveyor, lived in Boston, and had a large family of children. Hutchinson, i. Hist. Mass. 191. Savage, i. Winthrop, 284. Snow, Hist. Boston, 118. *PETER, Dedham, freeman 1642, was representative 1669 and 1670. JOHN Woodward, H. C. 1693, the minister of Norwich, was from Dedham. RALPH, one of the first deacons of the church in Hingham, was ordained 2 Feb. 1640. Lincoln, Hist. Hingham, 23, 45. RICHARD, Watertown, freeman 1635, d. 16 Feb. 1665. Rose, his wife, d. 6 Oct. 1662. ROBERT, Boston, a. 1640, [Snow] d. 21 Nov. 1653. He had sons, Smith, b. 1644; Robert, b. 1646. THOMAS, Roxbury, d. Oct. 1685.

WOODWORTH, HENRY, Massachusetts, was admitted freeman in 1642. Recompense Woodsworth, who is called in the Middlesex co. records, Bachelor of Arts, d. 12 July, 1679. WALTER, Scituate, 1634. The Hon. John Woodworth grad. at Y. C. 1788. Samuel C. Woodworth, known as a poet and editor, is a descendant from Walter.

WOODY, RICHARD, freeman 1642, was admitted an inhabitant of Boston, 1652. RICHARD, Boston, was admitted freeman in 1644.

WOOLLERY, RICHARD, Newbury 1679.

WOOLLEY, CHRISTOPHER, Concord 1666. Shattuck.

WOOLRIDGE, *JOHN, Dorchester, requested to be made free 19 Oct. 1630; admitted to the oath 1634, and was representative at the court 2 March, 1635.

WORCESTER, WILLIAM, the first minister of Salisbury, came from Salisbury, in England, [Coffin] and was admitted freeman 1640, d. 28 Oct. 1662. Mr. Savage, [ii. Winthrop, 390] having the choice of two dates for the day of the month, says 20 Oct. His wife Sarah d. 23 April, 1650, and he m. 22 Aug. 1650, Rebecca, widow of John Hall, and had been the widow of Henry Bylie. His children were, Samuel; William; Sarah. who d. 1661; Sarah, 2d, b. 1641; Timothy, b. 14 May, 1642, lived sometime in Newbury, and had a son Samuel b. there in 1691; Moses, b. 10 Nov. 1643; Sarah, 3d, b. 22 June, 1646; Elizabeth, b. 10 March 1648, d. 1649; Elizabeth, b. 9. Jan. 1650. This name exists in Conn., but the families there have written it *Wooster*. *SAMUEL,

son of the preceding, was admitted freeman 1670, settled in Bradford, which he represented in 1679, and died at Lynn, on his return
from Boston, 21 Feb. or April, 1680, leaving children, of whom
Francis, who d. 17 Dec. 1717, was father of Rev. Francis Worcester, of Sandwich, b. in June, 1698, d. in New-Hampshire, 14 Oct.
1783, æ. 85, whose son Noah Worcester, esq. b. 4 Oct. 1735, resided in Hollis, N. H. and d. 13 Aug. 1817, æ. 82, leaving a large
family, of whom four of the sons were clergymen, viz. Noah, D. D.,
of Brighton, Ms., the founder of the Mass. Peace Society ; Leonard,
of Peacham, Vt.; Thomas, of Salisbury, N. H. ; and Samuel, D.
D., of Fitchburg and Salem, Mass., who grad. at D. C. 1795, and
d. at Brainerd, in the country of the Cherokees, 7 June, 1821, æ.
51.   Joseph E. Worcester, member of the American Academy, and
author of many useful geographical and historical works, is of this
family, as are also Thomas, H. C. 1818, Samuel Austin, Vermont
Coll. 1819, Samuel Melancthon, H. C. 1822, Taylor Gilman, H. C.
1823, and Leonard, D. C. 1825, being all grandsons of Noah Webster, esq. of Hollis.

   WORDE, THOMAS, Massachusetts, freeman 1642.
   WORRALL, JAMES, Scituate 1638.   Coffin.
   WORSELY, BENJAMIN, Rhode Island 1663.
   WORTH, LIONEL, Newbury, d. 29 June, 1667, leaving a
number of children.   WILLIAM, brother to Lionel, was an early
settler of Nantucket.
   WORTHINGTON, NICHOLAS, came from Liverpool, England, and settled at Saybrook. [Tradition.]   Among his descendants may be named Colonel Thomas Worthington, late governour
of Ohio, Rev. William Worthington, H. C. 1716, Hon. John Worthington, LL. D., of Springfield, who grad. at Y. C. 1740, d. in
April, 1800, æ. 81, Daniel Worthington, of Colchester, Conn. who
had 9 sons and 10 daughters, and Erastus Worthington, esq. the
historian of Dedham.
   WOTTEN, JOHN, Portsmouth 1640.   Belknap,§i. Hist. N. H.
47.   Adams, Annals Portsmouth, 26, 395.   (See WALTON.]
   WRAY, DANIEL, Massachusetts, freeman 1634.
   WRIGHT, BENJAMIN, Guilford 1650.   EDWARD, Concord,
a. 1650, d. 1691.   There was an Edward Wright in Boston in 1657,
who d. in 1689, and a Captain Edward Wright, d. in Sudbury, 7
August, 1703.   GEORGE, Salem 1637, Braintree, freeman 1642,
and the first lieutenant there.   HENRY, Dorchester, freeman 1635,
had a son Samuel, born 1636.   ISAAC, Hingham, died in 1652.
ISAAC, LANCASTER, died in 1663.   *JOHN, Woburn, was
born a. 1601, representative 1648, had a son John, b. in 1646, who
was probably the John Wright of Chelmsford in 1666, unless the
father removed thither.   NICHOLAS, Lynn 1637, went to Sandwich.   Lewis.   PETER, Lynn 1637, removed to Sandwich 1638.
Ibid.   RICHARD, Lynn 1630, freeman 1634, was a captain, removed to Boston.   Prince, ii. Annals, 60.   Savage, ii. Winthrop,
116.   Snow, Hist. Boston, 58. Lewis. ||ROBERT, Boston, mem-
ber of the ar. co. 1643, had sons, John, b. 1645 ; Joseph, b. 1655.

SAMUEL, Sudbury, d. 21 August, 1644. SAMUEL, Springfield 1648, perhaps the same who, with his son Samuel, was at Northampton in 1658. THOMAS, Exeter 1639. WILLIAM, Sandwich, died 1646. WILLIAM, Plymouth 1623. Davis, Morton's Memo. 382. Twenty-five of the name had received the honours of the N. E. colleges in 1827.

WYATT, EDWARD, Massachusetts, freeman 1645. Widow Wyatt d. at Dorchester, 6 Feb. 1704, æ. 94, having been present " at the birth of 1000 or more children." JOHN, Ipswich 1638, d. 1665. Coffin.

WYBORNE, JAMES, Boston, d. 7 March, 1658. JOHN, Scituate 1660. THOMAS, Boston 1653, d. 2 Oct. 1656; had a son Nathaniel, b. in 1654. Howard Wyborn grad. at H. C. 1720.

WYER, NATHANIEL, Newbury 1637. Coffin. David Wyer, H. C. 1758, was a lawyer at Falmouth, Maine.

WYETH, HUMPHREY, Ipswich 1638. NICHOLAS, Cambridge 1648, whose wife was Rebecca, had children, Mary, b. 1649; Nicholas, b. 10 August, 1651; Mary, b. 1650; Martha, b. 1653; John, b. 15 July, 1655; William, b. 11 Jan. 1658. Several of the name have grad. at Harv. College.

WYLLYS, ‡†§GEORGE, son of Richard Wyllys, of Fenny-Compton, in Warwickshire, who d. 10 June, 1597, came to N. E. as early as 1638, and settled at Hartford, where he was elected a magistrate in 1639; deputy-governour 1641, and governour in 1642. He d. in March, 1644. He had two brothers, William and Richard. His descendants write the name as above, but on the family monuments at Fenny-Compton, for several successive generations, it is spelled *Willys*. SAMUEL, son of the preceding, was born in England, and probably at Fenny-Compton, in 1632, grad. at H. C. 1653, was elected a magistrate of Connecticut 1654, and continued in that office, a. 30 years; d. 30 May, 1709, æ. 76. He m. Mary, daughter of Gov. Haynes. Hezekiah Wyllys, his son, was secretary of Conn. from 1712 to his death, in 1734. His grandson, George Wyllys, b. 6 Oct. 1710, was secretary of Conn. from 1735 to his death, 24 April, 1796. Samuel Wyllys, son of the last, was b. 15 Jan. 1739, grad. at Y. C. 1758, succeeded his father as secretary; remained in office until 1809, and d. 9 June, 1823, being of the 10th generation from Richard Wyllys, of Napton, in the reign of Henry VIII.

WYMAN, FRANCIS, Woburn 1644, had a son Francis, who d. 26 April, 1676. JOHN, Woburn 1644. The descendants of these, probably brothers, have been somewhat numerous. Among them, are John Wyman, H. C. 1721; Ebenezer Wyman, H. C. 1731, minister of Union, Conn., Rufus Wyman, M. D., of Charlestown, a member of the American Academy, who grad. at H. C. 1799, and two others who grad. at H. College.

YALE, DAVID, descended from an ancient and wealthy family in Wales, came to N. E. and settled at Boston, and was admitted freeman 1640. His sons David and Theophilus were born at Boston, 18 Sept. 1645, and 14 Jan. 1651. Savage, ii. Winth. 262

THOMAS, New-Haven 1638, was brother to the preceding. His son Elihu was born at New-Haven, 5 April, 1648, went to England, a. 1658, and from thence at a. the age of 30 to the East-Indies, where he lived near 20 years, and acquired a large estate. He m. one of the natives, the widow of Gov Hinmers, by whom he had 3 daughters, Catharine, who m. Dudley North, commonly called Lord North; Ann, who m. Lord James Cavendish, and Ursula. After he returned to England, he was chosen governour of the East India company. He d. at Wrexham, in Wales, 8 July, 1721, æ. 73. Pres. Clap, Hist. Yale College, which derives its name from Gov. Yale, pp. 29, 30.

YEO, THOMAS, Boston, had a son Thomas, b. in 1654.

YEOMANS, EDWARD, Boston 1656, had a son Edward b. in 1657.

YORK, JAMES, Braintree 1647, had a son James, b. 14 June, 1640. RICHARD, Oyster-river [Durham, N. H.] 1652.

YOUNG, CHRISTOPHER, Salem, died a. 1647. JOSEPH, a mariner, was of Salem 1649. GEORGE, Scituate 1640. Coffin. JOHN, Charlestown, d. 29 Dec. 1672. ‡JOHN, a magistrate of New-Haven colony 1664. Perhaps this should be *Youngs*. RICHARD, Kittery, freeman 1652.

YOUNGLOVE, SAMUEL, Ipswich 1648. JOHN, Hadley, was admitted freeman 1675.

YOUNGS, JOHN, the first minister of South-Old, L. I., who had been a minister in Hingham, England, came to New-Haven with part of his church in 1640, and in October of that year commenced the settlement of South-Old, where he died in 1672, æ. 74. Wood, Hist. L. I. 34. JOHN, the eldest son of the preceding, was a colonel, and the sheriff of Yorkshire, in 1681, then embracing all Long-Island, and d. in 1698, æ. 75. Benjamin Youngs, his brother, was judge of the Suffolk (L. I.) court of common pleas, Joshua and Thomas Youngs were also judges of the same court. David Youngs, Y. C. 1741, was minister of Brookhaven from 1745 to his death in 1752. Ibid, 34, 35.

ZULLISH, DAVID, Massachusetts, was admitted freeman 1642. Savage, ii. Winthrop, 372.

APPENDIX.

CONTAINING ADDITIONS AND CORRECTIONS.

NAMES WHICH DO NOT APPEAR IN THE TEXT ARE ENCLOSED WITHIN BRACKETS.

ADAMS, ||THOMAS, of Braintree, Concord, and Chelmsford, was member of the ar. co. 1644. JEREMY, Cambridge, freeman 1635. THOMAS, freeman 1643.

ALLERTON, JOHN, one of the first pilgrims at Plymouth, d. in 1621. Prince, i. Annals, 86.

ALLIN. In the 3d line, *for* 1675, *read* 1671, and in the 5th line of this name, *after* graduates *insert* at H. C. John, the son recorded as born 4 Dec. 1639, was probably son of James Allen, and not of the Rev. John Allin.

AMADOWN, ROGER, probably d. at Rehoboth, 13 Nov. 1673.

AMES. In the 18th line, *for* Francker, *read* Franeker.

ANTRUM, THOMAS, Salem, member of the church 1639, freeman 1642, d. 1663.

APPLETON, SAMUEL, d. at Rowley. JOHN, Ipswich, had 4 daughters, viz. Elizabeth, who m. Richard Dummer, jr.; Priscilla, who m. a Capon; Sarah, who m. a Rogers; and Mary who m. Nath'l Thomas. John the eldest son of John Appleton, had daughters, Elizabeth, who m. Rev. Jabez Fitch; Margaret, who m. Rev. Pres. Edward Holyoke, and was mother to the venerable centenarian of Salem, and Priscilla, who m. Rev. Robert Ward. SAMUEL, Ipswich, was commander of the forces on Connecticut river in Philip's war in 1676, and in the expedition to Narraganset in Dec. of that year. His son Samuel m. Elizabeth Whittingham; had three daughters, Judith, who m. Samuel Wolcott of Windsor, Conn.; Hannah, who m. Wm. Downes, of Boston, and Susanna, who m. Nath'l Whipple.

[ARNOLD, JOHN, Massachusetts, was admitted freeman 1643.]

[ARTHUR, JOHN, Weymouth 1642.]

ASHLEY, ROBERT, Springfield, d. 29 Nov. 1682. [JOSEPH, Springfield, d. 18 May, 1698.]

[ASHTON, JAMES and THOMAS, were proprietors of Providence, a. 1639. Coffin.]

[ATHEARN, SIMON, New-Hampshire, about 1687.]

[ATKINS, HENRY, Yarmouth 1647, then of Plymouth, where his son Samuel was b. 1651; then of Eastham, where Isaac was b. 1657.]

AVERY, THOMAS, Salem, a blacksmith, was admitted freeman 1643.

[BABSON, JAMES, Gloucester 1664, was admitted freeman 1666.]

BACON, ‡NATHANIEL, m. Hannah Mayo 1642, and had sons, Nathaniel, b. 1645; Samuel, b. 1650; Jeremiah, b. 1659.

[BAGG, JOHN, Springfield, died 5 Sept. 1683. Rev. W. B. Sprague.]

BALDWIN, JOHN, Billerica, left sons, John, Jonathan, and Thomas, and daughters, Susanna, Phebe, and Mary.

BALL, FRANCIS, Springfield, d. 21 January, 1700. Rev. W. B. Sprague.

[BALLOU, MATURIN, was one of the proprietors of Providence as early as 1639. Coffin. Maturin Ballou was a Baptist preacher at Richmond, N. H. as early as 1770.]

[BARBER, THOMAS, Windsor 1640, was a Pequot soldier.]

BAREFOOTE, †WALTER, was of Great Island, now New-Castle, N. H. and d. about 1688.]

BARLOW, GEORGE, Exeter 1639, it appears was in 1652 of Saco, where he was a preacher, but forbidden in 1653, by the Court, to preach or prophecy there under the penalty of £10, for every offence. Greenleaf, Eccl. Sketches, 52.

BARNARD, ||MATTHEW, Boston. His son John, deacon of the 2d church, was probably father of Rev. John Barnard, H. C. 1700, who was b. at Boston, 6 Nov. 1681, and d. at Marblehead, 24 Jan. 1770. Rev. John Barnard of Andover, p. 26, line 7th, d. 14 June, 1758, æ. 68.

[BARSTOW, GEORGE, John, Joseph, and William, were of Scituate, as early as 1650.] MICHAEL, Watertown, was admitted freeman 1636.

BARTHOLOMEW, *HENRY, Salem, freeman 1637, d. 1692, æ. 85. His wife was Elizabeth, who d. 1 Sept. 1682, æ. 60. He had a number of children. Of those who survived him was Henry. Felt, Annals, 310. *WILLIAM, was admitted freeman 1635.

BARTLETT, JOHN, Newbury, was admitted freeman 1637.

BASCOM, THOMAS, was of Windsor 1640.

BASS, erase WILLIAM, Massachusetts, freeman 1638.

BATES, *EDWARD, Weymouth, freeman 1638. There were two of this name, one of whom was of Boston, and the| freeman of 1637.

BATTER, *EDMUND, was admitted freeman 1636. His first wife was Sarah, who with him joined the church as early as 1635. His 2d wife was Mary, daughter of Daniel Gookin. He left children, Edmund, Mary, Elizabeth, and Daniel. Felt, Annals, 281.

[BATTELLE, THOMAS, Dedham, was admitted freeman 1654. Ebenezer Battelle grad. at H. C. 1775, and died in 1818, æ. 64.] ROBERT, Boston, died 23 Dec. 1658. *Erase* the name *Battle*, 2 lines, p. 29.

[BATTING, WILLIAM. Saco, about 1659.]

BAYLEY, JOHN, jr. Newbury, was born a. 1615. His son James, b. in 1650, grad. at H. C. in 1669, was a preacher at Salem Village 1671, and finally settled, it is said in Roxbury, where he was a magistrate, and d. 17 Jan. 1707. Rev. James, of Weymouth, H. C. 1719, was son of James Bayley of Roxbury.

BEAMSLEY, ||WILLIAM, Boston 1632, admitted to the church 1634, freeman 1636, and probably member of ar. co. 1656. He d. 29 Sept. 1658.

BECK, ALEXANDER, was of Boston.

[BEIRCE, AUSTIN, Barnstable 1650, had sons Josiah, born 1651 ; James, b. 1660. This name continues in the old colony.]

BELCHER, ||ANDREW, d. before 1681. Elizabeth, his wife, d. 4 June 1680, æ. 61. His daughters m. respectively, a Blowers, a Remington, a Ballard, and Joseph Sill. His son Andrew was one of the council of safety 1689, [Hutch. i. Mass. 340] and one of the council of the province from May 1702, to 31 Oct. 1717, when he died, æ. 70 years, leaving one son, Jonathan, the governour of Mass., N. H., and N. J. His daughters should be stated as of Boston instead of Charlestown, excepting Sarah Fay, which should be Sarah Foye of Charlestown.

BENNETT. In the 4th line, *for* EDWARD, *read* EDMUND.

BISHOP, EDWARD, Salem 1645, was one of the founders of the church in Beverly 1667.

[BISSELL, JOHN, came from England with Rev. E. Hewett, and settled at Windsor as early as 1640.]

BLACKMAN, ADAM, was of Stratford instead of Strafford. BENJAMIN, H. C. 1663, was probably his son, and was a preacher and magistrate of Saco before 1688.

[BLACKMORE, WILLIAM, possibly the one of Lynn, died at Scituate, 21 April 1676.]

BLOOD, JAMES, Concord, freeman 1641. The authority for the first three lines, is Mr. Shattuck.

[BLUMFIELD, WILLIAM, Massachusetts, was admitted freeman 1635. Some of this name went early to New Jersey, where the name of *Bloomfield*, said to be the same, exists.]

BLUNT, WILLIAM, Andover. His sons were William, who d. 1738, æ. 67 ; Samuel, and Hanborough. The sons of William were David, Rev. John, Jonathan, and Ebenezer.

[BLUSH, ABRAHAM, Barnstable, had sons, Joseph, b. 1648 ; Abraham, b. 1654, and probably others.]

[BOLTWOOD, SAMUEL, Hadley 1672. Ebenezer Boltwood grad. at H. C. 1773.]

BONIGHTON. *Erase* this paragraph and *insert* the following :

BONYTHON, RICHARD, Saco 1636, a captain, and appointed assistant of the plantation there, 2 Sept. 1639, d. a. 1650. His daughter m. Richard Foxwell. John, his son, was of Casco 1658, and is supposed by Mr. Folsom to have been killed by the Indians, a. 1684, and the one commemorated in the distich in Sullivan's Hjst. of Maine, p. 368, although the author of that work considers Richard as the one who " went to Hockomocko."

[*BONDET, DANIEL,* minister of the French congregation in Oxford in 1691. Mather, ii. Magnalia, 382. Worcester Mag. ii. 363.]

[BOSWELL, SAMUEL, Bradford, a. 1663. Spofford, Gazetteer Mass. 163.]

BOWDITCH. The blank should be supplied with WILLIAM.
He d. 1682. See Felt's Annals Salem, 174, 271.

BOWMAN, NATHANIEL, of Watertown 1637, instead of
1687. He requested to be admitted freeman 19 Oct. 1630.

BOWSTREE, or BOWSTREETE, WILLIAM, Concord, was
admitted freeman 1639.

BRACKENBURY. *For* RICHARD, *read* WILLIAM, who
was admitted freeman 4 March, 1633. RICHARD, Salem, was
admitted freeman 14 May, 1634, and was probably one of the founders of the church in Beverly, and the one who d. in 1684, æ. 84.

BRADSTREET, JOHN, Salem, a. 1659. *Erase* this article.

BRATCHER, AUSTIN, d. in 1630.

BRENTON. 5th line of this name, *for* a. *read* before.

BREWSTER, NATHANIEL. From the new edition (the
third) of Hon. Mr. Wood's Hist. of the towns on Long-Island, p. 48,
it appears that Mr. Brewster was settled at Brookhaven in the fall
of 1665, instead of 1656, according to the former editions.

[BRIGHT, SAMUEL, Massachusetts, was admitted freeman in
1645.]

BROOKHAVEN, JOHN, a captain of Rhode-Island 1669.
1 Coll. Mass. Hist. Soc. v. 249.

BROWN, ‡HENRY, Rhode-Island, was an assistant 1652.
JAMES, Newbury, freeman 1637. ROBERT, Cambridge, freeman 1639. JOHN, and the first SAMUEL, both of Salem, were
brothers. Page 45th, line 15 from bottom, 36 should be 366.
THOMAS, Concord, freeman 1638. JAMES, Newbury, p. 44,
was admitted freeman in 1637.

BUCKLAND, THOMAS, freeman 1635, was of Windsor 1640.
WILLIAM, probably d. at Rehoboth, 1 Sept. 1679.

BULGAR, RICHARD. He was of Exeter in 1640. His name is
erroneously Biellyer, in Hazard's Collections, and in Coll. N. H.
Hist. Soc. i. 322, as John Kelly, esq. assures me.

BULKLEY, GERSHOM, was b. at Concord in Dec. 1636, died
at Weathersfield, 2 Dec. 1713, æ. 77. Shattuck, MS Hist. Concord. JOHN, freeman 1642.

[BULL, THOMAS, was an officer in the Pequot war 1637.
2 Coll. Mass. Hist. Soc. viii, 139.]

[BURR, JOHN, Massachusetts, and perhaps of Ipswich, was
admitted freeman 1631.]

[BURRAGE, WILLIAM, a preacher at Scarborough, a. 4 years
from 1684, and a selectman and town clerk.]

BUSS. In the 5th line, *erase* the comma *after* N. H. In the
11th line, *for* Lieut. Bass, *read* Lieut. Buss.

BUTLER, HENRY, who grad. at H. C. in 1651, is said to have
been a physician in Boston.

BUTTON, ‖JOHN, member of ar. co. 1643.

CARPENTER, JOSEPH, d. 6 May, 1675. [SAMUEL, sen.
Rehoboth, d. 20 Feb. 1683.]

CHAFFY, ‖MATTHEW, member of the ar. co. 1642.

CHAUNCY, ISRAEL, was of Stratford, instead of Stamford.

Rev. Mr. Field, in his Statistical Account of Middlesex County, Conn., says that Rev. Nathaniel, Y. C. 1702, the minister of Durham, in that state, from 1711 to 1756, was his son, but the family genealogy regards him as the son of Rev. Nathaniel, of Hatfield.

CHICHESTER, JAMES. One of this name was at Taunton in 1643.

[CHIPMAN, JOHN, Barnstable 1652, had sons John and Samuel, b. in 1657 and 1661.]

CHURCHILL, JOHN, Plymouth, died 1 Jan. 1663. His son Eleazar was b. 1652.]

CLARK, ‡DANIEL, magistrate of Conn., came from England with Rev. E. Hewett, a. 1639, and settled at Windsor. ||‡*THOMAS, Boston, was captain of the ar. co. in 1653, and 1665. On 62 page, 4th line, *for* captain *read* baptism.

COBB, HENRY. Six of his sons were, John and James, b. at Plymouth in 1632 and 1634 ; Gershom, b. at Scituate 1644, d. 24 June 1675 ; Eleazar, [?] b. 1648 ; Samuel, b. 1654, and Jona. b. 1660.

COBBETT. *Erase* the last two lines of this paragraph. *THOMAS*, freeman 1638.

COLE, ||SAMUEL, member of the ar. co. 1637.

CONVERSE, *EDWARD, Charlestown, freeman 1631.

COOK, AARON, perhaps of Windsor 1640. JOSEPH, came from Earle-Colne, or its vicinity to N. E. in Oct. 1635.

CORNEL. *Erase* in this paragraph, " James Cornall was a witness to the Indian Deed to Rev. John Wheelwright 1638."

COTTON. Page 71, *erase* " GEORGE, Springfield, died 17 December 1699," and *transfer* the date to the name of COLTON, GEORGE, p. 66. Rev, Seaborn Cotton, p. 70, had a son Roland, by a second wife, who grad. at H. C. 1696, and received the degree of M. D.

CROAD. In the 4th line, *for* Hampton, *read* Frampton,

[CROCKER, WILLIAM, Barnstable, had sons, John, b, 1637 ; Samuel, b. 1642; Job, 1644; Josiah, 1647 ; Eleazar, 1650; Joseph, 1654.]

CROFTE, GRIFFIN. This name in Savage, ii. Winthrop, 362, should be Griffin Craft, Roxbury, freeman 1631.

[CROSSMAN, ||ROBERT, member of the ar. co. 1644. One of this name was of Taunton, and had sons, John, Robert, Joseph, Nathaniel, Eleazar, and Samuel, b. there from 1653 to 1667.]

[CUNNINGHAM, PATRICK, Springfield, d. 12 Sept. 1685. Sprague.]

[CURTIS, GEORGE, Massachusetts, admitted freeman 1640.]

CUTTER. *Erase* " ROBERT, Massachusetts, was admitted freeman 1638," which should be Robert Cutler, of Charlestown.

DARVELL. It is somewhat doubtful whether this name should be Darvell or Darnell.

DAVENPORT, ||*RICHARD, captain, was freeman 1634, member of the ar. co. 1639.

[DAVIS, JOHN, Barnstable, m. Hannah Linnet, and had sons,

John, b. 1649 ; Samuel, b. 1651 ; Joseph and Benjamin, b. 1656 ; Simon, b. 1658.] JENKIN, Lynn, freeman 1637.

DAVISON, ||NICHOLAS, member of the ar. co. 1648.

DAVY, JOHN, Boston, freeman 1636.

DEARBORN. In 1st line, *for* form, *read* from.

[DEWEY, THOMAS, freeman 1634, removed to Windsor as early as 1640. 1 Coll. Mass. Hist. Soc. v. 168.]

DIMMOCK, THOMAS, Massachusetts, was admitted freeman 1636.

DINELY, WILLIAM, was admitted freeman 1637, instead of 1635.

DODGE. In the first line, *erase* GEORGE, Concord 1645, which should be DOWDY, GEORGE, freeman 1645, who was of Concord at that time.

[DODSON, ANTHONY, Scituate 1651, whose son Gershom was b. 1653.]

[DOTEN, JOHN, Plymouth, had sons, John, Edward and Jacob, b. in 1668, 1671, 1673. This is probably the same name with *Dotey*, which Mr. Prince [i. Annals, 86] assumes as the true spelling. Morton and the Old Colony records give the name *Doten*.

[DOUGHTY, JAMES, Scituate 1649.] Perhaps James was the preacher, whose name of baptism is conjectured to have been [SAMUEL ?]

DOWSE, FRANCIS, Boston, was admitted freeman 1641. LAWRENCE, freeman 1647.

DUNLEY, at the head of page 87, should be DUDLEY.

DUNSTER, HENRY. Mr. Whitman, p. 151, Hist. Sketch of the Ar. Co., gives one of this name as a member in 1640, although it seems hardly probable that he was the same person, who, the same year, was inducted into the office of president of Harvard College.

EAMES, *ANTHONY, Hingham, freeman 1637.

EATON, NATHANIEL, was born in England, a. 1609, came to N. E. as early as 1636, was a member of the church at Cambridge, from which he was excommunicated. He went to Virginia in 1640, and having arrived there, sent for his wife and children, who set out, but the vessel in which they took passage, was never heard of afterwards. It appears that one son, Benoni, was left behind, who, from the records of the Church of Cambridge, was living in 1658 in the family of Deacon Thomas Cheeseholme. Savage, i. Winthrop, 308—313. ii. 22. Mather, ii. Magnalia, 7, 8. MS Birth and Life of Rev. Thomas Shepard, 18mo. Church Records of Cambridge.

ELMES, RODOLPHUS, was of Scituate 1645, and had sons, John and Joseph, b. there in 1655 and 1658.

EMERSON, JOHN, (in the 13th line of the paragraph), who grad. at H. C. 1675, was probably the "worthy minister" at Berwick 1689, [Mather, ii. Magnalia, 511] who had a happy escape by declining an invitation to lodge at the house of Major Waldron at Dover, on the night of the 27th June, that year, when the Major and 22 of his family and neighbours were killed by the Indians. Dr. Belknap [i. Hist. N. H. 204] considers him as the future *minister* of New Castle and Portsmouth, not recollecting that *he* had not then graduated. He might have been the schoolmaster named in the text, who d. at Salem in 1712.

ENGLISH, *WILLIAM, Hampton, freeman 1642, representative 1646 and 1647.

EWELL, HENRY, Scituate, had sons Gershom and Ichabod, b. in 1650 and 1659.

FABENS. This name is written in old records Fabins, and was intended to be so spelled. *Fabgan* in the 2d. line, should be *Fabyan*.

FASSETT, JOHN. In an *original* copy of the list of freemen for 1654, this name is John *Farell*, and is put under Dedham. *Fassett* therefore should be erased.

FAUNCE, JOHN, Plymouth, d. 29 Nov. 1654.

FAWN, JOHN, Ipswich, instead of John Faunce, [ii. Savage, Winthrop, 365] was probably the freeman in 1635.

FENNER. The name of WILLIAM HARRIS should be William Harris.

FIRMING, GILES, Ipswich, was admitted freeman 1639, instead of 1634.

[FIELD, ROBERT, Saco, freeman 1653.]

FISKE, JAMES, freeman 1642. In the 22d line, John, son of Rev. John Fiske, was b. earlier than there stated, as from Allen's Hist. Chelmsford, p. 127, it appears that he m. Lydia Fletcher in 1666. He died a. 1700, without children. Ibid.

FITCH, JEREMIAH. *Erase* Lynn 1634. The one at Lynn, at that time removed to Reading 1644. A Jeremiah Fitch d. at Rehoboth, 15 Oct. 1676. ZACHARY, Lynn 1634, freeman 1638, removed to Reading.

FRARY, JOHN. The second one of this name was admitted freeman in 1656 instead of 1638.

FREEMAN. In lines 22 and 23, p. 113, *erase* "and lived at Watertown. His son Samuel was a deacon of the church."

FOWKES, HENRY, was admitted freeman in 1635 instead of 1645.

GALE. *Erase* the comma after HU, which is probably a contraction for Hugh or Humphrey.

GARDNER. In the 25th line, *for* Damasis, *read* Damaris ; *for* Sceth, *read* Seeth, and in 27th line, *before* 246, *insert* 229.

GIBBONS, *‖‡EDWARD, member of ar. co. 1637, was its captain in 1641, 1646 and 1654.

GIBBS. In the 17th line, *prefix* the numeral 7 to Henry, who had 3 sons, Henry and Josiah Willard, who are named, and William, (omitted) who d. at Philadelphia, 22 May, 1829, æ. 72.

GIBSON, JOHN, Cambridge, was admitted freeman 1637.

GILL, ARTHUR, was admitted freeman 1641, instead of 1631.

GODFREY. In the 6th line, *for* Broune *read* Browne.

GOFFE. In 1 and 2 line, p. 124, *erase* "He probably went to

341

Newbury, and d. 9 Dec. 1641," and *insert*, JOHN, Newbury, admitted freeman, 22 May, 1639, and d. 9 Dec. 1641.

GOODHUE, WILLIAM, Ipswich, was born about 1612.

GOOKIN. In the 6th line, *for* Thompson, *read* Tompson, which should be so read in line 19th, p. 160. In 15th line, *for* Butler, *read* Batter.

[GORHAM, JOHN, whose name is spelled in records and printed books, *Goram* and *Gorum*, appears to have resided in Barnstable, Plymouth, Marshfield, and Yarmouth, where his sons James, John, Joseph, and Jabez, were born in 1644, '51, '53, and 1656. He died of a fever at Swanzey, while in command of a company in Phillip's war, 5 Feb. 1676. I. Mather, Hist. Ind. War, 21. Plymouth Colony Records.]

GRAVES, THOMAS, Charlestown, was son of John Graves of Radcliffe, England, and was born 6 June, 1605.

[GRAY, EDWARD, Plymouth 1653. THOMAS, Plymouth, d. 7 June, 1654.]

GREEN, JOHN, p. 129, the freeman in 1654, was of Cambridge.

GREENHILL, SAMUEL, was admitted freeman 4 March, 1635.

GRIGSON. In the 4th line, *for* Grove *read* Cove.

GROSSE, ISAAC, removed to Exeter, and was one of the first rulers there.

GULLIVER, ANTHONY, Massachusetts, was admitted freeman 1666.

GUNNISON, *HUGH, was admitted freeman 1636.

HACKBURNE, ABRAHAM, Boston 1639, was admitted freeman 1645, instead of 1639.

[HACKET, JABEZ, Taunton, had sons, John, b. 1654; Jabez, b. 1656. Samuel, b. 1664.]

[HAMBLEN, JOHN, Barnstable, had sons, Bartholomew, b. 1642; John, b. 1644; Eleazar, b. 1649; Israel, b. 1655.]

HAMLIN, ‡GILES, was of Middletown, where he d. 1 Sept. 1689, æ. 67. His son John, an assistant and judge of Conn., died in 1733, æ. 74.

HANCOCK. In the 3d line, *for* 1655, *read* 1665.

HANFORD, THOMAS, minister of Norwalk, Conn. d. in 1696, æ. a. 80. MS letter, S. W. B.

[HARLOW, WILLIAM, Plymouth, had sons, William, Samuel, William, 2d, John and Nathaniel b. from 1650 to 1664.]

HARDING, ||ROBERT, member of the ar. co. 1637.

[HASEY, ||WILLIAM, member of the ar. co. 1652.]

HATCH, WILLIAM, Scituate, was an elder of the church, and d. 6 Nov. 1651. William and Walter, perhaps his sons, were of Plymouth in 1652.

HATHAWAY. The authority for this article probably relied on tradition, which, after the lapse of two centuries, is seldom entitled to much confidence, unless supported by written memorials. The article may be expunged, and the following substituted.

[HATHAWAY, ARTHUR, Plymouth, m. Sarah Cook 1652, and their son John was b. 1653.   JOHN, Barnstable, had a son John, b. in 1658, who, with his father, was probably of Taunton in 1689.   JOSEPH, Taunton, was admitted freeman in 1657.   Plymouth Colony Records, MS copy of Mr. Jackson, of Boston.]

HAWKINS, ||*THOMAS, member of the ar. co. 1638 instead of 1644, and representative 1639 and 1644.   [||THOMAS, member of the ar. co. 1649.]

HEYWOOD.   In the 6th line *for* Benone, *read* Benoni. GEORGE, Concord, wrote his name *Heaward*.   He was admitted freeman 1638.

HIGGINSON, JOHN, Salem, was admitted freeman 1636.

HILL.   In the 9th line, *for* Dorchester, *read* Bridgewater. ROGER, Saco, freeman 1653.   Folsom. ||*VALENTINE, was representative of Dover.

HILLIARD, HUGH, was admitted freeman in 1634 instead of 1644.

HILTON.   In the 5th line, *for* apprised, *read* appraised.   Catharine, the widow of Edward Hilton, d. 29 May, 1676.   *WILLIAM, Newbury, Dover, &c. was admitted freeman 1642.

HINCKLEY, ‡§THOMAS, m. Mary Richards 1641, and three of his sons, Samuel, Thomas, and Ebenezer, were b. in 1652, 54, and 62.

HINSDALE, ||ROBERT, was member of the ar. co. 1645.

[HOBBY, JOHN, Massachusetts, and probably Dorchester 1637, [Winthrop, ii. 348] may have been the ancestor to the Hobbys of Boston at the close of the 17 century.   Two of the name, Wensley and William, natives of Boston, grad. at H. C. in 1723 and 1725, the last of whom was minister of Reading.]

[HODGES, ANDREW, Massachusetts, was admitted freeman in 1641.

[HOLLAND, ANGELL, Boston, freeman 1636, had a son Thomas, b. in 1644.   CHRISTOPHER, Boston 1647, d. 4 March, 1704, æ. 91.   EDWARD, N. Hampshire 1664.   JEREMIAH, who grad. at H. C., went to England, and was a minister in Northamptonshire.   JOHN, Dorchester, freeman 1636.]

HOLYOKE, *EDWARD, Lynn, probably did not remove to Springfield, as he died at Rumney-Marsh [Chelsea].   See Lewis's Hist. Lynn, 28.

HOUGH, SAMUEL, m. a daughter of Rev. Z. Symmes.   He left one son, a minor.   His estate amounted to £1822, 7s, 5d.   This name continued in Boston many years, and now exists in Connecticut, N. Hampshire, and Vermont.

HOWE.   There having been two Edward Howes contemporary, and both representatives, a mistake occurs respecting the time of service of each.   *EDWARD, of Lynn, was admitted freeman, 8 Dec. 1636, and was representative at three courts, March, May, and Sept. 1638.   *EDWARD, Watertown, freeman 1634, was representative at five courts in 1635, 1636, and 1639.   In the 8th line of HOWE, *for* Edward, *read* Ephraim.

HOWLAND, JOHN, was upwards of 80 years. The Plymouth Colony Records say of him, that he was "an ancient professor of the ways of Christ; one of the first comers, and proved a useful instrument of good, and was the last man that was left that came in the May Flower." It seems that John Alden, who came in the May Flower was living until 1687.

HULL. In the 7th line, *after* Baptist church, *add* in Boston.

HUSSEY. In the 6th line, *for* left two, *read* had three, and *after* John, *insert* Joseph. Christopher Hussey, was cast away and lost on the coast of Florida in 1685. Lewis, Hist. Lynn, 29.

HUTCHINSON, ||SAMUEL, was member of the ar. co. 1652.

IDE, NICHOLAS, Rehoboth, had a son Nathaniel, born in 1678.

INES, MATTHIAS, was admitted freeman in 1636, instead of 1646.

JACKSON, EDMUND, Boston, died in 1683, having had four wives and 15 children. Three of his sons, Samuel, Jeremiah, and Edmund, survived him. In the 14th line from bottom, page 159, *for* the second 1640, *read* 1644, and *transpose* the b.

JAMES, EDWARD, should be EDMUND. FRANCIS, Hingham, was admitted freeman 1643.

JANVRIN, GEORGE, Portsmouth 1684, was the member of Mr. Moodey's Church, mentioned by Belknap, [i. Hist. N. H. 165] Alden, [Account of Rel. Soc. in 1 Coll. Mass. Hist. Soc. x.] and Adams, [Annals of Portsmouth, 78.] JOHN Janvrin, probably a descendant, grad. at H. C. 1728.

JEFTS, HENRY. This name is erroneously printed *Sciffs*, in 2 Coll. Mass. Hist. Soc. ii. 162.

JENKS, ||RICHARD, Boston, member of ar. co. 1666, was admitted to 2d church, Oct. 1682.

JENNER, THOMAS. Two of this name were admitted freemen, one in 1636, the other in 1639. The name of the last is spelled *Ginner* in the Colony Records, and *he* might have been the deputy from Weymouth 1640. The name existed in Boston many years, and Thomas Jenner was admitted member of the ar. co. 1673, and David Jenner grad. at H. C. in 1753.

JOHNSON, DAVY, was admitted freeman, 18 May 1631. HUMPHREY, had sons, John, Joseph, and Benjamin, b. in Scituate in 1653, 1655, and 1657. RICHARD, Lynn, and perhaps Salem, was freeman 1637. WILLIAM, Charlestown, was admitted freeman 1635.

JORDAN, ROBERT, was an Episcopal minister at Cape Elizabeth. He m. a daughter of John Winter, from whom he inherited a large landed estate. He removed to Portsmouth in 1676, and d. there three years after. Sullivan. Greenleaf, Eccl. Sketches, 224. Geo. Folsom, MS letter.

KEAINE, ||BENJAMIN, member of ar. co. 1638. CHRISTOPHER, (spelled *Cayne*,) was admitted freeman 1638.

KELLOND, THOMAS, Boston, had sons, John, Thomas, and Richard, baptized in 1673, 1675, and 1681.

KELLY, ABEL, Salem, was admitted freeman 1641. *RO-
GER, was of the Isles of Shoals as early as 1668.

KEMPTON, EPHRAIM, Scituate, d. 1655.   Sons Ephraim
and Manasseh were b. in 1645 and 1651. MANASSEH, Plymouth, d. 14 Jan. 1663.

KENRICK, JOHN, Boston and Newton, was admitted freeman
in 1640.   JOHN, of Ipswich, was probably the freeman of 1654.

KENT, JOHN, the freeman in 1654, was of Dedham. *Erase*,
therefore, in 13th and 14th lines, p. 168, " perhaps the freeman of
1654."

KILBURN, GEORGE, Rowley, was admitted freeman 1640,
instead of 1644.

KINGSWORTH, HENRY, should be KINGSNORTH, HEN-
RY. 1 Coll. Mass. Hist. Soc. x.

KIRBY, WILLIAM, Boston, freeman 1647.

KIRMAN, JOHN, Cambridge, was admitted freeman 1633.

KITCHEN, JOHN, Salem, freeman 1643, instead of 1642.

KITTREDGE. In the 6th line, *for* 1614, *read* 1714. ۱ The
early genealogy of the Kittredges may be found in the oldest book
[4to] of the records of births in Billerica.

KNIGHT, JOHN, Newbury, freeman 1636.   RICHARD, Boston, freeman 1642. [RICHARD, Portsmouth 1643. MS letter of
John Kelly, esq.]   ROBERT, Boston, d. 27 June, 1655.

KNOTT, GEORGE, Sandwich, d. in 1648.

LAKE, THOMAS, a captain and merchant of Boston, and member of the 2d church. He was a joint owner, with Major Clarke of
Boston, of the Island of Arrowsick, in Maine, where he had a house
and occasionally resided, and near which he was killed by the Indians, 14 August, 1675. Hubbard, Eastern Wars, 41, 42.   MS
Records of 2d Church in Boston.

LAMBERT, FRANCIS, Rowley, was admitted freeman 1640.

LANGHORNE.   In last line, *for* Patince, *read* Patience.

LARKHAM.   In first line, *for* Notham, *read* Northam. Those
of the name in Beverly, where it still exists, wrote it Larcom.

LAWES, FRANCIS, Salem, was admitted freeman in 1641, instead of 1637.

LEEDS, BENJAMIN, Dorchester, freeman 1645.   The Benjamin, freeman 1670, might be a son. RICHARD, Salem, freeman
1647.

[LEARNED, WILLIAM, freeman 1634, was early at Woburn,
and d. there, 5 April, 1646.]

[LEUSON, JOHN, Dedham, one of the founders of the church,
was admitted freeman 1638.]

LOCKWOOD, ROBERT, Watertown, freeman 1637.

LONG, ROBERT. Three of this name appear to have been
admitted freemen in 1635, 1636, and 1649, one of whom was member of the ar. co. in 1639.

LOWDER, RICHARD, freeman 1642.   Perhaps Lowden and
Lowder were the same name.

LOWELL.   From Percival Lowle, or Lowell, it is supposed descended Ebenezer Lowell, of Boston, who d. in 1711, aged a. 36, whose son John was born 14 March, 1704, grad. at H. C. 1721, was ordained at Newbury, 19 Jan. 1726, and d. 15 May, 1767, æ. 63. John, son of Rev. John Lowell, was b. at Newbury, 17 June, 1743, grad. at H. C. 1760, was a distinguished character ; a member of the Amer. Acad., LL. D., Judge of the U. S. District Court, and d. 6 May, 1802, leaving sons, *John*, LL. D., born 6 Oct. 1769, grad. at H. C. 1786; *Francis Cabot*, b. 7 April, 1775, the founder of the Waltham factory, and the proprietor of the Lowell factories, who d. 10 Aug. 1817, æ. 42, and *Charles*, D. D., b. 15 Aug. 1782, grad. at H. C. 1800, and was ordained over the West Church in Boston, 1 Jan. 1806.   JOHN, Boston 1655. I feel some doubt respecting this name and William Lowell, freeman 1642, [Savage, ii. Winthrop, 372] as there appears to have been a John Lovell or Louell of Boston, and a William Lovell of Dorchester, at these periods.

[LUDLOW, GEORGE, Massachusetts, requested freedom 19 Oct. 1630. Savage, ii. Winthrop, 361.]

LUKAR, ||[——] member of the ar. co. 1640, might be Henry or John Looker or Luker, who were very early at Salisbury.

LUSHER, *||‡ELEAZAR, Dorchester, member of the ar. co. 1638.

LYFORD.   In the 7th line, *for* Mordicai, *read* MORDECAI.

MARSH, GEORGE, Hingham, was admitted freeman 1636.

MATHIS, JOHN, freeman 1642.

MARSHALL.   In the 8th line, *for* Manshall, *read* Marshall.

MAVERICK, JOHN, Dorchester, was admitted freeman 18 May, 1631.

MAYHEW, THOMAS, Watertown, freeman 1634, instead of 1637.

MAYO, NATHANIEL, m. Hannah Prence, and had sons, Thomas, b. 1650; Nathaniel, b. 1652; Samuel, b. 1655, and Theophilus, b. 1659. [JOHN, probably a brother of Nathaniel, has sons, John, William, James, Samuel, and Nathaniel, b. after 1651.]

MELCHER, EDWARD, Portsmouth 1684. Belknap, i. Hist. N. H. 324.]

[MERRY, WALTER, Boston, was admitted freeman 1634.]

MILLER, THOMAS, Springfield, was killed by the Indians, 5 Oct. 1675. Sprague, Hist. Disc. 21.

MITCHELL.   In 1st and 2d lines, *erase* " was probably son of the following," and *insert* " Lincoln, Hist. Hingham."

MOORE, JOHN.   One of the three freemen of this name was member of the ar. co. 1638.

MORRIL, ||ISAAC, Roxbury, was member of the ar. co. 1638.

MOSELY, ||SAMUEL, member of the ar. co. 1671, and captain in Philip's War, might be son of Henry Modsley or Maudsley, of Braintree, if, as has been said, Modsley and Mosely are the same name.

MOTT, ADAM, was admitted freeman in 1636.

MOULTON. In the 13th line, *erase* " He was admitted freeman 1631."

[MUNINGS, MAHALEEL, was admitted to the 2d church, 27 Nov. 1659.]

[NETTLETON, JOHN, Killingworth, 1663. D. D. Field, Hist. Middlesex Co. 106.]

NEWBURY, *THOMAS, freeman 1634, was probably of Dorchester instead of Lynn. He was representative at the March and May sessions in 1635. RICHARD, was admitted freeman 1645, instead of 1655.

[NEWTON, RICHARD. A second Richard Newton was admitted freeman 1647.]

NICKERSON, WILLIAM, was probably the proprietor of considerable lands in Monamoy or Chatham, Mass. 1665. 1 Coll. Mass. Hist. Soc. viii. 151.

NODDLE, WILLIAM, was admitted freeman, 18 May, 1631.

NORTON, JOHN, Ipswich and Boston, freeman 1637.

NOYES. In the 12th line, p. 200, *for* Lym, *read* Lyme.

OAKMAN. *For* Mebzar, *read* Melzar.

ODLIN, JOHN, Boston, was admitted freeman 1634.

OLIVER. In the 11th line, John, the son of John Oliver, m. Susanna, and d. in 1683, leaving a son Sweet, b. in 1668, and baptized in the 2d church Boston, in 1678. The other children named in the 24th and 25th lines should be erased, as they belonged to another John Oliver. In the 8th line from the bottom, *erase* " He removed to Newbury, and d. in 1642," and *insert* " JOHN, Newbury, was b. a. 1616, came from the city of Bristol, and was living in Newbury in March, 1643. [Affidavit in 1st vol. of Suffolk Reg. of Deeds] but probably died soon after." In the 9th line, p. 212, *for* the preceding, *read* Peter. [THOMAS, Salem 1638, had a wife Mary, who gave the church there much disturbance. See Winthrop's i. Hist. N. E. 281, and Felt's Annals Salem, 117.]

[ORMSBY, JACOB, Rehoboth, d. 2 March 1677. JACOB, perhaps his son, d. 16 Feb. 1677.]

OWEN, THOMAS or WILLIAM, was probably the member of the ar. co. 1639.

PADDY, WILLIAM, Plymouth and Boston, d. in 1658 instead of 1653. Four of his sons were, John, b. 1643, perhaps the one who d. at Boston in 1663; Samuel, b. 1645; Joseph, b. and died 1649; and William, b. 1652. The William who was member of the ar. co. might be the preceding, and the one who, according to the Boston records, d. 11 Nov 1653, might be his son William, b. in 1652.

[PAINE, MOSES, who might, instead of the MOSES, freeman in 1647, be member of the ar. co., was admitted freeman in 1641.]

PAINTER. In the 3d and 4th line, *erase* " He came to N. E. in 1630."

PALFRAY. In 1st line, page 216, *after* years, *insert* since.

PARKMAN, ELIAS, Dorchester, was admitted freeman 1635.

[PARSONS, ROBERT, Lynn, was admitted freeman 1638.]

PEACOCK, RICHARD, Roxbury, was probably the freeman 1639, entered in the colony records under the name of *Richard Pococke*.

PEAKE, CHROSTOPHER, should be PEAKE, CHRISTO-PHER.

PECK, NATHANIEL. One of this name died at Rehoboth, 25 Aug. 1676.

PENTICUS, JOHN, the freeman 1640, was of Charlestown.

PERKINS, JOHN, who arrived in N. E. 5 Feb. 1631, was probably the person who was admitted freeman the 18th May following. Two others of the name of John Perkins were admitted freemen in 1633 and 1637. WILLIAM, probably the representative in 1644, was admitted freeman 1634.

[PERRY, ISAAC, Massachusetts, was admitted freeman 1633.]

PHILLIPS, JOHN, the deacon of the 2d church in Boston, d. in 1682. NICHOLAS, Weymouth, freeman 1640. WILLIAM, Charlestown, freeman 1640.

PIKE. In the 21st line, 230th page, *for* 1788, *read* 1688.

[POND, DANIEL, Dedham, was admitted freeman 1654.]

POPE, THOMAS, Yarmouth 1646, and Plymouth, had sons, Seth, Thomas, and John, b. in 1647, 1651, and 1652.]

PORTER. In the 3d line, *for* EDMUND, *read* EDWARD, and *erase* " Perhaps this name should be *Edward* Porter."

POWELL, MICHAEL, Boston, d. 28 Jan. 1673. In 1st line, p. 234, *erase* " Increase Mather."

PRATT. *For* ANTHONY, *read* ABRAHAM, who was probably connected with the Pratts of Plymouth. MATTHEW, Weymouth, freeman 1640 instead of 1651.

[PRESBURY, JOHN, Sandwich, died in 1648.]

PRIEST, JAMES. Two of this name appear to have been admitted freemen in 1643.

PYNCHON. In the 1st line, p. 238, *for* Edward, *read* Elizur.

QUINCY. In the 10th line, *for* Daiel, *read* Daniel.

RAINSBOROW, [——] Lord Clarendon [Hist. of the Rebellion, 3219] gives an account of his death in 1648.

BANDALL, WILLIAM, Scituate, had sons Joseph, William, John, and Job, b. from 1642 to 1654.

RAVENSDALE. In the 3d line, *for* 1656, *read* 1556.

RAWSON, EDWARD, d. at Dorchester, a. 1694. The inventory of his estate is dated 2 Feb. 1693, 4. His son Grindall, b. in 1658, m. Susan, daughter of Rev. John Wilson, of Medfield, and had 8 sons and 5 daughters. Family Genealogy.

READ, ROBERT, Exeter and Hampton, was probably one of the company lost in a boat going out from Hampton, 20 Oct. 1657. PHILIP, Weymouth, was admitted freeman 1654, instead of 1660.

[REEVES, THOMAS, Massachusetts, freeman 1645.]

RICHARDS, *||‡JOHN, Dorchester, removed to Boston, where he was admitted to the 2d church in 1664, and d. 2 April, 1694.

[RICHMOND, JOHN, Taunton, had sons, John, born 1656;

Thomas, b. 1658; Josiah, b. 1653; Edward, b. 1665; Samuel, b. 1668.]

ROBINSON, WILLIAM, Salem, was admitted freeman 27 Dec. 1642. WILLIAM, Dorchester, freeman 18 May, 1642. [RICH-ARD, Massachusetts, was admitted freeman in 1641.]

ROBY. *For* Heny, *read* HENRY. Many of this name in New-Hampshire have written the name *Robie.* HENRY, New-Hampshire d. in 1688, leaving wife Sarah, and sons Thomas, Samuel, Ichabod, and John.]

[ROGERS, JOSEPH, Sandwich, (probably the same who was at Plymouth 1623) was a lieutenant. His children were, Joseph, b. 1635; Thomas, b. 1638; John, b. 1642; Mary, b. 1644; James, b. 1648; Hannah, b. 1652.]

RUSSELL, JOHN, Cambridge, was admitted freeman 1636. After his name, in lines 23d and 24th, *erase* " may be the one called *sen.*, and admitted freeman in 1681." ‡*RICHARD, Charlestown, freeman 1641.

SARGENT, and SERGEANT, WILLIAM, Charlestown, pp. 254 and 258, was admitted freeman 1639.

[SAUNDERSON, ROBERT, Massachusetts, was admitted freeman 1639.]

[SAVORY, THOMAS, Plymouth, had sons, Moses, Samuel, and Thomas, b. in 1649, 1651, and 1652.]

SCARLET, JOHN, was member of the 2d church Boston, and d. 4 May, 1675. SAMUEL, of Boston 1665, a captain, was admitted freeman 1673.

SCOTTOW. In the 7th line, *for Scotts, read Scotto.*

SHED, DANIEL, was of Billerica as early as 1660. Two of his sons, Samuel and Nathan, were b. there in 1660 and 1668. He d. 27 July, 1708. Elizabeth, his wife, d. 17 Jan. 1700. His son Daniel, d. of small pox, in 1690, and John d. in 1737, æ. 81.

SHERBURNE. In the 10th line, *for* 1734, *read* 1774. Capt. [Samuel] Sherburne, of Portsmouth, a worthy officer, was killed at Macquoit in 1691. Belknap, i. Hist. N. H. 212.

SHERMAN, EDMUND, was probably of Watertown. JOHN, the captain, of Watertown, was a distinguished land surveyor. He was employed with Jonathan Ince in 1652, in finding the most northerly part of Merrimack river. See Belknap, i. Hist. N. H. 87. SAMUEL, Boston, was admitted freeman 1640.

SMITH, [HENRY, freeman 18 May, 1631. HENRY, freeman 1640.] One of these was probably Capt. Henry Smith of Springfield. In the 29th line, p. 267, *erase* " MATTHIAS, Massachusetts, freeman 1645," and *insert* " freeman 1645," in the next line, after Watertown. *THOMAS, the freeman 1633, and the representative 1635, was probably of Watertown, instead of Weymouth. THOMAS, of Salem, was admitted freeman 1637.

SOUTHCOT, RICHARD, appears to have been of Pascataqua 1639. J. Kelly, esq.

SPARHAWK. In the 4th line, p. 270, *for* 1665, *read* 1765.

SPENCER, *WILLIAM, was representative 5 years, from 1634 to 1638, inclusive.

[SPOONER, WILLIAM, an inhabitant of Plymouth in 1651.]

STEDMAN, JOHN, Cambridge, came over in 1639, with the family of Rev. Josse Glover, in whose employment he was, and from whose estate some of his children received legacies.

STEVENS. In the 15th line, *erase* Abbot, Hist. Andover, 21, and *insert* it after 71, in the 14th line.

STILEMAN, †ELIAS, 2d, was admitted freeman 1642, and probably member of the ar. co. 1645.

STOW, SAMUEL, the graduate at H. C. 1645, is said by Mr. Shattuck, [MS letter] to have been son of Thomas Stow, instead of John Stow of Roxbury. He went with two brothers to Middletown, Conn., where he was a preacher, a. 10 years. He died after 1697.

STUDSON, ROBERT, Scituate, had sons, Joseph, b. 1639; Benjamin, b. 1641; Thomas; Samuel, b. 1646; John, b. 1648; Robert, b. 1653.

[STURGES, EDWARD, Yarmouth 1648. JOSEPH, Yarmouth 1650.]

[STURTEVANT, SAMUEL, Plymouth 1650, had sons, John, Samuel, and James.]

TOOTHACHER, ROGER, should be TOOTHACKER, ROGER. In the records of Billerica, the name is spelled *Toothaker*.

[TULLY, JOHN, the author of almanacks from 1681 to 1702, was b. in the parish of Horley, in the county of Surry, England, a. 1639. He settled in Middletown, Conn., when a lad, and died 5 Oct. 1701. Field, Stat. Account of Middlesex co. 104.]

TYNG, ||‡EDWARD, jr. member of ar. co. 1668. ||‡JONATHAN, ar. co. 1670.

[VARNEY, THOMAS, Boston, was admitted to 2d church, 8 Jan. 1664.]

[VIXON, ROBERT, Eastham 1652. Copy of Plymouth Colony Records.]

WADE. In the 8th line, *erase* " also."

WALTON, GEORGE, New-Castle and Portsmouth, d. 1686, over 70 years.

[WALTER, THOMAS, father of Rev. Nehemiah Walter, lived in Boston, and was admitted member of the 2d church, 2 Nov. 1680.]

WAY, AARON, was of Boston, and admitted to the 2d church, 1660. RICHARD, also of Boston, was member of the 2d church, 1660.

[WEYMOUTH, WILLIAM, brother of Robert, of N. H. died 1654.]

WHITSON. Read this name WHISTON.

WILLARD. In the 13th line from the bottom, *for* presented, *read* preserved. In the 12th line, *after* folio volume, *insert* " of divinity." In the 4th line, p. 319, *for* Bideford, *read* Biddeford.

WOODBURY. In the 12th line, *for* Francistown, *read* Antrim.

WORCESTER, WILLIAM. In the last line but one, and in the last line of the article Worcester, *for* Noah Webster, esq. *read* Noah Worcester, esq.

YALE, ‖DAVID, Boston, was member of the ar. co. 1640.

[YATES, JOHN, Eastham 1655, had a son John.]

[YOUNG, JOHN, Plymouth, had a son John, b. 1647.]

To the following persons may be added or corrected the year of their admission as freemen of the Massachusetts Colony.

Allen, ‖*Bozoun, Hingham 1641; Allen, John, Charlestown, 1641; Allen, William, 1631; Archer, Henry, 1641; Armitage, Joseph, 1637; Aspinwall, Peter, 1637; Atkinson, Theodore, 1642; Barber, ‖*George, 1647; Bateman, William, 1642; Batchelor, John, Watertown 1635; Batchelor, Stephen, 1635; Bourne, Garrett, 1635; Bright, Henry, Watertown 1635; Buck, James, 1639; Buckminster, Thomas, 1646; Bunker, George, 1635; Bulfinch, John, 1642; Buttrick, William, 1647; Busby, Nicholas, 1638; Bulkley, John, 1642; Casely, William, 1637; Chapin, Samuel, 1641; Dassett, John, 1640; Dow, Henry, 1638; Draper, Roger, 1639; Ely, Nathaniel, 1635; Evans, Richard, 1645; Fellows, Samuel, 1645; Firnam, Henry, 1645; Fiske, Nathan, 1643; Fiske, *William, 1642; Foster, ‖*Hopestill, 1639; Fowler, Philip, 1634; Gay, John, (the 3d of the name) 1645; Genery, Lambert, 1645; Gott, Charles, 1631; Grafton, Joseph, 1637; Hastings, John, 1643; Healy, William, 1645; Heath, William, 1633; Hildreth, Richard, 1643; Holt, Nicholas, 1637; Hunt, William, Concord, 1641; Palmer, Walter, 1631; Parker, Thomas, Newbury, 1634; Parkman, Elias, Dorchester, 1635; Parmenter, John, 2d, 1643; Partridge, William, 1638; Payson, Giles, 1637; Peters, Hugh, 1636; Pierce, Robert, Dorchester 1642; Prentice, Valentine, 1632; Rawling, Richard, 1643; Ripley, William, 1642; Scales, William, 1640; Scott, Robert, 1636; Scott, Thomas, 1635; Shepard, Edward, 1643; Shore, Samson, 1642; Singletary, Richard, Newbury, 1638; Southwick, Lawrence, 1639; Spencer, Roger, 1652; Stanyan, Anthony, 1644; Steele, John, 1634; Stevens, John, 1641; Strong, John, 1637; Swain, Richard, 1640; Swan, Richard, 1638; Underhill, John, 1631; Wadsworth, William, 1632; Waite, Gamaliel, 1635; Waite, *John, the representative, was probably the freeman of 1647; Wales, Nathaniel, 1637; Warham, John, 1631; Warner, Daniel, 1641; Way, Richard, 1643; Wells, Richard, Lynn 1638; Wheatley, John, 1643; White, Nicholas, 1643; White, Thomas, 1640; White, William, Newbury and Haverhill 1642; Wenbourn, or Wenbane, William, 1644; Wilson, John, 1632.

ADDITIONAL EXPLANATIONS.

In arranging those of the same surname alphabetical order has generally been regarded, so that sons are sometimes placed before their fathers.

Each section or sentence beginning with a name in capitals is to be considered as a separate article, or distinct paragraph. It was at first intended that the work should be printed in such a manner that a separate paragraph should be allotted to every person printed in capitals, but the limits would not allow of it.

The children of the early settlers in many instances, from not having the necessary information, are entirely omitted; sometimes but an imperfect list of them is given, and frequently only the names of the sons are mentioned. Where numbered with Arabick numerals, the family is generally complete.

There are probably some errors in assigning the residence of freemen, and especially where there were several persons of the same name.

Dates, where copied by myself, and generally, if not always, when furnished by others, are made according to original records. Characters or marks, denoting office and station, are sometimes omitted by mistake, but not being very essential, their omission will not be here named.

A LIST OF NAMES FOUND AMONG THE FIRST SETTLERS OF NEW ENGLAND.

[Those names which are starred are not contained in Farmer's Genealogical Register, and concerning those which are not starred, additional facts are related. The article is prepared entirely from unpublished manuscripts, by Mr. S. G. Drake.]

ADAMS, SAMUEL, Chelmsford, authorized to solemnize marriages there, 1664.

ALLEN, BOZOUN, Boston, constable, 1680.

ALLIN, ONESIPHORUS,* Ipswich, 1679.

ALLYNE, THOMAS,* Barnstable, 1644, a witness to a sale of land by the Indian *Seacunk.*

ANDREWS, THOMAS,* and THOMAS JR.,* Dorchester, 1664.

ANGIER, ANDREW, first inhabitant at Dunston, Me. — ARTHUR, born about 1625.

ANNABLE, ANTHONY, Barnstable, 1644.

ARCHARD, SAMUEL,* church member, Salem, 1640.

ARDELL, RICHARD,* Boston, merchant, 1686.

ATWOOD, JOHN,* ensign, Boston, juror, 1686.

AVERY, WILLIAM* and JONATHAN,* members of the church, Dedham, 1677.

BAXTER, DANIEL, Salem, 1638. Carried the charter of R. Island from Boston to Newport, 1663. [*Farmer's MS.*]

BENTLEY, WILLIAM,* came to New England in the ship Arabella, Richard Sprague master; sailed from Gravesend, May 27, 1671.

BEZBEANE, JOHN,* Woburn, 1677.

BERRY, RICHARD,* Medford, 1636.

BLAKE, FRANCIS,* Dorchester, 1664. — WILLIAM,* — JAMES, a. 24 in 1677.

BLOWERS, JOHN, a. 36 in 1663, a lessee of an island in Boston harbor for seven years.

BOTT, ISAAC,* Boston, 1675.

BRADLEY, WILLIAM,* Dorchester, 1664.

BROUGHTON, THOMAS, Boston, 1655, petitions general court against imposing duties on importations.

BULL, WILLIAM, Charlestown, 1638, heard Squaw Sachem say then, that she had given all her lands to Mr. Gibbons; was 43 years of age in 1662.

CAPEN, BARNARD, witnesses the Indian deed of Dorchester, 1671; SAMUEL,* also a witness to the same.

CARPENTER, WILLIAM, Hingham, 1641, witnessed, and seems to have drawn the deed of a tract of land there from the Indians "to John Tower the elder." His autograph, and the instrument to which it is attached, are a most elegant specimen of the chirography of that age.

CHEEVER, EZEKIEL, married the widow of Capt. Lothrop, who was killed in Sudbury fight, before May 19, 1680.

CHILD, RICHARD,* Watertown, juror, 1680.

CHURCH, GARRETT, Watertown, 1636, aged 51 in 1662. — RICHARD, Plymouth, 1631; went there from Wessaguscussett.

CLARKE, JONAS, constable of Cambridge, 1680. — THEODORE,* York, 1663.

CLAY, NATHANIEL,* Dorchester, 1664.

COBB, HENRY, Barnstable, 1644.

COOK, GEORGE, Colonel, &c., Cambridge, Ms., in which place and vicinity he had large possessions; returned to England in or about the beginning of the Civil War, in which he took a part, went into Ireland, where he was killed in 1652. He was twice married, and left by one of his wives, two daughters: 1. MARY, m. to "her mother's younger brother," Mr. Samuel Annesley, 1681. In 1669 she resided at Martins in the Fields, London; in 1691 she resided with her husband in the city of Westminster. 2. ELIZABETH, m. 1st, Rev. John Quick, of St. Giles. Cripple Gate, London, and perhaps, 2ndly, Joseph Cawthorne.

CRISPE, BENJAMIN, "Misticke als Meadforde," 1636.

CURWIN, GEORGE, Salem, 1682, aged 70; went there near 44 years before.

CUSHIN, JEREMIAH,* Boston, juror, 1680.

DAVIS, LAWRENCE,* York, 1663.

DINSDALE, WILLIAM, aged 47 in 1663. Hired an island of John Leverett, in Boston harbor, for seven years.

DOGGETT, JOHN, Hingham. 1662, where he witnessed an Indian deed.

DURGIE, WILLIAM,* came to Ipswich, Nov. 9, 1663, and was then 33 years old. Had been in the W. Indies, and came here from thence. Wife, Martha. Perhaps this name is that since written *Durgin.*

EDGECOMBE, MILES,* a. 25, 1676. Was at "Black Point the day and tyme when nine of Winterharbor men were fighting with the Indians upon the sands opposite to the said place."

EEDY, JOHN,* Plymouth, left there to reside in Massachusetts, before Feb., 1632.

EUERS, MATHIAS,* Dorchester, 1664.

EVERETT, JOHN, Chelmsford, 1664, where he is authorized to unite people in marriage.

FOOTE, PASCO, Salem church. 1640.

FOSTER, JAMES,* Dorchester, constable, 1680.

FOX, THOMAS, Ms., about 52 in 1659, wife, Elinor.

FOXWELL, RICHARD, Dunston, Me., 1654.

FRANKLIN, BENJAMIN, Boston, before 1678, wife, Katherine.

FRIEND, JOHN, Salem, church memb., 1640.

GODDARD, GILES,* Boston, 1679, had wife and servants.

GRAY, JOHN,* buys Nantasket of the Indians, 1622.

GREENLEAFE, ENOCH,* Boston, saddler, 1693.

GREENOUGH, ROBERT,* Rowley, 1701.

GREEN, JOHN, Cambridge, juror, 1680. NATHANIEL, 1675.

HARROD, THOMAS,* Boston, juror, 1680.

HEWS, JEREMIAH,* Dorchester, 1664. — ELEAZER,* Dorchester.

HAUXWORTH, THOMAS,* Salisbury. Had a daughter married to Onesiphorus Page. His widow was living there, 1667.

HAYDEN, SAMUEL,* Dorchester or vicinity, 1666.

HILLS, JOSEPH, Medford, a. 60 in 1662. Capt. JAMES,* [HILL] grand juror, Boston, 1686.

HOAR, WILLIAM,* Boston, baker, 1679.

HODMAN, JOHN, Dorchester, 1679, born 1659.

HOOD, JEREMIAH,* Massachusetts, 1676.

HOPIN, STEVEN,* born 1626, Dorchester, in Capt. Roger Clapp's employ, 1642. Witness to Indian deed of Dorchester, (8: 4: 1649.)

HOUGHTON, RALPH, Lancaster, 1676, where he was constable, collector of taxes, treasurer, &c. There were at the same place in 1703, HENRY, JONAS, ROBERT, JOHN, SEN., JOHN, JR., JOSEPH and JACOB.

HOWARD, JACOB,* Dorchester, 1664.

HUDSON, WILLIAM, lived at "Wading River" in 1670, "where King Philip and Squamaug (brother of Josias deceased) met to settle the bounds between them, which had for some time been in dispute.

JOHNSON, EDWARD, a. 60 in 1660, at which time he gives evidence about land in Charlestown. FRANCIS, Marblehead, 1660, nephew of Mr. Christopher Coulson, a merchant adventurer of London.

JOYLIFFE, JOHN, Boston, will dated 1699-1700. Had a brother, Dr. GEORGE JOYLIFFE, in England; sisters, DOROTHY CANE, in England, MARTHA COOK, in England, REBECCA WOLCOTT, MARGARET DRAKE, and MARY BISS, "sometime wife of James Biss of Shepton Mallet, in the county of Somerset," Eng.

KEY, JOSHUA,* probably married a daughter of Capt. Thomas Lothrop, who was killed by the Indians in 1675, as his children received a legacy out of Lothrop's estate.

KING, THOMAS, was an inhabitant of Exeter, 1675.

KNIGHT, WALTER, aged 66 in 1653, at which time he was at Boston. The same person was at Nantasket in 1622.

JOHN, Charlestown, juror in the witch trials, 1680.

LATHAM, CARY, was born in 1612; Boston, 1663.

LAWRENCE, THOMAS, Hingham, 1661.

LOEPHELIN, PETER,* Frenchman, Boston, 1679.

LEACH, RICHARD, Salem, a. 60 in 1678, leased a farm of Gov. Endecott, 1657.

LONG, ROBERT, Marblehead, a. 70 in 1660.

LOTHROP, CAPT. THOMAS; his widow married Joseph Grafton, before May 19, 1680. After her decease, the property left her by Lothrop was ordered by court to the wife of Ezekiel Chever, and her issue, heirs of Capt. Lothrop. It is also ordered Mrs. Grafton to pay to the children of Joshua Key, £20.

LYON, PETER, Dorchester, 1664.

MARRINER, ANDREW,* Boston, 1693, leather dresser.

MATHER, TIMOTHY, Dorchester, 1667.

MAYHEW, THOMAS, hired a farm in Medford, 1636.

MELLEN, JOHN,* Charlestown, where he died before 1695.

MIDDLECOTT, MR. [RICHARD?] Boston, juror at trials for witchcraft, 1680.

MOKALL, JAMES,* b. 1660, Massachusetts, 1680.

MORSE, WILLIAM, Newbury; wife, Elizabeth, accused of practising witchcraft, finally acquitted at Boston, 1680.

MOSE, JOHN, Watertown, 1680, constable.

MOTT, NATHANIEL, a. 19, or thereabouts, in 1681.

NARAMORE, THOMAS,* Dorchester, 1664. Persons of this name are in N. Hampshire at this time

NEIGHBOR, JAMES,* Massachusetts, 1662.

ODIORNE, JOHN and PHILL., Portsmouth, N. H., 1657, subscribed toward the support of public worship.

PAGE, ONESIPHORUS,* Salisbury, 1667, married daughter of Thomas Hauxworth [Hawksworth].

PARSONS, MARK,* Sagadahock, 1665.

PATESHALL, ROBERT,* Boston, 1655, petitions General Court against duties on importations.

PEASLEE, JOSEPH, went to Haverhill before 1653.

PHILIPS, JOHN,* Massachusetts, 1630, styled servant, went to Plymouth, 1631.

POLE, WILLIAM,* Dorchester, 1649. The name is since written *Pool*.

PRAY, EPHRAIM,* born 1661, Dorchester, 1680.

RAINSFORD, SAMUEL,* Boston, killed with Capt. Turner, at Pawtucket, in Philip's war, leaving no relative in the country.

RICE, HENRY, Charlestown, juror, 1662.

RICHARD, GYLES,* SEN., Massachusetts, 1666.

ROBBINS, RICHARD, juror at trials for witchcraft, 1680.

ROOT, THOMAS, Lynn, 1674, where he attempted to gather a church.

RYALL, JOSEPH,* Charlestown, constable, 1680.

SAUNDERS, MARTIN,* born 1630, Boston, 1679.

SEALE, EPHRAIM,* Lieutenant, Boston, juror, 1686.

SEARES, JOHN,* Boston, Lieutenant, 1652.

SEWALL, HENRY, was residing at Manchester, Lancaster co., Eng, in 1623, only son of HENRY SEWALL, who came to N. England with his family, and settled in Newbury.

SHERBURNE, GEORGE, b. 1602, Portsmouth, 1650, m. Rebecca, dau. Ambrose Gibbins, and had children, SAMUEL, ELIZABETH, m. Tobias Lear, MARY, HENRY, JOHN, AMBROSE, SARAH, and REBECCA. [Farmer's MS.]

SIBLY, JOHN, church member, Salem, 1640.

SMITH, JOHN,* Barnstable, 1644.

SPRAGUE, SAMUEL.* Charlestown, 1695.

STILEMAN, ELIAS, Boston, constable, 1673.

STONE, JOHN,* Watertown, juror, 1680.

STUDSON, ROBERT,* one of the commissioners for settling the bounds between Plymouth and Massachusetts, 1664.

SUMNER, WILLIAM,* Dorchester, 1670.

SWAIN, JOHN,* Salisbury, b. 1633, Nantucket, 1703. A Lieutenant SWAIN had been under Major Appleton against the Indians at Narraganset, in 1675. He was afterwards a captain.

TAYLER, JOHN,* Shipcot, [Sheepscot,] 1665.

THAYER, RICHARD, Massachusetts, went to England, and returned in 1679.

TINKHAM, EPHRAIM, Massachusetts, 1666, at which time he was a witness to the sale of lands to Richard Thayer of Braintree, by the Indian chief *Josias*. He attests to it in 1678.

TOWER, JOHN, Hingham, buys a large tract of land of several Indians in that place; deed dated June 17, 1641. In an endorsement on said deed, (made by Ri: Bellingham, 19: 1: 1662-3,) JOHN TOWER is called senior. But in the TOWER GENEALOGICAL TREE there are assigned as the children of JOHN TOWER of Hingham, (1637) only AMBROSE, BENJAMIN, JONATHAN, HANNAH, and JEREMIAH.

TRAVIS, DANIEL,* "chiefe gunner in ye town of Boston, to salute shipps and look after ye artillery," at £5 per annum, 1680.

WAIT, JOHN, Charlestown, juror, 1662, [spelt *Wayte*,] Boston, juror at the trials for witchcraft, 1680. RICHARD, Boston, a. 82 in 1678. He was marshal. RICHARD, Springfield, 1680, wounded by Indians, Oct. 5, 1675.

WALES, JOHN,* and JOHN, JR.,* Dorchester, 1677.

WALKER, ROBERT, Boston, aged 72 in 1679. He came from Manchester, Eng., where he was living in 1623.

WAY, RICHARD, Lieutenant, Boston, juror, 1680. HENRY, Dorchester, 1664.

WEBB, THOMAS, came to N. England in 1671, in the ship Arabella, Capt. Richard Sprague, which sailed from Gravesend May 27.

WHITTINGHAM, RICHARD,* Charlestown, 1693; had been in England in 1691.

WILLEY, EDWARD,* Boston, juror, 1686.

WILLIAMS, WILLIAM,* Boston, 1675, wife, Johanna; was pressed to go against the Indians in Philip's war, and was killed at Medfield, leaving "four small children."

WILLIS, LAWRENCE,* Barnstable, 1644.

WINSOR, JOSHUA,* Boston, constable, 1686.

WISWALL, JOHN, Dorchester, witnesses a new deed of the town, (8: 4: 1649,) made "because ye old deed was something decayed with ill keeping."